PENGUIN BOOKS

THE LITERATURE OF THE UNITED STATES

Marcus Cunliffe, born in 1922, was University Professor at George Washington University, Washington D.C., from 1980 until his death in 1990. Educated at Oxford and Yale he was a lecturer and professor at Manchester University, and Professor of American Studies at the University of Sussex. His books include an interpretative essay on George Washington, an account of the United States in the early nineteenth century, a survey of *The American Presidency*, *Soldiers and Civilians: The Martial Spirit in America, 1775–1865*, and *Chattel Slavery and Wage Slavery*. *In Search of America: Transatlantic Essays 1951–1990* summarizes his lifetime curiosity about the United States and its place in the world.

Marcus Cunliffe

THE LITERATURE OF THE UNITED STATES

FOURTH EDITION

PENGUIN BOOKS

PENGUIN BOOKS

Published by the Penguin Group
Penguin Books Ltd, 27 Wrights Lane, London W8 5TZ, England
Penguin Books USA Inc., 375 Hudson Street, New York, New York 10014, USA
Penguin Books Australia Ltd, Ringwood, Victoria, Australia
Penguin Books Canada Ltd, 10 Alcorn Avenue, Toronto, Ontario, Canada M4V 3B2
Penguin Books (NZ) Ltd, 182–190 Wairau Road, Auckland 10, New Zealand

Penguin Books Ltd, Registered Offices: Harmondsworth, Middlesex, England

First published in Pelican Books 1954
Published with enlarged bibliography 1959
Second edition published 1961
Published with revisions 1964
Third edition published 1967
Published with revisions 1968, 1970
Fourth edition published 1986
Reprinted in Penguin Books 1991

3 5 7 9 10 8 6 4 2

Printed in England by Clays Ltd, St Ives plc
Set in Monophoto Photina

CONTENTS

ACKNOWLEDGEMENTS

I WISH to thank the following authors (and publishers) for permission to quote from them: Louise Bogan and the Noonday Press (New York), for 'Several Voices out of a Cloud'; E. E. Cummings, *Collected Poems* (New York, Harcourt, Brace and Company); Eyre and Spottiswoode, *Selected Poems* of John Crowe Ransom and *Poems 1920–1945* of Allen Tate; Faber and Faber, *Collected Poems* of Marianne Moore and *Selected Poems* of Wallace Stevens; Princeton University Press, *The Political Works of Edward Taylor*, edited by Thomas H. Johnson, copyright 1939, Rocklands Editions, copyright 1943, Princeton U.P.; and William Carlos Williams and New Directions (Norfolk, Conn.), for 'The Red Wheelbarrow' and others. I am indebted in other ways to scores of people – students, colleagues, scholars, friends, my former wife Mitzi. Most recently I would like to thank the George Washington University for a thoroughly congenial berth; Karen Greisman not only for typing the fourth edition but for doing much else to put it into shape – especially the index; and Phyllis Palmer for renewing one's faith in the American scene.

NOTE ON THE
FOURTH EDITION

THE FIRST edition of this book appeared in 1954. I was then teaching at Manchester University, which had introduced one of the earliest European programmes in American Studies. In those post-war years American literature was a relatively unfamiliar subject. Key works were often out of print or not stocked in academic libraries. Such handicaps were in a way a stimulus. There was a sense of pioneering. The dearth of material – text or monograph – encouraged one to conceive the subject in bold and simple outlines.

Even at that date they were probably too simple. In any case, everything has got more complicated during the last thirty years. Analytical and biographical commentary on American authors has grown enormously. Schools of criticism have come and gone, reputations have slid or climbed. There has been a disposition to revise or even deny conventional distinctions between 'good' and 'popular' writing, or between 'fiction' and 'fact'. And of course we have thirty additional years of American imaginative literature to reckon with – a large span of time in a history which, according to some people, only began to matter seriously in the 1840s, and which was of fairly minor interest to the rest of the world before about 1920.

At intervals I did revise the original text and bibliography. By degrees I found the patching process unsatisfactory. This fourth edition is almost a new book. Every chapter has been revised and extended. Extra chapters have been added, for example on women's and on Southern literature. The bibliography has been expanded and recast. The result is substantially longer and more up to date.

It is, however, still only a one-volume survey, obliged to cover the ground at a brisk pace. Some readers may as a result feel that the treatment of particular topics or authors is superficial. I have tried to avoid mere lists of names with one-sentence verdicts appended to each, and have been deliberately selective. Many good writers, especially of the last decade, are not even mentioned. The book, is, to repeat, a survey and not a biographical dictionary.

In one respect *The Literature of the United States* has not changed. It continues to blend biographical and socio-cultural information with stylistic and aesthetic observations. To a follower of certain current critical schools this may appear old-fashioned. Nor is any overall thesis proffered as a key to American literature. Such naïvety, if that is what it is, embodies an approach that I still find congenial. My reservations about a culturally based approach – that it tends to encourage an exaggerated emphasis on the unique or exceptional – have not fundamentally altered in the course of a generation. However, many people inside and outside the United States seem to agree as to the usefulness of a *comparative* emphasis, setting American literature alongside that of other societies.

My occasional recourse to comparison does supply a shape if not a thesis. Another frame is provided by the book's concern with what I have called the *people–public* conundrum: the recurrent American endeavour to reconcile culture and democracy, popular sovereignty and possibly unpopular literary modes. Such arguments appear unending, since they are both important and impossible to solve. (They are discussed, with reference to the nineteenth century, in Larzer Ziff, *Literary Democracy*, 1981.)

My book started out with a mainly British audience in mind. Over the years the actual readership broadened to embrace a number of countries, not least the United States. I now envisage the ideal reader as among three or four possible types. For the 'beginner' a sensible rule is to begin at the beginning of a book. If that does not seem to work, I recommend that he or she hop about, seeking an entry through some later chapter. The same method could also of course suit a well-informed reader, who may choose to sample chapters, or use the index in search of themes that run through several chapters. Whatever the in-between shade of knowledge and interest, *The Literature of the United States* does not have to be ingested from first to last. Chapters are on the whole self-contained. But there is no ban against reading in sequence from introduction to conclusion. A final small point. In common with many people I both like and dislike footnotes. Sometimes I have put them in, sometimes knocked them out. A scholar mentioned in the text but not footnoted can be tracked down in the bibliographical section at the back.

I

INTRODUCTION

━━━━━━━━━━

A HUNDRED years ago the Victorian poet-essayist Matthew Arnold pooh-poohed the view that there was any essential difference between English and American literature:

> I see advertised *The Primer of American Literature*. Imagine the face of Philip or Alexander at hearing of a Primer of Macedonian Literature! ... We are all contributories to one great literature – English literature.

A little later came a second British comment, from H. G. Wells (*A Modern Utopia*, 1905). Wells did not assume there were no national cultures. What he did was deplore the prevalence of nationalistic cultural claims:

> The idea of the fundamental nature of nationality is so ingrained in thought, with all the usual exaggeration of implication, that no one laughs at talk about Swedish painting or American literature.

In a saner world, apparently, people *would* laugh at such narrow or unfounded categories.

To the late twentieth century the issue may seem self-evidently settled. Perhaps there is still a question as to whether there is an American *language*. Whether there is an American *literature* is no longer in doubt. But for many decades after the War of Independence the matter was troublingly uncertain. Even before 1776 a goodish number of people were writing *in* the American colonies, and sometimes specifically *about* America, out of close knowledge and involvement. After the war they were Americans in a more precise sense: citizens of a nation whose new sovereignty was internationally recognized. When, though, would there be a genuine, fully fledged literature *of* America?

The almost slangy, debonair tone of Matthew Arnold infuriated certain Americans, Mark Twain among them. Yet a number of Americans were prepared to concede that in a way the Arnold or Wells attitudes might be correct. If language were the basic feature of a literature (as in ancient Greece and Rome, or in the parts of the modern world that spoke German or Italian, without necessarily corresponding to national boundaries or operating only within large nation-states), then whatever was written in English, wherever it was written, arguably belonged to 'English literature'.

Again, the United States was culturally an offshoot of Europe. The colonists were Europeans, together with the Africans or 'involuntary immigrants' brought in by the slave trade. White Americans were settlers, *colons* in the French term. Early artists who wished to depict the American continent symbolically did so by a rendering of some exotic native figure: perhaps an Indian princess with feathered garments and attendant alligators. But the symbolism was principally pictorial. The white American bore little kinship, actual or psychological, with the native inhabitant, whose enemy or at any rate supplanter he was. He appropriated a few useful nouns – *canoe, mocassin, pemmican, squash* – from Indian speech. Otherwise the colonists' main language was English. English was to continue to dominate: the United States became for most purposes a country of one language, unlike Canada or Belgium or Switzerland. British – or, more broadly, European – modes in every branch of literature and intellectual activity, and in music, art, and architecture, closely resembled those of the New World. Up to 1914 Europe usually set the patterns for the United States and for the rest of the world. Economically, America had an adverse balance of trade until the First World War, importing more than was exported. The same was true culturally.

Writing in America was therefore, in the estimation of a Matthew Arnold, subsumed within the 'one great literature – English literature'. To some degree that was also an international realm, not only because English speech covered the modern globe but because – the argument ran – great literature was necessarily universal in treatment. Homer, Virgil, Dante, Shakespeare, Cervantes transcended time and space. Genius carried no passport. Falstaff and Don Quixote were ageless. In the loftier reaches nationality or locality were supposedly almost immaterial. For the writer, talent and inspiration and purity of diction were the vital ingredients. Local, regional or national elements might add colour and flavour. But they were secondary, and likely to be prominent only in fiction – itself a brand of literature which many people in the eighteenth and nineteenth centuries regarded as secondary, in comparison with poetry, or with the elevation of thought and style characteristic of good theological, philosophical or historical discourse.

However, the Arnoldian contention was complacent, tending to applaud the nationalistic or parochial quality of things written by Englishmen (not omitting Shakespeare), while rebuking similar fervour in others. It showed little sympathy for the problems of non-English authors. The Scots, Welsh and Irish, unable for various reasons to confine themselves to their ancestral languages, might nevertheless feel confined by Englishness. John Dillon, a present-day scholar, speculates that a 'stimulus to linguistic exuberance' among the Irish may be 'the resolve to take the language of the British and do more with it than they can'. Yet 'praising an Irishman for his eloquence is like felicitating a black on his sense of rhythm. Eloquent we may be, but this eloquence was acquired at the price of our own language, and, to some extent, of our soul.'[1]

Australia, New Zealand and Canada are even more relevant to the American case. They too were offshoots of Europe, and in pioneer days even more subordinated to British modes, social as well as cultural. They too were white settler societies, proud of their rough-and-ready fraternalism, yet intermittently ashamed of their provincialism. They too, with the partial exception of New Zealand, were mainly hostile or indifferent to the aboriginal inhabitants. The Australian bandit Ned Kelly became a national folk-hero, akin to the American Billy the Kid, or to Jesse James. American true-life fiction, inelegant and authentic, such as Edgar W. Howe's *Story of a Country Town* (1883) or the early novels of Theodore Dreiser, found an Australian counterpart in the touching detail of Joseph Furphy's *Such is Life* (1902).

Similarly, Canadians say their country has historically felt uncomfortable with every other heritage or analogue, whether from Britain or France or from the big brother to the south. To Margaret Atwood, *survival* is the central theme of Canadian literature, just as *frontier* is a prime geographic metaphor for the United States, and *island* for England. *Survival* is the forlorn, minimal response of immigrants to a monotonous landscape in which winter is the 'real' season. European literature, says Atwood, is rich in images of *sex*, that of the United States in *killing*; whereas Canadian writing, a 'bush garden', is preoccupied with *being dead*.[2] Atwood cites a Canadian poet who speaks of the country as 'America's attic', and a

1. John Dillon, 'Antaeus and Hercules', in Leonard Michaels and Christopher Ricks, eds., *The State of the Language* (Berkeley, U of California P, 1980), 555.

2. Margaret Atwood, *Survival: A Thematic Guide to Canadian Literature* (Toronto, House of Anansi Press, 1972); and see *The Bush Garden: Essays on the Canadian Imagination* (Toronto, Anansi, 1971) by Northrop Frye. He has borrowed the vivid term 'bush garden' from Atwood – herself perhaps Canada's principal imaginative writer.

literary scholar who feels that 'no other country cares enough about us to give us back an image of ourselves that we can even resist'.

These comparisons remind us of the chronology of cultural evolution. Isolation, inwardness, self-criticism, the search for a usable past and for unifying symbols, the lure of expatriation for a young country's liveliest talent: these have been painful stages in the emergence of an American literature now widely known and respected. Bygone generations of Americans have passed along the same trails that other anglophone (or francophone) societies must later follow. A second point is that, in relation to Canada or the antipodes, the United States has enjoyed certain half-accidental advantages.

Both points are illustrated by the recurrent habit of enumerating the things left out of American life. The most famous of such lists occurs in Henry James's graceful evaluation of a predecessor. In his little biography *Nathaniel Hawthorne* (1879), James describes 'the items of high civilization as it exists in other countries, which are absent from the texture of American life, until it should become a wonder to know what was left':

No State, in the European sense of the word, and indeed barely a specific national name. No sovereign, no court, no personal loyalty, no aristocracy, no church, no clergy, no army, no diplomatic service, no country gentlemen, no palaces, no castles, nor manors . . . ; no great literature, no novels, no museums, no pictures, no political society, no sporting class – no Epsom or Ascot! . . . .

James is talking here of the America of about 1840, but he does not seem to believe any prodigious change took place during the next generation. He mentions too the preface to Hawthorne's *Marble Faun* (1860), also well known to students, which dwells upon the difficulty of concocting a romance 'about a country where there is no shadow, no antiquity, no mystery'. James Fenimore Cooper anticipates Henry James and Hawthorne with a similar 'no' catalogue (*Notions of the Americans*, 1828) to explain the recalcitrance of American material for the aspiring author:

There are no annals for the historian; no follies (beyond the most vulgar and commonplace) for the satirist; no manners for the dramatist; no obscure fictions for the writer of romance; no gross . . . offences against decorum for the moralist; nor any of the rich artificial auxiliaries of poetry.

Cooper in turn was preceded by Hector St John de Crèvecœur. In the celebrated essay 'What is an American?' (*Letters from an American Farmer*, 1782), Crèvecœur declares:

Here are no aristocratical families, no courts, no kings, no bishops, ... no great manufacturers employing thousands, no great refinements of luxury.

The annals of American literature contain other such lists. A final imaginary example comes from Edward Bellamy's *Looking Backward* (1888), a tale set in the America of AD 2000. The hero is introduced to '*Penthesilia*', a novel by the foremost author of this future time. He is greatly impressed, above all that 'not so much was in the book as what was left out of it':

The story-writers of my day would have deemed the making of bricks without straw a light task compared with the construction of a romance from which should be excluded all effects drawn from the contrast of wealth and poverty, education and ignorance, coarseness and refinement, high and low, all motives drawn from social pride ..., the desire of being richer or the fear of being poorer, together with sordid anxieties of any sort. ...

The usual list-assumptions assert that America is a social paradise – 'born in broad daylight', in Tocqueville's phrase – but that the novelist is left with rather thin material. Bellamy suggests that, on the contrary, unreformed nineteenth-century America displayed the same basic social iniquities as in Europe. As a result of the bloodless revolution imagined in *Looking Backward*, America actually becomes the classless paradise of previous legend. Since Bellamy is writing a Utopia, he insists that everything in AD 2000 is for the better, including the low-calorie, unsalted yet appetizing diet of new fiction.

Whatever the approach, these catalogues of exemption and renunciation convey a slightly chilly tedium. No wonder, we feel, that Henry James – comfortably installed in Queen Victoria's England – spoke of his subject as 'poor Hawthorne'. In fact they also acquired a tinge of self-pity. Challenged by Europeans, badgered by their own countrymen to produce the 'Great American Novel' that the nation's size, natural beauty and varied attainments seemed to specify, American writers, as the century wore on, resorted to excuses. There was, they said, no 'society' in any meaning of the word: hence a dearth of suitable material. American authors were neglected by the general public, which turned instead to imported literature, or read nothing at all. The absence of 'society' meant there was no patronage, public or private, to sustain native talent, whereas Europe abounded in royal pensions and snug sinecures.

So the excuses ran. The real circumstances were less grim. William

Charvat, the historian of American publishing, calculates that considerably more than half of American nineteenth-century authors were at one time or another in public employment. (The same can be said of artists, at least up to 1860: a sizeable number gained commissions to execute murals and sculptures for Congress and for state legislatures.) Several authors received senior diplomatic appointments (as ministers – the United States did not create ambassadorial rank until 1893). Among them were Washington Irving, George Bancroft, Edward Everett, John L. Motley, Bayard Taylor, James Russell Lowell, and the philologist George Perkins Marsh.[1] Consular posts, with less prestige yet a substantial revenue from official fees, were bestowed on a fair sprinkling of others. Hawthorne was appointed U.S. consul in Liverpool in 1853, after churning out a presidential campaign biography of the successful Democratic candidate, his old college classmate Franklin Pierce. He counted on the job to give him a surplus income that would permit years of future leisure. Other consular appointees included Hawthorne's editor friend John L. O'Sullivan, posted to Lisbon; Charles Edwards Lester, whose stay in Genoa furnished material for a torrent of books on European and American culture; Bret Harte (Glasgow and Krefeld, but domiciled in London); and William Dean Howells. Howells, having concocted a campaign biography of Abraham Lincoln in 1860, was rewarded with the Venice consulate, where he was able during the Civil War to begin a busy and prosperous career as cosmopolitan man of letters. In 1876 Howells obliged his fellow-Ohioan Rutherford B. Hayes with another presidential campaign biography, and was asked by the victorious Hayes administration whether he would like to be minister to Switzerland – an offer which he could by then refuse. Even the aloof Henry Adams indicated that he would consider a diplomatic position. The grandson and great-grandson of American presidents, Adams is said to have felt insulted when the only prospect dangled before him was to be U.S. minister in Guatemala City.

There were also internal and local appointments. It is customary to bewail the fate of Hawthorne, Herman Melville, Edwin Arlington Robinson and other American writers, eking out an existence as clerks in customhouses or, like Walt Whitman, drudging amid the federal bureaucracy in

1. Lecturing in the United States in 1852, the English novelist W. M. Thackeray praised the 'manly share in public life' of American men of letters, among whom he mentioned Irving, Bancroft and Everett (*Fraser's Magazine*, January 1853). See *The Profession of Authorship in America, 1800–1870: The Papers of William Charvat*, ed. Matthew J. Bruccoli (Columbus, Ohio State UP, 1968).

Washington D.C.[1] The most salient point is that such subsidies existed at all, in a land reputedly indifferent to the arts.

The exaggeration of the plight of the American author suggests a prolonged and complicated set of resentments, against Europe and against the homeland. Some of these grievances had to do with the greater fame and brio of civilization in Europe. The American visual or literary artist, in patriotic moments, proclaimed that the Old World was corrupt, snobbish and fettered by tradition. In Whitman's words:

> Come Muse migrate from Greece and Ionia,
> Cross out please those immensely overpaid accounts....

But it was difficult to sustain the pretended contrast between innovative America and outmoded Europe when, throughout the nineteenth century, the world's cultural avant-garde was stationed across the Atlantic. Almost every new development in style and genre was European in origin, including some of the very experiments which in theory ought to have been initiated in the land of liberty. The use of homely vernacular speech, for example, was pioneered in Scotland by Robert Burns. The lives of ordinary humble folk were chronicled in novels such as Walter Scott's *Heart of Midlothian* and in the poetry of William Wordsworth. George Bancroft's 'Office of the People in Art, Government and Religion' (1835) was a paean of praise for democracy. His actual instances of democratic literature, however, were all European. The patriotic Bancroft could not, or did not, cite a single American literary example of the new popular, non-aristocratic spirit.

Why was this? A possible explanation is that America was a classless society, or rather a society of one class, the middle. It therefore lacked either of the artistically picturesque if socially deplorable extremes, an aristocracy or a peasantry. In Cooper's words: 'I have never seen a nation so much alike ... as the people of the United States, and what is more, they are not only like each other, but ... remarkably like that which common sense tells them they ought to resemble.' Historians have amassed contrary evidence in order to show that classlessness is an American myth; that Afro-Americans and poor immigrants, not to mention native-born 'poor whites', constituted a sizeable underclass; and that it took many decades for American literature to concede the bias of a cultural

1. Another such figure is Lewis Gaylord Clark (1808–73), the long-time editor of New York's *Knickerbocker Magazine*, who in later days found the New York custom-house a snug harbour.

fable built around the native-born free male – the 'WASP' or White Anglo-Saxon Protestant.[1]

By definition, however, a myth is something widely believed, and therefore able to influence a community. The *idea* of middle-classness as the American norm fitted into the nation's democratic ideology, merging with both actual and imputed traditions of Puritan austerity. The democratic imperative encouraged American writers to portray their society in ideally simplified tableaux – virtuous toil reaping just rewards. It is clear that not all of them were as happy as George Bancroft with the constant emphasis upon democratic betterment, and the rosy view of human (or at any rate, American) nature which this entailed. Classlessness modulated into middle-classness, yes; but middle-classness was sometimes equated with *mediocrity*. The word *mediocre*, as employed by James Fenimore Cooper, was neutral; but it took on an unfavourable meaning: classlessness as worthlessness. Middle-classness also connoted conventionality or, in the worst guise, prurient conformism. The New York literatus Lewis Gaylord Clark is said to have been so ultra-refined that 'he wrote the name of a famous Dutch city thus: Rotterd—m'. Knut Hamsun, the Norwegian novelist who visited the United States in the 1880s, was acidly amused by the country's prudishness:

you do not find a single word of honest-to-goodness profanity even among the greatest American writers. . . . In every Yankee novel there is a villainous blackguard; now when this villain is called upon to swear, he expresses the word *hell* as *h* with a dash, the word *damned* as *d* with a dash. . . . Nor does American literature know anything about sex. . . . If by chance the old Adam comes out in fictional character, he appears in the . . . sugar-coated sensuality of a glance or a kiss, never as an overwhelming force . . .; Boston's vise is clamped around his neck. While American newspapers are flooded . . . . with stories of crime and rape, serious literature is almost forbidden to display a naked chair leg.[2]

Present-day American fiction might seem to have progressed, or rather regressed, from the tamely juvenile to the nastily 'adult', outdoing the newspapers in lurid explicitness. But the change was still almost undetectable in 1911, when the Spanish-American philosopher George Santayana presented his famous interpretation of the nation's 'genteel tradition'. He

1. These topics are explored in ch. 14 and to some extent in ch. 11 below.
2. L. G. Clark anecdote in Perry Miller, *The Raven and the Whale* (New York, Harcourt, Brace, 1956), 260; Knut Hamsun, *The Cultural Life of Modern America*, ed. and trans. Barbara G. Morgridge (Cambridge, MA, Harvard UP, 1969), 39.

saw a split between 'Will' and 'Intellect'. The former signified bustling modernism, the latter decorous conservatism:

This division may be found symbolised in American architecture: a neat reproduction of the colonial mansion – with some modern comforts introduced surreptitiously – stands beside the skyscraper. The American Will inhabits the skyscraper; the American Intellect inhabits the colonial mansion. The one is the sphere of the American man; the other, at least predominantly, of the American woman. The one is all aggressive enterprise; the other is all genteel tradition.[1]

The distinction, within the literary sphere, is more or less between what the twentieth-century critic Philip Rahv called 'redskin' and 'paleface' modes. It can be and has been disparagingly said that America has alternated between mindlessness and bodilessness, between the plethoric and the anaemic. Santayana, for instance, increasingly depressed in his Harvard milieu by what he considered New England's and America's cultural sterility, brushed aside the literature of New England Transcendentalism as 'a harvest of leaves' – something peculiarly dry, fruitless, and even idiotic.

Even by 1880, it is true, an exceptionally sympathetic and well-read European could have been aware of the diverse talent revealed in Poe, Emerson, Thoreau, Hawthorne, Melville and Whitman, not to mention the more prominent 'genteel tradition' contributions of Washington Irving, Oliver Wendell Holmes and Henry Wadsworth Longfellow. But one should not be too hard on a Matthew Arnold or an H. G. Wells: Americans themselves were slow to spot the authentic native utterance they quested and requested.

Nevertheless – to come back to the comparison with other ex-colonial literatures – the United States has in the long run derived great benefits from its special situation. From the negative view, it represented, like other settler societies, the periphery, the outer edges of civilization, as against the metropolitan glamour of the 'centres': London, Paris, Rome, Madrid. Being provinces, they were provincial. Worse still, some European *philosophes* developed the theory that the American continent represented a lower stage of evolution than that of Europe: for climatic and other environmental reasons, American fauna and flora (and human beings, aboriginal and – eventually – immigrant) were, it was alleged, comparatively weak and unattractive. There were in this deprived hemisphere no indigenous horses, sheep, or cattle, and very few songbirds.

1. Given as a lecture at Berkeley, CA; first published in Santayana's *Winds of Doctrine* (1913).

A powerful contrary view, however, saw the New World as magical, hopeful and delightful. Its tomatoes were recommended as aphrodisiac 'love-apples'. Its tobacco, while a noxious weed to some, became an indispensable solace to millions. Its potatoes and maize were to provide nourishment for people all over the globe. The 'noble savage' as a symbol of simple dignity was contrasted with the effete city-dweller – and located in the New World by Christopher Columbus. George Berkeley, an Irish-born Anglican bishop, dreamed of establishing a perfect college, in what could certainly have been a paradisial campus – Bermuda. In the 1720s, to support his project, Berkeley wrote a poem whose opening line ('Westward the course of Empire takes its way') became almost a cliché of optimistic prophecy. Berkeley's line was for example stamped on the cover of the first volume of Bancroft's immense *History of the United States*, which came out in 1834. There were other semi-providential assumptions, that the discovery of America had been left until a late stage of history in order to fulfil some grand purpose of the Almighty. Australasia never quite acquired such mythic glamour.

In this positive version the American continent was not peripheral but progressive. The backwoods were not backward, the provinces were merely biding their time and already nurtured the seeds of the future. The New World must necessarily supersede the Old. Such a vision was gratifying and stimulating for those in civilization's hinterlands. They could hug to themselves the consolation of their final destiny. Speaking of 'poor Hawthorne', Henry James said: 'one might enumerate the items of high civilization, as it exists in other countries, which are absent from ... American life, until it should become a wonder to know what was left.' James concluded:

The natural remark, in the almost lurid light of such an indictment, would be that if these things are left out, everything is left out. The American knows that a good deal remains; what it is that remains – that is his secret, his joke, as one may say.

Much of New World humour was built upon special ironies of this nature: the difference between American universalism and European pomposity, the discrepancy between the glorious 'frontier' of rhetoric and the frequent squalor of the actual Western scene – between America as the ultimate and America as the 'end' in the sense of *Endsville*. Such dualisms ('*paleface*' and '*redskin*', and so on) were indeed fundamental to American literature as a whole. Archetypes emerged: America as an innocent, not the 'old Adam' but an Adamic beginner full of wonderment, confronting experience; the hero as a wanderer, unsettled rather than a settler, on the way, on the road, a stranger, perhaps an orphan, the victim or beneficiary of amnesia, promised a destiny but with no specific destination. Often the setting is a journey; American fiction is concerned to plot the indefinite stages, after departure and before arrival. Often, as a result, the tale carries a poignant sense of something lost, or abandoned, or forgotten. What is still to happen remains problematic.

The literature of the United States fell heir to a mass of dualistic speculation and mythology. Originally this referred to the entire continent; in fact the first legends to reach the Old World were of the central and southern parts of the hemisphere. Most of the peoples of America have gone through more or less the same historical sequence: 'discovery', settler–Indian conflict and accommodation, slave-importation, colonial revolt, national independence, westward settlement, domestic strife or wars with neighbours, large-scale immigration, urbanization, industrial-ization. In several parts of the hemisphere, vividly distinct types appeared. The empty spaces of the *pampa*, with their nomadic native tribes, were evoked by the Argentine poet Esteban Echeverría (for example in 'The Captive', 1837). Another Argentine writer, Domingo Sarmiento, described (in *Facundo*, 1845) such frontiersmen as the *rastreador*, *baqueano* and *gaucho* – pathfinders, trappers, cowboys, outlaws. The *gaucho* was to be celebrated in the Argentine epic poem *Martín Fierro* (1872).

Nevertheless the United States annexed the New World's stock of legend, just as it took the name 'America' to itself – the part for the whole. Hispanic America, from Argentina to Mexico, was culturally overshadowed by the United States, as was Canada.

This is not a straightforward matter of cultural imperialism arising from economic power. The pervasiveness of the English language no doubt counts for a good deal. There were in the nineteenth century more people around the world familiar with English than with Spanish. Sarmiento himself seems to have grasped the literary potential of the *pampa* as a result of reading Cooper's *Last of the Mohicans* and *The Prairie*. Sarmiento also refers to Echeverría as a creator of New World themes. But Echeverría, who in any case wrote in Spanish, was a sophisticated intellectual who had lived in Paris. The myth aspects of the American hemisphere were to some extent created by European demand. Those expressed in English had a considerable advantage over Spanish or Portuguese. And in the nineteenth century the United States became a setting more symbolically satisfying than any other part of the continent. Canada was still attached to the British Crown. Brazil was an empire until the 1880s. The Argentina of which Sarmiento eventually became president had, in common with most Latin American countries, suffered from dictatorships. Only the United States appeared to present a clear, bold story of democratic-republican individuality.

Such was the curious, almost unlooked-for, consequence of a literary culture based on colonial and provincial factors. From the early days of white settlement, bad as well as good qualities were attributed to America. The legacy was equivocal. But in becoming independent the United States, by a sort of claimed primogeniture, emerged as the principal inheritor. In European eyes the native Americans often appeared as Calibans – uncouth savages. White settlers, too, often seemed uncouth: provincial nobodies. Little by little interpretation grew more thoughtful and more kind. The American as literary subject became more real *and* more mythic. He enlarged from nobody to everyman, from nonentity to universality.

In the late twentieth century the myth-advantage may be passing from the United States to other literatures – including, perhaps by some complex law of compensation, those of other American nations to north and south. Most of the chapters that follow, however, retrace the emergence of a literature *of* the United States: a development which took a long time. The 'American' quality was more easily discernible in fiction and drama than in poetry or expository prose. Because of that, novels and short stories have been made to bear the main interpretative burden. Generalizations about American literature, or even sometimes about the nation's whole ethos, tend to be glosses upon a group of fictional works.

Whether that is an adequate sample can be considered in later chapters. For the moment it is enough to note that, despite wrangling between schools of criticism, we can find broad bands of interpretative consensus. The following assertions have been common in American literary history (how far they are true is another matter):

American literature is 'different' or 'unique' (the difference usually measured as difference from the literature of England).

A major mark of 'difference' is the American conception of the novel as a 'romance'. According to this theory (propounded, for example, by Lionel Trilling and Richard Chase), English novels deal essentially with social conventions, while the most interesting achievements of American fiction lie not in realism, but (beginning perhaps with Charles Brockden Brown, and continuing with Poe, Hawthorne and Melville), in peculiarly abstract forms of 'romance'.

American literature often embodies rival sets of values. The title of Leo Marx's *The*

Machine in the Garden: Technology and the Pastoral Ideal in America (1964) indicates one such polarity. R. W. B. Lewis, *The American Adam* (1955), sees American authors as committed to a debate between the 'party of hope' (innocence) and the 'party of memory' (tragic pessimism), with a mediating third force, the 'party of irony', that refuses to opt for either extreme.

American literature is rich in symbols and codes, whether or not the artist fully realizes what is being attempted. These patterns exist in all literary forms, from Puritan theology to the complex poetry of Wallace Stevens and the esoteric fiction of Thomas Pynchon. An analysis of this sort is found in Charles S. Feidelson Jr., *Symbolism and American Literature* (1953). Another is in Richard Poirier, *A World Elsewhere: The Place of Style in American Literature* (1966), according to which major American writers have – far more than British ones – been preoccupied with metaphors of building, or 'structures' of mind and language.

A final, regional element deserves a preliminary mention. Leslie Fiedler has suggested there are four main types of American fiction – Westerns, Northerns, Easterns and Southerns – each corresponding symbolically to a geographic locale. The 'Western' exists as the name of a well-defined genre. It may have come into being through the popularity of Owen Wister's *The Virginian* (1902), which he dedicated to his friend and Harvard classmate President Theodore Roosevelt. The idea of the West as prototypically American goes back even further than Bishop Berkeley. The notion of a 'Southern' is also not hard to imagine; we have only to think, say, of a novel by William Faulkner that is set in Mississippi, or of some of the fiction of Eudora Welty or Robert Penn Warren. 'Northerns' and 'Easterns' are more conjectural, though ingeniously categorized by Fiedler. A 'Northern' is an urban story, an 'Eastern' at bottom an American copy of a European book.

However we define West, North and East, these regions still fit within the expected frame of 'American'. What of the 'Southern'? The old slaveholding South disagreed with the North, in 1860–65, to the extent of seceding from the Union and trying to win recognition as a separate nation. Has the South been in the past so far at odds with the rest of the country as to constitute an *un*-American society? If so, caution is called for in generalizing about the whole United States. Was the South in some respects 'European'? Did the 'Southern' reflect such an affinity or demonstrate other non-American attitudes? For discussion see chapter 13, 'Southland'.

II

COLONIAL AMERICA

WILLIAM BRADFORD (1590–1657)

Born in Yorkshire, England, into a fervently Puritan family and neighbourhood. Converted to Separatist principles in adolescence, he crossed to the Netherlands in 1609 with a band of associates. They remained in Holland (mostly in Leiden) until 1620, when the 'Pilgrim Fathers' sought the New World, reaching the mainland at a place they called Plymouth. Bradford soon became the first governor of 'Plymouth Plantation' and was re-elected annually for the best part of thirty years. He began writing his *History* in 1630, and completed his tale in 1650.

ANNE BRADSTREET (1612–72)

Born in the English Midlands, daughter of Thomas Dudley, a competent and well-placed man who was later governor of the Massachusetts Bay Colony. Married at sixteen to Simon Bradstreet (another subsequent governor of Massachusetts), she emigrated in 1630 with her parents and her husband. The Bradstreets lived in Ipswich ('Agawam') and then in Andover. Anne bore eight children. Managing a large household, she also found time to write poetry and meditative prose. A volume of her verse (*The Tenth Muse Lately Sprung Up in America*) was published in London in 1650, apparently without her consent.

EDWARD TAYLOR (1645–1729)

Born near Coventry in England, of a nonconformist family. Taylor's religious views excluded him from the possibility of ordination into the Church of England. He therefore came to Boston and entered Harvard College. On graduation (1671) he was appointed minister and physician to the frontier settlement of Westfield, Massachusetts, serving there for half a century. His poetry (mostly in 'God's Determinations' and 'Preparatory Meditations') remained in manuscript and was bequeathed to Taylor's grandson, Ezra Stiles, subsequently a president of Yale.

COTTON MATHER (1663–1728)

Born in Boston, Massachusetts, the son of Increase Mather (1639–1723), and grandson of Richard Mather (1596–1669) and John Cotton (1584–1652). He was thus by birth a member of the Bay Colony's ministerial and intellectual élite. Cleric, historian, scientist, polymath, a Fellow of the Royal Society, Mather was prodigiously learned, and the author of some five hundred publications. Among the best-known are *The Wonders of the Invisible World* (1693), an account of the Salem witchcraft trials; *Magnalia Christi Americana* (1702); *Bonifacius* (1710; usually known as *Essays to do Good*); *The Christian Philosopher* (1721); *An Account ... of Inoculating the Small-Pox* (1722); and *Manuductio ad Ministerium* (1726). Three times married, with thirteen children, Mather was both prominent and unpopular in his latter years. His father Increase lost the presidency of Harvard College. Enemies of the opinionated Mather dynasty made sure that Cotton was not allowed to inherit the Harvard appointment.

WILLIAM BYRD (1674–1744)

Born in Westover, Virginia, a James River plantation not far from the city of Richmond, which he himself laid out. He spent long periods in England, where he received his education, became a Fellow of the Royal Society, and was proud to claim acquaintance with various men of rank. His *History of the Dividing Line* was a travel journal (also now known in a different version, *The Secret History*) describing the adventures of a surveying party in 1728. He kept other shorthand journals and diaries. The *Secret Diary* has been published for the years 1709–12, 1717–21 and 1739–41. He held important offices in Virginia, embellished Westover, and when he died there owned nearly 180,000 acres of Southern land. Byrd was the cousin of Robert Beverley (c. 1673–1722), author of *The History and Present State of Virginia* (1705).

JONATHAN EDWARDS (1703–58)

Born in East Windsor, Connecticut, educated at Yale, and almost as precociously diverse as Cotton Mather. He remained at Yale, having graduated at sixteen, for further years of theological study. In 1726 he joined his grandfather, Solomon Stoddard, as Congregational pastor in Northampton, Massachusetts. After Stoddard's death (1729), Edwards had sole charge, and in a series of powerful sermons and treatises pleaded for the revival of religious fervour which actually took shape in the 'Great Awakening'. His strict zeal eventually displeased the Northampton parishioners. Dismissed by them (1750), he spent the next few years as missionary and pastor in the remote village of Stockbridge, and there wrote his great Calvinistic *Freedom of Will* (1754). In the last months of his life Edwards became president of the College of New Jersey (Princeton).

BENJAMIN FRANKLIN (1706–90)

Born in Boston, the tenth and youngest son of a soap-maker. Scantily educated, he was a printing apprentice at twelve to his brother James. Quarrelling with James, he ran away to Philadelphia (1723), sought work as a printer in London, returned to Philadelphia, and there (1728) set up his own printing business, which flourished, in conjunction with Franklin's activity in publishing the *Pennsylvania Gazette*, the annual *Poor Richard's Almanack* (1732–57), and many other pieces, together with involvement in civic affairs and in scientific experiments. He was in England (1757–62, 1763–75) as colonial agent; a member of the Continental Congress and postmaster-general (1776); a diplomat in Paris (1776–85); and a delegate to the Constitutional Convention of 1787. He wrote his (incomplete) *Autobiography* in intervals of relative leisure, beginning in 1771.

WILLIAM BARTRAM (1739–1823)

Born in Philadelphia, the son of the Quaker botanist–explorer John Bartram (1699–1777). The elder Bartram created the gardens outside Philadelphia described in Crèvecœur's *Letters from an American Farmer*. Botanist by appointment to George II and George III, he collected specimens for and corresponded with European naturalists, writing two books of travels, the *Observations* on a journey from Pennsylvania to Lake Ontario (1751), and *Description of East Florida* (1769). The son, William, continued these activities. His own principal work was *Travels through North and South Carolina, Georgia, East and West Florida* (1791), undertaken in 1776–8.

HECTOR ST JOHN CRÈVECŒUR (1735–1813)

Born in France, a gentleman of Normandy who served in French Canada as an officer under Montcalm, was wounded in the battle for Quebec (1759), and soon after entered the American colonies. He travelled widely, eventually settling with his American wife, Mehetable Tippet, on a farm in Orange County, New York. During the Revolution he left his farm and his wife, returning to France via London, where he left the manuscript of *Letters from an American Farmer*. These were published in London (1782), in English, and subsequently in Paris (*Lettres d'un cultivateur américain*, 1784, 1787) in a somewhat modified version. Crèvecœur was back in the United States as French consul, 1783–90, but then settled once more in France. Some early travels in western Pennsylvania and New York also appeared in French (1801). Other essays remained in manuscript until 1925 (*Sketches of Eighteenth-century America*).

II

COLONIAL AMERICA

———

ONE and three-quarter centuries in time, though only twenty miles of Virginia space, separated Jamestown and Yorktown. At Jamestown, in 1607, the English made their first serious lodgement in North America. At Yorktown, just across the peninsula, in 1781, Cornwallis's encircled army marched out to surrender to the Franco-American army commanded by George Washington, with the fife music of 'The World Turned Upside Down' sounding in their ears. It was not the end of British influence in America. Too much had been done that nothing could undo; in language, institutions and ways of thought the thirteen English colonies along the Atlantic fringe of the continent were bound to exhibit some of the characteristics of what Nathaniel Hawthorne, seventy years after Independence, still described as *Our Old Home*.

Nevertheless the colonists shared experiences that set them apart from England and Europe. They had to adapt themselves to unfamiliar climates and crops; to deal with the Indians; to chart and survey, clear and plant, and build and improvise. By the end of the colonial period conditions were less strange and more comfortable. Some floors, figurative and literal, were carpeted, where once the settlers had trodden on earth or clattered on bare boards. Yet in the first precarious years life was stark. William Bradford outlines the plight of the Pilgrim Fathers, landing at Plymouth Rock in 1620:

Being thus passed the vast ocean, and a sea of troubles before in their preparation ..., they had now no friends to welcome them, no inns to entertain or refresh their weatherbeaten bodies, no houses or much less towns to repair to, to seek for succour .... Besides, what could they see but a hideous and desolate wilderness, full of wild beasts and wild men? and what multitudes there might be of them they knew not. Neither could they, as it were, go up to the top of Pisgah, to view from this wilderness a more goodly country to feed their hopes; for which way soever they turned their eyes (save upward to the heavens) they could have little solace or content in respect to any outward objects. For summer being done, all things stand upon them with a weatherbeaten face....

In such circumstances, the early colonists could find little leisure for either the reading or the writing of polite literature. William Penn's advice to prospective emigrants in 1685 was: 'Be moderate in Expectation, count on Labour Before a Crop, and Cost before Gain.' His words apply to most of the colonial period, as far as literature is concerned. America produced no writer who merits comparison with Milton, Dryden, Pope, Swift, Sterne, Fielding – or with Bunyan and Jeremy Taylor, if we are to name men whose chief preoccupation was religion. Nor, in colonial times, did America expect to.

> Here first the duties of to-day, the lessons of the concrete,
> Wealth, order, travel, shelter, products, plenty....

the lines are Whitman's, from his 'The United States to Old World Critics'. But before the American Revolution there were no strictures from Old World critics, and no United States. There were only isolated colonies, on the edge of a wilderness, busily consolidating and extending their gains. They were not without cultivation, especially in New England, where what became Harvard College was founded as early as 1636,[1] with a printing press set up near by in 1639.[2] But on the whole the New World was content to accept the literary products of the Old, when it had time for them and if they seemed suitable. Though books were among the cargo of almost every ship from Europe, standards of taste were at first fairly austere in most colonial communities.

In the case of New England, the word 'Puritanism' has been used to sum up such standards. To some degree during the nineteenth century, 'Puritanism' was a rebuke. Historians such as George Bancroft, for example, and novelists including Hawthorne were not sure how to account for the Salem witchcraft trials of the 1690s in any enthusiastic interpretation of proto-'American' or 'democratic' behaviour. In the early twentieth century, Van Wyck Brooks began a long career as a literary critic by announcing (*The Wine of the Puritans*, 1908) that colonial New England, with its bleak religiosity and incipient commercialism, laid a curse upon literature and the arts from which America was still suffering. The

---

1. Other foundation dates for American colleges are: 1693, William and Mary (Williamsburg, Virginia); 1701, Yale (New Haven, Connecticut); 1746, Princeton (New Jersey); 1751, Pennsylvania (Philadelphia); 1754, Columbia (New York) and Dartmouth (Hanover, New Hampshire); 1764, Brown (Providence, Rhode Island).

2. No further presses were established in the colonies until the 1690s, when Philadelphia and New York had each acquired one. There were five presses in Boston by 1715.

Puritans, according to the familiar accusations of the 1920s, were joyless hypocrites. H. L. Mencken and other critics[1] relished such jokes as:

When the Pilgrim Fathers landed, they fell upon their knees – and then upon the aborigines.

They derived much amusement from the Puritan's scrutiny of God's purposes: as, for example, the speculations of John Winthrop (1588–1649) on the mice in his son's library, which nibbled away the Anglican prayer book but touched nothing else. They liked to jeer at colonial 'blue laws' (not noting that these were in large part the fabrication of the hostile Anglican minister Samuel Peters, in 1781). From the absence of the novel or the play in colonial New England and the sparseness of Puritan poetry, they concluded that American literature had been wellnigh throttled at birth.

Since the 1920s there has been a closer, more sympathetic examination of Puritan life and thought, led by the Harvard scholars Samuel Eliot Morison, Perry Miller, and Kenneth Murdock. It has been shown that, considering their difficult origins, the New England settlements produced a surprising quantity of literature (if – as we ought to do – we take literature to embrace theology, history and chronicles, private journals, and the like). Jonathan Edwards in particular has been put forward as an author of great intellectual distinction. The anti-Puritan attack was recklessly overstated. There is now a tendency to err in the opposite direction. The earlier onslaught involved the 'debunking' of ancestors *as* ancestors. Yet there may be an element of ancestor-worship in the high praise meted out to colonial literature, especially that of New England. American literary historians, in quest of the 'usable past' of Van Wyck Brooks's phrase, have naturally pushed the pedigree of their literature as far back as possible, and insisted on its integrity. They have also been concerned to establish the existence of a Puritan tradition. Their reinterpretation of colonial writing has been necessary; and the best scholars in the field have been careful not to make exaggerated claims. Historically speaking, colonial writing is of absorbing value. To assess its value *as literature* is more problematic.

In saying this, one is not denying the praiseworthy qualities of the Puritan mind (to leave out for the moment the colonies south of New

1. Writing in their magazine, the *American Mercury*, in 1925, Mencken and his friend George Jean Nathan defined Puritanism as 'the haunting fear that someone, somewhere, may be happy'.

England): courage, earnestness, sense of purpose, intellectual energy, and (*pace* Brooks and Mencken) robustness and even sprightliness. Nor is one asserting that there is no Puritan tradition: New England had a distinctive moral and social order whose influence spread over much of the United States. This was the 'Universal Yankee Nation' (a phrase first coined in the 1820s, in a political context) to which the Connecticut showman P. T. Barnum dedicated his memoirs (1855). But for *imaginative writers* the tradition, after the Revolution and until the twentieth century, seems not to have been a strong *positive* force. Apart from Hawthorne, and to a lesser extent Harriet Beecher Stowe, J. G. Whittier, and perhaps J. R. Lowell, which of the chief authors of the nineteenth century was deeply stirred by it? When he was past sixty Longfellow admitted he had not read Jonathan Edwards, though he meant to, and Longfellow, a professor of modern languages, was a cultivated man. In common with most of his contemporaries, he was more drawn to the literature of bygone Europe than to that of his own region. Again, it is perhaps both a cause and an effect of the tradition's discontinuity that several pieces of colonial writing had to wait so long to be brought out in print. The elder John Winthrop's *Journal* was not published until 1790, and not in complete form (as *The History of New England*) until 1825–6. The *History of Plymouth Plantation* by William Bradford, the manuscript of which disappeared during the Revolution – to reappear in England, in the library of the Bishop of London – was not printed in full until 1856. The journal of Sarah Kemble Knight (1666–1727) did not reach the public until 1829, nor the diary of Samuel Sewall (1652–1730) until 1878–82. The poems of Edward Taylor remained in manuscript until a number were printed in 1937. (Similar delays in the discovery and publication of work from the middle and southern colonies, as we shall see, affected understanding of the literary heritage of those regions.)

As for the qualities of New England writing, the Puritan atmosphere was discouraging to imaginative literature. The statement must not be made too strongly, for within a century of the first settlements the Puritan disciplines were a good deal relaxed. Moreover, in the colonies outside New England, where no strict theocracies had been set up, there was little evidence of a freer kind of literature – or indeed any kind of literature – until the end of the seventeenth century. But in New England itself, the first generations in the Calvinistic townships of Massachusetts and Connecticut wrote almost nothing for mere amusement. They regarded themselves as God's agents, sent under his 'wonder-working providence' to make homes for his chosen and to convert (or annihilate) the Indians – 'those miserable Salvages' whom, Cotton Mather concluded, 'probably the Devil decoy'd ... hither, in hopes that the Gospel of the Lord Jesus Christ would never come here to destroy or disturb his Absolute Empire over them'. They took for guides the Bible and their own consciences.

The early literature that emerged from such a God-centred world was heavily weighted, in subject and style, by religious considerations. The best writing was held to be that which best brought home to the average church members a full awareness of their perilous, probationary status on earth. As the Puritans condemned the images and incense of the Roman Church, so in literature they distrusted the highly coloured. A plain style was commended, without unnecessary ornament and without allusions that might pass over the heads of the unlettered. New England authors did not always confine themselves to their own roles. Look, for instance, at Nathaniel Ward's *The Simple Cobbler of Aggawam* (1647). Here is an extract from the part of this lively pamphlet which is devoted to women's fashions:

But when I hear a nugiperous gentledame inquire what dress the Queen is in this week, what the nudiustertian fashion of the court ... I look at her as the very gizzard of a trifle, the product of the quarter of a cipher, the epitome of nothing, fitter to be kicked, if she were of a kickable substance, than either honored or humored.

Or observe the endless classical references in *Magnalia Christi Americana* (1702), the compendium of ecclesiastical history written by Cotton Mather. Yet these are unusual cases. Nathaniel Ward (*c.* 1578–1652) did not emigrate to Massachusetts until he was in his fifties. And while classical references were indulged in by some Puritan scholars (together with such literary devices as the anagram[1]), Cotton Mather – who confessed to his diary[2] that 'proud thoughts fly-blow my best performances' – exhibits a special brand of pedantry, unrivalled in the colonies even by his learned father Increase Mather (1639–1723).

Otherwise, in general, New England writers relied upon the Bible. Not only did they clinch their arguments with biblical chapter and verse; they saw their whole situation in scriptural analogies, with themselves as the Jews and their enemies as the enemies of the Jews:

1. For instance: Thomas Dudley
                                  ah! old, must dye

an anagram of *c.* 1645 reprinted in H. S. Jantz, ed., *The First Century of New England Verse* (Worcester, MA, 1944), 34.

2. Cotton Mather's *Diary* was first published in 1911–12.

Accordingly when the *Noble Design* of carrying a Colony of *Chosen People* into an *American Wilderness*, was by *some* Eminent Persons undertaken, *This* Eminent Person was, by the Consent of all, *Chosen* for the *Moses*, who must be the Leader of so great an Undertaking. . . .

It seemed natural to Cotton Mather to refer thus to John Winthrop. The Bible furnished him and his contemporaries with images and illustrations to suit every occasion. It was their source-book, as, in a minor degree, the catalogues of Chippendale and his fellow-craftsmen in England subsequently provided designs for colonial cabinet-makers. In most ways it was an ennobling influence, which lent its great resonance to otherwise tame discourse. It has left its mark, for example, on the sturdy prose of William Bradford, whose *History* is one of the finest colonial works. Some scriptural allusions were exotic and mysterious, some homely or sharply pointed and therefore utilized by Tom Paine in his pamphlet *Common Sense* (1776). Some supplied names of people and places (*Salem* was an old name for Jerusalem; *Canaan* was the Promised Land between the Jordan and the Mediterranean). But in other ways Bible-reading may have limited writing, blurring and deadening the pages. Its superb phrases came too easily into the author's consciousness, and their formidable respectability ensured that they were used and used until they had weakened into cliché.

Perhaps the dominance of the King James Bible also helped to widen the chronological gulf between colonial and English literature. C. V. Wedgwood has suggested[1] that the language of the Authorized Version was already a century out of date when this Bible was published in 1611. New England authors, though often erudite men, were certainly not always acquainted with the work of English contemporaries. Taste, and hence style, were archaic. Edward Taylor, the best poet of colonial America, wrote metaphysical verse after its vogue had passed in England. Milton and Marvell reached few New England readers in their own lifetimes. The poems of Edmund Waller were not introduced into America (by Dr Benjamin Colman of Boston) until 1699, when Waller had been dead for twelve years. Increase Mather, the president of Harvard, seems not to have known the plays of Shakespeare and Ben Jonson, nor, more surprisingly, to have been familiar with *The Pilgrim's Progress* of John Bunyan.[2] Many years after their heyday at home, Addison and Steele were still carefully

1. *Seventeenth-century English Literature* (Oxford, 1950), 16.
2. See Thomas J. Wertenbaker, *The First Americans, 1607–90* (New York, 1927), 240–41. But Benjamin Franklin (1706–90), who spent his boyhood in Boston, tells in the *Autobiography* of his early enthusiasm for Bunyan's works, which were available in small, inexpensive editions.

imitated in America; and as Americans turned to political controversy in the second half of the eighteenth century, their reading of such seventeenth- and early eighteenth-century authors as Algernon Sidney, James Harrington, John Locke, Milton, Bacon, John Trenchard and Thomas Gordon may likewise have had some effect in anachronizing style.

Another factor which affected and circumscribed Puritan writing was the conviction that all events, however small, are contrived by God, or else the Devil. Sometimes a moving passage results, from the spectacle of strength in adversity, or from the serenity of the righteous – as in this charming excerpt from a pamphlet by Samuel Sewall, in which he meditates on the Book of Revelation, with special reference to Newburyport:

As long as . . . any Salmon, or Sturgeon shall swim in the streams of Merrimack; . . . as long as the Sea-Fowl shall know the time of their coming, and not neglect seasonably to visit the places of their acquaintance; as long as any Cattle shall be fed with the grass growing in the meadows, which do humbly bow down themselves before Turkey-Hill; . . . as long as any free and harmless Dove shall find a White Oak, or other tree within the Township, to perch, or feed, or build a nest upon; . . . as long as Nature shall not grow old and dote; but shall constantly remember to give the rows of Indian corn their education, by pairs: so long shall Christians be born there; and being first made meet, shall from thence be Translated, to be made partakers of the Inheritance of the Saints in Light.

Sewall, whose *Diary* is one of the most fascinating pieces of Puritan literature, clearly shows his love of place and of growing things; and the suggestion that Newburyport is only a halfway stage seems a merely conventional one. But in much other New England writing, especially of the seventeenth century, we are continually reminded of Winthrop's mice, or of Cotton Mather's decision, on losing the manuscript of some lectures, that 'Spectres, or Agents in the invisible World, were the Robbers'. The fascination with *typology* (the contrasting of Old Testament 'types' with their supposed New Testament 'antitypes') generated a literary–scholastic set of allusions of considerable intricacy. Human motive, on the other hand, is rarely analysed except in basic terms. Genuine emotion peeps through, often to be squeezed back by some orthodox piety. Thus, Anne Bradstreet, grieving for her dead child, writes:

> By nature trees do rot when they are grown
> And plums and apples thoroughly ripe do fall,
> And corn and grass are in their season mown,

> And time brings down what is both strong and tall.
> But plants new set to be eradicate,
> And buds new blown, to have so short a date,
> Is by his hand alone that guides nature and fate.

The last line is intolerably lame, all the more so after the two deeply felt lines that precede it. Similarly, Urian Oakes (c. 1631–81) touches a nerve of agony in these lines of his laborious 'Elegy upon the Death of the Reverend Mr Thomas' (1677):

> My dearest, inmost, bosom-friend is gone!
> Gone is my sweet companion, soul's delight!
> Now in an huddling crowd I'm all alone,
> And almost could bid all the world goodnight –

only to flatten their appeal by adding:

> Blest be my rock! God lives: oh let Him be,
> As He is, so all in all to me.

Again, Mary Rowlandson (c. 1635–c. 1678), a minister's wife captured by Indians in 1676, describes her experiences with dignity and simplicity, but includes in her narrative a tortuous analysis of God's purpose in allowing the Indians to accomplish a massacre.

Even in the form of allegory, fiction had no place in New England. Except for hymnody and the ballad, the *writing* of poetry was understandably held subordinate to religious purposes, such as private meditation. The *reading* of poetry, especially after 1700, was recommended within limits, perhaps as an aid to classical scholarship, or as a relaxation after serious study. Such a concession is offered by Cotton Mather in his *Manuductio* (1726), a handbook for divinity students. 'Be not so set upon poetry', he warned them, 'as to be always poring on the passionate pages. Let not what should be sauce, rather than food for you, engross all your application. Beware of a boundless appetite for the reading of the poems which now the rickety nation swarms withal....' There were dangers too of moral corruption, even more from poetry than from other forms: 'the powers of darkness have a library among us.' Among pestilential authors Mather mentioned 'Butler', presumably the English poet Samuel Butler, of *Hudibras* fame. For good measure, Mather adds: 'Most of the modern plays, as well as the romances, and novels and fictions, which are a sort of poems, do belong to the catalogue of this cursed library.' As for writing poetry, only two Puritan poets, Anne Bradstreet and Edward Taylor, have a major claim to notice; with Michael Wigglesworth (1631–1705) as a possible third because of his relative success during his own day. Wigglesworth gives a thorough demonstration of Calvinist doctrine in his lengthy *Day of Doom* (1662). The most notorious stanza of *The Day of Doom* is the one in which God settles the fate of those who, dying in infancy, 'never had good or bad effected pers'nally':

> A crime it is, therefore in bliss
> you may not hope to dwell;
> But unto you I shall allow
> the easiest room in Hell.
> The glorious King thus answering,
> they cease, and plead no longer:
> Their Consciences must needs confess
> his Reasons are the stronger.

These lines have been given undue prominence by anti-Puritan commentators. By and large, Wigglesworth's discussion is calmly reasonable in tone. Nevertheless, as poetry neither *The Day of Doom* nor any of his other theological verse treatises rises far above doggerel.

Anne Bradstreet is much more interesting, for her prose *Meditations* as well as for her poetry, which was published first in London (1650), as *The Tenth Muse Lately Sprung Up in America*. She thus anticipated the first English woman poet – Kathleen Philips, the 'Matchless Orinda' – by a year. Her achievement, as the mother of a family in early colonial America, was possibly even more remarkable than Orinda's – especially if one remembers John Winthrop's story of the young wife of a Puritan dignitary who, in 1645,

was fallen into a sad infirmity, the loss of her understanding and reason, which had been growing upon her divers years, by occasion of her giving herself wholly to reading and writing, and had written many books.... For if she had attended her household affairs, and such things as belong to women ... she had kept her wits.

More verse by Anne Bradstreet was published in 1678, posthumously; still more work, in prose as well as verse, remained unpublished until 1867. She was a woman of exceptional learning and sensibility, who had paid close attention to the poetic canon of her day. She produced highly competent groups of *Quaternions* – poems dealing with 'The Four Seasons', 'The Four Elements', 'The Four Monarchies' and so on. She moralized effectively, for example in 'The Flesh and the Spirit', a dialogue between two sisters:

> One Flesh was call'd, who had her eye

> On wordly wealth and vanity;
> The other Spirit, who did rear
> Her thoughts unto a higher sphere....

Anne Bradstreet was herself spiritedly spiritual. Her seemingly meek confession that 'Men can do best, and women know it well', and her apologies for her 'foolish, broken, blemish'd Muse', were accompanied by some mischievously witty remarks:

> I am obnoxious to each carping tongue
> Who says my hand a needle better fits,
> A poet's pen all scorn I should thus wrong,
> For such despite they cast on Female wits:
> If what I do prove well, it won't advance,
> They'l say it's stoln, or else it was by chance.

At the end of 'The Flesh and the Spirit' the high-minded sister declares:

> If I of Heaven may have my fill,
> Take thou the world, and all that will.

Yet, in other poems, she spoke of her own domestic world – husband, children, household – with tender and touching attachment.

A more dazzling talent, though unknown to the world until 1937, is that of Edward Taylor, who came to America in his twenties. He was probably by then already a devotee of English metaphysical poetry. No doubt, in the long isolation of his Massachusetts frontier community, he continued to ponder the example of Vaughan, Herbert and Crashaw. However, the only volume of poetry in English listed in Taylor's library was by Anne Bradstreet. Taylor was first and foremost a scholar–theologian. But – a paradox of Puritanism – this endowed him with a grammarian's gusto, a taste for elaborate rhetorical devices, some of them, such as the habit of repetition or 'amplification', well suited to versifying. His Harvard graduation poem of 1671 included the following scholastically whimsical lines:

> Here lies a Metonymy; there doth sculke
> An Irony; here underneath this bulke
> A Metaphore; Synecdoche doth reare
> And open publickly Shopwindows here.

The main mass of Taylor's manuscript verse consisted of some two hundred *Preparatory Meditations*, on the church's supreme sacrament, the communion or Lord's Supper; and, more polemical and militant, the verse statements of *Gods Determinations Touching His Elect*. Taylor also left some sermons, a long *Metrical History* of the Church, and a handful of more personal poems. One of them deals with the death of two of his children. He comforts himself that they have gone to heaven: 'I piecemeale pass to glory bright in them.'

The elaborated, inward, idiosyncrasy of Taylor's marvellous imperfect poetry prefigures Emily Dickinson, a New Englander of a later time who likewise held private communion:

> Thus in the usual coach of God's decree
> They bowl and swim
> To glory bright, if no hypocrisy
> Handed them in.

and

> Who would
> Wash with his blood my blots out? Crown his shell
> Or dress his golden cupboard with such ware?

Somehow Taylor, like Dickinson, is not cramped by environment. Conceding that such things are mere 'wits wantonings', nevertheless he revels in a catalogue of wonders (from *Meditation Fifty-Six, Second Series,* 1703):

> The clock of Strasburg, Dresden's table-sight,
> Regsamont's fly of steel about that flew,
> Turrian's wooden sparrows in a flight,
> And th'artificial man Aquinas slew,
> Mark Scaliota's lock and key and chain
> Drawn by a flea, in our Queen Betty's reign....

This is awkward poetry, but it has passages of magnificent imagery:

> Who laced and filleted the earth so fine
> With rivers like green ribbons smaragdine?
> Who made the seas its selvedge, and it locks
> Like a quilt ball within a silver box?
> Who spread its canopy? Or curtains spun?
> Who in this bowling alley bowled the sun?[1]

No other Puritan writer in America displayed such verbal riches; Cotton Mather, who himself wrote verse on occasion, probably came nearest. But

---

1. From the preface to *Gods Determinations Touching His Elect*.

if the bulk of New England writing was ponderous, it was rarely trivial. Even where its authors are lost in the intricacies of a sermon or of a historical chronicle, they are never altogether lost. William Stoughton (1631–1701) of Massachusetts declared that: 'God hath sifted a nation that he might send choice grain into this wilderness.' A like conviction pervades the writing of the seventeenth and early eighteenth centuries. In his *Phaenomena Quaedam Apocalyptica* (1697), Samuel Sewall predicts that New England will be the site of the New Jerusalem. The preacher grapples with his text, wasting no effort in wooing the audience; the chronicler sets down every detail, believing all to be of ultimate significance. This fixity of purpose is a chief strength of Puritan writing, and does much to redeem the stretches of crabbed or even absurd material in such works as Cotton Mather's *Magnalia*:

I write the wonders of the Christian religion, flying from the deprivations of Europe, to the American strand. . . .

A decisive battle is in progress; God watches for the outcome, and all posterity will speak of it. For as Mather (with a welcome touch of humour) says of the struggle with the Indians that went on from 1688 to 1698,

the author pretends that the famous history of the Trojan War itself comes behind our little history of the Indian War; for the best antiquaries have now confuted Homer; the walls of Troy were, it seems, all made of poet's paper; and the siege of the town, with the tragedies of the wooden horse, were all but a piece of poetry. And if a war between us and a handful of Indians do appear no more than a *Batrachomyomachia*[1] to the world abroad, yet unto us at home it hath been considerable enough to make an history.

Secularized, the Puritan attitude to the New World becomes the belief in futurity which has already been mentioned. The other side of Puritan thought – belief in what Thomas Hooker of Connecticut (1586–1647) called 'the unconceavable hainousness of the hellish nature of sin' – has had a weaker hold over the American mind, though its after-effects are still apparent in Hawthorne.

Indeed, its hold was slackening in New England by the early eighteenth century. The skull-and-crossbones crudely carved on the first tombstones was replaced by a winged cherub, and then even by attempts at portraiture. Jonathan Edwards, a theologian who belonged to a younger generation than Cotton Mather, struggled tremendously with himself and with his

1. 'Battle of the Frogs and Mice': an early Greek burlesque of Homer.

Northampton congregation to keep alive the grand, hopeful–hopeless tenor of ancestral thought. Yet the response he evoked was a little more hectic and a little less profound. A powerful revivalist, whose best-known work is a scarifying sermon, 'Sinners in the Hands of an Angry God' (1741), Edwards was also something of a philosopher on the eighteenth-century model, whose delight in nature has a pantheistic tinge:

God's excellency ... seemed to appear in every thing; in the sun, moon and stars; in the clouds, and blue sky; in the grass, flowers, trees; in the water, and all nature ... I often used to sit and view the moon for continuance; and in the day, spent much time in viewing the clouds and sky, to behold the sweet glory of God in these things....[1]

Though his *Freedom of Will* (1754)[2] might be regarded as a harsh document, the *Two Dissertations* (1765) of his last years breathe benevolence and gentleness.

Edwards may have had the most encompassing intellect in colonial New England. The Great Awakening that his preaching helped to stimulate seems almost an anachronism: could he truly believe, in the eighteenth century, that God was so fiercely and intimately concerned in the warfare with Satan? The typological schemes that Edwards, like Taylor, cherished could also be regarded as in a sense old-fashioned. Taylor, for example, had taken Christ to be the antitype of Adam, Moses and half a dozen other Old Testament figures. Edwards perceived types and symbols everywhere: 'almost everything ... that we have recorded in Scripture from Adam to Christ, was typical of Gospel things ... indeed the world was a typical world. And this is God's manner to make inferior things shadows of ... the most excellent; outward things shadows of spiritual....' Yet, as Ursula Brumm has shown, Edwards's millennial faith looked forwards as well as back. He extended typology, so that the New World of a potentially glorious future became the visionary antitype of the cruel Old World.

Mather and Edwards were prolific authors, from their precocious childhoods to their last days. They led busy, public lives, but these were the outcome of intense private communings. Introspection, and with it the habit of keeping a diary, was a common Puritan trait. From John Winthrop's *Journal* (maintained from 1630 to 1649) to *The Education of Henry*

1. *Personal Narrative* (c. 1740).
2. This was the book that led Boswell to say, 'The only relief I had was to forget it' – and Dr Johnson to pronounce that 'All theory is against the freedom of the will, all experience for it.' See Paul E. More, *Selected Shelburne Essays* (Oxford World's Classics, 1935), 250–51.

Adams (1907, privately printed), such records have been impressive features of New England literature, whether or not intended for publication. Samuel Sewall's journal has been mentioned. Different in tone, and highly diverting, is the brief journal of a trip made from Boston to New York and back, in 1704–5, by the forty-year-old widow Sarah Kemble Knight. To read her narrative is to pass into another world than that inhabited by the Winthrops and the Mathers:

Being at a merchant's house, in comes a tall country fellow...; he advanced to the middle of the room, makes an awkward nod, and spitting a large deal of aromatick tincture, he gave a scrape with his shovel-like shoe, leaving a small shovel full of dirt on the floor, made a full stop, hugging his pretty body with his hands under his arms, [and] stood staring round him, like a cat let out of a basket.

This is the tone of the eighteenth century in New England, relaxed and semi-secular, and marking the transition from Puritan to Yankee. We catch it again, more refined, in the cheerful accents of the Tory Minister Mather Byles (1707–88), Cotton Mather's nephew, whose lines[1] might serve as an epitaph of his uncle's regime:

> An hundred Journies now the Earth has run,
> In annual Circles, round the central Sun,
> Since the first ship the unpolish'd Letters bore
> Thro' the wide Ocean to the barb'rous Shore....
> Solid, and grave, and plain the Country stood,
> Inelegant, and rigorously good.

In more wryly apologetic form are lines by Richard Lewis, a schoolmaster–poet in Maryland, dedicated to Governor Calvert. Calvert had apparently described to him the culture and beauty of Italy. Maryland, Lewis lamented, was a different matter:

> While *Here*; rough Woods embrown the Hills and Plains,
> Mean are the *Buildings*, artless are the *Swains*....

Outside New England, a comparable urbanity could thus be found, along with a sometimes ribald, rural roughness, as in the satirical verse of *The Sot-Weed Factor*, printed in London in 1708: 'Sot-Weed' is tobacco. The author, Ebenezer Cook (*c.* 1672–1730), wrote scornfully of life in Maryland. Perhaps an Englishman, perhaps a Marylander, Cook was to furnish the theme of John Barth's *The Sot-Weed Factor* (1960), a clever

1. From 'To Pictorio, On the Sight of his Pictures' (1744).

pastiche of a picaresque novel featuring 'Ebenezer Cooke [sic], Gentleman, Poet and Laureate of the Province.' The real Cook, it must be said, does not appear to have enjoyed 'this Inhospitable Shoar':

> May Wrath Divine then lay these Regions waste
> Where no man's Faithful, or a Woman chaste.

In Pennsylvania, it is true, William Penn (1644–1718) wrote in the cool, charitable vein of the Quaker faith, while the colonies to the South were not without religious testimony. But by the mid eighteenth century the Quaker city of Philadelphia was beginning to represent commerce and the arts with some vigour; and, there or elsewhere, the New England combination of church, school, and town-meeting had never had an exact counterpart. In the Anglican colony of Virginia the secular tone is apparent in Robert Beverley's good-natured *History and Present State of Virginia* (1705), and – strikingly – in the pages of William Byrd of Westover. Byrd, a wealthy planter educated in England and resident there for long periods, had a home which was by colonial standards a mansion, with a library of 4,000 books (twice as many as Cotton Mather) and portraits of the English nobility hanging on his walls. He wrote various sprightly accounts of Virginia which remained in manuscript until 1841, when they were published. He also kept a shorthand diary, whose parts waited another hundred years for publication. Byrd has been described as an 'American Pepys' (nearly all American writers once had some such identification tag attached to them, often to their annoyance); and one thinks also of Boswell. The *Secret Diary* of Byrd, like Boswell's *London Journal*, reveals a man who is by turns shrewd and ingenuous. Certainly Byrd could not be taken for a Puritan; this is how he speaks of the first Virginia settlements, in his *History of the Dividing Line* (c. 1729):

From Kiquotan they extended themselves as far as James-Town, where like true Englishmen, they built a Church that cost no more than Fifty Pounds and a Tavern that cost Five Hundred.

And here is Byrd visiting some neighbours, in 1732:

I was carried into a room elegantly set off with pier glasses. . . . A brace of tame deer ran familiarly about the house, and one of them came to stare at me as a stranger. But unluckily spying his own figure in the glass, he made a spring over the tea table that stood under it and shattered the glass to pieces, and falling back upon the tea table, made a terrible fracas among the china. This exploit . . . surprised me, and perfectly frightened Mrs Spotswood.[1] But 'twas worth all the damage to show the moderation and good humour with which she bore this disaster.

By contrast, let us look at another domestic mishap that took place in Boston ninety years earlier, as described in John Winthrop's *Journal*:

A godly woman ..., dwelling sometime in London, brought with her a parcel of very fine linen of great value, which she set her heart too much upon, and had been at charge to have it all newly washed, and curiously folded and pressed, and so left it in press in her parlour over night. She had a negro maid went into the room very late, and let fall some snuff of the candle upon the linen, so as by the morning all the linen was burned to tinder.... But it pleased God that the loss of this linen did her much good, both in taking her heart from worldly comforts, and in preparing her for a far greater affliction by the untimely death of her husband, who was slain not long after at Isle of Providence.

This is in part a difference between Puritan Massachusetts and planter Virginia; but it is also the distance between one century and another. By the eve of the Revolution the colonies were established beyond possibility of failure. Daniel Boone had mounted the Pisgah of the Appalachians, and beheld thence the country of Kentucky. Samuel Mather, the last of the Mather dynasty, who died in 1785, was (to use a later idiom) a fourth-generation American. There were gentry and fine houses, though not many; there was litigation and slavery; there were several worthy colleges, and a quantity of schools. In Boston and Philadelphia, New York and Charleston (and in New Orleans, a French and now a Spanish city, not to join the United States until 1803), urban life brought urban refinements: newspapers and periodicals, libraries, clubs and societies, concerts, theatrical performances.[2] Urbanity could be a feature too of smaller towns, such as Annapolis, Maryland, where Dr Alexander Hamilton's 'Tuesday Club' held the meetings (1745–56) which he burlesqued in a fictionalized 'History'.

Colonial literature might henceforth develop in modest conjunction with that of the mother country: for there was little to distinguish it, seemingly, from that of England. It was clumsier; it lacked the excitement of a great metropolis; a few of its words were novel; some Indian names had crept among the scriptural and classical references. But its models were English – 'godlike Addison', 'thrice happy Dryden', and (above all)

1. The wife of Alexander Spotswood, governor of Virginia (1710–22).

2. Though in Boston, even at the end of the eighteenth century, performances had to be disguised as 'moral lectures'.

'heav'nly Pope'.[1] The colonial, one might say, had become the provincial;
in men like William Byrd and Mather Byles there was evident the typical
provincial yearning for London and all its glories. But since they were
still Englishmen, there was no need to apologize for their transatlantic
enthusiasms – until the Revolution set them under a new flag, making
them Americans.

In the years after the Seven Years War (or French and Indian War),
with Great Britain triumphant over the ancient Catholic and Bourbon
monarchy of France, the colonies had seemed securely set upon a modestly
prosperous evolution. The most famous American, Benjamin Franklin,
was to make a new reputation in Paris during the War of Independence,
as the first American minister. Plainly garbed, genial and unaffected, he
was taken as 'le bon Quaker' because he came from Pennsylvania, and as
the embodiment of the idea that the world's salvation might come from
the backwoods. In fact, of course, Franklin had spent nearly all his life in
cities: Boston, Philadelphia, London. A good part of his mature years had
passed contentedly in London, where he had served as a colonial agent.
In Britain he could count Adam Smith, Lord Kames, David Hume and
Edmund Burke among his friends. He was of the new age heralded by
writers such as Daniel Defoe: an age of commerce and common sense,
when deserving and ingenious persons might make their mark in, say,
journalism or publishing or the practical arts and sciences, as if they were
Defoe's hero Robinson Crusoe, creating an ordered, comfortable existence
out of the material to hand. Franklin achieved success in all these fields,
to a degree that has made D. H. Lawrence, and other critics, suspicious of
him. Lawrence disliked the prudential, calculating aspect of Franklin, as
evidenced in 'The Way to Wealth' (1758) and the aphorisms of his 'Poor
Richard' almanacs.

Possibly Franklin's literary gifts have indeed been overpraised by some
admirers. His maxims were as often as not – he himself never denied it –
adapted from other sources. The prose of his *Autobiography*, while plain
and effective, and at times engagingly humorous, is not an entire novelty.
In New England the almanacs of Nathaniel Ward preceded 'Poor Richard'.
From the mother country Franklin had the literary examples of Bunyan,
Swift, the *Spectator* and so on. But then, he did not present himself as a
man of letters. He was too busy with other things, and it was the

1. Although he was a vehemently patriotic American, the poet Joel Barlow, travelling in
Europe in 1788, made a pilgrimage to Pope's Twickenham home, to pay homage to a master.
James Woodress, *A Yankee's Odyssey* (Philadelphia, 1958), 99.

astonishing range of his activities which made him appear so exemplary an Anglo-American. William Byrd might have been a little lucky to be made a Fellow of the Royal Society: no one doubted that Benjamin Franklin merited the F. R. S. Until controversy became sharp he seemed as much a citizen of the Empire as an Irishman such as Burke, a Scotsman such as Hume, his half-American friend Benjamin Vaughan, or the English Unitarian clergyman–chemist Joseph Priestley. These men were all a little peripheral. They did not belong to the inner circles of power and elegance. But they were not negligible and did not feel so, although their brands of humour tended towards riposte, coded complaint, and even surrealist farce, as in William Byrd's *Secret History* account of his travels with 'Firebrand' and 'Meanwell' – an account which offers an ironic counterpart to the events recorded in his *Dividing Line*:

This being my Birth day, I adored the Goodness of Heaven, for having indulged me with so much Health and very uncommon happiness, in the Course of 54 years in which my Sins have been many, and my Sufferings few, my Opportunitys great, but my Improvements small. Firebrand and Meanwell had very high Words, after I went to Bed. . . , in which Conversation Meanwell show'd most Spirit, and Firebrand most arrogance and Ill Nature.

No doubt it amused Franklin to conceal his 'deep worldly wisdom and polished Italian tact ... under an air of Arcadian unaffectedness' – as Melville wrote of him,[1] or rather of the likeness between him and the patriarch Jacob. In this respect Franklin can be regarded as an early example of the American humorist. For there is an American 'joke' (to which Henry James referred) which derives its flavour from the blend of sophistication and savagery in American life. The European is more fascinated by America's primitive aspects, and if the American mythology contains a good deal of toughness and roughness, it may arguably have been put there by Europeans.[2] The American joke is to play up to the

1. *Israel Potter* (1855).

2. When her American friend Charles Eliot Norton sent some photographs of native scenery to the English novelist Elizabeth Gaskell, she told him disappointedly that she 'thought America would have been odder and more original; the underwood and tangle is just like England'. She had got a more satisfactory idea from a painting done by another Englishwoman, 'in some wild luxuriant terrific part of Virginia? in a gorge full of rich rank tropical vegetation – her husband keeping watch over her with loaded pistols because of the alligators infesting the stream. – Well! that picture did look like my idea of America' (1860). *Letters of Mrs Gaskell and Charles Eliot Norton* (Oxford, 1932), 51–2. Her friend, Barbara Leigh Smith, was married to a French physician, Dr Bodichon. Barbara Leigh Smith Bodichon, *An American Diary, 1857–8*, ed. Joseph W. Reed Jr. (London, 1972). The description was actually of Louisiana.

European (and Eastern) legend of the West. So the frontiersman spoke of himself as 'this chile' in deference to Rousseau's vision of the child of nature; so Buffalo Bill wrote dime novels about his own adventures; so, probably, Chicago gangsters enjoyed gangster movies; and so, to return to Franklin, this 'didactically waggish' man assured English readers that it was grand to see whales leap like salmon up the falls of Niagara.

The Philadelphia Quaker and botanist William Bartram (1739–1823) likewise wrote of America as Europeans liked to hear of it. 'Impelled by a restless spirit of curiosity, in pursuit of new productions of nature', and in order to look at Indian customs, Bartram made a lengthy journey into the South. His account was published in 1791, with the full title of *Travels through North and South Carolina, Georgia, East and West Florida, the Cherokee Country, the Extensive Territories of the Muscogulges, or Creek Confederacy, and the Country of the Chactaws.* Though Bartram's journey was undertaken during the Revolutionary War, there is no mention of the conflict. He seems immune, in a paradise almost empty of white men. The book conjures up a strange remote world, lush in vegetation and teeming with wild-life. The human inhabitants of this world converse in the tones of Rousseau: one settler

who was reclining on a bear-skin, spread under the shade of a Live Oak, smoking his pipe, rose and saluted me: 'Welcome, stranger; *I am indulging in the rational dictates of nature*, taking a little rest, having just come in from the chace and fishing.'[1]

Such passages alternate enchantingly with lists of plants and precise descriptions of new species. Unlike many travellers, Bartram makes light of personal discomforts; after a sleepless night spent alone in a swamp, surrounded by terrifying reptiles and tormented by mosquitoes, he greets the dawn with a brisk exclamation of relief, and pursues his investigations with the utmost good humour. How prosaic, and yet how magical, are such paragraphs as this:

... we should be ready to conclude all to be a visionary scene, were it not for the sparkling ponds and lakes, which ... gleam through the open forests, before us and on every side. ... And at last the imagination remains flattered and dubious, by their uniformity, being most circular or elliptical, and almost surrounded with expansive green meadows; and always a picturesque dark grove of live oak, magnolia, gordonia, and the fragrant orange, encircling a rocky shaded grotto of transparent water, on some border of the pond or lake; which, without the aid of any poetic fable, one

1. Italics mine.

48 THE LITERATURE OF THE UNITED STATES

might naturally suppose to be the sacred abode or temporary residence of the guardian spirit; but it is actually the possession and retreat of a thundering absolute crocodile.

The charm of a yeoman's middle landscape, embedded in the middle colony of Pennsylvania, was rendered with artful artlessness in Crèvecœur's *Letters from an American Farmer* (1782). Crèvecœur's narrator is presented as a simple, untravelled farmer of British stock, supposedly writing to a sophisticated English gentleman of his acquaintance. Only towards the end of the chronicles of rural life does the threat of revolutionary war impend, and only in a description of a brutal slave episode in South Carolina is there any serious blemish upon the American scene. The sturdy whalers of Nantucket (many of them Quakers); the botanizing Bartrams, son William and father John (also Quaker); the industrious Scottish immigrant, rewarded by acquiring his own farm: these and others form a composite 'new man', an American who is said by Crèvecœur to be fused, perhaps from several European stocks, in the abundance of Nature in America. Crèvecœur's New World is rural, bucolic, diligent, and peaceable. The immigrants are absorbed without difficulty. A favourable environment, since 'men are like plants', ensures full growth. It may promote too rank a growth among certain species (lawyers, religious zealots). But in general 'this great field of opportunity' produces the ideal, a land of landowners – the hopeful vision of a mild, diminutive (five-foot nothing) French gentleman, writing in the apparent calm of the early 1770s, and dedicating his idyll to a Paris *philosophe*, the Abbé Raynal.

There were indications of an evolving autonomy, such as the increasing use of the term 'American' to signify rather more than a mere geographical collectivity. Protests against excessive attachment to the British royal family were voiced in a swingeing Boston sermon by Jonathan Mayhew (1750), and in a pamphlet (1764) by the Boston lawyer James Otis. The bulk of formal literary comment, however, was as polite as polite could be. Francis Hopkinson, later a prominent lawyer and signatory of the Declaration of Independence, composed an almost sycophantic poetic 'exercise', performed at the 1762 commencement of the College of Philadelphia to salute the accession of George III:

> Bright ascending in the Skies
> See Britannia's Glory rise!

– – – –

Another George majestic fills the Throne,
And glad Britannia calls him all her own.

In this context Britannia's 'wide Domain' obviously takes in North America.

Nevertheless, on the eve of the Revolution – which was not generally foreseen – Americans were some way towards being a different people. In the northern colonies, for example, the promotional efforts of the Anglican church met with strenuous resistance. Among the resisters in New York were William Livingston and a couple of friends who in the 1750s made their views felt through a polemical journal known as *The Independent Reflector*. *The Reflector* was closely modelled on the British *Independent Whig* of a generation earlier – in other words, outspoken in a gentlemanly, Whiggish way. There is a nice doubleness about the name of Livingston's venture. One might argue that a 'reflector' cannot be 'independent'. Such a quibble would not have troubled Livingston and his friends. They were as yet not revolutionary in spirit, and one of the three did in fact remain loyal to the British Crown. The matter of deciding how to make a colonial reflector independent of a British image is discussed in the next chapter.

III

PROMISES AND PROBLEMS
OF INDEPENDENCE

―――――

HUGH HENRY BRACKENRIDGE (1748–1816)

Born in Scotland, the son of a farmer who emigrated to America in 1753. Hugh, a precocious child in Pennsylvania, taught school in his teens and entered the College of New Jersey (Princeton) at twenty. A classmate of James Madison and Philip Freneau, Brackenridge joined with them in literary activities. At graduation (1771) he and Freneau collaborated on a long poem, 'The Rising Glory of America'. During the War of Independence he served (1776–8) as chaplain in the Continental Army, attempted to edit a literary magazine in Philadelphia (1779), turned from theology to law, and moved to Pittsburgh (1781) to practise as lawyer. Then and later, Brackenridge tried to be both an ardent democrat and an upholder of leadership by well-educated, seasoned citizens. As such, he had a complicated involvement in the 'Whisky Rebellion' of 1794. Prominent in the local councils of Jeffersonian party politics, he was made (1799) a justice of the Pennsylvania Supreme Court. After humiliating encounters with the electorate, he had begun a poem in Hudibrastic rhyme ('The Modern Chevalier', 1788–9), but abandoned this versified satire for a prose narrative, *Modern Chivalry*, which came out in several volumes, intermittently (1792, 1793, 1797, 1804–5, and in collected, somewhat revised form, 1815). In 1801 he moved to Carlisle, Pennsylvania, his residence when he died.

JOHN TRUMBULL (1750–1831)

(Not to be confused with the painter of the same name, a second cousin), he was born in Connecticut. Precociously erudite and articulate, he graduated at the age of seventeen from Yale, where he was associated with Timothy Dwight and David Humphreys in arguing for a curricular reform making way for the study of modern literature. His valedictory oration discussed the 'Uses and Advantages of the Fine Arts'. He spent several more years at Yale as a tutor, writing essays and poetry (such as *The Progress of Dulness*, 1772–3). After an apprenticeship with John Adams in Boston (1773), Trumbull spent the rest of his life as a lawyer in New Haven and Hartford. His main contribution to the Revolution was a long Hudibrastic poem, *M'Fingal* (first two cantos 1775–6, two more 1782), poking fun at Tory-Loyalist arguments. Thereafter, as a member of the Hartford or Connecticut Wits, Trumbull became increasingly sceptical of democratic theory and practice, collaborating with Dwight and others in satirizing the disorganization of post-war America (*The Anarchiad: A New England Poem*, 1786–7), and in sporadic Federalist attacks upon Jeffersonian democracy (*The Echo*: verse satire written 1791–1805, published in collected form 1807).

TIMOTHY DWIGHT (1752–1817)

Born in Northampton, Massachusetts, grandson of Jonathan Edwards. He entered Yale at thirteen, and tutored there 1771–7. Dwight served briefly as army chaplain and was Congregational minister (1783–95) at Greenfield Hill, Connecticut, when he became president of Yale, holding the office until his death. A staunch churchman and moralist, Dwight was also an accomplished poet (*The Conquest of Canaan*, 1785; *Greenfield Hill*, 1794; *The Triumph of Infidelity*, 1798).

PHILIP FRENEAU (1752–1832)

Born in New York, of Huguenot ancestry; a Princeton classmate of James Madison and H. H. Brackenridge. As a student and in the opening stages of the American Revolution Freneau revealed a remarkably fluent gift for satirical verse. For part of the war years Freneau lived in the West Indies as secretary to a planter. Returning to the United States in 1780, he was held for several weeks in a British prison ship, an experience which heightened his hostility to the mother country. In 1784–90 he spent most of his time on voyages as a ship's captain, while continuing to publish (*Poems*, 1786; *Miscellaneous Works*, 1788). During the 1790s Freneau was mainly occupied in journalism, including editorship (1791–3) of the Jefferson-inspired *National Gazette*. The *Gazette*'s attacks on the supposedly monarchical tendencies of George Washington's administration led the President to call him 'that rascal Freneau'. After 1800 he resided in New Jersey, producing more collections of verse and some prose.

JOEL BARLOW (1754–1812)

Born in Connecticut, the son of a farmer of modest means, Barlow graduated from Yale (1778) after initial schooling at Dartmouth. He was a classmate of Noah Webster and, like him, turned first to schoolmastering. But his passion was poetry, and he began to conceive an American epic (eventually published 1786, as *The Vision of Columbus*). A friend secured him a commission as army chaplain, a semi-sinecure that left leisure for writing. Barlow's opinions were conventional enough to qualify him as one of the Hartford Wits. His ideas changed dramatically after 1788, when he went to France and lived through the events of the French Revolution, a friend of Thomas Paine and honorary French citizen (see his *Advice to the Privileged Orders*, 1792, similar in tone to Paine's *Rights of Man*). He accumulated a sizeable fortune through shrewd business deals, and after 1795 served his country as consul in Algiers. His fairly contented years in exile are charmingly commemorated in his 'Hasty Pudding' poem (1796). Barlow returned to America in 1805, living in elegant semi-retirement on the Kalorama estate he had purchased in Washington, D.C. A revised version of *The Vision* was published (1807) as *The Columbiad*. Appointed U.S. minister to France in 1811, he died in Poland, where he had gone in the hope of meeting Napoleon, to arrange a peace treaty.

NOAH WEBSTER (1758–1843)

Born in West Hartford, Connecticut, of an old but impoverished family. He attended Yale (1774–8), and on graduation tried various means – teaching, the law, literature – of establishing himself. With the achievement of American independence, in 1782–3, Webster began to produce patriotic essays on America's future greatness. He argued that this involved defining and sustaining a common American language. His first modest publication of this nature (1783) soon became known as *The American Spelling Book*, or 'blue-back Speller'. It formed part of Webster's *Grammatical Institute of the English Language* (1789). He combined philology and lexicography with teaching, law practice and journalism. His opinions became steadily more Federalist-conservative. Webster's *Compendious Dictionary of the English Language* (1806) was a pioneering venture but hardly 'compendious' in comparison with his major *American Dictionary of the English Language* (completed 1825, published in 2 vols., 1828; enlarged 1840). At his death the copyright of 'Webster' was acquired by the Merriam Company.

WILLIAM DUNLAP (1766–1839)

Born in New Jersey, the son of an Irish-born British army officer who became a retail merchant and was a perhaps semi-reluctant Loyalist during the Revolution. Dunlap, amazingly versatile, began a career at sixteen as portrait painter. Much impressed by Royall Tyler's play *The Contrast* (1787), he wrote his own version of an American comedy, *The Father; or, American Shandyism* (1789). It was the first of some thirty original plays, and he adapted thirty-five more, most of them translations from French and German playwrights. Dunlap's most successful plays were the blank-verse tragedy *André* (1798) and *The Italian Father* (1799; based on an Elizabethan comedy by Thomas Dekker). His other diverse yet not negligible works included a *Life of Charles Brockden Brown* (1815), a *History of the American Theatre* (1832) and a substantial *History of the Rise and Progress of the Arts of Design in the United States* (2 vols., 1834). Gregarious, open-minded, often impecunious, a patriot but not a chauvinist, he was greatly liked; and his likeability is evident in a three-volume selection of his journals, *The Diary of William Dunlap* (ed. Dorothy C. Barck, 1930).

CHARLES BROCKDEN BROWN (1771–1810)

Born in Philadelphia, of Quaker stock. Frail in physique, he became a prodigious reader during childhood. Without going to college, he prepared for law practice in a Philadelphia office, with increasing distaste, and under the influence of a Yale-educated medical student and poet, Elihu Hubbard Smith. Brown followed Smith to New York. Additionally influenced by reading radical literature, by William Godwin and others, he produced an extraordinary spate of fictional or semi-fictional works: *Alcuin* (1797), a dialogue on the position of women; *Wieland, or The Transformation* (1798); *Arthur Mervyn* (1799–1800); *Edgar Huntly* (1799); *Clara Howard* (1801), published in England as *Philip Stanley*; and *Jane Talbot* (1801). He was also a magazine editor (*The Monthly Magazine and American Review*, *The Literary Magazine and American Register*, which printed some of his fiction). By this time he was back in Philadelphia, where he died of tuberculosis.

III

PROMISES AND PROBLEMS
OF INDEPENDENCE

Colonial resistance to British imperial policies began to become vocal, and widespread, after the end of the French and Indian or Seven Years War in 1763. That war had deprived the French of Lower Canada, and prompted the government in Westminster to reassert authority over the colonies – including authority to tax them as a contribution to the cost of imperial defence.

The sequence of events leading to the Declaration of Independence (1776), and thence to the American triumph (Peace of Paris, 1783), do not concern us. In literary terms, the first point to stress is the combination of styles, traditions and expectations that seemed to work in favour of the colonies, and to the detriment of Great Britain.

Among these was the tradition of religious dissent, expressed on both sides of the Atlantic as antagonism to the alleged arrogance, greed, sloth and doctrinal unsoundness of the established Anglican church. In Britain, people who refused to subscribe to the Thirty-nine Articles of the Church of England (Roman Catholics, Quakers, and various other Protestant 'nonconformists') were excluded from Oxford and Cambridge, from Parliament, and from holding army and navy commissions. In the colonies, Anglicanism was established in Virginia and elsewhere. But 'dissent' was itself established, as Congregationalism, in New England; and such Protestantism, in orthodox British eyes, promoted dangerous forms of protest. The clergy of Massachusetts or Connecticut was, it was sometimes said, covertly republican in outlook. Political dissent therefore found a congenial climate.

The vocabulary of dissent, religious or secular, was eloquent, familiar and highly effective. Colonists who turned to pamphleteering could draw upon a rich Anglo-American heritage, in which the individual's own conscience supplied the ultimate sanction, and in which authority must always show itself to be founded in fairness. John Bunyan's *Pilgrim's Progress* (1678, 1684), a work closely read by young Benjamin Franklin, is a fine example of English nonconformist argument. In the prefatory verse 'Apology' Bunyan declares:

> By metaphors I speak; were not God's laws,
> His Gospel laws, in olden times held forth
> By types, shadows and metaphors? ...

Bunyan's parable, of a 'Dangerous Journey, and Safe Arrival at the Desired Country', presented 'Under the Similitude of a Dream', could easily be interpreted, like many such metaphorical stories, as a portrait of corrupt courtiers and politicians in far-off London. Thus, a despicable character named 'By-Ends', questioned by 'Christian' as to who are his kinfolk, answers:

Almost the whole town; and in particular, my Lord Turn-about, my Lord Timeserver, my Lord Fair-speech . . . , also Mr. Smoothman, Mr. Facing-both-ways, Mr. Anything, and the Parson of our parish, Mr. Two-tongues . . . ; and to tell you the truth, I am become a gentleman of good quality; yet my grandfather was but a waterman, looking one way and rowing another; and I got most of my estate by the same occupation.

Thomas Paine, an English Quaker of the same plain origins as Bunyan, was able to make excellent use of his libertarian heritage when he came to the colonies in 1774, aged thirty-seven, a frustrated man whose talents and angers all at once found an outlet. Paine's *Common Sense*, a tract first published anonymously (January 1776), brought together, or brought into the open, a cluster of 'American' themes. One was the practice, dating back to the Elizabethan era, of dwelling promotionally upon the colonies as an area certain to prosper, and therefore ideal for settlement. Another, semi-millennial theme was that of *translatio studii*: the belief, already voiced in Bishop Berkeley's 'Westward the course of empire', in an ordained movement of civilization in a westerly direction. Crèvecœur's version of *translatio*, written c. 1770, was: 'Americans are the western pilgrims, . . . carrying along with them that great mass of arts, sciences, vigour, and industry which began long since in the east; they will finish the great circle.' Providence had left the discovery and development of the American hemisphere for the opportune moment in human (or divine?) history. Geography conspired with other factors to ensure that the evolution of North America would be in every way grand. 'The mighty objects' a man beholds in America, as Paine was to maintain later (*The Rights of Man*, Part II, Introduction), 'act upon his mind by enlarging it, and he partakes of the greatness he contemplates'.

Kenneth Silverman has called this the 'Rising Glory' theme in American writing, exemplified in the 'Rising Glory of America' poem offered by Philip Freneau and Hugh H. Brackenridge as a Princeton graduation exercise in 1771, or John Trumbull's 'A Prospect of Our Future Glory', a Yale performance of about the same time, or William Smith's 1773 Philadelphia oration, which expressed his delight in anticipating 'the rising Grandeur of America; to trace the progress of the Arts, like that of the Sun, from East to West .... THAT *Day* hath even now more than dawned upon us.' Silverman cautions that the *translatio studii* was a standard literary allusion, and in these pre-Revolutionary utterances not necessarily a sign of resistance to Britain.[1] However, it was adapted by Paine and others as an additional justification for independence. In his fifteenth *Crisis* paper (1783), Paine exulted in the 'vast prospect before us'. Americans could now 'see it in our power to make a world happy'. During the same year Ezra Stiles, president of Yale, preached a sermon on 'The United States Elevated to Glory, and Honor', in which he expressed confidence that the 'fermentation and communion of nations' about to be created through immigration and universal trade 'will doubtless produce something very new, singular, and glorious'. The arts, he suggested, 'may be transplanted from Europe and Asia, and flourish in America with an augmented lustre'. Timothy Dwight carried the conception forward in an 'Address to the Genius of Columbia', urging the delegates to the 1787 Philadelphia constitutional convention to do their almost preternatural best:

> For this stupendous realm, this chosen race,
> With all the improvements of all lands its base,
> The glorious structure build. ...
> [On] freedom, science, arts, its stories shine,
> Unshaken pillars of a frame divine.

In *Common Sense* Paine, writing with the gruff clarity of English polemical prose, could invoke still other libertarian themes. There was the ancient appeal of country against town, of the pastoral or agricultural life against the artificial and often exploitative existences of townsmen. In a related guise this was the English antagonism of 'Country' and 'Court'. It represented plain, virtuous, industrious conduct in contrast to luxury, immorality and indolence; the godfearing against the godless; deserving poverty versus undeserving privilege and affluence. In such a morality play the

1. Kenneth Silverman, *A Cultural History of the American Revolution, ... 1763–1789* (New York, 1976), 228–35.

Americans took all the 'good' roles, assigning villainy and ineptitude to the mother country.

The colonists also thereby claimed the civic virtues of republicanism as their own. The republics from which they could construct an ancestry included those of Greece and Rome, the medieval Italian city states, the Dutch provinces, the cantons of Switzerland, and republican aspects of English history – notably the Cromwellian Commonwealth of the 1650s, after the beheading of Charles I. Related in some respects was the history of Anglo-Saxon England, according to Whig interpretations. Before the 'Norman yoke' was fastened upon England, it was said, there had been an essentially democratic, pre-feudal society. Anglo-Saxondom's great champion, King Alfred, exhibited none of the evils of later monarchy. With this lost, proto-republican realm in mind, Thomas Jefferson was eager to make the Anglo-Saxon language a branch of study in American colleges; and *Alfred* was the name given to the first vessel commissioned by the Continental Congress in the War of Independence.

Republicanism was an old half-dream. *Common Sense* echoed a venerable case-history of resistance to tyrants and of overt or covert anti-monarchical sentiment. Paine cited, for example, the Old Testament story (used by Jonathan Mayhew in a powerful New England sermon of 1750, on resistance to tyranny) of how the Jews foolishly asked the prophet Samuel to give them a king; how Samuel spoke with God; and how God reluctantly granted the request – so saddling the Jews with the dangerous institution of monarchy.

Paine himself was more concerned to attack monarchy than to describe republicanism – whose actual lineaments may not have been very clear to him or to American contemporaries. His onslaught, combining fury and mockery, general and particular denunciation, was brilliantly effective in demythologizing both monarchy and the supposedly wondrous British mixed constitution. It was left to James Madison and Alexander Hamilton (collaborators with John Jay in the eighty-five weekly 'Publius' essays of 1787–8 known as *The Federalist Papers*) to tackle a potentially awkward problem. Even admirers of republicanism usually stated that modern republics could function only in small communities and that republics were sooner or later swallowed up by larger, more aggressive powers. The counter-argument developed by Madison and Hamilton was that while such theories might apply to European history, the opposite would be true of America. The United States, a nation of republics, would flourish and indeed expand all the more successfully *because* of the republican principle.

This assertion rested upon the definition of a republic as a *representative* democracy: which is to say, one in which a large body of voters would choose a manageably small number of legislators to represent them, and entrust the business of government to the elective body instead of vainly attempting to run things by means of mass assembly.

In the verbal warfare of the Revolutionary era, therefore, the Americans were able to employ old British contentions as to constitutional liberty, turning them against the mother country like cannon or vessels captured in actual combat. And the colonists profited from new weapons of argument, with Paine again as a skilful adversary. In conventional imagery, Great Britain was the parent, and the colonies the offspring. In the British version of the controversy, parents are owed gratitude and obedience: they have reared their children from helpless infancy, protecting and educating the defenceless, unformed babes (as Britain could feel it had done during the century of intermittent conflict with France). The American retort, naturally enough, emphasized not deference and indebtedness but a rapidly attained maturity. Children become adult. As Paine asked, 'is it the interest of a man to be a boy all his life?', or, as Americans formulated the dispute, was Britain genuinely a parent? No, answered Paine. The mother country was at best a stepmother: more precisely, a wicked stepmother. Americans had no obligation to pay tribute to false, ungenerous parents. They were descended from every country in Europe and owed no especial allegiance to supposed elders who had maltreated them. The debate was pleasing to alert young authors, who sensed they were on the winning side. Whether or not they realized the full dimension of the parent–child analogy, they perhaps drew dividends from a profound change in the imaginative schemes of Europe–America during the second half of the eighteenth century. The novels of Samuel Richardson and other sources of the epoch lend themselves to the theory of a substantial shift in the relative jurisdiction of older and younger generations – the verdict generally going to the young, as being more likely to behave wisely and generously in the new circumstances of the 'modern' world.[1]

Another idea deserves a mention at this stage. It was all very well for the former British colonies to deny an obligation to the mother country. What of the mother tongue, the dominant English language of the thirteen mainland colonies (and of the other colonies – Jamaica, Bermuda, Upper

1. Jay Fliegelman, *Prodigals and Pilgrims: The American Revolution against Patriarchal Authority, 1750–1800* (Cambridge, MA, Cambridge UP, 1982).

Canada – they hoped would join them)? Literature involved language. In what language would the rising glory of America conduct discourse? Timothy Dwight composed an optimistic hymn in about 1778 (published 1793):

> Columbia, Columbia, to glory arise,
> The queen of the world, and child of the skies!
> Thy genius commands thee; with rapture behold,
> While ages on ages thy splendours unfold....

A little less vaguely, Dwight added:

> Fair Science her gates to thy sons shall unbar,
> And thy sons see thy morn hide the beams of her star.
> New bards, and new sages, unrival'd shall soar
> To fame, unextinguish'd, when time is no more.

This was yet another instance of *translatio* rhetoric. Any more specific statement, however, must address the linguistic issue of how America's bards and sages were to express themselves. The mother country had been repudiated: what of the mother tongue? Ezra Stiles touched on the matter in his 1783 'Glory and Honor' sermon. The immense size of the United States and its trade with all nations would, he predicted, make it a sort of cosmopolitan arbiter of proper language. English would be the 'prevailing and general language of North America'. But, as spoken and written in the United States, it would develop as a single norm, without fragmenting into provincial dialects. 'The English language', Stiles asserted, 'will grow up with the present American population into great purity and elegance.'

Pondering the problem a few years later, in the course of a voyage from Le Havre to Boston, a French admirer of the new nation concluded that since Americans detested the English and wished to 'erase every trace of their origin', they must 'introduce innovations into their language as they have in their constitution'. The brainwave of Brissot de Warville was that Americans ought deliberately to adopt French turns of phrase. In that way they 'will be drawn farther away from the English. They will create a language of their own; ... an American language.'[1]

There is little sign that Brissot's fanciful theory ever took effect. Some

1. J. P. Brissot de Warville, *New Travels in the United States of America, 1788*, trans. Mara Soceanu Vamos and Durand Echeverria, ed. D. Echeverria (Cambridge, MA, 1964), 78; and see A. Owen Aldridge, *Early American Literature: a Comparatist Approach* (Princeton, NJ, 1982), 186–208.

people speculate that residence in France may have done something to the prose style of Henry James, and possibly – in different ways – to that of Ernest Hemingway. But, in Brissot's own day, living in France seems not to have influenced the blunt cadences of Thomas Paine; nor are there conspicuous Gallicisms in the writing of Joel Barlow.

On the other hand, what Stiles merely alluded to became during the 1780s and 1790s the almost obsessive concern of that 'Schoolmaster to America', Noah Webster. In the closing stages of the Revolutionary War he began work on a 'speller' which was to form the first of three volumes comprising *A Grammatical Institute of the English Language*. He pushed his proposals with extraordinary tenacity, corresponding with and calling upon the leaders of every part of the country from George Washington down, and lecturing everywhere he could find an audience. At this stage Webster was a passionate nationalist. He insisted, in the preface to his *Spelling Book*, that America must eventually 'be as distinguished by the superiority of her literary improvements, as she is already by the liberality of her civil and ecclesiastical constitutions'. Europe had 'grown old in folly, corruption and tyranny', its literature in decline and its human nature 'debased':

It is the business of *Americans* to select the wisdom of all nations . . . , – to avoid their errors, – to embellish and improve the sciences, – to diffuse an uniformity and purity of language, – to add superior dignity to this infant Empire and to human nature.

To a Connecticut acquaintance he wrote: 'America must be as independent in *literature* as she is in *politics* – as famous for *arts* as for *arms*, – and it is not impossible but a person of my youth may have some influence in exciting a spirit of literary industry.'

Noah Webster's critics found his spirit of self-advertisement even more inflated than his prospectus for American cultural glory. Educated, impecunious, ambitious, Yankee, more energetic than charming (unlike, say, Barlow), Webster in the 1780s felt the surge of optimistic, patriotic pride. Along with other able young 'literary' men on the make, he wished to define, to stimulate, to control and, yes, to profit from, the country's growth. American greatness, he was convinced, depended upon unity and true independence. Unity in turn depended upon a common language for all of the 'confederated republics' of the United States (and upon universal, which is to say both widespread and standardized, education). The common language ought ideally to be 'American'. Such a language should incorporate words and usages peculiar to the United States. It ought to be purged of British corruptions or mistakes – for instance, the tendency to add an unnecessary *k* to the end of *musick*, *Gothick*, and so on. A pure language would establish consistent, logical, simple rules for spelling and pronunciation. American schoolbooks and dictionaries would abide by these 'American' rules, and would provide American instead of British place-names, anecdotes and other references.

Some of what Webster urged did win acceptance. The *u* disappeared from *color*, *parlor* and various other words. Endings in -*re* were changed to -*er*, so that *centre* became *center*. Other Websterian proposals failed to find favour/favor. He wished to drop the silent final *e* in words like *fugitive*; but although Webster's propaganda was never *tentativ*, the public response was *negative*. Most of his recommended reforms were in fact sensible. They were welcomed by Benjamin Franklin, who had himself worked out a phonetic basis for the language. A century later, the playwright George Bernard Shaw was likewise to urge a drastic simplification of English. None of their systems achieved any substantial success. Webster, however, was at first understandably sanguine. The newly independent nation seemed to provide a unique opportunity for mankind, as Paine said, to remake the world. In the process Webster was determined that his own primers and dictionaries should serve to educate and mould America.

The outcome was a disappointment. In 1800 he announced his plan for 'a Dictionary of the American Language'. The manifesto met some ridicule. Joseph Dennie in Philadelphia, editor of the new weekly *Port Folio*, compared the labours 'of Mr. Webster to that of a maniac gardener' who, instead of clearing away weeds, 'entwines them with his flowers'. A Boston pundit said: 'A language, arrived at its zenith, like ours, and copious and expressive in the extreme, requires no ... new words.' Colloquial barbarisms had no place in any dictionary. How could an American dictionary differ from a good English lexicon such as Samuel Johnson's (1755)? Webster's product 'must either be a dictionary of pure English words, and, in that case, superfluous ..., or else must contain vulgar, provincial words, unauthorized by good writers.'

Our sympathy may lie with Webster, as the apparent victim of hidebound resistance or of jealousy. Complaints from England about the American neologisms approved by Webster seem comical, when we have grown entirely accustomed – for instance – to *appreciation*, *caucus*, *lengthy*, *presidential*, *subsidize*. There seems to be good sense in the view (*Dissertations on the English Language*) that the closeness of European nations to one another was making their languages, too, come closer. Far-off America, however, would be less affected:

New associations of people, new combinations of ideas ..., and some intercourse with tribes wholly unknown in Europe will introduce new words into the American tongue. These causes will produce, in ... time, a language in North America as different from the future language of England as the modern Dutch, Spanish, and Swedish are from the German or from one another.

If this has not happened, a major reason could be that English English has fallen into the orbit of American English, unwilling or at any rate unable to resist 'Americanization'.

The American-ness of Noah Webster was undoubtedly manifest in his big *Dictionary* of 1828, which cited examples of proper usage from a quantity of American authors. 'It is with pride and satisfaction', said Webster's preface, 'that I can place them, as authorities, on the same page with ... Milton, Dryden, Addison.' The style of *The Federalist Papers*, of Joel Barlow, William Ellery Channing, Washington Irving and 'many other writings' in 'purity, in elegance, and in technical precision, is equalled only by that of the best British authors'.

From the vantage-point of the 1820s, or even a decade earlier, a reasonable 'pride and satisfaction' could be voiced by Webster's countrymen if they chose to call the roll of native writers, in poetry as well as prose. There was the exuberant satirical verse of John Trumbull's *M'Fingal*, a spoof on the speechifying of a New England Tory, tarred and feathered by the exasperated crowd, which ends with the victory of the 'Rebel Empire' and M'Fingal's flight into shameful exile. There were the caustic poems of Philip Freneau, jeering at British snobbery, stupidity and brutality. There were the attempted epics – Timothy Dwight's *Conquest of Canaan* and Barlow's *Vision of Columbus*. Dwight produced a sort of latter-day typological narrative: the Bible story of Joshua, seizing the Promised Land for the Israelites, implies an antitype in the shape of the American commander, George Washington. Barlow's *Vision*, equally grand in conception but less involute, pictured Christopher Columbus at the end of his life, disgraced, despondent and imprisoned. He is shown a vision of the evolution of the Americas as they are to be, long after his own death. He can die content in the knowledge that his New World is to become the home of republican liberty, with the United States in the vanguard. In another vein, there was *Greenfield Hill*, Dwight's affectionate tribute to the place of his home, to Connecticut and to a peaceful, modest, outdoor

America. In this seven-part poem, Dwight experimented with American-isms, explaining them in footnotes, and risking derision from commen-tators on both sides of the Atlantic. Another poem with a strong personal flavour was Barlow's 'Advice to a Raven in Russia', written in the last weeks of his life. He had supported the French Revolution, and as a keen francophile had refrained from adverse comment on the headlong career of Napoleon Bonaparte, which had toppled the *République* and substituted the *Empire*. The poem pictures a raven, feeding as a bird of prey upon the frozen dead who line the route of Napoleon's march on (and away from) Moscow. 'Black fool, why winter here?' Barlow asks the raven: the Emperor has provided carrion all over Europe:

> Each land lies reeking with its people slain
> And not a stream runs bloodless to the main.

In fiction, by the end of the century, Americans could name some minor curiosities such as *The Power of Sympathy* (1789), a novel based on an actual scandal, of a woman who committed suicide after being seduced by her brother-in-law. This work, sometimes attributed to Sarah Wentworth Morton, seems in fact to have been written by William Hill Brown (1765–93), a young Bostonian. Apart from its gossip interest it has some claim to be called the 'first American novel'. There were, however, more solid contributions to American fiction. *Modern Chivalry*, whose first volumes appeared in 1792, narrated the rambling, comic tale of Captain Farrago, an American gentleman, and his Irish 'bogtrotter' servant Teague O'Regan. The author, Hugh Henry Brackenridge, had obviously been in-fluenced by Cervantes's mock-epic *Don Quixote*, so that Farrago was in some degree an American version of the Spanish knight, and O'Regan a distant literary relative of Quixote's servant Sancho Panza. Most of Farrago's plans misfire, like those of Don Quixote. His ignorant 'man' wins elections, on the other hand, as Panza becomes governor of Barataria; and there is a hint in the final chapter of *Modern Chivalry* that Teague may be given an ambassadorial appointment (he has already been presented to President Washington). The parallel, though, is only approximate, as we shall see. In any case, scores of writers have imitated Cervantes. Another influence on Brackenridge was that of Laurence Sterne, the English clergyman whose *Tristram Shandy* and *Sentimental Journey* amused, titillated and mildly shocked Anglo-America with their air of garrulous, accidental impropriety – a style used, for example, in flirtatious letters sent by the New Englander James Lovell to Abigail, the wife of John Adams. She would enjoy the joke, up to some point at which she would reprimand him. He would reply pretending not to know why she was offended. Brackenridge was not alone, therefore, in utilizing Sterne's ingenious non-narrative.

A more subtle imagination, which fascinated contemporaries such as the English poet Percy Bysshe Shelley, was that of Charles Brockden Brown. During the 1790s Brown, determined to prove it was feasible for an American to live wholly as a man of letters, poured out half a dozen novels of intricate psychological suspense. His 'romances', which purported to be American in setting and in mood, were intended to show that prose fiction was a match for poetry in 'all the subtilities of ratiocination, the energies and ornaments of rhetoric, and the colours of description'. The prospectus for an early, lost novel (announced under the mysterious title of *Sky-Walk; or the Man Unknown to Himself*) avowed his interest in 'a sort of audaciousness of character'. The world was actually governed 'not by the simpleton' (such as Teague O'Regan?), 'but by the man of soaring passions and intellectual energy'. In fact Brown tried to reach both a popular and a sophisticated public, in a balancing act which was to be repeated half a century later by Herman Melville. Brown was obviously well read in European literature, including Gothic novels. But his endeavour was to domicile such tales of eerie melodrama in the very different setting of America. His solution in part was to internalize the narrative: that is, to analyse states of mind rather than to establish an exterior landscape of dungeons, castles, ghosts, revenges, and so on. In *Arthur Wieland*, Brown developed a tangle of intricate relationships and deceptions, some manipulated by a sinister ventriloquist named Carwin. Carwin himself, we discover from an incomplete manuscript, *Memoirs of Carwin, The Biloquist* (1798), is a farmer's son whose aspiring intelligence renders him corruptible. *Arthur Mervyn; or Memoirs of the Year 1793*, begins in Philadelphia, a city then in the grip of a yellow fever epidemic. The 'hero', Arthur, is a young man apparently dominated by a trickster named Welbeck. The second part of the novel casts doubts on whether Arthur Mervyn is the unspoiled country lad he claims to be. Brown's central figures suffer traumas of displacement, impoverishment, anonymity, bewilderment, shame, feared insanity. Guilt and innocence become ambiguous.

An American of the next generation, John Neal, remarked that Brown's fiction was marked by negations. There was 'no wit; no ... pleasantry; no passion; ... [and] a most penurious and bony invention.' Nevertheless, despite the further handicap of an unremarkable style, Brown secured one's attention, like a man 'who is altogether in earnest, and believes every word of his own story'. Neal added that Brown could make you feel that 'you had just parted with a man who *had* seen' what he described, 'a man who had been telling you of it' in real life – 'with his face flushed'. The authenticity, combined with tedium, of such testimony resembled that of evidence in some protracted lawsuit; and this comparison is unconsciously hinted at in Brown's confession to a friend, while he was a reluctant law student, of how much he hated to be 'encumbered with the rubbish of law', wading through 'its endless tautologies, its ... circuities, its lying assertions and hateful truths'. Yet, as this grumble shows, Brown was capable of acute and witty insight. He is the probable author, for example, of an article in the *Monthly Magazine and American Review* which gleefully parodied the solemn banalities, by way of sermon and funeral oration, that greeted the death of George Washington at the end of 1799. In the same magazine, which he edited, he had contributed an intriguing review article, 'Walstein's School of History', on an imaginary German scholar, and his imaginary pupil, Engel, whose biographical studies rest upon the realization that 'the causes that fashion men into instruments of happiness or misery are numerous, complex, and operate upon a wide surface'. Of these, 'opinions relative to property' are the immediate source of most of the world's stock of happiness and misery. Next comes sex. In fiction, 'love and marriage' have occupied the stage; and an attendant 'monotony and sentimental softness have hence arisen'.

Brown, then, was potentially a figure of considerable importance in the early history of his nation's literature, and possessed what some have seen as a peculiarly American psychological quirkiness. Brackenridge too could be described as a promising early candidate – anticipating, say, Melville's *Confidence Man* (1857) in this catechism from *Modern Chivalry*:

You are a man of books –
A little so.
What books have you read?
History, Divinity, Belles-lettres.
What is the characteristic of history?
Fiction.
Of novels?
Truth.

As for other branches of literature, there is argument over which is the first genuine 'American' play. There is little dispute that one of the earliest in the nation's independent history, Royall Tyler's *The Contrast* (1787), was a sparkling contender: still occasionally revived, and still worth the trouble. Tyler (1757–1826) was a New England lawyer who, it is said, attended the theatre for the first time in his life on a visit to New York, and happened to see a production of Sheridan's *School for Scandal*. According to the story Tyler was so stimulated that he devised a play of his own within a few weeks. *The Contrast* is obviously in Sheridan's genre. It is a social comedy in which genial semi-virtue triumphs over such minor sins as snobbery, hypocrisy and backbiting. Tyler ridicules the city's social climbers. The 'contrast' of the title is between these creatures, and Colonel Manly (manly by name and by nature) plus his ingenuous yet sturdy servant, Jonathan – the down-to-earth Yankee, who was to become a stereotype in American fiction and drama. The play's prologue begins:

> Exult each patriot heart! – this night is shown
> A piece, which we may fairly call our own;
> Where the proud titles of 'My Lord! Your Grace!'
> To humble Mr. and plain Sir give place.

But Tyler then discloses that his words are double-edged. There is no need to turn to foreign authors or plots, he says, when Americans are showing themselves only too quick to imitate the vices of Europe. Tyler's light satirical skills (usually concealed behind anonymity, or a pen-name) were deployed in amusing verse and prose composed, as 'Colon' and 'Spondee', in partnership with Joseph Dennie; in several more stage comedies, one of them based on Sancho Panza's natural talent as Governor of Barataria; and a picaresque novel, *The Algerine Captive* (1797).

As Royall Tyler was inspired by Sheridan, so William Dunlap was prompted by *The Contrast* to write another play set in New York, emphasizing native themes. Dunlap's prologue to *The Father, or American Shandyism* (1789) declared:

> The comick muse, pleas'd with her new abode,
> Steps forth in sportive tho' in moral mode;
> Proud of her dwelling in our new-made nation,
> She's set about a serious reformation,
> For, faith, she'd almost lost her reputation.

And one of the women characters remarks, with barbed humour, that New Yorkers are 'a match for the most polish'd people in Europe; we can shew you lawyers without common sense, soldiers without courage, gentlemen without politeness, and virtuous ladies without modesty.' Did Dunlap add that word 'virtuous' as a concession to the 'moral mode'? He was an admirer of the mock-genteel robustness of Laurence Sterne (as the play's title avows). At any rate Dunlap, in the course of his career, was to turn out plays by the dozen in every sort of style. His finest serious drama, *André* (1798), stands as the first American play to deal with the Revolution as a morally profound, rather than a mere solemnly moralized, occurrence.[1]

The tally of American literary publication would increase if we were to define 'literature' in the wide senses of the Revolutionary era, to embrace history, biography, theology, law, travel, and so on. This was the comprehensive interpretation, employed, for instance, in Samuel Lorenzo Knapp's *Lectures on American Literature* (1829), or in the 1828 *Dictionary* compiled by his friend Noah Webster, who affirmed that *literature* was almost synonymous with *learning*: it entailed a grasp of 'the ancient languages, ... history, grammar, rhetoric, logic, geography, &c. as well as of the sciences.' In such a reckoning, Chief Justice John Marshall's biography of George Washington might be deemed at least as significant as a novel or a volume of poems.

So far we have discussed the promises of American literature in the early years of independence: the pride, the high hopes, the eagerness of authors to make their mark and of critics to identify them as they emerged. It is generally admitted, however, that the promises were not fulfilled. At least, the fulfilment was delayed; *The American Renaissance* celebrated in F. O. Matthiessen's book of that title did not burgeon until the 1840s, with its greatest achievements in the years 1850–55. Before then, especially in the period from about 1780 to 1820, the results were disappointing to many American contemporaries. They were pounced upon with malicious pleasure – according to aggrieved Americans – by British commentators, or by anglophile and therefore disloyal Federalists.

A common argument, then, is that American literature got off to a good start, despite inevitable difficulties (the lack of libraries, periodicals, patronage, and so on in a new country still engaged in the primary tasks of establishing governments and clearing the wilderness); but that the nation's real if modest achievements were caricatured by hostile commen-

---

1. Joseph J. Ellis, *After the Revolution: Profiles of Early American Culture* (New York, Norton, 1979), 141–4; and see the references to the evolution of the André theme (the trial, conviction and hanging of a British officer, Major John André, a person of unusual courage, politeness and virtue), in American literature, in Michael Kammen, *A Season of Youth: The American Revolution and the Historical Imagination* (New York, Knopf, 1978).

tators. Certainly we can find sharp comment in abundance. The New England Federalist Fisher Ames made clear his view that, under American democracy as exemplified by President Jefferson, the prospects were bleak. Except for a few 'able works on our politics, we have no authors':

There is no scarcity of spelling-book makers, and authors of twelve-cent pamphlets; and we have ... a sort of literary nobility, whose works have grown to the dignity and size of an octavo volume. We have many writers who ... have the sense to understand what others have written. But a right perception of the genius of others is not genius; it is a sort of business talent.

'Has our country', he asked, 'produced one great original work of genius?' Similar doubts were expressed by Joseph Dennie, who shared with the increasingly pessimistic band of Connecticut Wits a fear that universal suffrage would be the ruin of America's fragile culture.

There were, too, many cutting references to American literature – or its absence – in the new, self-assured and highly successful British periodicals, the *Edinburgh Review* (1802) and the London *Quarterly Review* (1809), and subsequently in the monthly *Blackwood's Edinburgh Magazine* (1817). The *Edinburgh Review* (January 1810) insisted that 'liberty and competition have as yet done nothing to stimulate literary genius in these republican states.... Noah Webster, we are afraid, still occupies the first place in criticism, Timothy Dwight and Joel Barlow in poetry, and Mr Justice Marshall in history.' Except for the contributions of Benjamin Franklin, the United States had created nothing, 'either of the useful or the agreeable'. The *Quarterly Review* said of Americans in 1814: 'They have done nothing original; all that is good or new is done by foreigners, and yet they boast eternally.' This opinion was echoed in the *Edinburgh Review* (December 1818), by Sydney Smith. 'Literature the Americans have none – no native literature, we mean. It is all imported.... But why should the Americans write books, when a six weeks' passage brings them in our own tongue, our sense, science and genius, in bales and hogsheads?'

Smith soon made even more wounding observations, which were to become notorious. 'In the four quarters of the globe,' he inquired (*Edinburgh Review*, January 1820), 'who reads an American book?'

Considering their numbers,... and the favourable circumstances in which they have been placed, they have yet done marvellously little to ... show that their British blood has been exalted ... by their republican ... institutions.... During the thirty or forty years of their independence, they have done absolutely nothing for the

Sciences, for the Arts, for Literature, or even for the statesmanlike studies of politics, or political economy.

In the so-called 'War of the Quarterlies', Smith and his ilk were vigorously countered. One such retort was Robert Walsh's *Appeal from the Judgments of Great Britain Respecting the United States of America* (1819). James Kirke Paulding (1778–1860), a one-time associate of Washington Irving, made a career for some years out of sparring with British critics, in books like *A Sketch of Old England* (1922) and *John Bull in America; or, the New Munchausen* (1825), which almost obsessively cited and rebutted certain *Quarterly Review* phrases on American republicanism as epitomized in 'bundling, negro-driving, and dram-drinking' and in such evidently ludicrous 'poems as the Columbiad' by Barlow. (The *Quarterly* could, incidentally, have added to its taunt the claim that Barlow borrowed his conception from Milton, his metre from Pope, and his facts from the Scottish historian William Robertson. True, Robertson had never set foot in the New World to acquire material for his *History of America*. But then Charles Brockden Brown, who once wrote of a hermit in the wilds of Ohio, never crossed the Alleghenies.)

There *is* an unlikeable condescension in British pronouncements of this kind. It would be wrong, though, to maintain that in themselves they did serious harm. At most they were an irritant – and perhaps all the more irritating for the measure of truth they contained. Too much had been promised; the euphoria induced by independence had led to inflated claims, often couched in toplofty terms, with denunciations of British tyranny and predictions of Britain's impending downfall. Each side provoked the other; the Americans were not blameless. Freneau was not exactly conciliatory when he asked, with reference to Britain,

> Can we never be thought
> To have learning or grace
> Unless it be brought
> From that damnable place?

Nor was Noah Webster, when he informed his compatriots in 1789 that 'Great Britain ... should no longer be *our* standard, for the taste of her writers is already corrupted and her language on the decline.' How simple, if only Webster had been right.

But, a generation later, there was no sign that European corruption had impaired European literature. Was it possible even that literature, like the pearl, was a secretion caused by impurities in the body politic? Whitman was one of those who brushed aside the query with the assertion that America would invent a new *kind* of literature. But when, how and what? American writers appeared to cling to traditional and outmoded forms. William Wirt's *Letters of the British Spy* (1803) was modelled on the London *Spectator* of a hundred years back, and indeed contained a hero-worshipping chapter on Addison's irreproachable prose and moral sentiments. Combinations of national pride, democratic instinct and vernacular language were emanating from Europe rather than the United States. There was no American verse equivalent, other than an 'educated' production such as Barlow's 'Hasty Pudding', to Robert Burns's *Poems, Chiefly in the Scottish Dialect* (1786). On close inspection, Webster's project for an 'American' language seemed chimerical. It was to aim at a pure English and yet incorporate new American usage. It was to set a national (and eventually international) standard, ignoring or frowning upon dialect pronunciation and vocabulary – this when regional patterns were already firmly set, so that critics could accuse Webster of trying to impose New Englandisms on the rest of the country. One could reasonably argue that whatever emerged by way of a distinctive language or literature, the process might take several decades or even longer. But how long? The imminence of the brilliant 'rising glory' had been exaggerated. Foreigners had some justification for their jeers, as when London's *New Monthly Magazine* remarked (1821):

An American, unlike the rest of mankind, appeals to prophecy, and with Malthus in one hand and a map of the back country in the other, he boldly defies us to a comparison with America as she is to be, and chuckles in delight over the splendours the geometrical ratio is to shed over her story.

Moreover, the British reviewers were not persistently anti-American. The *Edinburgh* was in general Whig, and disposed to praise American libertarianism. The *Quarterly* was a Tory periodical, and perhaps more cranky on that account. But the reviewers specialized in a tone of severe omniscience, demolishing any and every book to which they took objection. The English poet John Keats was one of their victims; according to Byron, Keats's death was hastened by a savage piece on his *Endymion*:

> Who killed John Keats?
> 'I' says the Quarterly,
> So cruel and Tartarly,
> ' 'Twas one of my feats'.

And, to reiterate, they did have grounds for contending that, so far, American literature was more promise than performance.

Their case was bolstered by the shift in Noah Webster's opinion. In old age he felt that Americans were 'a degenerate and wicked people', ruined by their exposure to the democratic cant of Jefferson and Andrew Jackson. Webster had in fact lapsed into Federalist pessimism, so far as politics were concerned, as early as 1800. He never lost enthusiasm for his lexicography. But he did gradually abandon his belief in a separate American language. His final view was: 'Our language is the *English* and it is desirable that the language of the United States and Great Britain should continue to be the same, except so far as local circumstances, laws and institutions shall require a few peculiarities in each country.' After a visit to Europe in 1826 he vaunted his discovery that 'good usage in England accords almost wholly with good usage in this country'.

Is 'Federalism' the explanation? The furious partisan clashes of the 1790s undoubtedly served to divide American men of letters. Freneau and Barlow were found, with Tom Paine, on the Republican or Jeffersonian side. Trumbull, Stiles, Dwight and other New Englanders seemed to harden into conservative opposition. Thomas Green Fessenden (1771–1837), who in later years was to take young Nathaniel Hawthorne as a lodger at his Boston home, wrote Hudibrastic verse as 'Christopher Caustic'. His satiric doggerel, in the same vein as the Wits' *Anarchiad*, concentrated its fire on the Jeffersonians. Fessenden's *Democracy Unveiled: or Tyranny Stripped of the Garb of Patriotism* (1805) derided Thomas Jefferson's attachment to universal suffrage:

> Nature imposes her commands,
> There must be *heads*, as well as *hands*. . . .

Fessenden's family, like that of his friend Joseph Dennie, included kinfolk of Tory (Loyalist) sympathy. Dennie sometimes sounded like a self-styled cultural arbiter, as when he accused Franklin of being

The founder of that Grubstreet sect, who have . . . attempted to degrade literature to the level of vulgar capacities, and debase the polished and current language of books, by the vile alloy of provincial idioms, and colloquial barbarism, the shame of grammar, and akin to any language, rather than English.

Dennie's private comments occasionally go much further. In a letter to his parents (May 1800) he emphasized his 'settled attachment to *Englishmen* and English principles', and his abhorrence of the 'traitors' who instigated the Declaration of Independence. 'We are now tasting the bitter fruit of that baleful tree ..., to which the natural malignity of our rascal populace has given the increase.'

Nevertheless, Federalist tendencies among authors should not be judged in Jeffersonian terms. The Connecticut Wits ardently supported the cause of independence. They also supported the new Constitution of 1787, but that – despite anti-Federalist allegations – did not make them crave a return to monarchy. In the 1790s, appalled by the French Revolution, they expressed horror at the world's descent into atheism, violence, demagoguery, and new forms of despotism. To that extent they were suspicious of Jeffersonian 'Democracy' as they understood it. But by European standards they were themselves 'democratic' (though they preferred to be labelled 'republican'). The Napoleonic wars widened the gap between Jeffersonians and Federalists. The Federalists however were, with a few exceptions, by no means slavish in their alignment with the British or anti-Napoleonic side. There was, Noah Webster shrewdly suggested in 1808, rather a *competition in hatred* among Americans: dislike of France vying with dislike of Great Britain.

Some Federalists, of whom Fisher Ames is an example, expressed embarrassment at the braggart chauvinism, as they saw it, of the new nation. They were not lacking in patriotism, but only anxious to establish a better basis. Ames's misgivings were to be voiced for many years to come. The Harvard Phi Beta Kappa address of 1826 was delivered by Joseph Story, a Madison appointee to the Supreme Court. Justice Story said that Americans claimed 'an equality of voice and vote in the republic of letters.... We ask admission into the temple of fame, as joint heirs of the inheritance.' But it was not by 'a few vain boasts ... that we are to win our way to ... literary distinction.' He warned a probably sympathetic audience that, while there was no doubt of the vitality of America's tree-like roots and branches, the upper foliage was what mattered culturally. 'Never, never may ... our posterity have just occasion to speak of our country in the expressiveness of Indian rhetoric, "It is an aged hemlock; it is dead at the top."'

At the cultural level, the role of literature and scholarship in a democracy was acutely important, and not only to so-called conservatives. The periodicals that Brackenridge or Brown brought into being failed to survive. Educated Americans preferred the more substantial magazines of Britain. The rest apparently read nothing. In theory there were enough educated people to maintain a fair number of American writers. In practice they seemed dismayingly uninterested. Philip Freneau's despondent

'Author's Soliloquy' betrayed a painful nostalgia for a scene which he and his fellows had rejected:

> Thrice happy DRYDEN who could meet
> Some rival bard on every street:
> When all were bent on writing well,
> It was some credit to excel
> While those condemn'd to stand alone
> Can only by themselves be known.

Charles Brockden Brown's novels, as we have seen, possessed considerable merit, amounting potentially to that overworked attribute, 'genius'. The young man's initiation explored in *Arthur Mervyn* and in *Edgar Huntly* was to be a vastly significant theme for novelists. The actuality for Brown was nevertheless neglect – a greater neglect in his own country than in England. Recommending Brown's novels in the 1820s, Paulding admitted that most Americans had probably never heard of them, and he could do no more than wager on a 'future fame' for Brown, offering 'a bright contrast to the darkness in which he is now enveloped'.

One nagging, heretical doubt for American authors of every political persuasion was whether the mass of mankind possessed any appreciable degree of cultural sensibility or intelligence. If the doubt were well founded, it undermined the whole political basis of popular sovereignty – the view that the majority must necessarily be right – and therefore by implication raised the shocking problem of whether the Revolution might have been a mistake. Or perhaps if the majority were right on broad matters of political or moral judgement, it might be in error on matters of taste? An attempted way out of the difficulty was to differentiate the wholesomely from the crassly democratic. In *Democracy Unveiled*, Fessenden explained:

By 'people' I mean the great body of American farmers, merchants, mechanics, etc., who possessing habits of industry, and our primitive New England manners, may be considered as the *stamina* of republicanism. . . . I would make a distinction between the *people* and the *mob* or *populace*. By the latter I would designate certain of the lowest class in the community, who are alike destitute of property and of principle, and may . . . be styled the *rabble*.

The Philadelphia lawyer–author Charles Jared Ingersoll used a similar vocabulary in his *Inchiquin, The Jesuit's Letters* (1810), which purported to be the observations on the United States of an open-minded 'Unknown Foreigner'. *Inchiquin* said: 'There is no populace (plebs). All are people (populus). What in other countries is called the populace, a compost heap, whence germinate mobs, beggars, and tyrants, is not to be found in the towns; and there is no peasantry in the country. Were it not for the slaves of the south there would be but one rank.'[1] And in Herman Melville's *White-Jacket, or the World in a Man of War* (1850) the distinction is again pondered, in the course of a conversation between two seamen, plain Jack Chase and the poet Lemsford (a spokesman for the author?):

'Blast them, Jack, what they call the public is a monster, like the idol we saw in [Hawaii], with the head of a jackass, the body of a baboon, and the tail of a scorpion.'

'I don't like that,' said Jack; 'when I'm ashore, I myself am part of the public.'

'Your pardon, Jack; you are not. You are then a part of the people, just as you are aboard the frigate here. The public is one thing, Jack, and the people another.'

'You are right,' said Jack; '... The public and the people.

Aye, aye, my lads, let us hate the one and cleave to the other.'

The effort to separate good democracy from bad democracy was of limited utility. American writers of the Revolutionary era were unhappy to be forced into élitism. They resisted assertions such as that of their German contemporary Friedrich von Schiller, a man of very modest family whose talents elevated him into the gentry. *Vielen gefallen ist schlimm*, declared Schiller: *to please the many is bad*. How could an H. H. Brackenridge cope with the notion that the republic of letters was more fitly described as an aristocracy? In *Modern Chivalry* he tries in vain to straddle the issue. Captain Farrago is given a comical name and made to seem ineffectual. Yet most of the time Farrago is presented straightforwardly, as Brackenridge's persona – an honest, upright, educated citizen whose solid qualifications are undervalued by the *public/populace*. Farrago's servant Teague is a peasant, but without Sancho Panza's redeeming common sense. Teague is earthy in being a clod, in Brackenridge's unloving portrayal. He is thick, ignorant and devoid of appeal. Brackenridge's careful depiction of Irish brogue is intended to make the reader laugh at Teague, not laugh with him. Moreover, by the end of the book Farrago has after all done well; he has become 'governor', apparently of Pennsylvania, while there is no steady rise in his servant's fortunes. *Modern Chivalry* is a failure when set beside various books of its kind which seem to know where they are going.

1. The *Quarterly Review* (January 1814) made a sustained attack on *Inchiquin*. The claim that there was in the United States 'no patrician, no plebean, no third or middle class', served the reviewer as the excuse to ridicule American vulgarity: 'We knew, indeed, that there was no "Corinthian capital" above the shaft of the column, but we did not apprehend that there was any want of rough stone and rubbish at its base.' It should be remembered, though, that during 1814 the two countries were engaged in a real war.

In the main, Brown's novels too are, comparatively speaking, failures. Sometimes they seem to be all sub-plot and no main plot. Though ostensibly American, their landscape is almost as hypothetical and abstract as that of some of Edgar Allan Poe's tales. Brown's characters are usually said to be American, yet with European connections and experiences. Their native placing is indistinct. Arthur Mervyn, the raw country lad, speaks without a trace of dialect (we are told he had studied Latin, as if this would account for his gentleman's diction). Now and then one is tempted to think that Brown decrees insanity or psychological confusion for his characters because he senses they would otherwise lack motivation. As with much of the poetry of the era the author, like someone protractedly exercising on parallel bars, or on a rowing machine, may (one feels) derive more benefit than the audience.

The reasons for such relative lack of success are fascinating. Intelligent writers – Brackenridge, Brown, a dozen others – probably perceived that none of the conventional explanations was adequate; something still eluded analysis. European *philosophes* – Buffon, DePauw, Raynal – toyed with the theory of some fundamental process of deterioration, believed to be inexorably at work upon plants, animals and humans in the New World. To pay any serious heed to that fanciful supposition was self-defeating. Blaming Britain for everything, though an intermittent relief, was likewise ultimately a confession of defeat. The absence of an international copyright agreement was undoubtedly a handicap to American authors. It was annoying enough to famous British authors, such as Charles Dickens, whose works were pirated without royalty payments in America. For less well-established American authors the practice was ruinous. In the early 1840s, when conditions were aggravated by a financial depression, a Disraeli novel could be bought in the United States for half the price of one by James Fenimore Cooper; and a cheap edition of a Dickens novel went for ten cents where a Cooper one cost fifty. Doubly infuriating for American authors was the knowledge that pirate publishers, and even sincere citizens, used Jeffersonian rhetoric to contend that royalties were undemocratic: knowledge ought to be available to all.[1]

1. Thomas Carlyle and Ralph Waldo Emerson spent much time in trying to arrange safeguards for one another's publications. Carlyle wrote to his friend from London (3 April 1844): 'We have Pirates waiting for any American thing of mark, as you have for every British.... It is strange that men should feel themselves so entirely at liberty to steal, simply because there is no gallows to hang them for doing it.' For the contrary case, see Henry C. Carey, *Letters on International Copyright* (2nd edn., 1868).

The fault ought to be remedied, and if it could not be, then Americans had contrived their own literary suicide. Various other views were less grim, but brought no comfort to writers worried over their immediate livelihood; for their solution depended upon decades or generations of time. In the long run, for example, there might be a national publishing market instead of regions clustered round each large city. In the fullness of time (a phrase which tolled like a funeral bell for aspiring authors) – in the fullness of time there would be American magazines that managed to survive and thrive (the *Port Folio* was a rarity in that it stayed alive for a quarter-century). In the fullness of time libraries would be properly stocked. As it was, in 1820 Harvard College, the oldest in the United States, had a scant 20,000 volumes in its library: Göttingen University in Germany had 400,000.

Meanwhile, what of the rising glory? And what of the ambiguity of the origins of those first American *littérateurs?* Crèvecœur's most lyrical passages were written before the Revolution. He quit his farm in 1780, and though he returned to the United States for a few years, he came back as a Frenchman. In histories of the Revolution he figures not as a founding father of American literature but as a Loyalist, agonizing over his divided allegiances and (in his *Sketches*, first published in 1925) disposed to see things in more or less the same way as the New England Loyalist poet Jacob Bailey:

> A zealous father of sedition
> Took up the good man on suspicion
> Forced him without a grain of pity,
> Before th'inflexible committee.
> Committee men are dreadful things,
> More haughty far than Europe's kings;
> The latter mostly rule by laws,
> The first are governed by a Cause –[1]

Neither man, we can be fairly sure, wanted to be forced into either camp. Probably Joseph Dennie's parents had not either, nor the father of William Dunlap (who, as a retired British army officer, opted formally for the Crown during the War of Independence). William Dunlap himself steered a middle course. While still in his teens he made the acquaintance

1. Ray Palmer Baker, 'The Poetry of Jacob Bailey, Loyalist', *New England Quarterly* 2 (1929), 75. Bailey, a Harvard graduate who became an Anglican minister, went into exile in Nova Scotia.

of General Washington, by displaying his skills as a portrait painter. Then he went to London, in the shoes of Benjamin West, John Singleton Copley and other American artists, to study painting. On his return Dunlap transformed himself into a playwright. That was a workable compromise for a man of double loyalties, since theatre in the United States remained very much an Anglo-American enterprise.

Most writers of the Revolutionary age were more firmly committed to the American cause. There is no reason to think they regretted independence. All the same, their military commitment seems almost subordinate to literary preoccupation. Brackenridge, Barlow and Dwight served quite short enlistments as army chaplains; and of the trio only Dwight was truly a man of the cloth. Their chaplaincies gave them commissioned rank and leisure in which to write. John Trumbull and Noah Webster saw no military service. Philip Freneau had an idyllic life during the early part of the war in the Virgin Islands, and in the latter part, still based on the Caribbean, seems to have alternated delicious ease with interludes of privateering – a form of legalized piracy which could bring rich rewards. Their contribution, in other words, was literary rather than martial; and Freneau's fury at the British for confining him to a prison ship appears to have sprung from two grievances: that they treated him as a combatant, and that they did not treat him as an officer or gentleman.

That is not to say their testimony was insincere, or of no consequence. It was, however, tinged with grandiosity and vagueness. This was unavoidable. America's was a brand-new nationalism and so somewhat artificial and didactic. Poetic, dramatic and novelistic themes tended inevitably either to echo the familiar British discourse within which they had been nurtured, or else to sound declamatory, unspecific and hollow. Webster's larger prescriptions for an American language were a positive hindrance to authors in quest of authentic American idioms. Their dialect-speaking figures, such as Jonathan in *The Contrast*, somehow came out as oafish rather than admirable. Efforts at literary polish were often unduly dandified (Dennie's *Port Folio* pieces). Or their message was too complicatedly oblique. For example, William Wirt's *Letters of the British Spy*, like Ingersoll's *Inchiquin*, masqueraded as the work of a foreigner. Ingersoll's half-disguise was intended to let him praise the United States – a device laughed to scorn by the *Quarterly Review*. Wirt's contrary idea was to pretend to be a British Member of Parliament, surveying America with some disdain. His approach was more ingenious than Ingersoll's, and more widely popular. Nevertheless the effect is odd. Wirt's Englishman delivers strong criticisms, for instance, of the low standards of education in Virginia, with incidental comments that such failings are only to be expected in a republic. The supposed American editor adds footnotes objecting to these monarchical allusions. We thus have criticism of criticism – and yet are expected to think that the 'British Spy' is correct, even if for the wrong reasons.

None of these problems was insuperable. In sum, what they did signify was that cultural independence would take longer to achieve than political independence. And different weapons would have to be employed. America's literary maturity could not in any proper sense be 'declared', or 'fought for'. It would have to be earned and conceded. Middle ways would have to be found between the extremes of name-calling *Hurrapatriotismus* and subservience to British models. Americans were in fact to insist over and over again that they had escaped the literary thrall of the parent culture, or were about to do so. Ralph Waldo Emerson's 'American Scholar' address to Harvard Phi Beta Kappa association, a decade after Justice Story's, proclaimed that 'we have listened too long to the courtly muses of Europe'. Oliver Wendell Holmes described Emerson's stirring summons as America's Intellectual Declaration of Independence. It was, to be more accurate, a declaration of intent; and merely the most eloquent of many manifestos, several of them originating as Phi Beta Kappa performances. In his 'Remarks on National Literature' (1830), William Ellery Channing maintained that 'it were better to have no literature, than form ourselves unresistingly on a foreign one'. A little later, Edgar Allan Poe announced that 'we have at length arrived at that epoch when our literature ... must stand on its own merits or fall through its own defects. We have snapped asunder the leading-strings of our British Grandmamma.'

An obvious rejoinder was that a grandmother is not a foreigner. English literature and English language were not only a cultural inheritance but a continuing major factor for the United States. This was recognized if sometimes regretted in a number of contributions to Boston's *North American Review*, established in 1815 with the hope of attaining the stature of the British quarterlies. As one of the essayists on the *Review*, Walter Channing briskly assessed the 'delinquency' of American authors. He and William Tudor played with the seductive though delusive idea that Indian culture, including oratory, might form a basis for a 'native' white American style. Edward Everett in an 1821 article found himself arguing, as Walter Channing had done, that American English remained virtually indistinguishable from the mother tongue. Everett seemed uncertain whether this was a blessing or a curse, in his contention that

> our children's books are English; ... that our stage is supplied from England; that Byron, Campbell, Southey, Scott, are as familiar to us as their own countrymen; that we receive the first sheets of the new novel before the last one is thrown off at Edinburgh; that we reprint every English work of merit ...; and that the English version of the Scriptures is the great source whence the majority of Americans imbibe their English language. How, then, is it possible that we should not speak good English?

How indeed? But what would be 'good American'?

IV

A TRIO OF GENTLEMEN
Irving, Cooper, Poe

─────────

WASHINGTON IRVING (1783–1859)

Born in New York, youngest son of a Presbyterian merchant of Scottish background. He studied law, but was more attracted by the literary interests of his brothers William and Peter. He contributed 'Letters of Jonathan Oldstyle, Gent.' to a newspaper edited by Peter Irving. He travelled in Europe for his health, 1804–6. With his brothers and brother-in-law J. K. Paulding he brought out the *Salmagundi* essays, Federalist in outlook. His first important success was the *History of New York* (1809), purporting to be the work of one Diedrich Knickerbocker. Irving went to Europe in 1815, to assist in the family hardware business at Liverpool. He remained in Europe seventeen years, travelling extensively. Irving gained recognition with *The Sketch Book of Geoffrey Crayon, Gent.* (1819–20), and further popularity with such works as *Bracebridge Hall* (1822); *Tales of a Traveller* (1824); a biography of Columbus (1828); *A Chronicle of the Conquest of Granada* (1829); *The Alhambra* (1832). Back in the United States (1832–42), Irving wrote on American topics, including *A Tour on the Prairie* (1832). He returned to Europe (1842–6), at first as minister to Spain. On his return home, he devoted the remaining years to constant writing (lives of Goldsmith, Mahomet, and so on), culminating in the five-volume biography (1855–9) of George Washington.

JAMES FENIMORE COOPER (1789–1851)

Son of a prosperous landholder who founded Cooperstown, on Lake Otsego in New York state. Cooper was educated at Yale, but left without graduating. He went to sea, 1806–11, retired from the navy on marriage into the distinguished De Lancey family, and lived as a country gentleman. He began to write, with no serious professional intentions, at the age of thirty: his first novel, *Precaution* (1820), was followed by many other novels, histories, and so on. Cooper lived in Europe 1826–33. Later, at Cooperstown, he was involved in numerous libel actions, almost all successful, against a hostile press. His popularity declined, partly as a result of the notoriety thus gained, but he continued to write until his death. Cooper's best-known works are: *The Spy* (1821), *The Pioneers* (1823), *The Pilot* (1823), *The Last of the Mohicans* (1826), *The Prairie* (1827), *The Red Rover* (1827), *Gleanings in Europe*

(1837–8), *Homeward Bound* and *Home as Found* – published in England as *Eve Effingham* – (1838), *The Pathfinder* (1840), *The Deerslayer* (1841), *Satanstoe* (1845).

EDGAR ALLAN POE (1809–49)

Born in Boston, the son of itinerant actors. He was left an orphan in 1811, and taken into the home of a well-to-do merchant, John Allan of Richmond, Virginia. The Allans took him to England; he attended school there 1815–20. He quarrelled with Allan after their return to Richmond; they were never fully reconciled, and Poe was ignored in Allan's will when he died (1834). Poe spent brief periods at University of Virginia, in the U.S. Army (where he rose to the rank of sergeant-major), and as a cadet at West Point. After deliberately incurring dismissal from West Point, he supported himself as a man of letters in Baltimore, Richmond, New York, and Philadelphia. He was connected with various periodicals, including the *Southern Literary Messenger*. In 1836 he married his thirteen-year-old cousin Virginia Clemm, who died of tuberculosis (1846). After her death, he became more and more unbalanced, and died in Baltimore, after he was found lying delirious in the gutter. Poe published three volumes of poetry: *Tamerlane* (1827), *Al Aaraaf* (1829), *Poems* (1831). Thereafter, most of his work – poems, stories, and critical articles – first appeared in periodicals. The stories were first collected in *Tales of the Grotesque and Arabesque* (1840); others appeared in *Tales* (1845). Other writings included the metaphysical study *Eureka: A Prose Poem* (1848), and *The Narrative of Arthur Gordon Pym* (1838).

IV

A TRIO OF GENTLEMEN

WASHINGTON IRVING

WASHINGTON IRVING was the first man of letters from the United States to win an international reputation. He was closely followed by James Fenimore Cooper, and the reputation of the third author discussed in this chapter, Edgar Allan Poe, could likewise be described as international, though during his own lifetime his fame was far surpassed by that of Irving and Cooper. The case of Poe is somewhat special, yet he, like the others, reveals some of the complexities of being an American.

As for Irving:

He is not a learned man, and can write but meagrely and at second-hand on learned subjects; but he has a quick convertible talent that seizes lightly on the points of knowledge necessary to the illustration of a theme ... his gifted pen transmutes every thing into gold, and his own genial nature reflects its sunshine through his pages.

This is Irving's appraisal of Oliver Goldsmith, but it could have been written of Irving himself by his contemporaries, in Europe and at home, who so often called him the 'American Goldsmith', or spoke of him as a latter-day Addison or Steele. Most of those who met Irving liked him; Sir Walter Scott, Thomas Moore and a score of others testified to his personal charm, and agreed that his literary style matched his personality. As with Charles Lamb, something of his appeal was bound to evaporate when he died. When he was alive, not everyone rated him highly. To one satirist he was 'Dame Irving'; another writer defined him as 'Addison and water'; Maria Edgeworth said of his *Bracebridge Hall* that 'the workmanship surpasses the work. There is too much care and cost bestowed on petty objects.' The present-day reader is more likely to agree with Irving's critics than with his admirers. But it is worth our while to examine why he had such stature in his own day.

Poe offers a clue, in observing that

Irving is much overrated, and a nice distinction might be drawn between his just and his surreptitious and adventitious reputation – between what is due to the pioneer solely, and what to the writer.

It is the word pioneer that arrests us. What has a man like Irving, with 'his tame propriety and faultlessness of style' (Poe again), to do with pioneering? We can begin to answer the question with a sentence by Irving's biographer, Stanley Williams: 'Here was an American with a feather in his hand, instead of on his head':[1] a product of the New World who, emerging from a family in trade and from the callow literary circles of New York, managed to entertain the entire civilized world: an author who could please both his countrymen and the English – both exacting in their different ways. How he did so can be studied in the volume which brought him his renown.

The Sketch Book of Geoffrey Crayon, Gent., including 'The Author's Account of Himself' and 'L'Envoy', consists of thirty-four sketches. The great majority depict English scenes: 'The Inn Kitchen', 'Westminster Abbey', and so on. Cottages are thatched, churches ivied, forelocks tugged. Two essays only might be thought 'controversial'. One was a portrait of 'John Bull', the other about 'English Writers on America'. John Bull has his weaknesses, says Irving: 'he will contrive to argue every fault into a merit, and will frankly convict himself of being the honestest fellow in existence.' But Irving's amiable varnish shines over the subject; John Bull is after all, we learn, 'a sterling-hearted old blade'. As for the English writers (and their reviewers), whose accounts of America had stirred up so much trouble, Irving managed to make his reprimands acceptable by suggesting that instead of the gentlemen of England, who are such fair-minded observers, 'it has been left to the broken-down tradesman, the scheming adventurer, the wandering mechanic, the Manchester and Birmingham agent, to be her oracles respecting America'. Not a very good essay, it is a quite astonishingly tactful one.

Irving's persona is for the most part implied rather than avowed. Geoffrey Crayon is first and foremost a gentleman, and American in a secondary sense. Irving adopts the role of well-bred, intelligent traveller. Now and then he is the foreign traveller, as in Montesquieu's *Lettres Persanes* or Southey's *Letters from Espriella*, affecting to be puzzled by some oddity in the scene before him. But as an American, Irving is not really puzzled. He understands the English essence (as of course a Scottish

1. *The Life of Washington Irving* (2 vols., New York, 1935), i. 211.

observer might do – and Irving was of a Scottish family): indeed he is equipped to perceive more than does the average John Bull. In 'English Writers on America' he feels his way towards a successful Anglo-American formula. It embodies dignified protest at English misrepresentation of the United States; equally dignified pride in American achievement, and promise; a hint at British folly in alienating America; and a final assurance that England holds a special place for Americans, not as the still-acknowl-edged mother country but as a repository of good features despite sundry 'errors and absurdities'. Tact is the word. No wonder Irving was offered diplomatic appointments by his countrymen.

Of the few pieces in the *Sketch Book* that deal directly with America, one on 'Traits of Indian Character' is a conventional glimpse of the noble savage, who after the day's hunting 'wraps himself in the spoils of the bear, the panther, and the buffalo, and sleeps among the thunders of the cataract'. Another piece, the most famous and enduring in the whole book, tells the tale of Rip Van Winkle, the Dutchman bewitched in the Catskill Mountains, who after a twenty-year sleep makes his way back to his native village: an old man whose former cronies are all dead. Thanks to Irving, the New World was now beginning to pass on its myths and legends to the Old. Or so his contemporaries believed. In fact, as Irving hinted not too loudly, he had borrowed the story from a German tale, translating some of its paragraphs so literally as to lay himself open to the charge of plagiarism. And though he preserved the original Spanish setting in some of his other and later stories, similar objections were made: he had, it was said, simply moved his material from one language to another, and added some incidental ornament.

But the charge did not much harm Irving's place in popular esteem. How did he win his place, and merit the description of *pioneer*? The first, indispensable step was to go to Europe. The second was to secure approval by European readers, without forfeiting his right to be considered an American. This was an extremely difficult problem, and Irving came as near to a solution as was possible. He also indicated for American writers who followed him the necessary approaches to the problem. To begin with, style: it must be above all refined. For practical purposes, Irving saw, America had as yet no style of its own. British models must therefore be followed. Irving surpassed his models by evolving a fluent, graceful prose which made a successful passage from the eighteenth to the nineteenth century. Next, subject: if he had merely given himself over to describing Europe, his countrymen would have rejected him – as it was, they reminded him continually during his seventeen-year absence of his obligation to come back home again. However, he did more than merely describe the contemporary scene. He dug into folklore. Others were at work in the same vein; Scott, his friend and hero, had put the balladry of the borders to good use, and perhaps encouraged him to study German folk-literature. From German stories he passed to those of Spain. They were rich sources, and Irving explored them eagerly. His own land was deficient in such material; therefore he, like Ticknor and Everett and Longfellow, was driven to seek it in Europe. As later Americans searched diligently for old paintings and manuscripts, these pioneers hunted the neglected folk-past of the Old World.

Irving lacked a creative gift; he needed plots ready-made. Temperamentally, like Hawthorne, he preferred a plot out of the past; though, wanting a subject more superficial than Hawthorne, he sought for something colourful, whimsical, a little melancholy: something that hinted, not too sternly, at change and alteration. If America was born in broad daylight, Irving brought it an imported twilight. In *Bracebridge Hall*, to take one example, he concocted an American version ('The Storm-Ship') of the *Flying Dutchman* legend. It would be wrong to imply that Irving had any clear notion of inventing, single-handed, a set of American traditions. Rather, he tried to please simultaneously audiences on either side of the Atlantic. Rip, for example, is asleep throughout the American Revolution, never having been obliged to choose sides. Irving was born just early enough to escape the oppressive claims of nationality, and he was too equable to fret over the demands that were laid on him. When American material was of value he used it. He journeyed out into the Indian country, and wrote *A Tour of the Prairie* about his trip; he became interested in the development of the American West, and compiled a competent account in *Astoria* (1836). But he was no frontiersman, and too much the cosmopolitan to become one; enemies suggested that *Astoria* was proof of nothing but Irving's pleasure in the patronage of the millionaire fur-trader John Jacob Astor.

As Emerson saw, Irving and his American contemporaries were 'picturesque': a deeper power eluded them. His pioneering was a matter of setting the example for others to follow. He suggested lines of approach: he translated and adapted. He soothed native pride by becoming eminent. At the end, grinding out the enormous biography of George Washington, he was still a capable craftsman; however pedestrian the treatment, there was always the easy rhythm of the sentences, and the mild occasional

relief of a pleasantry. Though his glory was beginning to tarnish, he had
at any rate held out longer than most of his colleagues, men such as
William Cullen Bryant and Fitz-Greene Halleck, who had gone silent,
become journalists, or turned into bores.

Did Irving set the wrong example? Yes, if one visualizes the relationship
between America and Europe as a cops-and-robbers (or rather, snobs-
and-patriots) melodrama, in which the hero, in terms of literature, is the
one who stays home and nurtures his American vocabulary, while the
villain slips off to Europe to acquire an English accent and a mastery of
French menus. We may allow that Irving was something of a snob: or, as
he put it, a *Gent*. One of the few topics on which he expressed indignation
was the 'pale and bilious' taproom agitator, scheming to overturn John
Bull's household or Peter Stuyvesant's New York. Nor could he applaud
the equivalent in literature. He confided to his diary in 1817:

There is an endeavour among some of the writers of the day (who fortunately have
not any great weight) to introduce into poetry all the common colloquial phrases
and vulgar idioms – In their rage for simplicity they would be coarse and commonplace. Now the Language of poetry cannot be too pure and choice.

Granted he is speaking of poetry, not of prose, does this exhibit place
Irving among the renegades? Hardly. He was after all reared in a cultivated
family, doubly linked to Britain by kinship and by trade. His father, a New
York merchant, opted for American-ness: Washington Irving was named
after the national hero. But George Washington too was a gentleman; and
the Irvings, with a library of English and European literature, felt no
necessity to renounce their milieu, believing they could be internationalists
without disloyalty to the United States, that nation of nations. In his early
career Irving resourcefully – yet in a way effortlessly – blended a cheerful,
eighteenth-century clubman's wit with the satirical, anti-Jefferson sharp-
ness of the next generation's New York Federalism. He triumphed over
the seeming handicap of anachronism, at least in the *History of New York*
(1809). Sometimes its humour is uneven and off-centre, like that of
Brackenridge or Wirt. But in general its hilarious irreverence makes nearly
everything Irving wrote afterwards seem bland by comparison. The poet–
editor W. C. Bryant recalled how, required as a college student to recite a
passage from the *Knickerbocker's History*, he had collapsed in helpless
laughter, to the annoyance of his tutor. Some of its humour may now be
too local or 'historical', but much of the book is still funny, not least in a
peculiarly American sense of incongruity, and of bombast deflated: 'And

now the rosy blush of morn began to mantle in the east, and soon the rising sun, emerging from amidst golden and purple clouds, shed his blithesome rays on the tin weathercocks of Communipaw.'

There is a Twainian or Dickensian exuberance of language in the description of the curses of William the Testy, aimed at the Yankees 'for a set of dieven, shobbejacken, deugenieten, twistzoekeren, blaes-kaken, loosen-schalken, kakken-bedden, and a thousand other names, of which ... history does not make mention.' There is a wry wit, perhaps indicating an inheritance from Jonathan Swift and Laurence Sterne, in the fifth chapter, where with mock solemnity Irving reviews the justifications advanced by white settlers for dispossessing the American Indians – discovery, agriculture, civilization, and the final unanswerable 'RIGHT BY EXTERMINATION, or ... RIGHT BY GUNPOWDER.'

Only isolated paragraphs have just the Twain flavour; yet it is there, in 1809, sixty years before the publication of *Innocents Abroad*, in which 'native' American prose made a triumphant appearance. It is true also that Knickerbocker's burlesque saga is a young man's squib. But added years and personal worries are not enough to explain why Irving abandoned Knickerbocker and Salmagundi for Geoffrey Crayon, and in fresh editions of the *History* steadily pruned away what he now held to be its vulgarities. Nor is residence in Europe the explanation: that is to confuse cause and effect. The reason is simple: 1809 was not 1869. American prose could not survive until conditions were more favourable. More recent writers than Irving have been unable to accept the idea that a serious style could grow out of a burlesque intention. Is Irving so much to blame in judging his *History* a dead end, when it was only a false start?

JAMES FENIMORE COOPER

For Cooper, to be an American was indeed a complex fate. Unlike Irving – for whom, incidentally, he had no great regard – Cooper was by birth and still more by marriage a member of the American landed gentry. Staunchly patriotic, proud of his three years as a midshipman in the United States navy, he felt it to be his mission while in Europe to defend his countrymen from insult, and was hurt that they seemed so ungrateful for such efforts on their behalf as *Notions of the Americans* (1828) and *Letter to General Lafayette* (1831). Yet, while he condemned hereditary aristocracy, much preferred republicanism to monarchy, and rejoiced in his nation's warlike prowess, he held firmly to his notion of gentlemanliness, based upon property, good birth and upbringing, and paternal sway over the neighbouring community. Jefferson, an American 'gentleman' of the previous generation, had warned the young American against the lures of Europe:

If he goes to England, he learns drinking, horse racing, and boxing. These are the peculiarities of English education. The following circumstances are common to education in that, and the other countries of Europe. He acquires a fondness for European luxury and dissipation, and a contempt for the simplicity of his own country; he is fascinated with the privileges of the European aristocrats, and sees with abhorrence, the lovely equality which the poor enjoy with the rich, in his own country; . . . he recollects the voluptuary dress and arts of the European women, and pities and despises the chaste affections and simplicity of his own country . . . It appears to me, then, that an American, coming to Europe for education, loses in his knowledge, in his morals, in his health, in his habits, and in his happiness.[1]

Cooper had no hesitation in taking his children to France to be educated. Though he had remained, as he thought, sturdily American, he found it hard to conceal his distaste for American life when he returned. *Home as Found* is a caustic commentary on the failings of his native land: its mob-rule, its abusive and irresponsible press, its deference to Europe. Thus, a New York literary gathering lionizes a bluff sea-captain, under the mistaken impression that he is a famous British author:

'Ah!, the English are truly a great nation! How delightfully he smokes!'
  'I think he is much the most interesting man we have had out here,' observed Miss Annual, 'since the last bust of Scott!'

This observation had a particular edge for Cooper, who was so often told that he was the American Walter Scott. The compliment irritated him, for it assigned him a secondary status: no one would have dreamed, he knew, of speaking of Scott as the English Cooper. Pulled between two worlds, how could he cut the British 'leading-strings' to which he once referred and emerge as America's first great novelist? How was he to create a world large and various enough to form a novelist's territory: how write of American society when there was none?

The answer must inevitably refer to Europe. Cooper's first book, *Precaution*, was a deliberate attempt to improve on an imported novel which he had been reading aloud to his wife, and its setting was in English society. For his second novel, *The Spy*, he prefaced chapters with quotations

1. Letter to J. Bannister, Jr., 15 October 1785.

from Campbell's *Gertrude of Wyoming*. His third book, *The Pilot*, was meant to demonstrate that a better novel could be written about the sea than Scott's *The Pirate*; and in his introduction Cooper notes wryly that he has still other competition to face: the author 'will probably be told, that Smollett has done all this before him, and in a much better manner'.

Part of the solution to his problems lay in the American past. *The Spy* deals with the period of the American Revolution when the British occupied the port of New York, while Washington's men held the surrounding district. It is a satisfactory if not a great novel because it covers exciting events, and because it provides Cooper with a suitable social framework. Most of the British and American characters are gentlefolk, who have mixed socially before the fighting has begun. Cooper is thus able to stand on neutral ground, though he makes it plain that his patriotic sympathies are with the Americans. Both sides have their heroes, or at any rate their gentlemen. The result pleased British readers; it also pleased Americans, who were prepared to accept in a historical novel social pretensions which, by the era of Andrew Jackson, had become theoretically obnoxious. For somewhat similar reasons Cooper scored another success with *The Pilot*, in which John Paul Jones fights a complicated little sea-and-land war along the Yorkshire coast. Here again are British as well as American worthies.

The Pilot offered another solution to Cooper. He had been told, when venturing to criticize the evident lack of nautical experience revealed in Scott's *The Pirate*, that a novel which described life at sea in detail would bewilder the general reader. In disproving this contention he not only took for his own another field of adventure: he had a ready-made social order in miniature presented to him. For life on board ship, with all its customs and hierarchies, was a complete enough world, save that it lacked women. Though the details of seamanship might confuse the reader, shipboard life was in other respects sharply defined: as Melville was to insist, more forcibly than Cooper, it represented the whole human predicament:

Oh, shipmates and world-mates, all round! we the people suffer many abuses. Our gun-deck is full of complaints. In vain from Lieutenants do we appeal to the Captain; in vain – while on board our world-frigate – to the indefinite Navy Commissioners, so far out of sight aloft. Yet the worst of our evils we blindly inflict upon ourselves; our officers can not remove them, even if they would.[1]

1. *White-Jacket*.

If Cooper never reached this intensity of meaning, he too benefited as a novelist from the rigid differentiations of existence at sea. How blurred, by contrast, were the orders of society in Cooperstown; how unreal, in Melville's *Pierre*.[1] Cooper's sea stories are sometimes weakened by the necessity for a heroine. Beautiful young heiresses, with names like Alinda de Barberie, are not often found on ships; they can be introduced on board only by dint of strenuous plot manipulation. But if these improbable creatures appear in several of Cooper's sea stories, they fail to spoil the storms and gunfights which he describes with a masterly relish.

With *The Pioneers*, published in the same year as *The Pilot*, Cooper found his other and better-known theme: the American wilderness. Within this he had another social code, that of the Indians, to whom, despite their savagery, he attributes many of the traits of the white gentleman. He had no first-hand experience of Indian tribal life, though Otsego lake, where he lived and which he chose as the setting for *The Deerslayer*, had not long before been Indian country. Some of his ideas about Indian behaviour (including his prejudice against the Iroquois) were adopted from the writings of the Moravian missionary John Gottlieb Heckewelder. But his Indians, however idealized his account of them, were fascinating figures, to Europeans perhaps even more than to Americans. Equally fascinating was the landscape of the wilderness: the forests and lakes which were also to be the setting for Francis Parkman's great histories, and (in *The Prairie*) the open country across the Mississippi. The dynamic element was provided by the white man, intruding upon the Indian hunting-grounds, provoking wars, restless and even villainous, yet certain to conquer finally. Returning to Otsego after a long absence, Cooper noted in a letter that the encircling woods had been a good deal 'lacerated'. The word vividly expresses the process of white settlement. Even in the novels in which the Indians are holding their own, their future is heavy with foreboding. Sophistication wars with simplicity, with only one possible conclusion. Nor is it merely a clash between Indian and white man: in *The Pioneers* the parties to the struggle are society as represented by Judge Temple, and the wilderness as represented by the old white hunter, Natty Bumppo (or Leatherstocking).

This was the first of the Leatherstocking tales, five in all, which map out the life of the hunter. Natty, brave, kindly and illiterate, hovers between the two worlds of Indian and white man. Endowed with the forest skills

1. See pp. 151–2 below.

of the Redskin, the bosom friend of the Mohican chief Chingachgook ('pronounced Chicago, I think', Mark Twain commented), gently tolerant of Indian beliefs, he nevertheless retains some white characteristics: he would not think of marrying a girl of another colour, nor will he take scalps, though he accompanies Chingachgook on the war-path. In *The Last of the Mohicans*, Natty – under the name of Hawkeye – is shown at a slightly earlier stage, travelling with Chingachgook and his son Uncas, who are the only survivors of their tribe. A year later, Cooper published *The Prairie*, in which Natty, now an old man, has left his forests, driven out by the advance of civilization, and is living as a trapper on the western plains. The novel closes, quietly and poignantly, with the death of Natty.

He was too good a character to lose. Cooper revived him in *The Pathfinder* and *The Deerslayer*. In the latter, Natty is a young man on his first war-path, and in *The Pathfinder*, he and Chingachgook are still in their prime. But since the story has been told in reverse, we know that Natty is fated to wander the forests in isolation, until their laceration forces him to move westwards. At the end of *The Deerslayer*, fifteen years after the main events of the story, Natty revisits Glimmerglass (that is, Otsego). Here lived a girl who was in love with him; now the only reminder of her is a shred of faded ribbon, and her lake-cabin – a rotted ruin. The touch of the past stirs a strange anguish, in the reader as in Natty Bumppo.

Time's victory over the wilderness makes a large and vivid theme, and there is still strength in Cooper's writing. His defects have been mercilessly indicated by Mark Twain (in the essay entitled 'Fenimore Cooper's Literary Offences'). There are any number of improbabilities: for example, the fantastic punctuality of forest meetings between Natty and Chingachgook. Rescues are invariably delayed until the moment of extreme peril. Dialogue is often awkward; characters usually lack depth. Cooper's attempts at humour are somewhat lame, and he holds up the narrative with interminable stilted conversations, while the bushes fill up with hostile Indians. As Twain complained, there is little sensuous immediacy in Cooper; scene and characters are *imagined* rather than *visualized*. Where a passage calls for direct description, the novelist is apt to come between the reader and the situation. Thus Natty, spying on enemy Indians around a campfire,

saw at a glance that many of the warriors were absent. . . . Rivenoak, however, was present, being seated in the foreground of a *picture that Salvator Rosa would have delighted to draw*,[1] his swarthy features illuminated. . . .

1. Italics mine.

Cooper's allusion makes us lose touch with Natty, who has certainly never heard of Salvator Rosa. Yet while his style cannot be called supple, it is serviceable; we might apply to it Cooper's own words on the gait of one of his characters: 'There was nothing elastic in his tread, but he glided over the ground with enormous strides, and a body bent forward, without appearing to use exertion or know weariness.' Despite the passages of polite conversation, the movement of the plot is not fatally impeded. His stories possess the elementary and fundamental virtue of activity. Their end is never really in doubt, but one wants to know what will happen next; fortunes change with dizzy abruptness, like a game of snakes-and-ladders, till the firm final throw.

Why then, of his many writings, are only the Leatherstocking tales widely known, and why are these nowadays often found on the juvenile shelf? It can be noted, first, that some of his plots seem off-centre. We are provided with conventional heroes and heroines, but also with other characters of far greater interest, who steal most of the action. In *The Spy*, for instance, Harvey Birch is not adequately linked with the other characters; and in *The Prairie*, the hero and heroine are almost redundant. We come back to the word 'society', with its implications for Cooper as American novelist and American gentleman. Cooper cannot bring himself to make an orthodox hero out of anyone of inferior social status. At times he resorts to grotesque expedients to prove that his chosen ones have the necessary qualifications. In *The Pioneers*, Elizabeth Temple can have no truck with Oliver Edwards while he is thought to be a half-breed; but when he is found to be the grandson of old Major Effingham, and therefore 'a white man' in all senses of the term, the story proceeds to a fairy tale finale in which Oliver wins Elizabeth and half her father's wilderness kingdom.[1]

With Natty Bumppo the difficulty becomes crucial. So long as he is a free agent he can be admired, and serve as hero. But he does not belong to Indian society, and he can never be absorbed into white society without too closely defining his status. He can, thus, never marry. Of the two chances given him, that in *The Deerslayer* is reasonably plausible; if Judith

1. The problem of how to make a white gentleman out of a coloured hero exercised a good many nineteenth-century purveyors of fiction. In *Across the Plains*, Robert Louis Stevenson speaks of a favourite work of his childhood 'which appeared in *Cassell's Family Paper*, and was read aloud to me by my nurse. It narrated the doings of one Custaloga, the Indian brave, who, in the last chapter, very obligingly washed the paint off his face and became Sir Reginald Somebody-or-other; a trick I never forgave him. The idea of a man being an Indian brave, and then giving that up to be a baronet, was one which my mind rejected.'

Hutter is in love with him, his refusals to consider matrimony are explained by the simple fact that he is not in love with Judith. But in *The Pathfinder* Natty is himself in love, with Mabel Dunham, the daughter of an army sergeant. She is offered as heroine, with all sorts of apologies and qualifications (such as, that she is more refined than one might expect, because she has been in the care of an officer's widow). It is impossible, however, to trick Natty out in other colours than his familiar ones. He is illiterate; his origins are immitigably humble. So Natty must be rejected by Mabel.

Natty inhabits a kind of vacuum. His world is on the whole made wonderfully interesting. But it is insubstantial. The Cooper gentleman is a bore; the Cooper non-gentleman cannot be incorporated completely, since uncouth society in America could not, in Cooper's day – and especially for someone of Cooper's temperament – be considered a proper subject for a novel. As a result, Natty's moves constitute an evasion of society, a series of renunciations. Compare the Leatherstocking tales, or Cooper's sea stories, with the novels of his contemporary, Balzac. Balzac's is a dense and actual world; Cooper's, by contrast, is a mythological place, where in earlier times the knight-errant might have performed. It is the element of myth that makes the Bumppo stories more than mere adventure yarns. But in later times this element was to grow fainter and fainter; the adventure lost significance. In other words, the logical extension of Leatherstocking is the cowboy hero: the simple, manly person whose feats are brave and chivalrous, but who, since he is a knight without title or crest, has no place in society, and so must – according to the genre – ride off into the sunset, without having laid a finger on the rancher's daughter, let alone married her. Cooper's achievement, though, is remarkable. It could be argued that his view of the American wilderness is essentially that of a responsive European, as Bartram's had been a generation previously. Whether or not that is so, he did succeed in casting an enduring literary spell. Few today trouble to read Heckewelder, from whom Cooper drew his information, though his descriptions are no doubt more 'accurate'. It is the invented, mythological tincture that makes us still read Cooper, even if we usually leave his world behind with our childhoods. And though his novels of the sea have less of this capacity for magic, they too represent the power of Cooper to create fiction out of apparently unpromising material.

He is to be honoured also for an energy of invention almost as fierce if not as comprehensive as that of Balzac. Certain later novels, while conventional in treatment and unresolved in attitude, shed considerable light on the social dilemmas of Jacksonian America. Cooper, like other contemporaries, found it easier to be a Democrat than a democrat. In less extreme form, he suffered some of the anguish of Crèvecœur. Everyone knows the passages in Crèvecœur's *Letters from an American Farmer* which praise the simplicity and harmony of American life at its best. Far less familiar are the passages from the *Letters* and from Crèvecœur's *Sketches of Eighteenth-century America* which bewail the upheavals of the American Revolution:

Ambition, an exorbitant love of power and thirst of riches, a certain impatience of government, by some people called liberty – all these motives, clad under the garb of patriotism and even of constitutional reason, have been the secret but true foundation of this, as well as of many other revolutions.

The final chapters of Crèvecœur's *Sketches* take the form of dialogues between greedy, ignorant 'patriots' and dignified loyalists or would-be neutrals (of whom Crèvecœur was one).

The events of the America of the 1840s led Cooper into a comparable fictionalized, frustrated discussion of the excesses of popular democracy. The immediate occasion was New York's Anti-rent War. Some landlords still owned large estates, with titles going back as far as the seventeenth century. Most of them were good landlords who allowed tenant farmers to pay small rents, or no rents at all in times of financial difficulty. The tenants began to object to even the mildest aspects of landlordism: they were determined to possess their farms outright. Cooper, himself a landlord of sorts, was convinced that a basic principle of property was at stake. In his *Littlepage Manuscripts* trilogy (1845–6) he traced the history, from colonial times to his own day, of lands acquired by the Littlepage family. The tone of the first novel in the trilogy, *Satanstoe*, is cheerfully anecdotal. In the second, *The Chainbearer*, it becomes more ironical. The Yankee tenants, who eventually change the name of the old 'Satanstoe' settlement to 'Dibbletonborough', find Mordaunt Littlepage's devotion to the patriot side almost a cause for complaint. If he had been a loyalist they would have been able to seize his lands for themselves, under confiscation. The third novel, *The Redskins, or Indian and Injin*, is a caustic account of the squatter mentality. There are good Indians in the trilogy, men of simple honour; and there are false 'Injins', white men in mobs who disguise themselves as burlesque redskins to terrorize their betters. Mordaunt Littlepage's grandson is engaged in the Anti-rent War, though his defeat is inevitable.

Crèvecœur had been over the same ground seventy years earlier. He thinks of retreating from the white men's corrupt democracy, to live with good Indians. His demagogues, who bear names like Aaron Blue-Skin, are as meanly truculent as Cooper's Anti-renters. Cooper, in common with Crèvecœur, does not know the answer. The settlement of the wilderness was a worthy endeavour. Honour is important, and courage and justice. Yet where does true justice lie? Who properly owns any of this land? The Indians perhaps, but they have been defeated and dispossessed. If they are made to yield by stronger force, what is to save the landlords from an equivalent fate? All that Cooper is sure of, in so equivocal circumstances, is that things are deteriorating. The cycle obsesses him, as it was to obsess William Faulkner a century afterwards. Each is impelled to delve back into the past, in search of explanation and also of an elusive original perfection. Each is impelled to trace the story, whether of the Littlepage acres or those of Yoknapatawpha County, forwards and downwards to a present-day degradation. These transformations lie at the heart of much of American fiction, as do these ambiguous grapplings with the notions of progress and democracy. They are the substance, for example, of Hawthorne's *House of the Seven Gables*.

In some respects James Fenimore Cooper reveals the attitudes of a Federalist or Whig gentleman. His ideal America was a *representative republic*, like that expounded by James Madison in *Federalist* no. 10, rather than a free-for-all 'democracy' of the sort Madison decried. He feared the tyranny of the unthinking majority. In common with the H. H. Brackenridge of *Modern Chivalry*, Cooper felt that educated, seasoned, disinterested leaders with the habit of command could and must be found. He saw a worse threat to the health of the public, however, than Brackenridge's naïve ignoramus Teague O'Regan. This was the wily canting demagogue of the Steadfast Dodge or Aristabulus Bragg variety – lawyers, editors and politicians who hypocritically cater to the lowest instinct of the electorate.

Embittered by his own experiences, and dismayed by what he regarded as an alarming decline in republican virtue, Cooper occupied some of his last years with satire or fantasy on the disintegration of America. In addition to the sarcasms of *Homeward Bound* and *Home as Found* he produced *The Monikins* (1835) and *The Crater* (1848). *The Monikins* is a political allegory reminiscent of *Gulliver's Travels*, about three monkey kingdoms (England, France and the United States), portrayed respectively as Leaphigh, Leapthrough, and Leaplow. In this novel America is at least no worse than the other countries. But *The Crater* is a grim fable of an inverted republican Utopia. An idyllic society established by shipwrecked Americans as an island in the Pacific is ruined by enlargement, by litigation and religiosity and journalism and libertarianism. The island has come into existence through an earthquake. Cooper's denouement (revenge?) is to contrive a second earthquake that sinks the whole island and its squabbling cargo into the sea.

Cooper was an 'upper-class' American, as that word might be applied to George Washington or Thomas Jefferson. Yet the question of class is not simple, with reference either to American authors or to their writings. Cooper, Hawthorne and the bulk of their literary contemporaries, for example, supported the popular Democratic party of Andrew Jackson. Some of the early vernacular humorists, on the other hand, preferred the rival, supposedly 'aristocratic' Whig party – as did Abe Lincoln, the rising young lawyer–politician of Springfield, Illinois. Party affiliation was at best a very rough indicator of egalitarian sentiment, or otherwise.

In Cooper's plots, as we have seen, gentry weds with gentry, and race with race. The rightness of social hierarchy is made apparent; so is the coarseness and meanness of life without refinement. But he does not recommend any rigid social pyramid, on the British model, with hereditary titles and a vast gap between rich and poor. In these ways Cooper, like Irving, is not fundamentally at odds with the mass of his countrymen. To judge from literature at nearly all levels, America's was at heart a genteel culture, as noted in chapter 1 above – gentility modified yet not basically challenged by an ideological insistence upon 'democracy'. In association the two tendencies produce fictional or stage plots in which the hero is often of seemingly humble origin, and in which the baddies and boobies are people (American or foreign) pretending to be aristocrats. The latter are invariably routed. The hero not only demonstrates his integrity: he proves to have been well-born after all, or he rises out of the ranks of the poor in a standard, justificatory American success story. The rhetoric is patriotically egalitarian. The outcome, for virtuous characters, tends to be prosperity. Titular nobility is replaced by upward mobility. Though this is not always achieved in the heroes' own lifetime, it is guaranteed to their children. In J. K. Paulding's poem *The Backwoodsman* (1818), while the hero Basil starts out as a struggling farmer, he emigrates west from New York into the Ohio Valley, and does so well he ceases to work on the land:

> Old BASIL – for his head is now grown gray –
> Waxes in wealth and honours every day;
> Judge, general, congressman, and half a score
> Of goodly offices, and titles more....

A similar process operates in the Rev. Timothy Flint's novel *George Mason, the Young Backwoodsman* (1829), and in the middlebrow theatre of the day. European brands of snobbery are castigated. Country innocence is extolled over city sophistication: the main figure in Anna Cora Mowatt's amusing play *Fashion, or Life in New York* (1845) is a farmer symbolically named Adam Trueman. But there is a gulf between the grammatical characters and those who speak in dialect. Ungrammaticals can be treated, like Natty Bumppo, as nature's noblemen. But they usually remain outside the rules of proper society; and often they serve mainly comic purposes, as yokels or dupes.[1]

Gentlemanly assumptions did not therefore of themselves offend what was a mainly genteel culture. Cooper was unpopular with some people for what was thought to be arrogant personal behaviour, not for what his novels said. Irving's gentlemanliness, personal and authorial, was highly admired. Writers at odds with their society, as Cooper was in old age, were apt to stress their apartness in quasi-aristocratic language; and this might give offence. Or they were tempted into covert statements – satirical, allegorical – which masked their misgivings yet tended drastically to reduce the number of readers. Where does Poe fit into the scheme?

EDGAR ALLAN POE

WHATEVER might be said in disparagement of their work, it had to be admitted by contemporaries that Irving and Cooper were eminent men of letters. Poe never during his short life reached their level of eminence. 'Essentially a Magazinist', as he said of himself, he struggled among the ruck of writers in the immature literary circles of America. He jostled in the crush of minor celebrities, amid all those authors of 'genius', so overpraised (by Poe himself, on occasion): the Mrs Sigourneys and Frances Sargent Osgoods, and N. P. Willises and Thomas Holley Chiverses. In a

---

1. See Henry Nash Smith, *Virgin Land* (Cambridge, MA, 1950), 137–42, 224–6, and the same author's *Democracy and the Novel* (New York, 1978). On the theatre, see David Grimsted, *Melodrama Unveiled: American Theater and Culture, 1800–1850* (Chicago, 1968), especially ch. 9. Anna Mowatt's *Fashion* is reprinted in Richard Moody, ed., *Dramas from the American Theatre, 1762–1909* (New York, 1966), 309–47.

way, he was the 'Poor-Devil Author' of whom Washington Irving wrote a sympathetic sketch, the man who from vast dreams of literary fame descends to ignominious hack-work. Poverty dogged Poe also; successes as an editor – and he seems to have been a very good one – were obliterated by unstable acts; and he too had his hack-work: the spate of scrappy reviews, the arrestingly bad humorous pieces, the textbook on conchology. Yet Poe never became abject; like Oscar Wilde with the customs inspector, he had his genius to declare. This word, so debased in the periodicals of the day, he cherished with a passion that must have appeared out of place in the shabby offices and lodgings he inhabited. But time, denying the description to the host of his contemporaries, and even to Irving and Cooper, has rewarded his tenacity and applied it to Poe.

The verdict of posterity has not been utterly unanimous. Some of his own countrymen have tended to dismiss him as the 'jingle man' (Emerson's phrase) or else, while praising him, have said that he stands outside the main current (whatever that is) of American literature. Yet to many others there has been no question of his 'genius'. Tennyson conceded it; so did W. B. Yeats; and, above all, so have the French, from Baudelaire to Valéry. More than one American, involved in a literary conversation with a Frenchman, has heard the word *Edgarpo* produced as though it were both a talisman and a high compliment. In fact, *Edgarpo* is to the French almost another person than Edgar Allan Poe, as the English-speaking world knows him.

The casual reader thinks of Poe in connection with certain gripping stories; who has not, at one time or another, read 'The Gold Bug' or 'The Pit and the Pendulum'? We may remember details of a poem or two: Poe's 'Raven', croaking 'Nevermore', or his jangling 'Bells'; or know of

> the glory that was Greece
> And the grandeur that was Rome.

without necessarily being aware that they come from Poe's lines 'To Helen'. But if we refresh our memories of Poe's fifty poems and seventy stories, we may find ourselves agreeing with J. R. Lowell's verdict (in *Fables of a Critic*) that Poe is 'three-fifths genius and two-fifths sheer fudge'. We will perhaps agree with Whitman's opinion that Poe's verses 'belong among the electric lights of imaginative literature, brilliant and dazzling, but with no heat', and that they carry 'the rhyming art to excess'. *Mechanical* is a word often applied to Poe's poetry, and those who glance at his essays on prosody will perhaps think it is not inapt. These essays suggest that their author, in his insistence upon the craft of poetry, allowed its rules to triumph over him; that in eschewing 'truth' – 'the heresy of "The Didactic" ' – and seeking after 'beauty', 'purity', and 'melody', he too often lapses into doggerel. Strict with others (see, for example, his close examination of Elizabeth Barrett Browning), he is blind to faults in his own work. Thus in 'Ulalume' he rhymes 'kissed her' with 'sister' and 'vista'; in 'For Annie', 'Annie' is paired with 'many'. In these and other poems all the stops of prosody are pulled out, with shattering effect. 'Eulalie', for instance:

> I dwelt alone
> In a world of moan
> And my soul was a stagnant tide
> Till the fair and gentle Eulalie became my blushing bride –
> Till the yellow-haired young Eulalie became my smiling bride.

Mallarmé singled out the last line for especial praise; the English reader may find it or the others hard to savour. (To current taste, Poe's choice of names is singularly unfortunate. *Eulalie* seems excessively melodious; *Ligeia* and *Porphyrogene* might be proprietary medicines.) The opening lines of 'Lenore' are almost as bad as those from 'Eulalie':

> Ah, broken is the golden bowl! the spirit flown forever!
> Let the bell toll! – a saintly soul floats on the Stygian river;
> And, Guy de Vere, hast thou no tear? – weep now or nevermore!
> See! on yon drear and rigid bier low lies thy love, Lenore!

If we are to be flippant about such resounding stanzas, we may even catch premonitory likenesses. Is there not a hint of Rudyard Kipling's Suez in Poe's

> Far down within the dim West
> Where the good and the bad and worst and the best
> Have gone to their eternal rest –

or even of John Betjeman, connoisseur of Victorian and Edwardian England, in this couplet from 'Al Aaraaf':

> What guilty spirit, in what shrubbery dim,
> Heard not the stirring summons of that hymn?

But this is unfair to Poe. Even in the bad poems there are redeeming features. 'For Annie' offers

> Its old agitations
> Of myrtles and roses.

'The City in the Sea' has a haunting weirdness:

> Resignedly beneath the sky
> The melancholy waters lie.
> So blend the turrets and shadows there
> That all seems pendulous in air,
> While from a proud tower in the town
> Death looks gigantically down.

And if it is hard to appreciate any part of 'The Bells', 'The Raven', or the play-fragment 'Politian', there are shorter poems of compelling beauty. In the 'Sonnet – to Science', Poe laments the disappearance of magic:

> Hast thou not torn the Naiad from her flood,
> The Elfin from the green grass, and from me
> The summer dream beneath the tamarind tree?

One may object to 'Elfin', but the cry of the poem is authentic. So is that of 'Romance', whose second stanza begins:

> Of late, eternal Condor years
> So shake the very Heaven on high
> With tumult as they thunder by,
> I have no time for idle cares
> Through gazing on the unquiet sky –

though the poem continues with a regrettable poultry-plucking image:

> And when an hour with calmer wings
> Its down upon my spirit flings. . . .

'Alone' and 'A Dream within a Dream' are excellent poems. But we must take into account the rest of his writing to understand why he is thought a major figure.

Poe's stories form a more substantial claim to remembrance. If we leave out the comic ones, most of which are painful or even horrible (for instance, 'The Spectacles', in which a short-sighted man falls in love with a woman who proves to be his great-great-grandmother; or 'The Man Who Was Used Up', about a soldier so mutilated that he is like 'a large and exceedingly odd-looking bundle of something'),[1] they fall roughly into two kinds: those of horror and those of 'ratiocination'. Under the first head may be listed such stories as 'The Black Cat', 'The Cask of Amontillado', 'The Fall of the House of Usher', and 'Ligeia'; while the second group includes 'The Gold

---

1. For further comment on these see pp. 207–8 below.

Bug', 'The Purloined Letter', and so on. The distinction is not sharp; stories like 'The Murders in the Rue Morgue' combine the macabre with the methodical. Indeed all his stories have the special Poe flavour. Many are set in strange places – a ruined abbey, a castle on the Rhine – with elaborate and dimly or luridly lit décors. (His ideal room, as depicted in 'The Philosophy of Furniture', has window panes of crimson-tinted glass.) Things usually happen at night, or in unlit interiors. The heroes and heroines are of ancient and aristocratic lineage (rarely are they American): they are erudite and accomplished – yet doomed. In such particulars Poe hardly differs from the mass of sensational writers who used the trappings of the Gothic novel. The 'tale of effect' was by no means invented by Poe; he acknowledged the success of the examples that appeared in *Blackwood's Magazine*, and jibed at them in 'How to Write a Blackwood Article':

There was the 'Dead Alive', a capital thing! – the record of a gentleman's sensations when entombed before the breath was out of his body – full of taste, terror, sentiment, metaphysics, and erudition. You would have sworn that the writer had been born and brought up in a coffin.

This quotation suggests in part what lifts Poe out of the ruck: the quality of intelligence and self-awareness. His stories, as Baudelaire noted, show 'absurdity installing itself in the intellect, and governing it with a crushing logic'. Though the ghastliness is occasionally overdone,[1] it is made more nightmarish by the measured deliberation with which it is unfolded. Here we are reminded of Poe's own life – as when he could write (in a letter of 1848) of the visiting clergyman who 'stood smiling and bowing at the madman Poe!' It is the same terrible lucidity that makes his fiction better than melodrama. Calamity –

> the cloud that took the form
> (When the rest of heaven was blue)
> Of a demon in my view –

is inbred, not accidental: it cannot be averted. We may apply to Poe some lines of Baudelaire:

> Je suis les membres et la roue
> Et la victime et le bourreau.
>
> ————
>
> Je suis de mon coeur le vampire...

1. As in 'Ligeia', in which an artificially induced current of air keeps the draperies in constant motion. Theatrical devices such as this are discussed in Nathan B. Fagin, *The Histrionic Mr Poe* (Baltimore, 1949).

I am the vampire of my own heart: the hero in Poe's tales destroys himself. Yet his destruction involves others, particularly the heroine. 'The Philosophy of Composition', in which Poe analyses the structure of 'The Raven' and implies that he wrote it according to formula, includes this much-quoted passage:

I ask myself – 'Of all melancholy topics, what, according to the universal understanding of mankind, is the *most* melancholy?' Death – was the obvious reply. 'And when,' I said, 'is this most melancholy of topics most poetical?' From what I have already explained . . . the answer . . . is obvious – 'When it most closely allies itself to *Beauty*': the death, then, of a beautiful woman, is unquestionably, the most poetical topic in the world – and equally is it beyond doubt that the lips best suited for such topic are those of a bereaved lover.

There may appear little in this statement to startle; love and death run close together in the world's literature, and the death of a beautiful woman is the theme of the unhysterical Henry James, in *The Wings of the Dove*.

But Poe's deaths are of a special order. It is the no man's land between death and life that obsesses him, and the incestuous vampirism of the dead with the living. Ligeia and her husband; Roderick Usher and his twin sister Madeline; the painter and his wife in 'The Oval Portrait'; Berenice and her cousin; Morella and her nameless daughter – in all cases the dead return from unquiet graves, as Poe's own cousin-wife seemed to slip from life to death and back again. Only in 'Eleonora' do the dead relinquish their hold upon the living; but even here there have been ties across limbo. This is the desperation of Poe's story world: life ebbs away, swiftly and remorselessly, yet death does not bring peace. For him nothing is stable or sweet. Even his beautiful women are described as though they were corpses; they are human beings with marble poured over them, smooth, white, monumental, and a little gruesome – much like academic sculpture of the period.

In common with such sculpture, some of Poe's stories leave us indifferent, or seem repellent. 'Ligeia', which Poe thought his best grotesque story, is impaired by morbid self-pity and gimcrack Gothicism. Other stories have retained their sinister spell; and these are the ones which avoid vampirism, and concentrate upon various forms of suffering. Poe's imagination is in many respects that of a brilliant and neurotic child. Like a child, he shows off, he dreams of power. Like a child, he is vulnerable, not only to night-time fears (lamps blown out, waving curtains), but to the physical oppression of a giant-adult world, whose doors are too heavy to open, and whose locks too stiff to turn. (Many of his plots are claustrophobic, vertiginous: victims are walled in, entombed alive, sucked down into whirlpools.) To these anxieties we still respond. And we still read with pleasure his pieces of ratiocination. Though he sometimes exhibits to a naïve degree his pride in logic and learning, they are admirably constructed; and his mastermind, Auguste Dupin, is one of the very first in literature's endless procession of omniscient criminologists.

Poe's *Narrative of Arthur Gordon Pym* is his most sustained piece of imaginative storytelling. It was based on an account of an actual South Sea expedition. Such reports from the world's edges, with their evocation of the unknown, the marvellous and the ominous, exercised a powerful influence upon the sensibility of the age. In Poe's tale the matter-of-fact modulates into the sinister and supernatural. A young stowaway aboard a whaler becomes involved in a mutiny, then in a storm which claims the lives of almost the entire ship's company. At the end, the youngster and another survivor are borne in a canoe, through a dream landscape towards the South Pole, heading into a weird whiteness presided over by an immense white figure . . . here the narrative breaks off.

Anthologies usually omit Poe's satirical sketches – understandably, since the humour in them is often forced and misanthropic. They are also taken to be less representative of Poe, just as Cooper's *The Crater* is felt to be less typical than the Leatherstocking series. But in both cases the less familiar writings, complicatedly irascible and pessimistic, provide glimpses of covert uneasiness as to the supposed triumphant progress of modern man. Some of Poe's stories have made a new reputation in the realm of science fiction for their ingenious future-oriented post-mortems on American republicanism. In these Poe's gentleman persona has tinges of savant, aesthete, and nobleman (or, in the American version, Southern planter). The narrator dissociates himself from the democratic imperative, much as did the majority of European commentators, but to an extent unparalleled among American men of letters of his day (with the partial exception of certain minor Southern works, such as *The Partisan Leader*, 1836 – a prediction of despotism and civil war by the Virginia law professor Nathaniel Beverley Tucker).

'The Colloquy of Monos and Una' is an example of a fantasy in the shape of a philosophical dialogue. 'Mellonta Tauta', written near the end of Poe's life, is another:[1] Poe imagines a group of scholars aboard a balloon in the

---

1. 'Mellonta tauta', also used by Poe as epigraph for 'Monos and Una', is a rendering of a phrase from Sophocles: 'These things are in the future.'

year AD 2848, speculating as to the downfall of the vanished civilization of 'Amricca'. Poe adds the date 'April 1st', and in part the joke seems to be on pundits who theorize over-confidently, and inaccurately, on the basis of too few facts. But the humour is in the main superciliously bleak. The joke is on 'Amricca' rather than on academe. The narrator explains his initial scepticism at being told by a colleague that the 'ancient Amriccans *governed themselves!* – did anybody ever hear of such an absurdity? – that they existed in a sort of every-man-for-himself confederacy', like prairie dogs. Little by little, we gather, Amriccans discovered their system of democracy was unworkable. Mob rule (exemplified for Cooper by the Steadfast Dodges and their following) subverted the republic. Out of the resultant anarchy came the inevitable sequel – despotism.

A few poems, some stories and *Arthur Pym*: these are Poe's claim to fame as a creative writer. But in estimating his stature we must mention his critical essays. To compare them with the work of his master, Coleridge, is to realize Poe's limitations as a critic. He can be shrill and vindictive; too closely involved in the literary squabbles around him, he can castigate and praise for the wrong reasons. He smells out plagiarism with the fury of a witch-doctor. His insistence upon precision of language is apt to seem fussy; he was capable of occasional slack writing which he would not condone in others. His larger theories are impressionistic, and the philosophizing in *Eureka* is obscure. Nevertheless he is full of perceptive comment (on Macaulay, for example: 'We assent to what he says, too often because we so clearly understand what it is that he intends to say'). He takes his criticism seriously, pitching it on an ambitiously high level. Even if he is not always consistent, he provides theories for all that he has tried to write, theories that may serve others. Poetry should aim at beauty, but should be composed in obedience to rigorous technical standards. Like stories, poems achieve their maximum effect if they are fairly short; there is no place in Poe's system for the epic poem and not much for the three-decker novel. Perhaps his view that history's trend was towards 'the curt, the condensed, the pointed', was a rationalization of his own habit of writing for magazine publication; for the nineteenth century continued to absorb long novels despite his prophecy. As far as America is concerned, the important facts are that Poe had ideas and standards; that he brought a welcome professionalism to American letters; and that though he now and then 'tomahawked' innocent victims, it was good for native authors to be warned that literature was an exacting trade.

But we have still not grasped his full significance, and cannot do so without considering *Edgarpo*: the man whom Baudelaire and Mallarmé acclaimed so fervently and translated with such rich sympathy. It might indeed be argued that they invented *Edgarpo*; that in their version the pinchbeck became gold, the flamboyant vocabulary was identified as *poésie pure*: the harried magazinist appeared (to paraphrase Baudelaire) as the tragic young aristocrat, alone in a barbarous, gaslit America. We must admit that this figure does not altogether correspond to Edgar Allan Poe. It does, however, correspond to Poe as he wished to present himself to the world, and to certain real aspects of his work which align him rather with the symbolists of a later generation than with the Gothic writers of a previous one. Where his English and American (especially Bostonian) contemporaries sought to 'inculcate a moral', he pleaded for the 'poem written solely for the poem's sake'. Yet though 'with me poetry has been not a purpose, but a passion', intellect came to the rescue of imagination. Underlying the extravagances and vulgarities of Poe's fantasy world are hints of subtle, hitherto unanalysed correspondences and compulsions. We are accustomed by now in literature to the equation of one sense with another, or to be told that human behaviour is frequently cruel and irrational. To Baudelaire, on the other hand, it came with the excitement of a revelation to read, in Poe's *Marginalia*, that 'The orange ray of the spectrum and the buzz of the gnat ... affect me with nearly similar sensations'; and to be asked, in 'The Black Cat', 'Who has not, a hundred times, found himself committing a vile or a silly action, for no other reason than because he knows he should *not?*' For the French, such insights established Poe as one of the great forerunners of modern literature, and they came to venerate him as a symbolic figure as much as for his various discoveries. It has taken longer for the English-speaking world to view him thus; the delay, it could be said, is explicable in terms of the time that it took English verse to respond to the influences of the Continent. Baudelaire's *Fleurs du mal* was published in 1857; the only important volume of poetry to come out that year in England was Elizabeth Barrett Browning's *Aurora Leigh*. But Whitman, at any rate, though he disliked what Poe represented, was not blind to his inner meanings. In 1875, after the ceremony at Poe's grave for which Mallarmé contributed a famous sonnet, Whitman spoke of a dream he had had, of

one of those superb little schooner yachts I had often seen lying anchor'd, rocking so jauntily, in the waters around New York, or up Long Island sound – now flying uncontroll'd with torn sails and broken spars through the wild sleet and winds and waves of the night. On the deck was a slender, slight, beautiful figure, a dim man, apparently enjoying all the terror, the murk, and the dislocation of which he was the centre and the victim. That figure ... might stand for Edgar Poe, his spirit, his fortunes, and his poems....

His dream may recall to us Rimbaud's 'Le Bateau ivre', which itself derived from Poe. Poe and *Edgarpo*, word and echo, are in truth indistinguishable. Yes, perhaps he is more interesting to read *about* than to read; one may not enjoy his work, but one cannot ignore it. It has become part of us; we are his kin, and in this sense has the American poet Allen Tate spoken of him as 'Our Cousin, Mr Poe'.[1]

1. An article reprinted in *The Forlorn Demon* (Chicago, 1953).

V

New England's Day
Emerson, Thoreau, Hawthorne

─────────

Ralph Waldo Emerson (1803–82)

Born in Boston, son and grandson of ministers; educated at Boston Latin School and Harvard. He became pastor of the Second Church, Boston, 1829; he married Ellen Tucker, who died in 1831. In 1832 he resigned his pastorate, and made the first of three visits to Europe (other visits were in 1847 and 1872). On his return, he settled at Concord, Massachusetts; in 1835 he married Lydia Jackson, changing her name to 'Lydian' so that it would go better with 'Emerson'. He determined upon a career of writing and lecturing, and gradually achieved fame. He continued to live in Concord, though he was frequently in Boston, and absent on lecture tours. He kept himself as far as possible from public affairs, though he took his share of citizen duties in Concord, and acquired a heated interest in abolitionism during the 1850s. His works included: *Nature* (1836); the 'American Scholar' oration, Harvard (1837); the 'Divinity School' address, Harvard (1838); *Essays* (two series, 1841, 1844); *Poems* (1847); *Representative Men* (1850); *English Traits* (1856); *The Conduct of Life* (1860); *May Day* (verse, 1867); *Society and Solitude* (1870); *Letters and Social Aims* (1876).

Henry David Thoreau (1817–62)

Born in Concord, Massachusetts, son of an unsuccessful storekeeper who turned to the manufacture of pencils; educated at Harvard, where he was undistinguished but he read widely. After graduating, he had a brief skirmish with the teaching profession. He became friendly with Emerson, and lived in his house 1841–3. He spent a few months on Staten Island as tutor to Emerson's nephew. Thoreau became acquainted with New York writers and editors and placed one or two reviews, but was unhappy and ill at ease ('They say there is a *"Ladies' Companion"* that pays – but I would not write anything companionable'). Thoreau spent the rest of his life (unmarried) in the vicinity of Concord; in 1845–7, he built himself a hut by Walden Pond and lived there alone, reading, and writing in his journal. Returning to Concord, he divided his time between his journal, lectures, walks in the country, and surveying. In 1849 he published *A Week on the Concord and Merrimack Rivers*; also the essay 'Civil Disobedience' (originally called 'Resistance to Civil Government').

His other main work was *Walden* (1854); Thoreau also produced sundry essays and poems.

NATHANIEL HAWTHORNE (1804–64)

Born in Salem, Massachusetts, son of a sea captain who died in 1808. Hawthorne was educated at Bowdoin College, Maine, where he met Longfellow and Franklin Pierce (later President of the U.S.). On graduation, he lived in seclusion at Salem, where he wrote a novel (*Fanshawe*, published anonymously, 1828) and short stories, sketches, and so on (collected for book publication as *Twice-Told Tales*, 1837, 1842). He left Salem in 1836 to work in Boston, as a hack-writer and at Boston Custom House. In 1841 he joined Brook Farm community; in 1842, Hawthorne married Sophia Peabody, who was something of a transcendentalist ('Mr Emerson is Pure Tone'), and moved to the Old Manse at Concord. Further tales and sketches appeared in *Mosses from an Old Manse* (1846). During 1846–9, he worked as port-surveyor at Salem; afterwards he lived in the Berkshires (where he was friendly with Herman Melville). Hawthorne was in Liverpool, as American consul, 1853–7, then in Italy, and then he went back to Concord, 1860. Hawthorne's first great success was *The Scarlet Letter* (1850), followed by his other novels, *The House of the Seven Gables* (1851), *The Blithedale Romance* (1852), and *The Marble Faun* (1860). His other work included *The Snow Image* (short stories, 1851); books for children (*Tanglewood Tales* and so on); *Our Old Home* (1863), essays on England; and posthumous fragments.

NEW ENGLAND'S DAY

NEITHER Irving, Cooper, nor Poe liked New England. In his *History of New York* Irving pictured it as a region of unscrupulous Yankee traders with names like Preserved Fish. Cooper objected to its solemnity and self-righteousness. Poe's opinions were still more decided. Boston he referred to as 'Frogpondium': never was a man less proud of his birthplace. Frogpondium was the home of 'that ineffable buzzard', the *North American Review*, which since its foundation in 1815 had steadily grown in influence and assurance. This periodical, Poe thought, abetted New England writers in maintaining a mutual admiration society. In a review of J. R. Lowell's *Fable for Critics* he burst out:

It is a fashion among Mr Lowell's set to affect a belief that there is no such thing as Southern literature. Northerners . . . are cited by the dozen . . . , while Legaré, Simms, Longstreet, and others of equal note, are passed by in contemptuous silence. Mr L. cannot carry his frail honesty of opinion even so far South as New York. All whom he praises are Bostonians; other writers are barbarians. . . .

Regional pride apart, Poe had principled reasons for disliking the products of Frogpondium. He insisted that the writer was an artist, not a preacher; the literature of Boston and the New England hinterland was packed with moral sentiment – even that of Longfellow, whose work he in general admired. As for Emerson and the others whom Poe thought of as 'transcendentalists', they offended against every article of his creed. Contrast his observations on the nature of poetry with Emerson's journal entry of 1838, that 'the high poetry of the world from the beginning has been ethical, and it is the tendency of the ripe modern mind to produce it'. Or set against Poe's 'Philosophy of Composition' Emerson's instruction to the bard (in 'Merlin') that

> He shall not his brain encumber
> With the coil of rhythm and number.

'Mr Ralph Waldo Emerson', said Poe in his *Chapter on Autography*, 'belongs to a class of gentlemen with whom we have no patience whatsoever – the mystics for mysticism's sake. . . .' Elsewhere, giving sarcastic advice on how to imitate the 'tone transcendental', he said that its

merit consists in seeing into the nature of affairs a very great deal farther than anybody else. This second sight is very efficient when properly managed . . . Put in something about the Supernal Oneness. Don't say a syllable about the Infernal Twoness. Above all, study innuendo. Hint everything – assert nothing.

Poe's remarks form a good introduction to the New England writers, for he was right in detecting a special Boston tone. New England's history made for earnestness. The extremer Puritan mood had gone; around Boston itself Unitarianism – that 'feather-bed to catch a falling Christian' – had gained some hold; the wealthy merchant and shipowner were more interested in the solvency than the religious zeal of their clients. Yet the 'didactic heresy' still hovered over the scene. New England's culture was still religious; its men of letters were, in one sense, men of God, even if they preferred to speak of the deity as Nature, and if like Hawthorne they belonged to no church. Transcendentalism, as Perry Miller has said in his anthology of the movement, 'is most accurately to be defined as a religious demonstration'.[1] Interest in religion was not confined to New England; the nineteenth century saw religious controversy everywhere in the Western world, and the clash of dogma and secularism, the individual hesitations over unsatisfying alternatives, the succession of hard-fought rearguard actions: all these were staged in Europe with more *éclat* and intellectual weight. In New England it was rather a broadening of faith than a loss of faith which exercised the religiously minded; a search for limits, and – as always in American experience – an attempt to arrive at an attitude suitable to the variegated bustle of the American scene.

Towards the middle of the century Boston became, if not the hub of the universe (as Oliver Wendell Holmes genially described it), at any rate the cultural centre of the United States. Other cities – New York, New Orleans, Philadelphia – were larger; others again – Charleston, for example – had developed fairly elegant forms of society. But Boston took the lead, buttressed by nearby Harvard and nourished by the wealth its ships brought in. Private income matched public occasion; club, library, periodical, publishing house ran together. Much was still lacking. William Charvat, the historian of American publishing, has shown that before 1850 New York and Philadelphia both had bigger publishing hinterlands

1. *The Transcendentalists* (Cambridge, MA, 1950), 8.

than Boston. Until mid-century most of the work of New Englanders reached publication outside New England. The Boston firm of Ticknor and Fields, which combined promotional flair with a strong list of foreign and domestic authors, and managed to achieve nationwide distribution, was not founded until 1843. Boston's *Atlantic Monthly* was not launched until 1857; its New York rival, *Harper's*, had started in 1850. Henry James, in his ever so slightly patronizing biography of Hawthorne, evokes the hunger for culture that beset the parlours of Boston, where a volume of Flaxman's weak engravings from Dante could provide a whole evening's entertainment. It was, he stresses, a provincial place. But it had metropolitan qualities as well as ambitions, and the 'proper Bostonians' of the Boston–Cambridge axis, who will be discussed in chapter 7 below, were not negligible.

Here, however, we are concerned with New Englanders who were not, strictly speaking, Bostonians: who, indeed, resisted urban influences while undoubtedly drawing advantages from them in their rural homes. Hawthorne, visiting a family on a secluded New Hampshire island in 1852, saw on the parlour table a copy of Ruskin's *Pre-Raphaelitism* (published in England only the previous year), together with a tract on spiritualism. Many another New England home could have offered a similar choice of -isms. The young Harvard graduate, fresh from the Divinity School, carried his books and ideas to some quiet white township, and from his pulpit intimated truths which his predecessors would have at once condemned. If he wished to write, no grave financial difficulties stood in his way. The region around Boston, or behind any of New England's ports, was still unspoiled countryside, in which the aspiring writer could live for next to nothing, growing his own food (as Emerson, Thoreau and Hawthorne all did), and making now and then a journey to Boston to borrow books or meet an editor. An occasional article or lecture appearance would bring him in a useful few dollars and keep his name before the public, such as it was.

In this world of literate close-knit communities on the periphery of Boston, appeared the phenomenon of transcendentalism. It is an imprecise term, and hard to pin on to any of the major figures of the time. It originated in Kant's *Critique of Practical Reason* (1788): 'I call all knowledge *transcendental* which is concerned, not with objects, but with our mode of knowing objects....' But it reached the United States mainly in translation, and above all through the mediating influence of the Englishman Samuel Taylor Coleridge, particularly through his *Aids to Reflection* (1829).

Emerson, reminiscing on the wrongness of the notion that a doctrinaire set was attempting 'to establish certain opinions and inaugurate some movement in literature, philosophy, and religion', contended that there were

only here and there two or three men or women who read and wrote, each alone, with unusual vivacity. Perhaps they only agreed in having fallen upon Coleridge and Wordsworth and Goethe, then on Carlyle, with pleasure and sympathy. Otherwise, their education and reading were not marked, but had the American superficialness, and their studies were solitary.

Emerson did well to emphasize the isolation of these people, to whom no collective noun – 'group' or 'movement' – seems quite to apply. Loneliness and apartness have characterized the American author, from Poe's day onwards. Even exuberantly American authors such as Whitman have had surprisingly few friends with whom to associate professionally. In New England, if we except a circle of Bostonians, this has been especially true. It is easy to write of the literary activity of the time – the *Flowering of New England* of Van Wyck Brooks's title – as though its authors formed one big family. In a way, they did: Emerson, Thoreau, and Hawthorne lived for a while in the same village, Concord; and they and other personages pop continually in and out of one another's diaries and letters. Yet it would be less accurate to say that they knew one another than that they knew *of* one another. Each stood somewhat aside, a little critical of his companions, a little derisive, reluctant to commit himself. 'But how insular and pathetically solitary', Emerson confided to his journal, 'are all the people we know!' In the same source he notes that the happy author is the one who, ignoring public opinion, 'writes always to *the unknown friend*'. Of the known, he remarks that 'my friends and I are fishes in our habit. As for taking Thoreau's arm, I should as soon take the arm of an elm tree.' After Hawthorne's death, he reflects sadly that he has waited in the hope that he 'might one day conquer a friendship. . . . Now it appears that I waited too long.'

The point should be qualified with the reminder that America as a whole lacked Bohemias and artist colonies of the sort that could be found in France or Germany – above all in and around Paris. The New Englanders were perhaps less hearty than one or two of the New York coteries, but even those were tame by the standards of *la vie de bohème* in Europe. A second qualification is that a number of Transcendentalists did engage in communal and reformist activities. In not joining, Emerson and Thoreau were not entirely typical of those semi-kindred spirits who ran magazines, taught school, joined and even founded protest movements, and established the Brook Farm Utopian colony, which George Ripley heroically sustained from 1841 to 1847. Ripley, like Emerson, was a former Unitarian minister. Theodore Parker was one of the Boston Transcendentalists who hung on as a clergyman, though a somewhat unorthodox one; and he was an abolitionist. Nevertheless other people who were not sympathetic to these positions simultaneously laughed at the looseness of Transcendentalism, and exaggerated the unity of its proponents.

They were actually prepared to agree, as Emerson observed, on very little. Something emanating from certain German authors, and filtering through into England, attracted them and provided them with a loose philosophical structure. Transcendentalism suggested to them that theirs was a benevolent universe, which exhibited or could exhibit a steady movement towards perfection. In Tennyson's words:

> Yet I doubt not through the ages one increasing purpose runs,
> And the thoughts of men are widened with the process of the suns,

That much was European, and part of the humanitarian surge of the century, with its concomitant interest in education, in temperance, in abolitionism, in women's rights, in emigration to new countries. What was American about the movement – as expounded by Emerson, Thoreau, Parker, Margaret Fuller, Ripley, several of the Channing family, and others (including Whitman) – was the conviction that their country offered opportunities of a unique order. As the Mormons located Zion 'on this continent', so the transcendentalists were sure that only in America could the 'private man' expand to his full stature.

Transcendentalism has its comic aspects. Its wilder followers had little but good-heartedness and enthusiasm to commend them. One man who attended a transcendentalist meeting said, according to Emerson, that 'it seemed to him like going to heaven in a swing'. And 'at a knotty point in the discourse, a sympathetic Englishman with a squeaking voice interrupted with the question, "Mr Alcott, a lady near me desires to inquire whether omnipotence abnegates attribute?"' This was Amos Bronson Alcott, the father of Louisa May, who herself wrote an amusing account of 'Transcendental Wild Oats'. Alcott had a collection of 'orphic sayings', of which one on *Temptation* is a fair sample:

Greater is he, who is above temptation, than he, who having been tempted, overcomes. The latter but regains the state from which the former has not fallen. He who is tempted has sinned; temptation is impossible to the holy.

There is a staggering innocence in such a belief, as perhaps there was in the Utopian communities which the transcendentalists established at Brook Farm and Fruitlands. Such matters are for us, however, chiefly significant as a backcloth to the New England scene, and to the work of Emerson, Thoreau and Hawthorne, the three New Englanders implicated in transcendentalism who have a decisive claim to be read for their literary quality.

RALPH WALDO EMERSON

'MYSTICISM for mysticism's sake': these words of Poe were casually uttered. As did many others, he took Emerson for a type of the transcendentalists: the main culprit because the reputed leader. Certainly Emerson stated the transcendentalist outlook more fully than any of his fellows. His main beliefs were indicated fairly early in life, in three works: *Nature*, a small book of which only 500 copies were sold in twelve years; the 'American Scholar' lecture; and the Harvard 'Divinity School' address. He asserted that man and his world formed a perfect harmony, whose proofs were evident in every fact of nature and of human experience; and that the voices of orthodoxy, of tradition, of the past, were to be ignored in favour of one's own intuitive searchings. In a confusing terminology adapted from Coleridge, intuition was a feature of 'Reason', to be contrasted with 'Understanding' or conventional, logical, uninspired thought. 'Understanding' was the best that flat-footed, materialistic men could do. 'Reason' was the insight that bordered on the divine. 'Books', therefore, 'are for the scholar's idle times'; 'only so much do I know, as I have lived'. Man's primary task was to be true to himself; introspection, far from isolating him, would bring him out into the great arena of a common truth:

the deeper he dives into his privatest, secretest presentiment, to his wonder he finds this is the most acceptable, most public, and universally true. The people delight in it; the better part of every man feels, This is my music; this is myself.

Each Divinity School student was 'a newborn bard of the Holy Ghost', whom Emerson exhorted to 'cast behind you all conformity, and acquaint men at first hand with Deity'. The advice was considered shocking by the elders who heard his address; Deity had lost its definite article, and the place allotted it seemed too extra-curricular even for Unitarians, who were said only to require acceptance of 'the fatherhood of God, the brotherhood of Man, and the neighbourhood of Boston'. Life, it appeared, was a treasure hunt, with abundant clues and prizes for everybody. The chief prizes went to the most active and observant; power, activity, genius were all near-synonyms. The only disabilities – it would be too harsh to call them sins – were torpor, incuriosity, or some excess of temperament such as sensuality. Emerson did, though, have harsh words for the church's organization men, the cultus of priests who had made religion a dead thing and whose services were therefore best avoided. It is not surprising that his address delighted most of the younger auditors, but incensed the Unitarian leadership, for whom their denomination was not 'corpse-cold' but humanely reasonable.

These were the themes of the lifelong secular sermon which Emerson went on preaching after he himself had left the Unitarian ministry. There were, he said, happy correspondences to be found throughout existence. His journal for March 1852 has the entry:

Beauty. Little things are often filled with great beauty. The cigar makes visible the respiration of the body, an universal fact, of which the ebb and flow of the sea-tide is only one example.

Nature was the great source of inspiration, for him as for Wordsworth. Hawthorne, walking near Concord one summer afternoon, saw a figure among the trees,

and behold! it was Mr Emerson. He appeared to have had a pleasant time; for he said there were Muses in the woods to-day, and whispers to be heard in the breezes.

Out of such excursions Emerson derived material for his crowded journals; out of these and out of reading, for though he cautioned himself and others against books, he also told himself (in October 1842):

Thou shalt read Homer, Aeschylus, Sophocles, Euripides, Aristophanes, Plato, Proclus, Plotinus, Jamblichus, Porphyry, Aristotle, Virgil, Plutarch, Apuleius, Chaucer, Dante, Rabelais, Montaigne, Cervantes, Shakespeare, Jonson, Ford, Chapman, Beaumont and Fletcher, Bacon, Marvell, More, Milton, Molière, Swedenborg, Goethe.

And he did read them, as well as works by Coleridge, Wordsworth, Carlyle, and by oriental philosophers. Homer, Plato, Dante, Rabelais, Montaigne and Shakespeare particularly impressed him, to judge from his journal.

Emerson's journal, indeed, was his life's task. For over fifty years he set down in it his reflections, without any attempt at regularity, but giving great care to indexing the volumes (ten of them, produced in printed form). They were the raw material of his writing. He explained the process in a letter to Frederic Hedge:

The notes I collect in the course of a year, are so miscellaneous that when our people grow rabid for lectures, as they do periodically about December, I huddle all my old almanacks together & look in the encyclopaedia for the amplest cloak of a name whose folds will reach unto & cover extreme & fantastic things. Staid men & good scholars at first expressed mirth & then indignation at the audacity that baptised this gay rag bag English Literature, then Philosophy of History, then Human Culture, but now to effrontery so bottomless they even leave the path open.

Out of the journal came the lecture, out of the lecture series the volume of essays. His poems originated similarly, many of them attached to his essays as preliminary chants. Thus, the entry for 24 May 1847:

The days come and go like muffled and veiled figures sent from a distant friendly party, but they say nothing, and if we do not use the gifts they bring, they carry them as silently away –

becomes the poem 'Days', one of his best:

> Daughters of time, the hypocritic Days,
> Muffled and dumb like barefoot dervishes,
> And marching single in an endless file,
> Bring diadems and fagots in their hands.
> To each they offer gifts after his will,
> Bread, kingdoms, stars, and sky that holds them all.
> I, in my pleachèd garden, watched the pomp,
> Forgot my morning wishes, hastily
> Took a few herbs and apples, and the Day
> Turned and departed silent. I, too late,
> Under her solemn fillet saw the scorn.

Other instances could be cited, most of them representing less development of a germinal idea than is here apparent. But whether in essay or in poem, it was the central theme, 'the infinitude of the private man', which he sought to explore. Given a constant theme, any amount of variation seemed to him possible, without serious inconsistency or danger to consecutive reasoning. At twenty-one he wrote in his journal of those rare books – 'the Proverbs of Solomon, the Essays of Montaigne, and eminently the Essays of Bacon' – which 'collect and embody the wisdom of their times, and so mark the stages of human improvement'. He would like, he said, to add another volume to the series.

In his own terms he succeeded. Like his models he wrote in aphorism, achieving a quality as personal as, though very different from, that of Florio's translation of Montaigne (of which he was happy to think that Shakespeare and Ben Jonson possessed copies). His journal entries were sometimes anecdotes, sometimes references to nature ('When Edward and I struggled in vain to drag our big calf into the barn, the Irish girl put her finger into the calf's mouth, and led her in directly'), sometimes oblique and gnomic comments like the note on 'the days'. His lectures were an assembly of aphorisms, often admirably terse and unpompous, though not exactly in 'the language of the street' which he found so much more 'vascular and alive' than a page of the *North American Review*. Oratory dazzled Emerson: he paid tribute to Daniel Webster and Edward Everett, the great formal orators of his day. But he also noted that official utterances put the audience to sleep ('every man thinking more of his inconveniences than of the objects of the occasion'), while concrete fact and allusion woke them up. Fascinated by the organic properties of language ('the word made one with the thing'), he said that he would like to have been offered the professorship of rhetoric at some country college. That statement is an interesting clue to both his temperament and his literary method.

The lecture platform was the nearest that Emerson, a shy man lacking in 'animal spirits', could come to his fellows. The contact with the crowd exalted him; the rostrum separated him from too close identification. As a sea of upturned faces, they were Melville's *people*: good, generous, and free. When he mingled with them they turned into Melville's *public*: vulgar, property-engrossed, unreal. As he put it, 'I love man, not men.' 'Look into the stage-coach and see the faces!' he cried, in lines that recall T. S. Eliot's 'I had not thought death had undone so many':

Stand in State Street [Boston] and see the heads and the gait and gesture of the men; they are dooomed ghosts going under Judgement all day long.

Busy with his journal, however, or addressing a lyceum, he was untroubled. On the right social occasions, or in the tête-à-têtes which he professed to like best of all, he left an extraordinary impression of wisdom and goodness. 'A great benign soul' was the reaction of an intelligent observer who saw him in England in 1847. Mary Ann Evans ('George Eliot') met him on the same day. Emerson suddenly asked her to name the book she valued most. 'Rousseau's *Confessions*', George Eliot replied. 'So do I,' he said. 'There is a point of sympathy between us.' Certainly, too, the audiences of his day responded to him. J. R. Lowell wrote to a friend in 1867 that

Emerson's oration was more disjointed than usual, even with *him*. It began nowhere and ended everywhere, and yet ... it was all such stuff as stars are made of, and you couldn't help feeling that, if you waited awhile, all that was nebulous would be whirled into planets, and would assume the mathematical gravity of system. All through it, I felt something in me that cried, 'Ha, ha, to the sound of the trumpets!'

For us the rapture has gone; we are more likely to agree with the suggestion of Henry James, that whereas other writers 'give one a sense of having found their form' (Wordsworth for example), 'with Emerson we never lose the sense that he is still seeking it'. In such a light, it may be felt that his journal is only literature in embryo, his finished work stillborn. Though his sentences, Carlyle observed, were 'strong and simple', the Emersonian paragraph was 'a beautiful square *bag of duck-shot* held together by canvas'. Edward Bellamy, praising the compression of wit in Shakespeare's writing, said (in an 1876 review): 'There is not one word too much, while at the same time it stops short of the ellipses which make many of Emerson's sayings obscure through an excess of affectation of brevity.' When the theme is circumscribed, as in Emerson's delightful sketches of George Ripley and Thoreau, or in his perceptive *English Traits*, the product is more obviously pleasing than in the unconfined essay. His poems, with their awkward, unusual little lines,[1] are also open to objection. They are never ornately platitudinous, like the verse of most of his contemporaries. At times they are arrestingly bold:

> Things are in the saddle
> And ride mankind.

Often, however, they seem brittle and unmusical, or excessively didactic.

Is the want of form symptomatic of a larger deficiency in Emerson's thought? Its elements are as disparate as his sentences. Contradiction faces him at every turn. How to reconcile good with evil, the individual with society, the rival claims of nonconformity and neighbourliness, scholarship with intuition, the need to be up and doing with the equally imperative need to sit down and think? The charge against him is not that

1. Like that later American verbal pioneer, Gertrude Stein, he had a theory that phrase-rhythms should be determined by breathing. In his case, however, the theory may have arisen from the practice of oratory: in hers, she claimed to have learned from the water-drinking of her white poodle, Basket.

he naïvely sought to resolve these problems, but that he missed their serious implications by erecting contradiction into a system. Noting that such problems were stated in opposites, he concluded, in his earlier writings at least, that they were like cosmic see-saws; each opposite cancelled out the other. The notion of polarity seduced him. So, in 'Uriel' (Emerson's mild revenge on the Harvard Divinity School), we are told:

> Line in nature is not found;
> Unit and universe are round;
> In vain produced, all rays return;
> Evil will bless, and ice will burn.

Evil will bless, eventually. Or rather, as Mary Baker Eddy might almost have said, 'Evil is merely privative, not absolute: it is like cold, which is the privation of heat.' In the 'Ode Inscribed to W. H. Channing', after some sharp words on slavery, he finds the consolation that

> Foolish hands may mix and mar;
> Wise and sure the issues are.
> Round they roll till dark is light.

Is Congress corrupt? Corruption is a proof of energy, inseparable from it. Fate is merely 'unpenetrated causes'; 'no statement of the Universe can have any soundness which does not admit of its ascending effort'. Poe's worm is the Conqueror that at the last devours us; in Emerson's verse,

> striving to be man, the worm
> Mounts through all the spires of form.

For Emerson there is no cruel war of irreconcilable extremes; extremes nuzzle one another in their eagerness to come together. Mankind divides into pusher and pushed; but those who go under do so willingly, recognizing the superiority of the leader who has the *plus* of energy which they lack. We are not far here from the doctrine of the Superman, though it would have horrified Emerson.

The case against Emerson may seem convincing. Numerous passages in his essays exasperate or bewilder. There were, said John Jay Chapman, sudden deadnesses in Emerson, 'like the sick notes on a piano'. They suggest a person whose refinement, like that of certain other Americans, was excessive. Few authors came up to his standard. Hawthorne and Tennyson fell short; Shelley he dismissed in 1841, as 'wholly unaffecting to me'. Shelley thought of the poet as the supreme type of man, who must express a passionate awareness of the common human fate: 'the pains and pleasures of his species must become his own.' The thinly fastidious Emerson of our imagining, while he would have agreed in theory, stood apart in practice, separated from his fellow-beings by the walls of his reserve. 'Give all to Love', he advised in the peculiarly unattractive poem of that title – only, do not give all: be ready to relinquish the beloved. Marriage he obliquely commended (in 'Illusions') by arguing that even the worst marriages have compensations. Anti-slavery engaged him, yet as a somewhat abstract cause, and not as a publicly avowed concern until 1844. It has been charged that his love for his first wife was swayed by awareness that her family was a good deal richer than his own. It has been said too that during the Civil War, having convinced himself the cause was righteous, he protected his son from enlistment on the plea of ill-health (young Emerson, born in 1844, lived on until 1931).

Shelley was a rebel whose anarchism brought exile from his own country, and who yet had a clear sense of his purpose as a poet, and of the techniques of poetry. Emerson's rebellion might appear relatively painless. The American Scholar is a blurred figure, prophet (though not messiah) rather than poet. His chief equipment seems to be disinterested-ness. He moves in a void, without audience ('the literary man in this country', Emerson said in 1836, 'has no critic') and without literary antecedents, yet not urgently desiring them, since he believes the perform-ances of the artist, like the testimony of the inspired preacher, should be extempore.

The consequences of such beliefs have been unfortunate. If Emerson actually held them, one might trace a line from him down to the sloppy *bonhomie* of such a work as William Saroyan's *The Time of Your Life*. Or a connection might be seen with the inward and extempore performances of abstract expressionism ('action painting') in the America of the 1950s. In Emerson's day, before the full surge of the Industrial Revolution, the blend of oriental detachment and buoyant individualism seemed acceptable, and Lowell's remarks show this; for as Lowell wrote on another occasion, 'perhaps some of us hear more than the mere words, are moved by something deeper than the thoughts'. Later formulations, in the shape of determinism and nihilism, jar us. If, bearing these in mind, we turn back to Emerson, there are some strange correspondences. Thus the tough-guy morality of a famous statement by Hemingway seems foreshadowed by the gentle Emerson, for whom the name *Concord* might have served as a motto:

Good and bad are but names readily transferable to that or this; the only right is what is after my constitution, the only wrong, what is against it.

No wonder that to the critic Yvor Winters, a man of stern lucidity, Emerson's central doctrine – that of 'submission to emotion' – is inadmissible: 'it eliminates at a stroke both choice and the values that serve as a basis for choice.'

The case for Emerson is less easy to state.

One aspect of his enduring strength can be described, simply, as honesty. This is the aspect that endeared him to Carlyle. There was a shrewd Yankee in Emerson, a blunt fellow who could strip an occasion to its essence. His version of the Norman Conquest was: 'Twenty thousand thieves landed at Hastings.' Though his thoughts seemed to dodge about, his life was an unremitting effort to find the truth by being true to himself. He was a New England seer and seeker, both an accepter and a renouncer, a quiet man and a busy man, who liked 'dry light, and hard clouds, hard expressions, and hard manners'. He was a modest man of boundless ambition. 'Genius', he sighed, weary of a pursuit he could not abandon, 'is sacrificed to talent every day.' Again, 'Miscellany is as bad as drunkenness.'

The nonconforming aspect is worth stressing. Old John Quincy Adams was obviously prepared to loathe him at the end of the 1830s: this 'young man' who 'after failing in the every-day avocations of a Unitarian preacher and schoolmaster, starts a new doctrine of transcendentalism, declares all the old revelations ... worn out, and announces the approach of new revelations.... Garrison and the non-resistant abolitionists, Brownson and the Marat democrats, phrenology and animal magnetism, all come in, furnishing each some plausible rascality as an ingredient for the bubbling cauldron of religion and politics.' Ex-President Adams overstated Emerson's rebelliousness, lumping him with every current craze or cause. But there was an unbought, unbuyable quality in Emerson's cool detachment that struck people as rare, in fact perhaps awesome.

A more difficult aspect to grasp is Emerson's deliberate repudiation of the 'power of blackness'. Newton Arvin has pointed out that Emerson had to struggle toward serenity.[1] The cheerfulness he preached was always qualified by an awareness of the real world's iniquity. It was a non-tragic philosophy which, though perilously near to inanity, was derived from a close study of Platonic and neo-Platonic ideas, and from long meditation.

1. 'The House of Pain', repr. in Milton Konvitz and Stephen Whicher, eds., *Emerson: A Collection of Critical Essays* (Englewood Cliffs, NJ, 1962).

He did not assert that men were good and wise. He demanded that they be better – more candid, more equable, more capable of *seeing*. John Jay Chapman has said that 'Emerson represents a protest against the tyranny of democracy ... If a soul be taken and crushed by democracy till it utter a cry, that cry will be Emerson.' Though the remark tells us more about the perversely courageous Chapman than about Emerson, it contains an important clue. Emerson *was* religiously committed to democracy. 'The grey past, the white future': he *must* believe that men might achieve liberation from their false selves. They must be reborn into wholeness. If this faith proved empty, all was empty. But nothing in the pilgrimage was simple. Good and bad were impossible to separate. Money was a curse, but also the expression of improvement. Change was unsettling, but also imperative. American expansionism was a greedy phenomenon but had a kind of rightness. Jacksonian Democracy, in some ways contemptible, was nevertheless a generous faith. Where was the room in this for an absolute or a conventional morality? James Fenimore Cooper, wrestling with these problems, confessed to an angry defeat. Emerson's Scottish friend Carlyle, became a curmudgeon for whom the extension of political democracy was like tumbling over Niagara in a barrel. Emerson at the extreme end of his life turned soft. It was a preferable development. He had won through to a genuine serenity.

We cannot understand the America of the nineteenth century without coming to terms with Ralph Waldo Emerson. He drew on world-figures (Plato, Swedenborg, Shakespeare, Napoleon, and so on) for his *Representative Men*. Emerson was himself a representative American, as his countrymen gradually realized. There was his contrary mix of the exalted and the ordinary, in the immensities of what Quentin Anderson has termed 'the Imperial Self', together with the Emersonian miscellany of scholarship, datum and gossip. In some ways he is a nineteenth-century, 'ambidexter', Cotton Mather of an author, darting from the homely to the esoteric and back. He is a coiner of epigrams who endeavours to lift them into universality, like the Castilian proverbs that Cervantes loved – 'short sentences from long experience'. At his finest he is a marvellous writer. Here are two vivid examples: a stanza from 'Song of Nature', then a passage from the essay on 'Fate' in *The Conduct of Life*:

> Mine are the night and morning,
> The pits of air, the gulf of space,
> The sportive sun, the gibbous moon,
> The innumerable days.

From that lofty realm we turn to an evocation of horror which may have influenced a famous section in William James's *Varieties of Religious Experience* (1902).[1] Emerson says:

Nature is no sentimentalist.... The habit of snake and spider, the snap of the tiger, ... the crackle of the bones of his prey in the coils of the anaconda, – these are in the system, and our habits are like theirs. You have just dined, and, however scrupulously the slaughter-house is concealed..., there is complicity, ... race living at the expense of race.... Providence has a wild, rough, incalculable road to its end, and it is of no use to try to whitewash its huge, mixed instrumentalities, or to dress up that terrific benefactor in a clean shirt and white neckcloth of a student in divinity.

HENRY DAVID THOREAU

AT first glance no two authors seem closer than Emerson and Thoreau. Both lived in Concord, stirred by the same impulses. Like Emerson, the younger man – deeply struck by a reading of *Nature* – began to keep a journal, from which he culled items for publication. Like Emerson he preached the gospel of independence and the great outdoors. He was likewise affected by only one 'cause', that of anti-slavery. The two men even looked alike. It was natural, then, that Thoreau should be widely regarded as a disciple. Emerson himself, though he sought no relation as self-conscious as that of master–follower, felt that Thoreau's ideas were extensions of his own. J. R. Lowell, one of Thoreau's severest critics, spoke of him as picking up windfalls in Emerson's orchard.

In fact the two men had different personalities and somewhat different aspirations. What they had in common, it might be said, kept them apart. As the years passed contact became increasingly difficult. In May 1853 Thoreau wrote in his journal that he had 'talked, or tried to talk', with Emerson:

Lost my time – nay, almost my identity. He, assuming a false opposition where there

---

1. The passage in *Varieties of Religious Experience* comes in James's chapter on 'The Sick Soul': 'Our civilization is founded on the shambles.... Here on our very hearths and in our gardens the infernal cat plays with the panting mouse, or holds the hot bird fluttering in her jaws. Crocodiles and rattlesnakes and pythons are at this moment vessels of life as real as we are; ... and whenever they or other wild beasts clutch their living prey, the deadly horror which an agitated melancholiac feels is the literally right reaction....' James dwells more than Emerson upon the perils of the everyday; yet both men were well aware of what Calvinist ministers had meant by 'pitfalls': falls into the pit of damnation.

was no difference of opinion, talked to the wind – told me what I knew – and lost my time trying to imagine myself somebody else to oppose him.

At about the same time, Emerson was complaining to *his* journal that

as Webster could never speak without an antagonist, so Henry [Thoreau] does not feel himself except in opposition. He wants a fallacy to expose, a blunder to pillory, requires a little sense of victory, a roll of the drums, to call his powers into full exercise.

How revealing these two entries are: what wary, stiff-necked, no-surrender pride between the two nay-sayers! No wonder that neither liked novels, or that both wrote of friendship as something idealistic – and self-centred. How could the upright man be anything *but* self-centred?

Yet Thoreau has something to communicate that we miss in Emerson's writings. Even more wayward, he is also more robust. Emerson admired the ordinary skills of the world, the work done by hands, but a little wistfully; Thoreau had them at his fingertips, and could act as surveyor, farmer, or carpenter as well as any man in Concord. Emerson's feeling for nature was real enough; but in comparison with that of Thoreau it was limited and 'literary'. 'It seems', Emerson noted in 1851, 'as if all the young gentlemen and gentlewomen of America spent several years in lying on the grass and watching "the grand movements of the clouds in the summer sky" during this century'. The remark charmingly sums up the behaviour of an age of nature lovers, and it might apply in part to Thoreau. He, however, went further into the secrets of nature, not as a professional naturalist – it has been alleged that, for all his minute observation, he added nothing to existing knowledge of local flora and fauna – but as one entering a world denied to most men, merging into the scene like the faun of a classical mythology,[1] or like a sophisticated Bumppo.

The sophistication involved him in difficulties. He was an educated man, who contributed to the transcendentalist *Dial*, and participated in – or at any rate attended – transcendentalist 'conversations'. His problem was that of the complicated man seeking simplicity. He had to make a living, but one that would leave him free; he had to communicate his thoughts yet be sure the act led to no entanglements. Like Emerson he was concerned

1. A faun with his appetites well in check: see his fastidious chapter in *Walden*, 'Higher Laws', in which though he says, 'I love the wild not less than the good', he also declares: 'He is blessed who is assured that the animal is dying out in him day by day, and the divine being established.'

with the individual in relation to society, but in a special way. It was not a question of how the individual was to enter into a harsh, exclusive society, but of how he was to ward off an all too friendly and intrusive one. 'Wherever a man goes', he said in *Walden*, 'men will pursue and paw him with their dirty institutions, and, if they can, constrain him to belong to their desperate odd-fellow society.'

His answers to his various dilemmas were uncompromising. Never married, he had no commitment to provide for others. Part of a homogeneous community, he felt no need to seek a place in it. His place was understood despite himself: he was Henry, the son of John Thoreau, who had not shown a disposition to settle down. Though neighbours disapproved of his vagaries, they did not treat him with hostility, as they might have done a stranger. In few other communities could he have so organized affairs to suit himself. He could live in a civilized village, with men such as Emerson, Hawthorne and Alcott to talk to, and still find his beloved wilderness at the end of the street. Walden Pond, where he built his hut, was only a mile and a half from Concord, on land belonging to Emerson. Thoreau said in a sympathetic review that Carlyle

speaks of Nature with a certain unconscious pathos.... As we read his books here in New England, where there are potatoes enough, and every man can get his living peacefully and sportively as the birds and bees ... it seems to us as if by the world he often meant London ... the sorest place on the face of the earth.... Possibly a South African village might have furnished a more hopeful, and more exacting audience, or in the silence of ... the desert, he might have addressed himself more entirely to his true audience, posterity.

In his own case, Concord served for London or for the desert, according to which way he set his steps; and posterity was the audience he aimed at.

Such was Thoreau's situation. It called for resistance to various pressures, but none was heavy enough to cause serious discomfort. Those who dislike Thoreau have expressed irritation at the unfair ease of his solution. As did R. L. Stevenson, or J. R. Lowell, they have called him 'skulker', and told him he ought to have lived like the rest of his countrymen instead of withdrawing to a vantage-point that was half-hermitage, half-ambush. They have objected that it cost Thoreau little to be gaoled in Concord for refusing to pay poll-tax to a government he considered unjust, since a friend paid the tax on his behalf and had him promptly released – so that he could at once go off and gather huckleberries. They have argued that there was nothing very extreme in living in his Walden hut for a couple of years, almost within smell of his mother's cooking. Possibly, indeed, Thoreau, who at other times made adventurous forays into the Maine wilderness, confined himself to Walden out of sheer contrariness. This was an age of travel and travel literature, exemplified in the narratives of Richard Henry Dana (*Two Years Before the Mast*, 1840) and Francis Parkman (*The Oregon Trail*, 1849). Thoreau was a reader of travel literature. He may for example have been aware of *The Commerce of the Prairies* (1844), a lyrical yet factually precise and faintly misanthropic narrative by Josiah Gregg (1806–50), who ended by avowing his hope to return to the Great Plains, 'to spread my bed ... under the broad canopy of heaven, – there to seek to maintain undisturbed my confidence in men, by fraternizing with the little prairie dogs and wild colts, and the still wilder Indians. ...' At one point Thoreau declared his interest in the American West: 'I must walk toward Oregon, and not toward Europe.' At another point, however, he declared his utter indifference to the 'whole [westward] enterprise of this nation'. His wayward determination to be original may, then, have encouraged him to telescope the westering experience of various contemporaries into the cabin-building at Walden.

Critics of Thoreau have sometimes voiced distaste for the apparent sophistry of his 'Civil Disobedience' essay (which was to influence non-resistance advocates like Tolstoy and Gandhi), as when he announces:

I quietly declare war with the State, after my fashion, though I will still make use and get what advantage of her I can, as is usual in such cases.

Thoreau saw that his position was open to criticism. 'I know of no redeeming qualities in me,' he confessed at the age of twenty-four, 'but a sincere love for some things. ...' These are things in nature. He loves them completely, absorbedly, and without sentiment. Thoreau sits by a woodchuck for half an hour, talking to the creature:

He had a rather mild look. I spoke kindly to him. I reached checkerberry leaves to his mouth. I stretched my hands over him, though he turned up his head and still gritted a little. ... If I had had some food, I should have ended with stroking him at my leisure. ... A large, clumsy, burrowing squirrel. *Arctomys*, bear mouse. I respect him as one of the natives. ... His ancestors have lived here longer than mine.

He also has this feeling about two moose, surprised in the Maine Woods: they are the rightful owners of the wilderness. In a fine passage of the same narrative he regrets the wanton destruction of game and of timber:

Every creature is better alive than dead, men and moose and pine-trees.... It is the living spirit of the tree, not its spirit of turpentine, with which I sympathize, and which heals my cuts. It is as immortal as I am, and perchance will go as high a heaven, there to tower above me still.

J. R. Lowell, who accepted this piece for the *Atlantic Monthly*, enraged Thoreau by deleting the last sentence as too extravagant or too unorthodox for his readers. It was Thoreau's version of transcendentalism; and if he had too little contact with humanity to be a great imaginative writer, his close union with nature preserved him from most of the faults of transcendental literature. Work written deliberately for posterity tends to be ignored by posterity as well as by its own generation. The writer who is too much the seer becomes oracular and tries too hard to load each symbol-sentence with meaning. The *sententia* is apt to sound sententious. Thoreau usually saved himself by writing of what he knew: nature and his own character. Nature's innate rhythms gave shape to his writing and allowed it to flow by like the seasons, instead of coagulating around a series of 'thoughts'. In particular they gave shape to *Walden*, the work by which he is best known. The day-to-day account of how he lived – the food he cooked, the few people with whom he talked, the details of the Pond and its wild-life: these provide a firm base for his assaults upon conventional man: assaults delivered in a prose alert and trenchant like the best of Emerson:

Let us settle ourselves, and work and wedge our feet downward through the mud and slush of opinion ... through Paris and London, through New York and Boston and Concord, through Church and State, through poetry and philosophy and religion, till we come to a hard bottom and rocks in place, which we can call *reality*, and say This is, and no mistake....

Some circumstantial evidence is very strong, as when you find a trout in the milk....

Making the earth say beans instead of grass – this was my daily work.

Sometimes his writing has a metaphorical richness that reminds us of the debt Thoreau owes to such authors as Sir Thomas Browne:

Self-emancipation even in the West Indian provinces of the fancy and imagination – what Wilberforce is there to bring that about?

It has been said that with the exception of passages like this, Thoreau's style is conversational. Like Emerson's, though, it is not vernacular. It takes note of common speech, but not to reproduce it as Mark Twain does.

Rather, it has its own special sound, which is in part contemporary: Thoreau says of Carlyle's books that 'they are ... works of art only as the plough, and corn-mill, and steam-engine – not as pictures and statues'; and almost certainly he would like the statement to apply to his own pages. In part, too, his writing is reminiscent of the pamphleteering prose of a bygone England, as in the hammer-blow sentences of his 'Slavery in Massachusetts', or in 'A Plea for Captain John Brown', who 'died lately in the time of Cromwell, but he reappeared here'.

As for his few poems, they are in technique as unsatisfactory as Emerson's, while free from the mellifluous, proficient monotony of such verse as 'Thanatopsis' or 'To a Waterfowl' by William Cullen Bryant – Bryant (according to Lowell's *Fable for Critics*)

> as quiet, as cool, and as dignified,
> As a smooth, silent iceberg, that never is ignified.

Thoreau's lines have not fully made the transition from the prose of the journal to the form of verse. They rhyme too determinedly, ungainly as pairs tied together in a three-legged race. As in all the work that Thoreau managed to write during his fairly short life, they are on the *qui vive*. But their inadequacy brings us back to the general inadequacy of the literary world of Concord. Like Emerson, who said of Thoreau's poems that 'the thyme and marjoram are not yet honey', the younger man is a cleric without a pulpit, a scholar who condemns scholarship, a person with a rigorous conscience who recommends a kind of carefree anarchism. He is a Huckleberry Finn who has been to Harvard. The two sides are not fully united: we sympathize with his desire to live his life as well as utter it, but suspect him of a typically transcendentalist determination to eat his cake and have it too. As Emerson wishes to combine 'acquiescence and optimism', to be passive and dynamic by turns, so Thoreau shifts his ground, until one can understand Lowell's criticism (of *A Week on the Concord and Merrimack*) that 'we were bid to a river-party – not to be preached at'. But what preaching, and what a party! Thoreau's is magnificent literature almost in spite of itself; and in spite of one's sense that basically he has a low opinion of mankind as a species, so that there is a question as to whether people are worth saving, or capable of being saved from their purblind selves. Nevertheless *Walden* and his other writings are a memorable vision of a period and a place in America when men – some men – thought it possible to find the godhead in the nearby woods: or, with a pride that seems the more inordinate for its modesty, to be like Adam before the Fall. That vision has never ceased to tease the American imagination: and in noting its far-fetchedness we would be wrong to miss the enduring element of human aspiration which it shares with other such searches.

NATHANIEL HAWTHORNE

ONE afternoon in 1842, shortly after Hawthorne moved to Concord, he went on the river with Thoreau, to practise the management of a boat which he had bought from him. Hawthorne found himself quite unable to steer, though

Mr Thoreau had assured me that it was only necessary to will the boat to go in any particular direction, and she would immediately take that course, as if imbued with the spirit of the steersman. It may be so with him, but it is certainly not so with me. The boat seemed to be bewitched, and turned its head to every point of the compass except the right one.

The anecdote illuminates both men: Thoreau, the resolute and capable, who had made the boat with his own hands; Hawthorne, half-amused, half-rueful, all too conscious of the perversities of existence.

The differences between him and Thoreau or Emerson are well known. For them, nature was man's true home; to him nature was beautiful enough, but unconcerned with man. For them the age-old torment over sin, predestination and damnation was needless; these, as Emerson wrote in 'Spiritual Laws', 'never darken-across any man's road who did not go out of his way to seek them. These are the soul's mumps and measles.' For Hawthorne, once they entered a man's life, as they were more than likely to do, there was no road by which they could be avoided.

Why he differed thus is hard to say. Emerson had only to open his window to hear the shrieks of a madwoman confined near by. He lost his first-born son, Waldo; his young wife Ellen and two of his brothers died of tuberculosis, whose shadow also hung over Emerson's own adolescent years. Yet he discerned harmony wherever he looked. Hawthorne's own life was free enough from tragedy; yet he saw destiny's sombre operation all about him. The trite explanation is that Emerson was a transcendentalist, while Hawthorne, unable to accept transcendentalism's offers of emancipation, harked back to an earlier, grimmer New England. This explanation is of course too simple. Hawthorne did at least spend some months at Brook Farm, though he criticized its aims in *The Blithedale Romance*, and the larger implications of transcendentalism in 'The Celestial Railroad'. Nor was his gloom unrelieved: if he was haunted by his witch-hunting ancestor John Hathorne of Salem, he also delighted in the solid world of Trollope's novels. Moreover, his thought had something in common with that of Emerson and other transcendentalists. Like them, he sought the big in the little; as Emerson watching cigar-smoke thought of sea tides, so Hawthorne was forever speculating on the larger significance of some material fact or phenomenon:

Meditations about the main gas-pipe of a great city, – if the supply were to be stopped, what would happen? ... It might be made emblematical of something.

Emblem, symbol, moral, analogy, type, image: these are favourite words of Hawthorne, and he would surely have agreed with Emerson's statement that 'every natural fact is a symbol of some spiritual fact'.

But despite these resemblances, Emerson and Hawthorne are at variance in four important respects. First, Hawthorne's observations are usually of man in society, not of man in nature; and this though his theme is usually of a man in some way set apart: there is always a crowd in the offing. There was an oddly public side to Hawthorne's life, in part because he needed money and was obliged to use his Democratic party affiliation to seek custom-house work. The same concern led him to volunteer to compile a presidential campaign biography of his college classmate Franklin Pierce. Hawthorne's reward from the successful candidate was the consulate at Liverpool, which was regarded as the most lucrative of such political plums. He tried in vain to secure a consular post for Herman Melville. Although Hawthorne found the Liverpool appointment somewhat irksome, and rather less profitable than he had hoped, he derived a certain relish from holding an official position. Apart from the other gratifications, it gave him a ringside seat from which to observe the scene and amass the 300,000 words of his *English Notebooks* (first published in 1941).

Second, while it is possibly unfair to set Hawthorne's notebooks against Emerson's more highly wrought journal, they are strikingly less certain in emphasis. Hawthorne asks questions but rarely answers them: he gropes, with no confidence in the outcome. Third, as has been noted, he is concerned with blacker and bleaker problems than Emerson ever acknowledged. And fourth, he is a writer of fiction, far more occupied than Emerson with the technical questions of authorship. As such, and for temperamental reasons, he is a tentative writer, who speaks of his story-ideas as *hints*.

Could he have been more self-assured? That is the question which Henry

James poses in the biography of Hawthorne. Could a New Englander – or any American, at that time – write satisfactory fiction in and about a land that had so little experience of the art? Hawthorne's task was difficult: was it impossible? Cooper and Irving before him had to some extent succeeded, with the American as well as with the European scene; and in his own lifetime Poe built up imaginary worlds which were compelling if unreal. Perhaps Henry James over-stressed the lack of subject-matter, in his famous enumeration of the missing items in Hawthorne's America. As his notebooks show, Hawthorne had plenty of themes to think about. Society in New England, while possibly thin, was more substantial than that of Mark Twain's Missouri. Hawthorne's diffidence arises from a whole set of uncertainties. Cooper and Irving were not novelists from whom he could learn much; nor did he make any close study of Charles Brockden Brown, whose writings might conceivably have been helpful. Though the sermon, the poem or the private diary were familiar releases to the New Englander anxious to express himself, the novel was a suspect form. In the words (from the preface to *The Scarlet Letter*) which Hawthorne attributes to his ancestors:

'What is he?' murmurs one gray shadow of my forefathers to the other. 'A writer of story books! What kind of business in life, – what mode of glorifying God, of being serviceable to mankind in his day and generation, – may that be? Why the degenerate fellow might as well have been a fiddler!'

In Missouri a fiddler was a useful acquisition to society, and a newspaper humorist like Mark Twain was a welcome, even an honoured figure in a Western community. Hawthorne by comparison worked in the dark. New England was accustomed to didacticism in its literature, and unmitigated didacticism blights the novel. Yet Hawthorne brought himself up on two of the worst models for the would-be novelist as the nineteenth century understood the word: Bunyan and Spenser. Half of him entered the world of allegory and could never get out.

The other half remained in 'the ordinary world' (as he often calls it), closely interested in the gestures and motives of his fellow-men, and in the look of their New England world. This half of Hawthorne is somewhat unimaginative; the character sketches in his notebooks are a little prosaic. The people whose behaviour he jots down are not fully realized; he assembles them as a casting bureau collects actors, and they stand around as if waiting for lines to say.

Hawthorne's problem was to bring the two parts together, to contrive 'a neutral ground where the Actual and the Imaginary might meet'. It was complicated by his reluctance to bring them together in a gloomy place. He believed in the virtues of America, its cheerfulness and newness (in this aspect, he was more obviously patriotic than Emerson or Thoreau). His publishers and many readers urged him to step out into the sunlight. But he did not know how, when nearly all his symbols derived their force – in the words of Melville's review of *Mosses from an Old Manse* – from 'that Calvinistic sense of Innate Depravity and Original Sin, from whose visitations, . . . no deeply thinking mind is always and wholly free'. In *The Marble Faun* Hawthorne said of a building in Rome that

The prison-like, iron-barred windows, and the wide-arched, dismal entrance, . . . might impress [the artist] as far better worth his pencil than the newly painted pine boxes, in which – if he be an American – his countrymen live and thrive. But there is reason to suspect that a people are waning to decay and ruin the moment that their life becomes fascinating either in the poet's imagination or the painter's eye.

He could not admit that his own land had reached such a stage of corruption. It was a country, he said in the preface to *The Marble Faun*, 'where there is no shadow, no antiquity, no mystery . . . nor anything but a commonplace prosperity, in broad and simple daylight'. He did his best to achieve 'a mood half sportive and half thoughtful', so as to square Calvin with the cheerfulness of contemporary America. In 1850, for example, he noted down an idea for an article on cemeteries, with various mottoes, 'facetious or serious'. Some stories and sketches, some interludes in *The Blithedale Romance* and *The House of the Seven Gables*, his gentle mockery of thick-waisted domineering Englishwomen in *Our Old Home*, his books for children, and so on, did attain the lightness of heart and touch that he wished for. But he could not be facetious *and* serious, and where it was necessary to choose, the choice determined itself. It nearly always plunged him into the shadow and antiquity whose existence in 'my dear native land' he had denied.

The Actual and the Imaginary alternate in the 'hints for stories' which are scattered through his notebooks. At one extreme of psychological realism there is the sort of construction that interested Henry James:

A virtuous but giddy girl to attempt to play a trick on a man. He sees what she is about, and contrives matters so that she throws herself completely into his power, and is ruined, – all in jest.

At the other, preternatural extreme are such notes as:

A person to catch fire-flies, and to try to kindle his household fire with them. It would be symbolical of something.

or:

To personify winds of various characters.

Here we are back in the Imaginary with a vengeance. Other suggestions are: an insane reformer – a hero who never falls in love – a ghost by moonlight – thronged solitude – a body possessed by two spirits – return of images in a mirror – ice in the blood – a secret thing in public – a bloody footprint – an eating house with poisoned dishes. Some of them seem the stock-in-trade of horror-romance; and indeed Hawthorne was always in danger of tumbling over what he apologetically called the 'utmost verge of a precipitous absurdity'.

Year after year of his early manhood went by quietly and drably in Salem while, without much faith in his own talent, or much idea of where his notions might lead him, he turned out stories and sketches to exemplify the generalized jottings of his notebook. Sometimes he would destroy what he had written; if it was printed, it would often appear anonymously. Withdrawn, uneasy, commenting with a hurt humour on his lack of popularity with the public, he nevertheless began to make a reputation. Poe congratulated Hawthorne in one of his best reviews, where he outlined his belief in the short story as a literary medium. As Poe realized, and as *Twice-Told Tales* and *Mosses from an Old Manse* made apparent to others, this 'harmless Hawthorne' of Melville's phrase was producing work of a quite special weight. There were conventional essays ('Fire Worship', 'Buds and Bird Voices'); satirical excursions ('The Celestial Railroad'); and every kind of tale, from fantasy to tableaux of New England history. Among them certain stories stand out as remarkably powerful, their effect heightened by the refined, exact, undemonstrative prose in which they are narrated. In 'The Gentle Boy', for example, a Quaker child in an inimical New England settlement is stoned by the other children, and betrayed by one of them whom he has befriended. In 'Egotism; or, The Bosom Serpent', a man estranged from his wife is convinced that he has a live serpent inside him which perpetually gnaws at him. It leaves him only when he is able to meet his wife again and forget for a moment his obsession with his own ills.

An entry in Hawthorne's *American Notebooks* of the late 1830s says:

A young man in search of happiness, – to be personified by a figure whom he expects to meet in a crowd, and is to be recognized by various signs. All these signs are given by a figure in various garbs and actions, but he does not recognize that this is the sought-for person till too late.

Here is a variant on the theme of an earlier tale, one of Hawthorne's masterpieces, 'My Kinsman, Major Molineux'. Molineux, in colonial Boston, is the important figure who is to assist the career of a country boy, Robin, arriving in the city as a raw newcomer. No one will tell him where to find his relative – until the Major appears in the hands of a mob, tarred and feathered. Unthinkingly, Robin laughs with the rest at the spectacle of authority rendered helpless and ridiculous. At the end he accepts the advice of a bystander to remain in Boston and make his own way in the world. The author leaves us to wonder whether this democratic expedient is admirable, or merely inescapable. In the equally ambiguous story of an individual and a community, 'Young Goodman Brown', Hawthorne tells of an early New England in which his hero attends a witches' sabbath, to discover that the company includes not only all the prominent people of his township, but even his wife Faith. Pride, envy, remorse nag his characters; and the unthinking community shuts out the unusual individual. Yet there are virtuous people, and only one sin is unpardonable: that of wilful estrangement from the rest of humanity. This results in the suicide of Ethan Brand; causes Rappaccini to lose his daughter; and leads Reuben unwittingly to kill his son, as expiation for having long ago left Roger Malvin to die. Let Hawthorne but find a usable symbol, and he would erect it into a story.

One such symbol took firm hold. As early as 1837, in 'Endicott and the Red Cross', he mentioned, as one of a crowd in seventeenth-century Salem,

a young woman, with no mean share of beauty, whose doom it was to wear the letter A on the breast of her gown.... Sporting with her infamy, the lost and desperate creature had embroidered the fatal token in scarlet cloth, with golden thread and the nicest art of needlework; so that the capital A might have been thought to mean Admirable, or anything rather than Adulteress.

He reverted to the same symbol in a notebook entry seven years later, and in 1847 began work on what was to be his greatest achievement, *The Scarlet Letter*. Such letters were actually worn in colonial New England; instances have been recorded of a D for Drunkard, and of an I, signifying Incest. They furnished Hawthorne with just the combination of 'moral and material' that he could handle: here was a 'type' bodied forth: here was 'a secret thing in public'. However, despite its near-perfect construction, few great books have been more hesitantly produced. Worries over money prevented him from giving his whole mind to the story. He was troubled by its 'hell-fired' quality, and tried to make the book more attractive by supplying a lengthy preamble on the Salem Custom-house. Moreover, apart from his immature *Fanshawe*, Hawthorne had not written anything longer than magazine stories. If his publisher had not badgered him, it is possible that *The Scarlet Letter* would never have been completed as a novel.

Yet the finished work was a masterpiece. Instead of reading as an over-expanded sketch, as *The Marble Faun* does, it comes over as a concentrated, economical novel. There are only three chief characters, four if we include the child Pearl. The three are Pearl's mother, Hester Prynne the adulteress; her implacable old husband Roger; and Arthur Dimmesdale, the pious young minister who has fathered her child, and who, in failing to confess his sin, endures agonies of guilt. The voluptuous and maternal Hester, expiating her offence, survives to a tranquil old age; the two men are tortured and distorted, the one by conscience, the other by indulging sinfully in the sadistic luxury of revenge. In this one taut, subtle novel Hawthorne solves almost all his problems. Avoiding the a priori Americanism which is crudely contrasted with European depravity in *The Marble Faun*, he sets his trio in colonial Boston. He is able to make the past more real than his American present; when he deals with the latter the 'broad and simple daylight' seems to defeat him: it is the sense of the past that redeems *The House of the Seven Gables*. In that novel, and in *The Blithedale Romance*, he dodges round the question of contemporariness, insisting that they are 'romances', in which reality is to be done by mirrors.

Superb though *The Scarlet Letter* is, it does run into minor difficulties, concerned with his use of symbols. Poe, Henry James and Hawthorne himself have pointed out the authorial risks in dressing up characters to exemplify a theme which may be incompatible with 'actuality'. Emerson complained that 'Hawthorne invites his readers too much into his study, opens the process before them. As if the confectioner should say to his customers, "Now, let us make the cake".' It is what he does in the preface to *The Scarlet Letter*; and in the book itself he searches indefatigably for emblems. The central symbol of the letter worn on Hester's bosom is excellent, being both real and figurative. But Hawthorne cannot resist having a large A in the night sky, or on Dimmesdale's flesh. Too rarely does he trust himself to convey an idea: he must be heavily explicit. Thus, in 'The Gentle Boy':

The two females, as they held each a hand of Ibrahim, formed a practical allegory; it was rational piety and unbridled fanaticism contending for the empire of a young heart.

Suddenly a moving story has lapsed into public-monument cliché. At worst the fault destroys his fiction. 'The Birthmark' is ruined by a mixture of fact and fancy that becomes preposterous; so is 'Drowne's Wooden Image'. In *The Marble Faun* Donatello, with his problematical furry ears, is acceptable neither as a person nor as a symbol. Though *The Blithedale Romance* is a much better book, it too is marred by tiresome symbols. Zenobia's exotic flower and Westervelt's false teeth, like other obvious motifs of Hawthorne, may remind the reader of the alarm-clock crocodile in *Peter Pan*.

The Seven Gables comes next in stature to *The Scarlet Letter*; here Hawthorne deals with the crumbling old house and the malignant Pyncheons as novelist rather than allegorist. He is no more able than Cooper, or William Faulkner in a later generation, to answer finally whether Americans make too much of the past or too little of it. We are never quite sure in *The Seven Gables* of the efficacy of the curse supposedly visited upon the Pyncheons at the time of the Salem witch-trials of the 1690s. If it was a genuine curse, Matthew Maule must surely have been a genuine witch, whom the judges were right, given the standards of their age, to condemn to death? Is young Holgrave, the daguerreotypist who takes 'real' pictures of the modern scene, a true descendant of the Maules? If not, why not? Still, Hawthorne handles his pathetic characters with an acute sympathy, and his obnoxious ones with acute distaste. Victims and bullies are the types which he excels in drawing. The very limitations of Judge Pyncheon, his conceit, his thick-hided selfishness, made him the least symbolical and so the most solidly real of all of Hawthorne's characters. (This is not to say that reality was Hawthorne's only salvation; when he trusted himself wholeheartedly to fantasy, as in 'The Snow Image', he was sometimes highly successful.)

One other potential weakness, from which *The Scarlet Letter* is free, has to do with Hawthorne's view of 'ordinary people'. Ordinariness is his norm; what is extraordinary tends to be suspect. Human beings, he feels, should not tamper with one another. Chillingworth's sin, like Ethan Brand's, is to have 'violated, in cold blood, the sanctity of a human heart'. Any very strong interest or emotion, for Hawthorne, is next door to mania; the reforming zeal of Hollingsworth in *The Blithedale Romance* is only one step short of the madness of Rappaccini. This is what made Hawthorne unsympathetic to abolitionism. Defending the compromises of his Northern 'doughface' friend Franklin Pierce, he maintained that the 'great and sacred reality' of Union ought not to be put in jeopardy by divisive plans for slave emancipation. Those who stressed the moral wrong of slavery were in his eyes tainted with perfectionist arrogance, like so many Hollingsworths. Such reasoning can show Hawthorne as ungenerously conservative – an accusation which would rarely, if ever, fit Melville. Melville admires, even worships, intellectual and artistic talent. Not so Hawthorne, to judge from equivocal stories like 'Rappaccini's Daughter' and 'The Artist of the Beautiful'. Yet what is the novelist or artist but an extraordinary person who pries into the affairs of others? Hawthorne seems to deny his own vocation; and his position is the more ambiguous in that he does not like or at any rate feel at ease with 'ordinary people'. Mistrusting the intellectual, he also despises the boor. Try as he will, he cannot prevent the reader from preferring Ethan Brand to the cloddish villagers of the tale.

These shortcomings should be seen as consequences of Hawthorne's struggle to find his way in fiction without a guide. He has as much honesty as Emerson or Thoreau – which is to say a great deal – and he has a profounder knowledge than they of man's fate, and a correspondingly harder task as writer. Their lack of form represents the weakening of an older line of didactic communication; his lack of certainty represents the beginning of a new line of communication. Paradoxically, he made use of the past in proportion as they rejected it. For him, even in his theoretically sunlit America, there was no new start. As Chillingworth tells Hester,

My old faith ... comes back to me, and explains all that we do, and all we suffer. By thy first step awry thou didst plant the germ of evil; but since that moment, it has all been a dark necessity.

VI

MELVILLE AND WHITMAN

HERMAN MELVILLE (1819–91)

Born in New York City, the son of a prosperous importer who went bankrupt and died in 1832, leaving his widow and children (who moved to Albany, New York) to struggle along with the aid of relatives. Melville worked in a bank, taught school, and sailed as ship's boy to Liverpool and back before going to sea in 1841, in the whaler *Acushnet*, bound for the South Seas. In 1842 he deserted his ship in the Marquesas, encountered a cannibal tribe, and left the islands in an Australian whaler. After further adventures at Tahiti and Honolulu, Melville returned home in 1844 aboard the frigate *United States*. He began to write, using his sea experiences as basis: *Typee* (1846), *Omoo* (1847, in which year he also married), both well received; *Mardi, Redburn* (1849), *White-Jacket* (1850), *Moby-Dick* (1851), *Pierre* (1852). Of these, *Mardi* bewildered the public, *Moby-Dick* met with a disappointing reception, and *Pierre* was a complete failure. Thereafter, he gradually abandoned the effort to support himself by writing, though not until he had produced a number of stories, six of which appeared as *Piazza Tales* (1856), and two more novels, *Israel Potter* (1855) and *The Confidence Man* (1857). Melville turned to verse, most of it – including the long poem *Clarel* (1876) – privately printed. He worked in New York as customs inspector, 1866–85; then lived quietly in retirement, occupying his last months with *Billy Budd* (not published until 1924).

WALT WHITMAN (1819–92)

Born in Long Island, of mixed Dutch and Yankee stock. His father was a carpenter–builder, and in 1823 the family moved to the rapidly growing town of Brooklyn, across the East River from Manhattan. He left school in 1830, to work as a printer; he spent 1838–9 schoolteaching on Long Island, 1841–5 as a journalist, and 1846–7 as editor of the *Brooklyn Daily Eagle*. He disagreed with the Democratic party over political opinions; he was also regarded as a somewhat lazy editor. Out of a job in consequence, he made a brief trip in 1848 to New Orleans. In 1851–4 he worked as carpenter in Brooklyn, while keeping a notebook from which grew poems published as *Leaves of Grass* (1855). These were praised by Emerson and a few others, denounced by some reviewers, but in general aroused little attention. The second edition of *Leaves of Grass* appeared in 1856; the third in 1860. During 1863–5 he worked as clerk and volunteer hospital visitor in Washington, tending the Civil War wounded. *Drum Taps* appeared in 1865. Further editions of *Leaves of Grass* were published in 1867, 1871, 1872, 1876, 1881, 1889, 1892. He continued to work in Washington until 1873, when he suffered a paralytic stroke which left him semi-invalid for the rest of his life. *Democratic Vistas* (prose) was published in 1871. In 1879 he made a journey through the West and Middle West. *Specimen Days and Collect* (autobiographical notes) was published in 1882. In later years he was surrounded by disciples, and well known to men of letters, though still not to the general public. *November Boughs* (prose and verse) appeared in 1888. Whitman died in Camden, New Jersey, unmarried.

VI

MELVILLE AND WHITMAN

HERMAN MELVILLE

THOUGH Emerson and Hawthorne travelled to Europe they found literary sustenance, like Thoreau, in what lay under their noses. For all its limitations, New England nourished them, and along with other New Englanders they extracted a kind of genius from provincialism. Years at sea took Herman Melville far out of the familiar world of New York and Albany. Melville was not the only writer of the time who found the sea a rich source of metaphor. His contemporary, Flaubert, said in 1846 that 'the three finest things in creation are the sea, *Hamlet*, and Mozart's *Don Giovanni*'.[1] Perhaps Hawthorne would have benefited as a writer if he had accepted an offer once made to him to join in a voyage to the South Seas. Melville, unlike Hawthorne, actually made the voyage and was able to bolster his romantic flights with personal knowledge. The sea was for him not only a metaphor, it was also a real highway, along which real men earned their living. Indeed, in Melville's first books it is the reality – though a somewhat romantic one – that engages him. *Typee* pleased a public that was growing tired of travel narratives and sea yarns by presenting a fresh and exciting story couched as autobiography. And in fact, though some of the material was the product of Melville's imagination, he did not seem to regard the book as a novel. His preface claims an 'anxious desire to speak the unvarnished truth'. He equips the story with a map, and adds documentary chapters. (The title of the book as published in England – *Narrative of a Four Months' Residence Among the Natives of a Valley of the Marquesas Islands*; or, *A Peep at Polynesian Life* – was guaranteed to exclude it from the fiction shelves.) The style, as a whole, is that of the traveller on his best literary behaviour:

1. Compare Melville's observation (in a letter, 3 March 1849) that 'I love all men that *dive* ... the whole corps of intellectual thought-divers that have been diving & coming up again with bloodshot eyes since the world began', with Flaubert's 'I am the obscure and patient pearl-fisher, who returns from his dive empty-handed and blue in the face. Some fatal attraction draws me down into the depths of thought, down into those innermost recesses which never lose their fascination for the strong of heart.' (Letter to Louise Colet, 7 October 1846.)

Those who for the first time visit the South Seas, generally are surprised at the appearance of the islands when beheld from the sea. From the vague accounts we have of their beauty, many people are apt to picture to themselves enamelled and softly swelling plains, shaded over with delicious groves, and watered by purling brooks. . . .

Typee is an account, given in the first person, of the adventures of a young American who, with a companion (Toby), jumps ship. Making their way over a mountain range into an inland valley, the two find themselves among the cannibal Typees. Toby is able to leave, but the narrator is compelled to remain with the tribe. To his surprise and relief they treat him kindly. The story ends with his escape from the Typees; they pursue him into the sea, when he is picked up by a ship's boat. The point of this simple account lies in the contrast between the vices of civilization and the virtues of the supposedly barbarous natives, a beautiful and carefree group, with one of whom the young American conducts an idyllic though not very vivid love affair. But if the book has little creative interest, it does exhibit in rudimentary form nearly all the themes that Melville developed in his more ambitious writing. In *Typee* he deals with a voyage and a journey; he castigates white civilization (conventionally enough, with a reference to Rousseau) and its clutter of moral codes; he suggests that the wandering narrator can find satisfaction neither among his own people nor among the savages. And, although Toby's cheerful, extrovert character belies the description, Melville speaks of him as 'one of that class of rovers you sometimes meet at sea, who never reveal their origin, never allude to home, and go rambling over the world as if pursued by some mysterious fate they cannot possibly elude'. Here is sketched out the idea to which he returns in *Moby-Dick*, in the briefly glimpsed yet unforgettable figure of Bulkington.

In *Omoo* Melville takes up the narrative where he left it in *Typee* – with the escape of his hero. He establishes a more ominous atmosphere; for the young American is now in an ancient, condemned whaler, with a mutinous crew and a weak captain. After a death, one of the sailors prophesies that in three weeks not one-quarter of the men will be left aboard. The ship is apparently doomed. But the tension is dissipated, and a mutiny becomes a comic-opera situation, in which the only serious stress is laid upon the degradation of Tahiti. The islanders, their bodies ravaged by the white man's diseases and their culture destroyed by well-meaning missionaries, await extinction, chanting an old prophecy:

> The palm-tree shall grow,
> The coral shall spread,
> But man shall cease.

Again, however, cheerfulness breaks in, as the narrator (with his grotesque crony Dr Long Ghost) knocks about the islands as a beachcomber, until a convenient end can be made out of his decision to leave Tahiti in an American whaler.

Omoo reinforced the public's view of Melville as a writer of jocular and lively reminiscence. But *Mardi*, which followed hard on its heels, was another matter. *Mardi* begins straightforwardly, though the prose is markedly richer:

We are off! The courses and topsails are set; the coral-hung anchor swings from the bow: and together the three royals are given to the breeze, that follows us out to sea like the baying of a hound. Out spreads the canvas – alow, aloft – boom stretched, on both sides, with many a stun'sail; till like a hawk, with pinions poised, we shadow the sea with our sails, and reelingly cleeve the brine.

Two similes and one adverbial coinage in a short passage: these suggest the later Melville. But the tone is breezy, and though the narrator complains of boredom on this particular whaling voyage, there is no suggestion that he is anything other than an energetic, irresponsible young man, better educated than his shipmates but in no way alien to them. Soon the narrator – Taji, as he is called for the greater part of the book – decides to desert, and accomplishes this in a whaleboat, taking with him an old sailor. They head westward for a chain of islands in the Pacific; their various adventures are extravagant but still within the bounds of exuberant plausibility.

Then comes the change. As Taji sees land on the horizon, he also sights a native boat, manned by young warriors who prove to be the children of an old priest. He sits guarding a lovely white girl, Yillah, who is to be offered up as a sacrifice. Taji is determined to rescue her, and he kills the priest in doing so. Melville has abruptly and entirely altered his story; his prose becomes lushly melodramatic.

But he changes course again, as the voyagers reach the archipelago of Mardi, where Taji is welcomed as a demi-god and lives in bliss with Yillah, until she disappears. Determined to search the archipelago for her, he sets off on his quest in company with four Mardians, including the philosopher Babbalanja. Their journey with Taji occupies the greater part of the book, and for most of the account Yillah is only an excuse for travel: the interest is concentrated on what they see. True, there are reminders of Yillah: Taji is shadowed by three sons of the priest, who kill off a couple of characters that the author seems to have found superfluous. But these and other intimations are submerged in the flow of satire and speculation on the Mardian universe. The satire is uneven, and functions on different levels: some islands represent human follies (religious dogmatism, pride of birth), others represent actual countries ('Dominora' is England, 'Vivenza' the United States). The speculation likewise fluctuates from serious to facetious. Taji merges with the author as narrator, and for long periods is passed over, while Babbalanja and the rest wrangle over the meanings of existence. Occasionally Melville/Taji speculates on his own account, or sets down strange lyrical fantasies:

Dreams! dreams! golden dreams: endless and golden, as the flowery prairies, that stretch away from the Rio Sacramento . . . ; prairies like rounded eternities: jonquil leaves beaten out; and my dreams herd like buffaloes, browsing on round the world; and among them, I dash with my lance, to spear one ere they all flee.

He writes, as he says in the same chapter, as one possessed, intent – as he makes Babbalanja declare –

upon the essence of things; the mystery that lieth beyond; the elements of the tear which much laughter provoketh; that which is beneath the seeming; the precious pearl within the shaggy oyster.

As the book draws to an end, the voyagers have found the island of Serenia, where there is true love and peace. They call upon Taji to renounce his futile quest for Yillah; but he, discovering that she has been drowned in the whirlpool for which the priest intended her, sails out alone from the calm lagoon into the rough ocean, still pursued by the priest's sons. What began like a sea shanty has become a cry of anguish. From the reasonable world of Marryat or Cooper we have passed to one reminiscent of Poe's *Narrative of Arthur Gordon Pym*, which also begins reasonably, but ends in a weird commitment to disaster. Hawthorne attempts to dissociate himself from the headlong calamity which his fiction often records; but in Melville as in Poe there is a sort of hectic excess: the high spirits in the one, and the intellectuality in the other, engender hysteria. *Mardi* is an over-strained book, confused in aim. Yet it is extraordinarily interesting to study as a preliminary to the wonderful *Moby-Dick*.

   What Melville and Poe have in common is ambition, intellectual energy, a reaching for every kind of literary effect from poetry to parody, not omitting philosophy. Melville's comic talent is more genially abundant than that of Poe. In this context we remember that Melville was once approvingly described by Robert Louis Stevenson as 'a howling cheese'. A good instance of Melville's high-spirited fantasizing can be found in *Mardi* (chapter 24). An account of the amputation of someone's arm leads the author, somewhat in the mode of Laurence Sterne's *Tristram Shandy*, to reflect on other croppings of limbs out of history, and thence to Froissart's anecdotes of medieval knighthood. Mock-serious, Melville praises the era of 'gallant chevaliers' who 'died chivalric deaths'. Then he shifts to a comment halfway to the burlesque tone of Mark Twain's *Connecticut Yankee*: 'no sensible man . . . would exchange his warm fireside and muffins for a heroic bivouac, in a wild beechen wood, of a raw gusty morning in Normandy: every knight blowing his steel-gloved fingers, and vainly striving to cook his cold coffee in his helmet.' Yet such idiosyncrasy was not freakishly rare in the era of Melville and Poe: a point made by Perry Miller (*The Raven and the Whale*, 1956). The effort to be amusing yet profound, miscellaneous and essayistic, was exemplified in English authors such as W. M. Thackeray, and also by Melville's New York contemporary Cornelius Mathews, who shared with him an appetite (*Behemoth*, 1839; *Big Abel and the Little Manhattan*, 1845) for cosmology, allegory and so forth, combined with jocular narrative.

After *Mardi*, Melville continued to write, almost without pause. Aware perhaps that he had overreached himself as well as the public, he returned to some extent to the tone of *Typee* or *Omoo*. In *White-Jacket* he wrote what purported to be an account of his experiences aboard the American warship *United States*. And in *Redburn* he enlarged upon his first voyage, from New York to Liverpool and back. Again he presented himself as the bluff narrator of actual events, as though he could not trust himself with outright fiction. His prose, too, was simplified, though it had become more supple than that of *Typee*. Here is his child's-eye view of an oil-painting, from *Redburn*:

[It] represented a fat-looking, smoky fishing-boat, with three whiskerandoes in red caps, and their trousers legs rolled up, hauling in a seine. There was high French-like land in one corner, and a tumble-down grey light-house surmounting it. The waves were toasted brown, and the whole picture looked mellow and old. I used to think a piece of it might taste good.

Save for the word 'whiskerandoes', there is little to connect this admirably direct description with his Mardian flourishes.

Within a few years Melville had therefore written five books, none of which could be easily classified as a novel. The first three had dealt with the South Seas; but though there was plenty of shipboard incident in them, it was the islands that seemed chiefly to fascinate Melville – or rather, the whole tropical ambience of the area. His next books, *White-Jacket* and *Redburn*, moved out of the tropics, and though there is a long interlude ashore in *Redburn*, the two works show a considerable interest in the crews as social microcosms, and in the voyage (rather than the landfall) as an extended metaphor of man's destiny. He was reading widely and intensely during his first years of authorship. There are evidences of Dickens in his work, most noticeably in such later writings as 'Bartleby the Scrivener', in which the dull impersonality of the world of law and lawyers seems to echo the mood of *Bleak House*. Dickens, after all, was arguably the most important novelist in the United States from about 1840 to 1870: the most famous, the most inimitably (and therefore imitatedly) attractive, the most 'democratic'. One wonders too whether Melville may have read a jaunty, bawdy pamphlet written by an Englishman, Ned Ward, in the early eighteenth century. Somewhat scandalous publications of this sort, cheaply printed, had a wide circulation in the milieu of tavern or mess-deck. Ward irreverently summarized the typical styles of ships' officers in *The Wooden World Dissected; in the Character of a Ship of War*. The sketch of a ship's captain begins:

He is a Leviathan, or rather a kind of sea-god, whom the poor tars worship as the Indians do the devil, more through fear than affection; nay, some will have it, that he is more a devil than the devil himself.

Leaving aside such possible sources, it is clear that Melville gained most from Shakespeare, though the essayist Sir Thomas Browne also delighted him.

Moreover, he threw himself into an important new friendship, at a time when he had probably written one draft of his sixth book, on whaling. There are many indications in his previous work that, not content with conventional narrative, he wished his adventure tales to carry a greater load of significance. Until he read Hawthorne's stories, however, and made Hawthorne's acquaintance, there was no one to encourage him in what he called 'ontological heroics'. But in Hawthorne he discovered another fellow-American who was concerned with 'that which is beneath the seeming', and who used fiction as his medium. Though the friendship dwindled away, much to Melville's regret, it was a vital tonic to him while he was engaged on *Moby-Dick*. It may have led him to rewrite the book, on a deliberately higher plane of meaning. He dedicated *Moby-Dick* to Hawthorne, 'in token of my admiration for his genius'.

For *Moby-Dick* he chose a South Sea voyage in a whaler. In making this choice, and in sticking to the ship instead of roaming off among real or imagined islands, he provided himself with a firm social and occupational framework, such as he had recently established in *White-Jacket, or The World in a Man-of-War*. Anchored to actuality, he could let his imagination run free. Metaphysical inquiry came out of physical fact and not vice versa, as too often in Hawthorne. In the first draft it seems likely that the story was heavily documentary – as it still is, in certain chapters – and owed its origin to such narratives as that of Owen Chase. But in final form the hunt for whales focused on one in particular, the White Whale, Moby (*Mocha*) Dick; and on the obsessive hatred of Moby-Dick felt by the whaleship's captain, Ahab. The novel has tremendous power. It moves grandly through alternations of excitement and ease to the almost intolerable tension of the three-day chase of the White Whale, and the eventual, inevitable disaster when the whale kills Ahab, then smashes the *Pequod* as Owen Chase's *Essex* was smashed. The action writing is unsurpassable; here Melville's energy seems commensurate to the job in hand. His voyage, his seamen, their ship, their captain, the whale itself, are tangible: they possess weight, dimension, colour. What is added is a genuine dimension, not an erratic moralizing and groping after significances as in *Mardi*. There is, for example, nothing false in the fact that Ishmael, Ahab, Elijah, Gabriel, and others in the novel have scriptural names. Such names were natural in their New England context (as it was natural for the wife of Goodman Brown to be known as Faith), and Melville is thus legitimately able to suggest biblical analogies.

Ahab is in some ways a Hawthorne 'type'. In Hawthorne's tale 'The Great Carbuncle', we meet an 'aged Seeker' who, roaming the mountains in search of the precious object, has no hope of

enjoyment from it; that folly has passed long ago! I keep up the search for this accursed stone because the vain ambition of my youth has become a fate upon me in old age. The pursuit alone is my strength, – the energy of my soul, – the warmth of my blood, – and the pith and marrow of my bones! . . . Yet not to have my wasted lifetime back again would I give up my hopes of the Great Carbuncle! Having found it, I shall bear it to a certain cavern . . . and there, grasping it in my arms, lie down and die, and keep it buried with me forever.

This is the apart man, the demoniac dreamer – Dr Heidegger or Ethan Brand – doomed for his arrogant isolation. Since Hawthorne treats them as examples of error, their diabolism is often unconvincing; nor is it possible to take very seriously such objectives as a Great Carbuncle. But we are soon engrossed in the character and problems of Ahab, the 'grand, ungodly, godlike man' who, 'stricken, blasted, if he be', still 'has his humanities', and whose objective is a credible one. Ahab, like the Jonah of Father Mapple's magnificent sermon, sins through wilfulness, for 'if we obey God, we must disobey ourselves'. Yet courage and pride are – we learn in the same sermon – fine qualities: 'Delight is to him . . . who against the proud gods and commodores of this earth, ever stands forth his own inexorable self.' Hawthorne feels that all excess is to be deplored; Melville, with a more generous sense of human potentiality, insists that virtues and vices alike depend upon a certain excess. Ahab, then, is both hero and villain, dooming others where Taji dooms only himself.

  Moby-Dick is one of the world's great novels, whose richness increases with each new reading. But minor flaws link it with the other work of Melville's creative prime. In *Mardi*, though Taji is supposed to be the narrator, we lose our sense of who is telling the tale. In *Moby-Dick* the same confusion is apparent. The first sentence – 'Call me Ishmael' – has a premonitory rumble. However, Ishmael adopts a rollicking air, devil-may-care rather than bedevilled; he seems to be the same person as the author–narrator of Melville's previous books. 'God keep me from ever completing anything', he exclaims in chapter 32. 'This whole book is but a draught – nay, but the draught of a draught. Oh Time, Strength, Cash, and Patience.' This is surely an author's aside. Befriended by the native harpooner Queequeg, Ishmael does hint at a complexity more in keeping with his name when he says, 'No more my splintered heart and maddened hand were turned against the wolfish world'; but nothing else in the novel bears out this picture of the young man. In general, he is like the narrator of *Typee*, and his friendship with Queequeg seems a similar vindication of primitive values. But this theme is discarded, as though Melville finds Ishmael a nuisance. For twenty-eight chapters he relates the story. Then for three chapters (beginning with 'Enter Ahab; to Him, Stubb') it is clearly not Ishmael's story – he cannot be aware of the soliloquies of others – and though the novel reverts to Ishmael's narration, it frequently dispenses with him. Melville appears undecided who is in charge of the book, or what kind of book it is to be. His efforts at Shakespearean soliloquy can be construed as a grandiose attempt to enlarge its scope, and rescue it from

Ishmael's necessarily limited approach. An example is Ahab's encounter with the cabin-boy Pip (chapter 127) whom he has made crazy. Ahab: 'The Titans, they say, hummed snatches when chipping out the craters for volcanoes; and the grave-digger in the play sings, spade in hand. Dost thou never?' Pip answers in equally high-flown 'Elizabethan' diction. Certainly *Moby-Dick*, as it progresses, takes on majesty and assurance; one might say that Taji has been separated into his component parts, Ishmael and Ahab – though Ishmael and Melville still contend for the honours of narration.

These are, to repeat, minor flaws, like the puzzlingly brief allusions to 'one Bulkington', in whose eyes 'floated some reminiscences that did not seem to give him much joy' (chapters 3 and 23). They have nevertheless their interest when taken in relation to Melville's next novel, *Pierre; or, the Ambiguities*, which he wrote so soon afterwards that he must have had it in mind when completing *Moby-Dick*. Like *Mardi*, *Pierre* is resoundingly unsuccessful and curiously memorable. For the first time Melville leaves the sea and far-off places to write, in the third person, of contemporary America. Pierre is a young man whom fortune has endowed with looks, family, talent, and even a beautiful fiancée. Then another girl comes into his life, a strange creature who persuades him that she is the illegitimate daughter of his dead, revered father. Strongly drawn to her, Pierre is certain that his mother would never accept the girl, or the idea of her husband's guilt. In Hamlet-like torment – *Hamlet* is one of the books Pierre has been reading – and actuated by an insane high-mindedness, he takes his half-sister to New York, allowing everyone to believe that he has married her as the result of a sudden infatuation. The shock of this behaviour kills his mother and prostrates his fiancée. Penniless, installing his half-sister with him in shabby lodgings, he begins to write a book that is to earn them a living. But he writes in despair, and the result is a demented book that no publisher will handle. The story ends in a welter of gore, with the death of all the chief characters.

Much of *Pierre* is melodrama, interrupted by bouts of harsh facetious satire upon the literary and reforming circles of the day. Like many of Poe's protagonists, Pierre is a projection of the author, who likewise reveals the extent of the author's alienation from America. Formerly Melville had been an ardent democrat; he objected, for example, as Whitman does, to what he thought was a toadying to aristocracy in Shakespeare. Gradually, his democratic faith became more qualified, as the inanities of the public (partly in regard to his own work) and the revelation of human wickedness quenched his optimism. There are signs of an equivocal response in previous work. *White-Jacket*, for instance, protests at the undemocratic separation between officers and crew, much as Richard Henry Dana's *Two Years Before the Mast* (1840; an influence on Melville) had attacked the inhumanities of the American merchant navy. Yet in *White-Jacket* Melville seems to suggest that ordinary seamen misbehave when allowed ashore, and need the restraints of discipline. At any rate, Melville makes Pierre an aristocrat of the type of 1800, agonized and helpless in the America of 1850. Where he had previously tried to distinguish between the *people* and the *public*, he could now only offer to Pierre the consolation of a pamphlet by one 'Plotinus Plinlimmon'. This recommends virtuous expediency as the highest attainable goal of the average man, and for the exceptional man a goodness that is not much more rigorous: the whole tempered by a certain detachment. Nor is the pamphlet of any use to Pierre, since he mislays it, and since in any case he is no more rational than Taji or Ahab. What a collapse is evident in the Melville who only three years before could say in *Redburn* that

The other world beyond this, which was longed for by the devout before Columbus's time, was found in the New; and the deep-sea-lead, that first struck these soundings, brought up the soil of Earth's Paradise.

After *Pierre* Melville slowly relinquished his effort to live by the pen. For some years he continued to write prose, including a painfully desolate historical novel, *Israel Potter*, whose American narrator spends forty years of unmerited exile in London;[1] and *The Confidence Man*, in which the Melvillian voyage is made in that relatively humdrum craft, a Mississippi paddle-steamer. Melville's friend Hawthorne said of him, at about this period: 'He can neither believe, nor be comfortable in his unbelief; and he is too honest and courageous not to try to do one or the other.' *The Confidence Man* reveals this total perplexity. Everything in it is possibly something else, a masquerade, a paradox. The voyage in this instance is made on All Fools' Day, and the ship is sardonically named the *Fidèle*. A whole succession of tricksters or confidence men appear on the steamer – seemingly the same man in various guises. The readiness of Americans to deceive and be deceived was a richly promising theme, as Mark Twain was to show with his pair of travelling rogues in *Huckleberry Finn*. But

1. For the story of the original Israel Potter, whose autobiography was published in 1824, see Richard M. Dorson, ed., *American Rebels: Narratives of the Patriots* (New York, Pantheon, 1953).

Melville was not content with mere comedy, even of the most mocking sort. Preoccupied with truth and illusion, he leaves the reader in as much uncertainty as the *Fidèle*'s passengers. Is confidence wisdom or folly? What are we to take on trust – everything, nothing? If self-deception is a precondition of happiness, are swindlers necessary and even indispensable? Do drunkards blur reality, or come closer to it? The novel's message, like that of *Israel Potter* and of some of the short stories Melville wrote during the 1850s, seems to be a variant on Plotinus Plinlimmon. Secession was in the air; as Thoreau had declared his independence of society, and as the abolitionist Garrison had publicly burnt the American Constitution, so Melville implied that, if one were lucky, one might survive by becoming a spectator. Secession was not always possible, and never as smoothly accomplished as by Thoreau: 'Benito Cereno', caught in a web of evil, is so dominated by the sinister Negro slave Babo that he can only 'follow his leader' and die likewise. Or, having escaped, one might die, like 'Bartleby the Scrivener'. This is not to say that Melville had written himself out, or that his short stories of this period were all despairing. Indeed one of them, 'The Apple Tree Table', employs the hopeful image of the 'strong and beautiful bug' (eating its way out of wood that has been made into furniture) with which Thoreau ends *Walden*. But fine though some of them are, they are the work of a man who no longer wishes to grapple furiously with his universe.

A few years before the Civil War broke out in 1861, Melville turned from prose to poetry. Before his death he had written enough to fill a plump volume; and this excluding his long *Clarel*, which describes a symbolic as well as actual round-trip to the Holy Land. One might apply to Melville's verse the observation made by Emerson on Thoreau's – namely, that his genius was better than his talent. Perhaps only a dozen poems, and fragments of *Clarel*, are thoroughly satisfying, and not all of those are metrically impeccable. Yet they far transcend mere versifying. Some of the best are about the Civil War. To Melville, as to Whitman, it was a deeply tragic affair. In a way it proved him to have been right:

> Nature's dark side is heeded now
> (Ah! optimist-cheer disheartened flown)

– but a residual faith in America, which he has never altogether lost, makes him sadly conjecture that even with victory, it will be like 'man's latter fall':

>the Founders' dream shall flee.
>Age after age shall be
>As age after age has been.

Still, the conflict restores his sense of human grandeur. After the crisis is over, in the 1870s and 1880s, Melville's verse is mainly a counsel of acceptance. Sometimes, as in 'The Berg' or 'The Maldive Shark', it has a leaden melancholy; sometimes it rises to the gentle elegiac note of

>Where is the world we roved, Ned Bunn?

Last of all came *Billy Budd*, the long short story which provides a coda to Melville's life. In it he returns to the setting of a ship, with its rigid hierarchical discipline and its poetic overtones. (Billy has been 'impressed' in wartime from the *Rights of Man*, a symbolically named merchantman, aboard the seventy-four-gun H.M.S. *Indomitable*.) Melville returns too to a favourite early conception, of the Iago figure, the malign individual (Bland in *White-Jacket*, Jackson in *Redburn*) who acts from a pure sense of evil, and is therefore not the orthodox villain of fiction, but someone more to be pitied than hated. Claggart, the master-at-arms who falsely accuses the pure young Billy Budd of inciting mutiny, is struck dead by Billy, and therefore Billy is paired with him in retributive death. Claggart is evil, but his hatred for Billy is a subtly stated ambivalence. Perhaps too much has been made of the Christ-like nature of Billy, and of the Father-attributes of Captain Vere, in order to prove (according to one interpretation) that Melville had finally reached a Christian haven. No doubt Billy is supposed to be innocent, and Vere just. But Billy is too elementary a character to bear all the burdens that commentators have put upon him; perhaps Melville, his taste for excess gone, prefers to express the predicament of innocence in a historical parable of the imposition of order after egalitarian excesses.[1] Order is unfair, but it is comforting to the tired man. And surely *Billy Budd* has a passive, almost masochistic tone? Defeat, Melville seems to say, is inevitable for all: then why struggle, as did Taji, Ahab, Pierre? Rather, with Billy, summoning up a mournful, uncomprehending dignity like that of the Tahitians of *Omoo*,

1. *Billy Budd*, though set in the 1790s as an account of the British navy, also bears witness to Melville's long interest in an American drama of 1842 – an alleged mutiny aboard the U.S. brig-of-war *Somers*, which led to the hanging of three supposed culprits. One of the young officers who conducted the court martial was a cousin of Melville. Some Americans, in the controversy aroused by the *Somers* incident, accused the ship's officers of judicial murder. Others, including Longfellow and Dana, congratulated the captain on maintaining discipline in the face of threatened anarchy. Melville sympathized with his cousin.

> Just ease these darbies at the wrist,
> And roll me over fair.
> I am sleepy, and the oozy weeds about me twist.

This is the mood detectable in the correspondence of Melville's long fall away – the thirty years of custom-house employment, when he printed poetry at his own expense, endured the death of his two sons, and responded with flat politeness to the queries of an occasional appreciator or anthologist: a genius but almost forgotten.

WALT WHITMAN

MELVILLE's contemporary, Walt Whitman, was also a native of New York State. The two men have some qualities in common: a combination of exuberance and withdrawnness, of 'masculine' energy and 'feminine' (or homosexual) quiescence. Whitman's 'Mannahatta' –

> City of hurried and sparkling waters! city of spires and masts!
> City nested in bays! my city!

– sounds like the 'insular city of the Manhattoes, belted round by wharves', of the first chapter of *Moby-Dick*. In the same book Melville speaks as glowingly as Whitman of the democratic dignity 'in the arm that wields a pick or drives a spike'. Both men find endless interest in the sea: to Whitman it is a great rhythmic pulse, with a loose surge to which he compares the movement of his own poetry. And there are transcendental affirmations in Melville as in Whitman: 'O Nature, and O soul of man!' exclaims Ahab – 'how far beyond all utterance are your linked analogies! not the smallest atom stirs or lives on matter, but has its cunning duplicate in mind.'

But of course Melville and Whitman (who seem never to have met, and to have been indifferent to one another's work) are dissimilar in other ways. Though Melville, like Whitman, has a fullness and vigour which appear foreign to the New England temperament, he seems nevertheless much closer intellectually to his friend Hawthorne than to Whitman; beneath the sunlit surface of the waves are monsters, and the threat of shipwreck. We almost never find this sense of hidden calamity in Whitman: he, by contrast, is closer to Emerson, whose writings meant more to Whitman during his formative years than he later acknowledged. Two quotations, in each case from their notebooks, will suggest their affinity. First, Emerson:

I have been writing and speaking what were once called novelties, for twenty-five or thirty years, and have not now one disciple ... I delight in driving them from me. What could I do, if they came to me? – they would interrupt and encumber me. This is my boast that I have no school follower. I should account it a measure of the impurity of insight, if it did not create independence.

And Whitman:

I will not be a great philosopher, and found any school ... But I will take each man and woman of you to the window ... and my left arm shall hook you round the waist, and my right shall point you to the endless and beginningless road ... Not I – not God – can travel this road for you....

These are not identical utterances; but there is a marked resemblance. Indeed, for some time now it has been usual to praise Hawthorne and Melville for their 'awareness of evil' and point contemptuously to the lack of awareness displayed by the transcendentalists, and by Emerson in particular. One may agree with this rolling-out of the red carpet for the Awares: but must we simultaneously thrust the Unawares out at the back entrance? Perhaps criticism is a matter of perpetually being unfair to some and too fair to others. But it seems unnecessary, in lauding Hawthorne, to lambaste Whitman as Hawthorne's opposite 'in every respect', who 'did as much to ruin American poetry and prose as any single influence in America'.[1] Whitman, like any other great writer, is unique: he is nobody's opposite, except in an approximate way. However, his work *is* extremely uneven; and it is vulnerable to attack at the same points as those where New England transcendentalism is vulnerable. 'Transcendentalism means, says our accomplished Mrs B., with a wave of her hand, *a little beyond*.' We can pair this note, from Emerson's journal of 1836, with Whitman's explanation (in an anonymous review of his own poetry!) that the lines never seem 'finished and fixed' but are 'always suggesting something beyond'. Like Emerson, he is accused of being indiscriminately optimistic and formless. His purpose, in his own words, was 'mainly ... to put a *Person*, a human being (myself, in the latter half of the Nineteenth Century, in America,) freely, fully and truly on record.' He was to be 'the bard of personality', speaking for all Americans, and for mankind, since he knew other human beings were essentially the same as himself. Santayana objected that the doctrine was elementary, and that there was

1. Marius Bewley, *The Complex Fate: Hawthorne, Henry James and Some Other American Writers* (London, 1952).

no 'inside' to Whitman's perceptions. D. H. Lawrence, while praising much in Whitman, condemns his transcendental pretensions, making him say (in words that recall Poe's 'Supernal Oneness'): 'I am everything and everything is me and so we're all One in One Identity, like the Mundane Egg, which has been addled quite a while.'

Others have disliked aspects of Whitman not found in Emerson: his flamboyant patriotism, for instance (which may have been a family matter, since his father christened three of his brothers, in the fashion of the day, George Washington, Thomas Jefferson, and Andrew Jackson), and his equating of quantity with quality. The Southern poet Sidney Lanier said Whitman's argument seemed to be that 'because a prairie is wide, therefore debauchery is admirable, and because the Mississippi is long, therefore every American is God'. Lanier presumably had in mind such statements as this, from the 1855 preface to *Leaves of Grass*:

Here is not merely a nation but a teeming nation of nations. Here is action untied from strings necessarily blind to particulars and details magnificently moving in vast masses.

Or this from Whitman's 1856 'Letter to Emerson':

Of the twenty-four modern mammoth two-double, three-double, and four-double cylinder presses in the world, printing by steam, twenty-one of them are in the United States.

Such declarations remind us of Samuel Butler's comment that America should not have been discovered all at once, but in pieces, each about as big as France or Germany; and of Emerson's reflection that 'I expected [Whitman] to make the songs of the nation but he seems content to make the inventories'.

These inventories have been ridiculed and parodied. So has his vocabulary, which Emerson described as 'a remarkable mixture of the *Bhagavat-Geeta* and the *New York Herald*'. Or as Oliver Wendell Holmes remarked, with a mixture of amusement and reproof, the Good Gray Poet 'carried the principle of republicanism through the whole world of created objects'. Whitman overworked some words – *copious*, *orbic*; he made howlers (using *semitic* where he meant *seminal*). He invented strange terminations: *promulge*, *philosophs*, *literats*. He borrowed from other languages, especially French: *formules*, *delicatesse*, *trottoir*, *embouchure*, *Americano*, *cantabile*. He took words from phrenology: *amative*, *adhesive*. The results can be ludicrous:

The freshness and candour of their physiognomy, the copiousness and decision of
    their phrenology....

In thy resplendent coming literati, thy full-lung'd orators, thy sacerdotal bards,
    kosmic savans....

The same ample enthusiasm that led him to admire a large painting of
Custer's Last Stand permitted him to include lovely and laughable epithets
within the same line, and prevented him from pruning them in subsequent
editions. He revised constantly, but not always for the better.

At his worst Whitman seems preposterous. He flaunts his queer style
as a savage in a funny drawing might flaunt a top-hat retrieved from
somebody's dustbin. Surrounded in later life by disciples less odd only than
he, poseur, puffer, bearded ex-carpenter Christ-figure: this is the Whitman
about whom, for numbers of people, the main question was not whether
he was a fraud but whether he was a calculated or a self-deceived one.
Those who accord him a fair hearing, however, find his small defects,
though parts of the same whole, insignificant when set beside the magni-
tude of his achievement. Somehow this mediocre journalist, the writer of
pieces on Manifest Destiny and Decent Homes for Working-Men, conceived
his scheme of celebrating man and America in a thoroughly new and
appropriate form. Miscellaneous tastes and experiences went into its
development: the Quakerism of his mother's family; Shakespeare, and the
opera – the excitement of the sung or spoken word, communicated in a
public place; phrenology, which reassured him as to his own disposition;
the more permanently respectable sciences, where he, in somewhat the
same way as Emerson, discovered cosmic patterns; the trundling verse of
the popular English author Martin Farquhar Tupper; from France, George
Sand's *Consuelo*, and its sequel, *The Countess of Rudolstadt*, which may
have helped him to visualize his role of spokesman for mankind; Poe, who
argued the impossibility of the long poem; the crowds on Broadway, or on
the Brooklyn Ferry; the tides washing in from the Atlantic; the sweet
modulation of the seasons in the countryside; the feel of the great continent,
rolling interminably westward from the seaboard where he lived: these
and other ingredients went into the first edition of *Leaves of Grass*, which
appeared in New York in July 1855, when he was thirty-six.

It contained twelve poems, of which the most considerable was 'Song
of Myself'. Both the poems and the declamatory, deliberately under-
punctuated prose of the preface insisted on truths similar to those propounded by Emerson: the divineness of ordinary men and women, and

their share in the miraculous cyclical patterns of life. Otherwise the flavour was not Emersonian. Nor was that of subsequent, modified, and expanded editions of the book. They sometimes reveal the Emersonian benignity, especially in the early editions. But it is expressed differently: sometimes more stridently, sometimes with a joviality that can repel as much as Emerson's wintry abstractness, but almost always with a sensuous warmth to which one cannot remain indifferent. There is a morning gladness about Whitman that Emerson hardly ever manages to match:

To behold the day-break!
The little light fades the immense and diaphanous shadows,
The air tastes good to my palate....

I hear bravuras of birds, bustle of growing wheat, gossip of flames, clack of sticks cooking my meals....

The glories strung like beads on my smallest sights and hearings, on the walk in the street and the passage over the river –

Who can resist lines like these, or care to quibble whether they may be defined as verse? This, we feel with Whitman, 'is the meal equally set, this the meat for natural hunger'.

Even if we were to agree that its message is less profound than that of Hawthorne (though it is not), such poetry is only one aspect of Whitman. The comic Whitman of Max Beerbohm's cartoon altered, and grew more subtle. Yet even in his first editions Whitman is less noisy than critics have contended. He is a little detached, 'both in and out of the game'. He is curiously secretive for one who, according to hostile contemporary reviewers, liked to wash his dirty linen in public. 'Suggestiveness', he says, is the word that expresses the mood of his poems, in which 'every sentence and every passage tells of an interior not always seen'. An instinctive desire to camouflage homosexual tendencies may account in part for the obscurity of certain passages; at any rate they have nothing to do with the extroverted Whitman of legend:

Ever the hard unsunk ground,
Ever the eaters and drinkers, ever the upward and downward sun, ever the air and the ceaseless tides,
Ever myself and my neighbours, refreshing, wicked, real,
Ever the old inexplicable query, ever that thorn'd thumb, that breath of itches and thirsts,
Ever the vexer's hoot! hoot! till we find where the sly one hides and bring him forth,
Ever love, ever the sobbing liquid of life,

Ever the bandage under the chin, ever the trestles of death.

One could quote fifty passages as richly perplexing as this from 'Song of Myself'. Nor is he maintaining in that poem, or in his work as a whole, that there is no iniquity or pain in the world. 'Agonies', he says, 'are one of my changes of garments.' He is capable, too, of castigating his own country:

Let there be no suggestion above the suggestion of drudgery!
Let none be pointed toward his destination!

————

Let the sun and moon go! let scenery take the applause of the audience! let there be
    apathy under the stars!

'Respondez!', in which these lines occur, was left out of later editions; but its anger and dismay can be found in other poems, as well as in *Democratic Vistas*.

Whitman's moments of doubt have complex origins. Now and then, as semi-coded private notes reveal, he became alarmed at the intensity of his feeling for some young man, and warned himself to escape the imminent danger. More generally, he was preoccupied with the role of a writer in a democracy. He was convinced that America needed democratic bards. 'The greatest poet' is a prophet and prodigy, 'the president of regulation' and at least as important as the nation's political leaders. But, despite the self-promotion which he no doubt thought essential, Whitman failed to attain the renown he considered his due, and America's duty. As with Melville, the American people remained largely indifferent. The most terrible possibility, in which he was occasionally tempted to believe, was the old anti-democratic view that a democratic public was a mass of philistines. If that were so, Whitman's entire enterprise would have been in vain. A preferable alternative, as with Melville, was to try to distinguish between the good *people* and the corrupt or unreformed *public* – the latter he assailed in *Democratic Vistas*. Yet another consideration, also linking him with Melville, was the notion that perhaps he could conceal within the obvious, hearty, open-air, democratic message more subtle communications which might be audible only to a minority. We may wonder, though, why Whitman did not disarm criticism by toning down the explicitly 'physical' references that caused most offence. He did not object to revisions when a selection of his verse first appeared in England under the supervision of William Michael Rossetti. Why refuse to make this accommodation for American readers? Did he come to relish the combi-

nation of notoriety and neglect that marked the last decades? Did he adopt
a persona of exaggerated maleness, in speaking to his countrymen, for
reasons which he never fully understood?

Dismay is not a characteristic mood with him. Balancing his joy in the
'refreshing, wicked, real' properties of existence is his notion of immortality
in death:

The smallest sprout shows there is really no death,
And if ever there was it led forward life, and does not wait at the end to arrest it,
And ceas'd the moment life appear'd.

All goes onward and outward, nothing collapses,
And to die is different from what any one supposed, and luckier.

As Whitman grew older, death occupied his thoughts increasingly. It was,
as the biographer Justin Kaplan observes, his mantra. For him, death has
no sting; and indeed he began to make his *adieux* to life at a remarkably
early age. In 'The Wound-Dresser', written in his forties, he says:

An old man bending I come among new faces.

Perhaps the hospitals of the Civil War hastened the process; for, as a Greek
historian wrote, in time of peace the sons bury the fathers: in time of war
the fathers bury the sons. With Melville, Whitman is almost alone among
male authors of the period in grasping the tragic significance of the war.
He felt himself a parent, or sometimes perhaps an older brother, and as he
saw America stretched beneath the surgeon's knife, after enduring the
torment of the battlefields, he recorded his emotion in elegiac lines of
magnificent dignity:

Word over all, beautiful as the sky,
Beautiful that war and all its deeds of carnage must in time be utterly lost,
That the hands of the sisters Death and Night incessantly softly wash again, and
    ever again, this soil'd world.

The same tranquil maturity is revealed in his memorial tribute to the
assassinated President, Abraham Lincoln, 'When Lilacs Last in the Door-
yard Bloom'd'.

In the 1855 preface to *Leaves of Grass*, Whitman declares that 'of all
mankind the great poet is the equable man'. The same phrase recurs in
'By Blue Ontario's Shore'; and it is the word *equable* that best sums up
the peculiar temper of Whitman. Pride, he thinks, can and should be
accompanied by humility. Democracy, that proud estate, is symbolized by

the humblest of natural growths – the grass; his new man will speak in 'words simple as grass'. To him, the idea that life has the precise structure of classical architecture is a fiction; it is, rather, like a particular object in nature, with an organic form, that is nevertheless unexpected, asymmetrical, even wilful. In his vivid lecture on 'The Death of Abraham Lincoln' he says:

The main thing, the actual murder, transpired with the quiet and simplicity of any commonest occurrence – the bursting of a bud or pod in the growth of vegetation, for instance.

Far from ranting here – and how many would have resisted the opportunity? – Whitman explains the event as he does his own poems, in which things happen 'with what appear to be the same disregard of parts, and the same absence of special purpose, as in nature'. The poet, he said elsewhere, speaking of himself, conceals 'his rhythm and uniformity ... in the roots of his verses, not to be seen of themselves, but to break forth loosely as lilacs on a bush, and take shapes compact, as the shapes of melons, or chestnuts, or pears'. Regretting the lack of spontaneity and real sensuousness in other contemporary poets, he deplores in Tennyson

The odor of English social life ... pervading the pages like an invisible scent; the idleness, the traditions, the mannerisms, the stately *ennui*; the yearning of love, like a spinal marrow, inside of all; ... the old houses and furniture ... the moldy secrets everywhere; the verdure, the ivy on the walls, the moat, the English landscape outside, the buzzing fly in the sun inside the window pane.

Against this masterly evocation of airlessness we may put Whitman's view of the poet as one who 'judges not as the judge judges but as the sun falling around a helpless thing'.

Like any poet's theory of the poet's function, that is a personal testament. It is more diffuse than most, and we can agree with Whitman's critics that it is a dangerous counsel if it encourages the would-be American poet to rely too exclusively on bardic intuition. Whitman is least acceptable where most the Bard: as when he offers an antithesis between the Old and New Worlds, and glorifies the American pioneer, or insists that ordinary Americans will rise to greet their 'full-lung'd orators'. His America of mates and camerados can be a little embarrassing; and it is ironic that his one thoroughly conventional poem ('O Captain! My Captain!') is the only one known to the general public today. But if his most 'public' poetry is his weakest, there is something characteristically American, and not at all silly, in having made the effort to appeal to the multitude. Nor did his failure in this respect embitter him, although in the late prose of *Specimen Days* he paid a perceptive tribute to the great Scottish curmudgeon, Emerson's antagonist–friend Thomas Carlyle. Without Carlyle, said Whitman, the 'array of British thought ... would be like an army with no artillery. The show were still a gay and rich one – Byron, Scott, Tennyson, and many more – horsemen and rapid infantry, and banners flying – but the last heavy roar ... that settles fate and victory, would be lacking.' The military metaphor is not quite apposite for Whitman himself. Yet he shared with Carlyle an essential integrity, and a toughness of spirit, that reinforce his talent and help to confer the immortality which he accorded precedence over mere celebrity.

MORE NEW ENGLANDERS
The Brahmin Poets and Historians

HENRY WADSWORTH LONGFELLOW (1807–82)

Born in Portland, Maine, and educated at Bowdoin College, where he was a classmate of Hawthorne. He travelled during 1826–9 in France, Spain, Italy and Germany, and on returning was appointed professor of modern languages at Bowdoin (1829–35). After a further European visit in 1835, he became professor of French and Spanish at Harvard, in succession to Ticknor, and occupied the chair, though with growing reluctance, until 1854, when he resigned to devote himself entirely to literature. By then Longfellow was internationally known for such works in prose and verse as *Hyperion* (1839), *Voices of the Night* (1839), *The Spanish Student* (1843), and *Evangeline* (1847). His reputation grew steadily with the publication of *Hiawatha* (1855), *The Courtship of Miles Standish* (1858) and various later works. He was twice married, and both wives died in sad circumstances.

JAMES RUSSELL LOWELL (1819–91)

Born in Cambridge, Massachusetts, and educated at Harvard. In 1844 he married the ardent reformer Maria White, under whose influence he wrote various anti-slavery pieces. He won early recognition with *A Fable for Critics* and the first series of *Biglow Papers* (both 1848). Maria Lowell died in 1853; after her death his interest in reform waned. In 1855 he succeeded Longfellow at Harvard, and after an interval of some years began to pour out poems and essays. The first editor of the *Atlantic Monthly*, Lowell was also associated with the *North American Review*. He was minister to Spain (1877–80) and to England (1880–85).

OLIVER WENDELL HOLMES (1809–94)

Born in Cambridge, Massachusetts, and educated at Harvard, where, after medical study in France and teaching at Dartmouth, he became professor of anatomy and physiology (1847–82). He was prominent in most of the cultural and convivial activities of Boston and Cambridge; his local fame as *raconteur* and versifier spread abroad with the publication of *The Autocrat at the Breakfast-Table* (1858), *The Professor at the Breakfast-Table* (1860), *The Poet at the Breakfast-Table* (1872) and other works, including three novels and several volumes of verse. His son and namesake, O. W. Holmes, Jr. (1841–1935), was a no less distinguished Harvard figure, and a justice of the U.S. Supreme Court.

WILLIAM HICKLING PRESCOTT (1796–1859)

Born in Salem, Massachusetts, and educated at Harvard. Travelling in Europe (1815–17), he began to apply himself to historical research. After the success of his painstaking *History of Ferdinand and Isabella* (3 vols., 1838) – Longfellow described him as 'a striking example of what perseverance and concentration of one's powers will accomplish' – he embarked on his *History of the Conquest of Mexico* (3 vols., 1843), and followed it with his *Conquest of Peru* (2 vols., 1847). He had published 3 volumes of a history of Philip II when he died.

JOHN LOTHROP MOTLEY (1814–77)

Born in Boston, educated at Harvard. After two years of study in Germany, he worked at law in Boston, wrote two novels, *Morton's Hope* (1839) and *Merry Mount* (1849), and began to devote himself to the history of the Netherlands. His researches led to the publication of *The Rise of the Dutch Republic* (3 vols., 1856), *History of the United Netherlands* (4 vols., 1860, 1867), and *Life and Death of John of Barneveld* (2 vols., 1874). Motley was minister to Austria (1861–7) and to Britain (1869–70); he was recalled from the latter post through no fault of his own.

FRANCIS PARKMAN (1823–93)

Born in Boston, he was educated at Harvard, and travelled in Europe (1843–4) and to the American West (1846), where his strenuous life ruined his health, though it provided material for *Oregon Trail* (1849). Despite wretched health, he applied himself to his great series on the French and English struggles in colonial America. His *History of the Conspiracy of Pontiac* (1851) was followed after an interval by *Pioneers of France in the New World* (1865), and by six subsequent volumes, culminating in *A Half-Century of Conflict* (1892). He also wrote one novel, *Vassall Morton* (1856), and a book on horticulture – a subject in which he held a Harvard professorship.

MORE NEW ENGLANDERS

IN the decade or so after the Civil War, few would have mentioned Melville and Whitman, if they had been asked to list the chief living American authors. They would certainly have named Emerson, and perhaps the Quaker poet, John G. Whittier, both Massachusetts men. But pride of place would probably have been given to the writers associated not merely with Massachusetts in general, but with Boston (and Harvard, at nearby Cambridge) in particular. Their reputations, in their own day, were prodigious: a poem like Longfellow's 'Psalm of Life' was familiar equally to Baudelaire (as his sonnet 'Le Guignon' shows), and to a British soldier in the Crimea, heard to repeat one of its lines as he lay dying before Sebastopol.

Today it is otherwise. The historians are still treated with respect, but with the possible exception of Parkman they are no longer widely read. The poets, once so praised, are usually lumped together in our textbooks in one curt chapter. Poets and historians alike are put on the defensive, to be contrasted unfavourably with both Awares and Unawares. Did not Emerson remark in his journal (October 1841) that 'the view taken of Transcendentalism in State Street is that it will invalidate contracts'? Did he not note a few years later:

If Socrates were here, we could go and talk with him; but Longfellow, we cannot go and talk with him; there is a palace, and servants, and a row of bottles of different coloured wines, and wine glasses, and fine coats.

As for Longfellow, he wrote (December 1840) that 'there is in all Cambridge but one Transcendentalist, – and he a tutor! In the Theological School there is none of it; the infected class is gone.' The elder Richard Henry Dana of Boston, corresponding with his Vermont friend James Marsh in 1838, spoke disapprovingly of a current set of lectures by Emerson. 'That he has systematized his thoughts is hardly possible. I cannot find that he is bottomed on any thing.' Marsh, former president of the University of Vermont, concurred: Emerson's lectures, he said, 'must contain with scarcely a decent disguise nothing less than an Epicurean

Atheism dressed up in a style seducing and to many perhaps deceptive.'[1] Instead of the simple world of Concord, we have thus a picture not altogether unlike the one of Tennyson's England conjured up by Whitman. It is a Boston peopled either by businessmen or by *Brahmins* (the word was adopted by one of them, Oliver Wendell Holmes). These Brahmins were born with silver spoons protruding from their infant mouths, went to Harvard (or taught at it, usually both), had a distaste for democracy and the frontier, and for contemporary problems; they turned to Europe and the past for comfort, and failed to understand their own age or their own country; they were too refined.

So the charge runs, as levelled at the Brahmins by the literary historian Vernon L. Parrington, author of the still valuable but markedly 'Jeffersonian' *Main Currents in American Thought* (3 vols., 1927–30). Why have other scholars continued to hold New England's nineteenth-century library establishment in fairly low esteem? The very idea of Brahminism – the very idea! – has something to do with it. Since America has lacked a self-assured conservative tradition, the word *gentleman* has tended to be a term of abuse, first cousin to *snob*. To non-Bostonian Americans, the Brahmins have seemed both snobbish and parochial, too pleased with themselves and too eager to minister metaphorically (as Lowell and Motley did literally) to the Court of St James. F. L. Pattee, a professor in Pennsylvania, said with some justice that Barrett Wendell's *Literary History of America* (1900) should be renamed *A Literary History of Harvard University, with Incidental Glimpses of the Minor Writers of America*. By 1900, works with this sort of emphasis were just beginning to appear absurd; but they were irritating to non-Bostonians not so much for their absurdity as for the element of truth they contained. Boston, for much of the nineteenth century, was the intellectual capital of New England and accordingly (though New Yorkers, Philadelphians and others might dispute the claim) of the United States as a whole.

In the 1820s, a political writer coined the phrase 'The Universal Yankee Nation'. It remained alive for the next half-century in other contexts. The Connecticut showman Phineas T. Barnum (Connecticut Yankee, indeed) dedicated his memoirs to this 'Universal Yankee Nation'. In a survey of *American Men of Letters: Their Nature and Nurture* (1916), Edwin L. Clarke looked into the geographical and religious affiliations of 1,000 North

1. *Coleridge's American Disciples: The Selected Correspondence of James Marsh*, ed. John J. Duffy (Amherst, MA, 1973), 214–18.

American authors born up to 1850. He credited no less than 487 to N
England, as against 316 for the Middle Atlantic States (including New
York, New Jersey and Pennsylvania), 99 for the South Atlantic States, 53
for the East North Central, and so on. Of the 460 writers for whom there
was evidence of religious affiliation, 119 were Congregational and 49
Unitarian – both churches pre-eminently New England institutions. The
Yankee influence spread elsewhere, by direct and indirect means – through
the export of teachers and ministers, through publication, through the
lecture-circuit that carried easterners into the hinterland (lecturing, as
the joke went, for 'F.A.M.E. – Fifty [dollars] And My Expenses'), and
through the half-alliances of the American patriciate (which were, for
instance, to put Henry Adams as a Harvard undergraduate in touch with
Southern Lees, and Theodore Roosevelt with Owen Wister of Philadelphia).

During the middle third of the century, then, a considerable amount of
literary and scholarly talent was drawn to Boston; only in Boston could
you point to a group of families (Nortons, Lowells, Adamses, Holmeses,
Lodges) worthy to be mentioned with, say, the Huxleys, Darwins, Wedg-
woods and Stephens of Victorian England. A high proportion of the
contributions to the *Atlantic Monthly* were by Bostonians: Emerson tells a
story in 1868 of 'a meeting of the Atlantic Club, when the copies of the
new number of the *Atlantic* being brought in, every one rose eagerly to
get a copy, and then each sat down, and *read his own article*'. Here, we
may think, is the typical Boston inwardness. But where else could the
editor look for contributions? The *Atlantic* published W. D. Howells's first
venture, a poem; took a story from Sarah Orne Jewett when she was only
nineteen; and opened its pages to the young Henry James and to Mark
Twain. If it neglected Melville and Whitman, so did nearly every other
American periodical. Otherwise the *Atlantic* took what was available –
and the level of American literary merit was not always high in the years
following the Civil War. Boston, in fact, was an exasperating target. The
nearest thing to an American *Academy*, it was also less reactionary and
impervious than that word connotes. Many attacks, including Parrington's, have been unfair, and rather erratic; thus Parrington, while insisting
on the shortcomings of Oliver Wendell Holmes, makes him out to be a
charming and interesting figure.

One difficulty for the anti-Bostonians is that their enemies have a knack
of anticipating criticism and disarming it. Sensitive Bostonians were
almost masochistically aware of their defects. Henry Adams, who belonged
to a later generation but who spoke for the writers of 1820–70, said:

God knows that we knew our want of knowledge! the self-distrust became introspection – nervous self-consciousness – irritable dislike of America, and antipathy to Boston.... Improvised Europeans we were, and – Lord God – how thin![1]

How could one label an opponent as 'smug', after he has made such a confession? Again, though the Brahmins were on the whole well-to-do, they were not in intention frivolous. As Parrington admits, they were remarkably diligent. Though Longfellow was lucky in securing a professorship of modern languages at Harvard, he qualified himself carefully for the appointment. If not a great scholar, he was a cultivated man, widely read in several languages, and capable of considerable application. Lowell, who succeeded him in the chair, also merited the appointment. Holmes was an able medical man, who held a professorship of anatomy at Harvard Medical School for thirty-five years. Prescott, Motley and Parkman, the historians, conceived vast schemes, as did their fellow-historian George Bancroft, and carried them out to the limit of their powers. The Brahmins resisted the temptation to indolence as manfully as their ancestors warded off the snares of the Devil. Prescott and Parkman were severely handicapped by weak eyesight; yet, like the others, they lived up to the resolute sentiment of Longfellow's 'Psalm of Life':

> Let us, then, be up and doing,
> With a heart for any fate:
> Still achieving, still pursuing,
> Learn to labor and to wait.

Nor is the charge of over-refinement altogether applicable to the Brahmins. Some critics dwell on their expensive dinners and their cosy approval of one another, and contrast to their delicate literary stomachs the gutsy appetites of Twain or Whitman. Much has been made of Twain's icy reception at a Boston banquet of 1877 when he attempted to poke fun at Longfellow, Emerson and Whittier, and his speech fell humiliatingly flat. But the contrast, in some respects genuine, should not be exaggerated. Lowell, a thorough Brahmin, was active in the abolitionist cause; his dialect *Biglow Papers* constituted an important example of 'native' American literature. It was he who encouraged the Indiana novelist Edward Eggleston to write about backwoods settlements. Longfellow could be robust at times, as in this account (from his novel *Kavanagh*) of the visit to a New England village of

1. Or, as another Bostonian put it, 'The bother of the Yankee is that he rubs badly at the junction of soul and body.'

Mr Wilmerdings the butcher, standing beside his cart, and surrounded by five cats.... Mr Wilmerdings not only supplied the village with fresh provisions daily, but he likewise weighed all the babies. There was hardly a child that had not hung beneath his steelyards, tied in a silk handkerchief.... He had lately married a milliner, who sold 'Dunstable and eleven-braid, openwork and coloured straws', and their bridal tour had been to a neighbouring town to see a man hanged for murdering his wife. A pair of huge ox-horns branched from the gable of his slaughter-house, and near it stood the great pits of the tannery, which all the schoolboys thought were filled with blood!

Or, if we are to mention Mark Twain, he can be set against Oliver Wendell Holmes, who in 1861 published a novel, *Elsie Venner*, in which a savage dog, kicked by the hero in self-defence,

went bundling out of the open schoolhouse door with a most pitiable yelp, and his stump of a tail shut down as close as his owner ever shut the short, stubbed blade of his jack-knife.

In Twain's *Tom Sawyer* (1876), a poodle sits down on a pinch-bug during a church service and goes 'sailing up the aisle'. This originally continued 'with his tail shut down like a hasp'; but of this latter phrase Twain's friend and adviser W. D. Howells wrote in the margin of the manuscript, 'Awfully good but a little dirty'. The offending phrase was removed; and if Howells had not objected, it is quite likely that Twain would have cut it out himself, being less culturally self-assured, at that stage in his career, and therefore more anxious than the Brahmins to achieve 'good taste'.

In short, any simple version of the fastidious and un-American Brahmins is wrong. Even if we were to accept some of Parrington's criteria, it would be hard to condemn the Brahmins without condemning many other Americans. While none was an out-and-out abolitionist, they were closely concerned with the outcome of the struggle. Longfellow praised the outrageous John Brown in his diary; he and Holmes had sons wounded in the war. As for 'native' literature, even Parkman, despite his dislike of the masses, praised the *national* quality of books like *The Life of David Crockett*, and *The Big Bear of Arkansas*, 'which emanate from, or are adapted to, the unschooled classes of the people'; whereas, 'in the politer walks of literature, we find much grace of style, but very little originality of thought – productions which might as readily be taken for the work of an Englishman as of an American'.

In extenuating the Brahmins, there is a danger of erring in the opposite direction from Parrington. Where the poet-Brahmins are concerned, little of their work has retained its spell. We must beware, however, of attributing this thinness exclusively to Boston. Is there not, rather, a displacement of the poet which is almost as evident in nineteenth-century England as in America? Longfellow, Lowell, and Holmes were popular with the English public not because they deliberately aimed at it in an un-American fashion, but because their view of poetry closely corresponded to that approved in English (and American) parlours. The displacement in a writer such as Tennyson reveals itself in the gulf between his verse and his private conduct: the one so graceful, the other so gruffly compounded of tobacco, beer and slang. This is not to say that either Tennyson or the Brahmins were seriously worried by the fact that they did not write as they spoke – no writers ever *have*, exactly. But in the case of the Brahmins, neither the polite nor the popular idiom quite suited them. This was an all-American problem. Poetic norms were essentially the same throughout the United States. Perhaps New England's heritage of unsensuous integrity often made it unduly polite. In this sense we can agree with Parrington that the impression left by the Brahmins is of unwarranted refinement – the Anglo-American vice of the period, with extra Bostonian nuances that account for the Brahmin-poets' celebrity in their own day, and failure to communicate to ours.

What has Longfellow, the most successful of them all, to offer? In prose, flimsy novels like *Hyperion* and *Kavanagh*: priggish in sum, though with interludes of pleasant common sense. In verse, a great quantity, from little ditties to the ambitious long poems: *Evangeline*, *Hiawatha*, the translation of Dante. As Poe[1] and Whitman both testified (with reservations), Longfellow had abundant talent; there is no strain in his verse, for the meaning carried in it is always amply contained by the vocabulary and the metre. By contrast, technically Melville is the clumsiest of amateur poets, though the load of meaning is greater. Nor was Longfellow without originality, of a limited order. He rummaged busily in the attics of European literature, bringing to light much of interest. Like Irving, he did his best to supply America with its own folklore. In January 1840 he wrote that he had

broken ground in a new field; namely, ballads; beginning with the 'Wreck of the Schooner Hesperus', on the reef of Norman's Woe, in the great storm of a fortnight

---

1. Longfellow noted in his *Journal* (24 February 1847):

    In Hexameter sings serenely a Harvard Professor;
    In Pentameter him damns censorious Poe.

ago .... I think I shall write more. The *national ballad* is a virgin soil here in New England; and there are great materials.

He did write more, with gratifying results: few American schoolboys have escaped acquaintance with 'Paul Revere's Ride', to choose one example. But the *national* ballad, as such, made no real appeal to him; he was amused and sceptical at the endless argument on the need for a *national* literature. The juxtaposition was not America–Europe, but 'my ideal home-world of Poetry, and the outer tangible Prose world'. That the latter sometimes attracted him is shown by the quotation from *Kavanagh*. But the world of poesy was more his home, and whether he wrote of Europe or America, he did so without much desire for actuality. He never visited the American West and saw no need to do so: nor, on his own terms, can one blame him. When he wished to describe the Mississippi, in *Evangeline*, he was satisfied to go and look at Banvard's canvas panorama of the river, which happened to be touring the neighbourhood. His material for *Hiawatha* was taken in large part from the ethnologist Henry Rowe Schoolcraft, who had unwittingly mixed up the Iroquois leader Hiawatha with a Chippewa warrior; the metre for the poem – a metre to which he clung in face of unfavourable comment – came from Finland. When he wrote of his boyhood, in 'My Lost Youth', his memory of Portland, Maine, was prompted by lines from Dante. 'Siede la terra dove nato fui | Sulla marina', became 'Often I think of the beautiful town | That is seated by the sea'. And the chorus –

> A boy's will is the wind's will,
> And the thoughts of youth are long, long thoughts –

came from Herder's translation into German of a Lapland song:

> Knabenwille ist Windeswille
> Jünglings Gedanken lange Gedanken.

There is nothing wrong with such adaptations, which have been a godsend to some modern poets. But whereas with Ezra Pound and T. S. Eliot the adaptation (or direct quotation) is used purposely for its associative effect, with Longfellow it seems merely part of a miscellaneous literary stockpile. The reader is usually unaware that there has been something borrowed; even so, there is a slight odour of pot-pourri emanating from Longfellow. In *Hiawatha*, the Indians are not unreal because he failed to go and look at some actual redskins, but because they are the product of a romantic rather than a fiercely fresh imagination. Hence, they have 'dated' in a slightly ridiculous way, like bygone fashion-drawings. Parody can overwhelm them, as it fails to overwhelm a poet of Whitman's stature:

> He killed the noble Mudjokivis.
> Of the skin he made him mittens,
> Made them with the fur inside
> Put the inside skinside outside.

Time has been unkind to Longfellow; not for his Brahminism, but for an inability to transcend the requirements of his generation which he so admirably met. Emerson said of *Hiawatha*, with polite acuity, 'I have always one foremost satisfaction in reading your books – that I am safe. I am in variously skilful hands, but first of all they are safe hands.' True, certain stanzas by Longfellow seem to contradict the picture of him as invariably 'safe'. The last two verses of 'The Challenge' (1873) portrayed a sense of social injustice that led Jack London to cite them in his *People of the Abyss* (1903), an account of down-and-outs in the slums of England's capital. W. D. Howells, too, referred to the poem in his Utopian novel *Through the Eye of the Needle* (1907):

> There is a greater army
>   That besets us round with strife,
> A numberless, starving army,
>   At all the gates of life. . . .

> And there in the camp of famine,
>   In wind and cold and rain,
> Christ, the great Lord of the Army,
>   Lies dead upon the plain.

But as a character in Howells's novel indicates, these stanzas are almost concealed in a picturesquely 'historical' tale that 'begins in [Longfellow's] sweet old way, about some Spanish king who was killed before a city he was besieging, and one of his knights sallies out of the camp and challenges the people of the city ... as traitors. Then the poet breaks off, *apropos de rien*' – with the above two verses on the sufferings of the poor.

Lowell also has faded. Not all of his writing, though, has lost its colour. The *Fable for Critics* (1848) has witty and perceptive comments upon contemporary American writers, such as Whittier –

> A fervor of mind which knows no separation
> 'Twixt simple excitement and pure inspiration –

(and about Lowell himself, for in characteristic New England manner he is his own best critic). Some of the *Biglow Papers* have remained alive, with their quick, angry, or humorous comment on humankind. A few of his literary essays are good – those on Chaucer and Emerson, for instance – and most are readable. His work is fluent and rather felicitous. Poems and essays alike abound in neat turns of phrase, and epigrams that are immediately pleasing –

[Wordsworth] was the historian of Wordsworthshire

[Thoreau] watched Nature like a detective who is to go upon the stand –

though they will usually not bear a close scrutiny. For the last few years of his life he was America's most distinguished man of letters, to whom Oxford proffered a chair, and who was godfather to Adeline Stephen (better known, later, as Virginia Woolf).

Today Lowell is especially interesting in that his career illustrated all the main aspects of American literature of the period. As a young man he believed ardently in democracy and the anti-slavery cause. In his prime he was a Harvard professor, who also helped to edit the *Atlantic Monthly* and the *North American Review*. As an elderly figure he seemed conservative: a Brahmin who could write to Henry James that 'the best society I ever saw was in Cambridge, Mass., take it by and large'; who saw nothing in Whitman, and who regretted that Wordsworth 'did not earlier give himself to "the trade of classic niceties". It was this precisely which gives to the blank verse of Walter Savage Landor the severe dignity and reserved force . . . to which Wordsworth never attained.' As a cultivated gentleman, Lowell liked to feel cosmopolitan; European literature was an area in which he knew the best authors as he knew the best hotels and regional dishes, and his pages are crowded with literary allusions. The idea of a national American literature seemed to him as foolish as it did to Longfellow. He said in an ironical review of a minor American poet, James Gates Percival,

If that little dribble of an Avon had succeeded in engendering Shakespeare what a giant might we not look for from the mighty womb of Mississippi! Physical geography for the first time took her rightful place as the tenth and most inspiring Muse.

But as an American, Lowell never doubted that his country could give points to others. In the second series of the *Biglow Papers*, written during the Civil War, he addresses John Bull in accents that are far from anglophile:

> Why talk so dreffle big, John,
> Of honor when it meant
> You didn't care a fig, John,
> But jest for *ten per cent*?

And his essay 'On a Certain Condescension in Foreigners' makes plain
that he is an American, though with the appropriate quotations from
European literature at his elbow. In fact, like other Brahmins (and like
Cooper before him), he was impelled to defend gentility to his own
countrymen, and the ruggeder virtues of his native land to Europeans. As
he mellowed, he joined Holmes and the others under the Brahmin umbrella, in the belief that Boston–Cambridge offered the best of both worlds.
Yet as a writer he never fully occupied either, and never found an entirely
appropriate personal mode of expression. Thus, in 'Mason and Slidell: A
Yankee Idyll' are these lines:

> O strange New World, thet yit wast never young,
> Whose youth from thee by gripin' need was wrung,
> Brown foundlin' o' the woods, whose baby-bed
> Was prowled roun' by the Injun's cracklin' tread....

They are modified from lines in an earlier poem, 'The Power of Sound: A
Rhymed Lecture':

> O strange New World that yet wast never young,
> Whose youth from thee by tyrannous need was wrung,
> Brown foundling of the forest, with gaunt eyes,
> Orphan and heir of all the centuries....

Which is the better version? The one in dialect is more informal: *griping* is
a stronger word than *tyrannous*: yet the dialect does not sit very comfortably on the lines. *The Injun's cracklin' tread* is an unfortunate substitution;
and the dialect as a whole has a stagy sound. The speaker drops it a little
later, when he refers genteelly to the 'vassal ocean's mane', only to revert
to Yankeeisms. Both versions are dextrous, but neither is powerful. A
similar though less conspicuous duality marks other Brahmins, such as
Prescott the historian. Three generations of William Prescotts before him
had occupied his room at Harvard; there was a coat of arms on the family
plate; his style was hardly distinguishable from that of an Englishman;
and yet he was not an Englishman – he was a Yankee, whom the English
landscape makes homesick for a 'ragged fence, or an old stump ... to show
that man's hand had not been combing Nature's head so vigorously. I felt
I was not in my dear, wild America.'

Given a larger talent, Lowell might have overcome whatever handicap Brahminism imposed. As it was – and as perhaps the lines above suggest – verse-making came too easily to him. Stanza succeeds stanza, and still his nimble mind is not done with the theme. His much-praised 'Harvard Commemoration Ode' is too graceful, too felicitous through too many lines. It is in perfect taste; but the agony and the triumph are too readily explained. Lowell knew his fault; nearly twenty years before, he had written to Longfellow that when the *Fable for Critics* was finished he would abandon poetry for a while, since he could not 'write slowly enough'. But he never did. Henry James's memorial tribute to him is also implicitly a devastating comment on the civic culture of Boston in the twilight of the genteel tradition. James Russell Lowell, said James, 'carried style – the style of literature – into regions where we rarely look for it: into politics, of all places in the world, into diplomacy, into stammering, civic dinners, and ponderous anniversaries, into letters and notes and telegrams, into every turn of the hour – absolutely into conversation, where ... it ... disguised itself as intensely colloquial wit.'

The same can be said in general of Lowell's friend Oliver Wendell Holmes. He too could versify without effort, was keenly interested in language and dialect, adored puns and epigrams, and thought himself a gentleman. In addition he was a man of science: and, as befitted one who had produced an important treatise on puerperal fever, he was a little scornful of romantic notions. His favourite poets were Pope, Goldsmith and Campbell; both the bluffness and the elegance of their age appealed to him. 'Mysticism' he used as a term of reproach. 'The imaginative writer', he declared, 'is after effects, the scientific man is after truth.' He did not mean there was no room for imagination, but that it should be a whimsical subordinate to science. 'Life', his Autocrat said, 'is maintained by the respiration of oxygen and sentiments'; and Holmes's work is just such a medley. At one extreme comes his occasional verse, devised for dinner tables and college reunions, and his light conversation ('the whole art of love may be read in any Encyclopaedia under the title *Fortification*'); at the other, his interest in the application of scientific discovery to human behaviour. In his novels *Elsie Venner*, *The Guardian Angel*, and *A Mortal Antipathy* he mingles light-hearted local colour with themes that could be of great significance: all of them concerned with the extent to which men are free moral agents. Elsie Venner is an evil person, but the evil is inherited (grotesquely, as in a Hawthorne tale, from the rattlesnake venom which entered her mother's blood), and so she is 'not to blame'. The conduct of the principal characters in the other two novels is similarly predetermined. Are we, then, responsible for our own actions? Should society punish us? Such doubts, when coupled with the conviction that society was a sham, racked the great naturalist writers of the century's end.

But for Holmes, society was Boston, the city of which he was poet laureate. Private jokes, the ritualizing of talk and gustation, a hint of self-satisfaction, a tinge of inbred malice: these are not entirely unknown in Oxford and Cambridge. Perhaps they are concomitants of intellectual communities. At any rate it seems a little hard to blame Holmes and his Boston, especially as he loved the place, when we are told that American writers tend to emulate Whitman, in embracing the whole continent instead of an area of manageable size. Yet, exonerate Holmes as we may, we cannot make a great writer out of him. Even the best of his poems, 'The Deacon's Masterpiece; or, The Wonderful "One-Hoss Shay" ', is not much more than clever light verse; while the other poem by which he is chiefly known, 'The Chambered Nautilus', is – like Longfellow's 'Psalm of Life' – hortatory, melodious and flat. The novels of Holmes are not sufficiently concentrated; they show an inquisitive mind casting about in a variety of directions. The *Breakfast-Table* volumes have the same defect; after a few chapters one begins to fidget, and wonder why they are not as good as Sterne's *Tristram Shandy*, or the conversation-novels of the English author Thomas Love Peacock. They seem on a level with W. H. Mallock's *New Republic*, another English book of dialogues, but without the fun of guessing whom the characters represent. In the *Breakfast-Table* books the characters are Holmes and his sparring partners: and he floors them too infallibly, like an expert on a quiz programme.

Longfellow, Lowell, Holmes: all three, great men to their own age, have dwindled subsequently. There is not enough weight to their work. Helen Hunt Jackson, the vivacious writer and lifelong Amherst friend of Emily Dickinson, found the entire scene depressing in 1879. She wrote to an American in London: 'There is no such thing here … as a literary class.' The nation's businessmen 'think it is well to have a Longfellow and Whittier, and a few more like them, because other countries have authors – "a thing no country should be without," – but for anything beyond that? no! Their only feeling about literature is that it is an uncommonly poor way of making a living.'[1] For the quality of weight, and incidentally a degree of monetary success, we must turn to the Brahmin historians

1. Moncure D. Conway, *Autobiography* (2 vols., Boston, 1904), ii. 427–8.

Prescott, Motley and Parkman. With no financial need to engage in arduous work, they seem nevertheless to have yielded to the pressure of a New England atmosphere which compelled industry. (A Boston hostess is said to have replied to a visiting Englishman who complained to her that America had no leisure class, 'Oh yes we have, but *we* call them tramps'). The same atmosphere may have directed them into historical study. Motley would have preferred to be a novelist, but after two unsuccessful attempts, and some less unsuccessful efforts at literary criticism, he concluded that history (which demanded 'sappers and miners') rather than the novel (a task for 'lancers') should be his field. Parkman also tried his hand at a novel (*Vassall Morton*, 1856), but the stiffly autobiographical result made it clear that his talent must lie elsewhere. Whatever was missing in New England to inhibit creative writing can almost be said to have encouraged the scholar and critic, together with analysis of the self.

This trio of historians arrived at a suitable moment. The New World needed chroniclers. Historians like Jared Sparks and George Bancroft were celebrating the growth of American democracy. As Brahmins, however, Prescott, Motley and Parkman had little wish to engage directly in the political history of the United States; in doing so they might appear no better than party hacks. Casting about for a theme, the first two were drawn to Spanish history, an area of study which Irving and the Bostonian scholar George Ticknor had helped to popularize. Ticknor directed Prescott's early studies and was later to become his biographer; Irving relinquished to Prescott the theme of the conquest of Mexico by Cortés; and Prescott in turn assisted Motley in preparing his *Rise of the Dutch Republic*, though he was himself at work on a history of the reign of Philip II, and was hence allowing 'the cream of my subject' to be skimmed off.

Parkman chose differently. As an undergraduate with a strong taste for the outdoors, he had determined to write the story of early French activity in Canada. Then gradually, as his interest developed, he

enlarged the plan to include the whole course of the American conflict between France and England, or in other words, the history of the *American forest*; for this was the light in which I regarded it. My theme fascinated me, and I was haunted with wilderness images night and day.

So the three chose their subjects and set patiently to work. To all three history was a branch of literature. It was the drama of their themes – the expansion of Spain in the sixteenth century, the clash between democracy and tyranny in the Netherlands, 'the history of the American forest' – that enticed them. All, in fact, used the word *drama* to describe their aim. Though they set themselves high standards of accuracy and took great pains to accumulate material, they arranged their work so as to tell a story, hoping to make it as readable as the novels of Scott. They included chapters of social history, but wherever possible related their narrative to some outstanding figure: Cortés, William the Silent, Pontiac. Prescott, in his best book, *The Conquest of Mexico*, discusses in the preface whether he may not, in prolonging the drama past the fall of Mexico to the death of Cortés, have fallen into the error of 'a premature *dénouement*'; and trusts that he has preserved 'the *unity of interest*'.

In all three cases the combination of scholarship and dramatic interest is successful. From an American viewpoint, of course, the story is one with a happy ending, or evolution. As with Bancroft's history of the colonies and the American revolution, the pattern of history is progressive, and the Americans are in the van. Whites are at a higher stage of civilization than natives and bound therefore to conquer despite immense odds against them. Christians inevitably triumph over infidels, Protestants over Catholics, Teutons or Anglo-Saxons over Celts or Mediterranean types; and, gratifying for Bancroft, liberty-loving colonists wrest freedom from the world's next-best, the British. There are evidences of racial and religious prejudice in these histories, and (though not in Bancroft) of distaste for the *public*. Prescott's style, though in his diary he wrote 'bother euphony', is euphonious; bosoms swell with indignation, characters partake of bountiful collations, the 'polished nations' are contrasted to the 'barbarous' ones. Motley, for his part, makes his villains excessively villainous and his heroes wearisomely heroic. His William the Silent is a figure as awesome in his resolution and virtue as Bancroft's George Washington, or Prescott's Isabella. Motley, and Prescott to a lesser extent, is sometimes slipshod in handling his sources. Parkman occasionally allows a supercilious tone to creep into his writing. But these faults are far outweighed by the excitement of the themes and the narrative skill with which they are developed.

Parkman is the greatest of the three. He first attracted attention with his *Oregon Trail*, to give the book the title by which it is now known. In it he describes his experiences as a young Harvard graduate, among the Plains Indians, whom he visited at a time (1846) when they were still powerful, though in contact with white hunters and emigrant trains. He also unwittingly reveals his own temperament. He shows himself to be confident, almost compulsively addicted to hardship, somewhat contemptuous of the Indians, and considerably more so of the unkempt and uneducated white men whose wagons passed westward along the trails. The noble savage for him is at least half a myth. What may be called gentlemanly traits arouse Parkman's admiration; he likes his wilderness to be peopled by men of breeding. But they must be strong men: one of his favourite words is *manly*.

These predilections appear, though less obviously, in Parkman's major historical works, which run (chronologically) from *Pioneers of France in the New World* to *Montcalm and Wolfe*; *The Conspiracy of Pontiac* is not formally part of his great series. Reverencing veracity no less than virility, he criticizes Longfellow for sentimentalizing the Acadians (in *Evangeline*) and the Indians (in *Hiawatha*), and jeers at Cooper's improbabilities of plot. He avoids such pitfalls in his own writing. Knowing the ground of which he writes – one reason why, he believes, historians should write about their own countries – and ransacking the archives for documentary evidence, he erects his narrative on a firm basis of fact. Despite occasional errors and distortions discovered by recent scholars, Parkman is a highly competent historian. His interpretations are far less strained than those of Motley. His Protestant conviction that the English colonies represent a more enlightened, and therefore superior society to that of Catholic Canada, is offset by his admiration for the courage of such principal figures as La Salle, Frontenac and Montcalm. Indeed it is the pathos of their endeavour which fascinates him, and which gives his books such imaginative power. There is a hidden element of autobiography, as perhaps in all resonant historical writing. Parkman's heroes are lonely men, who act out their dramas in a setting whose wilderness immensity both dwarfs and ennobles whatever they achieve. Men like La Salle are also unpopular; their leadership is challenged by inferiors, and often ends in disgrace, betrayal, death. America repudiates the aristocrats who fashion its history: this is one of the buried themes in Parkman's *France and England in North America*. But it is handled with stoic understatement. His pages march on, direct and circumstantial. Before we dismiss the Brahmins as sweet and thin we must reckon with the transmuted passion of Parkman, who converted his wilderness dream and his Coriolanus-like sense of unappreciated heroism into a series of magnificently distanced narrative reports.

By the time he died in 1892, political power in his Boston had passed to the Irish. Feminists were steeling themselves for the long struggle to attain equality. To Parkman such transformations were disasters, undermining the fabric of his Universal Yankee Nation. When he wrote directly about social change (or rather, about means of averting it) he sounded narrow and cantankerous. When he took the continent for his stage, the record of strife and supersession achieved an epic sadness.

VIII

AMERICAN HUMOUR AND THE
RISE OF THE WEST
Mark Twain and His Predecessors

CHARLES FARRAR BROWNE ['ARTEMUS WARD'] (1832–67)

Born in Waterford, Maine. He worked as a newspaperman, in Ohio and New York City. His comic sketches for *Vanity Fair*, collected as *Artemus Ward, His Book* (1862), were favourites with President Abraham Lincoln. Ward also had a great comic success as a deadpan, rambling lecturer. He met Mark Twain in Virginia City, Nevada. Ward's writings and platform performances were a hit in London also: see the posthumous *Artemus Ward's Lectures* (1869). He died in London of tuberculosis.

GEORGE HORATIO DERBY ['JOHN PHOENIX'] (1823–61)

Born in Dedham, Massachusetts. He graduated from the U.S. Military Academy, West Point; was commissioned into the élite Topographical Engineers; served in the Mexican War; and was then stationed on the Pacific coast, 1849–56. His facetious and burlesque sketches were published as the popular *Phoenixiana* (1856), and (posthumously) *The Squibob Papers* (1865). He died in New York City.

GEORGE WASHINGTON HARRIS (1814–69)

Born in Allegheny City, Pennsylvania. As a child he moved to Knoxville, Tennessee, and became successively a metal-worker, riverboat captain, farmer, and business-man. Harris contributed humorous sketches to the New York *Spirit of the Times* and to local newspapers – the best-known of these were published as *Sut Lovingood's Yarns* (1867). He was strongly Confederate in his sympathies (he wrote derisively of 'Old Abe' Lincoln). Died in Tennessee, while travelling back from a business trip to Virginia.

FRANCIS BRET HARTE (1836–1902)

Born in Albany, New York, of partly Jewish Canadian immigrant stock. In 1854 he travelled to California with his younger sister, via the Panama Isthmus. He lived in Oakland and San Francisco, working as printer and journalist. He became editor of the new *Overland Monthly* (1868–70), where some of his most popular stories and poetry appeared. *The Luck of Roaring Camp and Other Stories* (1870) brought him an invitation to go East and contribute to *Atlantic Monthly*. He never again lived in California; consular appointments in Krefeld and Glasgow enabled Harte to base himself in London. His output as an author was considerable: *Condensed Novels* (1867; second series, 1902); *Gabriel Conroy* (1875–6), a novel; several dramatized versions of his stories, such as *Ah Sin*, 1877, in collaboration with Mark Twain; many subsequent collections of tales and verse. Harte died in London.

AUGUSTUS BALDWIN LONGSTREET (1790–1870)

Born in Augusta, Georgia, and educated at Yale and law school in Litchfield, Connecticut, but firmly Southern in outlook. Longstreet was a jurist, clergyman, and college president (for example at Emory College, 1839–48; University of Mississippi, 1849–56; and University of South Carolina, 1857–65). He published a semi-autobiographical novel of his Georgia upbringing, *Master William Mitten* (1864). His most popular work by far was *Georgia Scenes, Characters, and Incidents &c. in the First Half Century of the Republic* (1835), a medley of humorous pieces originally printed in two local papers in 1827.

THOMAS BANGS THORPE (1815–78)

Born in Westfield, Massachusetts, but lived for twenty years (1833–53) in Louisiana, where he was a newspaper editor. Thorpe served in the army in the Mexican War and was a colonel in the Union forces during the Civil War; he was also co-editor of *The Spirit of the Times*. Among many South-West frontier tales, his most famous was *The Big Bear of Arkansas* (1841). He was employed in his later years in the New York Custom-House.

SAMUEL LANGHORNE CLEMENS ['MARK TWAIN'] (1835–1910)

Born in Missouri, the son of John Marshall Clemens, a restless and unsuccessful lawyer–land-speculator, who settled (1839) at Hannibal, Missouri, on the Mississippi. He left school in 1847, on his father's death, to work as apprentice printer. He followed the printer's trade in Eastern and Middle Western cities, 1853–4; he journeyed to New Orleans in 1856, intending to make his fortune in Brazil, but abandoned the scheme and became a Mississippi river-pilot instead. This first part of his life furnished the basis of some of his best books: *The Adventures of Tom Sawyer* (1876), *Life on the Mississippi* (1883), and *The Adventures of Huckleberry Finn* (1884). After a short period as a Confederate volunteer, he spent the remainder of the Civil

War years in Nevada and San Francisco, writing humorous newspaper items under the pseudonym of 'Mark Twain', and establishing himself as a popular lecturer. He scored a great success with *The Innocents Abroad* (1869), a travelogue. In 1870 he married Olivia Langdon, and soon settled with her at Hartford, Connecticut. Twain wrote many books, nearly all well received, including *Roughing It* (1872); *The Gilded Age* (1873, in collaboration with his Hartford neighbour, C. D. Warner); *A Tramp Abroad* (1880); *The Prince and the Pauper* (1882); *A Connecticut Yankee in King Arthur's Court* (1889); *The Tragedy of Pudd'nhead Wilson* (1894), and *Personal Recollections of Joan of Arc* (1896), as well as many stories, sketches and articles.

AMERICAN HUMOUR AND THE RISE OF THE WEST

THE Brahmins, in writing and in person, upheld a polite America to Europeans. Europeans, for their part, responded; *The Times*, as Whitman quoted it in 'The Poet and his Program' (1881), said that the well-known American poets had 'caught the English tone and air and mood only too faithfully', and were 'accepted by the superficially cultivated English intelligence as readily as if they were English born'. They were read with enjoyment; yet their work was 'afflicted from first to last with a fatal want of raciness'. J. R. Lowell, for instance, 'can overflow with American humour when politics inspire his muse; but in the realm of pure poetry he is no more American than a Newdigate prizeman'. Here *The Times* is discussing the need for a native American literature much as the Americans themselves discussed it, and with something of the same inconsistency. For Longfellow and Lowell were New English (and so American) rather than English, and no more capable of writing like ruffians (except deliberately, as in the *Biglow Papers*) than Leslie Stephen or Matthew Arnold. When an American ruffian appeared, the English greeted him with delight, but regarded him (insultingly, to American eyes) as being thoroughly typical where Lowell and Longfellow were somehow slightly fraudulent. Thus, Motley was succeeded as minister to Great Britain, in 1870, by Robert C. Schenck, an Ohio politician and Civil War major-general: Motley, as a scholar and gentleman, had been an acceptable minister; Schenck became the hit of the London season by introducing draw poker, a game which he played with a consummate nerve born of long practice. Unfortunately, though, the general became involved in a dubious mining venture in which several British acquaintances lost heavily. He was recalled, and went to join the long list of English proofs that the Americans, however quaint, were uncivilized.

Nevertheless, the British were more willing than the majority of Americans to welcome signs of a really indigenous American literature (if only, in certain cases, to feed their own preconceptions of life in the United

States). Whitman, under the sponsorship of W. M. Rossetti, had been taken somewhat more seriously in England than at home. And in the years of the Civil War and after, the English appetite for authentic Americanism was fed. The lectures and *Punch* contributions of Artemus Ward; the personality of Joaquin (*né* Cincinnatus) Miller, 'The Byron of Oregon'; the mining-frontier poems and stories of Bret Harte; the aphorisms of Josh Billings; and the writings of Mark Twain: these burst upon the London scene with an explosive vitality comparable to that of the musical comedies of mid-twentieth-century America. As with *Oklahoma!* and *Annie Get Your Gun*, they were not everybody's dish. In his *American Literature* (1885), the Scottish critic John Nichol deprecated the 'degenerate style' of some American humour, singling out Mark Twain as one 'who has done perhaps more than any other living writer to lower the literary tone of English speaking people'. On the whole, though, British critics were kinder to 'Western' humour than were their colleagues in the Eastern United States, since, as Howells explained,

The West, when it began to put itself into literature, could do so without the sense ... of any older or politer world outside of it; whereas the East was always looking fearfully over its shoulder at Europe, and anxious to account for itself as well as represent itself.

'Western' or 'frontier' humour was not in fact confined to the West. Some of its characteristics were shared with New England or 'Down East' humour. The habit of hyperbole, for example (evident in Lowell's description of a wooden shingle 'painted so like marble that it sank in the water'), had been acquired by Easterners before it spread West. Artemus Ward, 'John Phoenix', and several other humorists came from the East. As a group – George Washington Harris, the creator of 'Sut Lovingood', is an exception – they were and portrayed themselves as moral, cultivated persons, Whigs rather than Democrats in political affiliation. Quite often they adopted an authorial pose as high-minded, literate narrators. The quoted tale, with its dialect, its deliberate mis-spellings (or cacography) and its rough-and-tumble, is set within this respectable frame, like a genre painting of some rural frolic – a corn-husking or a militia muster.

A. B. Longstreet's *Georgia Scenes* (1835), for example, establish an amusing contrast between the almost excessively 'correct' diction of the gentlemanly observer, and the homeliness or downright coarseness of what he observes – in which neither side is wholly sympathetic. The refined narrator of Longstreet's 'Georgia Theatrics' describes a brutal combat he overhears, which apparently ends with the gouging-out of the loser's eye. Horrified, he accosts the victor, only to be told: 'There a'nt nobody there, nor ha'nt been nother. I was just seein' how I could 'a' *fout*.' The narrator explains to the 'gentle reader' that this was true. The young man he had overheard was merely rehearsing an imaginary fight:

I went to the ground from which he had risen, and there were the prints of his two thumbs, plunged up to the balls in the mellow earth, about the distance of a man's eyes apart; and the ground around was broken up as if two stags had been engaged upon it.

By the same token, young Bret Harte was no Western he-man. Brought up in Brooklyn and New York City, precociously talented and bookish (as the parody–pastiches in his *Condensed Novels* were to reveal), he was an aesthete who had gained little first-hand experience of the mining camps about which he wrote. The Indiana-born Joaquin Miller, as *The Times* noticed, was nowhere near as rugged as his clothing and his demeanour indicated: his 'verse has fluency and movement and harmony, but as for the thought, his songs of the sierras might as well have been written in Holland.' East and West were as much states of mind as actual regions; and in this respect the East was inclined to repudiate its Western behaviour. John Hay came East from Indiana and it is difficult to reconcile the suave elder Hay, ambassador and Secretary of State, with the young man who endeared himself to the American and British publics with his *Pike County Ballads* (1871). The New York writer E. C. Stedman told a friend in 1873 that 'the whole country . . . is flooded, deluged, swamped, beneath a muddy tide of slang, vulgarity . . . impertinence, and buffoonery that is not wit': several critics had been no kinder to Hay's *Pike County* humour. Three years later an Eastern reviewer described a book by an Indiana author as the work of 'the invading Goths from over the mountains'.

The reviewer probably did not mean to imply that his quasi-Roman civilization was doomed. But it is worth looking at this Gothland in order to understand the Chief Goth, Mark Twain. The American Gothland included several dissimilar areas: the Old South-West, the mining frontier and the Pacific coast, to name only three that Twain knew. But we may speak loosely of the whole area as West or Frontier, to define parts of America still in process of settlement. Much of it was still or recently had been wilderness, thinly populated by Indians and white hunters and trappers. Life was hard for the settlers; they survived by developing self-reliance to an extraordinary degree, and in so doing developed a contempt for niceties of law, speech or social observance. Charles Dickens, touring America in 1842, met his first Westerner on a canal-boat making for Pittsburgh: a strange, scornful man who told the other passengers:

I'm from the brown forests of Mississippi, *I* am, and when the sun shines on me, it does shine – a little ... I'm a brown forester, I am ... There are no smooth skins where I live. We're rough men there.

Such men assembled a new vocabulary abounding in words like *absquatulate*, *flabbergast*, *rampageous*; and in vague, compendious terms like *fixings*, *notions*, *doings*, which covered a multitude of situations.

Frontier life could be lonely and empty. The solitude bred melancholy. John Nichol suggested that 'transatlantic humour ... is the rare efflorescence of a people habitually grave, whose insight is more clear than deep; it relies mainly on exaggeration, and a blending of jest and earnest, which has the effect, as in their Negro melodies, of singing comic words to a sad tune'. In other words, the optimism of the West became at times obligatory, almost to the verge of despair. Failure, because possible, was unthinkable. How could a straggling frontier village maintain its existence (as Lincoln's New Salem failed to do) unless you pretended that it was already a city?

Constance Rourke, in her *American Humour* (1931), says that 'the backwoodsman conquered the Indian, but the Indian also conquered him', by turning him into a somewhat similar savage, a taker of scalps and a prey to superstitious fears. True; yet the line of settlement moved fast: seventeen miles a year on average, according to Tocqueville. The steamboat and the railroad cut deep into the wilderness. What had lately been a frontier community swiftly acquired a newspaper (there were seven in Mark Twain's Hannibal), a school, a church, a law-office. Emerson thought it was religion that brought 'the piano ... so quickly into the shanty': Bret Harte assured him that, on the contrary, it was vice: 'It is the gamblers who bring in the music to California. It is the prostitute who brings in the New York fashions of dress there, and so throughout.'[1] Both no doubt had their effect; the American woman seemed ready to play her part, and the man to let her. Dickens, though affronted by American manners, had to admit that in all his travels he never saw 'a woman exposed to the slightest act of rudeness, incivility, or even inattention'. If the West glorified in being wild and woolly, it was also eager to be tame and cultivated. Dickens met a Choctaw chieftain who greatly admired *The*

1. A conversation with Harte noted in Emerson's journal, 18 October 1872.

Lady of the Lake and *Marmion*. Squalid mining towns put up opera houses, and paid to hear Oscar Wilde lecture on tastefulness. Tom Sawyer's robber gang finds itself raiding a Sunday-school picnic: and this on a Saturday, since the gang members' parents would not let them play on the Sabbath.

Constance Rourke's statement needs to be complemented with that of Tocqueville, who said of the backwoodsman that 'everything about him is wild, but he himself is the result of the labour and experience of eighteen centuries'. His frontier passed; forests were cleared and game slaughtered in a frenzy of waste. Everything changed; and in the midst of the hurrying, exuberant process there came moments of intense sadness. For a short while, flat-boats and horse-drawn barges were supreme on the inland waterways. Then the steamboats supplanted them. The 'old way' disappeared, leaving behind little more than the legend of Mike Fink, king of the flat-boatmen, and his cry: 'What's the use of improvements? Where's the fun, the frolicking, the fighting? Gone! all gone!' Artemus Ward caught the same mood in the 'jernal of a vyge' undertaken 'when I was a young man (in the Brite Lexington of yooth, when thar ain't no sich word as fale) on the Wabash Canawl'. He ends his account: 'This was in the days of Old Long Sign, be4 steembotes was goin round bustin their bilers & sendin people higher nor a kite. Them was happy days....' And the steamboats, though their reign was longer, were ephemeral craft. 'Pasteboard', as Thackeray called them, they consisted of 'an engine and $10,000 worth of fretwork', not built to last, since they were apt to reach a sudden end on a sandbar.

The Westerner's reaction to his environment was natural enough. The factitious and the short-lived could hardly be lamented in formal terms, but they could be laughed at. Though the frontier lacked a mythology, it was easy to invent one. These folk-heroes were supermen, but there was nothing portentous about them: they were comic figures, like Mike Fink, who could eat more, drink deeper, fight harder, and shoot straighter than any mortal. Davy Crockett, the hero of the South-West, had similar attributes: he was 'the darling branch of old Kentuck that can eat up a panther, hold a buffalo out to drink, and put a rifle-ball through the moon'. The growth of the Crockett legend shows how the self-conscious, even spurious aspects of the frontier could achieve a certain authenticity. For in life Davy Crockett was a backwoods mediocrity, who had a spell in Congress and then took a dislike to his party's President, Andrew Jackson. The rival, Whig party, anxious to capture the backwoods vote, seized upon Crockett, wrote his memoirs for him, and – embodying in them all kinds of existing swagger and tall tales – blew him up to monstrous proportions, as the 'half-hoss, half-alligator', that backwoodsmen had been calling themselves for a generation. Fortunately for his myth, he died at the Alamo, fighting for Texan independence, and so secured immortality.

Manufactured though his story was, it served a real need, in contriving a figure around whom legend might grow. Davy Crockett can scarcely be blamed for allowing himself to become a god: others, like Buffalo Bill and Wild Bill Hickok, did the same. The honorary title – Judge, Major, Colonel, even General – was a useful adjunct in myth-making. Sometimes the titles were genuine: true and false were intertwined, as when Kit Carson found among the wreckage of a wagon pillaged by Indians a dime novel relating the exploits of the Indian scout, Kit Carson. Print was a vital medium in defining the backwoods blend of crudeness and sophistication. Franklin and Twain are only two of a number of authors who got their start as apprentice printers. The typeset message was cheap, swift and effective. Sermons and orations were fully reported in newspapers, and reproduced copiously in pamphlet form. Paperback novels went everywhere. So, thanks to the exchange system, did unusual news items. Editors in places even smaller than Hannibal received complimentary or very cheap subscriptions to everyone else's newspapers, and were allowed to reprint any piece that took their fancy. An amusing tale could spread nationwide in a few weeks. The advent of the telegraph hastened the process. So did the railroad-building boom that began in the 1830s and lasted until the end of the century.

The element of fraud permeated American life and was a conspicuous element in American humour, from the Yankee pedlar with his wooden nutmegs to Bret Harte's poem of the Heathen Chinee who had twenty-four jacks stuffed in his sleeves. Life was competitive and offered endless opportunities for swindling. Dickens said that 'smartness' was extolled at the expense of honesty. Trollope found the same. 'You see,' he was told, 'on the frontier a man is bound to be smart. If he ain't smart he'd better go back East; – perhaps as far as Europe. He'll do there.'[1] The ugliness of fraud was made into a joke, and then even into a delight in deception. Humour softened a swindle as moonlight beautified the shapeless streets of the Western town. If everyone was something of a showman, nobody ultimately was victimized. You could not fool all of the people all of the time, because they were busy fooling one anoher. This was the theory,

1. Anthony Trollope, *North America* (London, 1862), i. 188.

and it seems to have worked. P. T. Barnum's successive hoaxes only brought him greater popularity, so long as he altered them often enough. Joaquin Miller claimed to have been wounded by an Indian arrow; if he sometimes limped with the wrong leg, as Ambrose Bierce alleged, it simply showed that his role needed more rehearsal. Miller worked hard at his part; later in life he toured a vaudeville circuit dressed in a Klondike outfit – a fur suit, with buttons made of gold nuggets. Probably none of his audience knew that he had once studied Latin and Greek. Or if they did, this was one more of the hilarious incongruities of America. Who could help but laugh at the non-existent towns, for instance, advertised with pictures that portrayed them as long-established communities? Laurence Oliphant, a British traveller, visited one in Wisconsin:

Having inspected the plan of the city in the land-office ..., we sallied forth to choose some lots ...; and having been particularly fascinated by the eligible position of some, situated within two doors of the bank, just round the corner of the grand hotel, opposite the wharf, fronting the principal square, and running back to Thompson Street – in fact, in the very thick of the business part of the town – we commenced cutting our way with billhooks through the dense forest ... called Third avenue ..., until we got to the bed of a rivulet, down which we turned through tangled underwood (by name West Street), until it lost itself in a bog, which was the principal square, upon the other side of which, covered with almost impenetrable bush, was the site of our lots.[1]

Some of this humour was surrealistic in its polysyllabic, mock-solemn, inverted logic. An example is Longstreet's 'The Debating Society'. The society was a group of young men who met to argue on some theme previously agreed upon – with the rule that every member must speak or pay a fine. A couple of the members managed to introduce the following nonsensical topic: 'WHETHER, AT PUBLIC ELECTIONS, SHOULD THE VOTES OF FACTION PREDOMINATE BY INTERNAL SUGGESTIONS OR THE BIAS OF JURISPRUDENCE?' They themselves spoke on opposite sides, with eloquence and pretended earnestness. Everyone else, struggling in vain with the 'question', was obliged to admit defeat and pay the fine. Another Longstreet tale is a hoax played on some amiable, gossipy Southern matrons by the narrator 'Baldwin' and his friend Ned Brace. Ned tells the ladies about 'two most excellent men, who became so much attached to each other that they actually got married ...; and no people could have lived happier or managed better than they did. And they raised a lovely parcel of

1. Laurence Oliphant, *Minnesota and the Far West* (Edinburgh, 1855), 159–60.

children; as fine a set as I ever saw, except their youngest son, Billy: he was a little wild, but, upon the whole, a right clever boy himself. . . .' They leave the matrons to puzzle over this information:

'We old women were talking about it last night after you went out, and none of us could make it out how they could have children; and I said . . . I would ask you how could it be? I suppose you won't mind telling an old woman how it was.'

'Certainly not, madam. They were both widowers before they fell in love with each other and got married.'

'The lackaday! I wonder none of us thought o' that. And they had children before they got married?'

'Yes, madam; they had none afterward that I heard of.'

We were here informed that our horses were in waiting, and we bade the good ladies farewell.

Apart from the sheer absurdity of the Ned Brace sketch, we can see that Western-style humour might have other uses. One was to poke fun at the otherwise sacred pieties of American life, above all the platitudes of patriotic democracy. Emily Dickinson, as a teenage student during the 'Manifest Destiny' excitements of the 1840s, composed a little spoof of a July the Fourth oratory. *The Squibob Papers* of John Phoenix contain another such, full-length oration. Longstreet's hoaxing debaters harangue their audience with tongue-in-cheek gusto:

The marble-hearted marauder might . . . hurl into thraldom the Votaries of Rational liberty . . . Crash after crash would be heard in quick succession, as the strong pillars of the republic give way, and Despotism would shout in hellish triumph amid the crumbling ruins. Anarchy would wave her bloody sceptre . . . , and the bloodhounds of civil war would lap the crimson gore of our most worthy citizens. . . .

Another use was to circumvent at least in some degree the taboos of the nation's 'Victorian' value system. Allusions to sexuality, or to most bodily functions, were excluded from respectable Anglo-American litera-ture. Masculine passions could perhaps be implicitly suggested, in veiled language. Female sexuality could not be mentioned. Nor of course could homosexuality, among males or females. The only licence allowed was in grotesquely oblique or comical formulations such as the Ned Brace sketch (in which the author himself may have been unaware of its possible meanings) – or, here and there, in the semi-disguise of dialect and cacography, as with Harris's Sut Lovingood. Sut is himself so uncouth as to be outside polite society, and therefore not to be held to its prohibitions – or perhaps, like some low-minded robot, to have broken loose from his inventor. Feeling that the Lovingood argot is practically impenetrable, Bernard DeVoto, F. O. Matthiessen and Brom Weber are among those who have produced simplified, modernized and occasionally bowdlerized versions. The results are unsatisfactory. One reason may be that Lovingood's opaque Tennessee idiom camouflaged statements that would have seemed outrageous in conventional diction. His plain English was anything but plain.

Sut is a bigot and a slob. He is cruel and utterly unromantic. But now and then he is capable of expressing sexual appeal with a power denied his refined contemporaries. In one tale Sut offends 'a right peart gal named Pop Baily' by two clumsy kisses; 'sez she, in a rale cat hiss, "If I had a blind mule that cudent fine its own stable door at two trials, I'd just cut its dad blasted throat, so I would."' A better-known sketch, 'Mrs Yardley's Quilting', offers a remarkably frank tribute to the attractive power of widows: 'They hes all been to Jamakey an' larnt how sugar's made, an' knows how to sweeten wif hit; an' by golly, they is always ready tu use hit. All yu hes tu du is tu find the spoon, an' then drink cumfort till yer blind.'

Comedy was not always simple, as we may see from the adroit recourses to it by Abraham Lincoln of the Old North-West. He effectively burlesqued military heroics, for instance, including his own brief service in the Black Hawk War. He was skilful as a lawyer and politician in citing humorous anecdotes to ridicule opponents and make his own arguments vivid. He was sensitive to the comedy of American place-names – and amused accordingly when he once paddled a canoe from Pekin to Havana without ever leaving Illinois. Matthew Arnold was repelled by the jumble of American names, especially the classical ones like Utica and Ithaca. Arnold's disapproval could be attributed to British stuffiness. But it is worth remembering that Bret Harte's first California efforts at literature sought to capitalize upon the exotic and romantic Spanish-speaking past. He thought the North American settlers greedy, murderous and uninteresting. The names of mining towns ('Dead Horse', 'Lost Mule', and the like) initially struck him as ugly and crude. It took some while for him to perceive, bolstered by praise from Eastern audiences, that he had struck a vein of literary gold in chronicling the inhabitants of Poker Flat and Roaring Camp. Picturesqueness, he discovered, was largely in the eye of the beholder; what was needed for literary fame was the right fortuitous combination of time, place and style. The West was about to consolidate and develop its previous partial annexation of older comic modes.

Among these the tall tale, which had been popular in America since Colonial days (there were twenty-four American editions of Baron Munchausen by 1835), spread West to reach inspired heights of mendacity: as in the story of the hunter who, charged by a bear and a moose at once, from opposite directions, fired at the sharp edge of a rock; the bullet split in two, killing both animals, while rock-splinters brought down a squirrel in a nearby tree. The recoil of his gun knocked the hunter into the river at whose edge he stood; climbing out of the water, he found his clothes full of fish.

The essence of the tall tale was that it was *told*. It required a narrator and an audience – fittingly, among a people who liked nothing better than to be lectured at, whether by hucksters, showmen, humorists, clergymen, Congressmen or authors. The English theatre agent Edward Hingston, to whom the subject was of obvious interest, said that

America is a lecture-hall on a very extensive scale. The rostrum extends in a straight line from Boston, through New York and Philadelphia, to Washington. There are raised seats on the first tier in the Alleghanies, and gallery accommodation on the top of the Rocky Mountains.

There may be some truth in the hyperbole of the morning drumbeat of the British army unceasingly encircling the globe; but yet more true is that the voice of the lecturer is never silent in the United States.

And Artemus Ward relates how

There was an execution in Ohio one day, and the Sheriff, before placing the rope round the murderer's neck, asked him if he had any remarks to make. 'If he hasn't,' said a well-known local orator, pushing his way rapidly through the dense crowd to the gallows – 'if our ill-starred fellow-citizen don't feel inclined to make a speech, and is in no hurry, I should like to avail myself of the present occasion to make some remarks on the necessity of a new protective tariff.'

Political oratory, especially of the spread-eagle sort with its gorgeous metaphors, became in burlesque moments, as we have seen, a variant of the tall tale. A great deal of frontier humour was professedly oral. Ward, Billings, Twain and others were successful public entertainers. Many of the comic ballads and tales of the genre purport to be monologues set down on paper.

These monologues were usually in dialect, sometimes introduced by another person who might be a neutral 'frame', or act as a foil or straight man. Or if the piece was supposedly a reminiscence or other type of essay, or set of joking aphorisms, it was often deliberately mis-spelt, as in Josh Billings's 'Out West!', which begins:

– Tha sa the praree chickens are so thik, out West, tha hav tew put up poles awl over the kuntry for them tew roost on.

[*They say the prairie chickens are so thick, out West, they have to put up poles all over the country for them to roost on.*]

– When tha bust up, out thare, tha pay their debts by jineing the church.

– It being agin the law tew carry consealed weepons, evry man carrys one in his hand.

– A man who don't kno how to play uker [*euchre*], would not be believed under oath.

Hingston was among the admirers of American humour who found such cacography tiresome. He conceded, however, that it could contribute to the humorist's pose of being a plain uneducated man, apt to mangle a Latin tag or a quotation from Shakespeare. Since the joke depended on the reader's knowledge of the correct form, the humour was less artless than it seemed. Yet with the passage of time it became increasingly free from the class-consciousness inherent in British humour of the same sort, in which the illiteracy of the speakers – servants, urchins, yokels, Irish navvies – made them figures to be laughed at rather than laughed with.

Hingston was right about the defects of the poorer sorts of Western humour. Not much has had lasting appeal. Puns exasperate after a while. (Are the Marx Brothers movies, with their S. J. Perelman scripts, really so funny at a third or fourth showing?) Tall tales have a certain sameness. Mis-spelling is a strain to read, and irritating when mechanically applied. The novelist George Meredith (*Essay on Comedy*, 1877) complained that the British public suffered from 'too many jesters kicking the dictionary around'. The sense of the comic was, he said, 'much blunted by . . . punning and using . . . Johnsonian polysyllables to treat of the infinitely little'. John Nichol laid the blame on *American* comic writers. He believed that in the United States, 'the anxiety to be national has led many . . . minor authors to make themselves ridiculous. To avoid walking like Englishmen they have gone on all fours: . . . tabooing the speech of Addison and Steele, they have delighted themselves with a jargon of strange tongues.' The 'Phunny Phellows' tended to harp on a repertoire of topics guaranteed to trigger an easy response: drunks, cowards, boasters, mothers-in-law, Mormon polygamy ('The girls in Salt Lake City marry [Brigham] Young, and often').

Such humour was not appreciated by everyone, even in the United States. Meredith distinguished between *agelasts* (non-laughers) and *hyper-*

gelasts ('the excessive laughers, who are as clappers on a bell, that may be rung by a breeze'). Hypergelasts not only joked excessively: their jokes were apt to deride poor, marginal or disadvantaged people – Indians, Jews, Negroes (slave or free), and women who showed any disposition to be militant. Feminists were portrayed as sex-starved spinsters; strong frontier females were commonly referred to as 'heifers'.

Nevertheless the best of Western humour resorted inventively to Nichol's 'strange tongues', in a jabberwocky akin to that of Edward Lear, Lewis Carroll and James Joyce. They broke through into an Anglo-American nonsense world, as in these reflections by B. P. Shillaber's Mrs Partington ('the American Mrs Malaprop'):

When I was young, if a girl only understood the rules of distraction, provision, multiplying, replenishing, and the common denunciator, and knew all about rivers and obituaries, the convents and dormitories, the provinces and the umpires, they had eddication enough. But now they have to study bottomy, algebery, and have to demonstrate supposition about the sycophants of circuses, tangents, and Diogenese of parallelogromy, to say nothing about the oxhides, corostics, and the abstruse triangles.

English humour had itself inherited standard themes stretching back to ancient Greece, where Aristotle analysed them and Menander exemplified them on the stage. Theorists of humour noted, for instance, the persistence of certain basic character-types, such as the *alazon* and the *eiron*, that stood respectively for overstatement (boasting, exaggeration) and for understatement (laconic and deflating rejoinders). Menander's Roman disciples, Plautus and Terence, turned his amusing situations into Latin. (From Plautus, Shakespeare borrowed the plot for his *Comedy of Errors* with its double set of identical twins.)

In the wake of this heritage came transatlantic humour. Jacksonian America sought to emulate, for instance, Europe's new humorous week-lies – *Charivari* (1832) in Paris, *Punch* (1841) in London, the *Fliegende Blätter* (1844) in Munich, *Kladderadatsch* (1848) in Berlin – though for some years the United States lagged behind in visual caricature. The first wave of American funny men to please both New York and London, Liverpool and Boston, adopted absurd pen-names. In England William Makepeace Thackeray once wrote as 'Michaelangelo Titmarsh'; Charles Dickens began as 'Boz', while his illustrator Hablot K. Browne was 'Phiz'. In America, David Ross Locke masqueraded as 'Petroleum V. Nasby', Robert Henry Newell turned into 'Orpheus C. Kerr' (an atrocious pun on the 'office-seeker' or job-hunter who pestered American presidents). Each sought his own particular patter, his 'fort' as Artemus Ward called it. Thus Ward, the creation of Charles F. Browne, spoke as a travelling showman with a battered display of waxwork effigies. The creator was sometimes taken over by his creation; Browne felt himself disappearing into Ward. Popular comic techniques were rapidly copied. Seba Smith, inventor of the homespun Yankee philosopher 'Major Jack Downing', soon faced dozens of imitations. Smith made Downing remark that he could only tell the real Major Jack by a scar on his left arm. Material by Billings and Ward was pirated by unscrupulous English publishers.

'Mark Twain' (Samuel L. Clemens) came up through these ranks. The elements of his early humour were all in being before he began to write. But for the spelling, these observations by Artemus Ward on the imminent Civil War might pass as Twain's:

I said the crisis had not only cum itself, but it had brought all its relations. It has cum ... with a evident intention of makin us a good visit. It's goin to take off its things and stop with us.

It was Twain who said:

Let us be thankful for the fools. But for them the rest of us could not succeed.

But Josh Billings had already had the same thought:

God save the phools! and dont let them run out, for if it want for them wise men couldn't get a livin.

A good deal of Clemens's humour, indeed, differs from that of Ward and the rest only in being funnier and more variegated. As a newspaperman out of Nevada and California, where he had recently adopted his pen-name (from the Mississippi leadman's cry for *two fathoms'* draught), he assiduously followed the techniques of the others. Twain's first resounding success was the tall tale of the 'celebrated jumping frog of Calaveras County', which he published in a New York paper in 1865 and which formed the nucleus of his first book, *The Celebrated Jumping Frog* (1867). The basic story had already been current in California for over a decade. What Twain did was to embellish and sharpen the anecdote. Clemens appears as the new persona 'Mark Twain', someone who is well educated yet rather naïve. The main narrator is someone else, who speaks with a Western drawl. There are deceptions within deceptions. Twain is in a way duped. So is the sturdy miner Jim Smiley, owner of the celebrated frog

'Daniel Webster' (a leading Whig politician) and of a bulldog named 'Andrew Jackson'; Smiley is bested by a laconic stranger who provokes a jumping contest by saying of 'Dan'l Webster', 'I don't see no p'ints about that frog that's any better'n any other frog.'[1]

Again, as Twain relates in *Roughing It*, he tried his hand at lecturing in San Francisco, in the Artemus Ward style of zany inconsequence. Ward's lecture posters had once read:

> Artemus Ward delivered lectures before
> ## ALL THE CROWNED HEADS OF
> ## EUROPE
> ever thought of delivering lectures

Twain's declared:

> Doors open at $7\frac{1}{2}$. The trouble will begin at 8.

To his relief and pleasure the lectures went down equally well with New York audiences. For the rest of his life, though with diminishing zest, Twain was almost always able to win applause as a platform orator or after-dinner speaker. A favourite device was deliberate repetition. In *Roughing It* Twain pretends to be exasperated at hearing four different people recount the same story about Horace Greeley (celebrated editor of the New York *Tribune*), each time in exactly the same words – and about an incident which, Twain asserts, never took place. In his posthumously published *Autobiography* Twain describes a comic lecture in which, accidentally-on-purpose, as if too nervous to know what he was doing, he repeated a story twice, then three times. The audience seemed unamused. At the fourth telling, however, there came a crash of laughter and applause. Twain recollects being congratulated on his audacious courage by no less a figure than the Boston Brahmin James Russell Lowell.

Twain's memory was not infallible. In old age he related what he claimed was an incident of his boyhood, but which had actually come from the 'autobiography' of Davy Crockett. In all likelihood it had been borrowed there from somewhere else, just as Twain's fascination with

---

1. The line is quoted by Penelope, the witty heroine of W. D. Howells's *The Rise of Silas Lapham* (1885), ch. 7.

twins and mistaken identities (in *The Prince and the Pauper*, 1881; and *Pudd'nhead Wilson*, 1894)[1] derives ultimately from the wellsprings of ancient Greek comedy. The point is that he Americanized and polished with unequalled verve.

We can follow Twain's evolution through his early work. In 1867 he secured a free trip as correspondent on an extensive chartered tour of Southern Europe and the Holy Land, aboard the *Quaker City*. The letters he contributed to New York and San Francisco newspapers were worked up into a book, *The Innocents Abroad, or the New Pilgrim's Progress* (1869). This book was an immediate hit, even if Bret Harte was a little condescending in the *Overland Monthly*, or if the anonymous *Atlantic Monthly* reviewer (W. D. Howells, who had not yet met Twain) referred to the author as 'Mr Clements'.

Twain was not the first person, American or otherwise, to draw attention to the grime and greed and superstition of parts of the Old World. The English philosopher Herbert Spencer had in his autobiography (1863) grumbled at the over-ratedness of Italian old masters. 'Were each of them', said Spencer, 'more or less approved as being good relatively to the mental culture of its age, which was characterized by crude ideas and sentiments..., I should agree that many ... deserve praise. But the applause given is *absolute* instead of *relative*; and the grossest absurdities ... are habitually passed over without remark.' So, to Spencer, the Sistine Chapel was too cluttered and the *Last Judgement* too 'busy'.

Twain made some similar remarks. He and his companions, he declared, became sick of hearing the name of Michelangelo, throughout Italy. As for Leonardo's *Last Supper*, in Milan, Twain considered it a 'mournful wreck'. New copies of old-master paintings were invariably 'superior ... to the original.... Maybe the originals were handsome when they were new, but they are not now.' Lake Tahoe far surpassed Como, or the Sea of Galilee. Florence's Arno might suffice as a river if it had some water. The old artists' 'nauseous adulation of princely patrons' was undemocratic. Abelard, the lover of Héloïse, was a dastardly seducer.

On the other hand, Twain paid tribute to a number of features, natural and man-made. Europeans knew how to relax without getting drunk. Paris was magnificent; so were French trains. As for the American tourists,

1. Also manifest in a famous 'interview' skit, admiringly discussed by the philosopher Henri Bergson in his essay *Laughter* (1900). Twain 'explains' to the interviewer: 'You see, we were twins ... and we got mixed in the bath-tub when we were only two weeks old, and one of us was drowned. But we didn't know which. Some think it was Bill. Some think it was me.'

they were capable of crass complacence. The elder members of the group were sanctimoniously Protestant. One harmless butt, a writer of bad verse whose real name was Bloodgood H. Cutter, was teasingly dubbed the 'poet lariat'. Americans as well as Europeans (and Arabs), then, came in for a share of derision together with a meed of praise. *Innocents Abroad* voiced the thoughts of the thousands of Americans who with glazed eye and aching feet followed the rule of their guide-book around Europe. Acknowledging that they were no connoisseurs, as the Twain persona was usually also willing to do, they appreciated a narrative which suggested that the compatriots of Uncle Sam had something better than refinement, and were not impressed – or at least were not bowled over. *A Tramp Abroad* (1880) was to be less proudly philistine, but made similar pleasantries about Americans in Europe.

Some of this humour has gone flat or sour. In *Innocents* and in *Roughing It* (1872), an account of adventure in the Far West and the Sandwich Islands – as subsequently in *Tom Sawyer* (1876) – the 'Noble Red Man' remained what he had been for Clemens/Twain in a facetious article of 1870: 'a good, fair, desirable subject for extermination if there ever was one'; a treacherous, bedraggled, subhuman creature wholly lacking in the qualities ascribed to him by Cooper or Longfellow, or in Helen Hunt Jackson's tragic romance *Ramona* (1884).

There is even a puzzle as to how Twain built so considerable a reputation upon early writings of comparatively limited scope and originality. His own promotional efforts must be taken into account. Even when he was an established author, he badgered people to review him favourably and to plug his books. Nor was he always prompt to admit what he had picked up from other humorists. Bret Harte began to win celebrity a little in advance of Twain, though a year younger. Twain made only one ambiguous allusion to Harte, in *Roughing It* (ch. 59): the other man, he remarked, was appointed editor of the *Californian* at $20 a week, while he was paid $12 by the same magazine. Some intense spirit of rivalry seems necessary to explain Twain's subsequent hatred of his one-time friend and colleague – an animus out of all proportion to Harte's actual defects.

More important is the place of comedy in the Anglo-American literary world of the nineteenth century. The first hugely successful humorous authors were Thackeray and Dickens. Both, as we have noted, started out with comic pseudonyms. Thackeray wrote for *Punch* and other magazines; Dickens was closely involved with papers and periodicals. Both were accomplished lecturers. In the same year, 1846, both happened to bring out travel books (Thackeray's *Journey from Cornhill to Grand Cairo*, Dickens's *Pictures from Italy*) which alternated between sober commentary and jaunty insouciance. Both of them loathed and satirized pomposity. Both men made lecture tours in the United States, and exploited their experience of America in various pieces – though neither greatly liked what he saw of the Great Republic. Both authors were prolific and versatile, experimenting with fact and fiction, with the historical and the contemporary. Both evolved from foolery to profounder studies of human nature. And each died in his prime, Thackeray in 1863 and Dickens in 1870.

There is no evidence that Mark Twain at once saw himself as the person to fill the vacuum left by their departure. At the beginning of the 1870s he was still in comparison a tiro. Perhaps, however, there is significance in a comment from *Roughing It* (ch. 55):

The matter that each editor of a daily paper in America writes in the course of a year would fill from four to eight bulky volumes like this book! Fancy what a library an editor's work would make, after twenty or thirty years . . . Yet people often marvel that Dickens, Scott, Bulwer, Dumas, etc., have been able to produce so many books. If these authors had wrought as voluminously as newspaper editors do, the result would be something to marvel at, indeed.

Twain himself, newly married, and embroiled in editorship to help support his new estate, may have felt a long way short of the lofty ease of recognized literati such as Oliver Wendell Holmes, about whom he was at that stage extravagantly complimentary.[1]

Yet there *was* a vacuum. Bret Harte, chronically hard up, waned in reputation as he wrote and lectured in haste for hard cash. The promising career of Artemus Ward was snuffed out in 1872, when Ward was in his mid-thirties. Chance favoured Samuel Langhorne Clemens. There was a continuing demand for humour, and a great increase in the market for American Western humour. Beyond and above that was a vast, widening international audience that wanted amusement, distraction and occasional flattery or reproof or uplift. This public craved novelty, yet liked

1. Ambrose Bierce, a fellow-member with Twain and Harte of San Francisco's rather flimsy literary bohemia, provided a humorous insult in an 1870 gossip item: 'Mark Twain . . . has got married. It was not the act of a desperate man . . . laboring under temporary insanity . . . , it was the cool methodical, culmination of human nature working in the heart of an orphan hankering for some one with a bank account to caress. . . . Well, that . . . long, bright smile will no more greet the early bar-keeper. . . . Poor Mark! he was a good scheme, but he couldn't be made to work.' Paul Fatout, *Ambrose Bierce: The Devil's Lexicographer* (Norman, U of Oklahoma P, 1951), 87–8.

to be able to associate some familiar 'name' with the literary product. It looked for such brand-recognition in a host of new monthly magazines. Among those merely on the American side of the ocean were *Harper's* (1850), the *Atlantic* (1857), *Galaxy* (1866), *Lippincott's* (1868), *Appleton's* (1869), *Scribner's* (1870), and *Century* (1881) – and there was to be a second wave of new periodicals in the 1890s.

The burgeoning middle-class audience liked to be offered fresh literary titbits each Christmas – an appetite busily catered to by Thackeray and Dickens, as in the latter's *Christmas Carol*. It sought diversion and enlightenment in the theatre and also in church, where a popular preacher like Henry Ward Beecher could draw a congregation (or 'house') of thousands. Beecher's Plymouth Church in Brooklyn had sponsored the *Quaker City* tour, and the prospect that he might himself join the trip had been used to stimulate bookings. An enterprising publisher commissioned the Rev. Beecher to produce a homiletic yet breezy novel, *Norwood, or, Village Life in New England* (1867), which netted handsome profits for the two of them. The general public continued to relish travelogues, historical novels, and love stories. In addition it began to appreciate tales of crime and detection. Charles Dickens, for example, was at work when he died on a murder story, *The Mystery of Edwin Drood*. One of the first of many authors to attempt to complete *Edwin Drood* was the American humorist Orpheus C. Kerr, although his version (*The Cloven Foot*, 1870) was peculiarly out of register.

Kerr's failure brings us back to Twain. A great opportunity lay open: to make an initial impact by way of humour. He was a quick learner. He had, moreover, served a quite lengthy apprenticeship. Twain is the probable author of a little comic sketch, signed 'S.L.C.', that got into print as early as 1852. The jumping frog tale brought him some attention in 1865. Even so, he was nearing thirty-five when *Innocents Abroad* came out in 1869. Dickens had reached celebrity with the *Pickwick Papers* at the age of twenty-four. It has been noticed that the early Mark Twain persona stresses youthful inexperience, not always in accordance with Clemens's own autobiography. The narrator of *Roughing It* claims to have been an untravelled youth when he set out by stagecoach for Nevada. The real Clemens had in fact already moved about a good deal, with a sojourn in New York. Again, in 'The Private History of a Campaign That Failed' (1887), Clemens/Twain presented a reminiscence of a short interlude with a Confederate volunteer unit in 1861 as a juvenile prank, though Clemens had actually been a man of twenty-five at the time.

There are probably several explanations for Twain's tendency to exaggerate his boyishness, and to use youthful males as the central figures in some of his finest work. One possible part-explanation is the desire of Clemens/Twain to assert a Dickens-like precocity: to appear before the public as Youth incarnate ('Youth' being a pet-name for him invented by his wife Livy).

The essential key to Twain's success, however, was sheer talent. Others might deem themselves rightful heirs to Charles Dickens. Only Twain had the requisite combination of inquisitiveness, sensibility, exuberance, ambition and verbal brilliance. In common with Dickens and Thackeray (and Melville) he was not a college graduate. Instead, he was miscellaneously but valuably engaged in occupations relating to the printed word, and also in jobs or pastimes that added to his hoard of information, his glossary of ordinary speech and gesture. Twain has been described as an uneven writer, rarely sure of where his books were taking him. It is true that even his best work reveals serious flaws. He often ran off the track. But that is also true of Dickens. Each suffered as well as benefited from an extravagantly rich imagination. Nevertheless, Twain was in some respects a highly professional author. Natural talent vouchsafed phrases of wonderfully easy wit, as when he said (in *Roughing It*) that a coconut palm resembled 'a feather duster struck by lightning'. Professional skill prompted him to revise his first drafts, working with a sure instinct to substitute the *mot juste* for the approximately suitable epithet.

Felicity in detail did not always sufficiently offset structural deficiencies. *The Gilded Age* was a novel satirizing the get-rich-quick years after the Civil War. The central character, 'Colonel' Beriah Sellers, is a visionary Micawber, forever dreaming up infallible projects to make himself and his friends millionaires. Twain is fierce enough with crooked Congressmen, but Sellers is too much a projection of the author (and perhaps the author's feckless father) to engage his wrath, although the 'Colonel' is basically no more honest than the Senators and lobbyists in Washington. There is a certain insane charm about Sellers. The very vastness of his schemes redeems them: they are on the Western scale (and Dickens, it may be said in passing, was right to ship Micawber off to Australia: his optimism needed the room of a frontier in which to spread itself). But apart from giving us Sellers, *The Gilded Age* is a confused book: its villains and its heroes are too easily interchangeable.

A Connecticut Yankee is similarly uneven, though for farcical invention it would be hard to beat the episodes in which the young man from contemporary Connecticut, equipped with such modern appliances as the bicycle, the telegraph, and the Colt revolver, comes to grips with a feudal never-never land. Twain intended to draw a contrast between Americanism (democracy, open-mindedness, energy) and the cruelty, stupidity, and superstition of the Old World. He meant to ridicule the England of his own day, and in particular a superciliousness he associated with Matthew Arnold. He meant to show the liberating magic of industrial technology. And of course he meant to be funny. Twain's countrymen thought he had succeeded in each of these aims. Some, including his illustrator Dan Beard, in addition regarded *A Connecticut Yankee* as an indirect attack upon such latter-day robber barons as the rascally Jay Gould. British critics were less enthusiastic; their national pride was hurt, but they could perhaps more easily discern inconsistencies. The burlesque element weakens the serious portions of the book. Like many of his contemporaries, Twain was not wholehearted in his praise of industrialism. At moments, instead of indicting King Arthur's England, he speaks of it with nostalgic affection, as when he recalls the Missouri of his boyhood. They are simple and fragrant, green vivid worlds, lost paradises. Twain's hero Hank Morgan is heartbroken at the end because he cannot get back to his Arthurian sweetheart. At other times, perhaps unwittingly, Twain implies that the industrial order is crude, greedy and destructive. Moreover, Morgan's growing contempt for mankind in the mass undermines the notion that there is any such thing as progress in world history.

If we are to deal purely with Twain the humorist, we have to fall back upon the details of his art. There are puns and word-plays: he knows the newspaper business 'from Alpha to Omaha'. There are all kinds of straight-faced exaggeration, of repetition, of anti-climax: as, of the man who 'had a wart on his nose and died in the hope of a glorious resurrection'. He is a master of travesty and invective.

Having said this, we have said very little about Twain's inner complexity. One facet is his enormous pessimism. Humour is, of course, perfectly compatible with sadness – as with the Negro songs which Twain loved – or with anger and disgust, as in the satire of Swift. The funny men were not all mere *farceurs*. American newspapermen have long been a special group, the licensed jesters and cynics at the court of public opinion; budding authors, budded authors, blown authors; consumers of late-night coffee, smokers of cigars, singers of ribald songs; lie- and cliché-detectors, disenchanted men; men somewhat detached from the world they watch.

As writers, they cherish economy, and witty phrases; they are often bitter, like Ambrose Bierce and Ring Lardner, but their rage at human folly has to be disguised and made entertaining.

Though he spent only part of his life as a newspaper humorist, Mark Twain had the newspaperman's outlook, coupled with immensely more talent than most. Gregarious, impatient of humbug and pomposity, adoring gadgets and technological improvements, absorbedly interested in the writer's craft, he loved the *people* and hated the *public*. An author, but not an intellectual, he was irritated by writing which he thought too cerebral. Henry James bored him; George Eliot and Hawthorne likewise, with their 'niggling analysis'. Jane Austen he would not read: he would read Poe only if somebody paid him.

Mark Twain and Poe: there is no need to enlarge on the gulf between them. There are, however, peculiar similarities that help to clarify the nature of Twain's pessimism. As a 'magazinist', Poe lived in a neighbouring world to that of the newspaper. Much of his work was done in a hurry; and his humorous sketches in particular were calculated to catch the public fancy. In general, they are bad: it is the quality of their badness that is interesting. They are shrill, strained, grotesque, even macabre; they are facetious in a knowing way; and they reveal a special fondness for cryptograms and hoaxes (as in 'The Balloon Hoax', or in 'Diddling Considered as One of the Exact Sciences'). Underlying them is a contempt of the author for his audience. He is cleverer than they; he knows exactly what their response will be to any given stimulus; they are vicious and gullible. For Poe people are not only unlovely: they are helpless. The universe, he maintains in *Eureka*, exhibits a perfect harmony; but, like that of his own story-plots, it is a hideous harmony. 'Cause and effect', says Emerson, '. . . seed and fruit, cannot be severed; for the effect already blooms in the cause, the end pre-exists in the means, the fruit in the seed.' Poe says: 'In the original unity of the first thing lies the secondary cause of all things, with the germ of their inevitable annihilation.' Here are completely different conclusions reached from similar premises. Men, says Poe, are the victims of a trap sprung long ago.

Twain comes far closer to Poe than to the equable Emerson. He, too, is often violent in his humour; he writes of bloodshed with an almost unholy glee, he makes ghastly fun out of the odour of corpses. There is, at times, an exaggeration in his work beyond what is called for in the scene in question: an exasperated rubbing of the reader's nose into unpleasantness. This cannot be explained away as a coarse Western deficiency; though his taste swung from joyous profanity to extremes of prudishness (as when he exclaims in horror at one of Titian's nudes, or at the misconduct of the poet Petrarch with his mistress Laura), Twain was a highly sensitive man, who, like Poe, had a quite unusual responsiveness to sounds and colours. Again like Poe, he was given to hoaxes. He has a similar histrionic sense of manipulating situations. He admires the resourceful person who diddles others (often, as with Huckleberry Finn, by ingenious lying), or the strong man who stands off a mob ('no mob', he writes in 'The United States of Lyncherdom', 'has any sand in the presence of a man known to be splendidly brave'). In either case, there is a latent scorn for mankind – 'this sackfull of small reptiles', as he describes humanity, as early in his career as 1871. And beneath this scorn there is a gloom which Twain cannot exorcize. It is a 'damned human race' in a not merely expletive sense. His short story, 'The Man that Corrupted Hadleyburg' (1900), tells of a practical joke of the grimmest kind, which proves the leading men of a whole town to be dishonest, and without defence except that 'it was ordered. All things are.' And in The Mysterious Stranger (1916, posthumous), Twain develops still further his long-held belief that free will is an illusion. His last message is not simply that the world has no virtue, but that it has no reality. Humanity is left 'wandering forlorn among the empty eternities'. The tall tale has here, as with the nuclear bomb explosions set off in the desert West, reached its ultimate.

Mark Twain was a determinist even before he wrote Huckleberry Finn. Yet he never ceased to scold the human race. Poe likewise, in his criticism, is forever nagging at other authors – a schoolmaster, who is aware that his class are dolts, and worse, who nevertheless strives to beat some sense into them. Twain, too, is something of the cynical pedagogue: though one of his San Francisco nicknames was 'the Wild Humorist of the Plains', he was also known as 'the Moral Phenomenon', and he insists over and over that his task is not buffoonery, but teaching (or even preaching). The difference between the two creative methods is enormous, though both stress with professional pride the deliberation with which they arrive at their effects. Poe eschews didacticism, and seeks an unreal beauty. Twain chooses burlesque: the public is to be coaxed and tickled into understanding.

No wonder his work is uneven. Part of him is coltish, part saturnine. Part of him revels in the chaos of Western life; for, as Howells wrote,

He had the Southwestern, the Lincolnian, the Elizabethan breadth of parlance, and

I was often hiding away . . . the letters in which he had loosed his bold fancy to stoop on rank suggestion; I could not bear to burn them, and I could not, after the first reading, quite bear to look at them.

This is the free-thinking, free-spoken, democratic Twain who girds at slavery, aristocracy and intolerance. But he has to come East to escape the last-named. Discussing Southern politics, he writes from Connecticut to a Missouri friend in 1876:

I think I comprehend their position there – perfect freedom to vote just as you choose, provided you choose to vote as *other people* think, social ostracism otherwise. . . . Fortunately a good deal of experience of men enabled me to choose my residence wisely. I live in the freest corner of the country.

– in other words, in the New England of Longfellow and Lowell. But the 'Eastern' Twain can be delicate to the point of prudery. And why campaign to overthrow aristocracy, if it is only to be replaced by mob-rule? What is the use of campaigning, if we are all the victims of circumstance? It seems appropriate that his pen-name, *Twain*, should suggest dualism; and that he should claim descent on his father's side from a regicide judge, and on his mother's from the earls of Durham.

There is fairly wide agreement that the classic Twain resides in the books in which neither farce nor bleakness has the upper hand, but which unite affection with intimate, remembered knowledge. Recent scholarship has also paid respectful attention to what Twain wrote in the last fifteen years of his life. The texts include various versions of *The Mysterious Stranger*; 'Three Thousand Years Among the Microbes', about a person (bizarrely nicknamed 'Huck') who has accidentally been transformed into an articulate cholera germ, living in a human bloodstream; and visions of the impending downfall of the Great Republic, from 'Glances at History'. Admirers of these late imaginings concede that the tone is pessimistic and the fantasy often wild. But – they inquire – do not humorists frequently appear misanthropic in their far-sightedness? It was jolly old Plautus who said that man is the wolf of man (*lupus est homo homini*), at least in reacting to strangers. And could not pessimistic wildness be attributed, if fatuously, to the great absurdists (Kafka, Beckett) of modern literature?

Less radically, a reasoned plea has been made to allot a high place in the Twain canon to the novel *Pudd'nhead Wilson*. Scholars praise it for the harsh aphorisms of the iconoclastic lawyer hero, David Wilson of Dawson's Landing, Missouri, in antebellum days; for the ironic plot, in which a nearly white 'black' baby is switched with a wholly white infant, the master becoming the slave and vice versa; and for Roxy, who may be the only three-dimensional female figure in Twain's fiction, and is one of the very few believable black women in mainstream nineteenth-century literature.

We may accept some of these contentions and still believe that Twain's comic mastery, unmistakably apparent in *Tom Sawyer*, reached a summit with *Life on the Mississippi* and *The Adventures of Huckleberry Finn*. In these books he wrote with warmth and accuracy of the life which was most vivid to him, the life of his boyhood river town and of the river. To Dickens, the Mississippi was a foul ditch 'running liquid mud', with 'nothing pleasant in its aspect, but the harmless lightning which flickers every night upon the dark horizon'. To Mark Twain, as a youngster and through the eye of reminiscence, it was all existence. Treacherous to the unaware, yet a haven to those (like Huck Finn) who know it, the Mississippi becomes in Twain's pages the symbol of the human journey. *Tom Sawyer* was a little too much the 'story of a bad boy' (equipped with an adult's dexterity) to be entirely satisfying, and *Life on the Mississippi* falls away in its final chapters, though the opening ones are magnificent. But *Huckleberry Finn*, apart from the Tom Sawyerish rescue of Jim, is perfect, the unforgettable portrait of a frontier boy.

Whether or not determinism is sound philosophy, it is a bad doctrine for a realistic novelist. He deals with ordinary people, and ordinary people do not *feel* their lives are predetermined, whatever the novelist may have decided on their behalf. If he imposes his view too firmly, his characters become listless puppets. In *Huckleberry Finn*, the characters are (in Whitman's words) 'refreshing, wicked, real'. Some of them, it is true, are caught, in apathetic squalor, in small-town brutality, in meaningless blood-feuds, or (like Jim) in Negro slavery. But Huck himself is still free, the natural being not yet ruined by an environment that seeks to mould him. He is able to free Jim from the immediate evil of slavery, though not from the disability of being black. But at the end, Huck, like Natty Bumppo, follows his instinct to stay loose from social conformity – though not to deny allegiance to a moral code he has pieced together for himself, in defiance of the laws and customs of church-going, slave-holding Missouri.

It is the American renunciation once more, in Huck's case unaccompanied by the asceticism of – say – Thoreau's choice. The New World is still new so long as it is possible to slip away into the wilderness, to live by the senses as wild animals do. Otherwise, there is nothing but the irrevocable movement known as progress – or sometimes in America as Manifest

Destiny. Commerce comes; churches and moralities; the falsehoods of the printed word and of the platform; humanity in herds, mobs, armies ('a company of soldiers is an offensive spectacle', said Emerson). Twain avoided some of these things: after a few weeks' soldiering in the Civil War, he lit out west for the Nevada Territory – but to join others in taming a wilderness, only to regret what he had done, in somehow despoiling the transcendental innocence, as pioneers must.

Everyone has heard the statement by Ernest Hemingway, that all of American literature comes from one great book, *Huckleberry Finn*. It is, no doubt correctly, taken as an acknowledgement of Hemingway's own debt to Twain; and more broadly as the opinion of an expert witness that Twain perfected for the writers of his nation a style (based on a concern for the truth of direct experience) exactly suited to the American ethos. According to this argument Twain's predecessors – Irving, Lowell, the Phunny Phellows – had moved somewhat tentatively towards the same goal. Their common approach had been through humour. Only in light, unaffected pieces, apparently, could Americans convey the informality of their national idiom, avoiding the ponderous Latinism of conventional utterance. Not until Twain, it seemed, was there much truth in the contention, as he expressed it, that

There is no such thing as 'the Queen's English'. The property has gone into the hands of a joint stock company and we own the bulk of the shares.

In his hands, comic jargon and dialect did become a fresh medium, visual, supple, deceptively simple, sounding like speech yet not quite spoken. His narrative persona – that of a sharp yet kindly onlooker, a spinner of yarns but fundamentally truthful – helped define a distinctive American confessional mode, embracing candour, irreverence, puzzlement, hurt, wise innocence. The novelist–critic Howells, who became Twain's dedicated friend, remarked that orthodox English, as written by the accepted masters, 'is scholarly and conscious; it knows who its grandfather was'. With Twain, *content*, like Western life, had a mongrel incongruity; but *form* began the lineage that led on to Hemingway and beyond.

However, something else needs to be said about style in Twain. At a surprisingly early stage in his career he expressed an uneasiness at being perceived as a mere clown or gag-man. Explanations for this worry have been proposed by Van Wyck Brooks and a string of later critics. Their theories include Twain's need and desire to please a mainly genteel public;

the self-censoring impulse within his dual personality; the subtle pressures exerted by Howells, by Twain's wife, and by their middlebrow Hartford neighbours, all encouraging him to purge himself of frontier coarseness (the same taint that many people detected in Abe Lincoln – so addicted to his 'little jokes'). To these may be added an innate sadness (also an aspect of Lincoln's temperament), intensified by personal disasters such as the death of an infant son, of two daughters, and of Livy.

All of these factors may be allowed some weight. But they should be qualified. Twain was an ambitious author. Great fame came to him. The charming old gentleman, white-haired and white-suited, was an international celebrity, who had travelled round the world and made many visits to Europe. Yale and Oxford gave him honorary degrees. At a sumptuous dinner in New York in 1905, to celebrate Twain's seventieth birthday, other celebrities vied with each other to pay tribute. Among them was the multi-millionaire Andrew Carnegie, who declared that Twain stood on a par with Sir Walter Scott (the supreme genius of Carnegie's native land): 'he has done everything that Scott did.' In the estimation of admirers, Twain stood also with Thackeray, Dickens, Dumas and Victor Hugo.

Such recognition was sublimely gratifying. Among other things, however, it was a vindication of Twain's wish to transcend and even to abandon the role of humorist – as Dickens had done. True, Twain never did entirely eradicate his jokester instincts: and this to the delight of his latter-day audiences, for whom he provided some brilliant speeches. Nevertheless, his emulatory spirit impelled him to vary his writing, in theme and in style. The modern classic authors had, for example, experimented with historical fiction. So did Twain, in *The Prince and the Pauper* and other books. He took the challenge seriously: the challenge, that is, of devising narrative and dialogue forms that were not in the dialect of his own time and place, and not burlesques. The result, in the view of Twain's best modern biographer, is a 'nerveless, bookish, conventional, totally denatured' language.[1]

The verdict may be just. But it does not do full justice to Twain's intention. It does not sufficiently recognize how comprehensive was Twain's sense of language, or his conception of the American share in the Anglo-American enterprise. Whatever his other uncertainties, Twain was

1. Justin Kaplan, *Mr Clemens and Mark Twain* (New York, Simon and Schuster, 1966; London, Cape, 1967), 239.

magisterially confident of his own grasp of good English. When he condemned pieces of writing (by Fenimore Cooper, or Matthew Arnold, or for that matter the sacred texts of Mormonism and Christian Science), he showed himself to be more provoked by bad English than by other faults. His analysis could be very funny; so could his comments on French and German material. The comic frame, however, should not conceal from us his linguistic astuteness. Twain was a fastidious stylist, and a grammarian. He faulted Cooper for grandiose imprecision, and Arnold among other British authors for supercilious sloppiness: and his case was unanswerable. He did not insist that they should write in dialect or in words of one syllable. His passion was for clarity, grace, professionalism.

To create such a style was perhaps Twain's ultimate aim. It could make people laugh, which was how he started out. It could make them weep, though with the danger of mawkishness as in the death-bed scenes of Dickens. It could, ideally, reach further than laughter or tears. Some part of Twain's fidgety malaise, especially after about 1890, can be attributed to the increasingly obsessive search for a flawless language. What it should then be used to express was a different problem. To the end Twain, having discarded many convictions, clung to this faith: beautiful literature could be created, and the creator would be an American – possibly a sort of Western Connecticut Yankee, a Hank Morgan blessed with leisure and equipped with a typewriter.

IX

REALISM IN PROSE
Howells to Dreiser

WILLIAM DEAN HOWELLS (1837–1920)

Born in Ohio, the son of a poor but well-educated printer. After several moves – one interlude of which is described in *A Boy's Town* (1890) – the family settled in Columbus. Here young Howells continued to educate himself, while writing for a newspaper. Appointed for services to the Republican party as consul to Venice (1861–5), he made the most of his opportunity to study Europe and its literature at first hand. Returning to America, he rapidly became one of its foremost novelists, essayists, and editors, working in Boston and later in New York.

HAMLIN GARLAND (1860–1940)

Born in Wisconsin, and spent some of his early years also in Iowa and South Dakota. After a high-school education, he made his way to Boston, where he decided to write of the region he knew, according to the 'veritist' technique described in his *Crumbling Idols* (1894). Perhaps never entirely wholehearted in his realism, he abandoned it by stages, and his last books dealt with spiritualism.

STEPHEN CRANE (1871–1900)

Born in New Jersey, and lived there and in New York State, achieving an erratic education combined with casual journalism. His first book, *Maggie* (1893), was published at his own expense, and largely ignored until the success of *The Red Badge of Courage* (1895). The last years of his brief life were restless; his experiences included newspaper work in Mexico, a filibustering expedition to Cuba (1896), war-reporting in Greece and Cuba, a spell of hectic country life in England, and eventual death of tuberculosis in Germany.

FRANK NORRIS (1870–1902)

Born in Chicago, Norris moved to San Francisco (1884) with his parents, who allowed him to study medieval art in Paris before he returned to attend the University of California. There he gradually forsook his early taste for romantic subjects and began to write realist fiction. In 1895–6 he acted as travel correspondent in South Africa; he reported the Spanish-American fighting in Cuba (1898); and became a publisher's reader in New York, producing a great deal of fiction before his sudden death.

JACK LONDON (1876–1916)

Born in San Francisco, of uncertain parentage, and raised along the waterfront, where he began at an early age to indulge his boundless appetite for adventure. Education was sandwiched in between journeys as a tramp and participation (1897) in the Klondike gold rush. His stories first appeared in book form with *The Son of the Wolf* (1900); thereafter, his many books reached an enormous public, whether his subject was socialism or the great outdoors, or both.

THEODORE DREISER (1871–1945)

Born in Indiana, the son of an impoverished German immigrant whose strong religious faith soon became repugnant to his son, and whose lack of financial acumen inspired in Dreiser an intense respect for wealth on the grand scale. Until middle age he worked for newspapers and periodicals, in several large cities of the U.S. He was a successful and well-paid editor, but only gradually did his novels achieve critical or popular favour. Widespread fame reached him with the publication of *An American Tragedy* (1925), a novel based upon an actual Adirondacks murder case of 1906.

IX

REALISM IN PROSE

In his *Devil's Dictionary*, Ambrose Bierce – that cynical *Ur*-Mencken – defined READING as

The general body of what one reads. In our country it consists, as a rule, of Indiana novels, short stories in 'dialect' and humor in slang.

Local-colour work, which he is in effect describing, aroused him only to facetiousness. REALISM, though, was another matter. It was, he said:

The art of depicting nature as it is seen by toads. The charm suffusing a landscape painted by a mole, or a story written by a measuring-worm.

This is the vocabulary of abuse. In fact, it is typical of the abuse that greeted those who called themselves 'realists'. The 'realists', for their part, replied with manifestoes which usually included the words *reality* (as opposed to *idealism*, *romanticism*, *sentimentality*), *truth* (frequently *unvarnished*), *honesty*, *accuracy*. They claimed to represent *real life*, *life as it is*. Such statements are unsatisfactory as definitions, since they beg the question of what is meant by *life* or *reality*. A clearer idea of 'realism' can be arrived at in terms of the material held suitable for the novelist:

So forgive me, once more, patient reader, if I offer you no tragedy in high life, no sentimental history of fashion and wealth, but only a little story about a woman who could not be a heroine.

Perhaps the humility of this passage gives away its early date. It comes from a short story published in 1861, by the New England writer Rose Terry Cooke. A decade or two later similar statements of intention were offered much more often and much less apologetically. 'Realism', then, entailed writing about the environment one knew, with strict regard to its actual properties – speech, dress, scene, behaviour. It had certain particularly American connotations. Henry James agreed with Bierce as to the prevalence of dialect 'in the subject-matter of the American fictions of the day'. No such predominance, he thought, 'exists in English, in French, in German work of the same order'. It seemed to him, however, part of 'the great general wave of curiosity on the subject of the soul aboundingly not civilized that has lately begun to well over the Anglo-Saxon globe and that has borne Mr Rudyard Kipling, say, so supremely high on its crest'.

It would be easy to write of the development of American realism as though it were a movement growing out of local colour by virtue of its greater sophistication, and then yielding in turn to the movement known as 'naturalism' – and all the while doing battle with the fiction writers grouped under the banner of 'romanticism'. Romance confronting reality: high life versus low, or at any rate middle, life: the exotic versus the demotic: the daydream versus broad daylight: sentimentality versus common sense. Easy, and not altogether wrong. For there were novelists of the time, like William Dean Howells, who avowed that they were 'realists', who explained the articles of their creed in the face of their opponents, who championed other writers whom they considered as allies, and who employed the metaphors of controversy – battles, skirmishes, camps, campaigns – as though a clear-cut literary war were in progress. And there were novelists like Francis Marion Crawford who, if they did not call themselves 'romanticists', nevertheless disagreed explicitly with Howells and his protégés. There *was* a cleavage: there is a wide difference of outlook and tone between Frances Hodgson Burnett's *Little Lord Fauntleroy* and Howells's *Indian Summer*, both published in 1886; or between Thomas Nelson Page's *In Ole Virginia* and Joseph Kirkland's *Zury, the Meanest Man in Spring County*, which appeared in the following year.

But on closer inspection the battle – to adopt the metaphor popular with literary historians as well as with Howells – seems to have been a confused affair, of civil strife, in which not all the combatants wore uniform or were certain of their war-aims. If we are to pick sides, to which does Ambrose Bierce belong? Or Henry James, who with Howells had been an early protagonist of 'realism', but who by 1886 was resident in England, and writing *The Princess Casamassima*? Can we agree with one critic that Mark Twain (whose *Huckleberry Finn* had come out in 1884) 'took to dealings with the romanticists ... after his single effective blow for the realists in *The Gilded Age* (1873)'?[1] What are we to make of Charles Dudley Warner (Twain's collaborator in that work), whom the same critic describes – justly enough – as a 'polite commentator'? It seems laughable to compare

1. Grant C. Knight, *The Critical Period in American Literature: 1890–1900* (Chapel Hill, NC, 1951), 169.

Warner with John Dos Passos; yet like Dos Passos he did create a trilogy about ill-gotten wealth and its miserable consequences. Again, the romanticists' leader, Marion Crawford, concocted thirty-odd novels set in such locales as fifteenth-century Venice and fourteenth-century Constantinople; but he also wrote seven about the contemporary American scene, including one (*An American Politician*, 1884) about the corruptions of the Gilded Age; and, although he did not altogether live up to his own advice, he told an interviewer in 1893 that the United States offered the novelist the richest field in the entire world. And if to write of past times and far-off places was to qualify as a romanticist, must one therefore condemn R. L. Stevenson and Rudyard Kipling, whose work Howells much admired? Or there is the case of 'Sidney Luska', whom Howells described in 1888 as 'a most delightful fellow, and a most ardent convert to realism'. 'Luska' was the pseudonym of the young author Henry Harland, who wrote novels about Jewish immigrants in New York. Only a couple of years later he suddenly abandoned his pseudonym and went to live in Europe, where he edited *The Yellow Book* and produced such elegant trifles as *Grey Roses* (1895 – a title which perfectly epitomizes what one thinks of as the decadent side of the 1890s), *The Cardinal's Snuff-Box* (1900), and *My Friend Prospero* (1903). What happened? Was the conversion followed by apostasy? Did the recruit (to mix metaphors) go over to the other army?

Yes, to some extent. But we miss much of the nature of realism if we speak exaggeratedly of victories and betrayals. 'Realism' is a label we cannot do without: it helps to isolate certain features common to a great deal of fiction written in the last third of the nineteenth century, including that of Henry James. But like other labels it is apt to acquire a false and tyrannical plausibility. It leads us to search for the lowest common denominators in literature, and to overlook or condemn more important factors. Perhaps this is why Howells praised Stephen Crane's *Maggie* (as an orthodox naturalistic novel which nobody read) and did not like Crane's *Red Badge of Courage* (a far better book, which could not be neatly labelled and which was popular with the general public). Perhaps, too, Howells was so grateful for allies that he did not look too closely into their war-aims. If he had, he might not have been so sure of Harland, who wrote of the New York Jews not *primarily* as the downtrodden poor, but as an exotic race who would add to the American stock a much-needed element of colour and creative imagination.

In fact, realism and romanticism were both expressions of their time. In an article defending Frank Norris, Howells said that his novels were a response to the needs of his generation: 'It is not for nothing that any novelist is born in one age.' He went on to deny the same necessity to 'that aoristic freak, the historical novelist'; but he erred in doing so, as his followers indicated, either consciously or unconsciously, in their work. Norris himself argued that the true romance lay in realism, and he was not merely playing with words.

Howells's comment reveals a self-consciousness characteristic of the period, and even more apparent in America than in the rest of the Western world, though Europe actually led the United States in artistic formulation of the fresh sensations and insights (impressionism, symbolism and so on) which are collectively referred to as 'the modern movement'. The year of *Little Lord Fauntleroy* and of Emily Dickinson's quiet death, 1886, was also the year of the Haymarket Massacre in Chicago; and, too, of the steel magnate Andrew Carnegie's *Triumphant Democracy*, in which he declared that 'the old nations of the earth creep on at a snail's pace; the Republic thunders past with the rush of an express'.

He was right in that America was altering with staggering rapidity. Between 1860 and 1900 its population soared from thirty-one to seventy-six million, and the balance began to shift from rural to urban living. Towns appeared overnight, and grew to cities within a decade. Chicago, the most spectacular example, was in 1833 a village of 350 inhabitants. By 1870, the 350 had increased to over 300,000; by 1880, to 500,000; and by 1890, to more than a million. The human scale seemed to vanish, as vast industrial enterprises reared themselves, only to be swallowed up by still vaster ones, knit together by complex financing by which the few enormously rich – Carnegie, Frick, Vanderbilt, Rockefeller, and their kind – apparently battened on everyone else, intensifying what Henry George (in his *Progress and Poverty*, 1879) called 'the contrast between the House of Have and the House of Want'. A helpless immigrant proletariat was squeezing into the slums of New York, Pittsburgh, Chicago, Detroit and a dozen other cities. Many of these immigrants were now coming, for the first time, from central and eastern Europe. Simple peasants from Italy, Jews from Polish ghettos, they were ill equipped to face their new world. Emma Lazarus, in the sonnet carved on the pedestal of the Statue of Liberty, spoke a welcome for Europe's tired and poor, the 'huddled masses yearning to breathe free'. The concept of free immigration was magnificent, the reality was inevitably less so. Nor did the native-born accept the fact with equanimity. How could a united nation emerge from such polyglot origins? Surely there must be a saturation-point; had it not been reached?

Henry James, visiting his homeland in 1904–5 after a long absence, was jolted to the depth of his being by Ellis Island, the immigrants' clearing-station, a 'visible act of ingurgitation on the part of our body politic and social'. 'This affirmed claim of the alien, however immeasurably alien, to share in one's supreme relation', gave him an acute sense of 'dispossession', and he could not help sighing for 'the luxury of some such close and sweet and *whole* national consciousness as that of the Switzer and the Scot'.

A fastidious person like James might think that little was left of the older, finer America. The ideal of democracy was mocked when the *nouveau riche* married his daughter into the aristocracy of Europe, and the bewildered immigrant placed his vote in the keeping of the ward-heeler. Nor was corruption confined to city politics: it thrived in state legislatures and in the federal government itself. As for rural America, the farmer was often as discontented as the urban poor whose ranks he swelled. Once the hero of Jefferson, the virtuous husbandman, he was now the *rube*, the *hick*, the *hayseed*. Agriculture over-extended itself as it reached into the rain-shadow of the Rockies. Angry and disappointed homesteaders found themselves prey to natural scourges – droughts, locusts, prairie fires – and to man-made evils: exorbitant freight rates, low prices, tight credit. Henry George, the author of *Progress and Poverty*, had seen the golden land of California parcelled out in a single generation of headlong acquisitiveness. He doubted whether any essential progress had been made. 'We have not abolished slavery', he declared (*Social Problems*, 1884). The chattel form had merely been replaced by wage slavery. 'Supposing we did legalize chattel slavery again, who would buy men when men can be hired so cheaply?'

In the 1890s Americans were told, too, that the frontier, the open zone of unsettled land, no longer existed. Even when the Mississippi formed the western limit of the United States, Jefferson had congratulated his fellow-citizens on 'possessing a chosen country, with room enough for our descendants, to the hundredth and thousandth generation'. But after less than a century it might seem that there was no more room; at any rate the ideal of illimitable westward territory was gone.

The establishment of monopolistic trusts seemed to reformers an alarm-ing and fundamentally un-American tendency. Not so, claimed the Yale sociologist William Graham Sumner, appealing to commonsense 'realism' to prove that life was necessarily a hard business. Sumner wrote in a clear, pungent prose. So did his opponent Henry Demarest Lloyd, as we may see

...in his attack on the Standard Oil Company, *Wealth Against Common-wealth* (1894):

– What we call Monopoly is Business at the end of its journey. The concentration of wealth, the wiping out of the middle classes, are other names for it. To get it is, in the world of affairs, the chief end of man. . . .

– It was an American idea to 'strike oil'. Those who knew it as the 'slime' of Genesis, or used it to stick together the bricks of the Tower of Babel, were content to take it as it rose, the easy gift of nature, oozing forth. . . . But the American struck it. . . .

– The market – the barrel that went to market – the freight rate that stopped the barrel that went to market – the railway king who made the rate that stopped the barrel that went to market – the greater king who whispered behind to the railway king to make the rate that stopped the barrel that went to market – this is the house that Jack unbuilt.

Puzzled by the rapidity of the changes overtaking their land, Americans groped for explanations and panaceas. Some were embodied in Utopian novels, of which Edward Bellamy's *Looking Backward: 2000–1887* is one of the few still remembered. Widely read and admired, by Mark Twain among others, *Looking Backward* (1888) puts its hero to sleep for a hundred and thirteen years. He wakes up in a Boston which has been cleansed of all its follies and miseries. Life is rational, benevolent and staid. Yet the book in its day had the force of a vision, and its comments on the unregenerate society of 1887 stand out boldly in their bland context. Thus the old order is compared to travel in a coach: the well-to-do are the passengers and the poor are the 'teams' which drag the coach along. In the Boston of A.D. 2000 when it rains the pavements are protected by waterproof awnings. The heroine says:

The private umbrella is Father's favourite figure to illustrate the old way when everybody lived for himself and his family. There is a nineteenth-century painting at the art gallery representing a crowd of people in the rain, each one holding his umbrella over himself and his wife, and giving his neighbors the drippings, which he claims must have been meant by the artist as a satire on his times.

Plunged back into a complacent dinner party in the Boston of 1887, and asked where he has been lately, the hero cries out:

I have been in Golgotha. I have seen Humanity hanging on a cross! Do none of you know what sights the sun and stars look down on in this city, that you can think and talk of anything else?[1]

1. This passage may have been appropriated by William Jennings Bryan for his impassioned 'Cross of Gold' speech at the Democratic party convention in 1896.

Bellamy secured less attention with a sequel, *Equality* (1897), in which the fictional devices are subordinate to a quite radical economic analysis. *Equality* is a dialogue rather than a novel. But it is more passionate than most of the fiction of the decade. Bellamy died the year after it was published, still in his early forties. He died of tuberculosis – a *fin de siècle* fate shared with a surprising number of ardent young contemporaries.

A more plaintive uneasiness was voiced by J. R. Lowell, in the wistful jingle of his poem 'Credidimus Jovem Regnare', published in the same year as *Looking Backward:*

> Men feel old systems cracking under 'em;
> Life saddens to a mere conundrum
> Which once Religion solved, but she
> Has lost – has Science found? – the key.

Many thought that science *had* found a key, in Darwin's theory of evolution. As expounded and popularized by Herbert Spencer, 'Social Darwinism' enjoyed a vogue with the general public, and made a considerable impression on such young writers as Hamlin Garland, Jack London and Theodore Dreiser. It was not a comforting revelation for all of them, but at least it seemed to fit the facts. In addition to providing a biological analogy for the struggle to survive that went on in the business world and in the teeming city streets, it lifted a load of guilt. Sins were no longer sins, if men's actions were determined by heredity and environment. Nor of course was it necessary to interpret Spencerian Darwinism as a pessimistic and passive doctrine. If progress was ensured, it did not matter that the method of improvement was predetermined. So long as the fittest *did* survive, and perfection came about after trial and error, it was possible to accept Darwinism as a scientific reinforcement of the poetic truth of Longfellow's 'Excelsior'. Man evolved upwards, though many perished in the process; and though, like the eager banner-carrying youth in Longfellow's poem, they might not have any clear idea of what they were doing.

Indeed, for the majority of Americans, whether or not they summoned Spencer to their aid, the era was one of great vitality. Grievances were aired, abuses bred reform. Those who were worst-off – ruined farmer or under-paid artisan – clung to the belief that they were still no worse-off than their European equivalents, and could look forward to a brighter future for their children. Yet the rate of change, though exhilarating, was disturbing. 'The Republic thunders past': it rushed past Americans, past the relatively tranquil country of their childhoods, depriving them of whatever had featured as their heritage, and revealing to them a tomorrow of further flux. For some it merely heightened the pleasurable, nostalgic ache of reminiscence. This is evident in a good deal of local-colour writing; so is the determination to set down the scene before one's eyes before it has altered irrevocably. Heartache for the time *Befo' de War* (the title of one of Thomas Nelson Page's books) was almost a chronic Southern emotion; but the whole country responded to the Southern fable of bygone gracious living, and extracted an agreeable melancholy from the Negro's plight,

> Still longing for the old plantation
> And for the old folks at home.

The words are by Stephen Foster, a Northerner who paid only one brief visit to the South.[1] He makes black people serve as a surrogate for white emotion. There is no harshness, no acknowledgement of wrong. The Negro, for Foster, is an innocent, exiled from a forgotten Africa (as white Americans were exiled from a forgotten Europe, and from the America of their childhoods), and now doubly exiled as he is taken away from his Old Kentucky Home to some new corner barren of association. As the past receded like the view from the observation car of Carnegie's express, Americans hankered after it a little, liking modernity in the bathroom – and the old world in the bookcase. Or, in relation to the United States, fascinated and rather envious of New England when they lived in regions further west, complaining of its outmoded conservatism, but secretly proud that the United States, also, had its antiquities.

W. D. Howells, whose career illustrates all the phases in the growth of realism, made no secret of his early respect for New England. A bookish little boy in Ohio, he determined to be a poet. At twenty-three he was able to head eastward for Boston, where the *Atlantic Monthly* had recently accepted one of his poems. Its editor, Lowell, gave him a dinner, attended also by Oliver Wendell Holmes and the publisher J. T. Fields. They were pleased with the young man; the meal, he wrote ecstatically to his father,

lasted four hours, . . . and involved an intoxication to me, as entire as that of Rhine wine. Lowell and Holmes both seemed to take me by the hand, and the Autocrat,

1. Foster (1826–64) is the composer of dozens of 'Negro' melodies, including 'My Old Kentucky Home' and 'Massa's in de Cold, Cold Ground', as well as 'Jeannie with the Light Brown Hair'.

about the time the coffee came in, began to talk about the apostolic succession. Tomorrow evening I am to take tea with him . . . .

After such encouragement it was natural for Howells to tell Fields, in the tone of his apostolic masters, that 'there is no place quite so good as Boston – God bless it!' By contrast, the more he saw of New York on this eastern pilgrimage, 'the more I did not like it'.

The Civil War found him in Italy, established as American consul in Venice (as the reward for a campaign biography of Abraham Lincoln). But though the experience put him closely in touch with European contemporary letters (a knowledge which he kept up to date for the rest of his life), Europe shocked him. His appreciation of Dickens, Heine and other Europeans was pushed firmly into a subordinate place in his new perspective. He wrote from Venice in 1862:

You will read . . . that life in Europe is more cheerful and social than ours. Lies, I say – or stupidities, which are almost as bad. . . . The pleasure which we have innocently in America, from our unrestrained and unconventional social intercourse, is guilty in Europe – brilliant men and women know something of it; but they are also guilty men and women . . . I think these things over a great deal . . . and the most earnest prayer that my heart can conceive is that America may grow more and more unlike Europe every day. I think when I return home I will go to Oregon – and live as far as possible from the influence of European civilization.

When Howells sent this letter he was no doubt homesick: one must make allowances for the fact that he was writing to his sister; and it may be noted that on his return to America he was soon installed not in Oregon but in Boston, as assistant editor of the *Atlantic*. But it is a genuine expression of Howells's belief in America's moral virtues. America's highest product, he thought, was the American girl, so gay and yet full of sensibility.[1] There was a Miss Wing in Ohio, for example, who when he was about to terminate a call said,

'Don't go, Mr. Howells, I'm about to sing for you, though you haven't asked me.' She is a glorious singer. I heard her at Dr Smith's, where she sang 'Excelsior' in a manner that made my heart ache. . . . So she sat down and sang. . . .[2]

It is tempting to ridicule such a scene; and Howells has been ridiculed for his famous statement that 'our novelists . . . concern themselves with the

---

1. The Boston wit Tom Appleton (Longfellow's brother-in-law) wrote in 1874 of 'that big exclamation mark behind her eyes which American girls have'.
2. *Life in Letters of William Dean Howells* (2 vols., London, 1929), i. 18.

more smiling aspects of life, which are the more American.... It is worth while, even at the risk of being called commonplace, to be true to our well-to-do actualities.' Mencken dismissed Howells as 'a contriver of pretty things', 'an Agnes Repplier in pantaloons'. Yet in the 1860s and 1870s, when Howells was evolving his creed, he was able to make such statements in complete sincerity: they were for him, quite simply, the truth.

Moreover, they enabled him to come to grips with realism, and to separate the disagreeable licence of contemporary European novelists from their underlying principles, of which he heartily approved. Howells would probably have smiled appreciatively at an 1876 newspaper review by Edward Bellamy: 'There are two sorts of French novels, the immoral and the moral. In the former the heroine commits adultery, in the latter, she comes as near to it as she can and miss it. Victor Cherbuliez writes the latter sort. His heroine often comes pretty near tripping, but generally maintains a precarious perpendicularity.' Realism in America, given the purer and more 'commonplace' nature of its society, meant writing about people of the kind to be met every day. These, the divine American average, were not murderers, seducers, burglars, prostitutes; nor princes in disguise, nor unwitting heirs to fortunes and estates. Coincidence operated only mildly in their lives, according to a sensible consideration of probability and not in obedience to the demands of romance. As young people, they fell in love, and often married. But there was no suggestion that two soul-mates had thus guaranteed one another unalloyed happiness. On the contrary, Howells was at pains to point out the limitations of his heroes and heroines – if one can call them that. If his characters fell in love, they might fall out of it (as in *A Chance Acquaintance*, 1873); or their marriage might end disastrously (as in *A Modern Instance*, 1881); or, as in *An Open-Eyed Conspiracy* (1897), a successful match might be mildly exasperating to the friends of the couple. This particular story concludes with a conversation between Mrs March and her novelist husband Basil. (For some reason Howells gave these favourite characters, who appear in no less than seven of his books, the same surname as that of the family in Louisa May Alcott's *Little Women*, 1868–9.) Mrs March says to him of an engaged couple:

'But isn't it always dreadful to see two people who have made up their minds to get married?'

'It's very common,' I suggested.

'That doesn't change the fact, or lessen the risk. She is very beautiful, and now he is in love with her beautiful girlhood. But after a while the girlhood will go.'

'And the girl will remain,' I said.

March/Howells seems to mean that the bride usually remains immature.

Apart from love and matrimony, the Americans whom Howells saw around him worried about their jobs, and about their position – for he never pretended that there was no class distinction in America: the plot of *A Chance Acquaintance* hinged upon the impossibility, for a young Bostonian, of moving out of his circle in order to marry a girl from what he regarded as a backwoods community. His Americans were confronted by moral decisions which were real to them, though of the domestic variety. Should a woman pursue a career? Apparently not, to judge from *Dr Breen's Practice* (1881), and *A Woman's Reason* (1883). Should a young girl (*Indian Summer*, 1886) marry a middle-aged man? She relinquishes him to a partner more appropriate.

Such was the world – largely a domestic world – that Howells set on paper, once he had decided that his principal interest lay in the novel. He seemed to turn naturally to novel-writing, as to most forms of literature in fact: for he never ceased entirely to be a poet; he wrote plays; he read widely, and wrote innumerable reviews and articles; and after a mere five years of work on the *Atlantic* he became its editor-in-chief. His first two books were travel accounts of Italy; his first novels were about travellers, or about Americans in relation to Venetians. At this stage he was very close to Henry James, with whom he maintained a lifelong friendship that did not prevent the two from criticizing one another. In 1880 they were 'those badly assorted Siamese twins, J. and H.', who 'treat intercontinental passion'.

But Howells soon began to concentrate upon the American scene, wrangling genially with James over the latter's decision to make Europe his base. Realism, for Howells, entailed living in and writing about the United States. Like Mark Twain, he resented comment by Matthew Arnold and other Englishmen, to the effect that the United States was without 'distinction'. Howells insisted that lack of distinction was exactly what distinguished democratic America. His pride and irritation may have combined with a professional's technical objections to rambling, amateurish narrative. At any rate he was sometimes more critical of English fiction (including that of Thackeray and Dickens) than of continental European. Vestiges of something that resembled anglophobia lingered in him for many years – perhaps until English recognition of his American worthiness was certified, in 1905, by means of an honorary degree from Oxford.

By the early 1880s Howells's brand of realism was in certain respects fixed. He was prepared to support anyone calling himself a realist, but though he read 'everything of Zola's that I can lay hands on', he said in 1882 that while 'the new school' was 'largely influenced by French fiction in form', 'it is the realism of Daudet rather than the realism of Zola that prevails with it, and it has a soul of its own which is above recording the rather brutish pursuit of a woman by a man, which seems to be the chief end of the French novelist'. Never wholly at ease with literature that could not safely be read aloud within the family circle, he saw little need to justify himself for not emulating Zola; American life as well as American taste was more refined than that of Paris. Europeans might extol the treatment of 'passion', he remarked in 1889. But there were several passions – grief, pity, ambition, hate, envy, devotion, friendship – all of which had 'a greater part in the drama of life than the passion of love, and infinitely greater than the passion of guilty love'. Moreover, in America fiction was read mainly by females, and to a large extent in magazines. The format dictated the content.

Choosing a few characters; relying not upon a formal plot but upon the presentation and solution of a problem (since he firmly believed, as a tenet of realism, that the novel's first object should be instruction rather than amusement); presenting his theme neatly and economically, in dialogue and not in the intrusive author-to-reader manner that irritated him in Thackeray; reproducing the look and sound of his situations with painstaking accuracy: Howells was, despite his faintly old-maidish quality, the most professional of writers, and the most generous of critics. Who else could have maintained an intimate friendship with two writers as unlike as Mark Twain and Henry James? On such a man – so warmly intelligent, so anxious to acknowledge new talent, so concerned for the unique moral standing of his country – the America of strikes and slums was bound to make a profound impression.

The Rise of Silas Lapham (1885) shows him at the height of his powers, before the spectacle of industrialized America had deeply perturbed him. Lapham is a self-made businessman living in Boston with his wife and two daughters, Penelope and Irene. The Laphams are emphatically not gentlefolk, though the daughters are more presentable than their parents. In contrast are the Coreys, an old Boston family in which the father is a witty dilettante and the mother a moderate snob. The son, Tom, is 'an energetic fellow . . . with the smallest amount of inspiration that can save a man from being commonplace'. (Much of Howells is a skirmish around the word *commonplace*, which he uses as a measure rather than a criticism.) The Laphams and the Coreys are thrown together when Tom, going into business, establishes himself in Lapham's firm, and then falls in love with one of the Lapham girls. The difference between the two families is a perfect theme for Howells; he makes this juxtaposition of polish and social barbarism comical yet touching, notably at a dinner party in which the Laphams are exposed to the Corey circle. He is brilliant too in developing a minor contrast, between Irene Lapham's charmless prettiness and her sister Penelope's unflirtatious, dry humour. Less successful is the storyline when Tom's attentions to the daughters are mistaken – Irene, believing him to be in love with her, falls in love with him, though in fact Tom is in love with Penelope. Here Howells is something of the doctrinaire, in his own harmless version of realism: his point that no serious harm is done in such cases has led him to contrive a sub-plot that seems a little implausible. One's withers are wrung, gently enough, while Howells is insisting that none *should* be.

The other main theme of the novel, to which Howells intended the title to refer, is the struggle within Lapham's mind when he runs into financial difficulties. Should he, on the brink of ruin, save himself by selling a property to an interested group, when he knows – though they do not – that it will soon become worthless? Rising above temptation, he keeps clean hands – and becomes a bankrupt. Or rather, by so doing he cleans his hands of a piece of sharp practice of earlier days, of which his wife's reminders have always kept him ashamedly aware.

A bare recital of the novel's themes gives no idea of its skill. High-minded in the kindest sense of the word, within its compass it is masterly. It flows; it is full of slyly observant, affectionate comment. Holmes's benevolent reference to the apostolic succession turned out to have been a remarkably good guess. For in Howells, Boston reached its silver age. As much as this age would permit, Howells exhibited Boston's far from contemptible traits: its erudition (as a boy, he studied five languages at once, on top of a day's work), its commitment to the written word, its prim honesty, its good-humoured knowledge of its own limits.[1]

Yet Howells left Boston for New York in the 1880s – a move that Alfred Kazin has called 'the great symbolic episode in the early history of American realism',[2] since in making it Howells showed that Boston was

1. For a witty reminiscence of Boston, see M. A. DeWolfe Howe, ed., *John Jay Chapman and His Letters* (Boston, 1937), 195.

2. *On Native Grounds* (New York, 1942), ix.

no longer the literary headquarters of America. New York was now more *real*. The *North American Review* had transferred itself to New York in 1878;[1] periodicals and publishing houses were flourishing there; it had, Howells told a friend, 'lots of interesting young painting and writing fellows, and the place is lordly free'. Ensconced as an editor of *Harper's Magazine*, and as an eminent novelist, he could be sure of an audience, and within certain limits speak out as he pleased.

He continued to speak out for realism, against romanticism, and against a new enemy – capitalism. It cost him nothing, emotionally, to attack romanticism, which was merely the flimsy veil that hid the features of American life. But could these features be fine, when capitalism was one of them? The constitutional debates at Philadelphia had been eloquent and profound; the debates over slavery had likewise engaged all America in a sober consideration of moral and social values. But with the end of the Civil War noble motives disappeared (Howells began to think); there was then 'no question but the minor question of civil-service reform to engage the idealist's fancy or the moralist's conscience. After the war we had, as no other people had in the world, the chance of devoting ourselves strictly to business, of buying cheap and selling dear.' Something had gone terribly wrong with the pure, uncomplicated America whose image had inspired his earlier realism; American life was now, he felt, 'a state of warfare and a game of chance, in which each man fights and bets against fearful odds'. The industrial brutality of the era – shown in such affairs as the Homestead strike of 1893, in Carnegie's Pennsylvania steel mills – sickened him. The execution of Chicago's Haymarket anarchists, on dubious evidence, was 'an atrocious piece of frenzy and cruelty for which we must stand ashamed forever before history'. He became a socialist in his principles if not in any political affiliation, with the Russian novelist–visionary Count Leo Tolstoy as his master. In such novels as the earnest *Hazard of New Fortunes* (1890), he described the moral decay of competitive society, and developed his Tolstoyan notion of the 'complicity' of all in the human predicament. The same truth was explored in *Annie Kilburn* (1889), which he called a 'cry for justice', and in his Utopian novel, *A Traveller*

1. Longfellow wrote of this event (in a letter of 30 October 1877): 'Osgood has sold or given and conveyed the North American into the hands of the Appletons. Henceforth it will be edited, printed, and published in New York. Mr Clarke, at the printing-office, said: "It is like parting with the New England Blarney-Stone." He might have said, in more classic language: "Troy has lost her Palladium." ' Samuel Longfellow, ed., *Final Memorials of Henry Wadsworth Longfellow* (London, 1887), 267.)

from Altruria (1894). In this he advocated socialism; yet as the name of his Utopia suggests, it was rather altruism that he aimed at, something which was not to be realized simply by espousing a political programme.

Howells never retracted his general attachment to socialism; he condemned the imperialism of the war with Spain in 1898, and as late as 1907 wrote *Through the Eye of the Needle*, as a sequel to *A Traveller from Altruria*, to describe the idyllic decency of life in this other country, a sort of once-and-future America. But he was not happy with the ideas of the time, any more than with the social unrest that bred them. He liked to argue, in Tolstoyan vein, that 'the author is, in the last analysis, merely a working-man'. An author's days are numbered when he begins to apologize for his *métier*; but Howells did not pursue his own work to the last analysis. As his comment reveals, he was worried about his responsibilities as America's most prominent realist. He postulated a divine average American. In the chaos of the 1890s, however, the average seemed to disappear; all that one could see, as literary fact, was the cleavage between the very rich and the very poor, the despoilers and the despoiled. He could not handle either group effectively; he was a cultivated man who could write of lack of cultivation in his characters, but as a *lack*, a deficiency, not as an absolute fact. Though the Darwinian metaphor appalled him, it did not spur him to write. He found it invigorating to speak of the struggle for realism, yet depressing to think of life itself as struggle.

He did his best, aware that many readers did not appreciate the understated ironies, the deliberately unsensational stretches of dialogue in, say, *The Landlord at Lion's Head* (1897), an acute portrayal of the relations between an artist, a businessman and a society girl. He showed courage in denouncing the furious prejudice manifest in the Haymarket trial, when other American authors were too timid to protest. 'Mr Howells', it was said, 'is more than democratic, he is anarchical.' This was of course a wild exaggeration. But it is an inadvertent tribute to Howells's range of sensitivity, and his inclination to commit himself to ideas of social justice. He did not, by later standards, go very far. From the cool detachment of his observer–narrator figure Basil March, he moved, so to speak, to being a semi-detached chronicler.

Howells, in other words, compromised by writing as he knew how – the majority of his novels published after the move to New York are not concerned with Darwinian strife – and by encouraging younger men, gulping down their prescriptions even when the medicine tasted sour. It did not always: the advent of realism was in many ways exciting and stimulating for the young author. If in *social* terms the modern era contradicted the moral idea to which Americans were attached, in *literary* terms it upheld the moral idea. American writers, as we have seen, had long maintained that they should deal with their own country, in its own idiom. In practice, though, they had fallen short. The language was somehow wrong, the time seemed too ordinary: no one was quite ready to bell the cat. Local-colour writing had done much to remedy this. Even so, in one important respect the local-colour novel nearly always failed to do justice to the American ideal. It could not, try as it would, make its hero and heroine humble people of the kind Whitman pictured. The hero and heroine might be poor, but they must be educated and genteel; half a century after Cooper, the convention was still in force.

Realism began to break it, partly by getting rid of the formal plot, with its obligatory 'hero' and 'heroine'. *Realism* is of course a word with many meanings, not all of them compatible. To the Norwegian-American author Hjalmar H. Boyesen, a realist was

a writer who adheres strictly to the logic of reality, as he sees it; who, aiming to portray the manners of his time, deals by preference with the normal, rather than the exceptional phases of life, and, to use Henry James's felicitous phrase, arouses not the pleasure of surprise, but that of recognition.

Photography, in a way; and in this way, Boyesen took Howells to be America's supreme cameraman. But in another essay Boyesen deplored the constraints placed upon the novelist by public taste, as embodied in magazine editors, who must shape their material according to the whim of the young female reader. 'She', he said, 'is the Iron Madonna who strangles in her fond embrace the American novelist; the Moloch upon whose altar he sacrifices willingly or unwillingly, his chances of greatness.' This arbiter with a whim of iron was not merely squeamish but indifferent to many public concerns. As a result, Boyesen thought, American novels almost ignored politics.[1] He could have noted, too, the curious delay in the appearance of realistic fiction about the Civil War. Ambrose Bierce's *Tales of Soldiers and Civilians*, for example, did not come out until 1891, twenty-six years after the end of the fighting,

What then was 'normal', and who decided? In *Crumbling Idols* (1894), Hamlin Garland spoke up for candour, integrity, a literature of the common

---

1. H. H. Boyesen, *Literary and Social Silhouettes* (New York, 1894), 46–9, 71–2.

man. Who, though, *was* the common man, or woman? Would they speak in dialect and be preoccupied with petty details? Could they ever be 'heroic'? Were they to be presented from the outside? Were their inner thoughts not perhaps more 'real'? Frank Norris, at the turn of the century, found realism as usually defined a humdrum affair: 'the drama of a broken teacup, the tragedy of a walk down the block, the excitement of an afternoon call, the adventure of an invitation to dinner'. There is indeed no single, simple 'logic of reality'.

Naturalism is almost as elusive, and sometimes used as a synonym for *realism*. For American literature, however, it makes sense to think of naturalism as a later phase, beginning in about 1890, though originating in France around 1870 with the first novels of Émile Zola. Zola's arguments on the scientific exactness of his fiction (*Le roman expérimental*, 1880) provided some of the doctrine for American authors. Their naturalism entailed much more emphasis than did Howellsian realism upon the underdog, the obscure human particle in the social mass, and upon existence as a perhaps unavailing struggle for survival. Howells, on behalf of his protégés, took a doyen's or dean's pleasure in the extension of subject-matter now opening up. The realist as naturalist could in theory deal with almost anything and anybody: slums, sharecroppers and home-steaders, labourers, strikers, criminals, prostitutes. Dismay at the grimness of the contemporary scene blended, among aspiring authors of the 1890s, with an excited sense of fresh material and fresh techniques. They tended to write with a heady confusion, unsure whether they were cheering on a revolution or mourning the collapse of America's ideal middle landscape; undecided whether their theme was *the people* or the *public*, or perhaps mankind in the grip of inexorable fate.

One such writer was Hamlin Garland ('the Ibsen of the West'), who came out of the prairie, a farmer's son. For the theme of his high-school graduation address he chose Horace Greeley's injunction – 'Go West, Young Man'. As soon as he was able, however, he went East, to Boston, as Howells had done before him. After the raw life of his boyhood, New England struck him as wonderfully old and interesting. But as he educated himself in the East (largely, it would seem, by giving lectures, picking up the subject as he went along), it was not romance that appealed to him, but Spencer, Henry George, Whitman, Taine, Max Nordau: anyone whose work appeared alive. In his middle twenties he began to write articles and short stories, his head in a whirl with hopes, theories, denunciations. At this stage he considered Howells and James trivial, while he hated 'Lowell,

Holmes, and other fossil representatives of classicism'. At twenty-seven he planned to deify the common people in a great work on 'Literary Democracy'.

By then he had revised his opinion of Howells, who befriended the rather bumptious young man and encouraged him to write of his own region as his radical inclinations prompted – of its resentment and envy of the city, its bleak poverty, its women old before their time. Garland was not quite the first American to view Western life with disenchantment. There had been Edward Eggleston's *The Hoosier School-Master* (1871), which deeply impressed Garland when he read it as a boy. And there was Edgar W. Howe's *The Story of a Country Town* (1883). Howe, a Kansas newspaper editor, published it at the age of thirty; yet it reads like the work of an old man whose hope is evaporated, leaving only a desire to get out of his system the joyless monotony of his existence. In this awkward, bitter, compulsive novel Howe makes one of the characters ask:

Haven't you noticed that when a Western man gets a considerable sum of money together, he goes East to live? Well, what does it mean except that the good sense which enabled him to make money teaches him that the society there is preferable to ours? . . . Men who are prosperous . . . do not come West, but it is the unfortunate, the poor, the indigent, the sick – the lower classes, in short – who came here to grow up with the country, having failed to grow up with the country where they came from.

A few years later Garland told an interviewer that

There is a mystic quality connected with free land, and it has always allured men into the West. I wanted to show that it is a myth.

When he went back to his family for a visit in 1887, he saw the Western farmers in one of the worst periods of their history. Howe's farmers had at least been relatively prosperous: Garland's were crushed with debt. He was a better writer than Howe, and in his earlier work was able to disguise his own limitations through the warmth of his pity for the farmer's lot, which he had managed to escape, and also through the excitement of applying the principles of realism. His own brand of this he chose to call 'veritism', to indicate that he stood somewhere between the realism of Howells and the older generation, and the naturalism of Zola, by which he was shocked. He wrote coarsely; his ear for dialogue, especially for polite discourse, was poor. But in the six stories called *Main-Travelled Roads* (1891) he conveyed with sincerity and dignity the atmosphere of heartbreaking drabness which enveloped people like his parents. 'A man like me', says one of his farmers, 'is helpless. Just like a fly in a pan of molasses. . . . The more he tears around the more liable he is to rip his legs off.'

In subsequent volumes Garland, a prolific writer, tended to spoil his histories by preaching populism or the single-tax remedies of Henry George. But gradually his interest in good causes ebbed away. His books had sold badly; much as he valued the opinion of Howells and other champions of realism, he craved success. Moreover, by 1900 he, like Howells, had grown accustomed if not entirely reconciled to the new America. The West now 'allured' him, not the flat land of Iowa or South Dakota, but the spectacular Rocky Mountain West. If it was a myth, he accepted it, and wrote copiously of it. He wrote too of his boyhood, each successive volume rosier and weaker than the previous one. Both he and Howells perhaps lived too long for their own good; tranquil old age, however well earned, seemed not to accord with the vigour of their best work. The brief careers of some writers who followed them formed a hectic contrast. Stephen Crane died at twenty-nine, Frank Norris at thirty-two, Jack London at forty; while Harold Frederic (who on the strength of at least one of his novels, *The Damnation of Theron Ware*,[1] can be included with these others) was dead at the age of forty-two.

In 1893 Crane published a little novel whose very title – *Maggie, a Girl of the Streets* – invited the literary world to side with him or against him. Howells and Garland, whom Crane once called his 'literary fathers', sided with him and gave him what support they could, though his defiance of middlebrow taste passed almost unnoticed by the middlebrow mass. Howells told Crane about the recently published poems of Emily Dickinson, and Crane produced some of his own – jerky, individual, full of unexpected images and epithets; as though Emily Dickinson had been jumbled together with the newspaper wit of Ambrose Bierce. Indeed, Crane was a newspaperman, and one of his poems discussed the matter:

> A newspaper is a court
> Where everyone is kindly and unfairly tried
> By a squalor of honest men.

But these were side-issues in the advancement of naturalism; Howells, when Crane was dead, felt that *Maggie* was 'the best thing he did'. *Maggie*, which Crane said 'tries to show that environment is a tremendous thing

1. 1896; published in England as *Illumination*.

in the world, and frequently shapes lives regardless', is important as a document in the history of naturalism.[1] It is spasmodic, melodramatic, grainy and yet poignant like a primitive film. Its most remarkable feature – a tersely vivid vocabulary similar to that in Crane's poems – has nothing to do with orthodox naturalism.

This feature Howells disliked in Crane's short stories, and in the latter's Civil War masterpiece, *The Red Badge of Courage*. War as a theme had hitherto hardly been treated by the American realists, with the honourable exception of J. W. DeForest's *Miss Ravenel's Conversion* (1867), which *Harper's Monthly* thought unsuitable for serial publication. Its horror, its enormity, its revelation of the brutality that lay beneath the surface of human beings: all these have made warfare a major topic for the modern movement – together with the obvious fact that in the twentieth century a great many men have had experience of it. Crane had none when he wrote *The Red Badge*. The Civil War, however, fascinated his generation, and subsequent generations of Americans. It was *their* war, something no European had known or could quite understand. Moreover, it was a modern war, a war mainly of civilians, not professionals; a war that was photographed, that depended on the factory and the railroad; a protracted, bloody, clumsy war; a war without romance in which, as Melville had perceived, 'a singe ran through lace and feather'.

Crane made his short amazing novel out of war, then, not out of farmers' woes or the iniquities of the great city. His dialogue is naturalistic ('We've helt 'em back; derned if we haven't'); the 'hero', Henry Fleming, is an ordinary youngster in the ranks, an uneducated farm-boy whose name is not even introduced until halfway through the book. He and his comrades are as helpless in other ways as Maggie was, alone in New York. Nobody wins; all is confusion. Collective pride, animosity, berserk fury account for what 'heroism' is displayed. Yet to discuss the novel as an example of naturalism is to miss its mood. Crane is preoccupied with the personal reaction to fear; so while Fleming, judged by his conversation, is loutish, his inward turmoil is that of a sensitive person (a discrepancy less evident

1. Several writers have suggested that *Maggie* must have been influenced by Zola's *L'Assommoir*. Possibly; but one can point to material nearer at hand: for example, to the sensationally popular sermons of the Brooklyn minister, De Witt Talmage, which were reprinted in 1885 as *The Night Side of New York Life*. In one of these sermons he asks his congregation to pity a poor prostitute ('Maggie'), for whom one of the few ways of escape is 'the street that leads to East river, at midnight, the end of the city dock, the moon shining down on the water making it look so smooth she wonders if it is deep enough. It is. No boatman near enough to hear the plunge . . . .' This is how Crane's Maggie ends her life.

in the book as printed than in the manuscript draft). Crane is also interested in the spectacle of war, which he describes with a painter's or poet's impressionistic responsiveness. A wound is a 'red badge'; fear is a 'red and green monster'. Everything is sharp, nervous, oddly gorgeous:

He stared ... at the leaves overhead, moving in a heraldic wind of the day....

The bugles called to each other like brazen gamecocks....

Each distant thicket seemed a strange porcupine with quills of flame....

The Red Badge ends on the somewhat unconvincing idea that though war is dreadful, the young man has finally overcome his fears, for the rest of the war. This is a conventionally happy ending, as Maggie's suicide is a conventionally unhappy one. However, the general sense of this brilliant book is that the world is a chaos whose only consolation lies in the tenuous fellowship between man and man. The conclusion is reinforced in Crane's best short story, 'The Open Boat', a rewritten account of a shipwreck which he himself experienced. Occasionally it is marred by a facetious phrase:

As soon as the correspondent touched the cold, comfortable sea-water in the bottom of the boat ... he was deep in sleep, despite the fact that his teeth played all the popular airs.

But it is a moving testimony to the tenderness of which men are capable, isolated in their frail boat, drifting towards a coastline where 'the furniture of the world' consisted of two lights. 'Otherwise there was nothing but waves.' And to the indifferent cruelty of the sea, which drowns one of the men at the moment the others are saved.

These quotations show how much romanticism there was in Crane, mingled with the racy, hard-boiled cynicism of the journalist. He was a Bohemian New Yorker, somewhat as Twain and Harte had been in San Francisco, living or dreaming existences that did not quite get into their books. Thus Crane spent his last few years with Cora Taylor, an educated, rebellious Bostonian whom he had met in Florida, where she was managing a brothel named (not by her) the Hotel de Dream. The two sides of his nature are both expressed in his crowded months as a war correspondent in Cuba and Greece. And as the newspaperman's role is one of the typical aspects of the American writer, so in a special way is that of the correspondent, travelling in strange and dangerous corners, 'both in and out of the game', no more fully committed than Whitman or Thoreau, testing himself isolatedly in an unfamiliar context.

Frank Norris also acted as a war correspondent, in Cuba and South Africa; and he likewise cannot be pinned down as a realist/naturalist. The copy of *The Octopus* that he gave to his wife is inscribed from 'Mr Norris, Esq. (The Boy Zola)!'; yet he told a friend the novel was 'the most romantic thing I've ever done'. His first published writing was an article on ancient armour; he would not at this stage have been amused by Bierce's definition of ARMOUR as 'the kind of clothing worn by a man whose tailor is a blacksmith'. But his first novels – *McTeague* (1899), *Vandover and the Brute* (1914, posthumously) and *Moran of the Lady Letty* (1898)[1] – bear many of the marks of Zolaesque naturalism. They abound in such adjectives as *vital, real, elemental, bestial*. Their characters are moulded by circumstance: creatures whose deepest instincts are animal, and who in moments of stress revert to brutishness. On the other hand Norris spoke of 'Romance' as something very different from sentimentality. In his usage 'Romance' embraced the 'wide world ..., and the unplumbed depths of the human heart, and the mystery of sex, ... and the black, unsearched penetralia of the soul of man'.

The alternating optimism and pessimism of the Darwinian literary attitude, plus an exoticism that links Norris with such men as Henry Harland, are to be seen in Norris's most ambitious effort, the uncompleted trilogy entitled *The Wheat*. The third part was never written; the second, a strong account of the Chicago wheat market, was published posthumously in 1903 as *The Pit*. The first part, *The Octopus* (1901), deals with the growing of wheat in California, and with the struggle between the farmers and the railroad which strangles them (hence the title). It rules their lives, dispossessing and killing those who stand in its way. The farmers band together to oppose it, but are beaten and ruined by the heartless machine. At the close of the book, a farmer's widow wanders the streets of San Francisco one foggy evening with her little daughter, penniless and starving. Her collapse and death are paired, in brief scenes, with an elaborate dinner party given in the same city, on the same evening, by one of the heads of the railroad.

All this is fiery radical writing. But it is robbed of some of its effect by a determinism especially noticeable in the later stages of the book, as in a curious conversation between a young poet and the president of the railroad, who easily convinces him (and is meant to convince the reader) that

1. Published in England as *Shanghaied*.

you are dealing with forces ... when you speak of Wheat and Railroads, not with men ... The Wheat is one force, the Railroad another, and there is the law that governs them – supply and demand. Men have little to do in the whole business.

However, Norris arrives at a benigner view, by celebrating the force of *growth*. He does this in a sub-plot of a mystical shepherd who, yearning for a lost love, discovers her again in the person of her daughter. There is, the shepherd concludes, no death; and, as on this human scale, so in a vaster way the immense fields of wheat prove the matter:

Untouched, unassailable, undefiled, that mighty world-force, that nourisher of nations, wrapped in a Nirvanic calm, indifferent to the human swarm, gigantic, resistless, moved onward in its appointed grooves....

Norris's rhetoric is not his strong suit, and to quote only from the more inflated passages in *The Octopus* does little justice to its narrative power. Though less gifted than Crane, he is still worth reading despite his doctrinaire confusion. Thus *The Pit*, like *The Octopus*, can be understood as an attempt to produce the 'Great American Novel' for which many people were calling in the 1890s. The Great American Novel had not yet appeared, according to critics. They were not sure what it would look like, or what it ought to look like. There was some agreement, however, that it must necessarily be long, detailed, truthful and uplifting. It must be conceived on a continental or even global scale, with a cast of thousands. In fact Norris's most effective novel, *McTeague*, was made into a movie 'epic' (*Greed*, 1924) by Erich von Stroheim, whose full version would have run for between eight and ten hours. McTeague, a dentist in San Francisco, is an inarticulate, amiably gross man who under stress degenerates into drunkenness and murder. Norris's novels anticipated by more than a decade the first huge enterprises of the motion-picture industry, such as D. W. Griffith's *Birth of a Nation* (1915) and *Intolerance* (1916), in being both dramatic and melodramatic, both grand and grandiose. Norris's plots were unsubtle, his philosophizings often crudely fatalistic. But he provided spectacle, combat, contrast, and 'passion' as that was to be interpreted in popular entertainment – namely as an impulse of well-nigh irresistible strength. Here is Norris's cinema-like treatment of the Chicago wheat market, from *The Pit*:

The trading would not begin for another half hour, but even now, the matter of the whirlpool, the growl of the Pit, was making itself felt.... From all over the immediate neighborhood they came, from ... hundreds of commission houses, from brokers' offices, from banks, from the tall, grey buildings of LaSalle Street.... And ... auxiliary currents set in from all the reach of the Great Northwest.... From the Southwest, St. Louis, Omaha, and Kansas City contributed to the volume. The Atlantic Seaboard, New York, and Boston and Philadelphia sent out their tributary streams; London, Liverpool, Paris, and Odessa merged influences.... The Pit was getting under way; the whirlpool was forming, and the sound of its courses was like the sound of the ocean in storm, heard at a distance.

Great American Novel? A big one, certainly. Some of the force of this particular extract has been lost through abbreviation. Some of Norris's effect depends, as with Whitman, upon enumeration. But where Whitman's lists are often lyrically evocative, Norris's tend to lapse into a kind of promotional brag, as in political oratory. Yet as with Whitman there is in Norris a likeable reaching-out, an urge to comprehend. This raises him above Henry B. Fuller (*The Cliff-Dwellers*, 1892; *With the Procession*, 1895) and Robert Herrick (*The Common Lot*, 1904; *Memoirs of an American Citizen*, 1905), two Chicago novelists who were intelligent and thoughtful, and wrote a more refined prose.

Norris died young, with much perhaps still to say. One suspects though that for most American authors of his generation, realism and naturalism created as many problems as they solved. At any rate the line of growth of realistic fiction was not straightforward. Commercial factors may have influenced Hamlin Garland to give up the effort to tell-the-truth-and-the-public-be-damned. Age, for Garland and others, may also have played a part; conservatism frequently accompanies greying hair. The possibility of having the best of both or all worlds is another consideration. Realism was sometimes equated with open-air life, as well as with the injunction to describe American scenery and speech. The most 'American' landscape was that of the West. Hence an inducement to write in the dialect of a Western state like Indiana, as Eggleston had patchily done in his *Hoosier School-Master*, and later in the *Hoosier Schoolboy* (1883). But the West was many wests, all in process of settlement and therefore of transformation into something very similar to the East. As literary material it was not easy to pin down. Mere geography – the Great Outdoors – was more inspiring to painters and poets than to novelists.

At any rate, the apparently promising realistic subject-matter of the West seemed to elude sustained pursuit, and to become sugar-coated. This happened for example to Maurice Thompson, whose *Hoosier Mosaics* (1875) contributed to the stock of 'Indiana novels' mentioned by Ambrose Bierce. Thompson's dialect sketches were greeted enthusiastically by Howells, who put work in Thompson's way. After some years, however,

Thompson turned on his champion with a shrill denunciation of naturalistic dogma. His own, and successful alternative was *Alice of Old Vincennes*
(1900), a historical novel of the Indiana (Wabash) frontier during the
War of Independence. *Alice* was 'realistic' in covering actual events, and
in portraying the heroine as a robust frontier girl, trained to ride and to
shoot, who has been brought up by a French backwoods trader. On the
other hand, she turns out to have been abducted in childhood from a
family of good stock; and this discovery makes her eligible to marry a
lieutenant who is both an officer and a gentleman. The result: a bestseller.

Similar compromises were arrived at by another popular Indiana writer,
Gene Stratton-Porter, who provided an additional success-ingredient in
the shape of adventurously winsome child characters (*Freckles*, 1904; *A
Girl of the Limberlost*, 1909). 'Freckles' is an orphan who has to fend for
himself. The plucky heroine of the second novel, a self-taught entomologist,
goes moth-hunting in the Limberlost swamp lands. But Freckles the
orphan proves to have a rich father, with whom he is reunited; and Nell
of the Limberlost, Freckles's comrade, collects on a commercial basis so as
to finance her future education. Such 'realism' became formulaic, and
respectable to a degree that must have dismayed Dean Howells.

Jack London, a Californian like Frank Norris, has even more energy,
and a greater narrative talent, together with some comparably ambivalent
attitudes to power and achievement. Friedrich Nietzsche, Karl Marx
and Herbert Spencer flavour his many novels and stories in a peculiar
vinaigrette. The Nordic peoples are on top, says London, and deservedly
so. They are the doers, the inventors, the warriors. 'Will the Indian, the
Negro, or the Mongol ever conquer the Teuton?' asks one of his characters.
'Surely not!' is the answer . . . 'All that the other races are not, the Anglo-
Saxon, or Teuton if you please, is.' Life is a struggle. The strong survive,
by natural selection; the weak go to the wall. This is the atavistic imperative
of *The Call of the Wild* (1903), in which a big dog returns to lead the wolf
pack from which his ancestors derived; and of *Before Adam* (1906), whose
narrator, in dreams, enters into the soul of a primitive forebear, Big Tooth.

On the other hand, London fictionally re-enacts the poverty, hardship,
and the education in socialism that characterized his own life as a boy and
young man along the wharfs of San Francisco bay and in the Klondike
gold rush of 1896. *People of the Abyss* (1903), indeed, recounts his actual
experiences among the down-and-outs of Edwardian England. London's
London is primarily the East End; the callousness of the rich West End
impresses him more than its historic splendours, *The Iron Heel* (1907), a

novel predicting a capitalistic revolution, has a protagonist with the unsubtle name of Ernest Everhard ('a superman, a blond beast such as Nietzsche described, and in addition he was aflame with democracy'). He is an idealized Jack London – big, handsome, eloquent, unconventional, a genius from out of the working class. Yet the novel expresses a passionate commitment by the superman to the underdog. Its harshness links *The Iron Heel* not with such relatively mild Utopian novels as *Looking Backward* and *Through the Eye of the Needle*, but rather with Ignatius Donnelly's *Caesar's Column* (1891). *Caesar's Column* was intended as a warning: society would go down in violent collapse if its abuses were not soon remedied. Donnelly and London both show a slightly sinister fascination with destruction on the grand scale. But *The Iron Heel* is less lurid and more consistently grim. Everhard is not so much a victor as a martyr, in an immensely protracted class-struggle.

Ambrose Bierce complained of a Jack London novel that it had 'a pretty bad style and no sense of proportion'. Yet it was 'a rattling good story in one way; something is "going on" all the time – not always what one would wish, but something'. This is a fair summary. The underlying 'philosophy' in London can be repellently crude. His racial theories seem crass in the extreme – for example, in 'The Unparalleled Invasion' (1914), a short story describing the annihilation of the entire Chinese population through bacterial warfare. One of London's pure-bred American toughs shows his dislike of a Latin American bullfight, in another story, by slaughtering several onlookers.

But there is something else in Jack London that transcends his *macho* attitudinizing. It is in part the quality to be found in the best of Ernest Hemingway: simplicity, dignity, courage. The consolations of life in the open air, above the snow-line or aboard a fishing boat, a long way from the cities; the desire to win through, the chances of defeat, the pathos of those unable to speak for themselves: these are the things London and Hemingway convey sometimes memorably. London's 'A Piece of Steak' (1911) is a fine picture of an ageing boxer, and *The Game* (1905) is an equally honest portrait of a young one. 'Told in the Drooling Ward' (1916) is a tender and perceptive glimpse of the world through the eyes of a mental defective.

Martin Eden (1909), a novel with a strong dose of autobiography, ends with the suicide of the hero, who has become weary of fame, wealth and love affairs after prior years of neglect. London himself was to commit suicide, like Hemingway, though at a considerably younger age. Both, it is clear, wanted to be recognized as important writers. Each, hating both 'society' and the general mass, tended to rid himself of other people in his fiction, by killing them off, or by making do with fewer and fewer characters, or by writing about non-humans, or by talking narcissistically about himself. Each wrote fantasies of war and destruction. Each had a genuine but incomplete involvement with radical political theory. London came an artistic cropper more often, because he wrote too fast, yet also because he was more willing to risk an image or a metaphor. Even in London's most slapdash performances there are signs of a poetic flair which he rarely allowed himself leisure to cultivate. To take one instance from a Yukon potboiler (*A Daughter of the Snows*, 1902), what could be more unexpected than this description of a man trapped by a wall of ice borne down a river in flood?:

The rainbow-wall curled up like a scroll, and in the convolutions of the scroll, like a bee in the many folds of a magnificent orchid, Tommy disappeared.

True, Tommy is a miserable coward. He deserves to die. But what an exquisite way to go.

In both London and Hemingway nobility of spirit was coupled with a curiously primitive intelligence. Each ultimately saw himself as a hunter, doomed to be hunted in his turn unless he acted first and took the decision into his own hands.

Howells had to work hard to convince himself and the public of the value of latter-day realism/naturalism. Perhaps Jack London's stress on red-blooded tribal instincts, or Norris's conscientious sexuality (for instance in *McTeague*) were honest and American. But realism had gone a long way from Howells's modest spectrum of virtue. Moral judgements had almost disappeared. Instead of good and bad, there were the weak and the strong. A few exceptional men might rise above circumstance: the majority were its slaves, women even more completely than men. Still, Norris was redeemed for Howells by his eager, sunny acquiescence; and there were vestiges of a moral code in London, who at any rate heartily approved of his strong men and despised his weaklings.

But Theodore Dreiser, whom Howells could not stomach, was another matter, as Norris enthusiastically recognized when he read Dreiser's first novel (*Sister Carrie*) for a publisher. The publisher, Frank Doubleday, backed away from his first acceptance, under pressure from his wife, and produced it so grudgingly that the small, unadvertised edition of 1900 was virtually suppressed. Though the book came out in England in 1901,

America had to wait another seven years to see it. Even then, Dreiser said, 'the outraged protests far outnumbered the plaudits'. Subsequent books were to meet with similar difficulties, so that Dreiser achieved no prominence as a novelist until the 1920s, by which time he was middle-aged. The question of his real ability was thus obscured, as in the case of James Branch Cabell's *Jurgen* (1919), by the question of his alleged obscenity; Mencken and his colleagues would defend the right of any book, however mediocre, to reach the public, and its unpopularity with their enemies became a criterion of its merit.

Sister Carrie was a naturalistic book in that it had the usual denominators. Carrie is a poor, pretty country girl who comes to Chicago, is tempted and seduced, by a commercial traveller and then by a restaurant manager. The first chapter is called 'The Magnet Attracting: A Waif Amid Forces'. Carrie cannot help herself; nor can her lovers, the second of whom ruins himself by stealing money and taking her to New York.

What upset Mrs Doubleday was the absence of a moral code. Carrie is passive, yet also resilient. She has a natural buoyancy, like a cork bobbing on water. She has vague regrets, but no anguished repentance. Retribution does not overtake her. She does not starve or lose her looks or become pregnant. She does not have to die, as the 'immoral' heroine does in Thomas Hardy's *Tess of the D'Urbervilles* (1891) or in Crane's *Maggie* (1893). There were a few precedents in European literature, notably *Esther Waters* (1894), by the Anglo-Irish writer George Moore. After an initial furore, Moore's novel had become something of a hit in London, with commendations from venerable arbiters such as William Ewart Gladstone. Esther is a servant girl who bears an illegitimate son and raises him to a reasonably proud manhood. But her tale was no true precedent for Dreiser. American firms had declined to publish *Esther Waters*. Scribner's professed to admire the book, but to confront an insuperable object in the 'plain-spokenness which our public finds objectionable and unnecessary'. In 1900 Dreiser was too plain-spoken, in his wordy ways, for America.

His philosophy, culled from Herbert Spencer and from determinist creeds, likewise failed at first to charm the American public. People are mere 'chemisms'; as Dreiser argues in *The Financier* (1912), 'We suffer for our temperaments, which we did not make, and for our weaknesses and lacks, which are no part of our willing or doing.' All of us crave affection and power; some men – notably the chief character in *The Financier* and *The Titan* (1914), its sequel – are innately powerful, but they are the exceptions: the vast majority are those who succumb to life's snares. This

Dreiser demonstrates at length, and with his customary mass of detail, in *An American Tragedy* (1925). The central character, a poor boy on the fringes of opulence, hopes to gain entry into the magic circle by getting rid of a girl whom he has made pregnant and who stands in his way. He is executed for a murder that he committed and yet did not commit, since the girl's death was in part accidental.

There is no suggestion here that Clyde Griffiths, the executed man, should have been acquitted. Dreiser does not know what should be done with him; he can only explain the awful absence of absolutes. Everybody and nobody is to blame. One thing is evident, for Dreiser: the moral and social codes of his America misrepresent the truths of human nature, and so does conventional fiction. Carrie is not punished for her immorality, as the contemporary reading public would have had her; like Dreiser's own sister, she is well treated by the man whose mistress she becomes. *Jennie Gerhardt* (1911), another 'fallen woman', behaves better than anyone else in the book.

There is considerable disagreement about Dreiser's stature as a novelist. His critics contend that he writes ponderously and pretentiously like the hack-journalist that for a long time he was, that his philosophy is elementary (even if he meant it to be elemental), and that his books are shapeless grey affairs. Irving Babbitt, while admitting that *An American Tragedy* is a harrowing novel, denies that it is a tragedy: 'We are harrowed to no purpose.' Lionel Trilling, in an essay on 'Reality in America',[1] maintains that Parrington and others have praised Dreiser's serious weaknesses because they have a false reverence for American authors who manage to seem not like men of letters.

Dreiser at his worst is certainly an abominable writer. 'Elephantine' has, as Charles C. Walcutt remarks, become almost a standard epithet to describe his style. Nor was he graceful in private life. His diaries, correspondence and memoirs, and reminiscences of those who knew him, reveal a person as unhandsome and undiscriminating as the typical characters in his fiction. Dreiser's novel *The 'Genius'* (1915) was withdrawn from publication when labelled obscene by the Society for the Prevention of Vice. Though their particular complaint now seems extravagant, it is hard to lament the book's near-demise. Eugene Witla, the main figure, arrives in Chicago as a naïve, good-looking youth from the small-town hinterland. He craves women, celebrity and 'culture', all of which he

1. Reprinted in Lionel Trilling, *The Liberal Imagination* (London, 1951).

associates with life in the metropolis. Dreiser also suggests that Witla has artistic talent that could amount to genius. A conflict is posited, though never made sharp, between money and art. Witla is successful as a magazine illustrator. This leads to a prosperous career in an advertising agency. But Witla also produces some oil paintings. They are apparently masterpieces, in a genre that intrigued Dreiser: that of the 'Ashcan School' or 'New York Realists'. The members of this group – Robert Henri, William Glackens, John Sloan, George Luks, Everett Shinn – specialized in bold, rough renderings of low-life scenes: boxers, wrestlers, music-halls, urban landscapes smeared with smoke and rain. No doubt Dreiser was aware that in 1907 the jury of the National Academy rejected some of the most ambitious canvases submitted by the Ashcan group. Great 'art' – his, Eugene's – offended people.

The theme is, however, fumbled and mislaid through scores of episodes during which Witla, a clumsily contrived authorial ego, goes up and down fortune's ladder. Towards the end the story focuses upon the death of Eugene's wife, and his own absorption in Christian Science. His life lacks shape; so does the novel, a pointless saga that is dreary to read. Words are misused ('pretentious' for 'ambitious', 'fearsome' for 'fearful'). Rooms that please Eugene are described in an utterly inappropriate vocabulary, as 'dainty', 'cosy', 'tasteful'.

This is the bad Dreiser, neither a primitive nor an aesthete, but a person of vagarious enthusiasms, sadly deficient in the coherence and unity which often lent authority to Ashcan paintings.

Dreiser's supporters, on the other hand, consider his clumsiness forgivable and even an asset. Dreiser – almost the first important American author not to have a British-sounding surname – is for them the first to catch the full atmosphere of 'modern' America. Europeans may study him: in fact, the English reviews of *Sister Carrie* were more sympathetic than the American ones. Nevertheless, only Americans, it is suggested, can fully share his intimation that it is all, so to speak, in the family. Most of what he chronicled *had* happened to his family – his tolerant mother and humourless father, his wayward sisters, his affable brother Paul. Paul wrote popular songs, the best-known of which ('On the Banks of the Wabash') Theodore Dreiser sometimes claimed to have given to Paul. The Dreisers were yet another Indiana product, or export.

Dreiser's native land *is* ungainly, indelicate, forlorn, rapacious, hyperactive. He gives American readers a relief from good manners, from the fatiguing sense imposed on them by European literature, of being among strangers: strangers who make them feel uncouth, who miss their jokes, who throw them back on to the conviction that though their pattern of life may be without pedigree, it is not to be derided. Dreiser exemplifies the complex, undeniable pattern: the maze of streets, fields, woods, rivers, railroads, stores, hotels, salons, noises, temperatures, appointments, songs, accents.

He is 'modern' – and this although his techniques often appear 'dated' and near-absurd, as do those of the cinema pioneers. This can perhaps best be grasped from his first novel, which he began to write at someone else's prompting, without forethought – at least as he remembered the inception of *Sister Carrie*. He set down the name on a sheet of paper: on the face of it not even a suitable name for what followed, since Carrie Meeber escapes from sisterly ties as soon as possible. The story flowed, with remarkable economy in its first pages, and with less subsequent turgidity than in later Dreiser novels. He had found his major theme: the dwarfing of human lives by an essentially inhuman, city environment.

Dreiser was of course not completely original: no one is. His greatest literary ancestor was the French novelist Honoré de Balzac, for whom Paris furnished the equivalent lure to Dreiser's Chicago and Manhattan. He acknowledged the indebtedness by having Carrie read Balzac's *Père Goriot* towards the end of her story. What Dreiser felt with fresh force, however, was the significance of the very absence of close personal relationships in American life – and this despite his continuing ties with his own kin. Family, religion, patriotism: none of the traditional bonds counts for much. Carrie and the men in her life obey the promptings of appetite. Chicago, for them and for Dreiser, connotes money, cultivation, power, sex, in one amalgamated aphrodisiac. This is a consumer society; almost every appetite can be satisfied at a price; and this satisfaction can be a kind of happiness. Mecca is Gomorrah, and vice versa. In place of old-time ethical rules, Dreiser's characters obey the practical, half-cynical wisdom embodied in the slogans of the street (*it's not what you know, it's who you know; the way to get along is to go along*).

The outcome is not admirable behaviour, but it is 'real' behaviour as most people recognize it, and presented with circumstantial weight in *Sister Carrie* and parts of other Dreiser novels. It has the neutral, leaden authenticity of the transcript of a trial, or of effective documentary journalism of the period (by Stephen Crane, for instance, and occasionally by Dreiser himself). Dreiser, in company with Norris and London, is bad when he indulges in superman fantasies, attempting to create 'big' characters (Witla; Cowperwood in *The Financier* and *The Titan*). When he loses objectivity he can lapse into silly displays of surrogate egotism – or into bar-room grossness, as in his many diary-references to sexual encounters. He calls them 'rounds', as if in boxing or golf.

Ultimately Dreiser is a paradox. His novels are often as formless as life itself, and therefore tedious. They tell of an America that Howells perhaps unconsciously set out to discover when he quit Boston for New York. The philanthropic, amiable Howells did not like what he began to find. The philandering, saturnine Dreiser took the national saturnalia more or less for granted.

Dreiser is not an altogether satisfactory figure on which to conclude a discussion of American realism. His work is, for example, difficult to place chronologically. *An American Tragedy* (1925), published in the same year as *The Great Gatsby*, relates to a murder case of 1906, on which Dreiser had accumulated clippings; but he had followed other cases during the 1890s. His last novel, *The Bulwark* (1946, posthumously) was equally long in gestation. Nor did Dreiser's ideological development keep in step with the times. He joined the Communist party at the very end of his life, years after the vogue for such conversions was over. By 1945, when Dreiser died, a great deal of realistic American fiction was in print that had not been significantly influenced by him. To Hemingway or Sinclair Lewis or John Steinbeck, Dreiser would have appeared old-fashioned.

Nevertheless, he plays a not insignificant part in the incarnations of realism, even if only a part. The whole history indeed is paradoxical. The demand for accurate delineations of *American* life antedated Dreiser, or Howells for that matter, and has persisted. Realism/naturalism is an enduring alternative to the opposite American tradition of symbolism. Yet it eludes precise definition. Complete objectivity is unattainable, and perhaps undesirable. The decision to devote one's fiction to extreme poverty would imply a preferential allegiance comparable to Howells's one-time concern with the middle-class average.

Moreover, reality can be private and psychological. If external existence is shapeless, the same can be said of internal thought processes. Experimental fiction was to become fascinated with stream-of-consciousness narration which represented a totally different perception of reality from that of the photographic recorders. In fact, the camera proved to be an excellent instrument for producing illusions. 'Motion pictures' were themselves an ingenious illusion. The 'logic of reality' can, as Malcolm Bradbury notes with reference to Stephen Crane, lead to an awareness of the world's fundamental *un*reality. 'It looked a wrong place to be a battlefield' is a reflection in Crane's *Red Badge of Courage* – prompting us also to wonder whether any place could be a suitable setting for a battle.[1] The illusionist Houdini, who specialized in miraculous escapes from padlocked milk cans and submerged crates, was only a couple of years younger than Dreiser, and the son of a Wisconsin clergyman named Weiss who (said Houdini) 'awoke one morning to find himself thrown upon the world ... with seven children to feed, ... and without any visible means of support. We thereon moved to Milwaukee, where such hardships and hunger became our lot that the less said on the subject, the better.'[2] He and Dreiser came from similar backgrounds, and in their respective fashions built careers upon early deprivation. For Houdini's brilliant magic, too, was achieved 'without any visible means'. In these ways, realism and naturalism were but stages in a debate still being carried on as to the connection between truth and fiction, art and artifice.

1. Malcolm Bradbury, 'Romance and Reality in *Maggie*', *Journal of American Studies* 3 (July 1969), 111–21; and see Bradbury, ' "Years of the Modern": The Rise of Realism and Naturalism', in Marcus Cunliffe, ed., *American Literature to 1900* (London, Barrie and Jenkins, 1973; Sphere Books, 1975; revised edn., 1986).

2. Walter B. Gibson and Morris N. Young, *Houdini's Fabulous Magic* (New York, Barnes and Noble, 1977), 196.

THE COSMOPOLITANS
James, Wharton, Adams, Stein

HENRY JAMES (1843–1916)

Born in New York, and educated privately by tutors and in Europe (1855–8) as well as in the resort town of Newport, Rhode Island. He studied law at Harvard, but abandoned this project in order to write critical articles and pieces of fiction, travelling frequently between Europe and his home in Cambridge, Massachusetts. From 1875 to the end of his life he lived in Europe, making two visits to the U.S. in the early 1880s and another – to furnish material for a commissioned travel book – in 1904–5. From 1889 to 1895 he was largely engrossed in the theatre; otherwise, his energies were concentrated chiefly upon fiction, though of all his writing perhaps only *Daisy Miller* (1879) excited the general public. His last visit to America was made in 1910–11. At the outbreak of the First World War, greatly stirred, he moved from his Sussex home to London, to assist in war work. He became a British citizen in 1915, and just before his death was awarded the Order of Merit.

EDITH NEWBOLD JONES WHARTON (1862–1937)

Born in New York, into a socially distinguished family, she was educated expensively at home and in Europe, before making an appropriate marriage. As she struggled to become a writer, her social situation grew increasingly irksome; and after 1910 she lived chiefly in France (gaining a divorce from her invalid husband in 1913). She travelled frequently and produced a steady flow of novels, short stories and works of elegant tourism. During the First World War she devoted herself wholeheartedly to relief work in France. *The Age of Innocence* (1920) brought her a Pulitzer prize and a fame she had not up until then known.

HENRY ADAMS (1838–1918)

Raised in the vicinity of Boston, Adams was educated at Harvard and in Germany. During the Civil War he lived in England, where his father was American minister and employed Henry as secretary. After writing a number of careful articles, he abandoned his vague ambition of a political career, and left Washington for Harvard (1870–77), where he was professor of history and edited the *North American Review*. He lived again in Washington, having married Marian Hooper in 1872, but after her suicide in 1885 he became increasingly restless, and travelled all over the world, returning to Washington intermittently, and keeping in touch with his friends through a voluminous correspondence.

GERTRUDE STEIN (1874–1946)

Born in Pittsburgh, of well-to-do German-Jewish stock, she was educated in California, in Europe, at Radcliffe (adjacent to Harvard), and at Johns Hopkins (Baltimore). Quitting her formal studies, she followed her brother Leo to Paris in 1902 and made it her permanent home, establishing a famous *salon* and writing steadily, though not always achieving publication. Her books include *Tender Buttons* (1914); *Geography and Plays* (1922); *The Making of Americans* (1925); *Lucy Church Amiably* (1930), a novel; *The Autobiography of Alice B. Toklas* (1933); *Four Saints in Three Acts* (1934), an opera libretto for the music of Virgil Thomson; *Picasso* (1938); *Paris France* (1940); and *Wars I Have Seen* (1945).

EZRA POUND (1885–1972)

Born in Idaho and educated in the eastern U.S., Pound was already set upon a literary career when he made his way to Italy and there quickly published his first poetry (*A Lume Spento*, 1908). As an aspiring scholar, he also intended to work on a doctoral thesis. His next books of poetry – scholarly, evocative, nostalgic yet 'modern' – dealt in part with medieval Provence, so as to establish a contrasting environment to that of modern times. He also for a while became an Imagist (or *Imagiste*) poet, and then a Vorticist. During these years he lived mainly in London, until he went to Paris (1920) and then to a permanent residence in Rapallo, Italy (1924). He befriended and promoted several artists and writers, including T. S. Eliot; corresponded vigorously with the editors of *Poetry* and *The Little Review*; poured out prose and verse; and began the publication of his vast serial poem, the *Cantos*, starting (1925) with *A Draft of XVI Cantos*. The idiosyncratic 'Jeffersonian Republicanism' expounded in these led Pound to proclaim his support for Mussolini's Fascist Italy, and to make broadcasts from wartime Italy. After the Allied victory (1945), he was charged with treason. Deemed insane (a verdict both charitable and dubious), he was confined to St Elizabeth's Hospital in Washington D.C. He continued to add to his *Cantos*. On release (1958) he returned to Italy, where he died.

THOMAS STEARNS ELIOT (1888–1965)

Born in St Louis, Missouri, the grandson of a New England Unitarian minister; educated at Harvard (1906–10, 1911–14) with an interlude in Paris. After further postgraduate research in Oxford, Eliot combined the writing of poetry and critical essays with employment in Lloyds Bank (to 1925), and then as a publisher (with Faber and Gwyer). His first book of poems, *Prufrock and Other Observations* (1917), was followed by more poetry, *The Sacred Wood* (essays, 1920), editorship of *The Criterion* (1922–9), and a volume of collected *Poems* (1925) that included 'The Waste Land'. In 1927 he became a British citizen and a full member of the (Episcopalian) Church of England. He returned to the U.S. in 1932–4, but otherwise made his home in London. Long fascinated by the theatre, he wrote a number of well-received verse plays (*Murder in the Cathedral*, 1935; *The Family Reunion*, 1939; *The Cocktail Party*, 1950). Among other 'Eliotic' work was *Old Possum's Book of Practical Cats* (1939) and the *Four Quartets* (1943). He was awarded the Nobel prize for literature in 1948.

X

THE COSMOPOLITANS

IN a letter of 1785 Thomas Jefferson expressed confidence that 'while we shall see multiplied instances of Europeans going to live in America, . . . no man living will ever see an instance of an American removing to settle in Europe, and continuing there'. This was already untrue of American painters. Benjamin West, having arrived in Italy in 1759, reached London four years later and remained there until his death in 1820. John Singleton Copley of Boston reached London in 1775 and stayed for forty years. Gilbert Stuart lived in England through the 1780s. John Trumbull, Robert Fulton and Patience Wright the 'wax sculptor' were other Americans who became familiar figures in the London art world. The list was to be greatly augmented during the nineteenth century. James McNeill Whistler and John Singer Sargent were probably better known in Europe than in their own country. The impressionist painter Mary Cassatt (1845–1926), daughter of a Philadelphia banker, established herself in Paris in 1874 as a permanent resident. In Rome and Florence, 'Yankee stone cutters' such as Horatio Greenough, Hiram Powers, Thomas Crawford and William Wetmore Story mingled with British and with other American artists and writers. Washington Allston produced a fictional account of American painters in Italy (*Monaldi*, published 1841 though written twenty years earlier). Hawthorne, collecting material for his novel *The Marble Faun* (published in England as *Transformation*), made dutiful notes on his impression of American artists' studios.

Authors as well as artists, then, streamed across the Atlantic. Irving and Cooper were among those who stayed so long that they risked alienating their American public. Jefferson's prediction was in part a declaration of patriotic pride, tinged with chauvinism (and in particular with anglophobia: he was more tolerant of French cultural styles). Up to about the Civil War, however, his forecast was on the whole to prove not absurdly sanguine.

During the early stages of independence various transfers of allegiance were still at the halfway stage. Copley's family was from Dublin; he chose the United States for his nation and London for his milieu. Washington

Irving's family still belonged on both sides of the Atlantic; an elder brother had been born in Scotland. When Irving lived in London one of his closest friends was the painter Charles R. Leslie, an American by nationality but born in England, and at home there by upbringing and temperament. In 1829 William Cullen Bryant addressed a poem to Thomas Cole, 'the Painter, Departing for Europe':

> Thine eyes shall see the light of distant skies;
> Yet, COLE! thy heart shall bear to Europe's strand
> A living image of our own bright land,
> Such as upon thy glorious canvas lies....

Cole, said Bryant, would gaze upon different, 'European' scenes. The poet begged his friend to keep his 'earlier, wilder image bright' and not to lose his essential recollection of America. These well-known lines contain a less well-known oddity: Cole (1801–48) was in fact a European, or more precisely an Englishman, accustomed to the moorland scenery of the north, who only came to the United States in 1819. Was his 'earlier, wilder image' American or British?

Again, there were obvious practical reasons why Americans should live in Europe. Painters, sculptors and musicians could derive important benefits, of the kind that impelled Europeans to base themselves in the respective centres of excellence. The availability of fine marble, of apprentice carvers, and skilled bronze-founders, that lured a Crawford or a Story to Rome also attracted the Danish sculptor Thorwaldsen. Cheapness of living could be an important consideration, not merely for artists and writers but for any people whose sophistication exceeded their income. Such was the case with the *rentier* parents of Edith Wharton (*née* Jones), who took her to Europe for six childhood years, partly in order to economize. Some Americans went abroad as journalists: the novelist Harold Frederic was London correspondent of the *New York Times*. Some were employed as editors and magazinists – positions that enabled Ambrose Bierce to extend his 1872 honeymoon trip to London to a four-year professional involvement. Numbers of Americans, as we have noted, secured consular and diplomatic posts.

Concern over copyright was another factor. Although the law and its interpretation varied during the nineteenth century, American authors could usually gain some protection against piratical British publishers by arranging for first publication in the United Kingdom, and sometimes by establishing residence there at the time of publication. As a result a good many American books, such as the early work of Herman Melville, were published in Britain before they appeared in the United States; and from Irving onwards, American writers were induced to consider living in Europe, at least intermittently, in the hope of safeguarding their revenues.

Others crossed the ocean to attend conferences, synods and reform gatherings; to give lectures; to gather material for travel books; to make cultural pilgrimages (for example, to the scenes of Sir Walter Scott's poems and tales); as celebrities (like Harriet Beecher Stowe); to attend foreign universities; or simply because, with the advent of steamships and railroads, travel grew cheaper, quicker and safer. Mark Twain made some thirty Atlantic crossings, for short or extended visits to Europe. On Bryant's sixth trip to Europe, in 1866, he reported that Rome, with more than two thousand American tourists, had become almost a 'Yankee city'. It is easier to list the American literary figures who did *not* go to Europe – Thoreau, Whittier, Whitman, Emily Dickinson – than the scores who *did*. The great majority, of course, were tourists or temporary visitors. Of those who stayed on, most retained a pride in the United States that brought them together for Fourth of July celebrations. The song 'Home, Sweet Home', written in Paris in the 1820s by the American expatriate John Howard Payne (1791–1852), can be regarded as an expression of poignant homesickness:

> 'Mid pleasure and palaces though we may roam,
> Be it ever so humble, there's no place like home.

Hawthorne called England *Our Old Home*, but his book of that name (1863) displayed no undue anglophilia. 'Not an Englishman of them all', Hawthorne said in his preface, 'ever spared America for courtesy's sake'; it would not 'contribute in the least if we were to besmear each other all over with butter and honey'.

Even after the Civil War, for the vast majority a spell in Europe implied no 'disloyalty'. Travel was largely a function of national wealth; and the fact that 90,000 tourists returned through the New York customs in 1891 was proof, above all, that America was now a rich country. What could be more natural than that she should spread herself: that she should scoop in art treasures, titled husbands, grouse moors, Loire châteaux? Or that some of her writers should join the Sargents and Whistlers who sought 'atmosphere' by living abroad? Those who lingered long in Europe were often cosmopolitan in their origins. Henry Harland, for example, was born of American parents in St Petersburg, and lived in Rome and Paris before going to the United States. Henry James had been a 'hotel child' in Europe. Francis Marion Crawford (1852–1920), the son of the sculptor Thomas Crawford, lived with his mother in Italy after his father's early death, had a French governess, and pursued his language studies in England, Germany, Italy, India and even at Harvard. Howard Sturgis (1855–1920), the author of *Belchamber* (1904), had New England parents but was born in London and spent most of his life abroad. Stuart Merrill (1863–1915), raised in Europe, domiciled himself in France and wrote mainly in French. If British authors such as Landor or the Brownings could settle themselves in foreign countries without incurring criticism, why should Americans meet with rebuke? Why should Theodore Roosevelt describe Henry James as a 'miserable little snob'?[1]

Such criticism was often crass. Perhaps it concealed innuendoes as to the 'effeminacy' of people who affected English accents and pretended to like poetry or ballet. What it also indicated was the recurrence of a test of Americanism, or a fear of insufficient revolutionary ardour, voiced as far back as 1776 by Thomas Paine. In *Common Sense* Paine categorized the types of colonist who were hesitant about breaking away from Britain:

Interested men, who are not to be trusted; weak men, who cannot see; prejudiced men, who will not see; and a certain set of moderate men, who think better of the European world than it deserves: and this last class, by an ill-judged deliberation, will be the cause of more calamities to this continent than all the other three.

That this last class still existed, and might even be more insidiously harmful than before, was a recurrent suspicion, a fear of defection voiced with new anger as the nineteenth century prepared to yield to the twentieth. By the 1920s expatriation had become a gesture so characteristic of American writers that Matthew Josephson, himself an example of the phenomenon, asked (*Portrait of the Artist as American*, 1930):

Is the emigration of intelligence to become an issue as absorbing as the immigration of strong muscle? With a greater frequency than ever our *illuminati* buy tickets for a more possible world, for a more breathable air.

And in the popular mind, to elect to live in Europe was to associate oneself with a curious amalgam of class-distinction, loose moral conduct, and ultra-radical political and economic programmes.

Such crude formulations hardly begin to explain that prodigiously gifted

---

1. James for his part once described Roosevelt as 'the mere monstrous embodiment of unprecedented resounding Noise'.

author Henry James. His almost equally perceptive brother William, the Harvard psychologist and philosopher, wrote to their sister Alice in 1889, that Henry's 'anglicisms are but "protective resemblances" – he's really, I won't say a Yankee, but a member of the James family, and has no other country'. Henry belonged to a uniquely articulate, sensitive and lively-minded family. Henry James Senior encouraged his children to be serious but not lugubrious, to be ambitious but unworldly: to endeavour according to individual light, trimmed by the friendly yet ruthless advice of the rest of the family. The result was exhilarating and even ennobling. It also imposed a pressure that revealed itself in the curious ailments which beset the children. These ailments, certainly in the cases of William and Henry, had something to do with their impulsion to excel, coupled with a difficulty in determining the desirable field of activity. Once they had chosen, family disposition bound them to unremitting effort.

In Henry's case, the choice was for literature. To begin with, he applied himself to the idea of realism; like his friend Howells, who invited him into the pages of the *Atlantic*, James thought of fiction as an art, with its own exacting forms and standards, not merely as a piece of narrative, still less as a disguised sermon. The line of the novel, Howells later said of James, ran to him from Hawthorne and George Eliot, not through the untidy though fascinating work of Thackeray and Dickens. This was to be a literature that aimed at psychological truth, conveyed with economy and precision.

It was natural that he should go to Paris to study his art in company with Turgenev (a Russian specimen of the expatriate), Zola, Daudet, Flaubert and the Goncourts. Despite their 'ferocious pessimism and their handling of unclean things', he had the deepest regard for their 'truly infernal intelligence' and honesty. Yet Paris left him unsatisfied: he sought for a form of society on which to focus his theories of fiction.

America would not do in this respect. James recognized that it might do for others: he admired Howells for making the most of the material to hand. But in his own view Americans in America were not enough. Too much was missing, as he explained in his book on Hawthorne; defending the book to Howells, he accepted as a truism 'the idea that it takes an old civilization to set a novelist in motion'. 'It is', he continued, 'on manners, customs, usages, habits, forms, upon all these things matured and established, that a novelist lives – they are the very stuff his work is made of.' He did not mean (though many of his irritated compatriots judged otherwise) that without aristocratic institutions a country could have no culture. He did mean that, as far as he was concerned, his writings had to be anchored in Europe. It was a matter of preferring the larger to the lesser view. Though a European might ignore America, an American must take Europe into account. How could a man 'who has the passion of observation and whose business is the study of human life' fail to opt for Europe-and-America, and be content with the meagreness of America alone?

When he had made up his mind, with deliberation, he settled in England. London was 'the biggest aggregation of human life – the most complete compendium of the world'. Like the English social scene as a whole, it had perspectives that the Continent seemed to lack. This is not to say that he was blind to the defects of Europe, or to the virtues of his own land. Like Howells he started with the notion, which he never entirely abandoned, that America was more innocent than Europe. If purity were the only thing at stake America won hands down. As a novelist, however, he had to show purity – which he valued very highly, in all its aspects – assailed and even overborne, by temptation, by greater sophistication, by cruelties and complexities of old-established social orders.

It is nevertheless the purity that he exalts and loves, even while he points to its downfall. His heroes and heroines seek perfection, as James sought it in his style, in his technique, and in the life about him. Like other Americans before and since, he conceived of an ideal and believed that it existed, or should exist. In America he found ideal aims suspended in a void. In Paris he found artistic integrity, in Italy a wonderful outward beauty of building and landscape, in England a system of society defined with an assumption of finality. But all of these were in some measure inadequate. The Continent was crumbling and corrupt; much of English life was 'grossly materialistic', and 'the British country-house' had 'at moments, for a cosmopolitanised American, an insuperable flatness'.

Even so, the conjunction of America and Europe gave James a rewarding theme. *Roderick Hudson*, his earliest real novel (1876), deals with the disintegration of a young American sculptor in Italy – a subject that Hawthorne, his predecessor in several ways, had handled with less assurance in *The Marble Faun*. In *The American* (1877), a finer study than *Roderick Hudson*, an American is confronted by Parisian society; Christopher Newman, a millionaire (and surely one of the most sympathetic pictures in literature of a *nouveau riche*), comes to Europe to seek its best, including a bride. He finds one, but loses her when her family decides that the connection would be ignoble. Newman, with a purity as genuine as theirs is perverted, renounces a chance to revenge himself, and quits Europe.

In *The Portrait of a Lady* (1881), one of James's greatest novels, he again explores the theme of an American's quest in Europe. Isabel Archer, a handsome and an intelligent girl, arrives in Europe as the ward of a rich aunt. An English suitor, Lord Warburton, proposes to her, but his advantages – name, appearance, kindness, an ancestral home – are not enough; she is able to refuse him in the assurance that something hardly to be defined, but far far better, awaits her. (It is the Emersonian attitude again: 'the nonchalance of boys who are sure of a dinner', which Emerson once spoke of as the 'healthy' response to human existence). Thinking that she has found her perfect person in Osmond, a cultivated man of American origins, she marries him – to discover by painful stages that he is a heartless snob who has taken her for her money. The only fine gesture possible is to accept her fate with dignity, which she does. The 'international theme' is handled here with great subtlety. James hints that his heroine's demands on life are inordinate, and that she is somewhat to blame for her own misfortune. But the Europe–America antithesis still holds. Whatever the minor faults of Isabel, her friend Henrietta, her admirer Goodwood, or of the others who are wholly American, they are *good* people; and the Americans who are not good – Osmond, Madame Merle – have been contaminated by Europe.

Perhaps we can detect a slightly irritated European reaction in an 1883 letter to an American friend from Max Müller, an Oxford orientalist in search of good current fiction. Which, he inquires, is the best of William Dean Howells's novels? He adds, possibly with James in mind: 'I want description of real American life – not that constant theme of American novels – international episodes – metamorphic confusions produced by American volcanoes breaking through the smooth and hard stratification of European society.' The Jamesian preference for 'international episodes' is, however, not a question of chauvinism, but rather a frame of reference that he is able to invest with vast significance. The fruit is eaten, the Eden so confidently glimpsed disappears among dark shadows. Virtue must be its own reward, for there is no other.

The international theme, though valuable to James, is not his only one. In the poignant novel *Washington Square* (1881) he is concerned with Americans in New York; the heroine rejects the chance of escape from an oppressive life as dutifully as Isabel Archer, if with less initial sensibility. In *The Bostonians* (1886), where he is again dealing with his own country, his reservations about America enter the very region in which America seems to him so much finer than Europe: the realm, that is, of illimitable hopes, especially those cherished by women. Women are important for James, as for Howells and Henry Adams; to a great extent he shared the belief of certain contemporaries that the American woman was superior to the male, in courage as well as in refinement. Yet in *The Bostonians* he attacks the American woman *qua* reformer (in this instance as advocate of women's rights) because he dislikes the shallow perfectionism of such movements and because they threaten 'the masculine character, the ability to dare and endure, to know and yet not fear reality, to look the world in the face and take it for what it is – a very queer and partly very base mixture'. These words may be taken as representative of James himself, with his constant injunction to live to the utmost, though in the book they are spoken by Basil Ransom. Ransom is a Southerner, and James opposes his conservatism to the arid radicalism of Boston. However, Ransom's ideas are vitiated by the 'false pride', the 'thread of moral tinsel' that runs through the Southern fabric; and though the novel ends with Ransom winning a Boston girl, James will concede them little likelihood of happiness together: perhaps one is too innocent, and the other too jaded.

It can be debated whether this ending, in which James so typically resists the reader's expectations, is a sign of genius or of an exasperating impalpability. There are indications in this novel, at any rate, that James was by now at one remove from American subjects. Its combination of light satire and sober criticism is not quite fused; he is remembering, improvising, theorizing. *The Princess Casamassima* (also 1886), a study of revolutionary or anarchist stirrings in London, as perceived by the dreamily sensitive Hyacinth Robinson, is a richer and more deeply felt book, with many flashes of James's gift for empathetic analysis. At one point, for example, Robinson feels 'the monstrosity of the great ulcers and sores of London – the sick, eternal misery crying, in the darkness, in vain, confronted with granaries and treasure-houses and palaces of delight where shameless satiety kept guard'. As a contrast to this almost preacher-like denunciation, we see young Robinson, who has been selected to commit an assassination, overtaken during a trip to Paris by 'a kind of desolation – a sense of everything that might hold one to the world, of the sweetness of not dying, the fascination of great cities, the charm of travel and discovery, the generosity of admiration. . . .'

Europe seems to have more 'reality' for James, and in most of his subsequent works Europe is the stage. America remains a convenient point of reference, a place to which characters may depart (as do Peter and Biddy Sherringham in *The Tragic Muse*, 1890), or from which they may arrive (as do Milly Theale in *The Wings of the Dove*, 1902, and Maggie Verver in *The Golden Bowl*, 1904), bringing with them America's special ambience. But the *mise-en-scène* is Europe, and was to remain Europe – if we except James's travel book, *The American Scene* (1907) – until his death. It was once fashionable to explain James as an exile whose work lost its firmness in proportion as his memory of the homeland grew indistinct. It is true that his writing became increasingly complex, but there is no need to suppose that he had lost his way. Indeed, he is unique among American authors, and rare in any group of writers, for a brilliance sustained through half a century. Nor does his comment upon America suggest a hopeless hankering after an actual country. On the contrary: *The American Scene* is clear evidence that he would not have known what to do with America as fictional material; while his short story 'The Jolly Corner' projects a horrifying vision of another James who stayed behind, to become evil. Rather, he depended on America for one element of his dialectic. It was the land of miracle from which might emerge princesses like Milly Theale, in the image of his own dead cousin, Minny Temple, whom he adored. James searched throughout his life for a literary equivalent to the James Family: if he could retrieve a simulacrum of family ties among European society, he had to present this society as more advanced than he knew it to be; and he still had to bring to it from an *imagined* America the spirituality of Minny Temple, or for that matter of his closer relatives.

As he grew older James had more and more, not less and less, to say. He became lonelier not because he lost touch with the United States, but because he lost touch with his audience, never large and never predominantly American. Attempts to find an audience through the medium of the London theatre ended in severe disappointment; brilliantly imagined novels like *The Princess Casamassima* received scant praise; and though he never faltered in his attachment to literature, he did reveal his perturbation in a number of stories about the isolation of the artist which recall Hawthorne's insights into the same theme. 'The Madonna of the Future' (1879) relates the failure of an American painter in Rome, who dreams so absorbedly of a masterpiece that he accomplishes nothing, and dies as obscurely as he has lived. In other stories James is concerned more directly with a writer such as himself – mature, dedicated, and known only to a few disciples amid the general indifference or hostility. This is the fate of 'The Author of "Beltraffio" ' (1884), and of the dying Dencombe in 'The Middle Years' (1895) – a title that James took later for a fragment of autobiography – who declares:

We work in the dark – we do what we can – we give what we have. Our doubt is our passion and our passion is our task. The rest is the madness of art.

His Oxford honorary D.Litt. citation called James *fecundissimus et facundissimus scriptor* – most prolific and most eloquent. He left behind him a steadily amassed *œuvre* of short stories, *nouvelles*, articles, plays, travel books, memoirs and novels, including two long unfinished works (*The Ivory Tower* and *The Sense of the Past*), that represents, in effort alone, an achievement of the most solid order. The additions and prefaces of the comprehensively revised 'New York' edition (24 vols., 1907–9) are in themselves a considerable labour, and yet another proof of James's unsparing devotion to his art. From comparative neglect, his reputation has soared.

But in his lifetime many thought him unreadable, or so comical as to excite parody (such as Max Beerbohm's 'Mote in the Middle Distance'). H. G. Wells, in *Boon*, likened Jamesian prose to a hippopotamus pushing a pea. His brother William found Henry's late or 'third manner' increasingly elaborate and pictured an exasperated reader protesting, 'Say it *out*, for God's sake, and have done with it.' His writing indeed still presents difficulties. The famous style of his latter years is perplexing not merely because it is the vehicle of intricate ideas and perceptions, but also as an arrangement of words. Often James's sentences are peculiarly opaque when there seems no reason why they should be. Here is one, from *The Wings of the Dove*:

It was wonderful for Milly how just to put it so made all its pieces fall at present quite properly into places.

A short sentence, with simple words. Yet the adverbial qualifications – *at present*, *quite properly* – clog it; and the unexpected *places*, instead of *place*, adds to one's faint bafflement. When we encounter thousands of such sentences, the effect is dazing, especially since James makes other heavy demands upon the reader. His themes are important, and clear: H. G. Wells complained that they are too clear, and too obtrusive. But in James's later work they are developed to a formidable degree of virtuosity. It is as though the reader is being escorted through a long art gallery by a companion whose interest in the exhibits is far more discriminating and enthusiastic, and whose scrutiny of each is therefore more prolonged and more exacting. Such companionship is improving; it is also tiring, and a little shaming. The spectator feels exposed to a test of sensibility, and tends either to exaggerate his or her appreciation, or else to withdraw in a huff. The most devoted admirer may occasionally long for the pace to be quicker, even if more superficial.

The problem does not always lie in the prose, or in the page-by-page narrative. James was usually a consummate stylist and an accurate observer, with a highly developed pictorial talent. There are felicities and sharpnesses on every page that remind us of his intention to be truthful, precise and even concise. Sometimes, especially in the later tales, one is troubled by James's carefully contrived narrative method, which often depends upon the introduction of a character–observer, someone *not* the author and *not* omniscient. The method is ingenious and has been used by many writers (for instance, in Scott Fitzgerald's *The Great Gatsby*, 1925). The snag in James is that this person tends to seem ineffectual, unconvincingly dedicated to the well-being of others, and almost pruriently inquisitive. In *The Golden Bowl*, Fanny Assingham and her pipe-puffing husband appear basically a pair of snoops.

Again, as Max Müller's reaction may suggest, Jamesian refinement can apparently rest upon a curious diagram of competing sensibilities and sets of virtue, in which the high score of one party is always being overtopped by the other. In part this is the 'international' theme, which tempts James to invoke hypersensitive dandified standards of conduct. Like other Americans, only more so, he protects himself against affront by out-gentrifying the gentry. He expects a degree of fineness that almost no one and nothing can attain. Such an attitude can lapse into preposterous pretension. Yet as T. S. Eliot recognized in writing on Henry James in 1918: 'It is the ... consummation of an American to become, not an Englishman, but a European – something which no born European, no person of any European nationality, can become.' Henry James aspired to such a condition – an exalted one.

Another valid comment is that James is not primarily a moralist or a thinker: he is a writer for whom the truth of art and the truth of life are the same thing. His characters' search for meanings in life is equated with the artist's creative processes. Both, for James, have their climax at fleeting, mysterious (though schemed-for) *moments* which constitute what he calls experience. His equation is of great interest and validity to other professionals, since it resembles their own viewpoint. But to the general reader (the *mostpeople* of E. E. Cummings's rather truculent coinage) the Jamesian 'passion' may seem precious. Just as he does not mean by passion what mostpeople mean, so his moments of 'experience' are often *not* experience as mostpeople think of it.

At any rate, in some of James's fiction motive seems to smother event, and the event when it does come – though sometimes in a magnificently explosive moment – is liable to disappoint because of its ambiguity and indirectness. Characters reach out to one another with the most delicate of antennae: something passes between them, beyond words: the reader thinks he understands, but he would give anything to *know*. What *was* 'the figure in the carpet'? What *was* Milly Theale's ailment? James will not tell. His refusal is deliberate; his obscurity has nothing to do with incompetence. It is a matter of the highest skill and can be convincingly defended (as F. O. Matthiessen has shown in *Henry James: the Major Phase*). Undoubtedly his ambiguity is superior to Hawthorne's. Hawthorne offers a supernatural phenomenon together with a possible material explanation, and thus frequently softens the blow too much. Where James is dealing with the supernatural – as in *The Turn of the Screw* (1898), or 'The Jolly Corner' – his ambiguity, offering the reader no vulgarly easy way out, has a tremendous impact. Where, however, it leaves the reader to make his way through a maze of possibilities, the characters become impalpable, and the defatigable reader retires from the contest, unequal to the James Family as Henry abstracted it.

It should be stressed that these remarks do not apply to the bulk of James's writing, though the seeds of his final method lie in his early work. And such books as *The Wings of the Dove* and *The Ambassadors* (1903), if failures, are Jamesian failures, which are still a great deal better than most writers' successes. James is *sui generis*; every one of his works, from the smallest story to the longest and most involute of novels, shows a consistent, unwinking gaze upon a humanity capable of abysmal treachery and evil, capable of undying loyalty and goodness: these chronicled with a degree of perception that no other novelist has surpassed. Finally, it must be said that James can also be very funny in his fastidiousness, as when he gossiped with brother William about his sense of Oxford dons: 'dreary, ill-favoured men, with local conversation and dirty hands'.

'Every great novel must first of all be based on a profound sense of moral values, and then constructed with a classical unity and economy of means.' The writer must 'bear in mind at each step that his business is not to ask what the situation would be likely to make of his characters, but what his characters, being what they are, would make of the situation'. These are, near enough, the views of Henry James. But the words are those of his close friend Edith Wharton. Like James, she felt out of touch with America; after divorcing her husband she lived in France. Like James, she preferred on the whole (with the exceptions of *Ethan Frome*, 1911, and *Summer*, 1917) to write of people in polite society. Both deal with the tension between the individual and the social framework. Neither author supposes that the social framework is ideal: James, as we have seen, imports his ideal from America, in the shape of the individual. Nevertheless the rules of his society, no matter how arbitrary or unsatisfactory, are observed: there is no doubt that they operate. By contrast, society for Edith Wharton is a collapsing affair. Its pressure, though real, is often crude and arbitrary; her leading characters tend to be people with grudges or handicaps that they cannot resolve.

Edith Wharton never achieved the detachment of her friend. If he belonged to any society, it was to the New York world of Washington Square or marginally to Massachusetts; yet the James Family, as Henry represented it, belonged everywhere and nowhere. Edith Wharton, however, was by upbringing quite definitely a member of older New York society. She was raised so as to become, after a season or two of dances and summers at Newport, one of its hostesses. An exceptionally intelligent girl, loving literature, she found her society intolerably narrow and uncultivated. Its standards were negative, though snobbish, and as soon as a newer aristocracy of wealth began to emerge in New York, the world of Edith Wharton fell apart. An old name counted for something, but not very much; more important was the money that made it possible for the *parvenus* to raise their mansions along Fifth Avenue. Her feeling about the fashionable scene of New York might be summed up as: 'it's not as good as it used to be, and what's more, it never was.' Sensitive and isolated in her youth, she regretted the rigidity of her upbringing, with its indifference to the creative life. On the other hand, what succeeded it was even worse. In either case a person like her was a misfit.

Given this frustrating basis, Edith Wharton made fine fiction from her material. She has a sharp eye for social absurdities, and compassion for the victims of social change. The sadness and stoic despairs of some of her characters no doubt acquired pathos in their presentation from her own unhappiness in marriage to an affluent, breezy, unintellectual Bostonian. In *Ethan Frome*, where her background is the barrenness not of New York society but of a New England farmstead, she draws an overpowering picture of human helplessness. The novels that deal with New York – *The House of Mirth* (1905), *The Custom of the Country* (1913), and *Hudson River Bracketed* (1928), to name only three – make convincing use of the author's special knowledge. Lily Bart (*The House of Mirth*) suffers because, despite her extravagance and frivolity, she is an honest person in a shoddy society. Ralph Marvell (*The Custom of the Country*) also goes under:

Ralph sometimes called his mother and grandfather the Aborigines, and likened them to those vanishing denizens of the American continent doomed to rapid extinction with the advance of the invading race. He was fond of describing Washington Square as the 'Reservation'....

The vulgarians with whom Lily and Ralph grapple unsuccessfully are accurately and acidly observed. She describes with precise disdain the social sins – of dress and décor and conversation – committed by philistines determined to make a splash. It seems appropriate that her first book dealt with interior decoration. She was a connoisseur of houses and gardens. Her moral judgements were in part aesthetic. She is a literary *grande dame* with resemblances to certain English novelists of class – Nancy Mitford or Evelyn Waugh – and has a similar mocking wit.

There is nothing tragic in Lily's downfall; nor in that of Ralph – with whom the author seems impatient, as she is with Lawrence Selden, the ineffectual friend of Lily Bart. There is usually no great *clash* in Edith Wharton: the new society ousts the old with contemptuous ease, and the individual is vanquished almost as much through his or her own weakness as from the power of society. The absence of a fully realized conflict is especially noticeable in her later novels. *Hudson River Bracketed* seems to grope for a non-existent norm. The hero, Vance Weston, is a young writer out of Euphoria, Illinois. Euphoria is crudely drawn, as though the author had borrowed her material from Sinclair Lewis (Vance's father, like Babbitt, is in real estate).[1] Where then is the norm, if not in the caricatured Euphoria? At first, apparently in an old house on the Hudson: 'this absurd house' was for Vance 'his embodiment of the Past'; it 'was to him the very emblem of man's long effort, was Chartres, the Parthenon, the Pyramids'. But then the house ceases to affect Vance, who buries himself in the teeming life of New York – is defeated by it – would like to return to his first love, poetry (Edith Wharton published two volumes of verse), but does not know where he stands – and at the end of the book has nothing left

1. She admired Lewis's sharp eye and ear, as demonstrated in *Main Street* (1920), and he dedicated *Babbitt* (1922) to her.

save a sense of vocation. Everything else, Edith Wharton implies, has gone for one of her generation: even the literary world of New York is singularly unappetizing. By 1928 the *parvenus* themselves have gone, almost, and Washington Square with its 'Aborigines' is not even a memory: for in *Hudson River Bracketed* a guide conducting a tour of the city shouts through his megaphone:

We are now approaching the only remaining private residence on Fifth Avenue, belonging to one of the old original society leaders known throughout the world as the Four Hundred.

Some years earlier, in *The Age of Innocence* (1920), Edith Wharton had produced a novel as finely nuanced as *The House of Mirth*, but with a gentler, more nostalgic, backwards glance upon the New York gentry of the 1870s, and upon the uncertainties of one of its products, Newland Archer. There is, he realizes, a kind of privileged, selfish innocence 'that seals the mind against imagination and the heart against experience'. Even by 1920, according to the young critic Edmund Wilson, Edith Wharton's elegant style was no longer quite 'American': its inflections were half-French.

Like Henry James, she uses the international theme, but with less effect. The drama that might lie in the marriage of the mid-Western Undine Spragg to a French aristocrat (in *The Custom of the Country*) is weakened by the fact that Undine is an odious character, incapable of a full relationship with anybody. Her husband's code therefore has only limited significance. To compare her stories and novels with those of James helps to define the scope of both: her considerable talent is exceeded by his. True, her aims were somewhat different; and while they were intimate friends, she had discreet reservations as to the stylistic luxuriance of the late or 'Old Pretender' phase of James. His *Portrait of a Lady*, a relatively early work, remained her favourite. However, in their exquisite versions of exile they were involved in a common search for a literary kingdom. *Kingdom* indeed: as their standards of conduct were lofty, so their vocabulary, like that of Emily Dickinson, acquired regal overtones. James's Milly Theale is a 'princess', Edith Wharton talks of 'thrones'. But the motive behind such words is austere rather than snobbish; perhaps the words for what they sought to convey did not exist, in uncontaminated clarity.

Henry Adams was another American with lofty expectations that his own time and country could not, or did not, fulfil. The Adams Family even outshone the James Family. Henry Adams's grandfather and great-grandfather had been Presidents of the United States, while his father was minister to England during the Civil War. There was every reason to suppose that Henry would try to emulate them.

He protested that he found it impossible to participate in American public life. Instead he became the most private of citizens, insisting on the enormity of his own failure, generalizing from the fate of the Adamses to the fate of the American nation, and – more widely still – to that of the entire globe. Henry's modesty has seemed to hostile critics a form of conceit on a gigantic scale. Cecil Spring Rice, an English diplomat who afterwards became a warm friend, on first acquaintance found Adams 'cynical' and 'vindictive'. Justice Oliver Wendell Holmes, when asked by the novelist Owen Wister, 'What was the matter with Henry Adams?', explained that 'he wanted it handed to him on a silver platter'. Adams and his well-born Boston wife Marian ('Clover') Hooper lived in their Washington years just across from the White House. They made clear their sense of superiority to all but a select few. Henry James, an old companion, probably used them as models for his short story 'Pandora'. In the story a character who sounds very much like Adams says, with reference to a dinner party: 'Hang it, . . . let us be vulgar and have some fun – let us invite the President.' (The President of the time was Rutherford B. Hayes of Ohio, whose wife 'Lemonade Lucy' was a temperance advocate. A Washington joke was that at White House receptions 'the water flowed like wine'.) And Mrs Adams was at least a match for her husband in the mode of amused disapproval. After visiting the Rome studio of the American expatriate sculptor W. W. Story she commented (in a letter to her father): 'Oh! how he [Story] does spoil nice blocks of white marble. Nothing but Sibyls on all sides, sitting, standing, legs crossed, legs uncrossed, and all with the same expression as if they smelt something wrong.'

Certainly there was in Adams a touch of *'roi ne puis, duc ne daigne'*. But like Henry James, he loved his country in his fashion. In middle age, busy as a journalist and historian in Washington, Henry Adams told his English crony Charles Milnes Gaskell that America was 'the only country now worth working for, or pleasant to work in'. He had been furious at what he considered to be British duplicity during the Civil War, and he continually criticized England for its crass materialism. As a young man he disliked France, and in later life, while he drew close to some aspects of French life, the general corruption of France provoked him to disgusted comment. Europe as a whole, he grumbled, was rotten; revolution was only a matter of time.

Nevertheless Adams became less and less at ease in America. For the last thirty years of his life he travelled incessantly, as if to escape the spectacle of a Washington full of dishonest barbarian representatives. 'West of the Alleghenies,' he wrote of America as it was in 1892, 'the whole country might have been swept clean, and could have been replaced in better form within one or two years.' He was not much more polite to the country east of the Alleghenies; and if he found Europe no better in many respects, the Old World did provide him with a solace of a kind he could not get at home.

But before he turned to Europe, Henry Adams did what he could with America. Like other Bostonians, he had the critical rather than the creative temperament. Summoning up truly Bostonian reserves of industry, he applied himself to American history of the early national period, when the nation was still taking shape and still, in his view, a promising experiment in democratic republicanism. On the way he published two novels, and biographies of Albert Gallatin and John Randolph, together with a couple of volumes of documents. His labours culminated in the nine-volume *History of the United States during the Administrations of Jefferson and Madison* (1889–91), portions of which he had printed privately in 1884–5 and 1888. William Dusinberre (*Henry Adams: The Myth of Failure*, 1980) argues that the *History* is Adams's greatest work, and that this has been lost to view because of the daunting length of the enterprise, but more particularly because of Adams's complicated subsequent acts of disguise and deprecation. There is no doubt of his devotion to literary skills (a passion shared with his historian brother Brooks, a tenacious editor–critic). We can see too how, like Prescott, Motley and Parkman, he regarded history as an important form of literature; and how, with the English historians Gibbon and Macaulay also on his mind, he wanted to compose a *literary*–historical masterwork.

On top of this ambition, however, and not necessarily in harmony with it, was Adams's concern with *scientific* history. Scientific history might mean the scrupulous use and weighing of sources, as enjoined upon students in the German university seminars he had attended. It might also signify a more abstract, global or even cosmic survey on the level of Comte or Darwin. At twenty-five he had speculated that 'the nations move by the same process *which has never been explained* but is evident in the ocean and air'. Thirty years later, in 'The Tendency of History', he spoke of 'the immortality that would be achieved by the man who should successfully apply Darwin's method to the facts of human history'. All of these aims went to the making of the *History*. The results are formidable, though not always perfectly blended. Adams wrote with elegant assurance, and close attention to documents. He introduced large theories – the comforting suggestion that Americans might have hit upon an energizing individualistic nationalism; the more austere theory that individuals were 'ants and bees', and even the leaders (Jefferson, Madison, Monroe) 'mere grasshoppers kicking and gesticulating on the middle of the Mississippi river' – history being 'simply social development along the lines of weakest resistance'.

At this stage he had probably not decided whether or not history contained significant patterns, in which the United States would figure importantly. Afterwards he arrived at a theory of history more grandly and consistently pessimistic. He lit upon the law of entropy, and fitted it to history to prove that human energy was being constantly and irrecoverably dissipated. Society, like any other organism, would run down, until a stage of stagnation was reached. This stage, Adams maintained, was not remote but imminent; for the modern scene was marked by tremendously rapid and ever-accelerating change. Adapting the Rule of Phase of the American scientist Willard Gibbs, he argued that human energy was being wasted at a rate subject to mathematical calculation. World history might thus be divided into three phases, of which the third or Electric phase, ushered in by the dynamos which he saw installed at the Chicago and Paris Expositions, would run from 1900 to 1917. There might be a fourth, Ethereal phase, that would 'bring Thought to the limit of its possibilities in the year 1921'.

One reaction is that Adams was wasting his own energy: the hypothesis is untrue, and there was no reason to take it seriously when he propounded it. But Adams loved analogies. As a poetic version of a disintegrating world, this one pleased him; and, tired of the current talk about history as science, he thought it worth while to put the matter to a test. In this, he acted rather like King Canute at the water's edge. Who knows whether Canute did not, in his innermost heart, think the waves *might* pause? And if they advanced, as was probable, he would have the pleasure of scolding his courtiers. So Adams with his fellow-historians. 'History', he said in a letter, 'will die if not irritated. The only service I can do to my profession is to serve as a flea.'

The tone is characteristically ironic. In a way it was how Adams had always sounded. The index in William H. Jordy's *Henry Adams: Scientific Historian* (1952), under *'snobbishness'*, says see *'aloofness'*. How much his disdain was shyness is hard to tell. What should be taken into account is the calamitous break in Adams's life after his wife committed suicide at the end of 1885. The later volumes of the *History* became drudgery, a labour of tormenting near-futility. Thereafter, quitting Washington, Adams fled from country to country, a wanderer disaffected not only with America but with the whole surge (as he saw it) of mankind towards oblivion. After her death he never directly mentioned Marian Hooper. His life with her is passed over entirely in *The Education of Henry Adams*. Eventually France became the nearest approximation to a home.

The Adams heritage, Henry's domestic experiences, his scientific hypotheses, the condition of the modern world: some combination of these stimulated him to produce two extraordinary books. History was a movement from unity to multiplicity; and in terms of human happiness, unity offered everything that multiplicity snatched away. Holidaying in 1895 in northern France, he found its atmosphere strangely attractive. Its village churches and great cathedrals filled him with delight. He plunged into the music, the poetry, and the philosophy of the twelfth and thirteenth centuries, and found peace: a peace he identified with Unity, in the figure of the Virgin Mary, and also Energy, in the shape of the temples men had raised to Her. Women had long exerted a powerful influence on Adams. After Marian's death he appears to have fallen in love with Elizabeth Cameron, the young wife of a Senator, and to have cherished her and her daughter Martha. The heroines of his two novels, *Democracy* (1880) and *Esther* (1884), count for more than the heroes – much more in *Esther*, which appeared under the pseudonym of 'Frances Snow Compton'. In the company of women, which he came to prefer, one could cling to the illusion that life was graceful and ordered: an illusion which vanished as soon as one met their harassed husbands.

This view of life, and his reverence for the great shrines of northern France, Adams voiced in *Mont-Saint-Michel and Chartres* (1904). From the eleventh-century masculinity of Mont-St-Michel, mankind passed to the twelfth century, growing gentler and more feminine, expressing itself in romances and in gothic architecture, with supreme effect in the cathedral of Chartres. This period was for Adams the finest in all history. He loved to speak of his ancestors as rooted in Normandy, an infinitely more congenial starting-place than Boston. In it, he could pay tribute to Woman (as, he noted, very few Americans except Whitman had done), and find relief from Law, from a Puritan deity and a mechanistic universe. *Mont-Saint-Michel* is a work of pure affection, and to call it Adams's form of expatriation is to stress how passionately Americans of his calibre have sought the great good place.

We might though take note of psycho-biographic theories according to which Adams's Virgin of Chartres signified either Marian (childless) or the Madonna-with-Child Elizabeth Cameron. A third hypothesis is that, consciously or not, Adams in *Mont-Saint-Michel* revealed a fascination with the story of Peter Abelard, a philosopher interested in 'truth' where scholastic method merely endeavoured to harmonize differing views. Abelard is dramatized as if he were a mischievous medieval Adams – an intellectual who irritated his peers. Abelard was humanized by his connection with the ultimate woman, Héloïse, as Adams with Marian Hooper. Abelard was castrated by her vengeful family (Adams was, more mildly, exposed to the disdain of Dr Hooper), and silenced by the authorities by indirect means. Abelard, finally, wrote a *Historia Calamitatum*, or history of calamities – a nice title for the later historical speculation of Henry Adams. Certainly the story of Abelard was well known in nineteenth-century America. He is discussed in C. S. Peirce's 1878 article on 'How to Make Our Ideas Clear', which William James praised as the first account of pragmatism. And in *Walden*, suggesting a kind of village Sorbonne for Concord, Thoreau said: 'Can we not hire some Abélard to lecture to us?' Henry Adams, proudly unhireable, is nevertheless conceivably a sort of Abelard.

At the other extreme is *The Education of Henry Adams*, with which the public first became acquainted in 1918, though it had been privately printed in 1907. The *Education* is intended as a study of twentieth-century multiplicity. An autobiography couched in the third person, it attempts to exhibit in Adams's own life the chaos of the Electric Phase, after the relative tranquillity of the Mechanical. Instead of the Virgin, man stands before the comfortless Dynamo. All is a delirium of change. If the *Education* were merely a lament for the past, it would be tedious; and the final chapters, in which Adams explains his theories without reference to his own life, are necessarily uninteresting to the average reader. But the book as a whole is a masterly contrivance, extravagantly humble, beautifully written, full of ideas and personalities. Is Henry Adams posturing? Yes; but his picture is convincing in the way that a work of art, artfully, convinces: this we believe is *a* veritable portrait of an era.

Hardly less enjoyment and insight are to be had from Adams's correspondence. He is one of the best letter-writers in the language, and whether he is describing the South Seas or the Arctic Circle, a book just read or an idea just conceived, he brings to them all an idiosyncratic and witty alertness that makes one more than ready to forgive him his pose of despair. Nor, of course, is it entirely a pose, or an attitude peculiar to him. Part of his problem was that of the small American intellectual patriciate. On their own terms, few honourable occupations existed. Politics and business had become unacceptable. There was as yet no properly defined professional career in government service. Preaching no longer appealed to people whose minds were refinedly sceptical. There remained the possibilities of medicine and law (which satisfied O. W. Holmes, father and son), journalism and scholarship. Henry did his best with the last two. There were, however, problems for other Americans than the educated gentry. Mark Twain, for example, developed as bleak a cosmology as anything in Henry Adams's scheme. Despair could be no less deep for a person living in the United States, as an 'inward expatriate', than for someone actually domiciled in Europe.

France was as useful to Gertrude Stein as to Henry Adams, though in a vastly different context. He came as a survivor (he said): she came as a forerunner, settling herself in Paris in 1902 and living there, or thereabouts, for more than forty years. In 1902 she was a quick-witted, well-to-do young woman who had studied psychology: she had been a pupil of William James, great brother of the great Henry. She was not an established writer, though early themes showed a certain originality. Among them was a piece about a young man, dragging his father by the hair through the orchard. 'Stop,' said the old man; 'I only dragged my father as far as this tree.' Henry Adams doubted whether there was any link between one generation and the next; Gertrude Stein felt that each new generation must inevitably war with the old. This knowledge gratified her, for unlike Adams she believed the future to be full of promise. With the aid of psychology she was to uncover truth. Previous American writers had had the same ambition. Yet though she sometimes used the vocabulary of, say, Howells – 'I am trying to be as commonplace as I can be' – she differed from the early realists as much as cubism from impressionism.

The comparison with painting is important. Her interest in psychology was in large part an interest in *language*. William James, who coined the expression 'stream of thought' (altered subsequently to 'stream of consciousness'), was struck by the way in which, in certain states of mind, words appeared to exert a supremacy over rational meaning. Under the influence of nitrous oxide, he found himself inventing impressively nonsensical propositions: 'There are no differences but differences of degree between different degrees of difference and no difference.' This is the philosopher's mind off the leash. Gertrude Stein was determined to cast her own mind off the leash. In Paris, through her brother Leo, she became intimate with obscure young artists who were to be among the foremost painters of the century. Picasso, Braque, Matisse, were doing in paint exactly what she was trying to do with words: to shatter convention, to let the medium triumph over the subject, to attain simplicity. The same thing was happening in contemporary music. In Paris all the arts evolved together, in a way unfamiliar to Adams's Boston, or Miss Stein's Pittsburgh (or Oakland, of which she said, 'there is no there there').

The revolt from the spirit of the *beaux-arts*, for her as for Picasso, meant two things as far as simplicity was concerned. First, art was to aim at the ultimate in economy. It was to be uncluttered, beautifully bare, as unemotional as the prose of Defoe (which Gertrude Stein greatly admired) but far more abstract. (Impatience with extrinsic subject-matter has been characteristic of the modern movement: for example, it led the American poet William Carlos Williams to argue that the novel is inferior as an art-form to the poem, since it cannot by its nature reach 'the underlying nudity'.) Second came a distrust of smoothness, a cult of crudity. In part this was inherent in the newness of what was being attempted:

Sure, she said, as Pablo [Picasso] once remarked, when you make a thing, it is so complicated making it that it is bound to be ugly, but those that do it after you they don't have to worry about making it and they can make it pretty, and so everybody can like it when the others make it.

Crudity was also a self-imposed condition, a result of refusing to take anything for granted:

So then I said I would begin again, I would not know what I knew about everything what I knew about anything.

Such was the background of Gertrude Stein's work. She set out to create a new literature that was to show 'the inside of things'. In some of her writing she tried to divorce words from their usual meanings, and to arrange them like objects in a cubist composition, simply for pleasure's sake:

I saw representative mistakes and glass cups, I saw a whole appearance of respectable refugees, I did not ask actors I asked pearls, I did not choose to ask trains, I was satisfied with celebrated ransoms.

In other work she described people and scenes in a language full of repetitions and banalities, like an abstraction of the common speech of uneducated people. She hoped thereby to convey the 'immediacy' of existence. Indeed, in *The Making of Americans* (written 1906–8, though not published until 1925), an enormously long and clumsy book, she thought she covered every facet of human nature. She first aroused interest beyond a circle of friends with *Three Lives* (1909), a volume suggested to her by a reading of Flaubert's *Trois Contes*. Two of her three tales – all of which are set in America – deal with elderly German servants, the third with a black girl, Melanctha. *Three Lives* is one of her most readable books, and as an experiment in methods of narration it is on the whole very successful. The complexities of Melanctha's life, her vague cravings and her unhappiness, are evoked largely in dialogue, and without condescension. Gertrude Stein's other well-known book, a highly entertaining and valuable record of her friendships, is *The Autobiography of Alice B. Toklas* (1933), an account of herself purportedly through the eyes of her companion–secretary Miss Toklas.

Much of her other work is difficult, not so much from obscurity – it is usually possible to see what Gertrude Stein is getting at, and her automatic writing is pleasing, in small quantities – as from repetition. Never was a creative writer so free with definitions and explanations. Some are shrewd; most are whimsical and arbitrary, suggesting bossiness rather than authority. Her emphasis is upon concentration, penetration. Nouns are only 'names' and are to be omitted where possible; the verb is what counts in a sentence. Punctuation is likewise a hindrance: out go question mark, colon, semicolon. Yet the result is not clarity but diffuse impenetrability. In limiting her vocabulary she achieves an occasional charming crispness in short statements (though often they are paraphrased from other people, including her brother Leo, who said of the absent-minded Miss Toklas that 'if I were a general I would never lose a battle, I would only mislay it'). But when she embarks on a lengthy exposition she flounders. In supposing that narration proceeds by a series of imperceptibly varied stages, like movement recorded by the frames in a strip of film, she ignores the vital question of pace: for though a film consists of a great number of images, it would be insupportable if these were to be examined one at a time: they have to be taken at the gallop to make any total effect. Gertrude Stein became obsessed with the process at the expense of the product. She is a writer's writer in several senses, and it is this that constitutes her importance in American literature.

For American literature has suffered from an under-dose of confidence and professional knowledge. Emerson sighed in vain for 'the friendly institution of the *Café*' in Boston, where writers could meet; fifty years later, Dreiser had no idea that other authors shared his interests, and might have helped him with *Sister Carrie*. To this under-dose Gertrude Stein added her over-dose. Massively confident, she was sure that *The Making of Americans* was 'the beginning, really the beginning of modern writing'. Many treated her as a joke, but for some young writers she was a person to believe in, if only as a technician. After the Armistice, they found her embedded in the cultural life of Paris, benign, omniscient and pleasantly American. She had been unashamedly sentimental over the doughboys, as she was to be about their G.I. sons; she read the Paris *Herald-Tribune* in preference to French newspapers (and gave the young Picasso a taste for the Katzenjammer Kids); General Grant was one of her heroes; she liked to play 'The Trail of the Lonesome Pine' on her gramophone: she *understood*. She talked to them professionally about the writer's problems. She conferred status upon the native idiom, serenely sure that the provincial gaucheries of America were close to the new mood of cosmopolitan literature, having in some ways anticipated it. To Eugene O'Neill, to Sherwood Anderson, to Ernest Hemingway (who proof-read for her, and wrote in 1923 that 'she has a wonderful head'[1]); to these and other Americans in their apprentice days she imparted the valuable assurance that the deliberately ingenuous, gangling, deadpan idiom of Mark Twain or of the American newspaper column was, with modifications, the ideal vehicle of the avant-garde. She is sometimes ranked second to Twain as a formative influence upon modern American prose.

Comparing her own people with the Spanish, Gertrude Stein once remarked that Americans

have no close contact with the earth such as most europeans have. Their materialism of existence, of possession, it is the materialism of action and abstraction.

Action and abstraction: *Huckleberry Finn* and *The Making of Americans*: the need to stay home and the need to get away from home in order to understand it. Or, 'America is my country' (as Miss Stein explains her own compromise) 'and Paris is my home town'. This dual tug is apparent in the earlier history of expatriation, making it impossible for most American

---

1. He said this to Edmund Wilson, who reprinted some perceptive early comments on Hemingway in *The Shores of Light* (London, 1952), 115–24. Perhaps because of her comments on him in *Alice B. Toklas*, Hemingway later expressed considerable dislike of Stein and her *ménage*, especially in his *A Moveable Feast* (1964).

writers to remain long abroad without incurring a guilty conscience, or to retain intact personalities in the face of European influence. Nineteenth-century writers tend to flounder and contradict themselves when discussing the problem. 'If I were in your position', Hawthorne writes to Longfellow in 1854, from Liverpool, 'I think that I should make my home on this side of the water, – though always with an indefinite and never-to-be-executed intention to go back and die in my native land.' Yet elsewhere, particularly in his more public utterances, Hawthorne speaks very differently. These wistful asides are only part of the story, for him and others.

The apparent paradox is that only when America became more authentically 'other', more American, could it afford to be more European – or more cosmopolitan. Viewed one way, the expatriation of Henry James or Gertrude Stein was a betrayal of American wholeness. Viewed another way, it was a mark of national confidence. Put in other terms, modernism in literature and the arts was markedly and even clamantly international – defying traditional boundaries, insisting upon the right and duty of creative spirits to be both actual and figurative travellers.

For such people, especially as long journeys became swifter and cheaper, permanent expatriation was not always essential. James Gibbons Huneker (1857–1921) studied music in Paris, wrote music criticism in his native Philadelphia, and then made his big move in 1886 to New York, which he called 'Cosmopolis'. Thereafter Manhattan was his base, and Europe a place to visit as often as possible. Mabel Dodge Luhan (1879–1962) started out in Buffalo, New York, emancipated herself by going to Italy in 1902, and on returning to the United States ten years later opened a *salon* in New York City. From there, in 1918, she transferred to Taos, New Mexico.

In two celebrated instances expatriation to Europe *was* the attempted solution. In 1908 Ezra Pound, budding poet and literary scholar, left America for Italy and then London, and eventually made Italy his permanent home. T. S. Eliot went to Oxford to study philosophy, stayed on in England and in 1927 became a British subject. Pound and Eliot both remained American in certain respects. Pound regarded himself as the international agent for American modern verse, vigorously promoting native talent and striving to educate his country in modernist modes. His detailed suggestions made an immense contribution to Eliot's early work, especially 'The Waste Land'. Eliot himself retained certain American turns of phrase and perhaps of attitude. They were in truth cosmopolitans, or 'Europeans' in the sense defined by Eliot in his memorial tribute to Henry

James. Nevertheless, Pound was actually tried for treason, after the Second World War, and Eliot, though less sharply assailed, was regarded by William Carlos Williams as one who had abandoned American values, preferring the royalist and other conservatisms of the Old World. The links between culture and nationalism were still apt to be entanglements. No one, however, could gainsay that American literature had moved a vast distance from its previous provincialism, into new realms of sophistication, verve and influence.

XI

WOMEN'S VOICES

MARGARET FULLER (1811–50)

Born in Cambridgeport, Massachusetts, and given a relentlessly thorough private education in languages and literature, mathematics and the Bible by her erudite father. On his death (1835) she had to seek employment, for example as a school-teacher, to support her family. She became involved with Transcendentalists, and she was a founder and editor of *The Dial* (1840), a quarterly periodical, and conducted weekly 'conversations' (1839–44) in a Boston *salon*. From these developed the material of her *Woman in the Nineteenth Century* (1845). In 1844–6, Fuller was in New York, as an increasingly rigorous critic for Horace Greeley's *Tribune*. For the *Tribune* she became European correspondent, living in Rome. She formed a sympathetic involvement with Italian patriotic and liberal movements, and she planned books on Mazzini and the Roman revolution of 1848–9. Her papers were, however, lost: she, her baby son and her husband, the Marchese Angelo Ossoli, were drowned in a shipwreck off the New York coast, as she sought to return to the United States. Some surviving work was published posthumously.

HARRIET BEECHER STOWE (1811–96)

Born in Connecticut, she moved with her father Lyman Beecher to Cincinnati (1832), where in 1836 she married Calvin E. Stowe, a professor in her father's theological seminary, and she became strongly opposed to slavery. Living thereafter in Maine, she wrote *Uncle Tom's Cabin* (1852), whose sensational success induced her to produce many other books, including another anti-slavery novel, *Dred, A Tale of the Great Dismal Swamp* (1856). For some years she was a resident of Hartford, Connecticut, on neighbourly terms with Mark Twain. Most of her later years were spent in Florida, where she had become interested in real-estate. Her views on careers for women were expressed in *My Wife and I* (1871); her life in Florida was described in *Palmetto Leaves* (1873).

EMILY DICKINSON (1830–86)

Born in Amherst, Massachusetts, where she spent nearly all her life, except for a year at the nearby Mount Holyoke Female Seminary. Gradually withdrawing into seclusion, she lived at home with her father, a well-to-do lawyer. Her small circle of friends and correspondents included the authors Helen Hunt Jackson and Mabel Loomis Todd, and the Harvard man of letters Thomas Wentworth Higginson, whose advice on her poetry she solicited, and who collaborated with M. L. Todd in editing her *Poems* (1890–91).

SARAH ORNE JEWETT (1849–1909)

Born in South Berwick, Maine, she began to write in her teens. Her first sketches, published as *Deephaven* (1877), were well received; others followed, and some novels and poems, most of them concerned with Maine. *The Country of the Pointed Firs* (1896) has remained her best-known work.

KATE [O'FLAHERTY] CHOPIN (1851–1904)

Born in St Louis, Missouri. She was French on her mother's side, and she married Oscar Chopin, a Louisiana Creole, and lived in New Orleans until his death (1882). Though she returned to St Louis, Creole and Cajun themes provided the chief material in such collections as *Bayou Folk* (1894) and *A Night in Acadie* (1897). Her most ambitious tale, *The Awakening* (1899), met with no better fate than Dreiser's *Sister Carrie* in the following year. Kate Chopin published no more books. Her reputation has been mainly posthumous.

WILLA CATHER (1873–1947)

Born in Virginia, she moved in childhood to Nebraska, and was a bright student at the University of Nebraska. She published poetry and short stories and worked as a journalist in Manhattan, until her first novels (*Alexander's Bridge*, 1912; *O Pioneers!*, 1913) established her as a prominent author. Successive novels, including *My Ántonia* (1918) and *The Professor's House* (1925), heightened her reputation, as did stories dealing with Catholicism in the New World (*Death Comes for the Archbishop*, 1927; *Shadows on the Rock*, 1937). Her observations on the craft of fiction are expressed in *Not Under Forty* (1936).

WOMEN'S VOICES

AMERICAN women writers – Anne Bradstreet, say, or Edith Wharton – figure in most chapters of this book. That is not surprising. Women have been present on the intellectual scene since the seventeenth century, prominent in American literature ever since the 1830s. Even in that early era they were achieving publication not only as novelists and essayists but as poets (for instance, Lydia Sigourney, 1791–1865) or dramatists (such as Anna Mowatt, 1819–70).

Given this prominence and diversity, why confine a number of them to a separate chapter? Such apparent segregation could be interpreted as a grouping of the second-rate within the ghetto of femaleness, and therefore as a denial rather than a recognition of the positive qualities of women's literature. Lydia Sigourney, the 'Sweet Singer of Hartford', has survived mainly as a figure of fun, dismissed as a laughably bad sentimental versifier. Many a student, too, has taken the part of Hawthorne, the writer of genius mortified to discover that his books were vastly outsold by those of a 'damned mob of scribbling women'. However we choose to define women's literature, one incontestable feature is the great spread of temperaments and approaches. Some women writers have shown relatively little interest in 'women's issues'. Matrimony, maternity and similar supposed concerns of women have bulked large for some but not for others.

Only since the 1960s, though, has the full richness of the history of this subject been grasped – including the extent of previous neglect, condescension and misunderstanding. Nor of course has the development been confined to the United States. The recognition of women's literature (and for that matter, art and scholarship) has been a worldwide process. Several, perhaps most, of the pioneers from whom American feminists have drawn inspiration are Europeans. In the early years of the new nation, Americans were stirred by an English manifesto, Mary Wollstonecraft's *Vindication of the Rights of Women* (1792). They have subsequently heard other British voices: those, for instance, of the Brontë sisters, Elizabeth Barrett Browning and 'George Eliot' in the nineteenth century, and of

Virginia Woolf in the twentieth. France has provided formidable examples, from Madame de Staël and 'George Sand' to Simone de Beauvoir.

Still, one might have expected American women themselves to set the pace. At least in regions such as New England and Pennsylvania, educated and articulate women seemed about to come forward in some numbers during the Revolution. 'Remember the ladies' was the celebrated admonition of John Adams's keen-witted wife Abigail in 1776, reminding him that a general declaration of equality ought to refer to both sexes. Her friend Mercy Otis Warren (1728–1814) was a poet, satirist and historian with radical views.[1]

They and their contemporaries felt that a new era in human rights had arrived. As Linda K. Kerber and Mary Beth Norton have shown, the rhetoric of American independence made great play with a notion of pristine New World republicanism, building upon ancient republican values – simplicity, frugality, modesty, integrity. In this rhetoric the role of American women was proclaimed to be central. All free citizens, male and female, were to be educated: otherwise Americans could not fulfil the solemn, novel duties of self-government. Sure enough, opportunities for women's education were greatly extended in the next decades. A national women's rights convention was held at Seneca Falls, New York, in 1848. By then, moves were under way in northern states to change the ancient *coverture* assumptions of Anglo-American common law, according to which women entering matrimony lost their separate identity (including property), passing under the baron and feme jurisdiction of their husbands. Women were moving into America's schoolrooms as teachers, and participating actively in reform campaigns, notably abolitionism and temperance. Moreover, Hawthorne's damned mob had begun to produce articles, poems and full-length works as early as the 1820s. Studies by Nina Baym and Mary Kelley reveal that the phenomenon was no figment of Hawthorne's imagination. A dozen American women were competing successfully for attention from editors and publishers. Lydia Maria Child (1802–80), the sister of the Transcendentalist minister Convers Francis, achieved more fame than he with her novels, and with vigorous essays on anti-slavery and other issues of the day. Another productive and prominent author was Catharine Maria Sedgwick (1789–1867), whose career began with the publication of her first novel, *A New-England Tale*,

1. Mercy Otis Warren was the sister of the lawyer patriot James Otis, and wife of the president of the Provincial Congress of Massachusetts.

in 1822, and continued for thirty-five years. Her historical novels, *Hope Leslie* (1827) and *The Linwoods* (1835), were especially admired. Sarah Josepha Hale (1788–1879) was a magazine editor for half a century, principally in directing *Godey's Lady's Book*, a monthly which occasionally printed pieces by Hawthorne, and by Emerson, Longfellow, Poe and others. Sarah Hale's own work included *Northwood: A Tale of New England* (1827; revised in 1852, with the addition of material on slavery).

By the time Nathaniel Hawthorne began to edge into print, professional women authors were already on the scene. Indeed he received important encouragement from the bluestocking Elizabeth Peabody (1804–94), his future sister-in-law. Admiring his early, anonymous tales, she invited him to her home in Salem, pulled strings to get him a custom-house appointment, and enthusiastically reviewed his subsequent work. Apart from her involvement with Transcendentalism, Elizabeth Peabody devised textbooks and courses so as to promote the study of history.

Nina Baym analyses the writing of a good many more women active between 1820 and 1870. Among them were Caroline Howard Gilman (1794–1888); Hannah Farnham Sawyer Lee (1780–1865); Emma Catherine Embury (1806–63); Louisa C. Tuthill (1799–1879); J. F. Cooper's daughter Susan Fenimore Cooper (1813–94); Maria McIntosh (1803–78), 'first of the popular women novelists of the mid-century'; E. D. E. N. Southworth (1819–99), a resident of Washington D.C. who set most of her novels in Virginia and Maryland; Caroline Lee Hentz (1800–1856), whose best-known though untypical novel *The Planter's Northern Bride* (1854) insists on the inflammatory nature of abolitionist agitation; Susan B. Warner (1819–85), who began to write under the pseudonym 'Elizabeth Wetherell' (sometimes in collaboration with her sister Anna), and whose *The Wide, Wide World* (1850) and *Queechy* (1852) would certainly nowadays be classified as 'bestsellers'; Maria Susanna Cummins (1827–66) of Salem, whose first novel *The Lamplighter* (1854) sold some 70,000 copies in its first year, and served to provoke the irritable complaint by Hawthorne; Ann Sophia Stephens (1813–86), a versatile contributor to popular magazines, in which a number of her stories were serialized, including the dime novel *Malaeska, The Indian Wife of the White Hunter* (1860); Mary Jane Holmes (1825–1907), the author of no less than thirty-nine novels, beginning with *Tempest and Sunshine* (1854); Sara Payson Willis Parton (1811–72), writing under the pen name 'Fanny Fern'; Augusta Jane Evans Wilson (1835–1909), a Southerner able to appeal to a nationwide audience with such novels as *Beulah* (1859), *Macaria* (1864) and – the most famous of all – *St. Elmo* (1867); and other women writers of fiction, not least Harriet Beecher Stowe, whose *Uncle Tom's Cabin* (1852) was an even greater bestseller.

There are various ways of assessing this material. Literary historians have in the past accepted that public response, measured in book sales, was *per se* an inference of mediocrity, as was copiousness of output: how could thirty-nine volumes lead anywhere but down? Such formulas tend to rate genius as inversely proportional to popular acclaim. Thus, Emily Dickinson is deemed a great poet in part *because* she was almost unknown during her lifetime.

Sentimentality is a common charge against the 'scribbling women'. Mary Jane Holmes's *'Lena Rivers* (1856), for instance, has been called a 'lachrymal classic'. One modern scholar, Ann Douglas, argues (*The Feminization of American Culture*, 1977) that with the shining exception of Margaret Fuller, writers of the Jacksonian era softened and trivialized national values; along with America's clergy, they promoted a marshmallow morality and thereby lost any genuine influence. Telling the culture what it wanted to hear instead of what it needed to hear, they relegated American women to subordinate, acquiescent roles, as advocates of mainstream religiosity and domesticity.

A less disparaging view is that of Mary Kelley (*Private Woman, Public Stage*, 1984). She regards the popular authors of the era as 'literary domestics'. By 'domestics' she does not mean *servants*. 'Literary domestics' in Kelley's usage are woman authors who willingly adopted the idea of a 'women's sphere': home, family, devotion, sensibility, sacrifice, salvation. Such values can be seen as 'republican', within the American context. The duty of the American female, that is, was defined within the domestic and moral realm. Her task was to make the home a sanctuary and a sanctum – a safe and peaceful place for harried males, and a sort of temple for the inculcation of Christian standards of conduct among those of tender years.

Whether that role was worth while, feasible, or actually accepted by women in Jackson's and Lincoln's America is open to dispute. It is clear that the American Revolution was in some respects a limited or conservative movement, hallowing rather than overturning family, church and other institutions. In such an environment, apparent improvements in opportunities for women were offset by conformist expectations, allowing even less room for unconventional behaviour than in Europe. Aristocratic privilege enabled some English ladies to flout middle-class standards; women intellectuals in Paris were not absolutely constrained by bourgeois codes. In the United States, however, increasing numbers of well-educated women seemed to be trapped by domesticity.

For all but the handful of out-and-out rebels, a reasonably satisfactory compromise could be reached. Kitchen, nursery, parlour, schoolroom, sick-bay, garden became their special domain. Their fiction or essays often idealized hearth and home, altar and prayer. An exchange of marriage vows supplied the happy ending for many a novel. Much of the fiction of the 'literary domestics' has dropped out of sight, and in truth not a great deal of it has powerful claims upon the attention of posterity. The 'good' characters are frequently goody-goody. Stereotypes recur, especially in inferior examples of the genre. There is for instance the Byronic model of hero (patterned perhaps on Mr Rochester in Charlotte Brontë's *Jane Eyre*); St Elmo, in the novel of that name, is arrogant and self-indulgent until shamed into reform by the heroine. Another standard figure is the middle-aged, charismatic clergyman, who inspires a not entirely asexual devotion among women parishioners. Such a figure appears in *Mercy Philbrick's Choice* (1876) by Helen Hunt Jackson. His ubiquity would seem to bear out Ann Douglas's 'feminization' theory – of an alliance of temperament, that is, between the minister of religion (male) and the ministering angel (female). Conventional pieties do abound in certain novels. Hawthorne's disapproval of *The Lamplighter* is understandable, given the profusion of such passages as this (ch. 48):

When he had gone, Gertrude lingered . . . to watch his retreating figure, just visible in the light of the waning moon; then returned to the parlor, drawing a long breath and saying, 'O, what a day this has been!' but checked herself, at the sight of Emily, who, kneeling by the sofa, with clasped hands, uplifted face, and with her white garments sweeping the floor, looked the very impersonation of purity and prayer.

Throwing one arm around her neck, Gertrude knelt . . . beside her, and together they sent up to the throne of God the incense of thanksgiving and praise!

The heroine of Augusta Jane Evans's *Beulah* awards Emerson's essays low marks for their fatalistic and irreligious tone. Edna, the heroine of the same author's *St. Elmo*, is advised by her minister friend not to go in for literature:

If you succeed after years of labor and anxiety . . . ., you will become a target for envy and malice and, possibly, for slander. Your own sex will be jealous of your eminence . . . ; and mine will either ridicule or barely tolerate you; for men detest female competitors in the Olympian game of literature.

Granted, then, that nineteenth-century women produced some work of indifferent quality, we should recognize other elements. The average level was not lower than that of male authors, who displayed their own brands of sentimentality and banality. Happy endings were not the hallmark of women's fiction. If the majority of women authors appeared to uphold genteelly conservative codes, they were acting as male mentors urged them to do. According to the well-placed littérateur Nathaniel Parker Willis:

> By the strong spirit's discipline,
>   By the fierce wrong forgiven,
> By all that wrings the heart of sin,
>   Is woman won to Heaven.

Willis himself did nothing to aid his sister Sara Payson Willis in her early struggle to establish herself. Yet in a way his complacent lines (so at variance with his actual playboy reputation) do define the temper of a considerable amount of women's literature. Nina Baym persuasively suggests that it embodies a genuine species of feminism. The heroine is frequently an orphan. She struggles to educate herself, and to live upon an intellectual as well as a spiritual plane. The cherished childhood reading of Edna in St. Elmo includes 'Plutarch's Lives and a worn school copy of Anthon's Classical Dictionary'. Despite the pessimistic counsel of her clergyman mentor, Edna Earl perseveres with her vein of literature and becomes a well-known author. The heroine of Mercy Philbrick's Choice achieves recognition as a poet; specimens of her work are incorporated in the novel.

Feminist attitudes are evident too in other features of women's fiction. The heroines of many stories are shown as courageous and high-minded. They withstand adversity and discouragement. If they eventually attain prosperity within matrimony, and richly deserve the reward, it is not their goal. On the contrary, their previous conduct is as stubbornly, even glacially high-minded as that of the heroines of Henry James. Male characters, at any rate the younger unregenerate ones, tend to be distinctly less admirable. Like the real-life N. P. Willis, in relation to his sister 'Fanny Fern', they seem generally selfish, patronizing and cowardly or dishonourable when under pressure. Sophy Burr, the spinster heroine of Helen Hunt Jackson's last novel, Zeph (1885), is markedly braver and more intelligent than the man she decides to redeem and marry.

In grumbling at the inflated reputation of *The Lamplighter*, Hawthorne nevertheless said that he admired the sketches of 'Fanny Fern' and that he would like to meet her. The success of *Fern Leaves from Fanny's Port Folio* (1853) was, he thought, well deserved. She wrote in haste for the magazines of the day. At the outset her need was frankly commercial. In common with the majority of the women authors of her era, she took to the pen out of necessity. Frances Trollope was an English example. Widowed, divorced, or struggling to support a family after the failure of a husband's business, or with older relatives to care for, the 'scribbling women' became professionals almost despite themselves. Fanny Fern made her mark with a vernacular, vivacious weekly column – the ancestor of a brand of madcap confessional whose twentieth-century practitioners include Dorothy Parker, Cornelia Otis Skinner, Betty MacDonald and Erma Bombeck. Louisa May Alcott (1832–88), a pioneer in the post–1865 vogue for juvenile fiction (stories about children or for children, or both), disclosed her talent for raillery in 'Transcendental Wild Oats', a reminiscence of her father Bronson Alcott, whose philosophic leisure was subsidized by her own literary labours. There are signs of mischievous wit in youthful writing by Emily Dickinson; in the responses of Caroline Sturgis, a New England friend of Margaret Fuller; and one can see why both men and women of spirit might have appreciated the less mawkish sketches of Sara Payson Willis, such as the picture of a lively woman married to a dull man, a person 'about as genial as the north side of a meeting-house'. She warns against a marriage of that nature: 'make no such shipwreck of yourself. . . . Owls kill humming-birds!'

Augusta Jane Evans would never qualify as a humorist. Her *Macaria* is a turgid defence of the Confederate cause, accusing Abraham Lincoln and his evil minions of fanaticism and tyranny. But it too is curiously tinged with feminism. We gather (ch. 32) that Southern women's 'appropriate work consists in moulding the manners and morals of the nation', which they can best do as Christian matrons – the American extrapolation of the republican ideal. Irene, the heiress heroine, is tirelessly occupied in good works, however, including the superintendence of an orphanage; and at the end of the novel, in a conversation with her artist friend Electra, she announces her intention to open a 'School of Design for Women'. The upheavals of the Civil War have left thousands of her sex without means of support. A reading of J. S. Mill's *Political Economy* (1848) has made Irene reflect on his observation that women are paid much less than men, because their employment opportunities are restricted. Hence, says Irene, 'in improving the condition of women, it is advisable to give them ... access to independent industrial pursuits, and extend the circle of their ... occupations'. This book and many another of the type indicate a perhaps unwittingly strong concern with the *is* and *ought* of women's life. There is a common tendency to present contradictory views, as Augusta Evans does. Fanny Fern, far more emancipated in her journalist persona, nevertheless disclaims outright feminism. After ridiculing a pompous English male, and telling him with pride that 'femality is wide awake, over here', she immediately distances herself from the agitators: 'I shall reach the goal just as quick, in my velvet shoes, as if I tramped on rough-shod, as they do, with their Woman's Rights Convention brogans!'

Apropos of Whitman's hospital-visiting, we have already cited the sad old epigram that whereas in time of peace the sons bury the fathers, in time of war the fathers bury the sons. In the context of the present chapter, such a statement looks astonishingly inadequate. Mothers too bury their sons. Wives, sweethearts and sisters likewise suffer agonies of bereavement all the sharper because of their helpless marginality in face of the male apparatus of organized belligerence.

Indeed, despite the length and grimness of the Civil War, the first formal masculine commemorations can sound oddly callous and superficial. For instance, the Rev. Horace Bushnell, in a widely read 1865 address, propounded a stoutly insensitive theory: the casualties of the war were actually an index of its importance. Real fighting entailed profuse exchanges of fire, not a conserving of supplies; the Civil War dead thus constituted its 'spent ammunition'. If women have traditionally been the chief mourners, this may be because their sorrow runs deeper, and their need to justify what is otherwise mere slaughter. Genuine grief and yearning for consolation underlie the gush of a novel like *Macaria*. Perhaps that is why it was popular in the post-war North, despite its uncompromising Southernness: women readers may have felt the book's real message was expressed in the subtitle, *Altars of Sacrifice*. By the same token, thousands of women throughout the reconstituted Union drew comfort from *The Gates Ajar* (1868), a novel by the young New Englander Elizabeth Stuart Phelps. She had been in love with a lieutenant killed at Antietam in 1862. The heroine of her story, Mary Cabot, has an adored brother killed in action. Disgusted by the consolatory pieties of conventional religion, she finally accepts the assurance of wise Aunt Winifred that she will be reunited with her brother in a heavenly kingdom that is an idealized version of life on earth. Not only will family and friends be

joined again, but they will (ch. 16) shake hands with the great dead –
'President Lincoln, or Mrs. Browning'.

And by extension, every death becomes a matter of concern, and
religious testimony, for women. Bereavement was of course not their
monopoly. Death-bed scenes, especially those involving children and
young people, were the stock-in-trade of the prominent male authors,
such as Charles Dickens. The death of little Eva, in Harriet Beecher Stowe's
Uncle Tom's Cabin, was not in itself a woman's 'statement'. Yet writing
by women captures with particular poignance the sensations of loss
associated with departure, absence, sickness, whether or not these in fact
entail a death. In the era of Dickens and Stowe, women are, both in fiction
and in real life, those who wave goodbye, gaze out to sea, wait for letters,
face betrayal and abandonment, tend the sick, mourn the death of the
infants they have borne. In Stowe's novel *The Minister's Wooing* (1859),
the heroine believes her fiancé has been drowned at sea – an experience
actually endured by Harriet's elder sister Catharine Beecher, and intensified by Harriet's own grief at the recent death by drowning of her
undergraduate son.

Edgar Allan Poe felt that 'the most poetical topic in the world' was 'the
death of a beautiful woman'. But what if such a woman were deemed
immoral? The behaviour attributed to George Sand, and sanctioned by
her in writing about fictional women, was solemnly deplored by American
reviewers. Handsome, sexually magnetic women existed in the United
States. They were tolerated and even admired if, like Miriam F. Leslie
(1836–1914) in New York, or Mabel Loomis Todd (1856–1932) in
Amherst, their allure was outwardly respectable; and this although they
were associated with the literary world.

But what if a female author–intellectual did not conform to social codes,
was forceful in expressing herself, and was not by ordinary standards
beautiful or winsome? Such was the case of the exceptionally clever and
articulate New England bluestocking Margaret Fuller. Her erudition was
not in question, nor her ability to speak and write. She acquired friends,
admirers and followers in the Boston–Cambridge milieu. When she became
a commentator for the New York *Tribune*, she escaped the anonymity
required of other contributors: her pieces were in effect 'signed' with an
asterisk – a symbol that at once identified her to those in the know. Such
strengths, and a somewhat shocking candour of sensuousness, are features
of the character Zenobia in Hawthorne's *Blithedale Romance*, which is
supposed to have been modelled upon Fuller.

In nineteenth-century fiction, sexual or other recklessness on the part of a woman almost always led to death: *her* death, for death was the wages of sin according to the established moral calculus. Zenobia commits suicide by drowning. Margaret Fuller's own accidental death by drowning, as she returned home from years of recklessness in Italy, probably prompted contemporaries to feel that her end was dramatically appropriate. Hers, apparently, was a figurative as well as a real shipwreck:

Thus there appears to have been a total collapse in poor Margaret, morally and intellectually; and tragic as her catastrophe was, Providence was after all, kind in putting her, and her clownish husband, and their child, on board that fated ship.

This harsh verdict, from Hawthorne's *French and Italian Notebooks*, records some gossip he picked up in Florence in 1858, and was obviously ready to believe. Her Italian husband, said Hawthorne, was almost illiterate, and 'without any pretensions to be a gentleman'. Her feeling for Ossoli must have been 'purely sensual'; his feeling for her 'could hardly have been even this, for she had not the charm of womanhood'. Margaret was a humbug, Hawthorne continued, though a talented one; she had 'lost all power of literary production, before she left Rome', and was not bringing back any manuscript 'History of the Roman Revolution'.

Emerson, who collaborated with two other editors to produce the two-volume posthumous *Memoirs of Margaret Fuller Ossoli* (1852), was less censorious than Hawthorne. But they omitted documents, including love letters, which embarrassed them, as if they too considered her scandalous. She had once tried to conduct a platonic flirtation with Emerson, yet was capable of brusque disagreement with him. Attempting to be generous in writing about her, Emerson was also truthful in confessing that he found her puzzling and sometimes disturbing – regally opinionated, but subject to emotional despairs, and agonized by the thought that 'a man's ambition with a woman's heart, is an evil lot'. He quoted revealing lines from a poem of hers, 'To the Moon':

> But if I steadfast gaze upon thy face,
> A human secret, like my own, I trace;
> For, through the woman's smile looks the male eye. . . .

It is hard to estimate what Margaret Fuller might have accomplished if there had been no shipwreck on Fire Island. Could she have faced down moralistic critics, as her great English contemporary George Eliot finally did? She herself recognized that she lacked the talent to write fiction, or lyric poetry on the level of Elizabeth Barrett Browning. Yet her memoirs and correspondence are poignantly alive; her journalism, while radically 'committed', is acute and informative; above all in the highly original *Woman in the Nineteenth Century*, she speculates with brilliant sympathy on questions of gender, friendship, talent and literary and social values. Her early observations sometimes strain too hard. But in Italy she went beyond Transcendental rhapsody, or precocious displays of her mastery of, say, Tasso and Goethe. She is a world away from, and in general above, the mass of conventional if competent 'scribbling women' of whom Hawthorne disapproved for different reasons. A comparable contemporary, perhaps, was the English author, traveller and intellectual Harriet Martineau, whom she met and admired in 1835. Martineau, however, was quick to discern the disabilities under which American women suffered. Perhaps Fuller could have survived and thrived, with the handsome unintellectual Ossoli; if so, the odds were probably more favourable for such a ménage in Europe. Back in Italy, she could conceivably have existed as a literary expatriate, writing for the *Tribune* and for posterity, her fame tinged with a degree of notoriety that stopped bearably short of ostracism. If she was high-strung, she had plenty of courage, and a love of life that grew with the years. There is little of Zenobia, for instance, in Fuller's mid-Western travel book, *Summer on the Lakes* (1844). Here she is at Niagara, seated beside the prodigious plunge of water:

A man came to take his first look. He walked up close to the fall, and after looking at it a moment, . . . as if thinking how he could best appropriate it for his own use, he spat into it.

In a less extreme sense, Harriet Beecher Stowe also stood out from the women writers of the century. Most of the 'literary domestics' expressed relatively conservative views. Stowe's first, spectacularly famous novel, *Uncle Tom's Cabin*, had some of the weaknesses of the middlebrow literature of the day: preachiness, sentimentality and so on. Uncle Tom has been derided as a caricature of black obsequiousness, so pious and loyal that he is mainly a white stereotype, far too good to be true. That is why the black writer James Baldwin called it 'Everybody's Protest Novel' – a basically prejudiced book calculated to make white liberals feel comfortably indignant.

Harriet Beecher Stowe was not immune to the covert prejudices of her society; Baldwin might have been right in seeing the 'protest novel' as a peculiarly American genre whose effect is to reassure readers that they are generous even if others are not. But *Uncle Tom's Cabin* is a better book than that. In the first place, it was so fiercely anti-slavery that it infuriated the South. Stowe did not write a commercially equivocal story, attempting to placate advocates as well as opponents of chattel slavery. The stereotypes in the novel do belong to the received wisdom of the day. But she was not absurd in assuming that some slaves were conditioned to behave like 'Uncle Toms', or that Christian worship was a powerful agency among black Americans. Nor did she pretend that misunderstanding and mistreatment of the Negroes were confined to Southerners. The villainous overseer, Simon Legree, is a Vermonter (though with a South Carolina name?), and there is an acid portrait of Miss Ophelia, a squeamish New England spinster who does not like to have any physical contact with black people. Mrs Stowe, the daughter, wife and sister of preachers of the Gospel, wrote a tract for the times, in the hope of arousing public sentiment. It might well have been as stilted as certain specimens of anti-slavery propaganda, or as the pro-slavery novels (such as *Aunt Phillis's Cabin*) published to counter her book. *Uncle Tom's Cabin* is a far better tale because the author, while caring passionately about her subject, brought to it an unusual energy, narrative power, and desire to be accurate. The death of Eva, a scene that made readers weep on both sides of the Atlantic, was indeed accurate in that it described something heartrendingly familiar in many a home, including that of Margaret Fuller, who as a child came home to find the nursemaid in tears, and to be told her little sister was dead ('I see yet that beauty of death! The highest achievements of sculpture are only the reminder of its severe sweetness').

Much of the more thoughtful argument about the book turned on the question of veracity. Could fiction be truthful? The point was discussed by the Southern sociologist George Frederick Holmes, reviewing Stowe in the *Southern Literary Messenger* (December 1852), and by the New England clergyman Nehemiah Adams in *A South-Side View of Slavery* (1854; ch. 13). What was the status of an imaginary account of plantation life? Stowe tried to refute such critics by producing a documentary *Key to Uncle Tom's Cabin*. The debate on those terms was never resolved; and of course it continues down to the present day; some people contend that ascertainable fact must be strictly adhered to, others that truth is relative or subjective, or most effectively conveyed through the medium of interpretative art.

Mrs Stowe never abandoned her own concern to be factually, psychologically and poetically truthful. Her sense of standards is evident in other less famous novels that draw upon her New England background. In them she portrays small, tense communities where religious observance and debate furnish the main fabric of existence – as indeed they did for the Beecher family. The characters in these books are serious, in that certain aspects of life are serious to them. Her villains – Aaron Burr in *The Minister's Wooing* (1859), Ellery Davenport in *Oldtown Folks* (1869) – are almost preposterous in the suavity of their sinfulness.

As a child she was forbidden to read any novels save those of Walter Scott. Cotton Mather's *Magnalia Christi Americana*, which she was encouraged to read, 'made me feel the very ground I trod on to be consecrated by some special dealing of God's providence'. Yet her clergyman father could throw off his dignity now and then. She recalled that he once shinned up a high chestnut tree that grew out over a precipice, 'then whirling himself over the abyss to beat down chestnuts for the children below'. Such incidents are rare in her novels. Their tone is reticent, as in Hawthorne, whom she rivals in her knowledge of the Puritan heritage. Still, as evocations of the New England scene, and of the Calvinist character, the books mentioned (together with *The Pearl of Orr's Island*, 1862, and *Poganuc People*, 1878), have a quality of circumstantial authenticity. Speech and dress and gestures are in exact focus. The closer these books come to description and analysis, the better they are. Thin as novels, they are strong sketches of an environment which she understood directly – not vicariously, as with the South of *Uncle Tom's Cabin*. In that novel, a certain staginess of presentation made it a suitable vehicle for the literal staginess of the dramatized version; travelling companies of 'Tommers' re-enacted Little Eva's demise, or Eliza's escape from the bloodhounds, before countless small-town audiences.

The 'documentary' side of Harriet Beecher Stowe's work can be described as local colour, though to say that is to note that local-colour fiction was already in existence before the Civil War. Certainly Stowe inspired New England's best writer in the genre, Sara Orne Jewett. As a girl Sarah Orne Jewett loved *The Pearl of Orr's Island*, a novel about the Maine coast, where she grew up, and which she soon began to depict, in short stories and then in novels. Her work is deliberately localized. Most of it deals with simple folk, on farms and in small towns that are never far from the sea. Most of her characters are women who have known one another all their lives. While they would not agree with Emerson that people 'who know the same thing are not long the best company for each other', they can be so laconic as to seem surly. This presents Sarah Orne Jewett with a problem in understatement. 'It is difficult', she realizes, 'to report the great events of New England; expression is so slight, and those few words which escape us in moments of deep feeling look but meagre on the printed page.' Much of their life is retrospection. Their settlements and harbours are on the decline, and deaths seem to outnumber births. (One whole island was in fact depopulated when its farm families departed for the Western gold-fields.) Not an obviously rewarding subject-matter for a novelist, it is exactly suited to Miss Jewett's gentle, economical talent.

Her best book, *The Country of the Pointed Firs* (1896), is a set of sketches about the imaginary Dunnet, a 'salt-aired, white-clap-boarded little town' observed by a narrator who can be taken as the author herself. Through Mrs Todd, the woman with whom she boards, the narrator enters unobtrusively into the lives of the townsfolk. Some of them have travelled far. Captain Littlepage has been to Hudson's Bay, and met an insane old Scotsman who believes he has discovered an Arctic Purgatory (comparable in its weird way to the Antarctic otherworld of Poe's *Arthur Gordon Pym*). Another inhabitant, Mrs Fosdick, sailed as a child in her father's ship:

'Ought to see them painted savages I've seen when I was young out in the South Sea Islands! That was the time for folks to travel, 'way back in the old whalin' days.... I used to return feelin' very slack an' behind the times, 'tis true,... but 'twas excitin', an' we always done extra well, and felt rich when we did get ashore.'

But they are elderly now; the world has drawn in upon them, and even the travelled ones are sure no place can compare with their own corner of Maine.

Sarah Orne Jewett's writing is as neat and unaffected as the homes of Dunnet, though like those homes it is relieved by an occasional decorative flourish. It balances between a rueful recognition of decay and a New England tartness which differentiates it sharply from the local colour of that other decaying region, the South:

There was an old house on the height ... – a mere shell of an old house, with empty windows that looked like blind eyes. The frost-bitten grass grew close about it like brown fur, and there was a single crooked bough of lilac holding its green leaves by the door.

'We'll just have a good piece of bread-an'-butter now,' said [Mrs Todd] ...., 'and then we'll hang up the basket on some peg inside the house out o' the way o' the sheep....'

Mary Wilkins Freeman (1852–1930), in such collections of stories as *A Humble Romance* (1887) and *A New England Nun* (1891), is another able chronicler of rural life in that region of the United States. Most of her tales are set in Massachusetts and deal principally with women. The New England aura is evident too in the work of America's greatest woman poet, Emily Dickinson, who partly by choice consigned herself to domestic obscurity in the small college town of Amherst. Nowhere but in such a compact, bookish community could an American woman be so tensely alone and yet so articulate, so buoyed up by the décor and the rules of existence: so aware of the contiguity of this world and the next. Or, one might add, so uneven and unfinished despite her genius. Here is the epitome of 'local' colour – writing that has shrunk in scale to the boundaries of a house, the surrounding garden, the view from the lawn or windows. Here is a sort of privileged seclusion (no domestic drudgery for Dickinson), that has on the one hand an almost agonized Calvinistic self-denial and, on the other, a transcendentally gratifying experience of communion with nature.

At her death Emily Dickinson left considerably more than a thousand unpublished poems and fragments. Only a few friends knew she had written them. Many were mere ideas for poems, jotted down on whatever scrap of paper lay to hand. Others had been revised with some care. All, however, were short poems, broken for the most part into four-line stanzas; and all have an unmistakable personal stamp. They are as compressed as a telegram. They are like oracular messages, but witty – jaunty at times – and sometimes trembling on the edge of whimsy. They have a scale of their own; the far-away and enormous are seen in terms of the humble and familiar, or vice versa. In her miniature world crumbs serve for a banquet; small creatures – fly, spider, bee, robin, butterfly – can loom immensely against the eye. Thus:

> The Crickets sang
> And set the Sun
> And Workmen finished one by one
> Their Seam the Day upon.

> The low Grass loaded with the Dew
> The Twilight stood, as Strangers do
> With Hat in Hand, polite and new
> To stay as if, or go.

> A Vastness, as a Neighbor, came,
> A Wisdom without Face, or Name,
> A Peace, as Hemispheres at home
> And so the Night became.

This poem, not among her finest, can be considered fairly typical. The prosody is erratic; there are conflicting images; the end, with its characteristic abnormal use of a verb, is abrupt and anticlimactic. Even so, as this particular poem shows, her work is extraordinarily rich and alert. *Cricket, workman, stranger, neighbour*: with these homely and small figures she tackles the coming of night. Yet, in the final stanza, the small has become 'a vastness', something prodigious and mysterious – 'a wisdom without face or name'. Notice also Emily Dickinson's acute susceptibility to *mood*, especially as affected by the change of light. Light reveals the subtle alteration of things, the sly or calamitous impermanence of mortal life:

> Presentiment – is that long Shadow – on the Lawn –
> Indicative that Suns go down –
> The Notice to the startled Grass
> That Darkness – is about to pass –

These lines form a complete poem. Another, in four stanzas, begins:

> There's a certain Slant of light,
> Winter Afternoons –
> That oppresses, like the Heft
> Of Cathedral Tunes –

and ends:

> When it comes, the Landscape listens –
> Shadows – hold their breath –
> When it goes, 'tis like the Distance
> On the look of Death –

The look of Death; she is preoccupied with death, the gateway to the next existence. It is conceived of as a special glory that has something, though not everything, in common with the conventional paradises offered in the hymns and sermons of her day, or with the Book of Revelation, which was among her favourite reading. Death means leisure, grandeur, recognition; it means being with the few, rare people whom it was not possible to know fully upon earth. The house is prelude to the tomb:

> We paused before a House that seemed
> A Swelling of the Ground –
> The Roof was scarcely visible –
> The Cornice – in the Ground –

Beyond the tomb, after the 'White Election', God presides over an opulent

kingdom whose splendours she denotes in words like *purple, royal, privilege,
emerald, diadem, courtier, Potosi, Himmaleh*. All help to reinforce her view
of immortality. Much of life is anguish endured in an ante-room to death;
as the 'empress of Calvary', she might have said with Whitman that

To die is different from what any one supposed, and luckier.

The poet is the keen observer who keeps life uncluttered as far as possible:
who,

> spreading wide my narrow hands
> To gather paradise,

catches whatever clues of Paradise are vouchsafed in the external world.
Nature supplies some hints, not of the transcendental order but altogether
more tantalizing and momentary:

> We spy the Forests and the Hills
> The Tents to Nature's Show
> Mistake the Outside for the in
> And mention what we saw.

It is the 'in' she watches for, the instantaneous flash when the mortal
seems about to pierce the veil. It happens, almost, when light changes, as
at the approach of a storm; or when seasons pass ('These behaviours of
the year hurt almost like music'); or above all when there is a death. At
such times she could feel that

> The Only News I know
> Is Bulletins all Day
> From Immortality.

In the poem 'Just lost, when I was saved!', an illness from which she has
recovered appears as an unsuccessful exploration:

> Therefore, as One returned, I feel,
> Odd secrets of the line to tell!
> Some Sailor, skirting foreign shores –
> Some pale Reporter, from the awful doors
> Before the Seal!

However, Emily Dickinson's vision of the next world is tempered by her
whimsical, domestic cast of mind; by what has been called the 'rococo' as
distinct from the 'sublime' element in her character.[1] Though she speaks

---

1. By Richard Chase, *Emily Dickinson* ('American Men of Letters'; London, 1952).

again and again of isolation in this world, she is not a mystic like St Teresa of Avila, or a religious poet like St John of the Cross. Dickinson flirts with eternity, she is coquettish with God, forgiving him his 'duplicity', sometimes distressingly coy:

> I hope the Father in the skies
> Will lift his little girl –
> Old-fashioned – naughty – everything –
> Over the stile of 'Pearl'.

God is a puzzling figure in her work. The Creator who may not know why he has created, he is 'burglar, banker, father', gentleman, duke, king: a being personified at times as Death, at other times as a sort of lover. Perhaps these are versions of the men with whom she may have been secretly in love, or of her own father. In correspondence with men, including her mentor Thomas Wentworth Higginson, there is a sort of display of plumage, the hint of a complex momentary courtship. It is possible to read some of her poems as covert avowals of affection, even passion.

Sometimes there is an edge too of New England humour, sometimes the recklessness evident in the behaviour of sensitive and unloved children. She takes amazing liberties with sacred themes. No wonder that Christina Rossetti, after praising Emily Dickinson's poetry, went on to deplore 'some of the religious, or rather irreligious pieces'. Perhaps the defect is not so much a matter of irreligion as of immaturity; a concern with the small and the familiar can approach garden-ornament whimsy, as when she signs her correspondence, 'Your Gnome'.

But the final impression is of a quick sensibility to the world around her and to the materials of her craft. Technically a poor poet, she does effective violence to vocabulary. Terms from many sources – law, geometry, engineering – are used to suit her purposes. Commonplace words come alive in new contexts, and she never hesitates to substitute parts of speech:

> Kingdoms like the orchard
> Flit russetly away.

At times her economy is that of New England idiom:

> And 'twas like midnight, some, –

The laconic *some* could only have been used by an American poet.

While she was not without friends, she keeps them at arm's length, so that she may discuss her affairs with a poet's abstraction (like Thoreau, who closed a letter by saying, 'You will perceive that I am as often talking to myself, perhaps, as speaking to you'). She never saw Mabel Loomis Todd face to face. Her relationship with Helen Hunt Jackson began with a mini-comedy of misunderstandings. 'The lawn is full of south and the odors tangle', she tells one correspondent, 'and I hear to-day for the first the river in the tree.' Again, 'If I feel physically as if the top of my head were taken off, I know that is poetry.' In her finest lines she has the magic of a major poet. The words

> Further in Summer than the Birds
> Pathetic from the Grass,

to take one example from hundreds, wonderfully defy analysis. Hawthorne whispers at us, as if he were deaf; Melville shouts, as if he suspected his *audience* were deaf; and Emily Dickinson too seems unsure how to pitch her work. But like the others, she draws strength from isolation.

In the spectrum of nineteenth-century writing by American women, Margaret Fuller is at the extreme opposite from the more primly mediocre 'literary domestics'. Fuller flouted convention in word and deed. Before the Civil War Harriet Beecher Stowe angered Southerners (and some in the North) by conveying her opposition to chattel slavery; but then, she was married, and pious; her abolitionist views became the American democratic orthodoxy; and, while the sales of her subsequent books disappointed her, she was in old age a firmly established authoress. The unorthodoxies of Emily Dickinson go deeper, perhaps. Harriet Beecher Stowe would have been as upset as Christina Rossetti if she could have seen, for instance, a Dickinson poem about the inefficacy of religion; once when people died

> They went to God's Right Hand –
> That Hand is amputated now
> And God cannot be found –

but such blasphemies were hidden from the public. Fanny Fern, while quick to recognize the sexual honesty of *Leaves of Grass*, could not jeopardize her popular following by becoming Whitman's outright champion.

Circumspection continued to mark the careers of most women writers, to an even greater degree than those of 'genteel tradition' men of letters. They cannot be blamed for persisting in approved forms of journalism, fiction and poetry, or for trying their hand at the newer fields of juvenile and humorous literature. Now and then an authentic statement of individual personality or social concern got into print. On the brink of the Civil War, when readers had other things on their mind, the *Atlantic Monthly* published the unsigned 'Life in the Iron Mills' by Rebecca Harding Davis (1831–1910). This tale of proletarian misery was to make a powerful impression, more than sixty years afterwards, on the youthful Tillie Olsen, the daughter of hard-pressed immigrant workers and later to be the author of *Tell Me a Riddle* (1961), *Yonnondio* (1974) and *Silences* (1978). Herself long denied the opportunity for peaceful composition, Olsen has often spoken of women *en masse* as prisoners of circumstance. In Rebecca Harding Davis's case authorship provided a productive and reasonably successful career. However, she increasingly conformed to the novelettish formulas of the market, to the detriment of her work; and – a further irony – she tended to be referred to as 'the mother of Richard Harding Davis', whose debonair journalism and fiction gradually overshadowed her own.

From the vantage-point of the late twentieth century, we can look back on a huge expansion of writing by women, in every field. Some of their achievements are described in later chapters. At the end of the nineteenth century, however, American women authors were with few exceptions regarded as versifiers rather than bards, and entertainers or uplifters rather than fabulists or prophets. True, so were the majority of American male authors. Yet the inhibiting factors for women narrowed their range even more.

Their extra handicaps can be illustrated from the fate of Kate Chopin. After being left a young widow with several children to raise, she began to write local-colour stories and sketches of life in Louisiana. *Bayou Folk* (1894) and *A Night in Acadie* (1897) were well received; and the more perceptive reviewers noted that she wrote with a cool, cosmopolitan assurance. Her novel *At Fault* (1890), according to Per Seyersted, was the first in America to 'deal with divorce ... in a tone that was not moralistic'. It did not sell many copies. But at least it aroused no scandal, unlike *The Awakening* (1899), an extraordinary piece of condensed, lyrical realism that seems to belong more to the spirit of *fin de siècle* Europe than to the moralistic prescriptions of literature in the United States. Edna Pontellier, the central character of the novel, is a 'modern' woman like Nora in Ibsen's *The Doll's House*. Restless as a matron housewife, fond enough of her husband but bored by domestic samenesses, she takes a lover; and finally, not so much from despair as from a romantic yearning for freedom and oblivion, she swims out alone into the sunlit sea, too far to turn back. In her last imaginings, about to sink,

Edna heard her father's voice and her sister Margaret's. She heard the barking of an old dog that was chained to the sycamore tree. The spurs of the cavalry officer clanged as he walked across the porch. There was the hum of bees, and the musky odor of pinks filled the air.

At the same period Kate Chopin dealt with the theme of sexual awakening (the 'meaning' of her novel's title) in a radiantly economical short story, 'The Storm'. But this time the reviewers scolded her, and some friends dropped her as an undesirable acquaintance. She lapsed into almost immediate obscurity. For half a century after her death in 1904, she was forgotten as if her name had been struck from the rolls.

For the average male, American women around 1900 were still what Edward Bellamy (in *Equality*, 1897, his sympathetic prediction of a forthcoming revolution in social and economic relations) called 'the religious sex'. Ex-President Grover Cleveland declared (*Ladies' Home Journal*, October 1905) that women's suffrage would be 'unwise', since women lacked 'the power of clear and logical reasoning' and were sometimes 'fitful and petulant' – even if their sulks were invariably 'the prelude to bright smiles and sunny endearments'. The foolishness of such opinions was galling to an intellectual like Charlotte Perkins Gilman (1860–1935), author of the icily controlled *Women and Economics* (1898) and of an anguished fictional sketch of a nervous breakdown, 'The Yellow Wall-Paper' (1891).

It was easier for men than for women to write airily of the circumstances of American women: to focus, for instance, on the undoubted fact that American society was producing quantities of young 'emancipated' women, whether or not their qualifications found any appropriate outlet outside the home. H. H. Boyesen (*Literary and Social Silhouettes*, 1894) christened the type the 'Aspiring Young Woman' – educated, earnest and charmless, like the woman student at Cornell University with whom he claimed to have had a waltz: 'Just as we swung out upon the floor she exploded this query in my ears: "Now, won't you be kind enough to give me, just in a few words, the gist of Spinoza's *Ethics?*" It did not surprise me afterwards to learn that she danced because it was good for the digestion.' William Dean Howells (who included 'The Yellow Wall-Paper' in a collection of *Great Modern American Stories*, 1920) was more generous. His Utopian novel *Through the Eye of the Needle* (1907) purported to be an account of the ideal world of Altruria seen by an American woman. She and her Altrurian diplomat husband, arriving there by sea, are greeted by flower-laden boats, each

not *manned*, but *girled* by six rowers, who pulled as true a stroke as I ever saw. When they caught sight of us, . . . they all stood their oars upright, and burst into a kind of welcome song: I had been dreading one of these stupid, banging salutes of ten or twenty guns, and you can imagine what a relief it was. They were great, splendid creatures, and tall as our millionaires' tallest daughters, and as strong-looking as any of our college-girl athletes. . . .

Magnificent women, yes – statuesque as the females drawn by Charles Dana Gibson, yet liberated from the social round within which 'Gibson girls' seemed to be trapped.

Howells imagined a freedom yet to be: and a freedom hard even to postulate in certain corners of the nation, as Kate Chopin discovered. Her younger Southern compatriot Ellen Glasgow (1874–1945), a sickly, nervous and lonely child in an impoverished, joyless Richmond family, grew up in the old Confederate capital among Virginians who 'did not publish, did not write, did not read'. She began to write novels like *The Battle-Ground* (1902) which enshrined yet by degrees questioned and then satirized what she was to call the 'sanctified fallacies' of her region. Among the fallacies which she was eventually to expose (for instance, in *Barren Ground*, 1925) were the 'womanly' obligations (domesticity) and prizes (wedded bliss to upright, prospering suitors). With *Barren Ground*, according to a slogan used by her publisher as an advertisement, 'Realism Crosses the Potomac'. It was palpably there to stay in the work of Eudora Welty of Mississippi and Flannery O'Connor (1925–64), women writers for whom local colour retained no vestige of moonlight and magnolias.

Realism crossed the Mississippi, too, with Willa Cather, who began life in Virginia but grew up on the Nebraska prairie. She was in a way Boyesen's Aspiring Young Woman – vigorous, hungry for culture, precociously talented, a campus personality who often wore men's hats, then a journalist in Pittsburgh and (for *McClure's Magazine*) in New York. Though she did not address her poetry, fiction or critical essays to the subject of love between women, in Cather's combination of public and private life she became an accomplished and recognized professional author who formed some abiding relationships with other women.

She is too richly versatile to be categorized in any restrictive sense as a woman writer, or for that matter a realist or local-colourist or regionalist.

She wrote of Scandinavian and central European immigrants toiling to survive as prairie farmers (*O Pioneers!*, 1913; *My Ántonia*, 1918); but also (*The Song of the Lark*, 1915) of musical and other creative talent seeking fulfilment in metropolitan milieux; of the continent's ancient Indian settlements, and of the endeavours of pioneering Catholic priests in the New World (*The Professor's House*, 1925; *Death Comes for the Archbishop*, 1927; *Shadows on the Rock*, 1931); of painful clashes over love and individual fulfilment (*My Mortal Enemy*, 1926; *Lucy Gayheart*, 1935); and (*Not Under Forty*, 1936) of the professional concerns of a writer who confessed indebtedness to predecessors as various as Flaubert, Henry James and Sarah Orne Jewett.

What she shared with all three was a dedication to the craft of words, a determination to catch the exact truth about particular people in particular habitats. Cather wrote with deceptive economy and lucidity. She did not sentimentalize the harsh, sometimes brutish existence of her farm folk, nor the achievements of refined and artistic people (realizing that their attainments exacted a price, from themselves or from others). With increasing age, she was less and less happy about what 'America' symbolized; it is perhaps significant that her borrowing of a title (*O Pioneers!*) from exuberantly patriotic lines by Whitman came early in her evolution. She valued tradition, integrity, sensibility. She was stirred accordingly by the relics of ancient civilizations, whether of Greece and Rome or of the Pueblo Indians of Colorado and New Mexico. She was distressed by the ephemeral and spurious aspects of modernity. And to the extent that timeless virtues were embodied in certain of her female characters, Willa Cather may justly be considered a woman writer. Ántonia Shimerda from Bohemia is a child in a squalid, broken family, works as a maid, and has a baby by a man who deserts her. Disgraced and humiliated, she eventually attains security and respect: deservedly, for 'she was a rich mine of life, like the founders of early races'. Such bald summaries leave out the special tone and timbre of Cather's writing, a musing, amused, elegiac womanhood wisdom.

THE COMING OF AGE
POETRY AND FICTION

By 1910 or so, the realist movement in prose that Howells had helped to inaugurate forty years before had lost much of its impetus. Crane, Norris and other promising authors were dead; Dreiser had apparently disappeared into hack journalism (though he reappeared with *Jennie Gerhardt*, in 1911); and Howells knew that to most young writers he was himself 'comparatively a dead cult'. A good deal of energy had been diverted into 'muckraking' literature like Gustavus Myers's *History of the Great American Fortunes* and Jane Addams's *Twenty Years at Hull-House* (an account of settlement work in Chicago), which were both published in 1910.

Yet if there was a temporary lull in the development of American fiction, there was plenty of life in other art-forms during these years when O. Henry was pouring out his slick and nimble stories of 'Bagdad-on-the-Subway'. In this same New York the photographer Alfred Stieglitz established his famous *salon* at 291 Fifth Avenue, and as early as 1908 was introducing to America some of the painters whom Gertrude Stein and her brother had discovered in Paris. Also in 1908, the 'Ashcan' school of American painters held a New York exhibition meant to show the public that realism need not be confined to the medium of the printed word. The critic James G. Huneker helped to inform the public of the revolutionary achievements of Diaghilev and the Ballet Russe, of Stravinsky and Debussy. Rumours of the London 'Imagists' came across the Atlantic. In 1913, New York had its chance, at the Armory Show of post-impressionist art, to see the work of the same artists that Roger Fry had introduced to London three years before, at the Grafton Galleries. Nor were these excitements confined to New York: the Armory Show, for example, was also sent to Chicago and Boston. The redoubtable American woman played her part. Though Gertrude Stein remained overseas, Mabel Dodge Luhan settled in New York in 1912, after a ten-year sojourn in Italy, determined to bring enlightenment to the United States. Amy Lowell was hardly less active in Boston, while in Chicago Harriet Monroe and Margaret Anderson were eager to do battle for the sake of culture. Isadora Duncan, the dancer from San Francisco, gloried in an enlightenment which others thought scandalous. Magazines came into being to voice the new sentiments in the air. In 1912 Harriet Monroe founded *Poetry: A Magazine of Verse* (a title whose seeming tautology made it clear that she was primarily interested in poetry, not in pieces *about* poetry). The year 1914 saw the beginning of Margaret Anderson's *Little Review* (like *Poetry*, a Chicago venture) and of the *New Republic*. In that year, too, H. L. Mencken and George Jean Nathan became joint editors of *The Smart Set*. The fiddles, as J. B. Yeats observed, were tuning up. More than most dates, 1912 defines the effective start of a rich era in American poetry, an era not interrupted by the European war which broke out in 1914. Though America joined the war in April 1917, its poets were able to continue what they had begun in the pre-war years (though the prose writers had to some extent to learn over again when the war was over).

One could say of 1912, in the words of the old song,

> There's a good time coming, and it's not far off –
> Been long, long, long on the way.

In that year several of the poets who were about to make their name had had to wait a long time for the moment. Edgar Lee Masters was forty-three, Robert Frost was thirty-seven, Carl Sandburg thirty-four, and Vachel Lindsay and Wallace Stevens both thirty-three. The 'new poetry', which came so much later than the comparable movement in prose, had thus had a lengthy gestation: it was no firework display of precocious talent. Nearly all its practitioners had cast about uncertainly, before finding the appropriate words and form.

Some poets never did quite fit together the necessary ingredients. The Southerner Sidney Lanier (1842–81) is one instance; another was Edwin Arlington Robinson (1869–1935). Robinson, a poet of New England and the exact contemporary of Edgar Lee Masters, came near to first-rateness but just missed it, perhaps because of too great isolation and obscurity in his formative years, perhaps from an unduly hesitant and fastidious reaction to his time. He was interested in Zola and in Hardy, and tried to write prose, modulating gradually by trial and error into his own poetic style. It was a painful, hangdog progress; although his first volume of poems was published (privately) in 1896, not until the 1920s did the public reward him. When it did, his success was considerable; he was three times a Pulitzer prize-winner. This very fact is indicative, perhaps, of the extent to which he fell short of true mastery. He had not altered greatly in these twenty-odd years: public taste moved forwards just far enough to accept him where it would not accept other 'modern' poets. His dour, questing, pessimistic poetry was sufficiently linked to conventional verse to pass for that, though a great deal better. Many of his early poems were portraits of lonely, wayward, confused men. They were subtle portraits, sometimes catching exactly the dry New England idiom. Such poems as 'Isaac and Archibald', 'Miniver Cheevy', 'Eros Turannos' and 'Mr Flood's Party' – to choose four deservedly fastened on by anthologists – have a wit and point underlaid by a deep perception of futility. He shows the human situation, however glossy the surfaces, to be complex and comfortless. Even in 'Miniver Cheevy', a comic poem in some ways –

> Miniver loved the Medici,
> Albeit he had never seen one;
> He would have sinned incessantly
> Could he have been one –

even here, the final note is one of failure:

> Miniver Cheevy, born too late,
> Scratched his head and kept on thinking;
> Miniver coughed, and called it fate,
> And kept on drinking.

Emily Dickinson (like Gerard Manley Hopkins) gives the sense of having come before her time; but Robinson, like Miniver Cheevy, suggests a man born too late – or supposing that he has been born too late. Something, we gather, is wrong; but neither his complaint nor his remedy is entirely satisfying. The New England dryness that is one of his strengths, preserving him from too literary a formulation, may also be a defect; one sometimes suspects that the reticence is not courage but drabness, concealing not despair but hollowness. There is a lack in Robinson of the contemporary awareness – not the ephemerally up-to-date quality of the bestselling novelist, but the profound one of the poet. He does not quite match theme and thought. His poems, despite their dignity and felicity, have an air of charade; and, especially in the popular Arthurian trilogy, of an unduly prolonged charade, whose answer is guessable after the first scene. Not wholly, possessedly sure of what he is about, not finding the way through, he becomes diffuse, lapsing into elegant paraphrase. A similar tonal uncertainty characterizes other poets of the time: the English Georgians, for example, and such Americans as William Vaughn Moody and Trumbull

Stickney, both of whom occasionally capture the modern manner, only to lose it again in a plethora of words.

Chicago led the movement when it came. The Chicago of Dreiser's *Sister Carrie*, Norris's *The Pit*, Henry B. Fuller's *The Cliff-Dwellers* (1893), Robert Herrick's *Memoirs of an American Citizen* (1905), or Upton Sinclair's *The Jungle* (1906), each depicting a harsh metropolis – was also a place of growing civic pride. The second city in the United States, Chicago saw no reason why it should not overhaul New York culturally as well as in population. In 1892 it acquired a university. In the following year Chicago hosted the huge World's Fair or Columbian Exposition; and in 1912 came Harriet Monroe's *Poetry*. Gratifyingly, its hinterland began to produce writers. The Illinois poets Carl Sandburg (1878–1967), Nicholas Vachel Lindsay (1879–1931) and Edgar Lee Masters (1869–1950), were destined to contribute to what can be called the American as distinct from the cosmopolitan movement in modern poetry. Brought up a thousand miles from the Atlantic, the trio considered themselves the more American on that account. All three were strongly drawn to Abraham Lincoln, also of Illinois: Lincoln the plain man, the martyr, the man of sorrows, epitome of America. Sandburg wrote a six-volume biography of his hero; Lindsay was born in Springfield, the town that Lincoln knew best; and Masters's lawyer father had been the partner of William Herndon, Lincoln's former partner in the same profession.

'In infancy I never heard of New England': so wrote Lindsay, and in essence the same was true of Masters and of Sandburg, the son of a Swedish immigrant. The Mississippi Valley was their heartland, in an emotional as well as in a geopolitical sense. Chicago was their metropolis, and their poetry aimed at catching the atmosphere of the central region of which it was the capital. Sandburg and Lindsay in particular tried to answer the great American *public–people* conundrum – that of making the ordinary extraordinary, of plucking significance out of common events.

The dangers were great when the effort was made. It was easy for the poet to slip into the rhetoric of the platform, to become excessively concerned with manliness, to surrender to a glib evocation of Western, pioneering America, to lose the individual in the crowd: in a word, to substitute for his private vision a public tableau. Nor was the language of the streets a simple thing to apply to poetry. Slang and dialect become quickly dated, or are unintelligible, or merely a hindrance to understanding; or can seem falsely 'folksy'. Sandburg and Lindsay began by identifying themselves as far as possible with the people; in fact, Sandburg grew from them, for he worked as a casual labourer before he started to write.

They were assisted in their efforts to create a poetry of and for the masses, first, by the sympathetic attitude of the modern movement towards 'anti-poetic' themes and vocabulary; second, by the genuine vitality of American popular speech; and third, by the special contribution of black America, not least the moods and techniques of jazz – that unique musical form which emerged not from the world of wine, women and song, but out of 'booze, brothels, and blues'.

With such aids the poetry of Carl Sandburg came into being. His first poems, published in 1904, were ignored. Ten years later, the poetry-reading world was ready for his verse. He won a prize for the poem 'Chicago'; possibly the award was influenced by the fact that it appeared in Harriet Monroe's magazine, and it praised the city. But when his *Chicago Poems* came out a couple of years later, the response to Sandburg was unmistakably enthusiastic. It was evident that he had learned from Whitman but was no mere echo of Whitman, despite the similarity of outlook. His poems, though some ran into long prose-like statements, were usually short, laconic and colloquial. They celebrated the clangour of Chicago, the sunlit prairie, the ordinary person:

> I speak of new cities and new people.
> I tell you the past is a bucket of ashes.
> I tell you yesterday is a wind gone down,
>   a sun dropped in the west.
> I tell you there is nothing in the world
>   only an ocean of to-morrows,
>   a sky of to-morrows.

Like Whitman, Sandburg concedes in these poems that the world has much ugliness and unhappiness. But he writes of injustice like an old-time radical; it makes him angry but not despondent. Basically he is content, for he is in love with his world and finds poetry in its commonest incidents – the baseball game, 'wop' or 'bohunk' workmen at their toil, prairie farm-life, city prostitutes, the jazz ecstasy of black musicians.

After sixty-five years not all of these poems have worn well. But on the whole they are still alive and immediate in a way that the poems of Robinson are not. They are warm-hearted yet not sentimental; their slang is a genuine idiom that fuses with Sandburg's tenderness to humanity:

> Take any streetful of people buying clothes and groceries, cheering
> a hero or throwing confetti and blowing tin horns ...

> tell me if the lovers are losers... tell me if any
> get any more than the lovers ... in the dust ... in
> the cool tombs.

Sandburg seemed to prove that one could make taut verse out of the most unpoetic of settings, and apply slang to serious themes to deepen, not to travesty them. Thus 'Ossawatomie', a poem from Sandburg's third volume (*Smoke and Steel*, 1920) which deals with John Brown, gains from its informality, as may be judged from the final stanza:

> They laid hands on him
> And the fool killers had a laugh
> And the necktie party was a go, by God.
> They laid hands on him and he was a goner.
>   They hammered him to pieces and he stood up.
> They buried him and he walked out of the grave, by God,
>   Asking again: Where did that blood come from?

Vachel Lindsay, in the fine poems among a collection of weaker whimsical or declamatory verse, had a comparable impact. As a young aspiring artist and poet, he dreamed comprehensively, determined 'to be the great singer of the Y.M.C.A. Army; to reconcile culture and manliness; to be by 1905 the biggest man in Chicago'. But Chicago knew nothing of him until 1913, when Harriet Monroe's magazine printed his 'General William Booth Enters Heaven' – a poem which proved he had accomplished the first and second of his three naïve ambitions. In the intervening years he had tramped America, 'trading rhymes for bread', likening himself to other wandering men: to 'Johnny Appleseed', who had roamed the Middle West, sowing the seeds of future orchards; to Daniel Boone, pioneering across the Appalachians into Kentucky; to the Barnum-like circus men; to travelling temperance reformers; to the gypsies; to the revivalist preachers, particularly the Campbellites who 'breathed fire, but they thought in granite'. These went to the making of his American hagiography, to which he added (besides Lincoln) John Brown, Andrew Jackson, Governor Altgeld of Illinois, the Democratic leader William Jennings Bryan and others. It was an album of enthusiasms which found room also for motion picture stars and for Keats, for Poe, Whitman, Twain, O. Henry. Out of them he evolved a form of heavily accented dramatic verse that he later called the Higher Vaudeville. It was meant to be read aloud, with the participation of an audience, as an evangelist at a camp-meeting would draw upon his congregation. 'General William Booth' was the first of these poems to reach a sophisticated public:

> Booth led boldly with his big bass drum –
> (Are you washed in the blood of the Lamb?)
> The Saints smiled gravely and they said: 'He's come.'
> (Are you washed in the blood of the Lamb?)

If these poems had been meant as a joke – if there had been the least hint of condescension – they would have been intolerable. However, they were meant seriously, and therefore Lindsay was able to encompass a delightful jocularity:

> His sweetheart and his mother were Christian and meek.
> They washed and ironed for Darius every week.
> One Thursday he met them at the door: –
> Paid them as usual, but acted sore.
>
> He said: – 'Your Daniel is a dead little pigeon.
> He's a good hard worker but he talks religion. . . .'

Like Sandburg, Lindsay learned from the Negroes. His father had read *Uncle Remus* aloud to him, there were black servants in their Springfield home, and he always considered himself part-Southerner: 'the inexplicable Mason and Dixon's line, deep-dyed and awful, ran straight through our hearts.' But he also envisaged an ideal Middle West, where people of every kind would live amiably together in some place neither village nor metropolis. His prose version of this was, so to speak, poetic – *The Golden Book of Springfield* (1920), a sweetly transfigured hometown. Lindsay's best poetry dealt with occasions when ordinary people are powerfully moved, by the glitter of costumed actors, the beat of a hymn tune, the histrionics of preacher or politician. Out of their brass-band garishness, their swing near to fraudulence and hysteria, he made a unique poetry:

> All the funny circus silks
> Of politics unfurled,
> Bartlett pears of romance that were honey at the cores,
> And torchlights down the street, to the end of the world.
>
> There were truths eternal in the gab and tittle-tattle.
> There were real heads broken in the fustian and the rattle.

The West – the world of 'tomorrows', of American myth – entered Lindsay's vision in a fantasy that was the fantasy of everyman in America. His vision was, when clear, endowed with an innocence that enabled him to produce a few enchanting poems for children ('The Moon's the North Wind's Cooky', 'Yet Gentle Will the Griffin Be') and that recalls the paintings of the Douanier Rousseau, in which gross matter of fact and world of dream so effortlessly merge.

Sandburg and Lindsay walked the tightrope; if the tension of their verse slackened, they were precipitated into prosiness, or sentimentality.

> I am the gutter dream,
> I am the golden dream

sang Lindsay's circus calliope. In some of his verse the miraculous combination collapsed. The same thing happened by degrees to Carl Sandburg, though he had a robuster talent and a more sustained career. Always stirred by the spectacle of the common man, by his sayings and his songs, Sandburg was able to voice these in his monumental life of Lincoln (2 vols., 1926; 4 more, 1939), and his *American Songbag* (1927) was a useful collection of popular ballads. In *The People, Yes* (1936) he tried with some success to state his faith in everyman by weaving together a miscellany of proverbs and wisecracks. But gradually, by a process of dilution, by the conquest of ordinariness over the poetic moment, Sandburg's writing became less memorable. The good tough concentration of his early verse yielded to incantatory repetition, and even (in *Remembrance Rock*, 1948) to a dropsical prose chronicling of the American epic.

There was a loss of touch too in the case of Edgar Lee Masters, the third local poet of the 'Chicago Renaissance' (*renaissance* is the wrong word, since it was Chicago's first birth of culture). All through his younger years Masters laboured at poetry of a conventional sort. Suddenly he found a new voice. His inspiration came from the Greek Anthology, with its brief epigrams and epitaphs; from a poignant sense of the incomplete lives led by people in the little towns of Illinois; and from the efforts of others, especially Carl Sandburg, at free verse. In 1914 he began to write the poems that form his *Spoon River Anthology*. They represent the self-spoken epitaphs of the citizens buried in an Illinois cemetery. The tone varies between an elegiac sadness, an occasional lyrical affirmation of life, and – the overwhelming impression of the book – a gaunt exposure of shame and disappointment. Husbands and wives, parents and their children tell 'what happened' from their own point of view. The epitaphs thus overlap, to build up a composite picture of a community in which the individual is isolated, yet involved with his fellows in common guilt, which somehow none could help:

> Oh many times did Ernest Hyde and I
> Argue about the freedom of the will.
> My favourite metaphor was Prickett's cow
> Roped out to grass, and free you know as far
> As the length of the rope.

But one day Prickett's cow breaks loose, and gores the speaker to death. As poetry, the *Spoon River Anthology* now seems undistinguished. As a comment on human nature, it is not on the whole profound. But in its time it was the most widely read document of the 'new poetry', and it has retained sufficient strength and sincerity for us to see why. Though his subsequent writing was marred by an unpleasantly denigratory outlook (for instance, in his 'debunking' biography of *Lincoln, the Man*, 1931), Masters contrived in *Spoon River* to do what Hamlin Garland and others had tried to do in prose. Masters, with Sandburg and Lindsay, assisted in widening the scope of poetry to a degree which would have seemed unthinkable to an earlier generation.

Another poet to win recognition at the same moment was Robert Frost, who although born in California regarded New England as his home, and made it the background of almost all his poetry. He was thirty-eight when, in 1913, he at last interested a publisher in his work. This was in England, where he had moved the previous year, to 'write and be poor without further scandal in the family'. With his first published volume (*A Boy's Will*), he established himself at once; his second (*North of Boston*, 1914) was still more successful; and on his return to America in 1915 he settled on a New Hampshire farm, where he continued to write and to grow in reputation.

Frost, whom some regard as America's finest poet of the century, was less obviously a product of the modern movement than the others mentioned above. Though his metres are varied, they are at first glance quite orthodox. He uses the speech of New England, but not as a vernacular intended to jolt the reader. The city – that intoxicating theme for the writer of his time – has little place in his work. He is the countryman, with the countryman's apparent conservatism; for rural life, with its heavy seasonal rhythm of growth and decay, imposes its own continuity on those who live amid it. Yet Frost's tone was 'modern': he could never be confused with Whittier, to name another poet of rural New England. He struck no attitudes; he made it clear that he was determined not to be poetical. The poetic element must come out of the scene as some extra and unbidden reward. Sandburg and Lindsay, while insisting on their share in everyday experience, thought of themselves (like Whitman) as *bards*, or at any rate minstrels. Frost on the other hand with pardonable exaggeration presented himself as primarily a farmer for whom poetry was a dividend. The farm was, he indicated, his anchor to reality, not local colour or a weekend gesture.

Frost's poetry cropped out of this farmer's world, which he learned how to render with what appeared to be perfect authenticity. His reticent, poor, dignified New Englanders are evoked in monologues a little like those of E. A. Robinson, or of Robert Browning, but with a difference. His people speak cautiously amid intervals of silence, making each word count. Volubility would be alien to them. They do not go on and on, as in Robinson, or explode as in Browning. Lonely farms, cold winters and all-too-brief summers; the imminence of failure, of the wilderness, of death – all give the sense of people living tensely. The tension comes out in the poetry; moments of relaxation have by contrast an almost extravagant gaiety. The hardihood, to repeat, is that of life in New Hampshire as such, not that imposed by the poet, though Frost describes it with a professional mastery.

But there is a distinction here that may suggest why Frost, though a beautiful writer, is not a poet of the highest rank. A poem, in his own words, 'begins in delight, it inclines to the impulse, it assumes direction with the first line laid down, it runs a course of lucky events, and ends in a clarification of life – not necessarily a great clarification ... but in a momentary stay against confusion. ... It finds its own name as it goes and discovers the best waiting for it in some final phrase at once wise and sad. ...' The final phrase is not a moral, but, rather, the crust of the loaf: the reader must cut his own sandwiches if he wants them. Another, indirect statement (or an attitude that Frost admires) lies in the final lines of his 'Oven Bird':

> The bird would cease and be as other birds
> But that he knows in singing not to sing,
> The question that he frames in all but words
> Is what to make of a diminished thing.

Once again we are at the dilemma; in his aversion to poetizing, the poet denies much of what was hitherto regarded as his material and his function. With Frost, the course of events is incomparably expressed: he cannot be beaten on home ground, as Randall Jarrell, a poet of a later generation, argues in a couple of magnificently appreciative essays.[1] But the clarification – the moment in which the poet must reveal himself, however unobtrusively, as poet – is sometimes too faint, or evasive, too much a mere shrug of the shoulders. Doubts are not allayed by Frost's more deliberate attempts at clarification, which seem to indicate that the stay is momentary: that he came to set more store by the matter-of-fact than by the deeper kinds of truth. In old age Frost, like Sandburg, became a white-haired sage of American letters. He was in demand on the lecture and seminar circuit, repeating his aphorisms as if they had just occurred to him. Thus, he remarked over and over again that free verse of the Sandburg type was 'like playing tennis with the net down'. Frost was the laureate invited to perform at the inaugural ceremony for President John F. Kennedy in January 1961. Unable to deliver the poem he had composed for the occasion, Frost recited instead one of his deservedly famous standard pieces:

> The land was ours before we were the land's.
> She was our land more than a hundred years
> Before we were her people.

Frost and the Midwesterners, while it would be misleading to stress their remoteness from world movements, were somewhat separated from the Eastern poets of the era whose development was urban and cosmopolitan. The Easterners had links with London and Paris (Frost, when in England, had lived in the country, not in London). New York, in its Greenwich Village section, offered them a more satisfying bohemia than that of Chicago, as well as the opportunity to become acquainted with parallel advances in art, music and the drama. Yet they had a certain amount in common with the Chicagoans; their solutions were different, their problems much the same. The verse of William Carlos Williams reveals some of the similarities and differences.

Williams, born in New Jersey, became a doctor and continued to practise his profession while also maintaining his existence as a poet. He made his poetry out of the stuff of life in Rutherford, New Jersey, but however coarse and prosaic his material, he transformed it with his poet's vision. Another poet, Wallace Stevens, has said of Williams that 'his passion for the anti-

1. Reprinted in Randall Jarrell, *Poetry and the Age* (New York, 1953).

poetic is a blood passion', and that yet one finds in his work 'the conjunction of the unreal and the real, the sentimental and the anti-poetic, the constant interaction of two opposites'. Here Williams differs from Frost, in his life and in his poetry; he recognized the cleavage between inner and outer experience (or between interpretation and experience), where Frost tended, in putting first things first, to put last things (eschatology) nowhere. Yet again the American conundrum. Williams did not always find the answer. One of his most praised short poems reads:

> so much depends
> upon
>
> a red wheel
> barrow
>
> glazed with rain
> water
>
> beside the white
> chickens

This has a glistening, child's-eye immediacy, and its structure is artfully artless. But if the poet confined himself to such impressions, we would soon tire of the demonstration. However, unlike Frost, Williams continued to improve because he brought to his themes the fierce concern of the poet as poet. He insisted upon the need for interpretation, and though for years condemned to the inbred obscurity of the little magazines (the ones that, in the joke-phrase, died to make verse free), he retained the fresh sense of the scene about him while refusing to simplify his response. He developed a close, affectionate knowledge of his fellows yet was not mawkish about them. They never became The People for him; and so as a statement of reality

> The beauty of
> the terrible faces
> of our nonentities

goes deeper than much of Sandburg, or than some of Frost. So do his lines on a baseball game:

> It is summer, it is the solstice
> the crowd is
> cheering, the crowd is laughing
> in detail
> permanently, seriously
> without thought

'No ideas', Williams has said, 'but in things': but he did not allow the *thing*,
despite the pre-1917 delight in emancipating itself from didactic and
decorative shackles, to pass itself off as the ultimate of poetry. He kept in
balance his busy life as a doctor; his Whitmanesque air of being a leisured
spectator; and a high degree of literary professionalism. The combination
made him, he said, an Objectivist. Certainly he was an abundant, endlessly
experimenting author. In his sixties, Dr Williams produced the first
instalments of *Paterson* (4 vols., 1946–51; a fifth vol., 1958), named after
a neighbouring New Jersey town. This long poem (with inserted prose
quotations) is apparently loose in structure. But that is of course also true
of other notable long poems of the twentieth century. *Paterson* was a
bravely individual version of a modern saga, linking past and present,
realism and fantasy, love of nature and a full awareness of industrial
blight – a medley recalling Sandburg's statement that life is a synthesis of
'hyacinths and biscuits'. Later instalments did not altogether sustain the
early promise of 'Paterson'. Williams is sometimes ungainly, snatching at
ideas or finding himself at the mercy of free-verse mannerisms of a kind
that never seduced Frost. His choppy lines and muttered diction can be
hard for non-Americans to understand. But he is a true poet, not least in
being so truly American.

As a medical student at the University of Pennsylvania, Williams became
friendly with two other young people who shared his interest in poetry.
One was Ezra Pound, late of Moscow, Idaho; the other, the daughter of an
astronomy professor, was Hilda Doolittle. Their friendship lasted, with
valuable results for Williams. Pound was a formidably precocious, irritating youth, utterly devoted to words and ideas. His devotion led him, and
likewise Hilda Doolittle, to London, where they made common cause with
a small group led by the philosopher T. E. Hulme and calling themselves
the Imagist(e)s. The group announced a new style of poetry which, in
Hulme's well-known phrase, was to be 'cheerful, dry, and sophisticated'.
Poetry was 'no more nor less than a mosaic of words, so great exactness
is required for each one'. *Mosaic* well describes the quality aimed at in
Imagist verse; for the laying of a mosaic calls for great care and technical
skill, and yet produces an effect of impressionist boldness – more exactly
of *pointillist* boldness, as in the painting of Seurat. Or as Pound expressed
the matter, 'the point of Imagisme is that it does not use images as
ornaments. The image is itself the speech.' What had been trimming was
now to be integrated in the poem, out of an extreme regard for economy
and concentration; formal metrical devices were to give place to 'the

sequence of the musical phrase'. At this stage Pound and the others
(Pound, always the disinterested bully, was soon dominating the group)
were mainly influenced not by symbolism but by the poetry of the Orient.
In Chinese and Japanese verse as they knew it through the translations of
Judith Gautier and from the work of the Boston Orientalist Ernest Fenollosa,
they found the perfect reticence: words distilled. Tremendously excited –
at this crucial period, in London as in Chicago, everything seemed 'new' –
they set out to achieve the quintessential in their own verse. Pound had
written a thirty-line poem, only to destroy it as a work of 'second intensity'.
Six months later he used the same theme – a moment of sudden emotion
at seeing beautiful faces in a station of the Paris métro – in a poem of
fifteen lines. After another year (the time-factor seems significant, as
though the process were akin to the ageing of a liqueur) he had reduced
the poem to its final two-line form:

> The apparition of these faces in the crowd;
> Petals on a wet, black bough.

Pound wrote a few other poems of similar 'intensity', and Hilda Doolittle
(who signed her work H. D. – compressing the very *name* of the poet) also
produced some solid, pleasing little Imagist pieces.

The movement soon attracted another American poet, the Bostonian
Amy Lowell (1874–1925), who arrived in London in the summer of 1914
with her mulberry-coloured car and two chauffeurs in matching livery.
Before long she was the leader of what Pound, now off on other scents,
including the Vorticist theories of Wyndham Lewis, described as
'Amygism'. For a while she was faithful to the cause. Then she too deserted
it, in favour of polyphonic prose. Too ebullient to confine herself to a
formula as restrictive as Imagism, she eventually wrote a biography of the
short life of John Keats that ran on for 1,160 pages.

Imagism was only a way-stage. Its limitations can be seen in the poem
by Pound quoted above, which is pared down beyond the point of
maximum intensity, until it has become a semi-private allusion. The image
in itself offers only frugal possibilities for poetry; in all but the most skilful
hands it is hardly more than the decorative flourish it came into being to
destroy. Still, it was an important way-stage, if not quite as novel as its
founders supposed, or as revolutionary as they hoped. As both a symptom
of change and a force for change in the world of poetry, the movement
had a passion and an exhilaration characteristic of the time. Its insistence
on economy and its advocacy of the free-verse line continued to be valuable

after the Imagists had scattered in their various directions. While the movement was active, it reached back into America, where Pound preached through the medium of Miss Monroe's *Poetry*.

A little after his Imagist phase, Pound also took advantage of Margaret Anderson's *Little Review* to make it too a stronghold of modernism. This he did from Europe, where he was firmly settled. Omnivorous as perhaps only an American can be, he sampled everything that could be of use to the New Poetry, helping to ensure that it should pass through its first joyful iconoclasms and experimental excesses, to attain maturity. French symbolism, the elegies of Sextus Propertius, Provençal balladry, Oriental verse techniques, Middle English: all these and other forms Pound incorporated in his poetry. His erudition exasperated the average reader, and was sometimes queried by the expert. His arrogance, after the First World War, led him into a Poundian type of fascism. Yet his unhandsome eccentricities do not detract from his vast exploratory significance. What he has meant to American poets, not to mention British ones, is attested in such books as the autobiography of William Carlos Williams. Pound rendered invaluable service to contemporaries, not by his wild denunciations of modern America, but by demonstrating that the professional poet, if he had the courage to renounce popular favour, could come out of Moscow, Idaho, and yet take the whole world for his province.

The poetry of Wallace Stevens (1879–1955) has, even more than that of Williams, the kind of technical excellence that Pound set as a goal. Wallace Stevens worked for an insurance company and became one of its senior officials; but the job bore only an antithetical relation to his writing. He spoke of himself as a romantic poet, using the epithet to define his innocently implicated relationship to the world about him: one who (said Stevens) 'still dwells in an ivory tower, but who insists that life there would be intolerable except for the fact that one has, from the top, such an exceptional view of the public dump and the advertising signs.... He is the hermit who dwells alone with the sun and the moon, and insists on taking a rotten newspaper.' Stevens did not like his own time, but he was not concerned to indict it (except indirectly), still less to propose a new order of society. His criticisms are of a special, exquisite order; but as his first published poems (in *Poetry*, 1914) showed, there was never anything sickly about him: he belonged to the modern movement, and was not a survivor from the Mauve Decade (as Thomas Beer christened the 1890s). Here is his 'Disillusionment of Ten O'Clock':

> The houses are haunted
> By white night-gowns.
> None are green,
> Or purple with green rings,
> Or green with yellow rings,
> None of them are strange,
> With socks of lace
> And beaded ceintures.
> People are not going
> To dream of baboons and periwinkles.
> Only, here and there, an old sailor,
> Drunk and asleep in his boots,
> Catches tigers
> In red weather.

Louis Untermeyer, a critic of the early 1920s who quoted this poem, scolded Stevens for playing with words as though they were trinkets. His verse does consort oddly with Sandburg, Lindsay, Masters or even Williams. One sees that Stevens is fond of colours; that they connote vitality and imagination, by contrast with the dull respectability of a white night-gown; that the imagery might be called artificial and far-fetched; that the scene described is not 'real', neither is the sailor a real sailor, though he might be cast as one in a ballet.

In subsequent poems Stevens sometimes led the reader a longer dance, down stranger avenues, approaching nonsense (as in his choice of titles – 'Le Monocle de Mon Oncle', 'The Paltry Nude Starts on a Spring Voyage' – that bear no apparent relation to the poem): approaching indeed the inconsequentialities of Dada and Surrealism. Meret Oppenheim, one of the Surrealists, made a cup (complete with saucer and spoon) out of fur. Some of Wallace Stevens's poems have a comparable effect; fur-teacup verse, they seem bizarrely 'useless' in that they offer the reader no advice or consolation, nothing but delight of a sophisticated order. Or, like certain eighteenth-century verse, or some of the poetry of the Sitwells, they present experience through the diffractive medium of a highly civilized sensibility.

Yet these remarks miss the import of Stevens. The view of the public dump matters to him; it represents poetry's 'fundamental and endless struggle with fact'. His 'fact' is usually not everybody's fact:

> Crow is realist. But, then,
> Oriole, also, may be realist.

Reality and imagination, and their interplay, are one of his main themes.

He is not impressed by Surrealism, because 'it invents without discovering. To make a clam play an accordion is to invent, not discover.' Poetry, he thinks, can and perhaps must reach reality by the unlikeliest routes, but not by jumping into the dark. All kinds of fragrance or scintillation are desirable, provided that the poet knows of the public dump of anti-poetic ordinariness. In these terms, it is clear that 'Disillusionment of Ten O'Clock' is not a mere exercise in colour-values, as Stevens's early critic grumbled. It will bear close investigation; it is entire; it comes out effortlessly, not with the squeezed gymnastic grunt of some Imagist verse of the same length. Though it has the flat bright air of a stage-set, it is much more than a décor. It makes sense; it is an excellent parable of dullness and poetic reality. In some of his later volumes (for instance *Auroras of Autumn*, 1950) his debate is a little too elaborate (like late Henry James) or too explicit – 'G. E. Moore at the spinet', Randall Jarrell has said. It is still the American conundrum, in which the poet seeks 'the gibberish of the vulgate', and tries 'by a peculiar speech to speak'

> The peculiar potency of the general,
> To compound the imagination's Latin with
> The *lingua franca et jocundissima*.

But the conundrum has rarely been so fastidiously treated. Wallace Stevens is one of the most accomplished poets of our century. Like Marianne Moore, whose work begins after the First World War, he ceased to be worried by crude equations of *people* and *public*. Taking for granted a craftsman's isolation that filled Melville with guilt and despair, he pursued his subtle goals with an adult tranquillity. Along with his more boisterous colleagues, he indicated that American poetry had come of age. There was no longer a cultural lag where Europe was concerned. Indeed, Pound, Gertrude Stein and some other expatriates (Hilda Doolittle, Laura Riding, Djuna Barnes) were prominent in the European avant-garde and beckoned on the rest. The main body of the American public followed far in rear, even further behind than the public in Britain or France; but this hardly perturbed the poets of the miraculous era. They could speak to one another in the little magazines. And they revelled in the old American game of deriding authority. Amy Lowell, a collateral descendant of J. R. Lowell, who 'had had that elderly gentleman held in front of [her] as a model ... all [her] life', was overjoyed at being told by someone that she was the better poet. While few others could have had so oppressive a connection with a previous generation, all shared her conviction that there was a revolution in progress.

Poetry and fiction were not exactly synchronic. Not until the Armistice of 1918, the peacemaking of 1919 (and the Eighteenth Amendment of the same year, which in theory made America a 'dry' nation), did the American prose-writer appear to enter a new age. In some ways this was a continuation of earlier movements. But the writers themselves did not think so; they acknowledged little kinship with pre-war writers, except perhaps Theodore Dreiser. Henry Adams had said that the generations in American history were discontinuous: the younger did not learn from the older one, nor could it. Few of Adams's contemporaries would have agreed with him. However, his *Education*, when published in a popular edition in 1918, made an immediate appeal to young people convinced that if they knew none of the answers, at any rate they had clues of which their parents had no inkling. Since they learned from Adams, who was old enough to be their collective grandfather, it might seem that he disproved his own theory. Such an objection, though, would have been met with the argument that Adams could make contact because he was out of touch with his own era. The post-war generation, the 'Lost Generation' – when had any age-group been so self-consciously aware of itself? – laid eager claim to lost souls from the past. In reviving such figures as Melville it apologized for the stupidity of its ancestors.

How much this belief in the uniqueness of the new generation, and of its problems, was due to the war, is hard to estimate. Undoubtedly the war was an enormous event. The puzzling factor, to Europeans, is the disproportionate nature of its effect upon Americans. In duration or cost (in lives, money, spiritual exhaustion) it meant comparatively little; the doughboys on the Western Front saw action for a mere four or five months. Yet disgust at the war, and revulsion from it, were almost universal in America: one reason why Edith Wharton fell out of favour as a novelist was that, in *The Marne* (1918) and *A Son at the Front* (1923), she actually spoke of the war as though it were a meaningful struggle. It was not only isolationists and partisan Republicans who opposed Wilson's Treaty of Versailles; he had no more clamorous critics than his former supporters, Herbert Croly, Walter Weyl and Walter Lippmann, who ran the *New Republic*. Americans had entered the fight under the assurance that it was a crusade ('Lafayette, we are here'), or at any rate in the expectation of fun and heroics in the Old World at the government's expense. They left the scene sure that they had been duped: that it was not, after all, their war. Many Europeans experienced and wrote of a similar disillusionment. But the American recoil was sharper. It was as though the sensitive doughboy passed overnight from the emotions of Rupert Brooke to those of Wilfred Owen, with the difference that instead of the tragic resignation of Owen he felt an almost personal affront and indignation. One of two things seemed to have happened in the Great War to the male American writer of the 1920s. Either he enlisted before the arrival of the main American forces (Hemingway, John Dos Passos, E. E. Cummings, all in ambulance units) – in which case he tended to conclude that the war was a nightmare which ought not to involve him. Or he failed to get overseas, like Scott Fitzgerald, or James T. Farrell's 'Studs Lonigan', or the cadet in William Faulkner's *Soldier's Pay*, or Faulkner himself, whose war service was confined to R.A.F. training in Canada. In that case he felt doubly cheated, having known only the backwash of disillusionment. In Dos Passos's *Three Soldiers* (1921), in Cummings's *The Enormous Room* (1922), and in some of Hemingway's work, the hero is an American, looking on at a war fought by other people, for slogans which he as a detached observer sees to be sham.

Things commonly believed in are false; the 'artist' is isolated from the rest of society: these were, in general, adopted as axioms by the writers of the Lost Generation. That they were negative statements was typical of an era of negations. They were, however, cheerful negations. The writers were not so hopelessly alienated as they chose to pretend. Or at least the novelists were not. For, quite apart from the comforting communion of the little magazines, which always seemed to find new backers, they received a surprising amount of support from the public they denounced. In fact, in broad issues the writers of fiction were not seriously at variance with their public. Plenty of Americans agreed with them that the war had been futile and horrible, that Prohibition was a mistake, that sex was important, that life in Paris or on the Riviera was more stimulating than life back home. They liked to have such topics described to them in pungent, economical prose. They recognized in the style of Sinclair Lewis or Ernest Hemingway something not too far removed from their own conversation, or from the newspaper column of their favourite sports-writer. (Many authors of the 1920s began as journalists; Ring Lardner in fact started as a sports-writer.)

Still, the writer insisted that there was an essential division between the genuine and the false, the sophisticated and what H. L. Mencken called the 'booboisie'. The cry of the writer in the post-war years was for liberty: liberty for individual self-expression. Freud contributed more than Marx to the ideology of the period, though the Marxian gospel did not seem incompatible. Freud (as popularly interpreted) gave scientific sanction to what the novelist and playwright wished to say. More, he assisted the biographer to pull authority down from its pedestal: the vogue of debunking biography set in. The imposing figures of past and present were exposed as sorry, thwarted wretches. The free soul must seek liberty: this was the categorical imperative of the 1920s as it had been for Thoreau, though with altered emphases. One must have sexual liberty; the 'Puritans' (the convenient term for unloved ancestors) had led warped lives because they refused the call of the flesh. So had the 'Victorians': the 1920s could not forgive a writer like Howells his lack of sexuality (for him, *intercourse* implied the prefix *social*: for them, *sexual*). To Sinclair Lewis, speaking in 1930, William Dean Howells had 'the code of a pious old maid whose greatest delight was to have tea at the vicarage'. Howells, said Lewis, echoing the argument of Van Wyck Brooks's *Ordeal of Mark Twain* (1920), had even managed to tame 'that fiery old savage' Twain, putting him into 'an intellectual frock coat and top hat'. Lewis was unfair; but Howells was a useful, perhaps indispensable scapegoat. In the new dispensation people must walk out of marriages that ceased to be satisfying, sexually or socially. The individual must go barefoot, metaphorically and even literally: the writings of the time are full of characters who take off their shoes, perhaps their clothes as well, to walk in the grass, to lie close to the soil. Civilization was oppressive: by contrast, one exalted the primitive. The Negro, with his 'dark laughter', was envied; black America supposedly held the clue to the art of living that the white world had forgotten. Mabel Dodge Luhan, a member of a rich and socially prominent family, who had lived in Italy before the war and in New York during it, went afterwards to New Mexico, where her fourth husband was a Taos Indian named Antonio.[1] Indeed, American women (who, like their British cousins, now had the vote) added powerfully to the emancipation of the decade. The richer they were, the more emphatic their gestures tended to be, since wealth enabled them to follow impulse wherever it led.

Yet the years after Armageddon were productive ones for the American novelist. The prose medium was admirably adapted to what the novelist

1. D. H. Lawrence lived for a while in the Taos colony; his widow continued to do so after his death in 1930.

had to say. The principal theme – that of secession from society – was one that had long engaged the American writer. Hitherto a somewhat native theme, it was now a formula that fitted the European scene, and one that European writers imitated. Like jazz and cocktails, it represented an American demeanour. It was youthful, frank, uncommitted and quick. Its extremes of high-spiritedness and glum disappointment expanded the horizons of a battered and jaded Europe.

Among American writers Sherwood Anderson (1876–1941) was the seceder *par excellence*. An Ohio businessman, married, he suffered a nervous breakdown and walked out on family and job. Establishing himself in Chicago, he began to write and at the age of forty, with the encouragement of Carl Sandburg and the Chicago author Floyd Dell, produced *Windy McPherson's Son* (1916), a novel about a man not unlike himself, who also abandons his business in order to 'find truth'. In one way or another this was to be Anderson's pattern for the rest of his career. As his novels and short stories were imagined variations on the theme of his own life, so in writing of his own life (*A Story-Teller's Story*, 1924; *Tar, a Midwest Childhood*, 1926) he made himself over in the desired image of the artist in revolt. Carl Sandburg and Gertrude Stein met in his work. With the one can be associated his eagerness to write of the Midwesterners from whom he came, whose speech was in his ears and whose worries he thought he deeply understood. Anderson's *Mid-American Chants* (1918), a volume of poetry, was a Sandburgian exercise. From Stein he derived technical benefit. He learned from her *Three Lives* and *Tender Buttons* (1914) the necessity for craftsmanship that made it a complicated process to tell the truth. Respect for technique, characteristic of the time, often saved him from the incoherence that lay near the heart of his subject. Yet, while he liked Gertrude Stein, with whom he became firm friends when he visited Paris in 1921, Anderson the former advertising copywriter was aware that her own writing failed to communicate. She was important, he wrote in 1922, 'not for the public but for the artist who happens to work with words as his material'.

How much he managed to learn of his craft was shown by his first widely successful book, *Winesburg, Ohio* (1919). This is a collection of stories, or sketches (it was always being denied that Anderson's stories were stories), about a small town of the kind Anderson knew from boyhood. Some of the characters are old, crabbed and eccentric, or borne down by failure. Others are restless adolescents. All – young, old and in-between – are puzzled people. They have been misunderstood, they seek to understand, they long for love and recognition; or else, wrapped in their obsessive fancies, they voice ideas though certain no one will listen to them. Winesburg contains them, as Spoon River cemetery holds its inhabitants. Their dreams burgeon when the streets have gone dark. The stories are given unity by their common setting, for most people in Winesburg know something of one another. Yet the closeness of acquaintance underlines the degree to which its citizens are remote from one another. A young reporter named George Willard enters the stories, in some as an actor, in others merely a confidant. His presence helps to correct the centrifugal tendency of Anderson's plots; and his departure from Winesburg at the end of the book, bound for the City on the morning train, gathers all the sketches together in a vision of escape.

The stories in *Winesburg* vary in merit. The young and their awkward love affairs are beautifully rendered, for the Andersonian yearning has exactly the quality of adolescence. Some of the elders, too, are sensitively defined – as in 'The Philosopher', where the half-mad Dr Percival declares that 'everyone in the world is Christ and they are all crucified'. The effect of the story lies in the fact that, while his assertion is almost ludicrously untrue of the doctor's immediate situation, it nevertheless contains a general truth.

Though Winesburg is a credible place, it is not Anderson's explanation of small-town life. He wrote the book in a Chicago lodging-house, and said that 'the hint for almost every character was taken from my fellow-lodgers ..., many of whom had never lived in a village'. To him Americans are the same wherever they officially reside. All are footloose, homeless seekers; few find what they are looking for. He explored the search for 'truth' through a succession of novels and stories. On the whole the stories are better; Anderson seems to think in episodes, and his novels are apt to consist of moments of perception set in long tracts of questioning. At his best, as in 'The Egg' and 'I Want to Know Why' (from the collection called *The Triumph of the Egg*, 1921) he gives memorable glimpses of impotence or grief, and yet manages to suggest some of the sensuous joy of living. The weakness in Anderson was his inability to develop sufficiently the main theme of aspiration towards liberty. One wearies of the perpetual questing of his characters, their reiterated insistence on the confusion of life and of their thoughts. Too often the confusion seems to have been in Anderson's own mind. Floyd Dell, reviewing *Windy McPherson's Son*, said that it was 'all through, an asking of the question which American literature has hardly as yet begun to ask: "What for?"' His generation believed in asking the questions and letting the answers take care of themselves; what he wrote therefore meant a great deal to the younger men who followed him.

Sherwood Anderson, as Alfred Kazin has said, made the novel something of a substitute for poetry and religion, whereas Sinclair Lewis (1885–1951) made it a branch of superior journalism. Anderson stressed the mystery and bafflement of life; Lewis recorded its details with the cynical expertise of a star reporter. In 1920, with the publication of his *Main Street*, which followed a series of novels that had attracted relatively little attention, he seemed to have struck a mortal blow at the 'booboisie', and to have done so by lifting realism to new heights of hilarious accuracy. An editor once characterized Dreiser's prose as 'moments of precision and passages of approximation'. To Lewis's world-wide audience, his precision was unvarying. Another blow, of no less weight, was delivered two years later in *Babbitt*. The first had dealt with small-town life, exposing the intolerable drabness, narrowness, and complacency of Gopher Prairie, Minnesota. The second performed a similar office for the American city ('Zenith') and for the businessmen who were so proud of their place in it. Only Mencken was able to assault stupidity and banality with so much verve; the novels of Lewis were wonderfully readable sermons to the kind of texts that Mencken gleefully printed in the 'Americana' column of the *American Mercury* – a magazine that he founded, with Nathan, in 1924. In Iowa or Nebraska or Alabama, somewhere outside the one or two great cities where the enlightened few contrived to endure, there were follies of a gorgeous nature that cried out for a satirist. This was Mencken's claim: and Lewis provided the satire. In *Arrowsmith* (1925) he portrayed the wanderings of an honest man through the idiocies and corruptions of America. In *Elmer Gantry* (1927) he focused upon the national appetite for fake religious movements. In *Dodsworth* (1929), which described the sufferings of an automobile manufacturer on his first trip to Europe, Lewis shifted his ground somewhat, to compare America with Europe (one of the stock obligations of the American novelist). Novels continued to flow from him; in 1930 he won the Nobel prize for literature (the first American to do so). But with successive books his touch became less sure, his criticism of America more perfunctory, until near the end of his life he startled a European audience by telling them, 'I wrote *Babbitt* not out of hatred for him but out of love.'

When one re-examines *Main Street* and *Babbitt* at this distance from their first appearance, it becomes clear that Lewis belonged in many ways to the people he castigated, that when he wrote of George Folansbee Babbitt, the 'realtor' of Zenith, he did not know whether he loved or hated him. Having subjected Gopher Prairie and Zenith to a merciless accounting; having laboured to convince the reader of the appalling silliness of their citizens; having shown the cruelty with which they treat the outsider: having done all this, Lewis lingers over his material, taking back half of what he has said. Thus in *Main Street* Carol Kennicott leaves her tiresome husband. So might Sherwood Anderson have ended a novel. But Lewis brings her back to Dr Kennicott – a solution he can make plausible only by suggesting that, after all, her husband is a sturdy, honest person, while Carol has been weak and self-centred. We see that, in comparison with Mencken or Ring Lardner (1885–1933; author of *You Know Me, Al*, 1916, and *How to Write Short Stories*, 1924), Lewis is basically much fonder of his America. It was raw, as he was raw when he found himself an undergraduate among smooth Eastern boys at Yale. But it is what he knows; and familiarity breeds affection as well as contempt. Perry Miller has noted that Lewis adored Dickens, and had nothing to do with Gertrude Stein or other prophets of the age. But perhaps the America of the 1920s held fewer resources for social satire than Dickens's England. At any rate, though Dickens had his faults, he rarely tried to pass a Mr Podsnap off as a Mr Pickwick. This is what Sinclair Lewis tends to do; his aim is divided, and his total effect therefore blurred, though each part may have the exactitude of a Sears, Roebuck catalogue. The *New Yorker*, when it started in 1925, frankly addressed itself to the 'caviar sophisticates' and 'not [to] the old lady in Dubuque'. Lewis was less certain about either his audience or his target; the impossible creature from Dubuque might turn out to be a relative, and he liked his relatives.

An attempted solution for Ernest Hemingway (1898–1961) was to avoid the orthodoxies of the American scene and to set his characters, even where they were Americans, in other contexts. The answer fitted his own experiences, as a Red Cross volunteer, and then after the Armistice as a correspondent covering the Graeco-Turkish imbroglio for a Canadian newspaper. The war-correspondent is free from all ties except the requirement to cable his story punctually to some far-off agency that pays him. A craftsman in words but not a city intellectual, he is a member of a secular order with its own special rules and immunities. Hemingway's early choice of career developed by stages towards the craft of fiction. When he arrived in Paris in 1922, bearing a letter of introduction from Sherwood Anderson to Gertrude Stein, he was a novice in the world of

letters, grateful when she and Ezra Pound blue-pencilled his first efforts
(some of them poems). It was she, according to Miss Stein, who first told
him about bullfighting. As late as 1926, when he parodied Sherwood
Anderson's *Dark Laughter* in his hilarious *Torrents of Spring*, Hemingway
still had a good deal of 'literature' to get out of his system. Dedicated to
Mencken and interlarded with quotations from Henry Fielding, his book
was full of skittish references to Henry James, the *American Mercury*,
Sinclair Lewis, and so on. He also still had the American scene, especially
the woods of northern Michigan where he had hunted and fished as a boy.
These are the setting of several of his first stories. The war, which haunted
him, was not yet a subject he could handle at depth. His first important
novel, *The Sun Also Rises* (1926),[1] treated it as the recent disaster which
nobody cared to talk about, though it had maimed his hero sexually and
had blighted the other characters in less evident ways.

The narrator–hero, Jake Barnes, is an American newspaperman working in Paris. He is in love with Lady Brett Ashley, a beautiful and
promiscuous woman who returns his love, as far as this is possible. The
other main characters are Brett's bankrupt fiancé Mike (a Scotsman), an
American writer friend of Jake's named Bill – and another American,
Robert Cohn. Jake, Bill, Mike and Brett form a circle of understanding from
which Cohn is excluded by an inability to share their code. This code of
behaviour, though rarely made explicit, is extremely important to
Hemingway; as Lady Brett says, 'It's sort of what we have instead of God.'
Obedience to the code, and departures from it, give shape to most of
Hemingway's writing. There is a resemblance here to Rudyard Kipling,
another novelist whose characters often find in action an outlet for an
almost mystical sense of commitment. On the surface the 'commitment'
of Jake and his associates does not amount to much. Their behaviour
could be called foolish and irresponsible; for example, they drink too much.
Yet those who are 'all right' can spot one another at once. They are usually
expert in certain subjects, but must never attitudinize. Understatement is
the rule; and Hemingway likes some Englishmen – Harris in *The Sun Also
Rises*, the big-game hunter in 'The Short Happy Life of Francis Macomber' –
for being reticent as well as competent. His favoured ones form a free-
masonry, with a joking conversation-slang of their own. A key word is
aficionado, applied here to those who know a great deal about bullfighting.
Jake and his friends meet at Pamplona for the bullfights; Jake has *aficion*,

1. Published in Britain as *Fiesta*.

and 'those who were aficionados could always get rooms even when the hotel was full'.

Outside the charmed circle stands Cohn. He is too voluble; he discusses his emotions. After a brief affair with Brett, he refuses to face with dignity that she no longer cares for him. He administers a thrashing to a young matador Brett has attracted, only to discover that the other man has somehow worsted him spiritually. Indeed, for Hemingway defeat is a more interesting condition than victory. Men all, sooner or later, go down to defeat: it is how they face the ordeal that determines their status. This is not to say that life holds no pleasures for Hemingway. He, and his characters, set great store by food and wine, sex, trout-fishing, skiing, shooting, and so on. But these are all tests of manhood, of *aficion*, in the autobiographical *Green Hills of Africa* (1935) Hemingway naïvely confesses just how much his sense of his own integrity depends upon the result of each day's pursuit of game. The ultimate test, for him as for Stephen Crane, is death. In war, badly wounded, Hemingway had felt its presence so close that nothing else afterwards could ever seem as real. He must push nearer and nearer to whatever truth its proximity held. For this reason the bullfight, in which the skirmish with death is ritualized, holds a peculiar prominence in his imagination: in fact he devoted a whole book (*Death in the Afternoon*, 1933) to the subject.

It has often been said that Hemingway handicapped himself by dealing with violent action rather than the act of intelligence: that he falsely equated expression with insincerity. It is true that he seems most at home with characters who say little. His code does at times appear absurd; in his poorer writing (as in *Across the River and Into the Trees*, 1950), knowledge degenerates into knowingness – on the level of what to tip a waiter – and courage is confused with the assertion of maleness. The nihilism of *The Sun Also Rises* and of its successor, *Farewell to Arms* (1929), seems a convincing statement of the mood of war and of the post-war years. The clipped understatement of the 1920s, suppressing emotion that might prove unbearable, hits the right note. The mere numbness of a Harry Morgan (*To Have and Have Not*, 1937) does not, in a later decade. Nor is the famous prose, with its purposely flat simplicity, altogether free from monotony. And Hemingway's dialogue has a little too much stylized repartee.

'They got a cure for that.'
'No, they haven't got a cure for anything.'[1]

1. 'A Pursuit Race', *Men Without Women* (1927).

Yet Hemingway's initial contribution, in novels and in the short stories of *In Our Time* (1924), *Men Without Women* (1927), and *Winner Take Nothing* (1933), had an extraordinary influence upon others: so much so that the innumerable imitations of Hemingway have almost spoiled one's palate for the genuine article. But on re-reading, his first novels and his best stories are still powerful and fresh. Rigorously confining himself to the matter in hand, refusing the aid of literary artifices, Hemingway extracts an amazing richness from his rare excursions below the surface of the narrative. In *A Farewell to Arms*, for example, the rhythm of the seasons is unobtrusively matched to the course of the campaign, with no editorializing from the author. Victory comes in the spring. In the autumn it is otherwise:

There was fighting for that mountain too, but it was not successful, and in the fall when the rains came the leaves all fell from the chestnut trees and the branches were bare and the trunks black with rain.

Equally effective is this brief mention of the blood dripping on to the hero from a dying soldier who lies on the stretcher above in an ambulance:

The drops fell very slowly, as they fall from an icicle after the sun has gone.

Hemingway was a careful writer who never hurried into print. Revealing (in *The Green Hills of Africa*) a curious embarrassment at the thought that he might be mistaken for an *artist*, he justified his occupation to himself as a *craft*, requiring the same careful apprenticeship as fishing or any other skill. (Though he did reveal in his choice of titles that he was aware of literature, taking them from Ecclesiastes, John Donne and so on.) If he was liable to exalt form to the detriment of content, he followed his craft faithfully. Within his own framework of motive and event he was a virtuoso. For instance, when he reproduces the speech of people who are not English, in *For Whom the Bell Tolls* (1940), he renders their words in an ingenious 'translated' English so as to remind the reader that they are actually speaking in Spanish. Again, in *For Whom the Bell Tolls* he shows himself perfectly able to handle educated characters whose emotions and ideas are complex. This book, though it contains some excellent writing, is not, however, his best. One never fully accepts the juxtaposition of the Hemingway-person in his writing with the simple man. Is the waiter really a friend? Does the peasant really respect the foreigner? Or is there something inadequate in this figure of the American-foreigner? What is he doing away from his own country, his own job? The journalist/ correspondent cannot reach to the heart of experience in a strange land.

Nor can the soldier, whose life is divided between the destruction at the front and the counterfeit gaiety of furlough. It is proxy living, in pidgin language.

Whether or not Hemingway pondered such problems, his short novel, *The Old Man and the Sea* (1952), avoids the insincerities that surround the concept of the *aficionado*. He tells of a Cuban fisherman who is a simple man but not a simpleton. The Cuban's fight with a great fish is in a way an illustration of the Hemingway code, but in a quite pure form. There is hardly a trace in it of the braggart sportsman, or of the sham lyricism that overcomes most non-Hispanic writers when they discuss the lives of the Latin poor. After *Across the River and Into the Trees*, Hemingway told an interviewer that

In writing I have moved through arithmetic, through plane geometry and algebra, and now I am in calculus.

At the time this sounded like the arrogance of a man who had become hopelessly entangled in his own legend. Indeed, it had an odd echo of Gertrude Stein. There was the same apparent delusion that technique could on its own transfigure the banality of what was being conveyed. *The Old Man* went some way towards justifying Hemingway's pride. Beginning, like Sherwood Anderson, with the notion of man shut off from his fellows, he passed somewhat unconvincingly (in *To Have and Have Not* and *For Whom the Bell Tolls*) to the assertion of human solidarity. In *The Old Man* he managed to tell a story of a man on his own that may be regarded as a parable for all humanity. Yet it was not the large novel Hemingway was rumoured to be producing. The only published works of his final years – years of depression, culminating in Hemingway's suicide in 1961 – were some distressingly slack and mannered pieces on Spanish bullfighters which might almost have been concocted by a parodist. One slim posthumous volume appeared: *A Moveable Feast* (1964), a memoir of Paris in the early 1920s. It is a sort of achievement: alive, precise, firmly shaped. The character sketches are tight with the sense of affection or antipathy, alliance or combat. He is nice about Ezra Pound and a few others, and amusing yet rather malicious on Gertrude Stein and Scott Fitzgerald. But this is a sad small book for Hemingway to have ended on. It is as if he were an old champion, turning over his scrapbook to comfort and hurt himself. The prose is 'in condition', the demeanour of an old man who tries to hold himself like a young one.

Like Anderson, Lewis and Hemingway, the writer Scott Fitzgerald grew up in the Middle West. Like Lewis he came East to college, though instead of Yale he chose Princeton. The Middle West was the place of origins: the destination for Fitzgerald was somewhere splendid, improvident, aristocratic, where everyone was (like himself and his wife) young, handsome, witty and free. His writing parallels his own experience to a poignant degree; both are the record of youth hunting for a perfection that does not exist. Fitzgerald longed for some central certainty, from which he could look upon the world, safe from hurt. He attended a university for the sons of well-to-do Easterners and strove to be a success among his classmates. In the army he envied those who had been in action and had thus entered the inner sanctum of danger. He wrote in a short story ('The Offshore Pirate'), of men coming out of the trenches, watched by the hero, that 'the sweat and mud they wore seemed only one of those ineffable symbols of aristocracy that were forever eluding him'.

Since Fitzgerald had been unable to adopt these symbols he concentrated upon others: in particular, upon the aristocracy of wealth. The very rich, as he told Hemingway and as he said in 'The Rich Boy', 'are different from you and me. They possess and enjoy early, and it does something to them'. What it did to them was not necessarily good, nor likely to endear them to the rest of the population. Fitzgerald knew this; and that the idea of American aristocracy was in large measure spurious, partly because the continuity essential to the aristocratic ideal was lacking in American life, where 'there was no norm, it was doubtful if there ever had been a norm'. Nevertheless, like Edith Wharton he clung to a conception of a specially privileged group while realizing with her that the actual group was worth little. But whereas her group served as a theoretical standard, a repository of good manners and fairly good behaviour against which to judge the shoddy conduct of the rest of society, Fitzgerald had no idea of contrasting one group against another. He was merely fascinated by the magic properties of wealth, and by the immunity it could purchase – immunity from everybody else who was an outsider. With wealth, and also youth, looks and success, which were part of aristocracy, one was an *aficionado* on the grand scale. All doors opened; all head-waiters were deferential; all boat-trains, liners, limousines, suites and mansions were available. One could follow the sun. Poverty was mean, grey, narrow; with money one could be generous, expansive, original. The minor disasters of life – the lost ticket, the wet holiday, the cramped quarters – could all be remedied. Largesse was a word that meant both a tip and a way of life.

It was an adolescent way of life, and perhaps Fitzgerald never entirely got away from it. Certainly his first books, the collections of stories (*Flappers and Philosophers*, 1920; *Tales of the Jazz Age*, 1922) and the novels (*This Side of Paradise*, 1920; *The Beautiful and the Damned*, 1922), are callow by comparison with his later work. His characters are too evidently projections of himself, dreaming extravagantly and extravagantly disappointed. The hero of *This Side of Paradise*, looking back gloomily over his twenty-four years, reflects: 'I know myself but that is all.' *All!* This hero, and the other young men and women, are almost wilfully immature. Fresh from fashionable schools and colleges, they have no desire to develop; development means growing old, and they clutch at their small score of years as though it were unthinkable to be over thirty. Their love affairs are febrile yet passionless; the idea of parenthood is repellent – how could any generation be younger than their own?

However, even at its most juvenile Fitzgerald's work was fluent and carefully constructed. From the first he meant to be a writer. If his characters seemed frivolous, and his own life equally so, Fitzgerald still regarded himself as a professional. He was, so to speak, seriously frivolous, as serious as Hemingway was behind the camouflage of stiff drinks and sporting gear. 'I know myself' was not altogether a brash claim. He had an astonishing knack of observing sensation while he indulged in it.

> The only way I can describe young Anson Hunter is to approach him as if he were a foreigner and cling stubbornly to my point of view. If I accept his for a moment I am lost – I have nothing to show but a preposterous movie.

That is how he approaches the theme of great wealth, in 'The Rich Boy'. Tempted by it, he struggles to maintain a detachment rendered difficult by the fact that he has nothing positive to offer in place of the chilly aplomb of 'the very rich'. Or rather, what he has to offer is confused in his mind with wealth. It is: joy, beauty, tenderness: all of which fade with age, for they are all aspects of youth.

In *The Great Gatsby* (1925) Fitzgerald shows wealth and youth at variance. Jay Gatsby, despite his huge house, his lavish parties, and his mysteriously dishonourable sources of income, is primarily a spokesman for youth. His life, despite its external clutter, is dedicated to the recovery and renewal of an early love affair with Daisy. It is for this pure end that he has amassed his fortune. But Daisy is married to Tom Buchanan; and they are 'the very rich'. Though Tom has a mistress, and Daisy has never forgotten Gatsby, their wealth has made them peculiarly invulnerable. In the end the Buchanans are still living together and Gatsby is dead, killed by a demented creature who does not realize that the Buchanans are to blame for his misfortunes. So the deluded faces the corrupt, and goes down to defeat. The set-up is slightly reminiscent of that in Henry James's *The American*, in which the trusting Christopher Newman discovers that his wealth is powerless against the entrenched assurance of the Bellegarde family. The clash of wills is more impressive in James's novel because the two sides are sharply differentiated, and neither can be called shoddy, as we may call the standards of Daisy or even of Gatsby. Nevertheless, *The Great Gatsby* is a dazzling novel. Fitzgerald really knows his world of wealth; and whether the characters are rich or not, the appearance, gestures and conversation of each are rendered with an exact and witty ease. The narrator – in the scene but, like Fitzgerald, not wholly of it – gives the story an extra dimension of detachment. Nick Carraway's under-employment in 'real' life accords with his necessary but unimportant recording function, within the structure of the book. Above all the book has a moving elegiac quality. Never completely suppressed even in the most brazen scenes, this quality wells up when the narrator remembers his Midwestern childhood, and again, finely, at the end, where Gatsby's effort to recapture the past and carry it into the future with him is related to the old American dream of a new world, when, three centuries earlier,

for a transitory enchanted moment man must have held his breath in the presence of this continent, ... face to face for the last time in history with something commensurate to his capacity for wonder.

After *The Great Gatsby* Fitzgerald produced acceptable short stories but did not finish another novel until *Tender is the Night* (1934). The reviewers of the socially conscious 1930s dismissed it as a hangover from a vanished era. Most of the expatriates were home again. The money had run out, Europe had turned sour. Fitzgerald wrote of an American expatriate, Dick Diver, disintegrating from too much money and from domestic problems, coming back to America at last not in repentance but to hide from abject failure. The reviewers were too hard on *Tender is the Night*, though recent critics have more than redressed the balance. In some respects it is superior to *Gatsby*; it is more ambitious and reveals an even more sensuously alert intelligence. But the intelligence is of a professional order. Fitzgerald has learned more fully how to construct a novel; he incorporates a wider range of characters; the varying pace and tone of his style afford a constant pleasure. Yet the early limitations have remained, and the elegiac note that sustains *Gatsby* is here flawed. There is a nobility in the errors of

Gatsby; there is a tinge of self-pity in those of Diver which seems to have been passed on unwittingly by the author. Nevertheless, one does not feel that *Tender is the Night* represents a dried-up talent, as critics alleged at the time. That Fitzgerald continued to hold on to his technical gift is demonstrated by his unfinished novel of Hollywood, *The Last Tycoon* (1941), as well as by the documents in the posthumous volume called *The Crack-up* (1945). Many American novelists have written themselves out, because they have been wedded to insubstantial themes and insufficiently devoted to their trade. If Fitzgerald had lived longer he might even have surpassed his rivalrous friend Hemingway in showing that professional intelligence can lead the writer towards a deeper knowledge.

Fitzgerald is, rightly or wrongly, associated with 'the Jazz Age' of the 1920s. The name of John Dos Passos is linked with the next decade, when he became one of America's most prominent novelists. Yet he had already made his name. Born in the same year as Fitzgerald, he displayed an equal precocity. His first novel, *One Man's Initiation – 1917*, was published in 1920, the same year as *This Side of Paradise*. With a second book, *Three Soldiers* (1921), Dos Passos took his place among the young writers (including the middle-aged young man, Sherwood Anderson) who were defining the character of their time. The hero of *Three Soldiers*, John Andrews, is a composer who enlists because he is tired of freedom and hopes 'to start rebuilding the fabric of his life, out of real things this time, out of work and comradeship and scorn'. Instead, military life, in America and then in France, arouses a wild repugnance in him. At the end, a deserter writing a piece of music inspired by Flaubert's *La Tentation de St Antoine*, he is arrested by the military police and marched off, leaving his unfinished score to blow away in the wind (instead of taking it with him like a sensible fellow). So, Dos Passos seems to imply, must all sensitive men suffer at the hands of the machine: the final chapter is called 'Under the Wheels'. The only gesture left to the Artist is secession – if the world will let him secede. This will be recognized as one of the typical situations of the early 1920s, when there was actually a little magazine called *Secession*. The Artist (including Dos Passos himself, a product of Harvard) is right, the world is wrong. John Andrews among the uniformed ranks is, in the words of the old joke, the only one in step.

How then was Dos Passos able to write the trilogy *U.S.A.*, which has been described as an example of 'the collectivist novel'? The answer is a commentary on the evolution of the American intellectual in his 'journeys between wars' (a phrase that Dos Passos used as a title for a collection of travel writings). Briefly, social protest supplanted aesthetic protest. The anger of the Artist at the materialism of American life modulated into the anger of the Radical at social injustices. Dos Passos did not become a 'proletarian' novelist; there had always been an element of radicalism in his work. From the beginning, he tried to represent both the lonely individual and the sensations of the crowd. In *Three Soldiers* he introduces three dissimilar, 'representative' men, as if to embrace the whole of American society. But two drop out, leaving the stage to Andrews, who in turn abandons his former interest in 'comradeship' to voice aesthetic protest.

In *Manhattan Transfer* (1925) the collectivist principle is more confidently tackled. Dos Passos now attempts to crowd New York into one book, by methods that foreshadow *U.S.A.* There is a multitude of characters, whose lives interweave, on various social levels; they are traced through twenty years, growing up, growing old, rising and falling in the success scale. The main narrative is doggedly prosaic, the dialogue painstakingly accurate. But there are passages of impressionist description. And there is still a principal character, Jimmy Herf, who is clearly a descendant of John Andrews. In some respects Herf is worse off. He is no longer the Artist, merely the Would-be Artist, intelligent but ineffectual. Still, at the end he secedes. In his case the act is not convincing; it is a reprieve happy-ending tacked on to a tale of trial and conviction. Others have been eaten up by the voracious city; Herf, walking out of it, away from his unimportant job and his broken marriage with only a few cents in his pocket, is a figure out of Sherwood Anderson mixed up in a metropolis from Dreiser.

In the *U.S.A.* trilogy (*The 42nd Parallel, 1919* and *The Big Money*, published in 1930, 1932 and 1936), Dos Passos covers the same ground with a larger sweep, taking all America into account. The narrative swings matter-of-factly from one to another of his many characters. Handsome, fraudulent public men; successful, frustrated women; those who drink themselves to disaster; radicals with their 'comradeship and scorn'; those who betray the workers; aesthetic poseurs: these and others are handled by Dos Passos with a circumstantial unloving competence. The narrative is accompanied by three diversifying devices, of which two – the Newsreels and the Biographies – emphasize the documentary nature of the trilogy, the concern of the 1930s to write of real gardens with real toads in them. The Newsreels are a medley of newspaper headlines, fragments of popular songs, and the like; the Biographies are brief, evocative sketches of important men and women who typify the periods covered by the work. The third device, that of the Camera Eye, is a survival from the aesthetic Dos Passos. Keeping pace chronologically (more or less) with the other parts, the Camera Eye sections, written in a prose-poetry with hints of E. E. Cummings and Gertrude Stein, look out on the crass scene from the viewpoint of a person one assumes to be the author.

As in *Manhattan Transfer*, but with an added anger and despair, *U.S.A.* covers the defeat of the individual on every front. The rich are all corrupt; even if (like some of Upton Sinclair's heroes) they give away all they have and join the poor, they do not find salvation. For though the poor may be decent people, they will accomplish nothing. Sacco and Vanzetti go to their death in spite of years of radical effort. The unjust triumph, only to sicken of their success. There are few happy people in this trilogy, whose tone grows progressively darker. In sum it is a massive indictment of America. It might be unreadably trite today if Dos Passos had merely asked his riddle, damned his capitalists, and then ended with a vision of the workers' paradise. But he comforts himself with no such easy hope. He concludes instead with a sketch of a nameless vagrant, not an Andrews or a Herf but an obscure citizen, trying to thumb a lift along a highway that will lead him nowhere.

U.S.A. is still a remarkable achievement in breadth, and as an attempt to incorporate within the framework of the novel everything from tabloid news to esoteric verse. But it is already slightly antiquated. A century hence it may appeal as a kind of academy-piece of the 1930s, large and workmanlike – a Frith's *Derby Day* done without joviality. It is readable; one likes the endless, crammed sensation, and one appreciates the effort to diversify the structure. But the cracks show; the less ambitious experiments of *Manhattan Transfer* are almost preferable. The Camera Eye, for example, is brilliant in parts, and its intention – presumably to leaven the mass with some evidence of sensibility – is laudable. But why call it by such an objective, 'documentary' name when it is such a subjective device? Why disconcert the reader by allowing it occasionally to cover the same scene as the narrative? And the handling of the characters is open to criticism. Some disappear just when they begin to be interesting; others linger on like guests after a party whose host is unable to get rid of them. And the Joycean habit of running words together – *rumbottle, fruitsteamer, icegrey* – is pointless, once the novelty has worn off. The honesty and the experimentations of *U.S.A.*, though, make it a good serious book, better than some subsequent novels by Dos Passos which exude a mellowly patriotic odour like those American tobaccos that are heavily flavoured with maple syrup.

The record of other writers active between the wars will be resumed in subsequent chapters. We may end this one by emphasizing how electric was the atmosphere in America in the coming-of-age years. To be more precise, it was creatively electric in a few cities, above all New York, rather than in the vast, often hostile hinterland. The positive charge was answered by a negative charge of equal voltage. In this crackling tension writers and artists thrilled to a fresh sense of reckless yet real potential. It is perfectly expressed in the *élan* of the old magazine *Vanity Fair*, and in Gilbert Seldes's book *The Seven Lively Arts*, first published in 1924. He wrote most of it in a friend's apartment in the Île St Louis in Paris. The arts in question were not necessarily an exact seven in number. Unfriendly critics doubted, in fact, whether much if anything in the book should properly be described as art. Seldes mentioned comic strips (for example, George Herriman's 'Krazy Kat'); motion pictures (notably Charles Chaplin's musical comedy); vaudeville; dancing; radio; and jazz. None of these was 'genteel'. He and such friends as John Peale Bishop and Edmund Wilson delighted in the newfound American irreverence and inventiveness, the discovery that artistic expression did not have to be 'artistic' or to have secured academy approval. Indeed the very *dis*approval of academic critics added to their relish in an indigenous set of American popular manifestations.

XIII

SOUTHLAND

AS EARLY as 1785, Thomas Jefferson of Virginia explained for the benefit of an inquiring Frenchman, the Marquis de Chastellux, that there were basic character differences within the United States. He set out his sense of the matter as a contrasting diagram:

In the North they are	*In the South they are*
cool	fiery
sober	Voluptuary
laborious	indolent
persevering	unsteady
jealous of their own liberties, and just to those of others	zealous for their own liberties, but trampling on those of others
interested	generous
chicaning	candid
superstitious and hypocritical in their religion	without attachment ... to any religion but that of the heart

Within a couple of years of the achievement of formal independence, the North–South debate is thus quite fully formulated. The Yankee is canny and canting, the Cavalier hot-blooded and harum-scarum. Emerson reiterated these truths (or stereotypes?) in his journal in 1837: 'The Southerner asks concerning any man, "How does he fight?" The Northerner asks, "What can he do?"' George William Curtis wrote in the same vein of well-to-do Americans summering at a resort hotel in Saratoga, New York, in the 1850s. There were, he said, the 'arctic' Bostonians and – a world away – the 'languid, cordial and careless Southerners'. In John William DeForest's *Miss Ravenel's Conversion* (written 1865, published 1867) one person explains the North–South difference as springing from 'a radical difference of purpose.... The pro-slavery South meant oligarchy and imitated the manners of the European nobility. The democratic North means equality.... It means general hard work, too, in consequence of which there is less chance to cultivate the graces.'

What Northerners called the Civil War, or War of Secession, and what Southerners preferred to call the War Between the States, broke out in 1861. By mid-century, Southern accounts of economic and temperamental separateness were sharpening appreciably. A speaker at V.M.I. (Virginia Military Institute) declared in 1857 that there were now two fundamentally different systems or civilizations, North and South: 'We possess a common language, and, in some part, a common ancestry; in these we resemble each other, and ... in nothing else.' On the brink of the secession crisis, a writer in the New Orleans *DeBow's Review* praised the cultured gallantry of Southern Cavaliers. New England Yankees, on the other hand, embodied 'the worst passions of the human heart' – 'diseased philanthropy, envy, hatred, fanaticism' and the like.

The extent of difference, and mutual antipathy, seem hard to gainsay. Climate, agriculture, the dearth of sizeable cities, and above all the expansion of plantation slavery, and the economic and ideological jostle between a chattel and a free labour system, reinforced the white South's perception of itself as embattled, in fact persecuted, yet – because Cotton was King – invincible. From the outset the Southern states within the new nation tended to focus sectional self-awareness upon their 'peculiar institution'. North of the Mason-Dixon line, the old states all began the emancipation of their relatively few enslaved blacks; territories in the upper Middle West excluded slavery altogether.

Yet we may wonder whether North and South were as starkly opposed before 1860 as their spokesmen asserted. Whitman was probably correct in claiming that most people in the pre-war North were anti-Negro rather than anti-slave. The small groups of active abolitionists were generally deplored and even abominated. A surprising number of Northern academics, clergymen, lawyers, doctors and journalists came South, intermarried, and adjusted themselves with apparent ease to Southern mores. One such person was the educator William H. McGuffey (1800–1873), Pennsylvanian by birth and author of the ubiquitous series of textbooks known as *Eclectic Readers*. McGuffey transferred from college administration in Ohio to spend the last twenty-eight years of his life in Charlottesville, as president of Mr Jefferson's University of Virginia – while also of course serving to standardize common-school curricula throughout the Union.

McGuffey's experience, by no means unusual, suggests that despite manifest antagonisms the two sections had many ties. These enabled the sections to sustain a discourse that was not always a shouting match, and to resume it after 1865. True, preoccupation with slavery, and the obligation to defend it or reconcile it within the Union's republican democratic creed, distorted and crimped the Old South's intellectual life. The painful effect upon sensitively erudite Southrons is revealed in Drew Gilpin Faust's group portrait, *A Sacred Circle*. One dissident Southerner, Hinton R. Helper, blamed slavery for his region's backwardness (*The Impending Crisis of the South*, 1857). Yet he pictured the South as in economic thrall to the free states, lagging far behind them in culture as measured by periodicals, publishing houses and colleges worthy of the name. Only Baltimore, a border city, could according to Helper claim any place among the nation's sophisticated metropolitan communities; even the fiercely 'Southern' *DeBow's Review* had to be printed and bound in Manhattan. William Gilmore Simms and Edgar Allan Poe trailed behind Northern contemporaries, said Helper, in quality as well as in reputation. Certainly they and other Southern authors felt isolated, and cold-shouldered by Northern literary arbiters.

Now and then a Southern antebellum novel or poem may have alienated Northern readers because of its sectional bias. But the grievance of Southern literati was not directly related to any notion of a censorship of taste exercised by the Northern publishing industry. In general authors and editors aimed at a national market, stratified perhaps by social class but otherwise homogeneous. The point is plausibly put in William R. Taylor's *Cavalier and Yankee*, an analysis of sectional literary modes. He sees North and South as complementary states of mind, as well as actual pieces of terrain. Each section could make the other a scapegoat for negative features of national life that were in reality not confined to any particular region. Commercialism or mob rule, say, could be treated as Northern vices, snobbery or brutishness as characteristically Southern. Conversely, these large generalizations could operate more positively. A Northern novelist could romanticize and gentrify a tale by locating it on a spacious Southern plantation.

Polarization of this type might be quite unreal – ignoring for example the diversity of milieux, between the upper states and those of the Deep South, between rich planter and poor farmer, or between the long-settled seaboard and the rough-and-tumble conditions of the frontier. Whatever their degree of accuracy, the important consideration is that stereotypes of the South shaped and were shaped by nationwide literary perceptions.

The process can be seen at work in the North, before and after the war. In 1850 Herman Melville was vastly impressed by Hawthorne's *Mosses from An Old Manse*, and the two became friends. Melville wrote an enthusiastic review of *Mosses*, concealing his authorship by pretending the piece was 'By a Virginian Spending July in Vermont'. Possibly he wished to hide his personal motives in eulogizing a friend. Presumably, though, his notion was to stress the all-American appeal of Hawthorne's work. Behold, a Massachusetts author, a Yankee, acclaimed by his symbolic opposite, a Virginia Cavalier! Where would be the thrill in announcing that New England was in receipt of congratulations from neighbouring New York?

As to post-war America, Vann Woodward remarks on the appearance of 'Confederate censors of Yankee morals' in several Northern literary works: Melville's long poem *Clarel* (1876), and three novels – *Democracy* (1880) by Henry Adams, Henry James's *The Bostonians* (1886), and W. D. Howells's *Hazard of New Fortunes* (1890). In each the Southerner is a gentlemanly ex-soldier, bearing within him a knowledge of suffering and defeat which it would be hardly possible to communicate to the strident, shallow gatherings of the Gilded Age. Yet, to the extent that Northerners seemed to pay attention to past events, the evidence of the printed word would indicate they were ready to forgive as well as forget the secession crisis. Journalists exploring the former Confederacy, as the New Englander Edward King did in *The Great South* (1875), appeared to accept much of the Southern contention – that Reconstruction was a humiliation and a disaster, that blacks were too ignorant to deserve the franchise, and too lazy to support themselves. At the same time, Southern writers began to supply the North's thriving monthly magazines with nostalgic reminiscence and romantic fiction. Thomas Nelson Page, Walter Hines Page (1855–1918) and Joel Chandler Harris were among the Southern authors who catered to an apparently insatiable appetite, on the part of a chiefly Northern readership, for legends of gracious hospitality, cavalier gallantry and picturesquely quaint or loyal darkies.

Inside the post-war South, literary prospects were indeed not bright, if authors were to seek to revive the old sectional call for a separate literature expressing the unique qualities of Dixie. Black authors were not in demand; for aspiring ex-slaves, getting an education and earning a livelihood came first. Their surrogate spokesmen were local-colourists like George Washington Cable (1844–1925) and Constance Fenimore Woolson (1840–94), who sympathized but did not quite empathize with non-whites, or the Uncle Remus narrator created by Joel Chandler Harris (1848–1908), a Georgia newspaperman of near-genius as a folklorist, yet also ambivalent in his feelings about black folk. Remus is a shrewd old man, delighting in the methods by which the underdog scores off those who are more powerful. Harris said: 'it needs no scientific investigation to show why the Negro selects as his hero the weakest and most harmless of all animals' – the rabbit, Brer Rabbit – 'and brings him out victorious in contests with the bear, the wolf, and the fox.' Harris claimed that his own favourite book was Oliver Goldsmith's *Vicar of Wakefield*, whose simplicity and 'air of extreme wonderment' had moved him all his life. To Joel Chandler Harris, literature came nearest to its true function when dealing with common people. Henry James's remarks on the barren tedium of Hawthorne's New England provoked Harris to furious rebuttal. In his own region the black presence gave everything an extra dimension. He was one of the first to convey this with any degree of subtlety, though never quite able to transcend a white Southern set of values.

The intricacy of black–white relations, and of white social structure, intrigued intelligent Southerners, but almost as if – for literary purposes – it were a confidential archive, material to be laid away for future use. More revelatory than any novel was the Georgia correspondence of the Jones family, a network of planters, clerics, doctors and lawyers, eventually edited by Robert Manson Myers as *The Children of Pride* (1975). The Joneses wrote affectionately, circumstantially, and on the whole earnestly, about deaths and marriages and sermons and crops and politics. During 1858–9, for example, the family head, a Presbyterian minister, exclaims: 'What a religion for the masses is popery! It . . . takes away the key of . . . knowledge from the people, rules them by superstition [and] . . . sanctifies them in sin.' His Harvard-educated son praises the author Richard Henry Dana, an acquaintance from Cambridge days, as 'the only abolitionist for whom I ever entertained any profound respect'. Mrs Jones says in a postscript to a son: 'The servants send many howdies.' A son-in-law describes a horseback excursion in Georgia:

As we rode up, Father spoke to a little Negro boy.

   'Howdy, John.'

   'My name is Norman, sir.'

   'Ah, yes – Norman!'

As we passed, someone asked Norman who we were.

   'I don't know,' was his reply, 'who he is. *But he know me.*'

Mary Boykin Miller Chesnut (1823–86), whose so-called *Diary from Dixie* was first published in 1905, was a witty Confederate socialite, married at seventeen to a wealthy and prominent South Carolinian who had been educated like his father at Princeton. Mary Chesnut's favourite author, among many familiar to her, was William Makepeace Thackeray. During the war years the Chesnuts were members of the Confederacy's governing élite; Mary was a close friend of Varina Davis, the wife of President Jefferson Davis. In the private journal she kept intermittently in 1861–5, Mary Chesnut tempered Southern patriotism with qualms about chattel slavery, moments of regret that her husband was not more dashing, and ironic amusement over indications of ambition and envy, and the juxtaposition of affairs of state with affairs of the heart. Thackeray's *Vanity Fair* was perhaps in her mind when she itemized the chatter and display of Confederate Richmond.

Even so, she missed its glamour in the diminished post-war atmosphere. An avid reader who yearned to be a writer also, Mrs Chesnut managed to produce drafts and chapters of no less than three novels. They show her searching for a persona, Thackerayishly skittish yet reflective, somewhere between the general and the personal. In her last years, ill and short of cash, she returned to her old Richmond notebooks. She had been trying to persuade former associates to edit her husband's papers. But Varina Davis's advice no doubt made sense: 'I think your diaries would sell better than any Confederate history of a grave character.... no one is so tired of Confederate history as the Confederates – they do not want to tell the truth or to hear it.' At any rate, Mary Chesnut recast and greatly amplified her wartime jottings, leaving at her death material amounting to nearly a million words. This labour received its first full posthumous publication, edited by C. Vann Woodward as *Mary Chesnut's Civil War* (1981), a century later. It is thus an elaborate artefact of the 1880s, purporting to consist of artless, hurried jottings of the 1860s. In a sense it is a concoction, of a kind likely to make academics uneasy. Historians can no longer straightforwardly cite Mary Chesnut as a source. Literary critics may be puzzled to define the nature of her 'Diary'. She deals with real people and events, more fully than in the actual wartime journal, yet in allusive, darting fragments, with references that demand close attention, and annotation.

She died in the same year as Emily Dickinson, in a matching obscurity. Mary Chesnut's posthumous work is, like Dickinson's, an astounding oddity – the imaginative feat of an unknown Southern artist on the brink of an invention actually closer to James Joyce's *Ulysses* than to *Vanity Fair*. Of course she and Joyce are very far apart. Mrs Chesnut was a rather prim romantic, who liked to flirt but was shocked to hear that George Eliot, an author she revered, was living out of wedlock. Joyce gave himself all the time in the world to weave together the memory and legend of a vanished Dublin. She, with a farm to run and a dying husband, had used up the stock of leisure supposedly available to Southern ladies of rank. The past, hateful and dear, remote and yet immanent, haunted them both. Their chronicles were scrap-albums, novels without conventional heroes, and without a plot but only epiphanies, and agitated movement within time and space. During the era known as Reconstruction Mary Chesnut composed her own 'reconstruction' of a fantasized nation, without a real culture to call its own: her private history of a war that failed.

Under Reconstruction there were hard times for old authors like Simms and for young ones like the poet–musician Sidney Lanier (1842–81), who had spent several months in a Union prison camp. A few, such as G. W. Cable (another ex-soldier), went north because they could not stomach white Southern racism; others because the living was easier in New York than in New Orleans or Charleston. Most people stayed put, perplexed to find words for their altered circumstances that made acceptable sense.

Confederates do not want to tell the truth or to hear it. Was Varina Davis correct? It is true that before the 1880s at least, few Americans, North or South, seemed impelled to record the sensations of the battlefield. Only a few pages of Lanier's novel *Tiger-Lilies* (1867) refer to his experiences as a soldier, though they offer perhaps the best American fictional insights into combat before Stephen Crane's *Red Badge of Courage* (1895), and include a memorable account of the celebrated 'rebel yell':

From the right of the ragged line now comes up a single long cry, as from the leader of a pack of hounds who has found the game. This cry has in it ... uncontrollable eagerness ..., together with a dry harsh quality that conveys an uncompromising hostility. It is the irresistible outflow of some fierce soul immeasurably enraged, and it is tinged with a jubilant tone, as if in anticipation of a speedy triumph and a satisfying revenge. It is a howl, a hoarse battle-cry, a cheer, and a congratulation, all in one.

Why had so many gone to their deaths? The claim that the South had fought for state rights ('The War Between the States') appealed to constitutionalists; Jefferson Davis and his Vice-President, Alexander H. Stephens, published exhaustive apologias along those lines. But this argument was at odds with the view that Davis and Stephens had stood at the head of a new *nation*, in a 'War for Southern Independence'. The

Confederacy had drawn together, too, in defence of slavery. The ingenious Virginian George Fitzhugh (1806–81) had claimed, for instance (in *Sociology for the South*, 1854, and *Cannibals All!*, 1857), that the 'peculiar institution', being humane and efficient, was destined to become universal. With emancipation such theories vanished from public discourse, though within a few years sentiment in the North seemed to agree with the white Southern assertion that Reconstruction was a big mistake, and black civic participation a catastrophe.

The resultant confusion of Southern thought is evident in the truncated career of Sidney Lanier. 'You have no idea', he told a Northern friend, 'how benighted we all are.' He resisted the idea of a 'Southern' brand of music or poetry. Though his creative and critical writings began to achieve recognition outside the South, like his predecessor Edgar Allan Poe he felt frighteningly untenured. Their comparable dreams – of chivalry, unearthly beauty, pure passionless women – were perhaps especially 'Southern' in being so loftily abstract. Like Poe, Lanier developed theories of prosody. Music and verse, he maintained in *The Science of English Verse* (1880), are governed by the same laws. Metre in poetry, he believed, obeyed the metronome: time, not accent, was the essential. As with Poe, Lanier strove to create poetry melodious as music:

> Oh, what is abroad in the marsh and the terminal sea?
>   Somehow my soul seems suddenly free
> From the weighing of fate and the sad discussion of sin,
>   By the length and the breadth and the sweep of the marshes of Glynn.

But his soul was not free in the post-war era. He echoed 'Lost Cause' rhetoric on ceremonial occasions, canonizing the Confederate generals, Robert E. Lee and 'Stonewall' Jackson. Lanier snatched at equivocal justificatory arguments, quoting Dr Arnold of Rugby in an article for the *Southern Magazine* (1871): 'Half a man's virtue is gone when he becomes a slave; the other half goes when he becomes *a slave broken loose*.' So much for Reconstruction! Beneath such sentiments, we may think, lay a profound malaise, embodied for instance in *John Lockwood's Mill* (1868), a novel Lanier never completed:

And, today we cannot labor, for there is here neither reward nor demand for labor. Our hope, our forgetfulness, our solace, has been drowned in some vile muddle or other of politics in which we had no part and no interest. . . .

The 'Lost Cause' was retrospective in tone, mourning the dead, extolling

Confederate valour, and tending to sentimentalize the days 'befo' de wah'. 'Marse Chan', a story by Thomas Nelson Page (1853–1922), narrated by a faithful body-servant, tells of the hero's battlefield death and the heroine's fervent dedication to his memory. This story first appeared in New York's *Century* magazine in 1884 (reprinted with other tales, 1887, *In Ole Virginia*). Little by little the South's theme became the 'Lost Cause Regained'. By 1898 Page could produce a nationwide bestseller, *Red Rock*, lauding the white South's wartime fortitude and resistance to Reconstruction.

Within a few more years, Southern 'redemption' was more vehemently upheld. Thomas Dixon (1864–1946), a Baptist minister in North Carolina, cited Scripture to crude effect in *The Leopard's Spots: A Romance of the White Man's Burden, 1865–1900* (1902), insisting on the folly of attempts to lift the Negro above an appropriately low station. His next novel, *The Clansman* (1905), presented the Ku Klux Klan as saviours of white racial purity; and Dixon's two lurid volumes furnished the plot for his friend D. W. Griffith's disagreeable epic film, *The Birth of a Nation* (1915).

Lanier did not live to witness the emergence of a different phenomenon, the 'New South' creed, which he might have half endorsed, half detested. The movement took its name from a speech, 'The New South', delivered in New York in 1886 by the Atlanta newspaper publisher Henry W. Grady (1850–89). Others before him had urged their region to apply the Northern economic model. A Vicksburg, Mississippi newspaper had said in 1881: 'We are in favor of the South, from the Potomac to the Rio Grande, being thoroughly and permanently Yankeeized.' Grady's ingratiating speech portrayed Abraham Lincoln as the ideal composite American, the 'sum of Puritan and Cavalier'. The South's future, said Grady, lay in becoming as democratic and industrious as the rest of the nation. The hero of *The Leopard's Spots*, while paying dutiful tribute to the Old South, 'worshipping the dead, and raising men rather than raising money', celebrated the imperial expansionism of Uncle Sam, in which the new white South would wholeheartedly collaborate.

The debate over Old and New involved also in some degree a clash between the planter aristocracy and the small farmers of the redneck South. The Populism of the 1890s held out the prospect of a crucial realignment of Southern society, linking sharecroppers and factory workers, black and white. In place of worker solidarity, however, came the 'Solid South', a one-party system pledged to white supremacy. Southern mythology, abetted by Northern publishers and readers, continued to conjure up images of cavaliers and cotillions, moonlight and magnolias, in the genre exploited by George Cary Eggleston (1839–1911) and John Esten Cooke (1830–86), for whom the Virginia gentleman, exemplified by Robert E. Lee, was a paragon of graceful integrity. Given such idealization, there was little room for dispassionate literary analysis. Ellen Glasgow of Richmond (1874–1945) was to bring her astringent intelligence to bear on the scene about her ('what the South needs now is – blood and irony'), but not with full force until the 1920s. Her Richmond contemporary James Branch Cabell (1879–1958), a dandified romanticist, had a streak of flippancy first apparent in *The Rivet in Grandfather's Neck* (1915), and then in the campy, many-volumed saga of the make-believe kingdom of Poictesme, whose Fellowship of the Silver Stallion could be construed as an obliquely irreverent reference to Lee and the 'gray ghosts' of Confederate cavalry.

In the decade or two before the 1914–18 war, however, the state of Southern writing almost deserved the doggerel lament of J. Gordon Coogler:

> Alas, poor South, her poets get fewer and fewer;
> She never was much given to literature.

The young firm of Doubleday, Page, which could boast of publishing Ellen Glasgow, Frank Norris and (with some hesitation) Dreiser's *Sister Carrie*, showed no embarrassment that its list should feature both *The Leopard's Spots* and Booker T. Washington's memoir *Up From Slavery* (1901).

Would the South ever escape from the disabling myths it had devised to rationalize caste-lines, staple-crop agriculture, the contradictory dream of state autonomy *and* Stars-and-Bars nationality, and the humiliation of Lee's surrender to Ulysses S. Grant at Appomattox? H. L. Mencken (1880–1956), the acerbic 'Sage of Baltimore', ridiculed the ill-educated, superstitious, Bible Belt provincialism of the 'Sahara of the Bozart' as a cultural desert, whose aridity was (he said) literally aggravated by the ratification of the Eighteenth (Prohibition) Amendment in 1919.

Yet by the middle 1920s an extraordinary Southern renaissance was under way. Poetry, fiction, history, belles-lettres began to pour out from cities, campuses and hamlets. One important collective manifesto was *I'll Take My Stand*, by 'Twelve Southerners', published in 1930. The subtitle of their symposium was *The South and the Agrarian Tradition*. They took their stand (borrowing the main title from the Confederacy's unofficial anthem, 'Dixie') for a 'Southern way of life against ... the American or prevailing way', and agreed that 'the best terms in which to present the distinction are contained in the phrase, Agrarian *versus* Industrial'. During the previous century 'agrarianism' had usually signified a proposal to redistribute landed property more equally. These modern Agrarians were, however, politically conservative rather than radical, belonging to the cultivated gentry. Their headquarters was at Vanderbilt University in Nashville, Tennessee; they had previously been known as the Fugitives, from the name of a stylish little magazine they edited from 1922 to 1925. John Crowe Ransom (1888–1974), a Vanderbilt poet–professor, had been a Rhodes Scholar at Oxford. Donald Davidson (1893–1968) was another member of the Vanderbilt faculty. Allen Tate (1899–1979) and Robert Penn Warren (1905–89), somewhat younger, were rapidly acquiring a reputation as talented men of letters.

Their protest was in a sense traditional. They were voicing ancient Southern grievances against the North. Their ancestors after all had proclaimed the superiority of a static economy, based on land and kinship, to what they saw as the soulless materialism of the North. In the old rhetoric, the Yankees of New England were accused of a particularly odious combination of religiosity and commercialism. The Agrarians reiterated the old attack in the guise of a denunciation of the 'New Humanism'.

The chief advocates of this movement were Irving Babbitt (1865–1933) and Paul Elmer More (1864–1937), professors of literature especially associated with Harvard, where Babbitt had once taught T. S. Eliot. Asserting the values of humanism, sometimes with 'new' as a prefix, they declared their hostility to the modernism of the 1920s. They invoked classical standards: taste, discipline, measure. According to Babbitt's argument, in *Rousseau and Romanticism* (1919) and *Democracy and Leadership* (1924), the malign influence of Rousseau and his disciples had carried personal whims to the point of chaos. Romantic individualism led to a denial of absolutes; self-expression had become the only norm. In life and in literature, what was needed was a return to ethical imperatives, an 'inner check'.

Opponents of the New Humanism complained that its opposition to modernity was futile and shrill. In *The Genteel Tradition at Bay* (1931) the philosopher George Santayana, a one-time Harvard colleague of Babbitt, took the Humanists' Platonic and Christian postulates as evidence that New England culture was exhausted. The Puritan and Transcendental heritage had finally produced – as Santayana implied in his novel *The Last*

Puritan (1936), and as Eliot said – minds 'refined beyond the point of civilization'.

Apart from ancestral antagonism, this is why the Southern Agrarians refused to support a position they might have been expected to admire. The introduction to *I'll Take My Stand* protested that

The 'Humanists' are too abstract. Humanism, properly speaking, is not an abstract system, but ... a kind of imaginatively balanced life lived out in a definite social tradition.... [We] believe that ... the genuine humanism was rooted in the agrarian life of the older South.... It was not an abstract moral 'check' derived from the classics....

Allen Tate, in his contribution to the symposium, said that

New England was one of those abstract-minded, sharp-witted trading societies that must be parasites in two ways: They must live economically on some agrarian class or country, and they must live spiritually likewise. New England lived economically on the South, culturally on England.

Certainly Tate and some of the others were fiercely proud of the South, and quite all-embracingly so. Mencken, himself a Baltimore brand of Confederate, was selectively Southern – celebrating the aristocratic virtues of the upper crust while jeering at the poor whites and their demagogic leaders. The Agrarians were prepared to embrace the plain folk as well as the planters. In 1925, all of Mencken's superb gifts of invective were brought into play to cover the Scopes trial in Dayton, Tennessee, at which a high-school biologist was charged with defiance of a state ban on the teaching of Darwinian evolution. What else could one expect, Mencken asked, of the 'gaping primates' of the Southern uplands, and their natural spokesman, the fundamentalist politician-windbag William Jennings Bryan? But the Agrarians were offended by such slurs. Some of them said the Scopes trial had convinced them that they were Southerners, first, foremost, and always.

Their South was a source of pride to them as gentlemen authors who would write books about Jackson, Lee, Davis – the great men of the Confederacy. On the other hand, their avant-garde literary impulses were both cosmopolitan and iconoclastic. The first editorial of *The Fugitive* (1922) announced that 'THE FUGITIVE flees from nothing faster than the high-caste Brahmins of the Old South.' Warren was, like Ransom, a Rhodes Scholar. Allen Tate was a poet–intellectual. When he embarked on a biography of Stonewall Jackson, and started to close letters with 'The Stars & Bars forever!' his friend Donald Davidson confessed astonishment.

Davidson, reviewing Tate's biography in 1928, said: 'One would think him more concerned about the French Symbolists, say, than the battle of Chancellorsville.'

They attempted to reconcile apparent anomalies. Tate thus insisted, a little perversely, that if New England leaned culturally upon England, the South did not. It had followed its own path, not out of sloth or backwardness but because it was mature: 'the South could be ignorant of Europe because it *was* Europe; that is to say, the South had taken root in a native soil.' Ransom's essay in *I'll Take My Stand* presented the South as 'unique on this continent for having founded and defended a culture which was according to the European principles of culture'. Davidson said: 'the specious theory that an "independent" country ought to originate an independent art, worthy of its national greatness, did not originate in the South.' Or, as Tate wrote in 1939, for a *Partisan Review* symposium, only a 'regional' writer like himself could comfortably absorb the whole literary heritage of Europe-*and*-America. The 'nationalist' writer, by contrast, either like Carl Sandburg 'naively assumes the "nationalism" of mere observation', or like the poet Hart Crane, author of *The Bridge* (1930), 'tries to pour myths into "America" from the top of his mind'.

By the 1920s, the conditions for a strong yet subtle literary revival were present. The Secession War had receded far enough into the past to be contemplated rather than raged or wept over. If white racial attitudes were still suffused with guilt and prejudice, the South had travelled some distance in self-understanding since the earliest phase of the Klan. Nor or course are racial and social justice guarantors or preconditions of first-rate literature: it is even tempting to argue the opposite case. What was decisive was the coming together of myth and actuality in workable mixes; and of the wish, the will and the means to convert experience into literature. Mary Chesnut's little vignettes, mingling romance and realism, were precursors. The generation of Tate and Warren was at last able to appreciate the poignance and the accuracy of this sort of perception (her 'diary' for 3 April 1865):

Saw Mr. Preston ride off. . . . Told him he looked like a crusader on his great white horse and William his squire. . . .

How different these men look on horseback – they are all consummate riders . . . – from the same men packed like sardines in dirty [railroad] cars.

Which cars are usually floating inch deep in . . . tobacco juice.

Confederates on horseback are magnificent centaurs: unhorsed and squeezed into freight wagons, they are squalidly ordinary. Which view is true? Both – was the answer available by the 1920s.

The answer gained confidence from the realization that the go-ahead, citified consumerism stereotyped as Yankee 'progress' found more and more critics. Northerners too – the Humanists among them – were beginning to deplore the consequences of the Machine Age. Allen Tate was not alone in supposing that the suicide of his friend Hart Crane in 1932 had something to do with the impossible pressures of the metropolis. Much of what was written by T. S. Eliot, or by the New York critic–historian Lewis Mumford, could be regarded as grist for the Agrarian mill. Southerners of almost any persuasion, from the cosmopolitan to the stay-at-home, could relish the paradox that their primitive region might be in the 'European' swim of things; and that others were coming round to their way of thought. According to Mary Chesnut her husband had remarked wryly, during the last days of the war, that he hoped to live long enough to see England and France become democratic republics, so that they too would learn 'how that sort of thing worked'. 'You are spiteful,' said one of his dinner companions. But with the passage of the decades, it appeared that people in the North, and in Europe, were as sceptical as Southerners like James Chesnut, Jr., about progress and democracy. Who truly believed in such slogans? Not Babbitt, not Mencken (according to his caustic *Notes on Democracy*, 1926), not crotchety Northerners such as John Jay Chapman and Albert Jay Nock. In that company the literati of the Southern Renaissance could pass as ultra-progressives – or, they might themselves have amusedly claimed, as Jeffersonians.

They were not quite fair to New England or to some other regions. The Agrarian view of the Southern past, in *I'll Take My Stand*, was somewhat euphemized and prettified, pretending for instance that the cotton, rice, sugar and tobacco plantations had been run by a modest 'squirearchy', and that the values transmitted by these bucolic ancestors would be betrayed if the South accepted industry (as it had already done in several places). Their South, in short, resembled W. B. Yeats's Ireland in being partly real and partly an invention. In Ireland and in the South (each stimulated too by having an intimate enemy to grapple with) what was probably imaginary contributed to the rich imaginative sum; both places had traditions amenable to every form of literature.

Perhaps it is wrong to speak of Agrarianism before speaking of individuals. The Agrarians were a motley group; and though the most famous among them – Ransom, Tate, Warren – may have contemplated dying in

Dixie, they eventually chose not to live there. Tate, never wholly committed to Agrarianism, for a while sought another allegiance by becoming a Roman Catholic. Nevertheless, they remained Southern in important ways.

John Crowe Ransom, the eldest, began in 1919 with a tentative little book, *Poems About God* – none of which he included in later collections. The subsequent *Chills and Fever* (1924) and *Two Gentlemen in Bonds* (1927) exemplified his 1941 definition ('*A poem is a logical structure* having a *local texture*'). The essay in which the definition occurs explains that particulars are a matter of texture, universals of structure, and that both are needed in a poem, as in a furnished house, in which 'the paint, the paper, the tapestry are texture'. Ransom was not a gaudy writer. But the word *tapestry* is a clue that his establishments are survivals from a bygone age. His rich, often archaic language speaks of old men, old places, the ancient mystery of death. The South, he knew, was crumbling; he said of it in his fine poem 'Antique Harvesters',

> Declension looks from our land, it is old.

Yet things should be, so to speak, time-honoured:

> True, it is said of our Lady, she ageth.
> But see, if you peep shrewdly, she hath not stooped;
> Take no thought of her servitors that have drooped,
> For we are nothing; and if one talk of death –
> Why, the ribs of the earth subsist frail as a breath
> If but God wearieth.

Allen Tate, an equally accomplished poet and critic, contemplated the South, and the world, with a mixture of regional piety and debonair distance. Tate's biographies of Stonewall Jackson and Jefferson Davis, while lacking the formidable weight and scale of Douglas Southall Freeman's studies of Lee and his generals, were as closely Southern in identification. His elegiac talents were more delicately deployed in the bittersweet 'Epistle' (1927) (dedicated to Edmund Wilson, 'a Syracusan domiciled at Rome'):

> Once we had marvelled country-wise,
> My friend. You know that light was brief.
> Mile after mile the cities rise
> Where brisk Adonis tied the sheaf.

The lightly classical tone is sustained in Tate's handsome 'Ode to the

Confederate Dead', his most anthologized poem. There are no words to speak at the desolate autumn scene, where history was once agonizingly made:

> We shall say only the leaves
> Flying, plunge and expire.

At times there is an edge of asperity or despair, as in 'Aeneas at Washington' (published in *The Mediterranean and Other Poems*, 1936):

> Stuck in the wet mire
> Four thousand leagues from the ninth buried city
> I thought of Troy, what we had built her for.

The Southern capacity to be immersed in the past, or incapacity *not* to be immersed in it (a difficulty inseparable from a duty, perhaps, and also from an astounding knack of recall): these layers of memory are assembled in Allen Tate's only novel, *The Fathers* (1938), which may come to be regarded as his masterwork. It is a tale of a Virginia family, overtaken by the Civil War, recounted long afterwards by an old man who on the eve of secession was a lad of fifteen. His brother-in-law is immoderate to the edge of insanity, his father a perfect gentleman, who disdains to save their house from destruction by disclosing to Yankee marauders that he is in fact a Unionist. In the introduction to a 1960 reprint of *The Fathers*, Arthur Mizener noted that the original edition 'sold respectably ..., perhaps because people expected it to be another *Gone With the Wind*, whereas it is ... the novel *Gone With the Wind* ought to have been'. Perhaps Fairfax County was not quite as intricately traditional in 1860–61 as Allen Tate made out; but the power of his art makes us feel it ought to have been.

His volumes of criticism, from *Reactionary Essays* (1936) to *The Forlorn Demon* (1953), resemble those of Ransom in courtly and erudite dicta. He and Ransom describe themselves as Aristotelian; they dislike 'Platonic' forms of literature which fail to make the fusion that Tate admires in John Donne, or in Emily Dickinson – a poet who '*perceives abstraction* and *thinks sensation*'. So, though they based themselves originally upon regional pride, they grew not into 'folksiness' but fastidiously away into a humanist abstraction married to poetic immediacy.

The most copious of the one-time Agrarians was Robert Penn Warren of Kentucky, author of ten novels, fifteen or more volumes of poetry, a play, and numerous biographies and critical studies. A long-time professor of English at Yale, he was a friend and colleague of Cleanth Brooks, the 'New

Critic' and Faulkner scholar. His prodigious energy, a zest for the Southern vernacular, and perhaps his readiness to accept the endemic nastiness of much of human nature, gave his writings their special tone. He may be the only author to have won Pulitzer prizes in the two categories of fiction and verse. His prize-winning novel *All the King's Men* (1946) examines the rise and fall of a Southern politician resembling Louisiana's Huey Long, governor and then U.S. senator, who was at work on a book called *My First Days in the White House* when he was assassinated in 1935. To many people Huey Long was an amoral, would-be dictator, a Southern-style Mussolini or even Hitler. But Warren declines to moralize; the protagonist Willie Stark is large in virtues as well as in faults. Good and evil are inseparable too in Warren's 'Ballad of Billie Potts', the plot of which parallels that of Albert Camus's play *Le Malentendu*. (A theme also mentioned in Camus's novel *L'Étranger*. One might compare the existentialism of Camus with Warren's depiction of a Southern wanderer, returning home to be reunited with his parents, who murder him before realizing who he is – or was.)

Warren's appetite for luridly intricate dramas of corruption and revenge was fed by the actual history of his region. His novel *World Enough and Time* (1950) took its plot from the 'Kentucky Tragedy' or 'Beauchamp Case' of 1825–6, a real-life story of seduction, retributive murder and attempted suicide that had already been exploited long before in American literature, notably in Poe's unfinished *Politian: A Tragedy* (1835–6) and in Simms's *Beauchampe* (1842) and *Charlemont* (1856). Warren exhumed another Kentucky horror-crime of the early nineteenth century in *Brother to Dragons* (1953), a 'tale in verse and voices', involving the murder of a black man by a nephew of Thomas Jefferson. They are in a way Southern scandals, whose vileness is not concealed by Warren. If he acts as judge and jury, however, he does not adopt the role of prosecuting attorney; he writes as an insider, as if to say, 'These are my people – God help us.'

Warren, like Brooks and every other fair-minded observer, recognizes the supreme importance of William Faulkner (1897–1962) as the embodiment of the idea of the South in literature. Faulkner, though never associated with Vanderbilt (or with Tennessee's other stronghold of gentlemanly culture, the University of the South at Sewanee), was no primitive. He too had travelled outside the South, training as a volunteer with the Royal Air Force in Canada. In his early Bohemian phase Faulkner lived briefly in New Orleans, where he met Sherwood Anderson, and in Europe; he published a small volume of verse (*The Marble Faun*, 1924); a tortuous first novel (*Soldier's Pay*, 1926) about a dying, disfigured war veteran and the generally discreditable responses that his return home arouses in the Georgia townsfolk; and a second experimental novel, *Mosquitoes* (1927). None of these proved much except Faulkner's wish to be a published author: they were mannered and derivative.

But then he settled for good in his hometown Oxford, Mississippi. Beginning with *Sartoris* (1929) nearly all his best fiction dealt with life in and around 'Jefferson' (an imaginary version of Oxford) in the mythical Yoknapatawpha County, Mississippi. He made the South his prime subject; or we could say the South *used* him, since his vision is obsessive and ambivalent. At one moment he is the Southern aristocrat, proud and courtly, watching his plantation fall prey to the avarice of an upstart. At another moment he seems to feel that the aristocrat is no better than the interloper, and may have only preceded him by a generation or two. The Southern tradition is sometimes cast into doubt, as something hateful or absurd. At still another moment Faulkner champions the illiterate poor white, or the Negro, or the Indians who inhabited the country before white and black ever appeared on the scene.

Faulkner's vision of the South is not merely complex but sometimes almost impossible to decode. In *The Sound and the Fury* (1929) there are four different narrative voices. We are introduced in it to the Compson family through the mind of the idiot Benjy. *Absalom, Absalom!* (1936) ranges in time from 1833, when Thomas Sutpen suddenly arrives in Yoknapatawpha, to 1910, when Quentin Compson and his Harvard roommate Shreve McCannon (a Canadian) are attempting, in the absence of sure knowledge, to work out just what chain of events led to the ruin and death of Sutpen in the 1860s. There are three chief narrators in the novel. Quentin, we have been told in *The Sound and the Fury*, is about to commit suicide, as a prelude to which he breaks the watch that is his guide to the dimension of present time....

However, in any one story or novel Faulkner is usually concerned with one particular facet of the vision. It is possible to state his position in broad terms, and along lines suggested by these words:

There are people who have an appetite for grief, pleasure is not strong enough and they crave pain, mithridatic stomachs which must be fed on poisoned bread, natures so doomed that no prosperity can soothe their ragged and dishevelled desolation.

The quotation, which might well be from Faulkner, actually comes from Emerson's essay on 'The Tragic' (1844). A key word in modernist fiction is *defeat*. Hemingway's people are defeated; so are Fitzgerald's, Dos Passos's, Farrell's. For the South *defeat* has special overtones. So does *secession*. Faulkner's people experience defeat but they do not secede in the sense of clearing out. Their ancestors attempted secession from the Union, only to lose what might in any case have been a sort of loss. The Civil War, the shattered economy, the emphasis on family, the closeness and exploitation of white–black relations: these have bound the South in a communion of defeat from which there is no escape except in death. This was Faulkner's lore, as for every other sensitive Southerner. For him another key word is *doom*. One should admit that some of his writing is wildly funny – for example the short story 'A Courtship', and the horse-trading episode in *The Hamlet* (1940). But the statement holds for nearly all of Faulkner if in certain works we substitute a somewhat lighter word – say *fatality*, also one much used by him.

His characters' involvement with one another is taken for granted by them. There is a Faulknerian 'code' which like Hemingway's has to do with courage, honour, duty. But Faulkner is even less explicit than Hemingway about what motivates his people. One can perceive, in track-ing through his chief cluster of novels – *The Sound and the Fury*, *As I Lay Dying* (1930), *Sanctuary* (1931), *Light in August* (1932), *Absalom, Absalom!* and 'The Bear' (a novelette, published in part in 1935, and fully in *Go Down, Moses*, 1942) – that the Faulkner code acts as a compulsion. Its servants could not do otherwise. Although some conduct arouses intense opposition, all parties to the quarrel grasp the general principles. Though many characters behave stupidly, obscurely, evilly, they show no hesi-tation. Their gestures seem prescribed and bold, even when negative – as when hunted men (in the story 'Red Leaves' or at the end of *Light in August*) cease to offer resistance. Violence and passivity are paired. At their most heated moments, Yoknapatawpha people often behave mechan-ically, like agents rather than actors. This frozen passion is conveyed in a fairly typical piece of Faulkner rhetoric, from *Light in August*:

He turned into the road at that slow and ponderous gallop, the two of them, man and beast, leaning a little stiffly forward as though in some juggernautish simulation of terrific speed though the actual speed itself was absent, as if in that cold and implacable and undeviating conviction of both omnipotence and clairvoyance of which they both partook known destination and speed were not necessary.

This is the rankly ornate Faulkner tone that has been called Dixie Gongor-ism.

The reader is in the position of an inexperienced judge, hearing an intricate tribal dispute; the evidence is thrown at him haphazard, some witnesses refuse to testify, and he fears that perhaps no verdict is feasible, since the litigants have different moral scruples from his own. The law, if any, lies in the accumulated custom of Yoknapatawpha. The remotest basis in time is the land, the wilderness so beautifully evoked in the long story 'The Bear'. Closest to the land are the Indians, of the period just before the white man drove them out. But they are already degenerate, with their slaves and ill-run plantations. Man has begun to ruin the wilderness, and has implanted upon it the curse of slavery. Everything else follows, as Faulkner would say, 'implacably': the inordinate pride, the distorted chivalry, the lost war, the mean commercial aftermath, the inescapable Negro presences, the rebellious sexuality of adolescent girls, the inbred anger of their brothers, the power of taboos, the well-founded suspicion that these are being flouted.

Out pours the tormented history of the South. Where people go by nicknames and ancestral names are handed on, it is not always easy to discover *who* is being talked about, in which generation. The Irish writer Sean O'Faolain complained with some justification that Faulkner, a writer of 'more genius than talent', is often unbearably wordy. O'Faolain suggests that life in Faulkner's Mississippi sounds much like life in County Cork – 'the same vanity of an old race; the same gnawing sense of old defeat; . . . a good deal of the same harsh folk-humour; the same acidity; . . . the same escape through sport and drink. There are, of course, differences. There is, for example, no escape in Ireland through sex.'[1] The comparison is illuminating, and the terms may be reversed. Consider for example the Faulknerian qualities (except for brevity) of Maria Edgeworth's novel *Castle Rackrent* (1800). She was a member of the Protestant landowning gentry in Ireland, comparable in status to Faulkner's great-grandfather Colonel William C. Falkner. Both novelists are well placed in their societies, yet aware of serious shortcomings. Edgeworth's narrator is Thady Quirk, 'Honest Thady', the garrulous, faithful, ingenuous steward of the Rackrent family ('I am proud to say, one of the most ancient in the kingdom', he naïvely announces), a brawling, litigious lot, either spendthrifts or misers. Thady's smart son Jason Quirk – as wily and grasping as Faulkner's Jason Compson – eventually becomes master of the Rackrent estates, such as

1. Sean O'Faolain, *The Vanishing Hero: Studies in Novelists of the Twenties* (London, Eyre and Spottiswoode, 1956), 101–3.

they are. *Castle Rackrent* is a tale of decline and meanness, brilliantly sharpened by its narrative structure.

Ireland and the American South are two regions on which time played many a trick. The consequences for literature have been manifold, but in balance powerfully and resonantly beneficial. Readers with no stake in the game whatsoever find Yoknapatawpha maddening yet mesmerizing. One of the clearest lessons in Faulkner is that the sin of pride dooms the ambitious families – the Sartorises, Sutpens and Compsons – while lowly blacks and poor whites endure. This pardon for humanity is not entirely persuasive. Sometimes Faulkner seems to say that only a mindless and animal indifference will enable people to survive – indifference like that of Lena Grove, a girl with an illegitimate baby, in *Light in August*, whose sheer wordless persistence gets her a man. Faulkner's portrayal of black house-servants seems to some readers tinged with paternalism. But Dilsey, the black woman who tends the pathetic or odious Compsons of *The Sound and the Fury*, and who has 'seed de first en de last', is given far greater moral strength than they.

Faulkner's 'modern' South was not an appetizing place, nor altogether convincing, as he wrote of it in *Sanctuary*, *Pylon* (1935) and *The Wild Palms* (1939). In some later novels and stories, such as *Intruder in the Dust* (1948), he seemed anxious to arrive at a 'liberal' position, akin to the affirmative tone of the Nobel prize speech he delivered in 1950. A shade of blandness crept into his otherwise hilarious chronicle of the rapacious, repellent, barely human Snopes family (*The Hamlet*, 1940; *The Town*, 1957; *The Mansion*, 1959). Possibly he came to regret the order and centrality imposed upon his Yoknapatawpha fiction by Malcolm Cowley's emphasis in *The Portable Faulkner* (1946). At any rate he made a grandiose effort to shift his *mise-en-scène* to a 1917 French army mutiny (*A Fable*, 1954) – a Christ-allegory in which a corporal with twelve companion-apostles tries to restore peace on earth. The Frenchman is martyred, along with two soldier-criminals, and his body disappears when the grave is hit by a shell.

Perhaps the true lesson is that Faulkner's South was always a state of mind as well as a geographical area – and therefore potentially universal. This at any rate was the almost paralysing legacy Faulkner left to the next generations of Southern authors. 'Getting out from under Faulkner', as Louis D. Rubin put it, was no easy matter; or in Flannery O'Connor's words: 'Nobody wants his mule and wagon stalled on the same track the Dixie Limited is roaring down.'

Modifying one's social and racial views was manageable for the majority of Southern intellectuals. The best of them had always sensed the ironies in the Dixie heritage. The Faulkner who had made Quentin Compson over-insist, '*I don't hate the South!*', could by degrees introduce sturdily rational characters like Gavin Stevens, and the black hero Lucas Beauchamp, with no lingering wisps of Southern Gothic. Warren too could modulate to mildly magnanimous 'Northern' discussions of race relations (*The Legacy of the Civil War*, 1961; *Who Speaks for the Negro?*, 1965). After all, the route had been opened in the 1930s by Howard Odum, Rupert Vance and the other Regionalist sociologists of Chapel Hill, who analysed the South as one among several compatible segments of a single American polity. W. J. Cash (*The Mind of the South*, 1941) produced a work of piety that was also, and perhaps predominantly, a critique of regional narcissism. The suicides of Cash and of James Agee (1909–55), poet, novelist, film critic and author of *Let Us Now Praise Famous Men* (1941), a lyric documentary on Alabama sharecroppers, suggest the transitional strain felt by certain Southerners, perhaps unable to resolve their anguish over personal/regional identity. Richard King writes acutely (*A Southern Renaissance*) of the searchings of such people, and of the Florida-born Lillian Smith (1897–1966), the radically unromantic author of *Strange Fruit* (1944), a harsh tale of an inter-racial love affair and a lynching, and *Killers of the Dream* (1949), a personal essay on racism. Perhaps it was easier for academics, especially if they were no longer domiciled in the Deep South. At any rate, transplanted historians such as David H. Donald, David M. Potter and C. Vann Woodward, while primarily concerned with their own region, seemed to flourish in the improved climate of Southern liberalism.

For a number of imaginative writers, however, the 'Dixie Limited' of William Faulkner loomed intimidatingly large, even though he himself shunned aggrandizing publicity. Faulknerian styles and themes influenced writers against their will or their conscious awareness. One recourse was to create pastiche, verging on parody and the 'camp'. The playwright Tennessee Williams dropped into this mode now and then, most notice-ably in articles and interviews discussing his technique. So, with more deliberate manipulation, did the precocious Truman Capote (1924–84). Beginning in elegant candour (*Other Voices, Other Rooms*, 1948), he tended thereafter to slip into glittery artifice (*Breakfast at Tiffany's*, 1958) – though with the somewhat equivocal exception of *In Cold Blood* (1965), Capote's much-ballyhooed, lucrative and yet sympathetic account of a pair of criminals and the Kansas family they murdered on their rounds.

Possibly some element of 'Dixie Gongorism', or more precisely of Faulknerian Family Gothic, found its way into the work of Carson McCullers (1917–67) and Flannery O'Connor (1925–64). McCullers, departing from Georgia for Manhattan in a debut as fey and precocious as Capote's, produced an excellent mass of short stories and novels, set in the rural South (*The Heart is a Lonely Hunter*, 1940; *Reflections in a Golden Eye*, 1941; *The Member of the Wedding*, 1946, which she turned into an effective play, subsequently filmed; *The Ballad of the Sad Café*, 1951, a collection of shorter work). Flannery O'Connor, also from Georgia, grew up a Roman Catholic. Her fiction, in Georgia and Tennessee, dealt with grotesque aspects in Southern behaviour, and more especially (*Wise Blood*, 1952; *The Violent Bear It Away*, 1960) with brands of religious fanaticism. Incurably and painfully ill in her final years, she wrote to friends with a cranky wit not unlike that of Henry James's invalid sister Alice James.

One could keep on listing 'Southern' writers almost *ad infinitum* – and begin to wonder how much birthplace and subject-matter really signified for some of them, or whether the many different Souths, real and imagined, can valuably be brought under one large category. For Erskine Caldwell (1903–87), the place which he made famous, and which made him famous, was at the outset the carnal, feckless *Tobacco Road* (1932) and *God's Little Acre* (1933) of the Georgia back country. James Dickey (1923–   ) produced a hillbilly-versus-city nightmare in his novel *Deliverance* (1970), set in more or less the same region.

For Thomas Wolfe (1900–38) of Asheville, North Carolina, the South was a place to start from. His romanticism encompassed Shelleyan and Keatsian literary and personal elements (his early death seemed appropriately romantic, in a literary context). There were Byronic tinges in his notion of the lonely Artist-genius, though these were probably picked up from his America of the 1920s. From the 1930s he no doubt derived reassurance that documentary copiousness was commendable. One can still think of other associative resemblances or influences: Rabelais, Whitman and James Joyce (Wolfe's education at Chapel Hill, and then at Harvard, made him in some ways remarkably sophisticated). But Thomas Wolfe is nobody but himself. His novels are a serial saga, lightly disguised, of Wolfe as 'Eugene Gant' or 'George Webber' – a boy and college student in North Carolina; a would-be playwright, then novelist; a wanderer in the North, in Europe, fidgetily back in New York and Brooklyn. During his last years he modified a little his passion to engulf life and literature. But only he could have said, with such deprecating innocence ('The Story of a Novel,' 1936), that

it is . . . more important to have known one hundred living men and women in New York, to have . . . got, somehow, at the root and source from which their lives came than to have seen or passed or talked with 7,000,000 people upon the city streets.

A mere hundred! No one but Wolfe could have referred (in the same essay) to a million-word manuscript as a 'skeleton of a book'. He knew that this was twice as long as *War and Peace*; yet despite the cutting that his devoted editor Maxwell Perkins nerved him to accomplish, he could not believe a single word was redundant. In four novels, two of them published posthumously, he showed that he considered his material as inexhaustible as life itself; for as he told Scott Fitzgerald, 'a great writer is not only a leaver-outer but also a putter-inner'. Wolfe, the South, mankind, seeks 'a stone, a leaf, an unfound door'. Americans are lost; home is a place they have grown away from (*You Can't Go Home Again* is one of Wolfe's titles), and not replaced with any other permanent or satisfying allegiance:

The deepest search in life . . . was man's search to find a father, . . . the image of a strength and wisdom external to his need and superior to his hunger . . . .

Southern rhetoric: Wolfe loved sonority, and high-flown words like *forever* and *nevermore*. His first book *Look Homeward Angel* (1929), generously praised by Sinclair Lewis in his Nobel prize address, is a stabbingly detailed portrait of childhood and adolescence, and the youth's craving to discover 'the lost lane-end into heaven' denied him by inelegant and thwarted parents. The subsequent novels, in their rich if frustrated promise, led Faulkner to say in 1955 that Wolfe was the 'finest failure' in modern American fiction, with himself second and Dos Passos third.

If Wolfe was one sort of Southerner, he had a few things in common with Richard Wright (1908–60): both lived abroad, though Wright for much longer. Both knew the pangs of expatriate exile. Wolfe, lonely and homesick in Europe, found himself remembering the sights, sounds and smells of bygone days: 'I discovered America during those years abroad out of my very need of her.' Living in Paris after the Second World War, Wright still wrote mainly of America.

Otherwise he and Wolfe were poles apart. Richard Wright, son of a black Mississippi sharecropper, was the South's hitherto silent (or silenced) voice: the missing black testimony which will be discussed in chapter 14 below. His scarifying autobiography *Black Boy* (1945) is a counterpart to *Look Homeward Angel*. It tells of growing up in Mississippi and Memphis; desperate efforts to gain an education under difficulties far greater than those of teacher-befriended Wolfe; working as a 'clean-up boy' in a cheap hotel; saving money by every means possible; and final escape, north to Chicago like a fugitive (of a non-Vanderbilt pattern), 'in a Jim Crow coach' and without a real home ever to go back to.

In the old North–South diagram the South had symbolized a set of good things: lordly grace, courage, courtesy, leisure, family and local ties, stability, love of the past. The reverse side was a set of antithetical vices: snobbery, brutality, affectation, laziness, parochialism, standpattism, mythologizing. Twentieth-century literature gained immeasurably, while keeping the *idea* of the South, by admitting its multifarious ambiguity. Perhaps the idea would ultimately lose all magic out of its very diversity, and its openness to parody. Could it, within its loosened conventions, make room for writing by blacks as well as about them; for feminist or 'womanist' interpretations; for the high-rise investment empires of Atlanta and Houston? In response to every article claiming that the South always had been different, and always would be, there was a contradictory assertion that the South, always less distinct than in legend, was becoming nearly indistinguishable from anywhere else in air-conditioned, conglomerate, suburbanite, U-Haul America.

The *idea* as a literary property would probably survive for some time to come, if with less panoply than in the Faulkner era. That was suggested, for instance by the commanding reputation enjoyed by Eudora Welty (1909–), who has been described by the fine South African author Nadine Gordimer as the best writer of short stories ever known in the United States. Welty's collections, most of them set in Mississippi, began with *A Curtain of Green* (1941) and went on to include also novels such as *Delta Wedding* (1946) and *The Ponder Heart* (1954). A dozen other veterans and newcomers could be named so as to demonstrate the continuing strength of Southern fiction (not to mention poetry). Several of these seem unquestionably 'Southern', by the criteria of birth, residence and subject-matter. This would appear true, for example, of Walker Percy (1916–90), nephew of the Mississippian poet William Alexander Percy (1885–1942). Walker Percy's first novel, *The Moviegoer* (1961), is set in New Orleans during the Mardi Gras carnival, and there is much talk about the South in his later novels, for example *The Last Gentleman* (1966). The short-story writer

Peter Taylor (1917–) was born in Nashville and deals with life in the upper South.

Contrary arguments? One is that on close inspection fewer and fewer writers seem to fill all the criteria. Eudora Welty's father was from the North, where she herself studied and worked for some years. Walker Percy's South was an object for a good deal of breezy satire, like the Maryland Eastern Shore of John Barth's early fiction. A second view, voiced by Nadine Gordimer in paying tribute to Eudora Welty, is that perhaps the neat, consumer South of modern times, while no doubt pleasanter to live in than Gothic Dixie, is rather an indeterminate, boring place. The Stars and Bars could amount to little more than a bumper-sticker emblem, along with HAVE A NICE DAY and THE LORD IS MY SHEPHERD.

The survival of the Southern ethos as such may not be of vast importance. Still, its vitality in the twentieth century indicates, first, the real complexity of American historical experience; second, the usefulness of an alternative décor or ideology, to enrich and challenge the representativeness of democratic America, Leader of the Free World; and, third, that *one* idea, deeply if not essentially associated with the South, is more compelling than ever. This is the idea of some terrible loss, sustained even by the victors in the modern world, through the mere passage of time. Much we consign casually to the limbo of yesterday, throwing bits of our existence away as garbage. Other objects – baby shoes, yearbooks, wedding china, vintage cars – we strive to preserve. We record ourselves ceaselessly for posterity, on tape and film. Computers and file cabinets, corporate and governmental, store our vital statistics, with a minuteness that would have amazed our forebears, and perhaps with an ominous implication of evidence for a trial, our trial. Whether we discard or collect, the present moment whisks away round the corner into a past perhaps close at hand, vivid, wrenching, irrecoverable. Nostalgia washes over us in waves. We cry, like Thomas Wolfe, *o lost and by the wind grieved ghost, come back . . . .* Or with Faulkner we ponder the might-have-beens, almost ready to believe it could have been different, Pickett's charge at Gettysburg might have succeeded, the South might have become a separate nation . . . Such emotions may be sentimental, self-pitying, superficial (ought we to grieve for the death of, say, a slapstick comedian or a pop star, ruined by drugs and money?). But, in life and in art, we seem to live increasingly by flashback. While that is so, the concept of the South will continue to haunt American literature.

AGAINST AND AFTER
THE GENTEEL TRADITION

'GENTEEL TRADITION' has various meanings. When the Spanish-American philosopher George Santayana used the term in 1911 he had in mind an enfeebled neo-Puritan idealism, prevalent throughout the United States but originally concentrated in New England. According to H. L. Mencken, American genteelism was hypocritical, moralistic, aesthetically and politically conservative, and limply anglophile. Others have noted the racial and religious bias of 'WASP' (White Anglo-Saxon Protestant) America.

In the early twentieth century the genteel or WASP tradition did appear to control the nation's cultural life. A representative figure of the literary establishment was Richard Watson Gilder, editor of *Scribner's* and *Century* magazines, an arbiter of taste who produced a book entitled *Grover Cleveland: A Record of Friendship* (1910), and who once declined to meet Robert Louis Stevenson, deeming him an immoral person. A stronghold of the establishment was the National Academy of Arts and Letters, founded in 1904. The Academy restricted membership to a maximum of fifty. Its first batch of nominees included William Dean Howells, the Secretary of State John Hay, and the stockbroker poet Edmund C. Stedman. Another Academy member, the Rev. Henry Van Dyke, a Princeton professor of English, was to gain notoriety by announcing that Sinclair Lewis was an unsuitable American recipient of the Nobel Prize.

Lewis retaliated vigorously against Van Dyke and the Academy in his Nobel acceptance speech. To him, and to other irreverent contemporaries, the pillars of the old establishment were pompously innocuous. 'One never remembers a character in the novels of these aloof and de-Americanized Americans', wrote H. L. Mencken ('The National Letters', 1920); 'one never encounters an idea in their essays; one never carries away a line out of their poetry. It is literature as an academic exercise....' The missing quality was 'gusto'. Henry Van Dyke was not without talent, but 'he is a

Presbyterian first and an artist second, which is just as comfortable as trying to be a Presbyterian first and a chorus girl second'.

There is indeed evidence to support the contention that the genteel tradition represented a deferentially Europeanized and anachronistic, East Coast and Ivy League mode. Thus, the preface to a run-of-the-mill *Introduction to American Literature* (1898), by Henry S. Pancoast, reveals a curious deprecatory complacence: 'when compared to that of many other nations America's total contribution to the world's literature is both inferior in character and insignificant in amount.' Pancoast's revised edition (1912) tacked on a perfunctory tally of 'modern' authors, among whom he did not name Theodore Dreiser. Conceding that New England's leadership appears to have been lost, he offers the comfort that the cultural burden may now be assumed by other regions to south and west; they will somehow strengthen America's cultural unity. Pancoast does not suggest the possibility of a distinctive literature of black America. The only Negro author he mentions is Paul Laurence Dunbar, in whose dialect poems he discerns 'deep democratic humanity':

> Whah's de da'kies, dem dat used to be a-dancin'
> Ev'ry night befo' de ole cabin do'?

As for non-WASP European immigrants, he insists that almost everywhere in the United States 'the great builders of our national literature trace their descent to the people of the British Isles'. The rule even holds for the recent flowering of literary talent in Indiana, where 'men of British stock' are the dominant element. Other stocks, Pancoast admits, do exist: 'it may not be long before American literature is enriched by Italian, Russian, Hungarian, or Pole.' But this is 'as yet, in the future'.

To impatient critics, then, America's 'learneries' (Ezra Pound's word) were culturally anaemic, and supercilious, and so was the National Academy. Despite themselves, we may think, the Academicians betrayed disagreeable prejudices, as in this ostensibly well-intentioned observation by Howells's protagonist Basil March (*A Hazard of New Fortunes*, 1890), who has been exploring in New York:

March noticed in these East Side travels . . . what must strike every observer returning to the city after a prolonged absence: the numerical subordination of the dominant race. . . . The small eyes, the high cheeks, the broad noses, the puff lips, the bare cue-filleted skulls of Russians, Poles, Czechs, Chinese, the furtive glitter of Italians, the blond dullness of Germans, the cold quiet of Scandinavians. . . .

Some years later Henry James (*The American Scene*, 1907) expressed the shock of a 'sensitive citizen' at the spectacle of Ellis Island, the immigrant station: the shock of having to 'share the sanctity of his American consciousness, the intimacy of his American patriotism, with the inconceivable alien'.

Nor, it is said, did America's belletrists feel comfortable in dealing with the native-born poor. They could handle the rural poor, treating such people as 'characters' or grotesques. The urban masses were another matter. Sympathy for their hardships rarely extended to cover strikes, unions or other demonstrations of solidarity. John Hay's *The Bread-Winners* (first serialized, anonymously, in *Century Magazine*, 1883–4) portrayed labour leaders as dangerous, wicked men. So did Francis Marion Crawford's *An American Politician*, a novel of the same period. Later fiction, such as *The Man of the Hour* (1905) by Alice French ('Octave Thanet'), while somewhat more sympathetic to labour problems, also condemned strikes, and blamed socialist or anarchist ideas upon foreign-born writers.

The record, however, needs to be clarified. In the first place, the guardians of the genteel tradition maintained a quite defensible position enunciated originally as far back as Noah Webster: the United States needed to be a country of one language. This, whether called 'English' or 'American', was a *common* language, an essential unifying or Americanizing feature for a society otherwise dangerously fragmented – the chief desire of outsiders was to become insiders, by conforming as rapidly and closely as possible to the tests of Americanism, among which the capacity to read and write English was fundamental.

In the second place, the racial and class attitudes of Academy members did not differ greatly from those of most authors usually classified as modernist or bohemian, at least in the late nineteenth and early twentieth century. There are tinges of anti-Semitism in the writings of Henry Adams, Henry James, Edith Wharton, Owen Wister and other upper-crust Easterners. On the other hand, Jews fare no better in Utopian and naturalistic fiction: consider the portrayal of Nathan Brederhagen in Ignatius Donnelly's *Caesar's Column*, Zerkow in Frank Norris's *McTeague* and S. Behrman in the same author's *The Octopus*. These authors emphasize the superiority of 'Nordic' or 'Anglo-Saxon' peoples. Westerners among them, such as Jack London, warned that Chinese and Japanese settlement was as much a peril as the inflow from Europe. There is a covert reluctance, in the frontier-thesis essays of the historian Frederick Jackson Turner, to attribute any significant contribution to the newer immigration. He showed little interest, for example, in the 'frontier' fiction of Willa Cather, whose *O Pioneers!* (1913) dealt with Swedish farmers in Nebraska, and whose *My Ántonia* (1918) sympathetically evoked the early struggles of Czech immigrants.

Furthermore, some of the leaders of the establishment at least made efforts to understand and even stimulate literary treatment of non-WASP America. Howells is a conspicuous example. He gave enthusiastic encouragement to the stories of Abraham Cahan (1860–1951), a Russian-Jewish intellectual who came to the United States in 1882 and initially worked for Yiddish papers in New York. Cahan tells how when he first submitted articles to the New York *Sun*, as a would-be freelance journalist, the editor in answering said: 'You use a word about which I must ask. What is a ghetto?' Howells badgered the magazines, with eventual success, to serialize Cahan's *Yekl: A Tale of the New York Ghetto* (1896). One editor returned the manuscript with the comment: 'You know, my dear Mr Howells, that our readers want a novel about richly dressed cavaliers and women, about love which begins ... while playing golf. How can a novel about a Jewish immigrant who becomes a tailor ... interest them?'

It is also worth noting that various ladies and gentlemen of letters took a lead in stirring the nation's social conscience. The New England poet–novelist Sarah Cleghorn (1876–1959), reared in refined comfort, spoke volumes in one quatrain on children employed in textile manufacturing:

> The golf links lie so near the mill
> That almost every day
> The laboring children can look out
> And see the men at play.

Walter A. Wyckoff (1865–1908), a Princeton graduate, worked his way west for two years as a day-labourer (*The Workers: An Experiment in Reality*, 2 vols., 1897–8). Another Princetonian, Ernest Poole (1880–1950), became involved in the lives of the proletariat through living in a New York settlement house. As a reporter in the Chicago stockyard strike of 1904 he recorded the story of a Lithuanian immigrant. This was published along with many such autobiographical sketches in *The Independent*, a religious weekly.[1] It may have formed the basis for Upton Sinclair's 'muckraking' novel *The Jungle* (1906), whose hero is also a Lithuanian-born stockyard worker. Another American of the professional classes who contributed to this *fin-de-siècle* 'discovery of poverty' was Josiah Flint

---

1. Leo Stein and Philip Taft, eds., *Workers Speak: Self Portraits* (New York, 1971), 69.

Willard (1869–1907), nephew of the temperance reformer Frances Willard. Writing as 'Josiah Flynt', he recounted his experiences as a vagrant in *Tramping with Tramps* (1899) and other books. Both Flynt's and Wyckoff's experiences were first published in *Century Magazine*, which was also hospitable to Sarah Cleghorn. Hutchins Hapgood (1869–1944), whose *Spirit of the Ghetto* (1902) has been described as 'the first authentic study by an outsider of the inner life of an American immigrant community',[1] was Harvard-educated and of old New England stock.

Dreiser's treatment of black Americans lends support to the argument that, at least in dealing with the non-white poor, there is no basic difference between the Academicians and non-traditional authors. Dreiser's early work includes a powerful fictionalized account of a lynching, 'Nigger Jeff' (1901; probably written 1895). But we are left to assume that the victim was probably guilty (of assaulting a white woman), and he is pictured as an almost mindless creature. The same can be said of Dreiser's description of a purportedly great 'Ashcan' painting done by the hero of his novel *The 'Genius'* (1915). It portrays a 'hulking, ungainly negro, a positively animal man, his ears thick and projecting, his lips fat, his nose flat, ... his whole body expressing brute strength and animal indifference to dirt and cold'.

Dreiser's intent of course is to be 'truthful', avoiding subjectivity or sentimentality. Such semi-documentary writing is apt, however, to produce blunt stereotypes of behaviour as perceived by insensitive whites. The tendency can be detected in even a more sensitive commentator. Of whom if not blacks (described but left unnamed) can Howells's Basil March be thinking when he refers to 'broad noses' and 'puff lips'?

In short, it will not do to blame America's genteel tradition for every supposed deficiency in the nation's imaginative literature. And it is an over-simplification to pretend that every problem was overcome, every inhibition swept away, with the overthrow of genteelly academic criteria. Howells has been particularly hard done by at the hands of a later generation. One suspects they did not trouble to read much, if any, of his fiction or review essays, and that his cautious treatment of sex annoyed them. They did not give him a fair hearing. But then, the process of disestablishing established reputations is age-old. In religious art the word *decollation* applies to paintings that show martyrdom by beheading (for instance, *The Decollation of St John the Baptist*). America's literary debunkers enjoyed themselves hugely at the expense of their predecessors. One

---

1. Moses Rischin, ed., *The Spirit of the Ghetto* (Cambridge, MA, 1967), vii.

can imagine a painting of a kneeling figure, behind whom stands an executioner with raised sword. Its title might be *The Decollation of William Dean Howells/Henry Van Dyke*.

For complex reasons, white American novelists were slow in dealing with immigrant and non-white people. They lagged behind writers in other countries, and behind the journalists and sociologists of the United States. Among the reasons for this tardiness are hesitation in accepting poverty as a fact of American experience, and an accompanying 'idealism' that held up before native writers the vision of a divine average American – a wholesome person of northern European antecedents, preferably blue-eyed, fair-haired and of course Protestant. Their view of Afro-Americans was adversely affected in the Gilded Age by the spread of 'retrogressionist' theories, as argued for instance in Philip A. Bruce's *The Plantation Negro as Freedman* (1889). Blacks, it was asserted, had regressed into 'barbarism' at an alarming rate since the removal of the disciplinary restraints imposed by chattel slavery.[1] Notions of racial differentiation and white superiority, bolstered by reports of seemingly reputable scientific research, influenced the underlying assumptions of imaginative literature.

To the extent that they were aware of such influences and sought to combat them, white authors tended to categorize non-WASPs as 'exotic'. 'Exotic' was a term used by Harriet Beecher Stowe as intended praise for Afro-Americans. It implied, however, that 'exotics' were outside the scope of an American author. As serious literary material they would have to be left to writers of their own provenance. Turn-of-the-century efforts to empathize with these outsiders usually seem stilted and condescending, no matter how well intentioned. Wyckoff among the labouring poor is in some sense Harun al-Rashid, a prince whose disguise can quite easily be penetrated. Jack London's seven weeks among London's East Enders prompts him to rate them, with Nietzschean finality, as a race of underlings. Upton Sinclair's Lithuanian immigrant Jurgis (*The Jungle*) is actually almost indistinguishable from a conventional American hero; he does not speak in dialect and his Catholicism is minimized. Sinclair's allusions to blacks in the novel – 'big bucks', one-time 'savages' – repeat the racial clichés of the era.[2] In general, native-born American writers devoted little attention, before the 1914–18 war, to this rich material.

1. Herbert G. Gutman, *The Black Family in Slavery and Freedom, 1750–1925* (Oxford, 1976), 531–44.

2. These points are developed in 'Upton Sinclair', a 1980 University of Sussex M.A. dissertation by T. Gilling.

As for the 'exotics' themselves, they too were inhibited. The pressure to Americanize, to conform to the melting-pot myth, induced them to grapple with more largely 'American' themes and thus (as they saw it) to escape the confining obscurity of writing about 'foreigners', especially if in a language other than English. In the act of applauding *Yekl*, Howells indicates as a test of Abraham Cahan's ultimate talent his ability to 'pass beyond his present environment into the larger American world'. It was hard in the circumstances for the foreign-born not to yearn for assimilation, and hence to adopt the stereotypes of their new home with what could be regarded as obsequious zeal. Mary Antin, brought as a girl to Boston by Russian-born parents, reveals (*The Promised Land*, 1911) how completely she has identified with the Yankees. She speaks of 'unkempt, half-washed, toiling, unaspiring foreigners', and pleads for tolerance of the 'greasy alien' who 'may have something to communicate ... when you two have learnt a common language'. But could the language possibly be other than English?

With inhibitions so subtle and yet so stringent, the alien cultures either yielded imitatively to Americanization, or remained alive in pockets of ethnicity whose impact on the 'larger American world' was accordingly negligible. Abraham Cahan's *The Rise of David Levinsky* (1917), perhaps the first full fictional assessment of an alien's spiritual balance (acknowledging minuses as well as pluses), took a longish while to emerge, and benefited from the existence of a New York Jewish enclave large enough to provide cultural sustenance in addition to psychological shelter. By the time *Levinsky* was published, Cahan was an eminent editor and writer, a kind of dean of Yiddish letters. Being also an acute observer, he brought a refreshing irony to the cloying conventions of acculturative autobiography. Thus Levinsky, fresh from Russia and struggling to make sense of the American scene, discovers a New World characteristic, 'the unsmiling smile.... It would flash up into a lifeless flame and forthwith go out again, leaving the face cold and stiff.' Taking English lessons, Levinsky comes across the statement that 'Kate had a smile for everybody.' It fascinates but dismays him: 'I had a disagreeable vision of a little girl ... grinning upon everybody she met.'

Dreiser was, in this regard, rather less of an outsider, but nevertheless a transitional figure. He grew up in a semi-immigrant milieu. German locutions found their way into his written English. Warner Berthoff suggests that the awkward phrasings and word-orders especially common in Dreiser's early efforts may be attributable to the hybrid Anglo-German

speech of his youth. By and large, though, the German-speaking Americans were by 1900 on the way to full Americanization, even if Howells
brings them in ('the blond dullness of Germans') to his catalogue of
foreignness. The Irish likewise were too long established, too numerous
and in some spheres already too successful to be treated in literature as
altogether alien or unwelcome. The day of unembarrassedly disdainful
caricature – as typified by Teague O'Regan in Brackenridge's *Modern
Chivalry* – had long gone. But Irish-American life in fiction was not fully
three-dimensional until the early 1930s, perhaps with James T. Farrell's
trilogy of *Studs Lonigan*. Until then, Irish-American characters in fiction
were commonly assigned minor, stereotyped roles as maidservants, eccen-
trics, warriors, vagabonds. (A partial exception was Finley Peter Dunne's
long run of newspaper sketches, featuring the astutely aphoristic 'Mr
Dooley' and his Chicago drinking companions – the saloon as *salon*.) The
transition was then swift. By the 1930s most authors of Irish extraction
had ceased to treat Irishness *per se* as a primary concern. Scott Fitzgerald
and John O'Hara, for instance, did not.

The cultural complications faced by foreign-born Europeans were paral-
leled but heightened in the case of black Americans. An important small
group of black writers had in fact reached the United States from Jamaica
and elsewhere in the Caribbean. But those came equipped with a mastery
of the language. The majority were long domiciled in the United States,
and while their speech retained or developed a sort of dialect, black English
was the mother tongue. The difficulties for Afro-Americans were racial
rather than linguistic. They were shut out from the democratic privileges
routinely claimed by white Americans, on account of colour where they
were 'free' Negroes, before the Civil War, and because of servitude where
they were chattel slaves. Before and after the Civil War, it was well-nigh
impossible for many blacks to get into print, let alone secure a proper
hearing. Poetry, fiction, stagecraft, travel, *belles-lettres*: the usual forms of
polite literature provided scant opportunity for aspiring 'people of colour'.
It is less surprising that few such writings were of high quality than that
any at all were created and published.

There is, for instance, an immense pathos in the history of George Moses
Horton (1797–*c*. 1883), born a slave in North Carolina. Horton taught
himself to read, and against all odds began to compose poems. A preface
to his first volume (*The Hope of Liberty*, 1829) explained on his behalf that
well-wishers were seeking to raise enough money to send the talented
'George' to colonize Liberia; 'his reading, which is done at night, and at

the usual intervals allowed to slaves, has been much employed on poetry, such as he could procure, this being the species of composition most interesting to him'. But not enough copies were sold to emancipate Horton: liberty remained only a hope. He spent the next thirty years as a college janitor at Chapel Hill, 'executing little commissions in verse from the students'. He published some extended editions, one under the title *Naked Genius*. A poem from this late collection, 'George Moses Horton, Myself' resignedly assumes that he is now too old to fulfil his youthful promise:

> My genius from a boy,
>   Has fluttered like a bird within my heart;
> But could not thus confined her powers employ,
>   Impatient to depart.

How bottled-up a 'Song of Myself' this is in comparison with that of magniloquent Walt Whitman, 'one of the roughs, a kosmos', claiming to be of the 'ouvrier class', but still several rungs above a slave bard on the social ladder.

Nor is it surprising that *Clotel, or the President's Daughter* (1853), a book usually described as the earliest novel by an American Negro,[1] failed to capture a vast audience. It was published in London where the author, William Wells Brown (1816–84), lived for some years as a writer and anti-slavery lecturer. Technically a fugitive slave, he had escaped north in Cincinnati, Ohio, the border city in which Harriet Beecher Stowe had first confronted the slave system of adjacent Kentucky. *Clotel*, like *Uncle Tom's Cabin*, can be called an abolitionist novel. In the English edition, though not in revised American versions (*Miralda*, 1860–61; *Clotelle*, 1864, 1867), the mother of the heroine is a slave housekeeper at Monticello; and the father of Clotel is Thomas Jefferson. Clotel drowns herself in the Potomac, within sight of the White House, to cheat pursuing slave-catchers of their prey. That novel, a play called *Escape, or A Leap for Freedom* (1858) and various autobiographical and historical works show Brown to have been fluently, ebulliently proud of his people. Established in Massachusetts with a medical practice, Dr Brown somehow found time for example to publish *The Black Man: His Antecedents, his Genius, and his Achievements* (1863).

He contributed, too, to the antebellum genre of the 'slave narrative'.

1. The title of first black novel *published in the United States* is claimed for *Our Nig; Or, Sketches from the Life of a Free Black* (1859), a strange semi-autobiographical fiction by Harriet Wilson (see the 1983 reprint, New York, Vintage, ed. Henry Louis Gates, Jr.).

These accounts were in their nature published in the North, usually under abolitionist auspices, to recount the escape into freedom of black 'runaways'. Since their tone was often pious, and their facts were not always verifiable, their reliability used to be questioned. Scholars now generally accept slave narratives, however, as testimony that may well represent the evangelical and libertarian style of self-educated slaves determined to make a new life in the free states, or under the British flag – in several instances ordained as clergymen.

One sample is *The Life of Josiah Henson, Formerly a Slave, Now an Inhabitant of Canada*, published as a pamphlet in 1849, and a probable source for the character of Uncle Tom in Harriet Beecher Stowe's novel. Benjamin Brawley, in *Early Negro American Writers* (1935), treats Henson with some scepticism, as a person who 'perhaps exploited himself unduly'. But there is the ring of truth in Henson's story of how, having been instructed by his master to take a group of Negroes from Maryland to Kentucky, in 1825, he resisted the temptation to turn his charges loose at Cincinnati, and how in later years he 'wrestled in prayer with God for forgiveness', for having consigned his fellow-beings to further slavery: 'my infatuation has seemed the unpardonable sin. . . . Those were my days of ignorance.'

More powerfully eloquent was the *Narrative of the Life of Frederick Douglass* (1845), which appeared in an expanded edition as *My Bondage and My Freedom* (1855), and in a third form as *Life and Times of Frederick Douglass* (1881). Also from Maryland, he was named by his slave mother Frederick Augustus Washington Bailey. Working in a Baltimore shipyard, he dropped the middle two names. Escaping north to New York and then the whaling port of New Bedford, Massachusetts (from which the *Pequod* set out, in Melville's *Moby-Dick*), he took the new surname of Douglass, adding a second 's' to the name of the heroic chief in Sir Walter Scott's *The Lady of the Lake*. Gradually shaping a new identity, Frederick Douglass (1817–95) became a superb orator and energetic editor, the most compelling black voice of the nineteenth century. 'What, to the American slave, is your 4th of July?' Douglass asked in an 1852 oration. He answered:

To him, your celebration is a sham; your boasted liberty, an unholy licence; your national greatness, swelling vanity; your sounds of rejoicing are empty and heartless; your denunciation of tyrants, brass fronted impudence. . . .

Despite such stinging words, Douglass, like other black spokesmen of the era, had acute difficulty in establishing his relationship to the world's racial hierarchy. He and Wells Brown spoke with such eloquent aplomb that unfriendly auditors denounced them as impostors – educated people pretending to be ex-slaves in order to make abolitionist propaganda. Inevitably they shared the uncertainty of the rest of America over how they should be designated. In the nineteenth century, 'nigger' was an insult, if used by whites, and 'negro' with a small 'n' not much better than off-hand slang terms such as 'darky'. 'Coloured', 'people of colour' and similar expressions seemed more polite. 'Black' was sometimes used, yet not thought suitable in every circumstance. After all, William Wells Brown and Frederick Douglass apparently had white fathers, as did the Negro educator Booker T. Washington (1856–1915). Douglass's second wife was white. Some enemies jeered that anti-slavery organizers liked platform speakers to be as 'primitively' black as possible. Other enemies shrugged off their attainments by arguing that, being partly white, it was only natural that a man like Frederick Douglass should develop into an accomplished speaker and writer.

White authors of the period commonly dealt with black characters in one or more of four ways. They might modify the degree of darkness – inventing for example a love affair doomed because the woman in the case is mulatto (invariably beautiful, often sexually alluring, usually light-skinned enough to 'pass' for white). That is the storyline of *The Octoroon* (1859), a popular play by the Irish-American dramatist Dion Boucicault (1820–90). It is embodied in the plot of Faulkner's *Absalom, Absalom!* Second, Negro characters might be shown as comically or lovably feckless, eaters of watermelon, strutters in finery, sometimes capable of deep loyalty but often cowardly and inconstant. Third, they might be lustful and dangerous, as in the stereotypes of Thomas Dixon's *The Clansman* ('His thick lips were drawn upward in an ugly leer and his sinister bead-eyes gleamed like a gorilla's. A single fierce leap and the black claws clutched the air slowly as if sinking into the soft white throat'). Fourth, a Negro tended to have only a walk-on part, or to 'stand for' something rather than to be a person, and so to disappear from the story, becoming perhaps 'invisible' as the black coachman does in Stephen Crane's short story 'The Monster' (1897).

Sadly but unavoidably, imaginative portrayals by black authors often fell into the same traps. Mary Antin, we have seen, wrote of European end-of-century immigrants as inferior beings. In William Wells Brown's *Clotel*, and in later revisions of the novel, the heroine is racially glamorized:

The appearance of Clotel on the auction block created a deep sensation amongst the crowd. There she stood, a complexion as white as most of those who were waiting with a wish to become her purchasers; her features as finely defined as any of her sex of pure Anglo-Saxon; ... her form tall and graceful, and her whole appearance indicating one superior to her position.

Despite the militant protest voiced in much of the book, Brown also pokes fun at an uppity slave named Sam, who works for a doctor and who boasts to other house-servants: 'I jist bin had my fortune told.... Aunt Winny told me I is to heb de prettiest yaller gal in town, and dat I is to be free.' Proud of his own supposedly light skin, Sam adds: 'I don't like to see dis malgemation of blacks and mulattoes, no how.'

In the next generation or two, similar conscious or unconscious pressures operated upon black American fiction. Paul Laurence Dunbar (1872–1906), reared in Ohio as the son of former slaves, produced a remarkable quantity of stories, novels and dialect verse before an early death of tuberculosis. But most of his tales employ white characters; and where black people are introduced, as in *The Fanatics* (1901), their role is subordinate and his representation playful or disapproving. Charles Waddell Chesnutt (1858–1932), who had a longer career, was also associated with Ohio. He wrote a biography of Frederick Douglass and usually concerned himself with racial themes. But most of his plots hinge on degrees of whiteness and the possibility of 'passing'. He had to press his publishers, who at first in fact passed him off as white, to let him write from the black viewpoint, even if this viewpoint were moderate and almost deprecatory. A third novelist, Sutton Griggs (1872–1930), combined writing and publishing with a career as a Baptist minister in Nashville, Tennessee. Griggs's *Imperium in Imperio* (1899), palpably aimed at a black readership, is fiercely critical of white and mulatto attitudes; revolutionists plan a separate Negro nation, beginning with the black annexation of Texas. From this anger, though, Griggs subsides into placatory tales with the general message that 'Good white people kin lead de cullud folks ef dey will jes' 'gree ter do so.' The old planter aristocracy is endowed by Griggs with no less grace but rather more authority than in the lilywhite fiction of Thomas Nelson Page.

For black Americans the perennial problem had been how to gain admission to the white culture. The 'accommodationist' position was restated by Booker T. Washington, head of a Negro vocational college at Tuskegee in Alabama. Washington, who had always lived in the South, was convinced that the way upwards for his people was through industry, temperance, thrift and religion. The freedman should walk before he ran, acquiring artisan skills that would make white people respect him. He should eschew militance, not campaigning for civil rights. His major opponent, W. E. Burghardt DuBois (1868–1963), was a Northerner with a Harvard Ph.D. and further study at the University of Berlin. DuBois came to feel that Washington's strategy would consign black Americans to a permanent underdog role. Far from gaining white respect, they were being shut into rigidly segregated existences. Lynchings averaged more than one hundred per annum. DuBois called for the 'Talented Tenth' of educated Negroes to supply leadership and inspiration. His intelligentsia, he explained in *The Souls of Black Folk* (1903), should teach their fellows how 'to be both a Negro and an American, without being cursed and spit upon'. How to achieve the necessary doubleness? Cultivated and cosmopolitan, DuBois insisted that he and his race should be able to commune with the great, timeless realm of art and philosophy, keeping company with Aristotle, Marcus Aurelius, Shakespeare, Balzac. On the other hand, there was a racial-territorial bond with Africa. He believed in the special genius of different races, and in the need for 'Pan-Africanism' to express the 'race spirit' inherent in Afro-Americans as well as their comrades elsewhere in the world.

By about 1910 such doctrines were beginning to attract widespread attention in black America, including of course that of the writers. The yearning to speak out certainly touched Paul Laurence Dunbar. His ballad 'The Haunted Oak' (1903) described a lynch mob:

> Oh, the judge, he wore a mask of black,
>   And the doctor one of white,
> And the minister, with his oldest son,
>   Was curiously bedight.

'We Wear the Mask' (1896) expressed the pain and perplexity of people forced to dissemble:

> We wear the mask that grins and lies,
> It hides our cheeks and shades our eyes,
> This debt we pay to human guile;
> With torn and bleeding hearts we smile,
> And mouth with myriad subtleties.

But as these lines indicate, Dunbar had technically been reared in the genteel tradition of versification. He knew of no suitable alternative models, other than dialect. Orthodox metre and vocabulary had a parlour primness. W. D. Howells, reviewing Dunbar's poems in 1896 with habitual geniality, urged him to have recourse to his own idiom, instead of 'literary English'. The best of Robert Burns, said Howells, was in his native dialect. Dunbar, however, felt that black poetry could hardly be 'exotic'. It would differ little from that of the whites. 'For two hundred and fifty years the environment of the Negro has been ... in every respect the same as that of all other Americans.'

Dunbar was not being timid, he was grappling with a double burden of racial and of linguistic definition, which for Negro writers of his generation might well appear unbearable. A decade or two brought new factors into play and with them, around 1920, the innovative surge of the 'Harlem Renaissance', in uptown Manhattan. Dunbar had urged black Americans not to abandon the rural South for the 'false ideals and unreal ambitions' of Northern city life. But the northward drift to the metropolis (Chicago, New York) increased momentum with the war years. By 1920 there were 100,000 Negroes in Harlem, once a heavily Irish and then a Jewish neighbourhood. The number doubled during the next decade.

Young Langston Hughes (1902–67), a budding poet from Missouri who had been excited by the work of Dunbar and of Carl Sandburg, decided to enroll as a student at Columbia University. He arrived in Manhattan in 1921:

I came up out of the subway at 135th and Lenox into the beginning of the Negro Renaissance.... That night I went to the Lincoln Theater across Lenox Avenue where maybe one of the Smiths – Bessie, Clara, Trixie, or Mamie – was singing the blues. As soon as I could, I made a beeline for *Shuffle Along*, the all-colored hit musical playing on 63rd Street....

James Weldon Johnson (1871–1938), author of the fictional *Autobiography of an Ex-Colored Man* (1912) and editor of the pioneer *Book of American Negro Poetry* (1922), called Harlem 'the Mecca for the sightseer, the pleasure seeker, the curious, the adventurous, the ... ambitious, and the talented of the entire Negro world'. Claude McKay (1890–1948), author of the novel *Home to Harlem* (1928), was drawn there from Jamaica. Zora Neale Hurston (*c*. 1901–60), novelist–folklorist–anthropologist, was Florida-born and, like Langston Hughes, came to New York to study at Columbia. Arna Bontemps (1902–73), born in Louisiana and educated in California, arrived in Harlem in 1924 to write poetry and fiction.

Not every black writer congregated in Harlem, or necessarily stayed put there. Jean Toomer (1894–1967) lived mainly in Washington, D.C., where he was born. Alain Locke (1886–1954), the first Negro Rhodes Scholar, grew up in Philadelphia and was long associated with Howard University in Washington as a philosophy professor. James Weldon Johnson's varied career took him to consular posts in central America, a roving commission as field secretary for the NAACP (National Association for the Advancement of Colored People, established in 1909), and a professorship of literature at Fisk University in Nashville. Langston Hughes, dropping out of Columbia, travelled abroad the poor man's way, as a merchant seaman. He subsisted for a while as a dishwasher in a Paris nightclub. Returning to America, he was working as a bus-boy in a Washington hotel, when he was 'discovered' by a literary guest, Vachel Lindsay, to whom he showed three of his poems.

Nevertheless Harlem was indeed 'Mecca' for what Alain Locke dubbed *The New Negro* (1925) – a person no longer an anxious apologist, painfully refined and longing to be white. Harlem was large enough to feel like a black capital, an *imperium in imperio*. Black music, dance, drama and art were flourishing there. In Hughes's Pigalle nightclub, 'the band was from Harlem'. James Weldon Johnson (as he recounts in his autobiography, *Along This Way*, 1933) stirred up some excitement as early as 1917 by arguing that (with the exception of American Indian artefacts, and skyscraper architecture), everything indigenously creative in American life was Negro. In music, there was not only the Negro spiritual but jazz, the expression of the culture outside its working hours:

At these times, the Negro drags his captors captive.... I have been amazed and amused watching white people dancing to a Negro band in a Harlem cabaret; attempting to throw off the crusts and layers of inhibitions ...; trying to work their way back into that jungle which was the original Garden of Eden; in a word, doing their best to pass for colored.

For Langston Hughes the place as he saw it shortly before the publication of his first book of poems, *Weary's Blues* (1926), was a melting-pot of black culture: 'Harlem of honey and chocolate and caramel and rum and vinegar and lemon and lime and gall.' It was, in the label of a novel of the same year by Carl Van Vechten, *Nigger Heaven* – a more ironic title than was realized by some of the public, whether or not they were aware that the author was white. 'Nigger Heaven' was an old slang term for the 'gods', the topmost, cheapest seats in a theatre. 'That's what Harlem is,' said Van Vechten. 'We sit ... in the gallery of this New York theatre and watch the white world ... down below us in the good seats.' Hence the 'vinegar' and 'gall' in Hughes's list: the whites owned most of the district and the best jobs were downtown. Well-meaning whites gushed about picturesque black savagery; this taste for primitivism was manifest in some avant-garde writing (Eugene O'Neill's *Emperor Jones* and *All God's Chillun*, Vachel Lindsay's 'The Congo'), and is perhaps even present in J. W. Johnson's reference to the 'jungle' of Eden.

At the time, however, hopes ran high. Some Harlemites, Hughes recollected in *The Big Sea* (1940), 'were sure the New Negro would lead a new life from then on in green pastures of tolerance created by Countee Cullen, [the actress] Ethel Waters, Claude McKay, Duke Ellington, Bojangles, and Alain Locke.' Cullen (1903–46), who was actually a native of Harlem, published three volumes of poetry in his early twenties. One four-line tribute to Paul Laurence Dunbar could be thought to express the distance which black America had travelled by 1925:

> Born of the sorrow of heart,
>   Mirth was a crown upon his head;
> Pride kept his twisted lips apart
>   In jest, to hide a heart that bled.

Married to the daughter of W. E. B. DuBois, Cullen seemed one of an irresistible élite – the Talented Tenth in fact. But his marriage did not last. Nor did the heady excitement of the first Negro Renaissance. There was, said Hughes, a Harlem 'vogue'; and such fads are temporary. Cullen had already in his volume *Color* (1925) conveyed a despairing sense that the New Negro was still kin to the Old Negro:

> Yet do I marvel at this curious thing:
> To make a poet black, and bid him sing!

What for instance should writers make of their African heritage? In a beautiful early poem, 'The Negro Speaks of Rivers' (1921), Langston Hughes brought the ancient world together with America, referring to the Euphrates, the Congo, the Nile *and* the Mississippi as 'ancient, dusky rivers' exemplifying the black soul. Marcus Garvey's 'back to Africa' movement was in full swing, under the title of the Universal Negro Improvement Association. But as Hughes emphasized in later verse, America was *not* an exotic, tropical land of 'chattering parrots Brilliant as the day': its reality was harsh and grey, like 125th Street in midwinter. A wealthy white patroness wanted him to collaborate with a Negro composer on a 'primitive' opera:

But unfortunately, I did not feel the rhythms of the primitive surging through me. . . . I was only an American Negro – who had loved the surface of Africa and the rhythms of Africa – but I was not Africa. I was Chicago and Kansas City and Broadway and Harlem.

Countee Cullen asked:

> What is Africa to me:
> Copper sun or scarlet sea . . .
> One three centuries removed
> From the scenes his fathers loved,
> Spicy grove, cinnamon tree,
> What is Africa to me?

Of all the works produced in the 1920s by what Wallace Thurman and Zora Neale Hurston impishly called the 'niggerati', one stands out from the rest in the critics' consensus: Jean Toomer's *Cane* (1923). Grandson of the adventurous P. B. S. Pinchback, who was acting governor of Louisiana during Reconstruction, Toomer grew up in a mainly white milieu. Racially, he noted in 1922, 'I seem to have (who knows for sure) seven blood mixtures: French, Dutch, Welsh, Negro, German, Jewish, and Indian. . . . I have lived equally amid the two race groups. Now white, now colored. From my own point of view I am . . . an American.' However, Sherwood Anderson and other admirers assumed that Toomer was, according to the American classification, black because he was not entirely white. Their assumption was reasonable, given the material of *Cane*. Its amalgam of prose and poetry, sketches and stories, belonged with the experimental modes of Gertrude Stein or James Joyce. But it was obviously semi-autobiographical. The first and third sections are set in rural Georgia, where 'Jean' (Eugene) taught for a few months at a black training school; the final section dramatizes the figure of 'Ralph Kabnis', a Northern intellectual much like Toomer. The vignettes of the middle section deal with Washington and Chicago. 'Seventh Street', for example, is portrayed as

a bastard of Prohibition and the war. A crude-boned, soft-skinned wedge of nigger life breathing its loafer air, jazz songs, and love, thrusting unconscious rhythms, black reddish blood into the white and white-washed wood of Washington. Wedges rust in soggy wood . . . Split it! In two! Again! Shred it!

Such passages struck his friends Sherwood Anderson and Waldo Frank as brilliant impressionism. *Cane* is an extraordinary assemblage, indeed. Like E. E. Cummings's *The Enormous Room* (1922), it does not fit into any of the usual compartments of literature; the final section, for example, had started out as a one-act play. *Cane* sold few copies; Toomer never published another book; and this one accordingly seemed mysteriously isolated. Some critics have seen it as a forerunner of other works, anticipating themes that could be more confidently restated by Richard Wright (1908–60) and Ralph Ellison (1914–). Thus, *Cane* introduces a solitary old black man whose home is a cellar – a notion of subterranean exile developed in Wright's 'The Man Who Lived Underground' and more comprehensively in Ellison's *Invisible Man*. The Kabnis portion of *Cane* includes a timeserving college president, Samuel Hanby, who sounds like a caricatured Booker T. Washington and a model for Ellison's two-faced black educator Dr Bledsoe.

It is probably truer to admit, however, that the initial influence of *Cane* was minor; and that the agonizing predicaments of Eugene Pinchback Toomer, which gave the book a curious quality of alternating avowal and denial, account for his inability to contribute further. He could agree with Northern friends of whatever background that 'pseudo-urbanized' people, Negroes perhaps especially, lost their roots. He could thrill to the lushness of the Georgia countryside, and the sensuousness of black girls; and try to believe that 'the Dixie Pike has grown from a goat path in Africa'. Dreaming though that a generous new era would embrace *all* races, and merge them into one another for mutual benefit, he was soon made to realize that he could not in the America of the 1920s opt to be both black and white (and Jewish and Indian, and so on). To his horror, he was suspect to both. Within a decade of the publication of *Cane*, married to a white woman, he was denying that he was in any real sense a Negro. Though he continued to write, he turned his energies towards ecumenical religion. Who is entitled to fault him for doing so?

The 1930s and 1940s saw the emergence of Toomer's more greatly gifted successors Richard Wright and Ralph Ellison, who met in Harlem and were for a while close friends. Wright, whose Mississippi sharecropper father abandoned the family, escaped north to Chicago by dint of desperate effort, and found work there as a post-office sorter. Wintertime Chicago – a cruel contrast, in temperature at least, to the steamy South – was the setting of his first novel, *Lawd Today*, finished probably in 1937 (when Wright moved to New York, as Harlem correspondent for the *Daily Worker*) but not published until 1963.

In that posthumous work, in his first book of four novellas, *Uncle Tom's Children* (1938), and his 'big' novel *Native Son* (1940), Wright wrestled with the main issue of blackness, instead of the intricate but relatively minor issue of near-whiteness that understandably preoccupied Toomer. It was a main issue for much of the 'Second Black Renaissance' that began with Wright. One of its principal forms, Roger Rosenblatt observes, following the theory of Franz Fanon (*Black Skin, White Masks*, 1967) is a 'reversal of reason'. The person classed as black in a white society feels impelled to behave contradictorily, grotesquely, even horribly, as if to confirm the society's dire expectations. There is, however, an accompanying and often self-hating awareness of 'how their lives, given the proper circumstances, ought to look turned around and right side up'.[1]

Jake, the central figure in *Lawd Today*, convinced that he will never be allowed to prosper in a white world, daydreams of winning at the numbers game, or in a hand of cards. Relaxed only in the company of male cronies, he mistreats his wife, loses the money he has recklessly borrowed, and is on the brink of losing his job – all this in one day, which (we learn from interpolated radio commentary), is 12 February, birthday of the Great Emancipator, Abraham Lincoln. 'Big Boy Leaves Home' in *Uncle Tom's Children* begins with the carefree decision of four black boys to ignore a 'No Trespassing Sign' and go swimming. The white owner, believing that the naked boys meant to molest a white woman, kills two of them. In self-defence, 'Big Boy' seizes the man's gun and shoots him. He and his remaining friend Bobo flee from a vengeful mob. Bobo is caught, mutilated, and burned to death. Big Boy survives, hiding in a hole from which he gazes upon the killing of Bobo. Black neighbours will smuggle him out of the South. But his destination, Chicago, will for Big Boy be no more the promised land than it is for Jake. Nor for Bigger Thomas, the hero-villain-victim of *Native Son*, whose nightmare experiences could almost be the sequel (Big into Bigger). Hired as chauffeur by a rich, 'liberal' family, Bigger kills their daughter in a panic contretemps which occurs despite himself. Falling ineluctably into his stereotype, he behaves with a mounting, furious brutality. He decapitates the daughter, consumes her remains in the family furnace, murders his black girl out of fear she will betray him, is arrested, put on trial, and convicted. The prosecutor's remorseless indictment makes the trial of Bigger Thomas, butcher-cum-sex-fiend, a hideously aggravated version of the trial of Clyde Griffith in Dreiser's *An American Tragedy*.

Unlike Toomer, Wright continued to publish. *Black Boy* (1945) was a

1. Roger Rosenblatt, *Black Fiction* (Harvard UP, 1974), 18–19.

grim memoir of childhood and youth in the Deep South. When it came out he had just broken with the Communist party, though he had never been an orthodoxly docile member. Soon after, he became an expatriate in France (a route also taken by the black authors Chester B. Himes and James Baldwin). Wright's *The Outsider* (1953) shows the intellectualizing effects of the existentialist philosophy of Albert Camus and Jean-Paul Sartre. He interested himself in West Africa, in racial questions everywhere.

But he did not quite repeat the sensational success of *Native Son*, which for some reason stirred up a good deal more debate than Chester Himes's comparably desperate novel, *If He Hollers Let Him Go* (1945); and *Native Son* disturbed some black Americans, including Ellison and his younger colleague James Baldwin (1924–87). Baldwin's 1949 essay, 'Everybody's Protest Novel', was mainly an attack on *Uncle Tom's Cabin* – for him a spurious, sentimental exercise, profoundly anti-black and oddly predisposed to violent incidents. Black, said Baldwin, was the colour equated in such literature with inhumanity. Moving to *Native Son*, he suggested that 'Bigger is Uncle Tom's descendant.... Bigger's tragedy is that ... he admits the possibility of his being sub-human....'

Whether Baldwin regarded this as entirely Harriet Beecher Stowe's fault or partly Wright's is not clear. One senses an ambivalence in writers coming after Wright: recognition of his standing, admiration of his bluntness, disapproval of Wright's deterministic (possibly Marxist) conception of a degraded black proletariat. Ellison (in *Shadow and Act*, 1964) complained that in *Native Son* 'environment is all'; and he shared the discomfort of other critics at a passage in *Black Boy* in which Wright spoke of the 'essential bleakness' and 'cultural barrenness' of black life in America.

Richard Wright does not deserve to be relegated to a minor place in the history of American black fiction. The force of his best writing depended upon the narrative thrust at least as much as on starkness of situation. Even if a little crudely, Wright did (for instance in *Uncle Tom's Children*) suggest the necessity and possibility of willed resistance. He did seek to render a fairly wide variety of black idioms. Thus there is a hilarious exchange (in *Lawd Today*) of the 'dirty dozens', the black ritual of hyperbolic insult. Violent rage is moreover a feature of certain mythological heroes such as Hercules (who in one story kills his wife and children).

Nevertheless the writer generally said to have produced the Great American Novel (subdivision Black) is Ralph [Waldo] Ellison (1914–   ), born in Oklahoma and named after the R. W. Emerson whose surname sounds so like his own. Ellison's *The Invisible Man* (1952) gained his every kind of recognition – prizes, volumes of exegesis, honorary degrees, a Schweitzer chair at New York University. And not surprisingly: *The Invisible Man* is long, complex and ambitious, starting for instance with epigraphs from Melville's *Benito Cereno* and T. S. Eliot's *Family Reunion*, and allusions to Edgar Allan Poe and Louis Armstrong. Ellison went to Tuskegee to study music, not long after the demise of its famous founder, Booker T. Washington. From teachers there he heard of Alain Locke's *New Negro*, and Eliot's 'The Waste Land'. He was also, less inspiringly, brought in contact with a textbook by the Chicago sociologists Robert Park and E. W. Burgess which decreed:

The Negro is, by natural disposition, neither an intellectual nor an idealist, like the Jew; nor a brooding introspective, like the East Indian; nor a pioneer and frontiersman, like the Anglo-Saxon. He is primarily an artist, loving life for its own sake. His metier is expression, rather than action. He is, so to speak, the lady among the races.

Lacking the money to pay for his fourth, senior year at Tuskegee, Ellison went north to Harlem in 1936, where he met Langston Hughes as well as Wright, kept up with his music and took classes in sculpture. The Federal Writers' Project rescued him from starvation in the Depression. It helped define for Ellison his pre-eminent aim – to write, not to play music or carve stone. FWP assignments allowed him to collect black folklore on Harlem street corners: to record, for example, the evasions or defiances of Rabbit and Bear, or the exploits of the black superman–burglar, Sweet the Monkey, invincible because he could make himself invisible.

Ellison began to publish short stories, and by degrees to assemble the materials for his big book. These were eclectic – jazz instrumentalism (Armstrong, Charlie Parker); literary technique (Dostoyevsky, Henry James, Twain, Faulkner, Joyce); anthropology and cultural history (Lord Raglan's *The Hero* developed the intriguing argument that the great figures of the remote past were mythological inventions); and presumably H. G. Wells's *The Invisible Man* (1897), or at any rate the 1933 film version of the novel, starring Claude Rains as a sophisticated, and doomed, simulacrum of Sweet the Monkey.

The Invisible Man begins with magisterial simplicity: 'I am an invisible man. ... I am invisible, understand, simply because people refuse to see me.' It ends with the intimation that the narrator, who went underground by accident and stayed there to take stock, is about to emerge again, 'since there's a possibility that even an invisible man has a socially responsible role to play'. The last sentence of the book is a question:

Who knows but that, on the lower frequencies, I speak for you?

It remains the most intricately symbolic work of fiction by a Negro American, a piece of virtuoso literature that blends the formal and the vernacular with a brio akin to that of Saul Bellow's contemporaneous *Adventures of Augie March* (1953). *The Invisible Man* might be viewed as a black *Bildungsroman* – a novel about a youth's development into manhood, with semi-autobiographical allusions. It begins at a college resembling Tuskegee and closes with a riot in Harlem. The (nameless) hero encounters every sort of black response to America – subservience, irony, militance – and various forms of white concern, from paternalistic uplift ('learn about [Emerson], for he was important to your people') and Communist manipulativeness to prurient fantasies held by white women about black men. The opening chapters in particular are charged with sardonic, surrealistic energy.

Yet conception and execution do not make a perfect fit. We start with the narrator as a student, eager and bewildered. His final declaration of a new social purpose is unconvincingly rhetorical; and he fluctuates between passive recorder, the stock anti-hero of modernist literature to whom things are done, and a supposedly engaged, effective and articulate person. Among other things the narrator seems not only without women friends – isolation is of course a 'given' of the book – but to have no interest in the possibility of such relationships. The notion of 'invisibility' becomes something of an artifice.

These are the defects of a serious and intricate work that made Ralph Ellison a celebrity – *the* Negro author of the 1950s, in tandem with James Baldwin – but left him with an even larger responsibility. He was now expected to generate another major work which, in view of the artful implications of 'universality' in *The Invisible Man*, might perhaps stand as the Great American Novel (Open category). Who better equipped? Ellison was in truth a seasoned and subtle craftsman, cosmopolitan in his literary ancestry. During the 1960s and 1970s, a book of essays (*Shadow and Act*, 1964) emphasized, he felt himself to be broadly 'Negro' (with a culture embracing the past of Europe and America) rather than 'black', if that meant pretending to be a predominantly *African* Afro-American. Like James Weldon Johnson he was ready to believe that the worthwhile American art-forms were Negro creations. But for him it did not follow that everything created by white civilizations was at best irrelevant, at worst insidious.

He produced several sections of the 'damned big book' that was to follow and possibly surpass *Invisible Man*. Sometimes known as the 'Hickman Stories', they deal with a black Southern evangelist and former jazz trombonist, the Rev. Alonzo Zuber Hickman, and an orphan boy, Bliss, mainly (wholly?) white, whom he adopts and rears. Bliss, reaching manhood, disappears, reappearing eventually as Senator Sunraider, an unquestioned white and a spokesman for white supremacy. These episodes were far from inadequate. But Ralph Ellison gradually ceased to speak of a completion date, as if what he were wrestling with was an 'Invisible Novel'.

If so, conceivably the demands put upon him *qua* twentieth-century Artist were excessive, and therefore inhibiting. It is also possible that he was unhappy with the insistence of the 1960s on being indeed *Afro*-American, 'black' rather than 'Negro', and maybe 'Black' rather than 'black'. James Baldwin, whose *Go Tell It On the Mountain* (1953) evoked an earlier Harlem, began to capture the altered, clamant mood in volumes of essays (*Nobody Knows My Name*, 1961; *The Fire Next Time*, 1963), in a play (*Blues for Mr Charlie*, 1965), and in fiction such as *Tell Me How Long the Train's Been Gone* (1968). Ellison's position, apparently, was closer to that of the black poet–novelist Owen Dodson, who said in an interview that 'the black writer has no obligation to "blackness" ', or perhaps that of the poet Gwendolyn Brooks (1917–   ). Her first books (*A Street in Bronzeville*, 1945; *Annie Allen*, 1949) were unconcerned with direct protest, though she shifted to a fiercer involvement in later work (*The Riot*, 1969). By 1970, having given a reading in a Chicago bar, along with younger black poets, she admitted her heightened desire to 'write poetry – and it won't be Ezra Pound poetry . . . – that will be exciting to such people'.

Whatever his inner thoughts, the evident reality of the 1960s was a mounting radicalism and vehemence that left Ralph Ellison out of the picture for the new wave of black authors, and eventually engulfed even James Baldwin. Alice Walker (1944–   ), who won a Pulitzer fiction prize for *The Color Purple* (1983), acknowledges the lessons she learned from other writers (*In Search of Our Mothers' Gardens*, 1983). Neither Ellison nor Baldwin figures in the tally.

Nor initially did LeRoi Jones (1934–   ), in his first incarnation a Greenwich Village poet with a white wife. Incensed by old injustices that suddenly seemed intolerable in the era of Southern Ku-Klux-Klannishness,

of Vietnam, of Eldridge Cleaver's *Soul on Ice* (1968), and of the murders of
Malcolm X and Martin Luther King, LeRoi Jones and many with him
changed direction. Shedding his former life, he renamed himself Imamu
Amiri Baraka. His writing became more impassioned, less 'literary',
reaching towards 'black dada nihilismus'. In the hectic confessional novel
The System of Dante's Hell (1965), Jones pondered the dominance of the
white world, including the literary culture it insists upon conferring
('the quick new jersey speech, full of italian idiom, and the invention
of the jews'), and sought a way towards the exclusively non-white
lifestyle embodied in a collection which he edited with Larry Neal, *Black
Fire: An Anthology of Afro-American Writing* (1968). As Imamu Baraka,
immersed in the actuality of New Jersey power politics, he moved away
(or on) from the craft of literature.

The positive side of such militance was the emphasis on 'black is
beautiful' (instead of ugly); the fascination with an African ancestry, and
with Arabic civilizations; and a deep affection for black music, whether of
Armstrong and Ellington in the older dispensation or John Coltrane and
Thelonius Monk in a newer one. Much in the angry denunciation of white
culture was justified, not least because it was what whites were saying
guiltily about themselves; much was perhaps therapeutic.

For a long while, the history of race relations had been paternalistic, in
the style of white Southern scholars like Ulrich B. Phillips who dwelt upon
the good things done *for* blacks. In a second, reformist phase, white
historians (Stanley Elkins, Kenneth Stampp) deplored the bad things done
to slaves. With the 1960s began a third emphasis, by black historians
(such as John W. Blassingame) as well as white ones (for instance, Herbert
Gutman, Lawrence W. Levine), on mainly good things done *by* blacks on
their own behalf. Blassingame's *The Slave Community* (1972), conceding
that the pressures of chattel slavery might engender an outwardly servile
'Sambo' temperament, argued that two other types were equally familiar
on antebellum plantations: a ferociously intransigent 'Nat', whom over-
seers dare not punish, and a middling 'Jack' personality, neither obsequious nor truculent.

Such scholarship perhaps risked understating the degradations of slavery: if blacks were so resiliently sturdy, where was the deep harm done
them? It was nevertheless a necessary correction of the previous over-
emphasis on white activity, and a worthwhile attempt to tackle the
problem of a pervasive white control and influence. Whites ('honkies'
in the hostile slang popularized in the 1960s) started to define black

entertainment in their own terms with the 'nigger minstrel' shows of the antebellum era, and continued (as black critics saw the matter) to cash in on black musical genius (jazz, blues, bop) via Elvis Presley, the Beatles and the Rolling Stones. The plantation songs of Stephen Foster were concocted by someone who was a white Northerner. The lyrics of 'Waitin' for the Robert E. Lee' (1912) were the creation of L. Wolfe Gilbert, who had been born in Russia; those of 'Is It True What They Say About Dixie?' (1936) were by the Romanian immigrant Sammy Lerner. The opera *Porgy and Bess* (1935), about black folk in Charleston, South Carolina, was the result of a collaboration between DuBose and Dorothy Heyward and George and Ira Gershwin, all of them white. Another white author, Roark Bradford, wrote mainly about Negroes; his dialect renderings of Old Testament stories were turned into the hit play *Green Pastures* (1930), set in Louisiana, by Marc Connelly of Pennsylvania.

The most complex case of all was *Uncle Tom's Cabin*. Harriet Beecher Stowe's novel might be resented or ridiculed but could not be ignored. If 'Uncle Tom' was a caricature, it still took root as a term of reproach within the Negro world. *Uncle Tom's Cabin* and its main episodes – the persecution of Tom, wicked Simon Legree, the death of Eva, the escape across the ice of Eliza – are firmly lodged in the psyche of black even more than white America. Ishmael Reed (1938–) begins his scintillating historical pastiche *Flight to Canada* (1976) with a quick mention:

> I have done my Liza leap
> & am safe in the arms
> of Canada, so
> Ain't no use your Slave
> Catchers waitin on me. . . .

In other words, whites seemed to have formulated and to continue to control the very language of racial identity. The novelist William Styron, according to black critics, appropriated a black hero in a historical novel, *The Confessions of Nat Turner* (1968), and demeaned the Afro-American heritage by making Turner a neurotic intellectual obsessed with a white girl. Whatever the justice of the complaint, Styron had got there first. Similarly, Scott Joplin was mythicized in E. L. Doctorow's *Ragtime* (1975). Why should such subjects not be left to black authors? How could Afro-Americans avoid the white embrace when their approved authors were rewarded with philanthropic bounty from Spingarn, Rosenwald, Pulitzer and Guggenheim awards? For those who wished to see it that way, there was an absurd yet fitting reversal in the career of Ralph Ellison. He, and his protagonist in *The Invisible Man*, had as students been subject to a dictatorial flunkey of a college head, a sort of sergeant-major or butler who bullied his juniors and salaamed to his superiors. Having himself become a man of distinction, Ellison was rewarded with a university chair named after Albert Schweitzer, white musician–medico who had spent a saintly life as missionary to the natives of equatorial Gabon . . . .

'Black pride' thrilled to the African alternative, stimulated by Alex Haley's reconstruction (*Roots*, 1976) of a family history going back to Gambia, and passing across the Atlantic to the landfall of a slave-ship at Annapolis in 1767. A proud resentment underlay the development of Don Lee (1942–), who declared that 'Black poetry in its purest form is diametrically opposed to white poetry', and that 'We are Afrikan people in America, defining ourselves from the positive (Afrikan) toward the negative (American).' Comparable emotions boiled up in the poetic manifestos of several black women poets – Sonia Sanchez, Nikki Giovanni ('Blessed be machine guns in Black hands'), Carolyn Rodgers, who maintained that to 'write well' was to surrender to white regulation, and that the words 'poem' and 'poet' were unusably white: she opted instead for 'song' and 'singer'.

The attempt at extreme disaffiliation was in a sense self-defeating. Afro-Americans proved for most purposes to be more American than Afro. To learn Swahili was a brave gesture. But that tongue was of small utility, even in the heart of Harlem or some other centre of black population; it was never a 'purely' African language; and it had not been common in West Africa where the slave trade operated. To learn Arabic was an equally serious commitment, of marginal value for ordinary American purposes. To choose to stay within a ghetto was not ultimately much more satisfying than to be compelled to remain there.

Circumstances changed, and fashions too. Black leadership, exposed to scrutiny from feminists, began to be perceived as swaggeringly sexist. Alice Walker, more interested in heroines than in heroes, delighted in a 1937 novel by Zora Neale Hurston, *Their Eyes Were Watching God*, that few male commentators, including black ones, had properly recognized. Black feminism itself altered in growing. Alice Walker coined the word 'womanist' to express its comprehensive context ('a woman who . . . appreciates and prefers women's culture . . . and women's strength. . . . Traditionally capable, as in "Mama, I'm walking to Canada and I'm taking you and a bunch of other slaves with me." Reply: "It wouldn't be the first time." '). Playing upon the title of her Pulitzer prize novel *The Color Purple* (1983), she offered a further definition: 'Womanist is to feminist as purple to lavender.' In the realm described by Alice Walker, or in the novels of Toni Morrison (*Sula*, 1973; *Song of Solomon*, 1978; *Tar Baby*, 1981), men were not absent, they were secondary, unreliable, John the Conquerors who usually missed the boat. The effect was to recast the presentation of blackness in America.

There was a further evolution, foreshadowed in Toomer, in Ellison, and in other prose or poetry (for instance, by Langston Hughes) that caught the patterns of street talk or aspired to the tone and rhythm of black music. It flouted conventional white syntax and spelling (though of course creative destruction of language was a feature of twentieth-century experimental or modernist writing in white cultures). This could be employed to signify affront, as in the poems of Lee, Sanchez and Giovanni. It could also, however, be wildly non-realistic – a literature of *comédie noire* in more senses than one, like Chester Himes's *Pinktoes* (1961), or his somewhat less outlandish thriller *Cotton Comes to Harlem* (1965; published the previous year in French as *Retour en Afrique*), about two black detectives named Coffin Ed and Grave Digger.

The most copiously inventive examples of 'black dada' came from Ishmael Reed. One of the influences he avowed was the semi-surrealist fiction of Nathanael West, in particular *The Dream Life of Balso Snell* (1931); West's burlesque inversion of American success stories, *A Cool Million* (1934), could also have served. A second, big influence upon him came from the necromantic visions of Caribbean voodoo, black-Americanized in New Orleans. Reed's book of poems *Conjure* (1972) offers a manifesto of 'Neo-HooDoo' (his coinage) – 'a "Lost American Church" updated':

Neo-Hoodoos would rather 'shake that thing' than be stiff and erect.... [Students of American Culture] are uptight closet Jeho-vah revisionists. They would assert the American and East Indian and Chinese thing before they would the Black thing. Their spiritual leaders Ezra Pound and T. S. Eliot hated Africa and 'Darkies'.

But Reed's HooDoo is more high-spiritedly miscellaneous than these statements might suggest. *Yellow Back Radio Broke-Down* (1969), his second novel, is a wickedly funny, headlong extravaganza, about a black cowboy–magician, the Loop Garoo Kid; a supervillain tycoon Drag Gibson; an elegant Indian, Chief Showcase; and others:

O Chief Showcase, he said weakly, good of you to come and visit me before I ride off into the eternal sunset.

Think nothing of it Drag, I was on my way back from Paris and I stopped off at that makeshift acreage they call the Capitol.

There is a challenge to *white* pride in Ishmael Reed's writings, implicit and quite often explicit. The genteel tradition, in any conceivable guise, is knocked down and sent up. The tone is that of a hyped-up 'Mr Simple' (as portrayed with deadpan Socratic wit by Langston Hughes), and akin to the variously comic-ironic-macaronic styles of, say, Dick Gregory, Richard Pryor and Eddie Murphy. Reed's *Flight to Canada* is a 'counterfactual' improvisation, approximately of the era of the Civil War. The author, or *an* author (such details are left to float), is one Raven Quickskill. Quickskill's lover is Princess Quaw Quaw Tralaralara, a 'Third World belle'.

In Reed's absurdist universe black and Indian (Native American) easily make common cause – more easily by far than the 'suffragettes' (feminists) whom he pokes fun at. But he is aware of the tragi-farce of competition between the different non-WASP groups inside the United States. How does the Afro-American saga of enslavement and survival match up against the antecedent Amerindian heritage of dispossession and destruction? Indian tradition has an indigenous authority greater than that claimable by blacks or whites. The Indian is unique in being both more of an outsider than most Americans, black or white, and more an authentic insider than anybody. His ghetto is a reservation, or remnant of his own land. He is, so to speak, low man on his own totem pole. Such, for instance, is the message of *House Made of Dawn* (1968), by N. Scott Momaday, a grave folkloristic novel about a Kiowa youth who cannot endure life in mainstream America, away from his own people.

Ishmael Reed attempts too to make a joke of the one-upmanship rivalry of blacks and immigrants, in particular Jewish immigrants. In the ahistorical satiric buffoonery of *Flight to Canada* (ch. 9), Raven Quickskill escapes from a pair of 'Nebraska Tracers' wishing to return him to slavery. Dashing into the Slave Hole Café in Emancipation City, he encounters the 'Immigrant' Mel Leer, a former indentured servant now fully at liberty. When Raven mentions his plight ('two guys just tried to confiscate me'), the Immigrant answers impatiently:

'Your people think that you corner the market on the business of atrocity. My relatives were dragged through the streets of St. Petersburg, weren't permitted to go to school in Moscow, were pogrommed in Poland. . . . Your people haven't suffered that much. I can prove it, statistically.'

Quickskill retorts: 'Nobody has suffered as much as my people.' Angered, the Immigrant responds: 'Don't tell me that lie.'

This, to repeat, is in fun. Being unhampered by strict fidelity to fact and chronology, it bypasses the Holocaust of the 1930s and 1940s or the subsequent history of Israel. In Reed's *comédie noire* the stereotypical Jew is a fast-talking *allrightnik* – a person who is no sooner off the boat than he begins an all-too smooth adjustment to American ways. More outspoken hostility is evident in statements by Imamu Baraka and other black militants.

The conflict is fraught with ironies. Jews have generally felt that their own acceptance in America was slow and painful: they were almost shut out from faculty appointments at prestigious institutions, until the end of the Second World War, and no Jew achieved wide recognition as a *serious* writer (excluding 'funny men' such as S. J. Perelman) until the 1940s. They themselves had been treated, they felt, as grotesques ('Ikey' and 'Hymie' in magazine jokes) or as monsters (like the 'Lecherous Jew' Leo Frank, lynched in 1913 by an Atlanta mob for a rape and murder he had in fact not committed). They had accordingly given encouragement and money to other unpopular groups in the United States. The swing of the Jewish magazine *Commentary* away from liberal causes at the end of the 1960s was in part probably a reaction to the anti-Semitic pronouncements now emanating from black spokesmen and occasionally from aggrieved white 'ethnics' ('PIGS' or 'Poles, Italians, Greeks, Slavs', in one crude acronym).

But this is to anticipate our story of the place of Jewish literature in the whole ferment of American modernism. Back in the 1930s, the harsh logistics of the Depression bore upon Jewish as well as upon Negro intellectuals, pushing some towards the Communist party, and more of them into jobs – manual, clerical, creative, whatever was being provided under state or federal auspices. For a while, ideology (and mainly of a radical order) seemed more crucial than race or other considerations. Some reputations became entangled in political controversy. Michael Gold (1894–1967; the pseudonym of Itzok or Irwin Granich), playwright and novelist, was praised for his *Jews Without Money* (1930) in Sinclair Lewis's Nobel prize acceptance speech of that year. *Jews Without Money* dealt with 'old-country people', enduring the crowding and squalor, the cockroaches and prostitution, of the Lower East Side. Gold's own view of American literature had just been made plain in a review dismissing the fiction and plays of Thornton Wilder ('genteel bourgeoisie'). Albert Maltz (1908–85), a Brooklynite whose parents had been born in Lithuania and Poland, was also an active Marxist novelist–playwright (his first major fiction, *The Underground Stream* – another underground! – was published in 1940), who worked as a Hollywood scriptwriter in the 1940s and was eventually blacklisted.

After the 1940s these authors dropped into obscurity for one reason or another. In retrospect, most of the American class-conflict literature of the 1930s sounds heavily didactic. A standard example of the protest novel is *Marching! Marching!* (1935) by Clara Weatherwax. Other works seem unduly neglected. *Call It Sleep* (1934) by Henry Roth, who had been brought to Manhattan as a baby, from Galicia, and whose novel is couched in a sort of translated Yiddish, enjoyed a revival of interest in the 1960s. Daniel Fuchs's trilogy about poor Jews in Brooklyn, beginning with *Summer in Williamsburg* (1934), also dropped out of print. The plays of Clifford Odets had a greater impact in their day; as Arnold Goldman notes, they explore one of the deepest concerns of ethnic immigrants – 'the reaction of the first generation American to the "migration" made by his parents'. What, in other words, is the actual 'meltability' of non-WASP people?[1]

Jewishness is certainly a concern of some of the fiction and drama of the 1930s, usually as a double problem of poverty and acculturation. It is of course a central feature of memoirs of that era such as Alfred Kazin's *A Walker in the City* (1951). In the next, more affluent phase, a sort of post-Depression depression characterized several novels (Arthur Miller, *Focus*, 1945; Laura Z. Hobson, *Gentleman's Agreement*, 1947; Saul Bellow, *The Victim*, 1947; Herman Wouk, *Marjorie Morningstar*, 1955; Myron Kaufman, *Remember Me to God*, 1957), in which veiled or occasionally blatant anti-Semitism was a 'problem', or in which the issue was how far to seek to retain Jewish religious and family ties. These vary in quality. The best, Bellow's *Victim*, is a subtle account of a good-natured, rather fussy Jew persecuted by an obnoxious, half-mad yet pathetic, self-proclaimedly WASP person who insists that the Jew is to blame for the wreck of his hopes. The question of which of the two is the true victim is left open.

By the 1950s Jewishness became a big theme in American culture. Gentile prejudice was one sub-topic. Jewish self-dislike, real or alleged,

1. Arnold Goldman, 'A Remnant to Escape: The American Writer and the Minority Group', in Marcus Cunliffe, ed., *American Literature since 1900* (London, Barrie and Jenkins, and Sphere Books, 1975), 318; and see Michael Novak, *The Rise of the Unmeltable Ethnics* (New York, Macmillan, 1973).

was also analysed. What for instance was at stake when a Jew changed his or her name, as Nathan Weinstein metamorphosed himself into Nathanael West – a subjective anti-Semitism, or a prudent decision to 'pass' (much easier for a white Jew than for an Afro-American) in order to make a better living out of mainstream America? Was being Jewish a 'minority' condition, and in that sense of minor interest for the majority of readers? The point was discussed, for instance, with reference to J. D. Salinger's *The Catcher in the Rye* (1951), and more especially his stories of the Glass family (the 'Glass Menagerie'), *Franny and Zooey* (1961) and *Raise High the Roof Beam* (1963). Salinger (1919–) was Jewish; the Glass children were reportedly Jewish-Irish, but no more 'Jewish' in behaviour than Holden Caulfield, the teenage protagonist of *Catcher in the Rye*. Did these writings suffer from a resultant blurring and idealizing? Or was something else in train – the emergence of outsider-Jewishness as a symbolic universalized condition of modern man, displaced, urbanized, sensitive, highly verbal, self-deprecating, ruefully humorous, highly conscious of the predicaments he is powerless to save, the fate he cannot run from?

Overall, the commonest awareness of Jewishness in the 1950s was of how prominent people of Jewish background were in American cultural and intellectual life: Miller, Odets and Lillian Hellman in drama; Karl Shapiro, Delmore Schwartz, Howard Nemerov in poetry; Bellow, Norman Mailer, Bernard Malamud, Isaac B. Singer, Budd Schulberg, Irwin Shaw, Joseph Heller, E. L. Doctorow, Edward L. Wallant, Tillie Olsen, Cynthia Ozick, Philip Roth in fiction; in critical and philosophical analysis a host more – Edward Shils, Sidney Hook, Philip Rieff, Lionel Trilling, Hannah Arendt, Susan Sontag, Leslie Fiedler, Daniel Bell, Alfred Kazin; in historical scholarship Richard Hofstadter, Oscar Handlin, Daniel J. Boorstin, David Landes, Fritz Stern; and so on and so on, in music or mathematics, sculpture or semiotics. This awareness was after about 1950 rarely described in terms of an invasion, a perversion or a diminution of American civilization, although it might be covertly resented here and there, by white Southerners, or less glamorous immigrant stock, or black nationalists.

A corollary is that within a decade of the end of the Second World War, Jewishness had won so extraordinary an acceptance that much of it was incorporated into American-ness, as if it had always been ensconced within the culture. In some respects, of course, this was not a myth. European high culture had for longer than a century owed much to Jewish musicians, scientists and philosophers. The prophets of modernism – Sigmund Freud, say, Franz Kafka, Marc Chagall – were likewise often Jewish. American-Jewish interpreters of modern ideas and aesthetics, such as Lionel Trilling and Meyer Schapiro, seemed able to assimilate the new to the traditional: to conduct themselves as exemplary custodians of Culture with a capital C while also presenting the case for modes that appeared to be fundamentally non- or anti-traditional. A much discussed book of the 1950s, Will Herberg's *Protestant-Catholic-Jew* (1956), claimed that the old era of WASP supremacy was over, in the religious sphere; the three main faiths constituted a tripod, each enjoying formal parity with the others. Via Hollywood, Broadway, and the ministrations of humorists from S. J. Perelman to Woody Allen, as well as of poets, dramatists and novelists, Jewish themes and Yiddish locutions became attached to and affected the natural repertoire. In a 1944 symposium Isaac Rosenfeld summed up the curious process by which the Jewish writer, a minority figure, was becoming a majority spokesman. In the weird world of the twentieth century, he said, 'the outsider often finds himself the perfect insider'.

'Jewish literature' is in a sense an artificial category, akin to such synthetic genres as the 'political novel' or the 'business play'. In the 1944 symposium Trilling avowed that there was nothing in his 'professional intellectual life' which he could 'specifically trace back to my Jewish birth and rearing'; while Alfred Kazin distinguished between the old Judaism of Eastern Europe, immensely rich in associations, and the (to him) generally uninspiring condition of Jewish culture.[1] For some authors, notably Norman Mailer, Jewishness may have been an identifying element but clearly has not been *the* intentional frame of their thought. The Jewish characters in Mailer's first novel, *The Naked and the Dead* (1948), are of relatively minor importance. At the other extreme, Isaac B. Singer wrote in Yiddish, about people for whom it is also their prime language. In between could be ranged novelists whose concern with Jewish subject-matter might vary from book to book, or might be significant yet not dominant. It counted for a good deal in the four novels of Edward L. Wallant (1926–62), *The Human Season* (1960), *The Pawnbroker* (1961), *The Tenants of Moonbloom* (1963), and *The Children at the Gate* (1964). *The Natural* (1952), the first novel by Bernard Malamud (1914–86), was a folkloristic fantasy about baseball, whose hero Roy Hobbs is from Middle America, not Middle Europe. In his second novel, *The Assistant* (1957), on

1. Judd L. Teller, *Strangers and Natives: The Evolution of the American Jew from 1921 to the Present* (New York, Delacorte Press, 1968), 255–6.

the other hand, or in *The Fixer* (1966), about anti-Semitic paranoia in Tsarist Russia, or in a number of short stories, Malamud did produce literature that could be labelled 'Jewish'. Saul Bellow (1915–   ) resembles Malamud in often but not invariably taking Jewishness as a prime element in the narrative tone or the conduct of people. Bellow's first novel, *Dangling Man* (1944), is a generalized meditation, torpid-existentialist in mood, by an American waiting to be called for military service in 1942–3. It has no specific connection to Jewish questions: 'Joseph', whose study of the eighteenth-century Enlightenment has been suspended, has an acute distaste for modern times, like most of Bellow's subsequent protagonists, but is not particularly appalled by the misfortunes of the Jews. Nevertheless Bellow translated Singer's story 'Gimpel the Fool' from Yiddish to English (1953), edited *Great Jewish Short Stories* (1963), and in 1967 covered the Six-Day War in Israel as a correspondent. Perhaps he is then a 'Jewish' writer, as Frank McConnell observes, in the same degree to which Graham Greene was a 'Catholic' novelist.

A difference, linking Bellow with Malamud or Mailer or possibly with the poet Allen Ginsberg, is that all of them in their individual ways have developed techniques of writing-as-talk (confession, harangue, invective) that depart radically from the well-behaved, consistent locutions of the genteel tradition. Bellow's individual tone might be termed the soliloquacious, Mailer's perhaps Brooklyn Gongorism. They and others use polysyllables, sometimes because they need to use complex words for complex ideas, sometimes for ironic purposes – for example counterpointing vernacular vocabulary, so that academe and street talk are blended in a highly seasoned casserole. Various effects can be achieved by such juxtapositions: the deflation of oneself or others, bittersweet reflections on life's deceptions, surrealist or supernatural flashes, autodidactic solemnities. This quality is in some broad sense Jewish. It is embodied, for instance, in the kind of Yiddish proverbs on which Augie March and other characters have been reared – 'if grandma had wheels she'd be a car', 'sleep faster, we need the pillows'. It is the quick, nonchalant wit that Malamud claimed to have learned from studying Charlie Chaplin: 'The rhythm, the snap of comedy; the reserved comic presence – that beautiful distancing; the funny with sad; the surprise of surprise.' William Dean Howells and a number of his contemporaries wrote well enough: none wrote quite like that.

MODERNIST AND POST-MODERNIST
MODES: FICTION AND POETRY

———————

IN the textbooks twentieth-century American literary history is often carved into decades. In such formulae, the 1920s figure as a self-contained era, sharply differentiated from the 1930s. Each is labelled accordingly – 'Jazz Age', 'Great Depression'. Similar decisiveness is attributed to other dates and eras: post-1945, the Fifties, the Sixties and so on.

These are of course crude simplifications. Individual lives stretch over several decades and cannot be so neatly compartmentalized. There is no spectacular changing of the cultural guard with each *lustrum*. Nevertheless there were considerable shifts in the national mood, affecting writers (above all novelists and dramatists), even more conspicuously than the rest of the population. The majority were in the 1920s concerned with their craft or with private activities rather than with social issues. A strong dollar made sojourns in Europe attractively feasible for a flock of Scott Fitzgerald's contemporaries. But the economic slump at the close of the 1920s, Fitzgerald's 'Crack-Up', ushered in the 'American jitters' – so named by his Princeton classmate Edmund Wilson. During the next decade, as Franklin D. Roosevelt's New Deal wrestled with a persistently malfunctioning economy, most of the expatriates came home. In 1932 Roosevelt was Democratic candidate for President, campaigning against the incumbent Republican President, Herbert Hoover. By then a sizeable group of authors and intellectuals, including Wilson and Sherwood Anderson, were prepared to announce their conviction that *laissez-faire* capitalism could not resolve the crisis of the time. Some recommended support for the Communist party in the 1932 presidential election. In the early 1930s Marxist ideas had a fairly wide appeal within the United States. The radical weekly *New Masses* (1926–48), under the galvanizing editorship of Michael Gold, won support from some of the nation's liveliest writers and artists. John Reed Clubs and Writers' Congresses produced manifestos affirming solidarity with 'workers', and the duty of the intelligentsia to enlist in the class struggle.

In this respect there was a dramatic change in the American *Zeitgeist*; for a while, as Daniel Aaron has shown, there were 'Writers on the Left', whose emotional radicalism tinged the literature of the era. Up until then, American fiction had had relatively little to say about the poor and the exploited. Before the Depression, Upton Sinclair was one of the few active authors to attack social wrongs in fictional form (*Oil!*, 1927; *Boston*, 1928). Now, many joined him in depicting the lives of sharecroppers, hoboes and union organizers. Allegiance with the underdog was reaffirmed during the Spanish Civil War of 1936–9, when Russia aided the Spanish Republican government, and Hitler and Mussolini backed the right-wing rising led by General Franco.

The passions of the decade touched the work even of non-signers and non-joiners like William Faulkner and Ernest Hemingway. Faulkner was affected at the outset because his Mississippi hometown was broke, and he with it. Obliged to cast about for a livelihood, he spent time as a scriptwriter in Hollywood, an occupation that also helped rescue Fitzgerald from financial ruin. In 1937 Hemingway's *To Have and Have Not* indicated an alignment with people in trouble. Harry Morgan, the novel's hero, loses his steady source of income – renting his Florida fishing boat out to wealthy sportsmen – under the influence of the Depression. Morgan is forced into illegal and dangerous enterprises; fatally wounded in the course of one of these, he utters a dying dictum, in favour of 'solidarity': 'One man alone ain't got ... no chance.' A similar message is proclaimed in Hemingway's Spanish war journalism, and in his novel of the conflict, *For Whom the Bell Tolls* (1940); its title comes from a sermon of the poet John Donne: 'No man is an Island ... ; every man is a piece of the Continent. ... And therefore never send to know for whom the bell tolls; It tolls for thee.'

The Depression was, however, much more immediately pictured in work by other novelists, especially the *U.S.A.* trilogy by John Dos Passos. Although *The 42nd Parallel*, *1919* and *The Big Money* deal mainly with the previous two decades, they came out in the 1930s. The final scene of *The Big Money* (1936) is of a nameless unemployed vagrant or 'vag', trying to hitch-hike across a continent whose luckier citizens seem unaware of him. He envies those passing overhead in the swift luxury of an airliner and reflects on the useless success slogans on which his generation was reared: 'went to school, books said opportunity, ads promised speed, own your own home, shine bigger than your neighbour. ...' *Let Us Now Praise Famous Men* (1941), by the Tennessee author James Agee (1905–55), with photographs by Walker Evans, chronicled the hardscrabble labours of white sharecroppers in Alabama; it was written in the mid-1930s on an assignment for *Fortune* magazine (whose readers were more likely to be travelling first-class than to be thumbing rides and sleeping rough).

The naturalistic writer James T. Farrell (1904–79) began his exploration of the bleak life of young Irish-Americans in Southside Chicago with the *Studs Lonigan* trilogy (1932–5). His *Note on Literary Criticism* (1936) avowed an attachment to Marxism while expressing repugnance for left-wing clichés. Farrell's characters, in other words, suffer principally from spiritual impoverishment; depression rather than Depression is their problem.

Nor was the 1930s fiction of John Steinbeck (1902–68) genuinely 'proletarian', although Steinbeck seemed to catch the very essence of those years of dispossession, bewilderment and comradeship in his widely admired novels *In Dubious Battle* (1936), *Of Mice and Men* (1937) and *The Grapes of Wrath* (1939). The last two were made into remarkable films – a reminder that Hollywood too was ready to vary its 'escape' entertainments with 'messages' in the vein of social realism.

Yet when all this has been said, the tinge of radicalism in the Depression is less striking than the failure of extreme ideas to take any deep hold. Creative talent remained basically idiosyncratic. Faulkner and Hemingway, given the material circumstances of the period, were by and large singularly unresponsive to the preoccupations of here and now. Faulkner in the 1930s wrote chiefly of the Southern past, Hemingway of bullfights and safaris. There was no banner-carrying by the humorist James Thurber (1894–1961) or by his fellow-fantasists Robert Benchley (1889–1945), S. J. Perelman (1904–79) and Nathanael West (1903–40). Writers might wish to express solidarity with blue-collar America. But then, most had never regarded themselves as gentleman aesthetes. The 1930s could revive an old national tradition of the artist as craftsman and patriot, and another tolerated if not always welcome tradition of the writer as mischief-maker. The manifestos of 1932–3 soon proved to have little in common with the dutiful rhetoric of Old World communism, although a few Americans did continue to imbibe Stalinist propaganda. The first issue of *Americana* (November 1932), a raucous publication edited by Gilbert Seldes and friends, announced that 'our civilization exudes a miasmic stench'. These self-described 'laughing morticians' recommended a 'decent but rapid burial', yet were 'unconditionally opposed to Comrade Stalin'. Again, *Partisan Review*, beginning as a Communist magazine in 1934, emerged a few years afterwards with a quite different brand of partisanship.

Sentimental conceptions of the Russian experiment ('I have seen the future and it works', in the famously deluded tribute of Lincoln Steffens) were weakened by revelations of the rigged Moscow trials and by the shock of the Nazi–Soviet pact in 1939. But domestic factors were more crucial. The WPA (Works Progress Administration) and other New Deal agencies found work for thousands of needy creative talents. Writers compiled densely circumstantial city and state guide-books, and recorded the reminiscences of venerable black survivors who had been born into slavery. Photographers registered the pathos, patience and importance of obscure American lives.

Eminent authors could get along and even prosper without government patronage. Of the total of literature and art engendered during the Depression very little was federally commissioned. Some of it was undeniably mediocre. Some – occasionally in Agee and Steinbeck, more frequently in the tales and plays of William Saroyan or in Sandburg's less successful verse – trembled on the edge of People-worship. But much was honestly affectionate, to a degree that perhaps surprised the writers themselves. Amid dismay and hardship, the Depression stimulated a discovery of America for authors who had somehow never learned to love their country. Thus, by the end of the decade Dos Passos was starting to celebrate rather than admonish. Van Wyck Brooks, previously a sceptical analyst of American literary failings, won a Pulitzer prize for *The Flowering of New England* (1936), a mellow evocation of Emerson and Longfellow and their regional companions in the republic of letters. Constance Rourke's *American Humor: A Study of the National Character* (1931) was a comparably reassuring study. The poet Carl Sandburg completed his vast folkloristic biography of Abraham Lincoln in 1939 with four volumes on the Civil War years, abridging them to a single volume (*Storm Over the Land*) in 1942.

By then there was a new war storm, beginning in Europe in September 1939. The vexed issue of American intervention was finally resolved with the Japanese assault on Pearl Harbor in December 1941; the United States declared war on the Axis powers. Another huge heave of the *Zeitgeist*. Rearmament ended the Depression. The millions of unemployed were reclad in military uniform. Ideological controversy seemed suddenly straightforward: Stalinist Russia was an ally, together with the British Commonwealth, France and China: the good against the bad. One argument did flare up among the American literati. The poet Archibald MacLeish (1892–1982) scolded his fellow authors (*The Irresponsibles*,

1940) for their supposed recent failure to behave like patriotic democrats. In *The Literary Fallacy* (1944; a set of lectures given in 1943), Bernard De Voto extended the indictment. During the 1920s, he claimed, H. L. Mencken, Sinclair Lewis, Hemingway, Dos Passos, Faulkner and their associates had misrepresented the national ethos:

Instead of studying American life, literature denounced it. Instead of working to understand American life, literature repudiated it. . . . The society was rugged, lively, and vital, but literature became increasingly debilitated, capricious, querulous, and irrelevant.

In the 1930s too, 'it was writers, not the American people, who believed that the promise of American life had ended': a dig at MacLeish for his previous past-tense lament that 'America was Promises'.

To judge from the responses to a 1939 *Partisan Review* symposium on 'The Situation in American Writing', intellectuals certainly emphasized their right and duty to stand apart, as far as possible, from public occasions. To the question, 'What do you think the responsibilities of writers in general are when and if war comes?', none answered with patriotic zeal. Sherwood Anderson supposed he was an 'isolationist': 'I do not believe in any war.' James T. Farrell was cynical over war aims: 'Of course, many tell us that the British Navy is required to protect our freedom. But this is one joke that the Farrells, the Brennans, the Kellys, the Sullivans, the O'Tooles, the Sweeneys, the Gannons, the Bannons, and the Murphys could never get the point of.' Gertrude Stein replied with her special blend of silliness and sense: 'most probably there will not be another general European war, the more America thinks there is going to be one the more suspicious the Continent gets and the less likely they are to fight.' If war nevertheless came, 'the writers would have to fight too like anybody else, some will like it and some will not'.

Irresponsibles? Such reactions probably did not differ greatly from those of writers in Britain or France. But as world conflict loomed over America, and finally enveloped her, these squabbles dwindled to nothing. In the harsh words of Allen Tate's 'Ode to Our Young Pro-Consuls of the Air' (1943):

> Once more the country calls
> From sleep, as from his doom,
>   Each citizen to take
>   His modest stake
> Where the sky falls
> With a Pacific boom.

In the early 1940s there was no immediate impression of new authors or techniques. Already established figures – Steinbeck, Hemingway, Sinclair Lewis – continued to develop their familiar magics, though with greater stress upon the dramas of war. Older poets (including E. E. Cummings and Marianne Moore), whose careers will be discussed later in the chapter, likewise wrote in the idioms associated with their names. New names gradually appeared. Here again *Partisan Review* is a fascinating guide. The *Partisan Reader* (1946), an anthology of the magazine's first ten years, included work by Tate, Cummings, Moore, Eliot, W. C. Williams, Wallace Stevens, Katherine Anne Porter and other substantial figures. Among them, however, appeared new names: stories by Delmore Schwartz, Saul Bellow, Paul Goodman and Mary McCarthy; poetry by John Berryman, Randall Jarrell, Karl Shapiro and Robert Lowell; essays by Dwight Macdonald, Lionel Trilling, Philip Rahv, Harold Rosenberg. Not many of their pieces referred directly to the Second World War; people directly involved in its Pacific, North African or European theatres did not have the contemplative leisure that nurtures literature; and perhaps the *Partisan* editors were not agog to print reports from the battlefield.

At any rate, by the close of the decade several of the newer names mentioned above were much talked of; and the literature of war, which always takes time to ripen, was beginning to proliferate. One of the first fictional responses was *A Walk in the Sun* (1944) by Harry Brown (1917–), a sharply observed tale of an army patrol in Italy – the scene also of novels by Alfred Hayes (1911–85), including *The Girl on Via Flaminia* (1949). James Gould Cozzens (1903–78), already a veteran novelist, caught the public eye with *Guard of Honor* (1948), a novel about the military, or more precisely about aviators in training, on a Southern air-base. Actual combat in the air was in these years most grippingly rendered in certain poems, most notably in Jarrell's 'Death of the Ball Turret Gunner':

> Six miles from earth, loosed from its dream of life,
> I woke to black flak and the nightmare fighters.
> When I died they washed me out of the turret with a hose

– a poem whose power survives constant anthologizing.

There were to be many more portrayals of the Second World War, and the world of the armed forces. In poetry, Louis Simpson (1923–), who had been in Normandy with an airborne division, hauntingly recaptured the incongruous terrors of combat:

> The watchers in their leopard suits
> Waited till it was time,
> And aimed between the belt and boot
> And let the barrel climb.

There were also various presentations, some comparable to *Guard of Honor*, about command and subordination (or insubordination): John P. Marquand's *Melville Goodwin, U.S.A.* (1951), a story of a professional soldier, and in the same year Herman Wouk's naval drama *The Caine Mutiny*, and James Jones's *From Here to Eternity*, an account of barrack life in Hawaii on the eve of Pearl Harbor. Jones (1921–77) based his novel on his own service memories, moving the conflict forwards in *The Thin Red Line* (1962).

By general reckoning, however, the 'biggest' war novel was also one of the first: *The Naked and the Dead* (1948) by Norman Mailer, an author then in his mid-twenties who put his wartime experiences to ambitious use. As Harry Brown does in *A Walk in the Sun*, Mailer deals with men in an infantry patrol, whose worst time comes when they are operating on their own in no man's land. *The Naked and the Dead* now has something of the air of a historic monument, or Exhibit 'A' in the case of Mailer versus the world of falsehoods. There is a formulaic element in making an army squad a cross-section of Americans. General Cummings, the officer in charge of this particular campaign, is allowed to deliver long harangues, somewhat in the vein of Ayn Rand, as to the need for authority in a civilization gone soft. Yet the mix of talk and violence, the vehement vitality of the narrative, impressed innumerable readers, made Mailer an overnight celebrity, and – as he was to complain – saddled him with the reputation of 'war novelist' who was expected to stay within the same idiom.

Mailer's next novels, *Barbary Shore* (1951) and *The Deer Park* (1955), were not about war as such, although their exploration of power, corruption and suppression develops concerns common to all of Mailer's writing. Critics were generally, in the nature of their trade, critical. His new books failed to become bestsellers. Mailer sought to explain himself to interviewers, the public, and himself, in *Advertisements for Myself* (1959), a self-annotated collection of stories and articles. He had, he explained, been an anarchist when he wrote *The Naked and the Dead*. America was cancerous, figuratively and actually – a notion which he was to reiterate. The Cold War inquisitions of Senator Joseph McCarthy typified a government of mindless bullies.

Again, *Advertisements for Myself* was not a book for the mass audience. Some readers found it stridently egocentric (Woody Allen was later to joke that Mailer had bequeathed his ego, as a unique organ, for medical research). Why should Mailer suppose that his diagnoses were accurate, or important? Could he not see that his recent novels seemed almost to exult in the depravities he deplored? Was there a disturbing ambiguity in Mailer's attitude to power? Someone said of the hyperactive Theodore Roosevelt that he could not help trying to dominate or assimilate every occasion: at a wedding he wished to be both bride and groom. Perhaps Mailer had a similar craving for omnipresence and omnipotence. His literary aspirations were apparently boundless: Mailer began to speak of himself as if he were a heavyweight pugilist in contention for a world title, and to refer to other authors such as Hemingway or Dostoyevsky as championship rivals. Detractors found him immodest in every sense of the word. Mailer's prose struck them as overblown and flashy, a customized extravaganza like a pop star's limousine.

On the other hand, Mailer's quite sizeable band of admirers felt that if his ego was large, so was his talent. The Mailer style – hyperbolic, idiosyncratic, confessional – had an unmistakable 'signature'. Mailer's journalism was never that of the journeyman; it was opinionated because he had opinions, and was willing to admit they were hunches rather than hypotheses, matters on which he might change his mind. Mailer was a fast talker yet not a pontificator. His boasting was candid and good-humoured. In *Advertisements*, 'The White Negro' mock-modestly claimed to offer merely 'superficial reflections', but proved to be a dazzling specu-lation on the 'new breed of . . . urban adventurers who drifted out at night' as 'hipsters', people 'looking for action with a black man's code to fit their facts'. The 'hipster' (a term which Mailer did not invent but did effectively annex) was a reckless existentialist, living for the moment, on the edge, sexually alive. 'If a hipster has a fall, it is to death or jail':

The poet is his natural consort . . . , even as the criminal, the hip hoodlum, and the boxer are the heart of knowledge for the hipster. . . .

There was an attractive pugnacity in Mailer's reply to a symposium on 'Our Country and Our Culture'. Many of the nation's intelligentsia, he said, had 'moved their economic luggage from the WPA to the Luce chain' – that is, to write for *Time* or *Life*. The major novelists, among whom he named Dos Passos, Faulkner and Hemingway, had travelled from alienation to the verge of 'proselytizing for the American Century'. Their work since 1945 was 'barren and flat. . . . they sound now like a collective *pater familias*'.

Also in *Advertisements* were 'The Man Who Studied Yoga', an extraordinary fragment of a projected fictional epic, and a second savagely compelling fragment, 'The Time of Her Time', on sexual attraction combined with repugnance. In short, the braggadocio and the bravura of *Advertisements* were almost impossible to separate. A generation afterwards, it looks as though Mailer's true gifts lay not at all in poetry, nor (to judge from *An American Dream*, 1965, *Why Are We In Vietnam?*, 1967, or subsequent imaginings) in fiction, but in the mock-grandiose first-person-singular testimony of *Advertisements*, of *Cannibals and Christians* (1966), and above all of *The Armies of the Night* (1968) and *Miami and the Siege of Chicago* (1968). In these last two memoir-manifestos Mailer projected himself as observer *and* participant, reporting the street warfare waged between police and demonstrators, a Hemingwayish correspondent though with rather more deprecatory humour than that displayed by the paramilitary Papa Hemingway of 1944–5. These were marvellously effective communiqués; the delirium around the Pentagon and in Chicago's Grant Park had a perfect counterpart in Mailer's copious, high-flown, absurdist rhetoric.

His were among the best histories of a hysterical era, when the notion of objectivity seemed both unattainable and undesirable. Mailer's claim to represent the society's inner reality sounded, in the 1960s, at least as good as anyone else's, given that the culture had gone crazy. Mailer's hipster apocalypses were on a grander scale than the ultimately feckless and garrulous semi-fictional rovings of Beat authors, likeable though these were in the best rhapsodies of Jack Kerouac (1922–69), especially *On the Road* (1957) and *The Dharma Bums* (1958). As critics gradually began to take Mailer more or less at his own ingratiatingly self-centred evaluation, they could perceive him as less narcissistic than Kerouac; less involved in homosexual diabolism if less outrageously experimental than the William Burroughs of *The Naked Lunch* (1959) and *Nova Express* (1964); less whimsically 'Californian' than the Richard Brautigan of *Trout Fishing in America* (1967) and *In Watermelon Sugar* (1968); and less playfully surrealistic than his almost exact contemporary Kurt Vonnegut (1922–) in *The Sirens of Titan* (1959), *Cat's Cradle* (1963) and *God Bless You, Mr Rosewater* (1965).

Again, Mailer's claims on behalf of 'factoid' prose (somewhere between fact and fiction) proved palatable to other Americans. Norman Podhoretz, editor of the monthly magazine *Commentary*, argued that much of the best 'creative' writing was now in the form of high-level personal journalism. 'Documentary' literature was not of course altogether new. James Agee's *Let Us Now Praise Famous Men* (1936), unpublished for some years, was achieving a cultish fame; and the *New Yorker* tradition of long 'profiles' and investigative essays, revitalized by John Hersey's *Hiroshima* (1946), had not yet by the 1960s started to lapse into wordiness: the *New Yorker* relish for fact had not, so to speak, declined into the factuous. The unforced verisimilitude of interviews by Studs Terkel (1922–   ), in *Division Street, America* (1966) and *Hard Times* (1970), reinforced the general respect for the apparently non-judgemental, unvarnished truth.

At any rate Podhoretz was not the only one to prefer the Norman Mailer of, say, *The Presidential Papers* (1963) to the swaggering fictive persona of *An American Dream*, or to be more moved by James Baldwin's essays than by his novels. Others found the critical essays of Mary McCarthy (1912–89) acute and incisive where her novel *The Group* (1963) struck them as factually cluttered and gossipy. Not everyone would agree with the magazine-pundit position of Podhoretz. Randall Jarrell observed in *A Sad Heart at the Supermarket* (1962):

Our age is the age of articles: we buy articles in stores, read articles in magazines, exist among the interstices of articles: of columns, interviews, photographic essays, documentaries; of facts condensed into headlines or expanded into non-fiction best-sellers; of real facts about real people.

Jarrell might have added that we read books made up, like his own, from articles previously printed in magazines. Or we might add on his behalf that Jarrell, a beautiful poet, was an equally fine critic. He was certainly correct in noting, with Podhoretz, the quantity of sub-genres. The interview had been resorted to in earlier days: Howells and Twain grew accustomed to providing instant copy for young men with shorthand notebooks. But the interview form grew more and more conspicuous in the twentieth century's periodical culture. Perhaps editors and readers were indulgent to its loose intrusiveness because they sensed the age's craving for 'human interest', updates, being in the know.

Mailer, then, emerged as a master of the ambiguous art of candour-by-limelight, imagining himself as an astronaut (*Of a Fire on the Moon*, 1970); a boxing trainer (*The Fight*, 1975); and, in a 'true-life novel', the condemned murderer Gary Gilmore (*The Executioner's Song*, 1979). Violent crime was a favourite theme for such predecessors as Dickens and Dostoyevsky; Henry James had been thrilled by a mysterious child-murder in Victorian England. Truman Capote's *In Cold Blood* (1965), another 'non-fiction novel', stood as a recent, oddly empathetic account of two criminals, their four Kansas victims, and the murderers' eventual execution – with Capote, as it were, in at the kill. All sorts of variations were possible, it became clear, when the distinction was blurred between objective 'truth' and supposition, between authors and characters. E. L. Doctorow (1931–   ) wrote *The Book of Daniel* (1971) as a fiction unmistakably based upon the son of Ethel and Julius Rosenberg, real-life Americans executed for espionage. Doctorow followed with *Ragtime* (1975), in which public figures of Theodore Roosevelt's time mingled with an invented generalized 'Family'.

One risk was of losing a necessary basic awareness that while fact and fiction did overlap, there *was* an important difference. Another potential weakness, illustrated in Mailer's more clamorous moods, was of denying that some behaviour *was* vile: murderers were perhaps unfortunate, perhaps to a degree victimized, perhaps highly intelligent, but never admirable. Finally, the emphasis upon the individual artist could become portentous, bloated, boring. The enlarged ego, like a swollen liver or spleen, is in itself an object of merely pathological interest. The problem in part may derive from a modern conception of the author as Artist, Entertainer, Prophet: a conception liable to persuade certain writers or painters that their task is prodigious, unprecedented, and possibly thankless. Members of a permanent counter-culture, they nevertheless count upon a degree of popular recognition and even celebrity. For them the public–people conundrum takes on a complexity dwarfing that of such ancestors as Cooper, Hawthorne and Melville. In the United States of the middle and later twentieth century, young authors were apt to receive two equally destructive messages: that they were geniuses on the brink of a great career, and that they were liable to be authors of one book only. When their early work brought praise, the strain of success could be worse than the strain of failure. A painful instance is the disintegration of the greatly talented poet, critic and short-story writer Delmore Schwartz (1913–66; see *The World Is a Wedding*, 1948).

Another perturbing example is that of Jerome D. Salinger (1919–   ), who during the 1950s was hugely acclaimed and who then slipped into almost complete silence. Between *The Catcher in the Rye* (1951) and *Franny and Zooey* (1961), plus a few subsequent stories, Salinger seemed *the* voice of the youthful, middle-class, urban American. In his environment war and depression are far away. Salinger's favourite people are children and adolescents; few of his adults retain any true feelings. *The Catcher in the Rye* surveys Manhattan and its hinterland through the eyes of an incoherent but likeably honest teenager, Holden Caulfield. In the cluster of stories that deal with a family named Glass – the 'Glass Menagerie', as it has been facetiously labelled – the family structure is more intricate. The brothers and sisters are highly intelligent; but like Holden Caulfield they are disgusted by the insincere catchwords that pass for serious discourse. They possess a quasi-religious feeling for exaltation, combining Christian mysticism and Zen Buddhism – a formula which was appealing in its heyday but which before long seemed as *passé* as the slang and pop music of the era. Salinger's achievement, peculiarly right for its first audiences, has tended to be expressed in obituary terms: namely, that after producing a modern version of *Huckleberry Finn* (the modern author's inevitable if unconscious quest?), and some other delightful fables, he opted for silence. It may be an odd commentary on our civilization that such withdrawal, like that of the even more mysteriously unreachable novelist Thomas Pynchon, should be cited as proof positive of the death of the creative faculty.

Such retirements or abdications cast into yet sharper relief the career of Saul Bellow (1915–), Nobel prize winner and – for most readers – foremost living, producing American novelist. His third book, *The Adventures of Augie March* (1953), was indeed talked of in American critical hyperbole as a modern match for *The Adventures of Huckleberry Finn*, with the presumption that Bellow intended the challenge implicit in his title. Or some felt there was a kinship with Whitman's *Song of Myself*. At any rate there seemed a Twainian or Whitmanesque talkative flair, a jocular citified knowingness sustained from the very beginning –

I am an American, Chicago-born – Chicago, that somber city – and go at things as I have taught myself, free-style, and will make the record in my own way: first to knock, first admitted; sometimes an innocent knock, sometimes a not so innocent

– to the concluding sentences:

Why, I am a sort of Columbus of those near-at-hand and believe you can come to them in this immediate *terra incognita* that spreads out in every gaze. I may well be a flop at this line of endeavor. Columbus too thought he was a flop, probably, when they sent him back in chains. Which didn't prove there was no America.

Augie March, a departure from Bellow's *Dangling Man* and *The Victim*, was large, assured, and loose and variegated in plot. Not surprisingly, reviewers called it 'picaresque'. As more novels and tales appeared from Bellow, some critics thought they could discern a rhythm of work. Was there for instance an alternation between short (*Seize the Day*, 1956) and long (*Henderson the Rain King*, 1959)? Did Chicago stand for him as a home city, a manageable place, where New York City signified frenetic, brutal megalopolis (*Mr Sammler's Planet*, 1970)?

Continuities and developments are probably more worth looking for than contrasts. Thus, Bellow's stories, and his main characters, are much concerned with ideas. Philip Rahv once claimed that there were no intellectuals but only he-men and Babbitts in American fiction.[1] With the emergence of Bellow the generalization ceased to hold. The hero of *Dangling Man*, awaiting a military call-up, tries to sustain his previous involvement in figures of the Enlightenment. Augie plunges into 'St Simon, Comte, Marx, and Engels'. The narrator of *Herzog* (1964) compiles scintillatingly erudite letters (which he never posts) to famous persons, including the illustrious dead; and he has in mind a book about the intellectual consequences of the demise of romanticism. Mr Sammler is a refugee scholar closely acquainted during the 1930s with the London intellectual bohemia. The protagonist of *Dean's December* (1982) is a Chicago professor–administrator. Such people are restlessly alert questioners, seeking final answers to fundamental problems, although they are too savvy not to suspect that the answers will not be forthcoming. Part of Bellow's accomplishment lies in his ability to handle these dialogues (often monologues) deftly and wittily yet not superficially.

True, he has been faulted for writing talk-shows rather than novels. Not enough happens, it has been complained, in the typical Bellow story – with the exception of *Henderson the Rain King*; and it is said that what does happen seems abrupt and unmotivated. Certainly the republic of letters, and academe, are at the source of Bellow's inquiry; he studied anthropology as a student, and held an appointment in social thought at the University of Chicago. Literary and scholarly allusions abound. The name of the hero of *Herzog*, Moses Herzog, appears to have been taken from a passing reference in James Joyce's *Ulysses*, not to mention the Joycean conception of Leopold Bloom, a Jewish city-wanderer. Von Humboldt Fleisher, the dead, disaster-prone genius of *Humboldt's Gift*, seems clearly

---

1. 'The Cult of Experience in American Writing', in Rahv's *Image and Idea* (Norfolk, CT, New Directions, 1949), 9.

based on Bellow's one-time friend Delmore Schwartz. But why not? Bellow's reflections upon burnt-out authors, and their country's curious pride in a tally going back as far as Edgar Allan Poe, do not depend for their effect on our knowing about Schwartz. For involution of literary allusiveness, Saul Bellow is pellucidly above-board when compared to *The Recognitions* of William Gaddis (1922–   ), an exploration of deception in the art world that plays tricks with the palindrome 'trade ye no mere moneyed art'. The same can be said of some of the fiction of the philosopher William Gass (1924–   ); or of such elaborations by the scholar–novelist John Barth (1930–   ) as *Giles Goat-Boy, or The Revised New Syllabus* (1966) and *Lost in the Funhouse* (1968); or the almost perversely esoteric problem novels of Vladimir Nabokov (1899–1977), *Pale Fire* (1962) and *Ada or Ardor* (1969).

Bellow's intellectualizing is often high-spirited, but almost never playful. Ideas are not games to him but attempts to encompass truth; and this even in the case of the boisterous Henderson, barging about Africa (another Twainian echo? Henderson is a kind of latter-day Hank Morgan, wrecking 'backward' peoples with well-intentioned technology). In a way Bellow has been on the side of culture, values, great books, since the early portrait of Joseph in *Dangling Man*, 'a graduate of the University of Wisconsin – major, History', and disapprover of modern 'hardboileddom' whose Hemingways 'fly planes or fight bulls or catch tarpon' instead of reading and pondering. It is reasonable to suppose that Joseph, Augie, Herzog, Charlie Citrine *et al.*, down to the Dr Shawmut of *Him with His Foot in His Mouth* (1984), hold views generally acceptable to their creator. Bellow's own pronouncements convey an acidly ironic distaste for counter-cultural America as entire as that of Shawmut, for whom Allen Ginsberg is the bard of 'bottom-line materialistic eroticism'; Ginsberg the screwball Confessor, whose line has proved attractive to Americans because they are suckers for 'sincerity and authenticity'.

This *ne plus ultra* on Bellow's part has made him a target for criticism, by Leslie Fiedler among others (a compliment Bellow has returned). He has been depicted as a modernist, unwilling – like, say, Mary McCarthy, Nelson Algren, Bernard Malamud, John Cheever or John Updike – to cross the border into the wilder terrain of post-modernism. Modernist authors, in such an alignment, may have brilliant gifts, and some capacity to experiment, yet nevertheless owe allegiance to canons of fiction established two or three centuries ago. Contrasting post-modernists – Mailer, say,

Barth, Thomas Pynchon, Burroughs, the John Rechy of *City of Night* (1963) and *The Sexual Outlaw* (1978), possibly the later Philip Roth, possibly Joseph Heller – are thought to have been far readier to explode or subvert the truth-and-worth premises of traditional fiction. The distinction is of course approximate, and has as much to do with symbolic items and gestures as with particular literary modes. Even so, there is an evident tendency to view Saul Bellow as a chief magistrate of American letters, out of touch with the scene around him; and he has indeed sounded increasingly magisterial or decanal since the clashes of the Vietnam era. But if one has to hear *ex cathedra* judgements, no one can deliver them with greater authority and sardonic elegance.

Dangling Man ends before Joseph has actually gone into the army. After the first flurry of sensitive or tough-guy combat yarns, the Second World War dropped into the background, yielding place to the Cold War and the Korean War, and at length the Vietnam War, not to mention the overwhelmingly civilian preoccupations of stateside America. It took time to digest the martial violence of 1941–5, and to find a means of expressing its inner significance. The first deeply cogitated expression of this came from Joseph Heller (1923–   ). He had served in the Mediterranean as a young airman. In *Catch 22* (1961) Heller's segment of the war is visualized as *comédie noire*, a slapstick story with some real blood. The senior commanders seek glory and promotion; a supply officer runs the base as the headquarters of a vast black-market operation, in pursuance of which he arranges the bombing of his own field; and the aviators, victimized by idiots and rascals, are left with no war aim except individual survival. Yossarian, the bombardier hero, determined to fly no more missions, pretends to be insane. The 'Catch 22' of the title is a crazily ingenious casuistry designed to thwart him. Captain Yossarian, it is ruled, does not wish to be killed. This is a quite natural instinct. Therefore he is not insane. Therefore he must continue to fly as directed, even though his senior officer Cathcart is risking men's lives to no purpose. Yossarian takes the only way out: he deserts to Sweden. The grim surrealism of *Catch 22* reverses the moral of Herman Wouk's *Caine Mutiny* (1951), in which a commander's incompetence is deemed not to entitle subordinates to disobey his orders. Heller's deep cynicism and inventiveness made his novel seem a profound comment upon not only the Second World War but also the sophistries of Vietnam. During the 1960s numbers of young Americans, choosing not to dangle and be drafted, emulated Yossarian in heading for Sweden or Canada.

Heller's next novels (*Something Happened*, 1974; *Good as Gold*, 1979; *God Knows*, 1984) brought out the ugly-hilarious aspects of corporate business, of bureaucratic Washington, and – this the burlesque turn of *God Knows* – the comic angst of an ageing Jewish impresario, cast as the Old Testament King David but holding forth in the idiom of the 1980s. As pre-Revolutionary France was called 'a despotism tempered by songs', the America of Heller is an absurdity tempered by fantastic gags. Yet, while Heller's fiction (and plays) have a post-modernist irrealism, his view of war interestingly enough remains within the same tradition as that established after the First World War, by the Dos Passos of *Three Soldiers*, Hemingway's *Farewell to Arms*, and *The Enormous Room* (1922) of E. E. Cummings, whose protagonists all want to escape from the brutal pressures of the state-in-arms.

The message of entropy had become more intricate by 1973, when Thomas Pynchon (1937–   ), already the author of the enigmatic, end-of-the-world *V* (1963) and *The Crying of Lot 49* (1966), produced *Gravity's Rainbow*. Pynchon's cult following, intrigued by the parodic and philosophical richness of the earlier work, and his absolute avoidance of personal publicity, turned eagerly to the exegesis of the dense new work. The title refers to the arc of the V2 rocket, Germany's secret weapon, which was deployed against Antwerp and London in the closing months of the Second World War. In that respect, *Gravity's Rainbow* is a war novel. According to older conceptions, it is not a novel at all but an immense assortment of anecdotes, puzzles, pastiches and counterfactual prophecies. Its plots and sub-plots are conspiracies (hence the 'Gunpowder Plot') rather than stories, each yielding to some huger scheme of doom by entropy. The war itself, we are assured by a German military scientist, is not really about politics or ideology: it is brought about quite impersonally by the imperatives of high technology. Bellow's Dr Shawmut ridicules the psychopathic vision of universal conspiracy – 'supercapitalism and its carcinogenic petrochemical technology' – which he attributes to Ginsberg. The talk of 'Star Wars' or SDI (Strategic Defence Initiative) scenarios in the 1980s makes the war fables of Heller and Pynchon (and for that matter of Mailer's general in *The Naked and the Dead*, fascinated by gun trajectories) seem hardly more unimaginable than the so-called real thing.

The point can be restated in support of post-modernist fiction as a whole. Why, say its advocates, labour to construct three-dimensional characters and credible stories? Are they not mere constructs, which moreover delude us as to the actual determinants of our world? What can we mean, incidentally, by 'our' world? Even if we knew who 'we' are, why assume that we have any control over 'our' ('their'?) planet?

Answers must be matter-of-fact, though that is to beg the question ('what is fact?'): for without question-begging, and an obstinate attention to a perception of everyday 'life', we have nothing to hang on to, and do not need to read any more fiction that reiterates how lost we are. Here, crudely, is a justification for continuing to read what might be called non-post-modernist fiction, by Bellow or Updike or Eudora Welty or Peter Taylor or Joan Didion or Walker Percy or Alison Lurie or Jayne Anne Phillips, or indeed by the superbly gifted Philip Roth, who has been back and forth across the reality border like a restless, conscience-stricken shepherd (his *alter ego* Zuckerman bears the brunt of Roth's formulation of a difficult question: if fiction is not meant to do good, is it not liable to do harm?). All of these and other writers catch at truths of the senses and the mind by which we live, however precariously. They report to us, 'in depth' (as the jargon of the late twentieth century puts it), on the only world we inhabit day by day, while we are still here. This too has been the domain of American poetry during the same span of time. Within its particular concerns, comparable disagreements have held the field.

Chapter 12 suggested that the beginnings of modern poetry in the United States were partly 'native' and partly 'cosmopolitan' – a division that corresponds to the 'redskin'–'paleface' dualism discerned by Philip Rahv in American literature as a whole. Certain poets continued after 1918 to stress the American-ness of their activity. Others took it for granted.

The issue gradually ceased to matter greatly. In 1920, however, William Carlos Williams called his one-time friend Ezra Pound 'the best enemy United States verse has'. With Pound he associated T. S. Eliot, who had lived in England since 1914 and who in 1927 was to become a British citizen. Williams charged that Pound and Eliot had harmed American poetry by kowtowing to Europe, 'content with the connotations of their masters'. Williams, Sandburg and others had meanwhile remained at home, striving to create a 'western dialect'. Williams, who was to become an inspiration for a later generation of home-bred bards, never quite got over this apparent defection. The native effort, he asserted in his *Autobiography* (1951), was impeded by Eliot's 'The Waste Land' (1922) which 'gave the poem back to the academics'.

Pound's counter-argument, expressed to Williams back in 1917, was that native American verse, when left without external stimulus, lapsed into 'fizz, swish, gabble of verbiage'. There was some truth in both positions. Pound too could be accused, in the more esoteric of his *Cantos* and other poetry, of an extreme, even rabid pedantry. Yet he did work indefatigably to bring the Old and New Worlds together; and unlike Eliot of the bowler hat and British mannerisms, Pound remained as shaggily 'Western' as the Joaquin Miller of 1870. The great contributions of his fellow-American poets have usually been *both* native and cosmopolitan, gradually achieving a mastery of 'the American voice-box' and a modernist capacity to blend the formal (European) and the colloquial (American).

E. E. Cummings (1894–1962) was among the most spectacular native innovators. The autobiographical prose of his first book, *The Enormous Room*, fashioned a distinctively eccentric idiom in which to express his romantic anarchism;

To the left and right through lean oblongs of stained glass burst dirty burglars of moonlight.

I will get upon the soonness of the train and ride into the now of Paris.

Cummings's first published verse, *Tulips and Chimneys* (1923), seemed dazzlingly assured in its praise of the individual, and disdain for those he later dismissed as 'mostpeople':

Mostpeople have less in common with ourselves than the squarerootofminusone. You and I are human beings: mostpeople are snobs. . . .

He began too to invent typographical tricks to indicate measures of time:

```
                              pho
            nographisrunn
     ingd o    w,    n        phonograph
                              stopS.
```

'Mr Lowercase Highbrow', as an imaginary interlocutor addressed him, became 'e. e. cummings', and in several further volumes of verse continued to conjure with syntax and typography. In these, love is supreme, 'wonderful one times one', and 'soonness' still the prelude to the fulfilment of 'now'. Life in Cummings's poetry is a series of unfolding discoveries: 'Always the beautiful answer who asks a more beautiful question.' The series is 'growth'.

Eventually, critics queried whether there was enough growth in Cummings, despite his technical ingenuity. Yet if his poetry in sum seemed

more amusing than profound, no one excelled him in conveying the lilt
and gaiety of the world as he kept recommending it:

> anyone lived in a pretty how town
> (with up so floating many bells down)
> spring summer autumn winter
> he sang his didn't he danced his did.

Cummings was to early modern poetry what the American artist Alexander Calder was to sculpture. At their best – Cummings in words and
Calder with his mobiles – they made art as delightful as a merry-go-round,
rotating and rising and falling in holiday sunshine.

Marianne Moore (1887–1972), like T. S. Eliot a native of St Louis, was
almost as cosmopolitan as he, though she lived mainly in New York and
had a passion for her local baseball team, the dear departed Brooklyn
Dodgers. Original and scrupulous, she went her own way with none of
the haste, heat and errors that often mark the so-called poetic temperament. Her *Collected Poems* (1951) and *Complete Poems* (1967) include only
the works she cared to preserve after severe pruning. Most of them are in
even stanzas, the lines regulated by syllabic counting. Rhymes are pulled
gently out of the poem. End-rhymes are sometimes made by breaking a
word in the middle:

> Priorities were cradled in this region not
> noted for humility; spot
> that has high-singing frogs, cotton-mouth snakes and cot-
> ton-fields....

The sense runs on across the form like a design painted over tiles. Her
subjects are an anthology of unexpected things, a poet's scrapbook of
clocks and jewels and living creatures, from sources both everyday and
recondite. Her observation has the exactness of an old botanical or
zoological engraving. Here is a stanza from 'The Jerboa':

> By fifths and sevenths,
> in leaps of two lengths,
> like the uneven notes
> of the Bedouin flute, it stops its gleaning
> on little wheel castors, and makes fern-seed
> foot-prints with kangaroo speed.

She can describe an ostrich or an elephant with equal felicity. Her meaning
is condensed, and she adopts a 'hybrid' technique of quoting directly from
her sources. Marianne Moore's world is full of delicate, exotic objects. Her

affection for them is akin to Whitman's rejoicing in 'the pismire . . . , and a grain of sand, and the egg of the wren' – except that her admiration must be deduced from the meticulous commentary. With Wallace Stevens, whose verse has been likened to hers, Marianne Moore is a subtle poet; she selects her material for a serious purpose, not for illustration or embroidery. Indeed a poem like 'Those Various Scalpels' seems to catalogue details so as to query their ultimate value, in a manner reminiscent of the Puritan poet Edward Taylor. For other professional poets – Eliot, Williams, Cummings, Stevens, Elizabeth Bishop – Marianne Moore's work constitutes (in W. H. Auden's words) 'a treasure which all future English poets will be able to plunder'.

The precocious brilliance of Hart Crane (1899–1932) was cut short by suicide. Marianne Moore's first slim volume was published in 1921 (in London) when she was thirty-four. Crane had had a poem accepted by Margaret Anderson's *Little Review* in 1916, when he was only half that age. When 'The Waste Land' appeared in 1922 Crane was already an established poet. He knew it for a great work but was, like W. C. Williams, troubled. Eliot appeared to hold out little hope for the twentieth century – and, therefore, for America, the most contemporary of lands. Crane himself intended to move 'towards a more positive, or (if I must put it so in a skeptical age) ecstatic goal'. The poems in *White Buildings* reveal how earnestly he was seeking the goal, which he tried to reach conclusively in the long testament to American-ness called *The Bridge* (1930).

Its main symbol was Brooklyn Bridge, the bold old structure over New York's East River built by the Roeblings. Whitman before him, and before the bridge was in place, had written magnificently of 'Crossing Brooklyn Ferry' as a joy to be savoured by others fifty or a hundred years hence. Whitman is the principal hero of *The Bridge*; it is to him that Crane speaks in the splendid section 'Cape Hatteras'. Both men were fascinated by the ocean highway to the new continent. But Crane's America is different from Whitman's; the Machine Age has arrived, the task of poetry is to 'absorb the machine, i.e. *acclimatize* it as naturally and casually as trees, cattle, galleons, castles' (an oddly 'poetic' agglomeration), 'and all other human associations of the past'. Crane's 'ecstasy' was sought by adding to the old America the new scene, in which

> spouting pillars spoor the evening sky,
> Under the looming stacks of the gigantic power house
> Stars prick the eyes with sharp ammoniac proverbs,

and in which the Wright Brothers had conquered space. Dynamos and aircraft were to be synthesized with more traditionally folkloreish items. Some of these were possibly suggested to him by William Carlos Williams's prose experiment, *In the American Grain* (1925). Crane's list included Columbus, Cortés, Pocahontas, Rip Van Winkle, Poe and Melville, who were introduced as significant figures from a usable American past.

The Bridge contains gorgeous poetry. However, the 'American' elements are a disparate batch: the synthesis fails. Crane's exultant lyricism clashes with moods of despair and disconsolate loneliness. There are marvellous outdoor lines, as in the 'Cutty Sark' section, on

> Pennants, parabolas –
> Clipper dreams indelible and ranging,
> baronial white on lucky blue!

But these word-intoxicated, Dylan Thomasish passages contrast with those such as 'The Tunnel', a subway plunge that makes him ask the self-destructive Poe

> why do I often meet your visage here,
> Your eyes like agate lanterns – on and on
> Below the toothpaste and the dandruff ads?

Though Crane invokes Whitman, the homeless figure of Poe haunts much of the poem. The rhythm of the dynamos is the pulse of nightmare. The airman crashes, and even wills his downfall, like the mad expatriate Harry Crosby, whom Crane addresses in 'The Cloud Juggler':

> Expose vaunted validities that yawn
> Past pleasantries. . . .

Some of these last poems, from the Caribbean, are as good as the best of *The Bridge*. But soon after composing them, Crane jumped to his death from a New York bound ship.

On the whole, American modern poets preferred to accept life's dissonances rather than cast about for a reconciling formula. Of those who, like Crane, tried to incorporate the national past, the most successful was Stephen Vincent Benét, whose *John Brown's Body* (1928) was a narrative chronicle with a similar brio to that of the English poet John Masefield. Both were popular with the general public, and for that reason perhaps under-rated by their peers. The Californian Robinson Jeffers (1887–1962) was another poet with a taste for long verse narratives, bleaker in mood than Benét's. Jeffers based some of these on themes from antiquity, deriving from them 'a more ideal and also more normal beauty, because the myths of our own race were never developed, and have been alienated from us'. In shorter poems, loving the ocean and wild animals as much as he disliked 'mostpeople', Jeffers looked forward to a future, possibly on the far side of some immense catastrophe, with

> The cities gone down, the people fewer and the hawks more numerous,
> The rivers mouth to source pure; when the two-footed
> Mammal, being someways one of the nobler animals, regains
> The dignity of room, the value of rareness.

Much of the interest of American poets in conservative, or at least non-American, approaches owed its impetus to Ezra Pound and T. S. Eliot. They were the wandering scholars of poetic modernism, the young men from civilization's periphery. Free from Europe's insularities, they were subjects of a universal republic or, perhaps better, holy empire of letters. Pound arrived on the European scene ahead of Eliot. The movements in which he involved himself, such as Imagism and Vorticism, had an edge of iconoclasm that he never quite outgrew. His early sources – Browning, Yeats, Villon – were of a slightly antecedent order to those of Eliot. For Eliot, as Pound admiringly noted, while deeply read in the past, also acquired the cultural equipment of a complete modern. True, when Eliot became acquainted with Pound, in the opening stages of the First World War, his education was not finished. The dedication of 'The Waste Land' to Pound acknowledged that he owed much to Pound's preliminary explorations, and to Pound's editorial scrutiny while the poem was in composition.

By the end of the war they were in agreement, Pound recollected, 'that the dilution of *vers libre*, Amygism, Lee Masterism, general floppiness, had gone too far and that some counter-current must be set going.... Results: poems in Mr. Eliot's *second* volume, also "H. S. Mauberley." Divergence later.'

The poems by Eliot to which Pound referred were published in 1920, as was his own *Hugh Selwyn Mauberley*. These, and 'The Waste Land', were a world away from Amy Lowell, Edgar Lee Masters and 'general floppiness'. They sensed the tragedy of the war much more fully than most of their 'native' contemporaries; and their modernity included a conviction that the past composed (as Eliot said in 1917) a 'simultaneous order' with the present. Hence their borrowings from other eras and tongues.

However, as Pound remarked, he and Eliot diverged. In 1920 Eliot published a volume of essays entitled *The Sacred Wood*, which included the famous piece on 'Tradition and the Individual Talent'. The same year saw the publication of essays by Pound under the name *Instigations*. The difference in titles is characteristic. For Pound nothing was quite sacred. In earlier years he instructed his books to

> Greet the grave and stodgy,
> Salute them with your thumbs at your noses.

He was, so to speak, an anti-clerical lover of cathedrals, an iconoclast in pursuit of iconography. In Eliot's historical scheme the mind of Europe changes generation by generation, but 'abandons nothing *en route*'. In Pound's scheme (which also includes Asia) certain periods are so exciting that he relives them in his work. In common with Browning, he is very much a poet of *monologue* – someone, himself or a character, is usually *talking* – and often his aim is to speak familiarly out of some bygone era as though it were today. His fine poem 'Provincia Deserta' ends:

> I have walked over these roads;
> I have thought of them living.

Both he and Eliot had an enormous respect for Dante. But where Eliot was impressed by the mental unity of Dante's Christendom, Pound seemed more interested in the freshness of Dante's world. The *Divine Comedy*, he says, was written 'to MAKE PEOPLE THINK' – as though it might have had *Instigations* as a subtitle. Pound's *Cantos*, as their name declares, have their source in Dante. Like the *Divine Comedy*, they were to consist of 100 cantos. Some of Dante's persons – Arnaut Daniel, Brunetto Latini, Bertrand de Born, Ulysses – figure in them. But they are not a record of spiritual progress. The redemption offered is primarily economic: redemption, that is, from the sin of usury, the medieval sin that Pound applies as his measure and explanation for much of man's history. Anger replaces humility; Pound's hell, Eliot has well said, is for other people. The Christian tradition means little to Pound; he relies upon the wisdom of Confucius, or of the early leaders of his own country, Jefferson and John Adams. His learning consists of innumerable gobbets that form a Poundian *Summa* of human experience.

While Pound's system makes sense, it is ultimately incoherent. And this despite almost unrivalled poetic talent. The trouble is not that Pound created a private vision. Other men – W. B. Yeats, for example – have done the same; and one does not demand of them an itemized catalogue, as though their work were a property up for auction. Idiosyncrasy appears a prerequisite for major imaginative *oeuvres* of our time; at any rate, 'public' visions have lacked intensity. Nor can it be said that Pound was flighty; his convictions were developed and sustained through half a century. For some other writers he was tremendously important. There is no rule as to how private an author may be. Yet Pound's privacy had a hostile and aberrant quality. On some days the estate is open to the public; on others trespassers will be prosecuted.

The poetry and criticism of T. S. Eliot by contrast always had an air of cool maturity. His academic beginnings took in Harvard, the Sorbonne, Germany and Oxford; poetic study included the French symbolists (particularly Jules Laforgue) and the English metaphysical authors. He learned from Dante, Blake, Ben Jonson, Baudelaire. His intellect was matched by a subtle poetic talent; and consequently, whatever he wrote, from the first poems like 'The Love Song of J. Alfred Prufrock' (1915), swiftly took rank as a modern classic. For a generation, Eliot was almost universally regarded as the foremost living poet of the English language. His emphasis on tradition therefore had a considerable effect upon contemporaries. Even in early and lightly ironic work, his criticism had nothing of hysteria or manifesto about it. As 'Gerontion', or as Tiresias in 'The Waste Land', he spoke in the person of an old man while yet a young one. By 1927, he described himself in the essays *For Lancelot Andrewes* as 'classicist in literature, royalist in politics, and Anglo-Catholic in religion'. Edmund Wilson objected that Eliot had 'evolved for himself an aristocratic myth' that had no more plausibility than other private systems: than that, for example, of Ezra Pound.

The difference, as T. S. Eliot's subsequent writing made clear, is that his own system was firmly defined, and eminently reasonable to those who also adhered to the Christian faith. Those who found his gravity oppressive had to reckon with the fact that his poetic genius continued to evolve. His dryness did not become aridity, but was rather of the quality ascribed to certain champagnes. Though he exasperated William Carlos Williams by seeming to reject his background, he made amends writing appreciatively of *Huckleberry Finn* acknowledging that, born not far down-river from Mark Twain's Hannibal, he had retained a memory of the Mississippi. Moreover, his interest in the possibilities of poetic drama does not square with the accusation that he was a would-be aristocrat. Experiments in this medium, starting with *Sweeney Agonistes, an Aristophanic Melodrama* (printed in *The Criterion*, 1926–7), progressed through *The Rock* (1934), *Murder in the Cathedral* (1935), *The Family Reunion* (1939) and *The Cocktail Party* (1950), towards an ideal of 'that collaboration of the audience with the artist which is necessary in all art and most obviously in dramatic art'. These words came from an essay that he wrote on 'Marie Lloyd' as far back as 1923. He was aware that he had not attained the ideal, and that a fastidious dogmatism made some of his work unduly glum. Yet there was majesty in the *Four Quartets* (1943); and the whimsical wit of *Old Possum's Book of Practical Cats* (1939), by a twist that Eliot would probably have relished, brought him posthumous celebrity as the 'author' of the hit musical *Cats*.

In 1948 Eliot was awarded the Nobel prize for literature. Pound, who still had nearly a quarter of a century left to live, was shut up in St Elizabeth's Hospital in Washington D.C. His support for Mussolini's Fascist régime had left him open to the charge of treason (a fate portrayed in Kurt Vonnegut's novel *Mother Night*, 1961). By a kinder twist than that of Heller's hero in *Catch 22*, Pound had in reverse been ruled insane, and therefore *not* responsible for whatever he might have said. St Elizabeth's was his asylum in a double sense – a place of confinement and a refuge. A jury (of writers) including Eliot, Conrad Aiken, Léonie Adams, Louise Bogan, Auden, Allen Tate and Robert Penn Warren, conferred the Bollingen prize upon Pound for his *Pisan Cantos* (nos. 74–84, 1948). An uproar resulted. Pound toiled away in semi-seclusion until 1958, when Robert Frost and other old comrades secured his release, enabling him to return to his and Dante's homeland, Italy.

By then another generation of American poets was emerging. Two of its members, Karl Shapiro (1913–) and Robert Lowell (1917–77), were in fact on the Bollingen panel. But they had also the preoccupations of their own age-group: coming out of the war (in which Lowell had been a conscientious objector), assimilating the America of Harry Truman and Dwight D. Eisenhower, earning a livelihood (less difficult than in the 1930s), finding the best words and metres to convey their necessarily singular experiences. Shapiro, for example, took a strong dislike to the cultural old guard represented by Eliot, Pound and Stevens – and was subsequently to complain of the inflated reputation of Robert Lowell. As with every literary generation, friendship could turn sour, for a tangle of personal and professional reasons.

Whether or not Lowell deserved his pre-eminence, by the early 1960s he was the most talked-about poet in America. In his formative years he rebelled against his New England family ties, Calvinism, and the authority of the state and its military establishment. He nevertheless looked for acceptable guidance, making himself a pupil-acolyte of John Crowe Ransom and Allen Tate, and becoming for a while a convert to Roman Catholicism. Two early collections, *Lord Weary's Castle* (1946) and *The Mills of the Kavanaghs* (1951), displayed a remarkable variety of verse forms; they were albums of New England, evoking old Puritan anguishes, newer landscapes, seas lunging at the rocky coast. Years of groping followed, while Lowell alternately sought and evaded tranquillity in his personal life. In his poetry, he strove to break loose from what he now felt to be an excessively 'influenced' and literary diction. The poems of *Life Studies* (1959) indeed achieved a fresh confessional-conversational immediacy; and their effect was heightened in the distraught yet easy verse of *For the Union Dead* (1964). He discussed his despairs and unhingeings; he spoke of and to other poets (Elizabeth Bishop, Delmore Schwartz, Hart Crane); he charted the decline from the flawed but precious past to the ugliness or emptiness of his own day.

> The stone statues of the abstract Union Soldier
> grow slimmer and younger each year –
> wasp-waisted, they doze over muskets
> and muse through their sideburns. . . .

In the 1950s Lowell wanted to arrive at a poetry as unabashedly personal as that of Allen Ginsberg's *Howl* or perhaps of W. D. Snodgrass's *Heart's Needle* (1959). In the 1960s the 'willed disloyalty' of his earlier life was renewed in scornful criticisms of great-power bullying ('top-heavy Goliath in full armor'), and in the symbolic march on the Pentagon described by his fellow-demonstrator Norman Mailer in *Armies of the Night*. Lowell also experimented (*Imitations*, 1961) with free adaptations of the verse of sundry ancient, medieval and modern poets from Homer to Pasternak. He wrote three one-act plays based on stories by Hawthorne and Melville. And in what was to be his last decade he wrote a quantity of autobiographical and meditative poems (*Notebooks*, *History*, *For Lizzie and Harriet*, *Day by Day*) – painfully introspective, with flashes of the vanity we may think we can detect in the self-condemnations of his Puritan forebears.

Lowell's was, however, one among many talents in what appears in retrospect an extraordinary era for American poetry. The formal skills of Richard Wilbur (1921–   ), fastidious and erudite and felicitous, have never been repudiated by him in favour of some rawer mode: skills masterfully deployed in translations (for example, of Molière's *Tartuffe*) much closer to their original than the borrowings of Lowell, or of Ezra Pound. Theodore Roethke (1908–63), who was as racked in temperament as Lowell, lacked some of the latter's thematic versatility, but compensated with a gnomic, rapturous intensity in certain unforgettable (and usually short) poems. In these Roethke reverts to his salad days as a gardener's son, and then still further back to pre-verbal infancy. His two finest collections, *The Lost Son* (1948) and *Praise to the End!* (1951), are full of mysterious incantations –

> Up over a viaduct I came, to the snakes and sticks of another winter,
> A two-legged dog hunting a new horizon of howls –

and of enchanting, remembered sensuousness:

> To have the whole air!
> The light, the full sun
> Coming down on the flowerheads,
> The tendrils turning slowly,
> A slow snail-lifting, liquescent;
> To be by the rose
> Rising slowly out of its bed,
> Still as a child in its first loneliness....

Delmore Schwartz, Lowell, Roethke lived on the edge of calamity. So to a degree did Randall Jarrell. So, with a vengeance, did John Berryman (1914–72), who like his father before him ended in suicide; 'really we had the same life', Lowell wrote in a memorial reminiscence. What they had in common, poetically, was a beginning in polished, rather mimetic versification; immersion in the early American heritage (for Berryman, *Homage to Mistress Bradstreet*, a passionate invocation to the Puritan poet in a long sequence of eight-line stanzas, published in book form in 1956); love-troubles (*Berryman's Sonnets*, published somewhat belatedly in 1967, even more self-recriminatory, self-exonerating than Lowell's *Life Studies*); and the search for a candid and congenial persona. Berryman's voices were first heard in the 1950s, in magazines. They were gathered in book form, with various titles, as his *Dream Songs*. 'This great Pierrot's universe', Lowell said of the first volume, *77 Dream Songs* (1964), 'is more tearful and funny than we can bear.' Allen Tate found their idiom 'wholly original'. In Berryman's own explanation, the 'poem in progress' was essentially about an imaginary character ... named Henry, a white American in early middle age and sometimes in blackface, who has suffered an irreversible loss and talks about himself sometimes in the first person, sometimes in the third, sometimes even in the second; he has a friend, never named, who addresses him as Mr. Bones and variants thereof.

Henry is Berryman but not completely so. The friend, who poses as a minstrel comic, teases and questions with impunity and immunity; it is Henry who pays the price of being a modern man, 'goatish', 'adult and difficult', drawing nearer to death's abyss, mourning the demise of Delmore. In later *Dream Songs* there are also caustic commentaries on the megalomaniacs of Washington D.C., and on the behaviour expected of university bards. Daniel Hoffman (1923–   ), himself an accomplished writer whose work includes a book-length poem on Philadelphia (*Brotherly Love*, 1980), points out that Berryman once produced a brilliant analysis of Stephen Crane, and that two of Crane's key characters (Fleming in *The Red Badge of Courage*, and the mutilated coachman in 'The Monster') were christened 'Henry'. So the supposition is that Berryman's 'Henry Pussycat', 'Henry Hankovitch', and so on, had a literary ancestry their creator took into account.

Twentieth-century American poetry teems with practitioners and programmes. To categorize them as divisible into 'paleface' and 'redskin' is a gross simplification. Lowell and Berryman, as we have seen, combined their quest of vernacular modes with their relish for cosmopolis. Nevertheless, William Carlos Williams (as Eric Mottram convincingly maintains[1]) was a giant figure in American poetry from the 1920s through to the 1960s, not only for his own poetry and opinions but because of the inspiration others drew from him. One of the most senior was the Objectivist Louis Zukofsky (1904–78). Objectivism, a doctrine especially prominent in the 1930s, insisted on beginning with a particular object and freely associating outward from that (compare Williams: 'not in ideas but in things'). The voice in such a concept is not merely vernacular rather than poetic: the very form of verse is, so to speak, con*vers*ation.

From Objectivism naturally enough developed 'projective' or 'open field' verse, exemplified in the *Maximus* poems of Charles Olson (1910–70). Olson, a powerfully eloquent theoretician and organizer, with something of the selfless managerial busy quality of Ezra Pound, became rector and

1. 'Sixties American Poetry', *Sphere History of Literature in the English Language*, vol. 9, *American Literature since 1900*, ed. Marcus Cunliffe (revised edn, London, Sphere, 1987), pp. 276–8.

chancellor of Black Mountain College, an experimental college set up in North Carolina. One of Olson's students and devotees was Robert Creeley (1926–). Another exponent of 'open field' writing was Robert Duncan (1919–88), a one-time teacher at Black Mountain; and Denise Levertov (1923–) also studied there. They were in general suspicious of Lowell, feeling that he had not truly understood the notion of poetic phrasing as organically determined by speaking and breathing. They believed that Olson was a more original and important writer. They tended to ally themselves with, or at least to sympathize with, Beat poets (Ginsberg, and also Gregory Corso and Lawrence Ferlinghetti), and other California-based writers such as Kenneth Rexroth; and with some of the New York poets, notably the Frank O'Hara of *Lunch Poems* (1964) and John Ashbery (1927– ; *Self-Portrait in a Convex Mirror*, 1975), who in turn were attuned to Manhattan's avant-garde art scene.

If most novelists failed to secure fame and fortune, the same was even more true of American poets. Their public was minute, their financial rewards negligible. Poetry thrived chiefly on campuses or in big cities, and sometimes in places where audiences had retained an appetite for performances of words with music. There were, however, a quantity of little magazines, and scores of little groups endowed with enthusiasm and knowledge, and sometimes (it must be said) with sectarian hostility to the creations of other practitioners. Hovering about the abodes of fiction and poetry was a third form, literary criticism, itself kaleidoscopically various and continually modifying, excommunicating and heralding. Some felt that its role was parasitic, others that it was important but apt to claim too much for itself; it was nominally their servant, but an imperious one, like a butler in a household whose inhabitants he considers badly need instruction in how to conduct themselves.

The American Theatre

THE American plays written in the first decades of independence can be seen as brave attempts to speak to and for a mass audience, proud of its un-European democracy. Colonel Manly, in Royall Tyler's *The Contrast* (1787), exemplifies his name by urging the republican virtues ('probity, virtue, honour') upon his compatriots. In Mordecai M. Noah's *The Grecian Captive* (1822), a Greek insurgent enthusiastically greets an American naval officer:

Let me embrace thee! Thou art from the country of a Washington..., who gave freedom and glory to the Western world. Sacred be his name – illustrious his example.

The officer replies:

I thank you, sir, and may you establish in Greece a free and happy republic, founded upon the only true basis, virtue, law, and liberty.

Frequently in nineteenth-century performances of such plays, as we learn from David Grimsted's *Melodrama Unveiled*, the central theme is the unimportance of inherited rank or wealth. A peasant hero in a play of 1838, in love with a high-born lady, has no doubt that he deserves her and will eventually win her:

> Nature's pure element comes through my veins....
> I stand a balance in the scale with kings,
> With all their bloated blood.

French or Germans were given comical accents. Europeans with titles were portrayed either as fops or villains. Adam Trueman, a sturdy farmer in Anna Mowatt's *Fashion* (1845), insists that although there is no formal aristocracy in the United States, 'we *have* kings, princes, and nobles in abundance – of *Nature's stamp* ... – we have honest men, warm-hearted and brave, and we have women – gentle, fair, and true, to whom no *title* could add *nobility*'. Social problems were likewise dramatized before American audiences, as in W. H. Smith's *The Drunkard* (1850) and in

George L. Aiken's phenomenally successful version of *Uncle Tom's Cabin*, which began its almost perpetual run in 1852.

Even if some suspicion of the supposedly loose morals of the playhouse lingered among strictly reared Americans, theatre-going was a prime entertainment and edification for city-dwellers like Walt Whitman. Charades and amateur theatricals were equally common. Oliver Wendell Holmes, in *The Autocrat of the Breakfast-Table* (1858), cites a verse prologue written by him for such an occasion. It epitomizes the popular expectations of the era:

> Here every foundling finds its lost mamma;
> Every rogue, repentant, melts his stern papa;
> Misers relent, the spendthrift's debts are paid,
> The cheats are taken in the traps they laid....

All difficulties are triumphantly resolved in the fifth act:

> – When the poor hero flounders in despair,
> Some dear lost uncle turns up millionaire, –
> Clasps the young scapegrace with paternal joy,
> Sobs on his neck, 'My *boy*! MY BOY!! M Y B O Y !!!'

On closer inspection, however, the assumptions of nineteenth-century popular drama in the United States appear little different from those of the London theatre. There too, as W. M. Thackeray remarked, the pit and gallery hissed at titled depravity and applauded the plainer, self-made styles of hero and heroine. British plots usually rewarded the good characters by enriching them, and by proving lovers to be of suitably respectable and compatible social rank. But then, essentially the same attitudes – including attitudes to race and creed – pervaded the American theatre. In Holmes's verse, the lost uncle is a millionaire; his nephew will be affluent, and his bride every inch a lady, even if not a Lady.

Theatre in the United States a century ago was still fundamentally the same as in Britain. In both countries it mirrored the values of a middling, bourgeois audience. Personnel as well as plots were Anglo-American, with a constant and easy transatlantic traffic of plays, casts and managements. And, perhaps even more than in Britain, American drama of the nineteenth century subordinated text to technique.

At the level of mass entertainment, America did introduce stage shows of considerable vitality. The Negro minstrel show, for example, had developed by 1850 into a formalized three-part amusement that retained its verve for a generation or so. The burlesque (or 'burleycue') performance that emerged a little later was also loosely organized in three parts, each with its characteristic routines and vulgarities. Vaudeville, the American equivalent of the Victorian music-hall, managed to be robust without the bumps-and-grinds coarseness that accompanied burlesque.

The legitimate theatre, however, produced very few plays of permanent interest. It was an age when the actor and the producer counted for more than the playwright. The big names were those of men like Edwin Forrest, or the Anglo-American Booths, Jeffersons, Boucicaults, Sotherns, and Barrymores, or the actor-manager 'play-doctor' David Belasco. But the play itself was not the thing. Often it was imported from Europe. It seems typical that *Our American Cousin*, the play at which Abraham Lincoln was assassinated in 1865, had been written by an Englishman, Tom Taylor. Often a successful play was an adaptation of a novel – *Uncle Tom's Cabin*, *St. Elmo* and *The Gilded Age* are instances – and so not initially conceived in terms of the stage. Where an author like W. D. Howells wrote directly for the theatre, he brought no startling novelty to the medium. The public, as Henry James discovered painfully in London, demanded melodrama lavishly staged. It liked large casts, romantic plots and spectacular effects; it applauded patriotic sentiments but did not insist on seeing American plays. The absence before 1891 of an adequate international copyright put native playwrights at an added disadvantage, and the growth of syndicates and circuits made it still more difficult for the young author to gain a hearing. Thus in 1881, the year of Ibsen's *Ghosts*, the American theatre was represented by *La Belle Russe*, a play concocted by Belasco out of two written by other authors. His melodrama was set in England and first advertised, for reasons of prestige, as 'from the French'. In 1888, the year of Strindberg's *Miss Julie*, Belasco collaborated with Daniel Frohman to write and stage a piece entitled *Lord Chumley*. Belasco had a genuine theatrical talent – shortly afterwards he directed a striking production of Sophocles' *Electra* – but there was a vast gulf between his long span of achievements and those of the new realism of Ibsen and Strindberg, Hauptmann and Sudermann, or of George Bernard Shaw (whose first play, *Widowers' Houses*, was put on in 1892).

The American theatre, then, lagged behind that of the Continent, or even of England. In 1900 there was little indication that the United States would make important contributions to world theatre. There were, it is true, some signs of life in the early years of this century. The opening of the New Theatre in Chicago in 1906, and of a similarly named venture three years later in New York, marked a welcome though abortive attempt to encourage experimental drama. In 1905 George Pierce Baker was able to start the course in play-writing that later grew into the famous '47 Workshop' at Harvard. The poet–dramatist William Vaughn Moody was beginning, in *The Great Divide* (1906) and *The Faith Healer* (1909), to feel his way towards adult theatre. Though he died in 1910, something of his sensitive and intelligent approach was evident in two plays of that year. One, by his former pupil Josephine Peabody, was *The Piper*, a verse drama on the theme of the Pied Piper of Hamelin that was chosen from a large field for production at the new Stratford Memorial Theatre. The other, by Moody's friend Percy MacKaye, was *The Scarecrow*, a dramatization of Hawthorne's fantastic story 'Feathertop'.

But the awakening of the American theatre was not accomplished through poetic drama or through adaptations like MacKaye's. It was not enough merely to emphasize the role of the playwright: there had to be a decisive break with the formulaic conventions of the commercial theatre. By the start of the First World War, the necessary conditions for such a break were present. The Little Theatre movement had got under way; throughout America small groups of amateurs were eager to try out new plays, the shorter and simpler the better. In 1915 artists and writers who made up a summer colony on Cape Cod, Massachusetts, banded together to amuse themselves under the name of the Provincetown Players. Their first stage was the porch of a building. Next summer, the young playwright Eugene O'Neill (1888–1953) came to Provincetown and was soon one of the leaders of the group. The son of a successful actor of the old school, he knew the theatre from early childhood on. But he did not make it his livelihood until he had explored the world outside. He abandoned undergraduate life at Princeton for a spell of prospecting with a mining expedition in Honduras. Later, an enthusiasm for Conrad and Jack London whetted his appetite for adventure at sea. He shipped as a seaman to Buenos Aires; to South Africa and back to the Argentine; to New York, and from there on several voyages to England. There were intermittent illnesses, and periods of beachcombing, followed by experience as a newspaper reporter. In the winter of 1913–14 he wrote several plays, among them the one-act *Bound East for Cardiff*. Next, he joined G. P. Baker's 47 Workshop; and thence, via Greenwich Village, he reached Provincetown, where *Bound East* was performed in 1916, the first of a long run of work staged by the Players.

This was the beginning of a remarkable era in the American theatre.

New York was the centre of activity, though there was plenty of life in other places. The Provincetown Players maintained a little theatre in Greenwich Village, and were able to keep in existence during 1917–18, when the United States was at war. By 1920 they were sufficiently developed to stage some full-length plays in addition to the one-act pieces of the modest early days. Though audiences were far smaller than those of commercial theatres, they were enthusiastic ones. Free from box-office obligations, the Players could be as experimental as they liked. With them the playwright came into his own; for by 1925 they had produced no fewer than ninety-three plays by forty-seven different authors. The authors, nearly all American, included Edna Ferber and Edna St Vincent Millay.

Moreover, there were other theatre-groups in New York. The Washington Square Players had been formed in 1914, with similar experimental aims. Their run of one-act plays was interrupted by the war, but they reappeared in 1919 as the Theatre Guild. By 1925, they had prospered enough to build their own Guild Theatre; and here, before the Guild gradually became too conservative, there were many distinguished productions of American and European plays. It was they who performed Eugene O'Neill's *Marco Millions* (1928), *Mourning Becomes Electra* (1931), and *Ah, Wilderness!* (1933); and he had been one of the Guild's founding members. Some of his plays were also presented by the Neighborhood Playhouse, which was built and endowed for an amateur company in 1915, though after the war it was taken over by professionals.

Other large cities had kindred groups. None of these, of course, ousted the commercial theatre. Easily the most popular American play of the 1920s was *Abie's Irish Rose* (1924), which ran in New York for more than 2,500 performances. No play by O'Neill came anywhere near such commercial success. However, the small experimental theatres indirectly influenced Broadway, and their playwrights became known to a wide public. Few people troubled to remember that *Abie's Irish Rose* was the work of one Anne Nicholls; many had heard of O'Neill.

As the nation's first important playwright, he did a great deal to establish the modes of the modern theatre in the United States. His work illustrates some of the main trends in modern American drama. One striking feature is the combination of deliberately drab prose realism and of boldly inventive expressionist technique. It is as though Henrik Ibsen and Bertolt Brecht had come together in the same person. In a sense, they had. When O'Neill began to write, American drama still had to make for itself the discoveries that Ibsen had indicated a whole generation previously. Yet by the end of the war European drama was branching out into expressionist fantasies like Georg Kaiser's *Gas* and Karel Čapek's *R. U. R.* Eugene O'Neill and his colleagues telescoped the whole process into a few years; American drama caught up with Europe almost overnight.

The first necessity was to establish an Ibsen-like psychological and visual realism, in place of the theatricality that dominated the American theatre. Instead of elaborate drawing-room or scenic sets, O'Neill substituted (in such plays as *Bound East for Cardiff* and *The Moon of the Caribbees*) the deck or forecastle of a tramp steamer. Instead of complicated plots, full of coincidence and high-minded stubbornness, O'Neill offered a seaman dying unheroically in his bunk, or an unromantic debauch with native women and native liquor. Instead of stilted dialogue and melodramatic 'asides', O'Neill's rough characters spoke in the idiom of their situation. It was 'the gibberish of the vulgate' adapted to the theatre; and although O'Neill moved a long way on from *Bound East*, a late play like *The Iceman Cometh* (1946), set in a Bowery saloon, showed that his sense of common talk was one of his more permanent assets. His feeling for eloquent speech was never so sure; he said in a letter about his *Mourning Becomes Electra*,

It needed great language.... I haven't got that. And, by way of self-consolation, I don't think, from the evidence of all that is being written today, that great language is possible for anyone living in the discordant, broken, faithless rhythm of our time. The best one can do is to be pathetically eloquent by one's moving, dramatic inarticulations!

In consequence, most of his plays are disappointing to read. They are flat on the printed page, and at a casual glance the detailed stage directions – when they call for realistic settings – seem not very different from directions for the kind of play O'Neill's father had acted in.

But there are essential differences. O'Neill considered himself a serious playwright. His realism began as a fresh attitude to the possibilities of drama. So did his expressionist tendencies, which began to reveal themselves quite early. *The Moon of the Caribbees* (1918), for example, was gruffly matter-of-fact; yet the offstage native chanting foreshadowed more ambitious efforts on his part at expressionism. *Beyond the Horizon* (1920) was a realistic, or naturalistic, play; but *The Emperor Jones*, produced in the same year, brought Brecht into the picture along with Ibsen – although O'Neill says that when he wrote it he had never heard of expressionism. Tom-toms beat in the background, almost throughout the play; there are several sets intended not to be lifelike but to create a mood, and at the end of one scene 'the walls of the forest fold in'; the cast includes a group of 'Little Formless Fears' (each like a black 'grubworm about the size of a creeping child'), as well as a number of shadowy Negro figures, among whom Brutus Jones in his delirium of fear passes backwards in time to primeval Congo origins. Several subsequent plays employed expressionist devices. In *All God's Chillun Got Wings* (1924), O'Neill introduces the theme of black–white relationships with a contrasted street scene:

People pass, black and white, the Negroes frankly participants in the spirit of Spring, the whites laughing constrainedly, awkward in natural emotion. . . . From the street of the whites a high-pitched, nasal tenor sings the chorus of 'Only a Bird in a Gilded Cage'. On the street of the blacks a Negro strikes up the chorus of 'I Guess I'll Have to Telegraph My Baby'. As this singing ends, there is laughter, distinctive in quality, from both streets.

A Congo mask on the wall of a room has a special relevance; and the walls keep closing in, as in Poe's 'The Pit and the Pendulum', to heighten the oppressive emotions of the couple who live within them. In *The Great God Brown* (1926) the principal characters wear masks, which are removed from time to time and even transferred from one person (Dion Anthony: Dionysus and St Anthony warring in the same man) to another (Brown: a 'visionless demi-god of our new materialistic myth'). In *Lazarus Laughed* (1927) masked choruses represent seven stages of life and seven different types of person, each type clad in a distinctive colour, so that there are forty-nine combinations of 'period and type'. This play was beyond the scope of most little theatres. So was *Strange Interlude* (1928), a drama of Wagnerian length in which the inner thoughts of the characters (often at variance with their conversation) are exposed by means of asides. And in the trilogy *Mourning Becomes Electra*, another ambitious venture, O'Neill seeks an extra dimension of significance by retelling the Greek legend in American circumstances. The end of the Civil War is equated with the downfall of Troy; Agamemnon is recognizable as Brigadier Ezra Mannon, Clytemnestra as Mannon's wife Christine, their son Orin as Orestes, their daughter Lavinia as Electra, and so on. Their porticoed New England house is an appropriately classical setting; the local townsfolk serve as a chorus.

For twenty years O'Neill wrote with prodigal energy. There were naturalistic pieces such as *Anna Christie* (1921) and *Desire Under the Elms* (1924), and experimental efforts like *The Hairy Ape* (1922), *Marco Millions*

(1928) and *Dynamo* (1929). Several failed to please the public, and the success of others may have depended largely on the brilliant stagings that were a feature of the expressionist drama of the 1920s. After 1934 O'Neill retired to his study, and though he continued to write, no new play of his was performed until *The Iceman Cometh*, twelve years later. A year afterwards he wrote *A Moon for the Misbegotten*. But then O'Neill was faced by serious illness, which culminated in his death in 1953, and his final work did not reach the stage during his lifetime.

Taken as a whole, his plays grope for the deeper meanings that underlie 'the discordant, broken, faithless rhythm of our time'. O'Neill said he was not interested in the relation between man and man – the superficial material of the majority of plays – but 'in the relation between man and God'. By 'God' he appears to have meant various things. In general, he has been concerned with humanity's frustrated craving for fulfilment – the Sherwood Anderson query of 'What *for*?' His technical experiments show him trying to overcome not only the limits of prose language but also limitations of outlook. His plays are sometimes more earnest than profound, more complicated than subtle. The early pieces have a rough, earnest dignity. He was still capable of achieving a wonderful greyness and graininess, reminiscent of the texture of an enlarged photograph, in subsequent work, especially when he resorted to autobiography. *Long Day's Journey into Night*, written in 1940 and produced in 1956, is perhaps his masterpiece. It is a long, tormented, touching family story, quite devoid of expressionist chic. The members of the family, unmistakably drawn from his own life, have a terrible authenticity that enlarges them. Most of O'Neill's later plays, on the other hand, while effective in stagecraft, seem to deal with small people. In *Lazarus Laughed* he spoke of men as 'those haunted heroes'. But the majority of his characters are not heroic; haunted by Freudian and biological ghosts, they are caught in a universal grubbiness. There is no grandeur, for instance, in the characters of *The Great God Brown*, or in those of *Strange Interlude*. The ambitious *Mourning Becomes Electra* trilogy acquires a certain loftiness from its Greek overtones. But even here, as O'Neill himself felt, there is a deficiency. Though strong melodrama, it is not quite tragedy. Since such characters lack stature, their affirmations are not fully convincing. The laughter of Lazarus, or of the Negroes in *All God's Chillun*, rings a little false. Love, Life, and O'Neill's other synonyms for God seem perpetually out of reach, impossible aspirations on which to ring down the curtain.

Nevertheless there is greatness in O'Neill. He did more than any other man to transform the American theatre, and his influence spread throughout Europe. He was unquestionably the foremost American dramatist of his era. He has more weight, for instance, than such relatively orthodox and skilful playwrights as Sidney Howard, S. N. Behrman, and Philip Barry (all products of the 47 Workshop); or than Robert Sherwood, Moss Hart, and George S. Kaufman. Howard's *They Knew What They Wanted* (1924) and *The Silver Cord* (1926) deal tenderly and accurately with the problems of a young woman married by a trick to an old man, and of excessive maternalism. Behrman's *Biography* (1932) is a polished comedy of the repercussions when a popular, unconventional woman is persuaded to write her memoirs. Philip Barry (1896–1949), besides writing dextrous pieces for the commercial theatre, tried his hand at more difficult themes. His *Hotel Universe* (1930), a play about American expatriates and their involved affairs, has an elderly mystic whose importance for the other characters is akin to that of the psychoanalyst Harcourt O'Reilly in T. S. Eliot's *The Cocktail Party*. Barry's *Here Come the Clowns* (1938) is an ingenious allegory of right and wrong. As for Robert Sherwood (1896–1955), his *The Road to Rome* (1927) is a brittle comedy of Hannibal's invasion; *The Petrified Forest* (1935) is a well contrived, eventful play that is also equipped, or laden, with 'messages'; and *Idiot's Delight* (1936) pictures the scene in a European resort hotel after a war has broken out – the cast includes a pacifist and a wicked manufacturer of munitions. Hart and Kaufman collaborated successfully on such fast-moving comedies as *You Can't Take It With You* (1936) and *The Man Who Came to Dinner* (1939).

Several of these plays are better written than O'Neill's work, in that the dialogue is neater and more felicitous. Yet none has his intensity. A similar conclusion can be reached about other American expressionist performances of the 1920s, however exciting they seemed at the time. There was Elmer Rice's *The Adding Machine* (1923). As a mere youngster, Rice (1892–1967) had attracted attention nine years before with *On Trial*, a murder play that borrowed the motion-picture device of the flashback to tell its story. Subsequent plays, some of them performed by a New York group called the Morningside Players, were not particularly unusual. *The Adding Machine*, however, was manifestly experimental. Its principal 'character' is a characterless accountant, Mr Zero; some other characters are known by numbers only. Executed for the murder of his employer, he finds himself working an adding machine in the Elysian Fields, only to be returned to earth at the end of the play, to undergo another miserable cycle of existence, and then another and another, until he will eventually become the utterly soul-less slave of his machine.

Or there was John Howard Lawson's *Roger Bloomer*, produced in the same year as *The Adding Machine*, with a symbolic ballet and abstract settings. In 1925 Lawson (1895–1977) presented in *Processional* what he called a 'jazz symphony of American life'. Gilbert Seldes's *The Seven Lively Arts* (1924) had given a vivacious, sympathetic account of the movies, the comic strip, vaudeville, and other popular art-forms. Other intellectuals – E. E. Cummings and Edmund Wilson among them – shared Seldes's enthusiasm for these indigenous amusements. So did Lawson, whose *Processional* was a spectacular expressionist vaudeville, a 'variety' show with serious overtones, based upon the very notion of America's ethnic and ideological variety. Gifted stage designers like Robert Edmond Jones and Norman Bel Geddes did much to assist the impact of the modern drama.

Expressionist techniques did not die out with the 1920s but, like other aspects of the theatre, they were modified by the Depression years. Even more than the novel, American drama changed with the times. As in the novel, Freud yielded place to Marx. For the spiritual liberty of the individual, authors substituted the theme of economic injustice. Some American critics, in a penitentially anti-Communist frame of mind, seemed impelled in the Cold War aftermath to reject plays that had been formerly applauded, as 'tendentious', 'propagandist', and so on. Perhaps they are; yet we would be wrong to overlook their effectiveness, or to under-estimate the liveliness of American drama in the Roosevelt era. It did the orthodox theatre no harm to become concerned a little more closely with economic realities. Thus, Sidney Kingsley's *Dead End* (1935) owed its success in part to a spectacular setting that included a tank of water, representing New York's East River, into which urchins dived and re-emerged dripping wet. But this lavishness was given a point; Kingsley's intention is indicated by his epigraph from Tom Paine: 'The contrast of affluence and wretchedness is like dead and living bodies chained together.'

Such contrasts also offered excellent opportunities for satire. The theatre responded with some delightful productions: the musical play *Of Thee I Sing* (1931), by George and Ira Gershwin, and the revue *Pins and Needles* (1937), staged by the International Ladies Garment Workers Union and then sent on a nationwide tour, to enable all America to enjoy sharp and sprightly numbers like 'Sing Me a Song of Social Significance'. Maxwell Anderson's musical comedy *Knickerbocker Holiday* (1938) made fanciful fun of Washington Irving's old comic creation, Peter Stuyvesant, and was aided by Kurt Weill's bittersweet score.

Another consequence of the Depression was an increased interest in *American* dramatic material. This was evident in several ways. There was a general turning homewards. The novelist–playwright Thornton Wilder (1897–1975), for instance, had written during the 1920s of other places and epochs. He had then examined *The Bridge of San Luis Rey* (1927); he now looked at *Our Town* (1938), a charmingly relaxed 'experimental' play about 'Grover's Corners, New Hampshire' in the early years of this century. It begins without curtain or scenery; when the audience is seated, the stage manager enters, arranges bits of furniture, and finally introduces the play. There are interjections from actors planted in the auditorium; one asks, 'Is there no one in town aware of social injustice and industrial inequality?' – but it is clear that Thornton Wilder is not bothered by such questions. His small-town is, unlike Spoon River or Winesburg, a homely community, bathed in the warm light of retrospection. (*The Skin of Our Teeth*, 1942, with similar merits, suffers from a certain cosmic cuteness.)

Affection for America's regional corners was not entirely new. 'Folk drama' had grown up in the 1920s, and had had forerunners – Frank Murdoch's *Davy Crockett* (1872), to mention only one. The movement for folk drama, which was centred in college and little theatres, verged upon the artificial. Yeats or J. M. Synge could draw upon an ancient folk-heritage: America's was a patchy affair of yesterday. The Red Indians might be considered as the American *folk*; but they had been belatedly co-opted for the role, and could not properly fill it. When Frederick H. Koch founded the Dakota Playmakers at the University of North Dakota, in 1910, he did his best to extract material from that bare region. He found the task easier among the uplands of North Carolina, to whose university he transferred in 1918. His Carolina Playmakers consisted of students who performed plays specially written for them and produced by Professor Koch. As an undergraduate at North Carolina, Thomas Wolfe had first become interested in drama. The Playmakers' most successful author was Paul Green (1894–   ), a colleague of Koch who wrote plays about Negroes, planters and poor whites. The most famous, *In Abraham's Bosom* (1926), ends in a lynching: this regional movement was more avowedly. liberal than that of the Tennessee Agrarians.

Though the South had a richer folk-past than other areas, it had no monopoly of folk-drama. At Cornell University, Alexander Drummond accumulated a repertory of plays based on the history of New York State;

while Lynn Riggs (1899–1954) dealt with the white and Indian folk-ways of his native Oklahoma. His *Green Grow the Lilacs* (1931) formed the basis of the Rodgers and Hammerstein musical comedy *Oklahoma!* (1943). Riggs hoped 'to recapture in a kind of nostalgic glow' the atmosphere of 'the old folk songs and ballads'. But this atmosphere was undoubtedly strongest and most genuinely alive among black Americans, whether in the South or in New York's Harlem. In New York during the 1920s there was a succession of Negro plays (some under the auspices of the Ethiopian Art Players, formed in 1923) and of swift-paced, high-spirited black musicals like *Chocolate Dandies* and *From Dixie to Broadway* (both 1924). *The Green Pastures* (1930) by Marc Connelly (1890–1980) has been criticized as a folksy, white man's concoction of black religious sentiment. Even so, its all-black cast, its version of black colloquial speech and its Negro spirituals brought it close to a poeticized folk drama as Synge or García Lorca might have understood the term. DuBose and Dorothy Heyward's novel *Porgy* (1925) was also a white view of black life; but as dramatized by the Heywards it too made excellent theatre, and as a folk opera done by the Gershwin brothers, *Porgy and Bess* (1935) has been deservedly famous.

Negro productions were a notable feature of the dazzling though short-lived Federal Theatre, which, like the Federal Writers' Project, was an offshoot of the New Deal WPA, organized in 1935 to allay the effects of severe unemployment. While writers were engaged in compiling guide-books and folklore narratives, actors and producers and stage-hands and dramatists were rescued by the Federal Theatre. Under its auspices the abundantly gifted young producer Orson Welles staged his Negro *Macbeth* (1936), in a tropical Haitian setting, before leaving the project to found his own Mercury Theatre. The Chicago Theatre Project's black *Swing Mikado* (1939) was such a hit that in the same year the commercial stage imitated the idea in *Hot Mikado*. The efforts of the Federal Theatre were usually on a more modest scale. Its companies put on performances in every part of the United States, ranging from puppet shows and vaudeville to Shakespeare and Euripides. Sometimes they played to audiences who had never before seen a theatre show.

They staged miracle and morality plays; and they invented a technique – the 'Living Newspaper' – that combined the methods of radio features and documentary cinema in what could be regarded as modern morality plays. *Triple-A Plowed Under* tackled the woes of the farmer who could not find a market for his crops; *One-third of a Nation* commented bluntly on America's housing conditions. Other samples of the Living Newspaper were equally effective. But they were frankly hostile to American capitalism, and the Federal Theatre as a whole fell under suspicion as a collective enterprise wasting the taxpayer's money. After prolonged argument, its Congressional appropriation was ended in the summer of 1939, and this astonishing movement came to an abrupt end less than four years after it had been initiated.

The modern morality play, with God and the Devil supplanted by class warfare, flourished in the unmistakably Marxist productions of New York's Theatre Union, and in the Group Theatre that grew out of the Theatre Guild at the end of the 1920s. The Group Theatre discovered Clifford Odets (1906–63). His *Waiting for Lefty* and *Awake and Sing* (both produced in 1935, though the latter was an earlier work) established him as a passionately sincere author fully in sympathy with the Group Theatre's ideas of ensemble acting as they had learned them from Stanislavsky and the Moscow Art Theatre. A longish one-act piece, *Waiting for Lefty* is an almost perfect example of a proletarian morality play. The stage is the platform of a union meeting; there are violent speeches and noisy interjections; half a dozen simple episodes are interspersed to show the lives of the committee members, and how each came to be present. At this distance the propaganda seems crude, the notes for production doubly so: 'Do not hesitate to use music wherever possible. It is very valuable in emotionally stirring an audience.' But the play, in common with Odets's other best work, is curiously moving. The stage can stand more didacticism than the novel, provided that the handling is not stagy. Odets avoids staginess. And his principal weapon has nothing to do with propaganda. It is his sense of American talk. His dialogue crackles with life. His villainous capitalists now sound a little absurd; his working men do not: their words are – as Emerson said of their predecessors' speech – 'vascular and alive'. This mastery of the common idiom has been one of the main assets of the American theatre.

By contrast, experiments at verse drama have looked anaemic. Perhaps that is not the word to define Wallace Stevens's early *Carlos among the Candles* and *Three Travellers Watch a Sunrise* (produced in 1917 and 1920 respectively). But they could never be popular with a wide audience; they are poetry, but they are not drama. The word drama could be applied to the poetic plays of Maxwell Anderson. They are worthy efforts, yet even *Winterset* (1935), the most powerful, does not gain much from its verse. The verse plays of Archibald MacLeish (1892–1982), some of them for radio, were competent in construction and ambitious in intent. But the older ones sounded a shade tinny; while the more recent *JB* (1958) – based on the Biblical story of Job, and performed on Broadway with great acclaim – is hollow, despite the author's technical authority.

In retrospect, the richest era of the American theatre was perhaps that of 1945–60. O'Neill's last plays, written earlier, were now being performed. They were accompanied by the new work of America's two other major twentieth-century playwrights, Tennessee Williams and Arthur Miller. The period saw, too, an explosion of musical comedy (*On the Town*, 1944; *Carousel*, 1945; *Kiss Me, Kate*, 1948; *South Pacific*, 1949; *Guys and Dolls*, 1950; *The King and I*, 1951; *Candide*, 1956; *West Side Story*, 1957), most of them smash hits; the development of 'Method Acting', principally under the aegis of Lee Strasberg, who took over direction of the new Actors' Studio from Elia Kazan in 1949; the optimistic beginnings of 'Off-Broadway', in which inexpensive productions could assimilate to American circumstances the post-war European experimentation of Samuel Beckett, Eugène Ionesco and Jean Genet; the fast-paced humour and improvisations of Lenny Bruce, Mort Sahl, or Elaine May and Mike Nichols; the apparent durability of established playwrights like Odets (*The Big Knife*, 1948) and Lillian Hellman (*Toys in the Attic*, 1960); and the emergence of successful new ones such as William Inge (*Come Back Little Sheba*, 1950; *Picnic*, 1953; *Bus Stop*, 1955).

In all this hum of activity, the greatest excitement accompanied the first Broadway productions of Williams and Miller. Tennessee Williams (1911–83) had begun to write in the middle of the Depression, winning a Group Theatre award back in 1939, and enduring the ignominy of a Theatre Guild flop with his *Battle of Angels* (1940). Perhaps the desire to escape from earlier, unpropitious selves led the young man to drop his given names, Thomas Lanier, in favour of 'Tennessee', and to assume a more flatteringly precocious birth-year, 1914, instead of the real 1911.

Evasions of 'truth', undershot by the intimation that pretence may be preferable to 'real' existence, constituted a central theme in O'Neill's *The Iceman Cometh*; and in the Panglossian 'gosh isn't everything great?' mode of G. S. Kaufman's *You Can't Take It With You* (1936), or William Saroyan's *The Time of Your Life* (1939), which were rewarded with Pulitzer prizes. Williams's *The Glass Menagerie* (1945), in both exposing and sympathizing with the protective make-believe of psychically disabled people, offered his audiences half-naturalistic half-expressionist encounters. It had a shattering effect, for example, upon the aspiring playwright William Inge, who saw *Menagerie* on its pre-New York run and found it 'so deeply moving that I felt ... ashamed for having led so unproductive a life'. A Streetcar Named Desire (1947) confirmed Williams's ability to wring pathos from failures of interaction. In such settings voluble matrons nag timid offspring; callous or thuggish men shrug off the possibility of intimacy with women, for whom their appetite is temporary, their distaste permanent. In Williams, Southern romanticism figures as a debased gentility. His Southern belles, traditionally renowned for being ladylike, slip into promiscuity, or in middle age vainly seek suitors for unloved daughters. He extended and consolidated his anti-romantic domain with Cat on a Hot Tin Roof (1955) and The Night of the Iguana (1961), among a number of plays. Several were derived from his own short stories; several were turned into Hollywood movies, Baby Doll (1956) being indeed a film first and last. He was, among other things, an adept chooser of titles. As names like The Rose Tattoo and Sweet Bird of Youth suggested, he had a taste for a wistful-extravagant, semi-poetic rhetoric that could be admired by audiences as genuine poetry, or more sophisticatedly interpreted by them as exposing Southern claptrap. Thus Blanche DuBois, in A Streetcar Named Desire:

then the searchlight which had been turned on the world was turned off again and never for one moment since has there been any light that's stronger than this – kitchen – candle. . . .

Arthur Miller's apprenticeship, like that of Tennessee Williams, occupied a longish span of years. One of his plays 'bombed' on Broadway in 1944; Focus (1945), a novel about anti-Semitism, suggested that his future might lie in fiction rather than the theatre. He began to achieve fame in 1947, with the production of All My Sons, a doggedly accusatory, Ibsenite story of a dishonest wartime manufacturer, and the punishments that befall him.

In 1949, Miller's Death of a Salesman won popular and critical acclaim with its portrait of Willy Loman, ageing salesman whose sands have run out and who ends in suicide. 'Attention must be paid', says Miller of his forlorn, once glib protagonist, his nobody of an everyman. Death of a Salesman, in company with Williams's two most admired plays, has secured an unquestioned place in the nation's theatrical repertoire. A 1983 revival, with Dustin Hoffman in the Loman role initiated by Lee J. Cobb, differed in style yet gripped the audience as tightly as a generation earlier; and the play proved capable of casting a spell in societies as far removed as China. The Crucible (1953), Miller's parable of the McCarthyite anti-Communist 'witch hunt', a re-enactment of the Salem witch trials of

THE LITERATURE OF THE UNITED STATES

1692, also seems destined to join the canon of 'classic' American theatre. *A View from the Bridge* (1955) was likewise respectfully received, as evidence that Miller was a serious playwright seeking to bring out universal significances in local incidents. In *A View*, Eddy Carbone endeavours to exonerate himself from the neighbourhood accusations that he is an informer. 'Such a sealed fate', Miller announced by way of introduction to the play, 'cannot be accepted': Eddy dies heroically refusing to be prejudged, out of a social necessity which the author insists upon.

The Williams–Miller duo created drama that was stylized yet realistic, with 'strong' confrontations and climaxes, and some lyrical or angry declamation, and whose subject was little people assailed by circumstances which threatened to overwhelm them. Using 'theatre poetry' (stage effects) and an intermittently heightened dialogue, they inverted the cheerful pieties of the American Dream. Their heroes and heroines, rarely heroic in the old sense of exemplary, recognized distinction, usually went down to defeat. Such outcomes blended the radical gloom of the Depression with more complex psychological theories as to the sad lot of sexually or ethically misplaced persons, hard put to survive in the world of the Lonely Crowd and the Organization Man.

Miller and Williams were joined in the later 1950s by a third much-discussed playwright, Edward Albee (1928–   ), whose first, short plays, *The Zoo Story* (1958) and *The Sandbox* (1959), had their premières in Berlin. Terse, stylized, half surrealist in the approved new European manner, they led to the New York production of *The American Dream* (1961), which Albee described as 'a stand against the fiction that everything in this slipping land of ours is peachy-keen. Is the play offensive? I certainly hope so; it was my intention to offend – as well as amuse and entertain.' At the same period, in an imaginary dialogue *Fam and Yam*, between a Young American Playwright and a Famous American Playwright – a transition which Albee himself was in process of making – he commented with ironic detachment on the operations of the celebrity system.

Edward Albee's transition was complete with the Broadway success of *Who's Afraid of Virginia Woolf?* (1962), a long but tightly written squabble between a professor and his wife, who have a high, accurate, wounding disregard for one another. Albee explained his play thus: '*Who's Afraid of Virginia Woolf?* means "Who's Afraid of the Big, Bad Wolf?" means "Who's Afraid of living life without false illusions?"' – another essay, apparently in the genre of inverted optimism developed by O'Neill, Williams and

Miller. The critic Diana Trilling found significance in the names of the main characters of *Who's Afraid of Virginia Woolf?*: 'George' and 'Martha', she suggested, were grotesque latter-day simulacra of George and Martha Washington.[1] Some years later, in the bicentennial year 1976, Albee said this reading was correct; the play was 'an examination of whether or not we, as a society, have failed the principles of the American Revolution'.

By 1976 the United States was no longer in the forefront of world drama. In the next decade its reputation continued to decline. True, the leading dramatists were still at work (though Williams died in 1983). Agents were still booking blocks of seats for popular plays (those, say, of Neil Simon) and for hit musicals like *Annie* and *A Chorus Line*. But most of the admired authors (Harold Pinter, Tom Stoppard, Michael Frayn) were English; and so were spectaculars such as *Nicholas Nickleby* and *Cats* – a field once monopolized by American composers, librettists and directors.

What happened? A part of the explanation may lie in the shortcomings of American playwrights, in the face of social and commercial pressures that no doubt contributed to the suicide of Inge and the disintegration of Williams. As each became a *Fam*, author and public reciprocally posited a flow of masterpieces, each to be recognizably the work of the star author, yet to represent and advance upon his or her previous play, and in that respect a new departure. Williams varied his settings and his character types, in an almost dazzling sequence. But in the process, reaching towards Gothic horrors of incest, castration and cannibalism, he seemed increasingly close to self-parody – misfits about misfits, full of wispy dream sequences and obtrusive symbols. Arthur Miller produced less and stayed closer to the pattern of recapitulated worry he had used to such effect in *Death of a Salesman*. However, Miller's subsequent plays, such as *After the Fall* and *Incident at Vichy* (both 1964), suffered like Williams's from being either too obviously or too improbably motivated. Albee, with a greater verbal agility than Williams or Miller, also seemed to become trapped in a theatricality consisting (as in *Tiny Alice*, 1964) of unpleasant exchanges between improbable people. Highly intelligent, and prepared to risk genuinely new approaches (*Box–Mao–Box*, 1968), he faced the *Fam* fate of being typed as the creator of a single famous play, and rationed to one only – *Who's Afraid of Virginia Woolf?*

But why did the playwrights not rise to the opportunities that seemed

1. See her article in *Edward Albee*, ed. C. W. E. Bigsby (Englewood Cliffs, NJ, Prentice-Hall, 1975).

to be reanimating the European theatre? Critics claimed that once again, as in the nineteenth century, the play itself was subordinate to the techniques of acting and directing, of design, and lighting and sound effects. It could also be argued that such experimentation, with the stimulus it offered to adventurous new authors, was the only truly imaginative part of the American theatre world after the late 1950s. Where would it have been without Joseph Papp? This regally independent impresario began his Shakespearian Theatre workshop in 1952, in a disused church, opened an outdoor summer season of Shakespeare in 1956, and in 1967 expanded into the Public Theatre, with two stages, downtown in the Old Astor Library. Contemporary with Papp was the Living Theatre, founded by Julian Beck and the German-born Judith Malina, which devised productions of shocking detachment, like Jack Gelber's *The Connection* (1959), a play about heroin addicts waiting not for Lefty but for the arrival of a pusher bringing them their fix, and Kenneth H. Brown's *The Brig* (1963), a picture of licensed brutality in a military prison. New York engendered several other groups: the Caffe Cino, a coffee-house theatre, La Mama Experimental Theatre (notable for such work by Claude van Itallie as *America Hurrah!*), Joseph Chaikin's Open Theatre (1963), the Judson Poets' Theatre (started in a Baptist church in 1961), and the street performances of the Bread and Puppet Theatre, a Christian-Socialist collective inspired by the German artist-evangelist Peter Schumann.

This tally does not suggest that the New York theatre scene was moribund. Cheerful analyses add the trite reminder that Manhattan is not America. Drama companies have become established in cities including Minneapolis and Washington D.C.; campus productions, summer stock and other activities are widespread. In New York itself, one may marvel at the exuberance of the Off-Off-Broadway movement, causing little theatres to sprout along the East Side and in Greenwich Village and adjacent SoHo. Among the newer writers associated with the Off-Off-Broadway phenomenon are Ronald Ribman, Sam Shepard (starting with *Cowboys* in 1964 when he was only twenty-one), Lanford Wilson, David Rabe (who began with two 1971 plays about the Vietnam war), Megan Terry (*Viet Rock*, 1966) and Rosalyn Drexler.

Add the scarifying 'theatre of assault' productions of *Dutchman, The Toilet* and *The Slave* (all 1964), by LeRoi Jones (who renamed himself Imamu Amiri Baraka); the hit of 1959, Lorraine Hansberry's *A Raisin in the Sun*, set in the Chicago ghetto but much less disturbing to white audiences;

and another black play, James Baldwin's *Blues for Mister Charlie* (1964), in mood somewhere between LeRoi Jones's ferocity and Hansberry's family drama. Add to these manifestations efforts to secure plays from such distinguished literati as Saul Bellow (for instance, *The Last Analysis*, 1964; the hero is an old comedian, trying to rescue himself from nonentity by re-enacting his psychic history) and Robert Lowell (whose three verse plays *The Old Glory*, 1964, were based on Hawthorne's stories 'Endicott and the Red Cross' and 'My Kinsman, Major Molineux', and on Melville's novella 'Benito Cereno'). Make a sum of this diverse enterprise and it may seem peevish to complain of the decline of the American theatre.

On the pessimistic side, there is the disappointing evolution, or non-evolution, of both *Fams* and *Yams*. So many bright débuts fade into albums of newspaper clippings. So many techniques, professedly revolutionary, turn out to be essentially the same as before, or to impair the magic of the word. Much blame, for example, has been attached to the Method Studio for generating mannered stars instead of ensemble companies, and grandiosely fuzzy stuff ultimately destined for Broadway and Hollywood.

The relations between cinema and live theatre defy quick summary. Cinematic concepts may have been more beneficial than harmful for playwrights. Williams and Miller seemed at times equally at home with stage and with screen. Film versions of their plays and those of others, including *Long Day's Journey* and *Who's Afraid of Virginia Woolf?*, were often excellent. On the other hand, Hollywood lured away theatre talent: Robert Edmond Jones and Clifford Odets are two cases among many. The worst effects of Hollywood and Broadway for legitimate theatre were economic. Production costs, inflated too by restrictive union practices, soared in the 1940s and after. Producers and backers became increasingly reliant upon probable hits (top writers, top actors, top prices), including revivals, and more and more reluctant to risk an investment in unknown or unorthodox offerings. The Broadway theatre district gradually shrank, until half its old strongholds were dark. Success was fatal: the same paradox soon began to spoil Off-Broadway. Off-Broadway companies attempted to mount uncommercial productions on inexpensive premises. A number of these enterprises found favour with the public. Willy-nilly 'commercial', they transferred to Broadway; or Broadway giantism infected their approach. Another exodus became necessary, from Off-Broadway to Off-Off-Broadway: the very terms are revealing.

Yearning for the Great American Play, as people had once done for the Great American Novel, those keenly concerned with theatre missed the way, ending up frequently with mere bigness (of budget and ballyhoo) or with the so-called 'flop *d'estime*'. Frank Rich, in the *New York Times* 'arts and leisure' section, noted (19 February 1984) that only theatre critics were now discussing stage productions. Scholarly journals might talk about fiction, or about cinema, rarely about plays:

Even essayists who once examined new American plays (or wrote them) – writers like Susan Sontag, Elizabeth Hardwick, Gore Vidal or Mary McCarthy – have long since stopped caring. Perhaps the most extreme expression of this animus comes from the director and author Jonathan Miller, . . . in a recently published interview. Asked 'What importance does Broadway have to Theatre?' he replies: 'I don't think Broadway matters at all. . . . People don't go to Broadway to have serious theatrical experiences.'

Where else should they go? The answer was unclear. Out of town, occasionally – say to Chicago. Possibly Off-Off-Broadway. London? Certainly not television or radio, unless imported.

AMERICA AND THE WORD

REAGAN rhetoric of the mid-1980s boasted of a rebirth of American pride and primacy. The 1984 Olympic Games in Los Angeles appeared to Americans to justify the cry of 'We're No. 1!' The same claim could be made, to judge from the tally of Nobel awards, for American pre-eminence in the natural and social sciences.

In literature, however, the perception was rather of decline. The sag in the reputation of American theatre has been described in Chapter 16 above. Among the poets none seemed to excite both the *cognoscenti* and the general public. No figure was being named as on a par with the late Robert Lowell, except possibly John Ashbery; in the book supplements and little magazines, high praise was mainly reserved for *European* poets – Seamus Heaney, Philip Larkin, Ted Hughes, Zbigniew Herbert, or younger figures. Indeed except among people paid to expound and review 'literature', drama and poetry hardly came into the reckoning. For most people fiction and literature had become almost interchangeable terms. Yet in fiction too there was a sense of let-down, in the face of, say, Norman Mailer's *Ancient Evenings* or his *Tough Guys Don't Dance*, or of recent works by John Barth and Philip Roth. Ralph Ellison and James Baldwin, written about and interviewed, were otherwise almost silent. So was Thomas Pynchon – a cult figure but apparently not about to delight and mystify his following with any substantial new work. Kurt Vonnegut was usually referred to as an author past his peak. Richard Brautigan, another winsomely surrealistic 'fabulator', dropped away from the celebrity he had gained with *Trout-Fishing in America* (1967) and *In Watermelon Sugar* (1968), and committed suicide in 1984. Truman Capote, scrabbling to recover the *éclat* of earlier years, also died wretchedly in 1984. Several American critics discerned greater imaginative originality, and weight, in the novels of foreigners such as the Czech writer Milan Kundera, or the Latin-American 'El Boom' of Carlos Fuentes, Gabriel García Márquez and Mario Vargas Llosa. In literary criticism's newest reaches the inspiration, if that is the term, was largely French.

A comprehensively pessimistic interpretation might be that the whole

culture of the United States was in decline, whether moving 'from barbarism to decadence' or involved in some other dismal sequence. Could it be
that the U.S. was, to mix cultural and economic metaphor, a nationwide
'Rust Bowl' of literary or other products unable to compete with more
desirable designs from elsewhere? The writer George Steiner regards the
'death of language', the loss of beauty and precision in the use of words,
as a main symptom of cultural disintegration. Certainly there are plenty
of examples of verbal insensitivity in the America of the 1980s. Some could
be blamed upon the 'gobbledegook' of military or civilian bureaucrats,
with their propensity to add unnecessary words ('a rainstorm activity
situation'), or upon the euphemism and obfuscation resorted to by
'spokespersons' (whose children would in winter presumably build snow-
persons?), 'communicators' and 'information specialists'.

The whole society could be seen as in the grip of a disease of advanced
capitalism (galloping consumption, or consumerism), in which every
aspect of life including culture inevitably conformed to the pressures of
the market economy. Such is the thesis of Charles Newman, in a special
issue of the periodical *Salmagundi* ('The Post-Modern Aura', summer
1984). Budget considerations, says Newman, determine not only the
production of literature but its very forms and tones. Along these lines,
we may speculate that planned obsolescence is almost as evident in
culture, both avant-garde and popular, as in dress and interior decoration.
With each new year magazines manufacture lists of who and what is
supposedly 'in' and 'out' – for literature no less than for vogues in colour
shades or running shoes or items of cuisine. In literature, it could be
claimed, the only writings to escape the system are those too financially
insignificant to enter the reckoning, like figures to the right of the decimal
point.

Apart from such uncommercial offerings it might appear, as George
Steiner argued in a previous issue of *Salmagundi*, that American literature
had reached the level of mere merchandise, being virtually unaffected by
the historic inhibitions that serve to sustain cultural endeavour in other
societies. Undoubtedly there were causes for concern. Back in 1820 the
Rev. Sydney Smith gave offence by asking, 'Who in the four corners of the
world reads an American book?' The late twentieth century might ruefully
paraphrase the question as: 'Who in the four corners of the United States
reads an American book?' Perhaps, it was suggested, more people were
writing books than were reading them. Many Americans of the 1980s
apparently did not in effect read books at all, once liberated from the

compulsions of school. Fewer new titles were published annually in the United States than in Britain, France or Germany. Good bookshops, especially second-hand ones, were increasingly rare, even in large cities. As an industry, publishing was unstable; its houses collapsed, merged, were swallowed up by conglomerates; profits depended more and more upon 'tie-ins' such as movie rights and television mini-series.

What status could the printed word retain against such battalions, with their commodity imperatives? The dominance of the 'media' is conveyed in a language glossary provided by David Marc (*Demographic Vistas: Television in American Culture*, 1984) – a detached analysis, by the way, not a diatribe. In TV vocabulary, any home with a set in working order was a *HUT* ('household using TV' – over 98 per cent of American homes). *MOR* ('middle of the road') referred to successful compromises in entertainment. *F & Q Scores* were said to be basic assessments for casting and salary (*F* being the performer's 'familiarity' rating, and *Q* his or her 'love' or popularity score). Talk of the *Entropy Curve* revealed the industry's awareness that any series would gradually suffer from decay: hence *Series Maintenance Studies*, designed to stave off collapse as long as possible. Another grandiose term, *Cosmology*, covers the entire 'teletext' of a TV show, including spin-offs or shows derived from the master-series.

In the balance-sheet universe authors themselves, on all levels, were products to be packaged and promoted with regard to their audience or market, and their estimated shelf-life. The costs of merchandising thereby continued to increase, and so too the sales-number of copies required to recover the original investment. There were spectacular successes, it is true; everyone knew of the prime instances, such as the nearly $2 million paid in a paperback auction for the rights to E. L. Doctorow's novel *Ragtime* (1975). There was the sudden bonanza for William Kennedy (1928–   ), with the appearance of *Ironweed* (1983), the third volume of a fiction trilogy set in Albany, New York, during the 1930s (the previous two volumes were *Legs* and *Billy Phelan's Greatest Game*). After years without fame or fortune, Kennedy all at once had both: book prizes, film contracts, foundation grants. A similar glory came to Elmore Leonard (1925–   ), who had been publishing without renown for several years before the appearance of his novel *Glitz* (1985).

For a disenchanted observer, these examples simply reinforced the argument that publishing was a business, calculating and yet often incompetent like most others – and like most others, torn between the need to play safe and the desire to gamble on novelty. A handful of famous and therefore safely accredited authors dominated the book clubs, review pages, display windows and bestseller lists. Their prominence was in a sense achieved at the expense of the general ruck of authors, whose volumes of fiction or verse or scholarship went almost unnoticed, and within a couple of years were being disposed of as cut-price 'remainders'. William Kennedy and Elmore Leonard no doubt deserved the recognition belatedly accorded them. But the delay cast doubt on the whole selection process; and the rewards seemed as irrational as the previous neglect. The gap between haves and have-nots was as wide as ever.

Not only did discussion of established authors monopolize the review columns: reviewers tended to be lavish in praise. An example from outside fiction was *The March of Folly* (1984), by Barbara Tuchman. This study was distinctly inferior to other admirable historical works by her. No matter: old reputation and promotional momentum carried the book up the charts and on to the literati's coffee-tables.

A possible consequence of all-or-nothing literary *éclat* was the seeming anxiety of authors to produce 'big' books: blockbusters in length, and often portentously apocalyptic in approach. True, Barbara Tuchman's *March of Folly* was not a mammoth in wordage, but it took in nearly the whole span of human history, viewing the record of governmental error with Olympian severity. 'Big' novels by well-regarded writers similarly seemed to aim at 'serious spectacle', indeed at literary catastrophism. Mailer's *Ancient Evenings* bore a prodigious self-inflicted burden of significance. So did two more evidently appealing novels: William Styron's *Sophie's Choice* (1979) and John Irving's *Hotel New Hampshire* (1981), both of which encompassed the 'important' topic for late-twentieth-century authors of concentration camps and mass slaughter.

Various non-economic explanations were also put forward for the apparent decline in American literature. One was that academe and the old avant-garde were to blame for the slump in 'high culture'. Too many authors were on campus payrolls, it was said, and therefore tempted (like John Barth, and W. H. Gass, and perhaps Joyce Carol Oates) to become word-spinningly precious. Others, the 'tarmac professors', were travelling pundits, in a milieu hardly less hermetic. As for literary scholarship, Yale and other powerful centres were accused of having committed themselves to narcissistic exercises in deconstruction and post-structuralism, which were of no interest to the reading public (to the extent that that abstraction remained in being at all), and which raised the problem of why one should listen to university teachers. If interpretation was subjective, relative, and never definitive, why not do the job oneself, like a home-handyman with a do-it-yourself kit?

Is the Great Republic past its peak? That might be a verdict, with supporting material from *Salmagundi*, or from the fiftieth anniversary number of *Partisan Review*, in which a large number of intellectuals sought to make sense of the world since the era of Franklin Roosevelt and Adolf Hitler. We might wonder what kind of cultural values existed for, say, a 1980s executive employed in a satellite-communications firm. His job was to rent out to clients segments of 'real time', or else of 'real real time'. He would probably pride himself on getting home early enough to share 'quality time' with his children, and would then watch a 'prime time' television programme with his spouse. Did any profound emotions stir in the breast (to pick another figure of the epoch) of a presidential appointee in Washington, D.C., whose talk was of 'facilities', and 'capabilities', and for whom 'opportunism' was only a quick way to express 'readiness to seize an opportunity', rather than (in its old meaning) a type of shoddy moral conduct?

Unrelieved pessimism about America – the blaming or piacular mode, in the vocabulary of the sociologist Durkheim – misses out much. One salutary reflection is that, while things may conceivably be getting worse, they are not doing so unprecedentedly. According to a 1970s joke, the decline in American integrity could be measured in the gap between George Washington, who could not tell a lie, and Richard Nixon, who could not tell the truth (or who, in an alternative version, could not tell the difference). But this joke was current a hundred years earlier, during the Grant administration of the 1870s; and perhaps it went even further back. Ultra-Federalists in Jeffersonian America spoke as though the country were irrecoverably ruined; to one of them, the New Englander Fisher Ames, democracy was 'an illuminated hell' (a nice anticipatory description of Times Square in Manhattan?). Edgar Allan Poe, reviewing a verse satire called *The Quacks of Helicon* in 1841, complained of 'the universal corruption and rigmarole amid which we gasp for breath', with special reference to the cliques and 'puffery' of American literary culture. Walt Whitman's *Democratic Vistas*, a prose jeremiad published in 1871, argued that

our New World Democracy, however great a success in ... materialistic development ... and in a certain highly-deceptive superficial popular intellectuality, is, so far, an almost complete failure in ... really grand religious, moral, literary, and esthetic results.... It is as if we were somehow being endowed with a vast and more and more thoroughly appointed body, and then left with little or no soul.

Not only Poe and Whitman, but Hawthorne, Melville and Henry James pondered their inability to win popularity. Their writings were surely not talentless: could it be that they were too *good* for the audience? In James's novel *The Bostonians* (1886; ch. 33), the hero Basil Ransom is made to reflect upon current literary standards: on, for example, the sort of article 'for which there was more and more demand – fluent, pretty, third-rate palaver, conscious or unconscious, perfected humbug; the stupid, gregarious, gullible public, the enlightened democracy of his native land, could swallow unlimited draughts of it'.[1]

Old as well as modern American authors have tended also to suspect their publishers of incompetence and malpractice. Hawthorne's outspoken sister-in-law Elizabeth Palmer Peabody (regarded by some as a model for Miss Birdseye, in *The Bostonians*) convinced herself that the Boston firm of Ticknor and Fields had short-changed the novelist.

As for the twentieth century, its early bestseller lists look as market-oriented as those of the 1980s. The non-fiction favourites of the 1920s were largely devoted, like those of today, to food and self-help. Hemingway, Fitzgerald and Faulkner never appeared during the inter-war years high up on the lists, if on them at all. In other words, breast-beating about any supposedly new or permanent American decline usually runs to unhistorical excess.

More positively, it is possible to argue that such lamentations rest upon a restrictive definition of literature as 'classic'. Several decades ago Van Wyck Brooks popularized the 'highbrow'–'lowbrow' distinction, maintaining that within the United States the former was unduly fastidious and the latter unduly crude. But American exponents of 'high culture' have long been uncomfortable with the notion of exclusiveness. What Gilbert Seldes called *The Seven Lively Arts* (1924) – jazz, vaudeville, film comedy, strip-cartoons and so on – delighted intellectuals such as Seldes's friend Edmund Wilson. Seldes was himself a sophisticate; he wrote his book on the Île St Louis in Paris. Critics go astray, said Seldes, when they make false comparisons: thus, if they argue that 'in literature the taste of

---

1. The novelist's philosopher brother William James was concerned too. Trying to praise Henry's new novel *The Tragic Muse* (in a letter of 26 June 1890), William wrote: 'As for the question of the size of your public, I tremble. The work is too refined, too elaborate and minute ... to appeal to any but the select few.'

Europe is far beyond ours, on the ground that Harold Bell Wright [author of *The Winning of Barbara Worth*, 1911, and other bestsellers] is the typical American author and Conrad and Anatole France and Tolstoy the typical European. I mean that this is possible if a critic has never heard of the work of Nat Gould and William Le Queux in England, for instance.'

Leslie Fiedler (1917–   ), an appreciative interpreter of the current scene, argued in *What Was Literature?* (1982), and in previous works, that 'high culture' was a patronizing and deadening conception. To him, as to the French 'literary anthropologist' Roland Barthes, popular culture is a revealing part of its society and it deserves close attention. Modernism's great figures – James Joyce, Ezra Pound, T. S. Eliot, Thomas Mann – were in this light members of a privileged caste, even if they appeared to be rebelling against some previous canon. They were in several senses bookish, and ideal for exegesis by professional scholars; high culture was for the highly cultured, and called into being its own high priesthood. Fiedler – amiably conceding that it had taken him a while to arrive at this point – would now wish to open up the canon, moving from criticism's traditional concern with ethics and aesthetics to *ekstasis* or 'ecstatics'. He would ask why certain books dismissed as 'mere' bestsellers – Harriet Beecher Stowe's *Uncle Tom's Cabin* (1852) or Margaret Mitchell's *Gone With the Wind* (1936) – continue to grip the imagination, when other popular works drop out of sight. The aim would be to understand the work, and its place in the collective cultural myth, not to assess it severely as being far down on some orthodox order of merit.

Fiedler's impatience with established modernism is obviously attuned to the mood of the late twentieth century. For a variety of reasons, scholars began to be fascinated by hectically 'bad' authors, such as Mason Locke Weems (1759–1825), book-peddler and biographer of George Washington, and the Philadelphia melodramatist George Lippard (1822–54). There was a revival or emergence of interest, as earlier chapters indicate, in fiction and poetry by women and by non-white authors. The trend did not, it should be said, appear to be overturning traditional assessments: a 1983 poll, conducted among literary historians and critics, placed Twain and Whitman first equal in a greatest-writer ranking, closely followed by Hawthorne, Emerson and Melville. T. S. Eliot beat out Ernest Hemingway for tenth place. There were two women on the list of twenty-one authors (Emily Dickinson at no. 10, Harriet Beecher Stowe at 15) and no black authors.

But then, the sample was small, the respondents senior, and writers had to be dead to be eligible. Any survey of twentieth-century American literature aiming at comprehensiveness would be bound to emphasize genres not easily classifiable as highbrow or lowbrow, though certainly popular with a mixed readership. These categories would include humour, crime and detection, fantasy and science fiction. In themselves they are of course not new. Twain and his predecessors established fairly distinctive forms of American humour more than a century ago. Poe is invariably cited as a founder of detective fiction. The fascination with violent crime and subsequent punishment goes back still further. Poe, Twain and others, European and American, are likewise placed in the lineage of writers intrigued by the supernatural and the grotesque.

However, all such genres remained very much alive, and strengthened the contention of Fiedler that, for a large area of literature, the division between venerated 'classic' and brushed-aside 'popular' work was extremely hard to define. Perhaps it was not altogether meaningless. After all, Seldes seemed to exclude Harold Bell Wright from his notion of desirable popular culture. Not every bestseller, it appeared, was 'lively' or worthy of respect.

Thus, in the field of humour there was a great deal of standardized 'sitcom' (situation comedy), 'one-liner' gag-writing and the like, emanating from Hollywood and TV rather than from the printed page. But even here the frontiers were blurred. Woody Allen's films were far better known than his books, but not necessarily superior. His acute sense of claptrap, however presented, belonged to a friskily alert tradition of parody, pastiche and wordplay, demonstrated by such older masters as S. J. Perelman, Peter De Vries and Russell Baker, and in newer authors: the mockery, for instance, of Prudence Crowther and Veronica Geng, and the amiable folkish wit of Garrison Keillor, Calvin Trillin and Roy Blount, Jr. All in one way or another demonstrate the 'discriminating irreverence' that Mark Twain once extolled (apropos of American journalism) as 'the creator and protector of human liberty', in contradistinction to the humourless deference that accompanied 'all forms of human slavery, bodily and mental'.

Not all these humorists reached a wide audience. But they were not obscure either: several wrote under the prosperous auspices of the *New Yorker*. However, crime and fantasy were represented by a number of American authors both widely and highly admired: or so one might judge from bestseller lists and from the well-thumbed paperbacks on offer in second-hand bookstores and at neighbourhood yard or garage sales.

Among admirably proficient crime and mystery writers, for example, were Ross Macdonald (a pseudonym for the Canadian-born Kenneth Millar); George V. Higgins, whose first book was *The Friends of Eddie Coyle* (1971); Amanda Cross (pseudonym of Carolyn G. Heilbrun, a New York professor of literature); and – with his new-found fame – Elmore Leonard. Behind them lay the increasingly formidable aegis of Dashiell Hammett (1894– 1961) and Raymond Chandler (1888–1959), the creators of 'hard-boiled' detective fiction. Not only did the stories and novels of Hammett and Chandler grow stronger with the years (a rough-and-ready gauge of 'classic' status): somehow they fused with their filmed versions. Each reinforced the other. Hammett's book *The Maltese Falcon* (1930) became yet more powerful when in due course its characters reappeared on the screen as Humphrey Bogart, Sidney Greenstreet and Peter Lorre. In a multitude of ways, that is, post-modernist literature defied conventional categorization. The cinema was for almost all levels of audience of at least equal importance to the printed word. In some senses it was the successor-enemy, killing off the appetite for books and periodicals. Indeed it was also arguably hastening the death of the theatre. A film critic, David Denby, put the point with scathing candour ('Theaterphobia: A Moviegoer on Broadway', *The Atlantic*, January 1985), having suffered through a season of Manhattan stage offerings. On the other hand, 'legitimate' theatre itself, as instanced by the plays of Sam Shepard and David Mamet, assimilated some of the fluid shifts and dissolves of cinema; and so did fiction. The screen was both supplanter and revivifier of stage and page.

Horror, the supernatural and the fantastic were likewise displayed both in print and on the television or cinema screen. The popular serials known as 'soap operas' were joined by 'space opera'. *Star Trek*, *Star Wars* and *2001* were – given their considerable variation – broadly congruous with a great range of published fables. In the international field of science fiction the American pioneers had included Hugo Gernsback (1884–1967), who began in 1926 to promote 'scientifiction' through the periodical *Amazing Stories*. *Astounding Stories* (1937; altered in 1960 to *Analog*) was another outlet, featuring, for instance, the fiction of Robert A. Heinlein (1907–   ), author of *The Moon is a Harsh Mistress* (1967).

The satirical possibilities of 'Sci-Fi' were demonstrated in *The Space Merchants* (1953), by Frederick Pohl and Cyril Kornbluth, which portrayed a solar system controlled by advertising agencies and dedicated to their hucksterish creeds. Linguistic as well as spatial explorations were the feature of *Babel-17*, *Dhalgren* and other novels by Samuel R. Delany, down to *Stars in My Pocket Like Grains of Sand* (1985). Ursula LeGuin used outer space, notably in *The Left Hand of Darkness* and *The Dispossessed* (both 1974), as a setting in which to make plausible an anthropology of alternative, basically 'human' societies. Philip K. Dick (1928–82) produced a variety of hypothesized worlds, some of them set in a counterfactual terrestrial future, as in *Do Androids Dream of Electric Sheep?*, or *The Man in the High Castle* (1962), which pictured a United States defeated in the Second World War, its West coast subsequently under Japanese occupation and its East under German rule.

'Counterfactual' writing – fiction about alterations in the known record of the past, sometimes with reference to an altered *future* – has a peculiar fascination for our age, as confidence in absolutes, verifiabilities and happy outcomes ebbs away. Gore Vidal (1925–   ) has been a resourceful experimenter, in fictive historical novels – *Burr* (1973), *Lincoln* (1984) – and with greater audacity in fantastic visions such as *Duluth* (1983), an American nightmare not improbably remote in time or space or ethos. Another author, Russell Hoban (1925–   ), expatriated in England, might come to be regarded as an American master of magic and apocalypse. Earlier fantasies by Hoban (*The Lion of Boaz-Jachin and Jachin-Boaz*, 1973; *Kleinzeit*, 1974, perhaps the only novel to make London's Underground railway a principal character) developed into *Riddley Walker* (1980), his extraordinary evocation of post-nuclear England whose inhabitants speak a garbled tongue that the reader gradually learns to understand and almost to adopt. Hoban is an American *and* an English writer, embodying a heritage of American grotesque and English whimsicality: a merger, say, of *Connecticut Yankee* and *News from Nowhere*, or of Ambrose Bierce and Richard Jefferies.

The vogue for 'counterfactual' fiction (of which E. L. Doctorow's *Ragtime* was also an example) had several possible implications. One was that 'truth' was unfindable, and probably non-existent. Evidence, values, standards, were contingent and subjective. Fiction and fact were not widely separated: hence Norman Mailer's coinages 'faction' and 'factoid', to describe the interpenetration between reporting and inventing, between the 'I'-narrator as the author and some imagined surrogate character.

Again, perhaps there was no longer any point in trying to follow the formulae of the past. The novelist Diane Johnson (1934–   ), discussing such other novelists as Don DeLillo (*White Noise*, 1984) and Jay McInerney (*Bright Lights, Big City*) in the *New York Review of Books* (14 March, 1985), speculates that it may now be almost impossible to produce novels in the distinguished old tradition 'from Gulliver to Greene', when there were 'novels of the person' in society or the universe, 'making his or her way, and making judgments on it'. Post-modern stories tend to be extravagantly conjectural and conspiratorial. Have old terms like 'poetic licence' lost their meaning? Reality itself, or our conception of it, seems crazily unreal; so why bother with the old subterfuges of supposedly lifelike storytelling? Why not 'stories', such as those of Raymond Carver, or Donald Barthelme or Frederick Barthelme, that dispense almost entirely with 'plot', 'viewpoint', 'moral' and the like? Why not cease to pretend that there is any 'canon' at all – or, at least, any hierarchy of literary types?

In the past, for example, pornography was either deplored or ignored in polite circles. If mentioned at all in print by Anglo-Americans, the scandalous work was usually described as dangerously *foreign* matter. Disraeli alludes somewhere to an Englishwoman who 'guanoed [that is, soiled] her mind by reading French novels'. For Americans, Europe was regarded as the home of the dirty book, and Paris the world capital of depravity. The first American works to challenge this dominance – Henry Miller's *Tropic of Cancer* (1934) and *Black Spring* (1936), Vladimir Nabokov's *Lolita* (1955), Terry Southern's *Candy* (1955) – were fittingly enough first published in Paris, and only after some delay re-published in the United States. *Tropic of Cancer*, for instance, did not come out in Miller's own country until 1961. By then the genteel tradition was beginning to recede from the nation's collective memory. Permissiveness in print, and soon in the cinema, was assumed by initially scandalous works – William Burroughs's *The Naked Lunch* (1959), John Rechy's *City of Night* (1963), Gore Vidal's *Myra Breçkinridge* (1968), John Updike's *Couples* (1968), *Portnoy's Complaint* (1969) by Philip Roth – in which homosexuality, transvestism, extramarital encounters and obsessive masturbation were treated with unabashed comical explicitness. The 'free speech' movement of the 1960s sometimes in practice signalized a 'filthy speech' movement – the right to give public utterance to America's rich vocabulary, ghetto-inspired in part, of obscene insult. Whatever law-and-order backlash was generated by conservative outrage at the campus rebellions of the Vietnam era, the reaction did not in the 1980s have any marked effect upon cultural codes: they continued to resist or elude censorship.

Did this mean that, for good or ill, the conventions of American literature were utterly changed from what had previously (and fairly recently) obtained? Big changes had unmistakably taken place. One feature re-marked on by the critic Jonathan Yardley (*Washington Post*, 16 May

1983), was that every current author whose 'serious' fiction he admired happened to be a woman:

When the American Book Awards were handed out last month, all three fiction prizes went to women (two of whom, incidentally, are black) and so did the award for biography; this was not a gesture in the direction of feminism, but an accurate representation of the state of American letters.

Their prominence, even at the 'serious' level, was not entirely unprecedented. Edith Wharton, Willa Cather, Flannery O'Connor and Eudora Welty were famously active over the previous eighty years. A sensible if unexciting conclusion may be that much was altered, and that the *perception* of drastic change was marked; but that certain needs and demands seemed permanent. Commercialism, as we have seen, had deep roots. So, perhaps, with contrary yearnings for uplifting tales, for felicity of language, for heroes and heroines capable of exhibiting the 'grace under pressure' of Hemingway's definition of courage. The appetite for rousing adventure was apparently as strong as ever, and for sympathetic biographies, whether of writers or of public figures. Recent well-received lives of Twain, Hemingway and Robert Lowell, of Andrew Jackson and Abraham Lincoln, Theodore Roosevelt, Walter Lippmann and Lyndon B. Johnson, were not uncritical. They revealed flaws and failures, and the decade's appetite for impropriety and for psychological interpretation. Yet they differed from the debunking exercises of the 1920s. The new biographies tended to be comprehensively large; the importance of their subjects was suggested by the very weight of investigative attention that had been paid. Here, they seemed to testify, was a person who *counted* in the sum of things.

Such testimony was also sometimes a tribute to celebrity and power, and therefore not free from the pressures of the marketplace. Indeed, not surprisingly, the American ethos affected every kind of work, no matter what its provenance. A good many first novels and stories were put together with remarkable proficiency and sophistication – benefiting in a number of instances from creative writing workshops. One instance was *Stones for Ibarra*, by Harriet Doerr (1910–   ), winner of the 1984 American Book Award; this first novel was nurtured within the Graduate Fiction programme at Stanford University. Jefferson Morley, speaking of the elegant 'significance' conveyed by a novelist like Bobbie Ann Mason (1940–   ), remarked that 'when a Bobbie Ann Mason character opens the refrigerator and sees a ham, it is bathed in the soft florescent glow of the Iowa Writers' Workshop, and we're supposed to hear the bell of Meaning go ting-a-ling'.

There was too a certain sameness within each shift of the *Zeitgeist*. At one moment a dozen impressive talents were devoted to 'metafiction' or 'irrealism' (terms demonstrated in Joe David Bellamy's anthology *Superfiction*, 1975). A few years later, less fantasized narratives seemed to prevail, whether in fiction or the 'new art of personal reportage' presented by Norman Sims in another selection (*The Literary Journalists*, 1984), of pieces by John McPhee, Joan Didion, Tom Wolfe, Tracy Kidder and others.

Poetry too appeared responsive (self-consciously, unconsciously? both, if that is possible) to some sense of the century's lateness. Each guide to the 'contemporary' dated itself with dismaying rapidity, even though the individual poets surveyed there might be serious, gifted and versatile. The Knopf Poetry series of the 1980s included no work by established writers of middle years (David Wagoner, Carolyn Kizer, Anthony Hecht, John Hollander), although the featured poets (Marilyn Hacker, Mary Joe Salter, Brad Leithauser, Amy Clampitt and a dozen more) were not palpably in revolt against previous modes. Amy Clampitt's two volumes (*The Kingfisher*, 1983; *What the Light Was Like*, 1985) acknowledged a deep indebtedness to predecessors, including Keats, along with a sort of 1980s blue-jeans personalism.

Obviously enough, no simple generalization will cover all aspects of literature in present-day America. One can identify American writing of the 1980s without necessarily being able to explain why its tone separates it from that of other countries, or from statements made by Americans a mere twenty years ago. There is perhaps a general American twentieth-century awareness, pragmatic-irreverent-perturbed, of being both free and lost – of entering a world in which (Santayana said in *The Genteel Tradition*, 1911) 'nothing will have been disproved, but everything will have been abandoned'. The national culture tends as a result to oscillate between exhilaration and dismay: to be unsure whether, spiritually speaking, it is prosperity or the great crash that lies just around the corner.

FURTHER READING

(UP stands for University Press. Two-letter abbreviations have been used for American states: MA for Massachusetts, CT for Connecticut, NC for North Carolina, and so on, in keeping with the new convention. In most cases only one place of publication is given, though many publishers in the United States have a London office. The date of publication is that of the first edition, though significant later editions are also noticed. Since books now go in and out of print with dismaying rapidity, no attempt has been made to incorporate references to paperback editions. The different versions of a book can be checked from *Books in Print*, available at libraries and some bookshops.)

GENERAL WORKS

(a) PERIODICALS

The following scholarly magazines and yearbooks are particularly useful for American literature, sometimes within the broader context of American Studies: *American Literary Realism*, *American Literature*, *American Quarterly*, *American Studies International*, *Early American Literature*, *[Jahrbuch für] Amerikastudien* (German), *Journal of American Studies* (British), *New England Quarterly*, *Nineteenth-Century Fiction*, *Studi Americani* (Italian). A number of volumes of essays have been produced under the auspices of the European Association of American Studies and the Netherlands Association of American Studies, most of them ed. Rob Kroes.

(b) REFERENCE AND BIBLIOGRAPHIES

Of the periodicals listed above, *American Quarterly* and *American Studies International* devote considerable space to bibliographies. Some of those in *ASI* have been collected, ed. Robert H. Walker. *ASI* bibliographies include, for instance, Grant Webster on literary criticism (vol. 20, no. 1, Autumn 1981); Louis D. Rubin on Southern literature (vol. 21, no. 2, April 1983); Charles A. Carpenter on American drama (vol. 21, no. 5, October 1983); and Richard M. Cook and Richard Ruland on American literature, 1910–30 (vol. 22, no. 1, April 1984).

There are good introductions and booklists in Dennis Welland, ed., *The United States: A Companion to American Studies* (London, Methuen, 1974; revised edn.

1977), and in Malcolm Bradbury and Howard Temperley, eds., *Introduction to American Studies* (London, Longman, 1981). The most compendiously helpful bibliographical and descriptive books are Clarence Gohdes and Sanford E. Marovitz, *Bibliographical Guide to the Study of the Literature of the U.S.A.* (Durham, NC, Duke UP, 1959; 5th revised edn., 1984), and James D. Hart, *Oxford Companion to American Literature* (NY, Oxford UP, 1941; 5th edn., 1983). See also the *Cambridge Handbook of American Literature* (1986), produced by the American Culture centre of Columbia University. There are several valuable Goldentree bibliographies, under the general editorship of O. B. Hardison, Jr. (published successively by Meredith, Appleton-Century-Crofts, and Harlan Davidson): e.g., C. Hugh Holman, comp., *The American Novel through Henry James* (1966) and Harry H. Clark, *American Literature: Poe through Garland* (1971). Among other important guides are Lewis Leary's *American Literature: A Study and Research Guide* (NY, St Martin's Press, 1976), and his three vols. (1954, 1970, 1979) covering *Articles on American Literature, 1900–1975* (Durham, NC, Duke UP); Robert A. Rees and Earl N. Harbert, eds., *Fifteen American Authors Before 1900: Bibliographic Essays on Research and Criticism* (Madison, U of Wisconsin P, 1971); and James E. Woodress, ed., *Eight American Authors: A Review of Research and Criticism* (NY, Norton, 1963; revised edn., 1971).

There is compact information in Malcolm Bradbury, Eric Mottram and Jean Franco, eds., *The Penguin Companion to Literature: American and Latin-American* (Harmondsworth, 1971), and in Louis D. Rubin's *Bibliographical Guide to the Study of Southern Literature* (Baton Rouge, LA, Louisiana State UP, 1969).

The bibliographical volume of Robert E. Spiller, ed., *Literary History of the United States* (NY, Macmillan, 1948; 4th edn., 2 vols., 1974) is important. Among other valuable reference collections are the *Dictionary of Literary Biography* (Detroit, MI, Gale Research Co., 1978–   ), which by 1985 totalled more than 30 vols., most of them covering American material (e.g. vol. 30, *American Historians, 1607–1865*, 1984; vol. 31, *American Colonial Writers, 1735–1781*, 1984). The series also includes Afro-American fiction writers and dramatists, post–1955, ed. Thadious M. Davis and Trudier Harris. See also James A. Levernier and Douglas R. Wilmes, eds., *American Writers Before 1800: A Biographical and Critical Dictionary* (3 vols., Westport, CT, Greenwood Press, 1983).

(c) SETS AND ANTHOLOGIES

Several paperback publishers (Penguin, Viking Portable, New American Library, Bantam, etc.) have strong lists of 'classic' authors, especially for American fiction. Multi-volume edns. are in progress for Hawthorne, Melville, Whitman and others.

Geoffrey Moore's anthology of American poetry, *The Penguin Book of American Verse* (1977), is excellent. *American Literature in Context* (London, Methuen), under the general editorship of Arnold Goldman, covers the field in 4 vols., combining readings and analysis (*1620–1830* by Stephen Fender; *1830–1865* by Brian

Harding; *1865–1900* by Andrew Hook; *1900–1930* by Ann Massa). Norton and Wiley are among the publishers who have brought out generous 2–vol. course-books of American literary material. Edmund Wilson's compilation, *The Shock of Recognition* (repr. NY, Farrar Straus, 1955; London, W. H. Allen, 1956) contains several books in one, including J. R. Lowell's *Fable for Critics* and D. H. Lawrence's brilliantly opinionated *Studies in Classic American Literature* (1924). Among antholo-gies of literary criticism are Philip Rahv, ed., *Literature in America* (NY, Meridian, 1957); Charles Feidelson Jr. and Paul Brodtkorb Jr., eds., *Interpretations of American Literature* (NY, Oxford UP, 1959); Morton D. Zabel, ed., *Literary Opinion in America* (2 vols., NY, Harper, 3rd edn., 1962); and Richard Ruland, ed., *The Native Muse* and *The Storied Land* (NY, Dutton, 1972; 1976), two vols. of comment by American writers under the general title *Theories of American Literature*. The Library of America (NY, in progress) is issuing exemplary edns. of literary classics, on the model of the *Pléiade* set of French literature, as uncluttered as possible with editorial apparatus. It includes two magnificent vols. of literary criticism by Henry James, and a fine comprehensive *Essays and Reviews* by Edgar Allan Poe. One interesting approach is that of Stephen Fender, *The American Long Poem: An Annotated Selection* (London, Arnold, 1977), ranging from Whitman to William Carlos Williams. Another, running from Irving and Poe to Edward Bellamy and Jack London, is H. Bruce Franklin, *Future Perfect: American Science Fiction of the Nineteenth Century* (NY, Oxford UP, 1966; revised edn., 1978). Creative writing and literary criticism, *c.* 1945–77, are surveyed in Daniel Hoffman, ed., *Harvard Guide to Contemporary American Writing* (Cambridge, MA, Harvard UP, 1979).

(d) General Histories and Interpretations

Aaron, Daniel, *The Unwritten War: American Writers and the Civil War* (NY, Oxford UP, 1973).

Aichinger, Peter, *The American Soldier in Fiction, 1880–1963* (Ames, IA, Iowa State UP, 1975).

Anderson, Quentin, *The Imperial Self: An Essay in American Literary and Cultural History* (NY, Knopf, 1971).

Baym, Nina, *Novels, Readers and Reviewers in Antebellum America*, (Ithaca, NY, Cornell UP, 1984).

Bell, Michael D., *The Development of American Romance: The Sacrifice of Relation* (Chicago, IL, Chicago UP, 1980). Covers Brown, Irving, Poe, Hawthorne, Melville.

Bercovitch, Sacvan, *The American Jeremiad* (Madison, WI, U of Wisconsin P, 1978); ed., *The American Puritan Imagination: Essays in Revaluation* (Cambridge, Cambridge UP, 1974).

Bewley, Marius, *The Eccentric Design: Form in the Classic American Novel* (London, Chatto, 1959; NY, Columbia UP, 1963).

Brooks, Van Wyck, *Makers and Finders: A History of the Writer in America* (NY,

Dutton, and London, Dent, 1937–52). Anecdotally informative 5-vol. set, of which the best may be *The Flowering of New England*.

Budd, Louis J., Cady, E. H., and Anderson, C. L., eds., *Towards a New American Literary History: Essays in Honor of Arlin Turner* (Durham, NC, Duke UP, 1980). Wide in scope.

Bush, Clive, *The Dream of Reason: American Consciousness and Cultural Achievement from Independence to the Civil War* (NY, St Martin's Press, 1978).

Chase, Richard, *The American Novel and Its Tradition* (NY, Doubleday, 1957).

Donoghue, Denis, *Connoisseurs of Chaos: Ideas of Order in Modern American Poetry* (London, Faber, 1966).

Duffey, Bernard I., *Poetry in America: Expression and Its Values in the Times of Bryant, Whitman, and Pound* (Durham, NC, Duke UP, 1978).

Feidelson, Charles S., Jr., *Symbolism and American Literature* (Chicago, IL, Chicago UP, 1953).

Ferguson, Robert A., *Law and Letters in American Culture* (Cambridge, MA, Harvard UP, 1984).

Fiedler, Leslie A., *Love and Death in the American Novel* (NY, Criterion, 1960; revised edn. 1966).

Gilmore, Michael T., *The Middle Way: Puritanism and Ideology in American Romantic Fiction* (New Brunswick, NJ, Rutgers UP, 1977). On Hawthorne, Melville, Henry James.

Green, Martin, *Re-appraisals: Some Commonsense Readings in American Literature* (London, Hugh Evelyn, 1963). Insouciantly unorthodox.

Guttmann, Allen, *The Conservative Tradition in America* (NY, Oxford UP, 1967).

Hoffman, Daniel G., *Form and Fable in American Fiction* (NY, Oxford UP, 1961).

Hubbell, Jay B., *The South in American Literature, 1607–1900* (Durham, NC, Duke UP, 1954). Compendious.

Jones, Howard M., *The Theory of American Literature* (Ithaca, NY, Cornell UP, 1948; new edn. 1965). Fashions in literary history.

Kasson, John F., *Civilizing the Machine: Technology and Republican Values in America, 1776–1900* (NY, Penguin, 1977). Particularly interesting on Twain.

Kaul, A. N., *The American Vision: Actual and Ideal Society in Nineteenth-century Fiction* (New Haven, CT, Yale UP, 1963).

Kazin, Alfred, *On Native Grounds: ... Modern American Prose Literature* (NY, Reynal and Hitchcock, 1942); *An American Procession* (NY, Knopf, 1984) – literature *c.* 1830–1930.

Kolodny, Annette, *The Lay of the Land: Metaphor as Experience and History in American Life and Literature* (Chapel Hill, NC, U of North Carolina P, 1975).

Levin, Harry, *The Power of Blackness: Hawthorne, Poe, Melville* (NY, Knopf, 1958).

Lewis, R. W. B., *The American Adam: Innocence, Tragedy, and Tradition in the Nineteenth Century* (Chicago, IL, Chicago UP, 1955).

Lindberg, Gary, *The Confidence Man in American Literature* (NY, Oxford UP, 1982). Benjamin Franklin to John Barth.

Lively, Robert C., *Fiction Fights the Civil War* (Chapel Hill, NC, U of North Carolina P, 1957).

Marx, Leo, *The Machine in the Garden: Technology and the Pastoral Ideal in America* (NY, Oxford UP, 1964).

Miller, Perry, *Nature's Nation* (Cambridge, MA, Harvard UP, 1967). Essays on American literature and culture.

Millgate, Michael, *American Social Fiction: James to Cozzens* (Edinburgh, Oliver and Boyd, and NY, Barnes and Noble, 1964).

Mills, Nicolaus, *American and English Fiction in the Nineteenth Century: An Antigenre Critique and Comparison* (Bloomington, IN, Indiana UP, 1973).

Parrington, Vernon L., *Main Currents in American Thought* (3 vols., NY, Harcourt Brace, 1927–30). Despite limitations, still a masterly treatment, 'Progressive' in tone.

Pearce, Roy H., *The Continuity of American Poetry* (Princeton, NJ, Princeton UP, 1961).

Poirier, Richard, *A World Elsewhere: The Place of Style in American Literature* (NY, Oxford UP, 1966).

Porte, Joel, *The Romance in America: Studies in Cooper, Poe, Hawthorne, Melville, and James* (Middletown, CT, Wesleyan UP, 1969).

Pryse, Marjorie, *The Mark and the Knowledge: Social Stigma in Classical American Fiction* (Columbus, OH, Ohio State UP, 1979).

Seelye, John, *Prophetic Waters: The River in Early American Life and Literature* (NY, Oxford UP, 1977).

Slotkin, Richard, *Regeneration Through Violence: The Mythology of the American Frontier, 1600–1860* (Middletown, CT, Wesleyan UP, 1973).

Smith, Henry N., *Virgin Land: The American West as Symbol and Myth* (Cambridge, MA, Harvard UP, 1950); *Democracy and the Novel: Popular Resistance to Classic American Writers* (NY, Oxford UP, 1978).

Stovall, Floyd, *The Development of American Literary Criticism* (Chapel Hill, NC, U of North Carolina P, 1955).

Strout, Cushing, *The Veracious Imagination: Essays on American History, Literature, and Biography* (Middletown, CT, Wesleyan UP, 1981). Intriguingly varied discussion, e.g. of William James and psychobiography, and of the 'antihistorical' novel exemplified by E. L. Doctorow's *Ragtime*.

Sundquist, Eric, *Home as Found: Authority and Genealogy in Nineteenth-Century American Literature* (Baltimore, MD, Johns Hopkins UP, 1979).

Tanner, Tony, *The Reign of Wonder: Naïvety and Reality in American Literature* (Cambridge, Cambridge UP, 1965).

Taylor, William R., *Cavalier and Yankee: The Old South and American National Character* (NY, Braziller, 1961).

Tichi, Cecelia, *New World, New Earth: Environmental Reform in American Literature from the Puritans through Whitman* (New Haven, CT, Yale UP, 1979).

Walker, Marshall, *The Literature of the United States of America* (London, Macmillan, 1983).

Watts, Emily S., *The Poetry of American Women from 1632 to 1945* (Austin, TX, U of Texas P, 1977).

Wilson, Edmund, *Patriotic Gore: Studies in the Literature of the American Civil War* (NY, Oxford UP, 1962).

Winters, Yvor, *In Defense of Reason* (Denver, CO, Allan Swallow, 1947).

Ziff, Larzer, *Literary Democracy: The Declaration of Cultural Independence in America* (NY, Viking, 1981; Penguin, 1982). Covers *c.* 1830–70; essays not only on 'classic' authors but on George Lippard, Sut Lovingood, Margaret Fuller, etc.

(e) TIES WITH OTHER COUNTRIES

This theme is well covered in Gohdes and Marovitz, *Bibliographical Guide to ... the Literature of the USA.* The period since 1945 has seen the emergence of good general surveys of American literature (e.g. by Cyrille Arnavon in French, and Carlo Izzo in Italian), as well as monographs by such excellent scholars as Ursula Brumm in Germany, Roger Asselineau in France, and Brita Lindberg-Seyersted in Norway, not to mention the sizeable contributions from anglophone countries. A recent Italian instance is Mario Maffi, *La giungla e il grattacielo: gli scrittori e il sogno americano, 1865–1920* (Bari, Laterza, 1981). Here is a sample of broad analyses:

Blumenthal, Henry, *American and French Culture, 1800–1900* (Baton Rouge, LA, Louisiana State UP, 1975).

Brooks, Van Wyck, *The Dream of Arcadia: American Writers and Artists in Italy, 1760–1915* (NY, Dutton, and London, Dent, 1958).

Brown, Deming, *Soviet Attitudes Towards American Writing* (Princeton, NJ, Princeton UP, 1962).

Conrad, Peter, *Imagining America* (NY, New York UP, 1980). British writers and what they made of the U.S., according to Conrad.

Denny, Margaret, and Gilman, William H., eds., *The American Writer and the European Tradition* (Minneapolis, MN, U of Minnesota P, 1950).

Gohdes, Clarence, *American Literature in Nineteenth-Century England* (NY, Columbia UP, 1944; repr. Carbondale, IL, U of Southern Illinois P, 1963).

Lease, Benjamin, *Anglo-American Encounters: England and the Rise of American Literature* (Cambridge, Cambridge UP, 1981). Covers *c.* 1800–1890, Irving to Whitman.

Pachter, Marc, and Wein, Frances, eds., *Abroad in America: Visitors to the New Nation, 1776–1914* (Reading, MA, Addison-Wesley, 1976). Includes several authors.

Pochmann, Henry A., *German Culture in America: Philosophical and Literary Influences, 1600–1900* (Madison, WI, U of Wisconsin P, 1956).

Williams, Stanley T., *The Spanish Background of American Literature* (2 vols., New Haven, CT, Yale UP, 1955).

(For other titles see the bibliography below to ch. 10, 'The Cosmopolitans'.)

CHAPTER II: COLONIAL AMERICA
Several of these titles are also useful for ch. 3.

Aldridge, A. Owen, *Early American Literature: A Comparatist Approach* (Princeton, NJ, Princeton UP, 1982). Especially relevant for Bradstreet and Taylor.

Bercovitch, Sacvan, *Puritan Origins of the American Self* (New Haven, CT, Yale UP, 1975).

Boorstin, Daniel J., *The Americans: The Colonial Experience* (NY, Random House, 1958).

Brumm, Ursula, *American Thought and Religious Typology* (New Brunswick, NJ, Rutgers UP, 1970; first pub. in German 1963).

Caldwell, Priscilla, *The Puritan Conversion Narrative: The Beginnings of American Expression* (Cambridge, Cambridge UP, 1983).

Davis, Richard B., *Intellectual Life in the Colonial South* (3 vols., Knoxville, TN, U of Tennessee P, 1978).

Elliott, Emory, ed., *American Colonial Writers, 1735–1781* and *American Writers of the Early Republic* (vols. 31 and 37 of the Gale Co. *Dictionary of Literary Biography*).

Emerson, Everett H., ed., *Major Writers of Early American Literature* (Madison, WI, U of Wisconsin P, 1972). Includes essays on Bradford, Bradstreet, Taylor, Cotton Mather, William Byrd, Jonathan Edwards, Franklin, Freneau and Charles Brockden Brown. *American Literature, 1764–1789* (Madison, U of Wisconsin P, 1977). Jefferson and Crèvecœur are among individual figures treated.

Gilmore, Michael T., ed., *Early American Literature: A Collection of Critical Essays* (Englewood Cliffs, NJ, Prentice-Hall, 1981). Essays on, e.g., Puritan poetics; Edwards and typology; Paine's *Common Sense*.

Jones, Howard M., *O Strange New World: American Culture: The Formative Years* (NY, Viking, 1964).

Miller, Perry, *The New England Mind: The Seventeenth Century* (Cambridge, MA, Harvard UP, 1939); *The New England Mind: From Colony to Province* (Harvard, 1953); ed., *The American Puritans: Their Prose and Poetry* (Garden City, NY, Doubleday, 1956).

Morison, Samuel E., *Intellectual Life in Early New England* (Cambridge, MA, Harvard UP, 1956).

Murdock, Kenneth B., *Literature and Theology in Colonial New England* (Cambridge, MA, Harvard UP, 1949).

Silverman, Kenneth, *A Cultural History of the American Revolution ... 1763–1789* (NY, Crowell, 1976); *The Life and Times of Cotton Mather* (NY, Harper and Row, 1984).

Tyler, Moses C., *A History of American Literature, 1607–1765* (originally 2 vols., 1897; abridged U of Chicago P, 1967); *The Literary History of the American Revolution, 1763–1783* (2 vols., 1897; available in shortened versions). Still a reliable scholar.

Ziff, Larzer, *Puritanism in America: New Culture in a New World* (NY,Viking, 1975).

CHAPTER III: PROMISES AND PROBLEMS OF INDEPENDENCE
See also references for ch. 2.

Brissot, J. P. de Warville, *New Travels in the United States of America, 1788*, ed. Durand Echeverria (Cambridge, MA, Harvard UP, 1964).

Cady, E. H., ed., *Literature of the Early Republic* (NY, Rinehart, 1950).

Elliott, Emory, *Revolutionary Writers: Literature and Authority in the New Republic, 1725–1810* (NY, Oxford UP, 1982).

Ellis, Harold M., *Joseph Dennie and His Circle: A Study in American Literature from 1792 to 1812* (Austin, TX, 1915; repr. NY, AMS Press, 1971).

Ellis, Joseph J., *After the Revolution: Profiles of Early American Culture* (NY, Norton, 1979). Good material on Brackenridge and Noah Webster.

Fliegelman, Jay, *Prodigals and Pilgrims: The American Revolution Against Patriarchal Authority, 1750–1800* (Cambridge, Cambridge UP, 1982).

Kammen, Michael, *A Season of Youth: The American Revolution and the Historical Imagination* (NY, Knopf, 1978).

Kerber, Linda K., *Federalists in Dissent: Imagery and Ideology in Jeffersonian America* (Ithaca, NY, Cornell UP, 1970). See e.g. comments on Webster.

Leary, Lewis, *That Rascal Freneau: A Study in Literary Failure* (New Brunswick, NJ, Rutgers UP, 1941). *Soundings: Some Early American Writers* (Athens, GA, U of Georgia P, 1975). Includes essays on Royall Tyler, Freneau, Brackenridge, William Dunlap and Joseph Dennie, as well as more obscure figures.

McLean, Albert Jr., *William Cullen Bryant* (Twayne's U.S. Author Series, hereafter referred to as TUSAS; distributed NY, Grosset and Dunlap, 1964).

Newlin, Claude M., *The Life and Writings of Hugh Henry Brackenridge* (Princeton, NJ, Princeton UP, 1932).

Nye, Russel B., *American Literary History, 1607–1830* (NY, Knopf, 1970).

Nye, R. B., and Grabo, N. S., eds., *American Thought and Writing*, vol. 2, *The Revolution and the Early Republic* (Boston, Houghton Mifflin, Riverside Editions, 1965).

Parrington, Vernon L., ed., *The Connecticut Wits* (1926; repr. NY, Crowell, 1969, with foreword by Kenneth Silverman).

Philbrick, Thomas, *St John de Crèvecœur* (NY, Twayne, TUSAS, 1970).

Ringe, Donald A., *Charles Brockden Brown* (NY, Twayne, TUSAS, 1966).

Rollins, Richard M., *The Long Journey of Noah Webster* (Philadelphia, PA, U of Pennsylvania P, 1980).

Roth, Martin, *Comedy and America: The Lost World of Washington Irving* (Port Washington, NY, Kennikat, 1976).

Spencer, Benjamin T., *The Quest for Nationality: An American Literary Campaign* (Syracuse, NY, Syracuse UP, 1957).

Spiller, Robert E., ed., *The American Literary Revolution, 1787–1837* (Garden City, NY, Doubleday, 1967).

Stone, Alfred E., ed., Crèvecœur, *Letters from an American Farmer* and *Sketches of 18th-Century America* (NY, Penguin, 1981).

Warfel, Harry R., *Noah Webster: Schoolmaster to America* (NY, Macmillan, 1936).

Woodress, James L., *A Yankee's Odyssey: The Life of Joel Barlow* (Philadelphia, PA, Lippincott, 1958).

CHAPTER IV: A TRIO OF GENTLEMEN

Beard, James F., ed., *Letters and Journals of James Fenimore Cooper* (6 vols., Cambridge, MA, Harvard UP, 1960–68).

Davidson, Edward H., *Poe: A Critical Study* (Cambridge, MA, Harvard UP, 1967).

Grossman, James, *James Fenimore Cooper* (NY, Sloane, 1949).

Hedges, William L., *Washington Irving: An American Study, 1802–1832* (Baltimore, MD, Johns Hopkins UP, 1965).

McClary, Ben H., ed., *Washington Irving and the House of Murray* (Knoxville, TN, U of Tennessee P, 1969).

McWilliams, John P. Jr., *Political Justice in a Republic: James Fenimore Cooper's America* (Berkeley, CA, U of California P, 1973).

Miller, Perry, *The Raven and the Whale: The War of Wits and Words in the Era of Poe and Melville* (NY, Harcourt Brace, 1956).

Nevius, Blake, *Cooper's Landscapes: An Essay on the Picturesque Vision* (Berkeley, CA, U of California P, 1976).

Ostrom, John W., ed., *The Letters of Edgar Allan Poe* (2 vols., Cambridge, MA, Harvard UP, 1948).

Quinn, Patrick F., *The French Face of Edgar Poe* (Carbondale, IL, U of Southern Illinois P, 1957).

Railton, Stephen, *Fenimore Cooper: A Study of His Life and Imagination* (Princeton, NJ, Princeton UP, 1978).

Reichart, Walter A., *Washington Irving and Germany* (Ann Arbor, MI, U of Michigan P, 1957).

Symons, Julian, *The Tell-Tale Heart: The Life and Works of Edgar Allan Poe* (NY, Harper and Row, 1978).

Williams, Stanley T., *The Life of Washington Irving* (2 vols., NY, Oxford UP, 1935).

CHAPTER V: NEW ENGLAND'S DAY

Allen, Gay W., *Waldo Emerson: A Biography* (NY, Viking, 1981).

Baym, Nina, *The Shape of Hawthorne's Career* (Ithaca, NY, Cornell UP, 1976).

Boller, Paul F. Jr., *American Transcendentalism, 1830–1860: An Intellectual Inquiry* (NY, Putnam's, 1975).

Brodhead, Richard H., *Hawthorne, Melville, and the Novel* (Chicago, IL, Chicago UP, 1976).

Emerson, Ralph Waldo, *Early Lectures*, ed. Stephen E. Whicher and Robert E. Spiller (3 vols., Cambridge, MA, Harvard UP, 1959–72); *Emerson in His Journals*, ed. Joel Porte (Cambridge, MA, Harvard UP, 1982).

Gollin, Rita, *Nathaniel Hawthorne and the Truth of Dreams* (Baton Rouge, LA, Louisiana State UP, 1979).

Hochfield, George, ed., *Selected Writings of the American Transcendentalists* (NY, New American Library, 1966).

Hutchison, William R., *The Transcendentalist Ministers* (New Haven, CT, Yale UP, 1959).

McWilliams, John P. Jr., *Hawthorne, Melville, and the American Character: A Looking Glass Business* (Cambridge, Cambridge UP, 1984).

Matthiessen, F. O., *American Renaissance: Art and Expression in the Age of Emerson and Whitman* (NY, Oxford UP, 1941).

Mellow, James R., *Nathaniel Hawthorne in His Times* (Boston, MA, Houghton Mifflin, 1980).

Meyer, Michael, *Several More Lives to Live: Thoreau's Political Reputation in America* (Westport, CT, Greenwood, 1977).

Miller, Perry, ed., *The Transcendentalists: An Anthology* (Cambridge, MA, Harvard UP, 1950); also *The Transcendentalists: Their Prose and Poetry* (1957; repr. Baltimore, MD, Johns Hopkins UP).

Rose, Anne C., *Transcendentalism as a Social Movement, 1830–1850* (New Haven, CT, Yale UP, 1982).

Thoreau, Henry, *Collected Poems*, ed. Carl Bode (enlarged edn., Baltimore, MD, Johns Hopkins UP, 1964).

Turner, Arlin, *Nathaniel Hawthorne: A Biography* (NY, Oxford UP, 1980).

Waggoner, Hyatt H., *Emerson as Poet* (Princeton, NJ, Princeton UP, 1974).

Whicher, Stephen F., *Freedom and Fate: An Inner Life of Ralph Waldo Emerson* (Philadelphia, PA, U of Pennsylvania P, 1953).

CHAPTER VI: MELVILLE AND WHITMAN

Allen, Gay W., *The Solitary Singer: A Critical Biography of Walt Whitman* (1955; revised edn., NY, New York UP, 1967); *The New Walt Whitman Handbook* (NY, New York UP, 1975).

Asselineau, Roger, *L'Évolution de Whitman* (Paris, Didier, 1954); trans. as *The Evolution of Walt Whitman* (2 vols., Harvard UP and Oxford UP, 1960, 1962).

Branch, Watson G., ed.,*Melville: The Critical Heritage* (London, Routledge and Kegan Paul, 1974).

Chase, Richard, *Walt Whitman Reconsidered* (NY, Sloane, 1955).

Davis, Merrell R. and Gilman, William H., eds., *The Letters of Herman Melville* (New Haven, CT, Yale UP, 1960).

Kaplan, Justin, *Walt Whitman: A Life* (NY, Simon and Schuster, 1980).

Leyda, Jay, *The Melville Log: A Documentary Life of Herman Melville* (2 vols., NY, Harcourt Brace, 1951; supplement, 1969).

Murphy, Francis, ed., *Walt Whitman: A Critical Anthology* (Harmondsworth, Penguin, 1969).

Solomon, Pearl, *Dickens and Melville in Their Time* (NY, Columbia UP, 1975).

Zweig, Paul, *Walt Whitman: The Making of the Poet* (NY, Basic Books, 1984).

CHAPTER VII: MORE NEW ENGLANDERS

Arms, George, *The Fields Were Green* (Stanford, CA, Stanford UP, 1953).

Arvin, Newton, *Longfellow: His Life and Work* (Boston, MA, Little Brown, 1963).

Brooks, Van Wyck, *New England: Indian Summer, 1865–1915* (NY, Dutton, 1940).

Canary, Robert H., *George Bancroft* (NY, Twayne, TUSAS, 1974).

Doughty, Howard N., *Francis Parkman* (NY, Macmillan, 1962).

Duberman, Martin, *James Russell Lowell* (Boston, MA, Houghton Mifflin, 1966).

Levin, David, *History as Romantic Art: Bancroft, Prescott, Motley, Parkman* (Stanford, CA, Stanford UP, 1959).

Pollard, John A., *John Greenleaf Whittier, Friend of Man* (Boston, MA, Houghton Mifflin, 1949).

Story, Ronald, *The Forging of an Aristocracy: Harvard and the Boston Upper Class, 1800–1870* (Middletown, CT, Wesleyan UP, 1980).

Tilton, Eleanor M., *Amiable Autocrat: A Biography of Doctor Oliver Wendell Holmes* (NY, Schuman, 1947).

CHAPTER VIII: AMERICAN HUMOUR AND THE RISE OF THE WEST

Andrews, Kenneth R., *Nook Farm: Mark Twain's Hartford Circle* (Cambridge, MA, Harvard UP, 1950).

Asselineau, Roger, *The Literary Reputation of Mark Twain from 1910 to 1950* (1954; repr. Westport, CT, Greenwood, 1971).

Baetzhold, Howard G., *Mark Twain and John Bull: The British Connection* (Bloomington, IN, Indiana UP, 1970).

Blair, Walter, *Horse Sense in American Humor from Benjamin Franklin to Ogden Nash* (NY, Russell and Russell, 1962); *Native American Humor, 1800–1900* (NY, American Book Co., 1937); *Tall Tale America* (NY, Coward-McCann, 1944).

Blair, Walter and Hill, Hamlin, *America's Humor, From Poor Richard to Doonesbury* (NY, Oxford UP, 1978).

Bridgman, Richard, *The Colloquial Style in America* (NY, Oxford UP, 1966).

Fender, Stephen, *Plotting the Golden West: American Literature and the Rhetoric of the California Trail* (Cambridge, Cambridge UP, 1982).

Fussell, Edwin, *Frontier: American Literature and the American West* (Princeton, NJ, Princeton UP, 1965).

Gibson, William M., *The Art of Mark Twain* (NY, Oxford UP, 1976).

Howells, William D., *My Mark Twain: Reminiscences and Criticism* (NY, Harper, 1910).

Kaplan, Justin, *Mr Clemens and Mark Twain* (NY, Simon and Schuster, 1966).

Ketterer, David, ed., *The Science Fiction of Mark Twain* (Hamden, CT, Archon, 1984).

Lynn, Kenneth S., *Mark Twain and Southwestern Humor* (Boston, Little Brown, 1959).

Rourke, Constance, *American Humor: A Study of the National Character* (NY, Harcourt Brace, 1931; repr. 1947, 1953).

Salomon, Roger B., *Twain and the Image of History* (New Haven, CT, Yale UP, 1961).

Smith, Henry N., *Mark Twain: The Development of a Writer* (Cambridge, MA, Harvard UP, 1962).

Welland, Dennis, *Mark Twain in England* (Atlantic Highlands, NJ, Humanities Press, 1978).

CHAPTER IX: REALISM IN PROSE

Berryman, John, *Stephen Crane* (London, Methuen, 1950).

Berthoff, Warner, *The Ferment of Realism: American Literature, 1884–1919* (NY, Free Press, 1965).

Cady, Edwin H., *The Road to Realism* and *The Realist at War* (2 vols., Syracuse, NY, Syracuse UP, 1956, 1958). A biography of Howells.

Conn, Peter, *The Divided Mind: Ideology and Imagination in America, 1898–1917* (Cambridge, Cambridge UP, 1983).

Duffey, Bernard, *The Chicago Renaissance in American Letters* (East Lansing, MI, Michigan State UP, 1954).

Geismar, Maxwell, *Rebels and Ancestors, 1890–1915* (Boston, Houghton Mifflin, 1953).

Gelfant, Blanche H., *The American City Novel* (Norman, OK, U of Oklahoma P, 1954).

Hoffman, Daniel G., *The Poetry of Stephen Crane* (NY, Columbia UP, 1957).

Holloway, Jean, *Hamlin Garland: A Biography* (Austin, TX, U of Texas P, 1960).

Langford, Gerald, *Alias O. Henry: A Biography of William Sidney Porter* (NY, Macmillan, 1957).

Lynn, Kenneth S., *Howells: An American Life* (NY, Harcourt Brace Jovanovitch, 1971).

Martin, Jay, *Harvests of Change: American Literature, 1865–1914* (Englewood Cliffs, NJ, Prentice-Hall, 1967).

Martin, Ronald E., *American Literature and the Universe of Force* (Durham, NC, Duke UP, 1981). Henry Adams, Norris, London, Dreiser, etc.

Moers, Ellen, *Two Dreisers: The Man and the Novelist* (London, Thames and Hudson, 1970).

Pizer, Donald, *Realism and Naturalism in Nineteenth-Century American Literature* (Carbondale, IL, U of Southern Illinois P, 1966; revised edn., 1984); ed., *American Thought and Writing: The 1890s* (Boston, Houghton Mifflin, 1972).

Roemer, Kenneth M., *The Obsolete Necessity: America in Utopian Writings, 1888–1900* (Kent, OH, Kent State UP, 1976).

Schneider, Robert W., *Five Novelists of the Progressive Era* (NY, Columbia UP, 1965).

Seyersted, Per, *Kate Chopin: A Critical Biography* (Baton Rouge, LA, Louisiana State UP, 1969); *Hjalmar Hjorth Boyesen: From Norwegian Romantic to American Realist* (Oslo, Solum Forlag; Atlantic Highlands, NJ, Humanities Press, 1984).

Sinclair, Andrew, *Jack: A Biography of Jack London* (NY, Harper and Row, 1977).

Spindler, Michael, *American Literature and Social Change: William Dean Howells to Arthur Miller* (Bloomington, IN, Indiana UP, 1984).

Stallman, R. W., *Stephen Crane: A Biography* (NY, Braziller, 1968).

Sundquist, Eric, ed., *American Realism: New Essays* (Baltimore, MD, Johns Hopkins UP, 1982).

Walcutt, Charles C., *American Naturalism: A Divided Stream* (Minneapolis, MN, U of Minnesota P, 1956).

Walker, Robert H., *The Poet and the Gilded Age: Social Themes in Late Nineteenth-Century American Verse* (Philadelphia, PA, U of Pennsylvania P, 1963).

Ziff, Larzer, *The American 1890s: Life and Times of a Lost Generation* (NY, Viking, 1966).

CHAPTER X: THE COSMOPOLITANS

Anderson, Charles R., *Person, Place and Thing in Henry James's Novels* (Durham, NC, Duke UP, 1977).

Bell, Millicent, *Edith Wharton and Henry James: The Story of Their Friendship* (NY, Braziller, 1965).

Bradbury, Malcolm, *The Expatriate Tradition in American Literature* (London, British Association for American Studies, Pamphlets in American Studies no. 9, 1982).

Brinnin, John M., *The Third Rose: Gertrude Stein and Her World* (Boston, Atlantic-Little Brown, 1959).

Dusinberre, William, *Henry Adams: The Myth of Failure* (Charlottesville, VA, U of Virginia P, 1980).

Earnest, Ernest, *Expatriates and Patriots: American Artists, Scholars, and Writers in Europe* (Durham, NC, Duke UP, 1968).

Edel, Leon, *Henry James* (5 vols., Philadelphia, PA, Lippincott, 1953–72).

Jordy, William H., *Henry Adams, Scientific Historian* (New Haven, CT, Yale UP, 1952).

Levenson, J. C., *The Mind and Art of Henry Adams* (Boston, Houghton Mifflin, 1957).

Lewis, R. W. B., *Edith Wharton: A Biography* (NY, Harper and Row, 1975).

Matthiessen, F. O., ed., *The James Family* (NY, Knopf, 1947).

Nagel, Paul C., *Descent from Glory: Four Generations of the John Adams Family* (NY, Oxford UP, 1983).

Page, Norman, ed., *Henry James: Interviews and Recollections* (London, Macmillan, 1984).

Perosa, Sergio, *Henry James and the Experimental Novel* (Charlottesville, VA, U of Virginia P, 1978).

Samuels, Ernest, *The Young Henry Adams; Henry Adams: The Middle Years; The Major Phase* (Cambridge, MA, Harvard UP, 1948, 1958, 1964).

Strout, Cushing, *The American Image of the Old World* (NY, Harper and Row, 1963).

Weintraub, Stanley, *London Yankees: Portraits of American Writers and Artists in England, 1898–1914* (NY, Harcourt Brace Jovanovitch, 1979).

Wickes, George, *Americans in Paris, 1903–1939* (Garden City, NY, Doubleday, 1969).

CHAPTER XI: WOMEN'S VOICES

See also the periodicals *Signs*, *Feminist Studies*, *Women's Studies* and *Women's Review of Books*.

Allen, Margaret V., *The Achievement of Margaret Fuller* (University Park, PA, Pennsylvania State UP, 1979).

Ammons, Elizabeth, ed., *Critical Essays on Harriet Beecher Stowe* (Boston, MA, G. K. Hall, 1980).

Appel, Alfred Jr., *A Season of Dreams: The Fiction of Eudora Welty* (Baton Rouge, LA, Louisiana State UP, 1965).

Auerbach, Nina, *Communities of Women: An Idea in Fiction* (Cambridge, MA, Harvard UP, 1978).

Baym, Nina, *Woman's Fiction: A Guide to Novels by and about Women in America, 1820–1870* (Ithaca, NY, Cornell UP, 1978).

Brown, Herbert R., *The Sentimental Novel in America, 1789–1860* (Durham, NC, Duke UP, 1942).

Carr, Virginia S., *The Lonely Hunter: A Biography of Carson McCullers* (NY, Doubleday, 1975).

Chevigny, Bell G., *The Woman and the Myth: Margaret Fuller's Life and Writings* (Old Westbury, NY, Feminist Press, 1976).

Conrad, Susan P., *Perish the Thought: Intellectual Women in Romantic America, 1830–1860* (NY, Oxford UP, 1976).

Douglas, Ann, *The Feminization of American Culture* (NY, Knopf, 1977).

Fetterley, Judith, *The Resisting Reader: A Feminist Approach to American Fiction* (Bloomington, IN, Indiana UP, 1978).

Foster, Edward H., *Catharine Maria Sedgwick* (NY, Twayne, 1974).

Gelpi, Barbara C., and Albert, eds., *Adrienne Rich's Poetry* (NY, Norton, 1975).

Gilbert, Sandra M., and Gubar, Susan, *The Madwoman in the Attic: The Woman Writer and the Nineteenth-Century Literary Imagination* (New Haven, CT, Yale UP, 1979); eds., *Shakespeare's Sisters: Feminist Essays on Women Poets* (Bloomington, IN, Indiana UP, 1979).

Givner, Joan, *Katherine Anne Porter: A Life* (NY, Simon and Schuster, 1982).

Godbold, E. Stanley, *Ellen Glasgow and the Woman Within* (Baton Rouge, LA, Louisiana State UP, 1972).

Hardwick, Elizabeth, *Seduction and Betrayal: Women and Literature* (NY, Random House, 1974). Mainly on European writers.

Howard, Maureen, ed., *Seven American Women Writers of the Twentieth Century* (Minneapolis, MN, U of Minnesota P, 1977).

Keller, Karl, *The Only Kangaroo Among the Beauty: Emily Dickinson and America* (Baltimore, MD, Johns Hopkins UP, 1980).

Kelley, Mary, *Private Woman, Public Stage: Literary Domesticity in Nineteenth-Century America* (NY, Oxford UP, 1984).

Kerber, Linda K., *Women of the Republic: Intellect and Ideology in Revolutionary America* (Chapel Hill, NC, U of N. Carolina P, 1980).

Lewis, R. W. B., *Edith Wharton: A Biography* (NY, Harper and Row, 1975).

Lindberg-Seyersted, Brita, *The Voice of the Poet: Aspects of Style in the Poetry of Emily Dickinson* (Cambridge, MA, Harvard UP, 1968).

Moers, Ellen, *Literary Women: The Great Writers* (Garden City, NY, Doubleday, 1976).

Norton, Mary B., *Liberty's Daughters: The Revolutionary Experience of American Women, 1750–1800* (Boston, MA, Little Brown, 1980).

Papashvily, Helen W., *All the Happy Endings* (NY, Harper and Row, 1956).

Pollak, Vivian R., *Dickinson: The Anxiety of Gender* (Ithaca, NY, Cornell UP, 1984).

Robinson, Janice S., *H. D. The Life and Work of an American Poet* [Hilda Doolittle] (Boston, MA, Houghton Mifflin, 1982).

St Armand, Barton L., *Emily Dickinson and her Culture: The Soul's Society* (Cambridge, MA, Cambridge UP, 1984).

Saxton, Martha, *Louisa May: A Modern Biography of Louisa May Alcott* (Boston, MA, Houghton Mifflin, 1977).

Sewall, Richard B., *The Life of Emily Dickinson* (2 vols., NY, Farrar Straus and Giroux, 1974).

Seyersted, Per, *Kate Chopin: A Critical Biography* (Baton Rouge, LA, Louisiana State UP, 1969).

Slote, Bernice, and Faulkner, Virginia, eds., *The Art of Willa Cather* (Lincoln, NB, U of Nebraska P, 1974).

Strouse, Jean, *Alice James: A Biography* (Boston, MA, Houghton Mifflin, 1980).

Walters, Dorothy, *Flannery O'Connor* (Boston, MA, Twayne, 1973).

Watts, Emily S., *The Poetry of American Women from 1632 to 1945* (Austin, TX, U of Texas P, 1977).

Wolff, Cynthia G., *A Feast of Words: The Triumph of Edith Wharton* (NY, Oxford UP, 1977).

CHAPTER XII: THE COMING OF AGE

See also references for ch. 9.

Baker, Carlos H., *Ernest Hemingway: A Life Story* (NY, Scribner's, 1969).

Bloom, Harold, *Wallace Stevens: The Poems of Our Climate* (Ithaca, NY, Cornell UP, 1977).

Bode, Carl, *Mencken* (Carbondale, IL, S. Illinois UP, 1969).

Bradbury, Malcolm, *The Modern American Novel* (NY, Oxford UP, 1983).

Bradbury, M., and Palmer, D., eds., *The American Novel in the Nineteen Twenties* (London, Stratford-on-Avon Studies, 1971).

Brower, Reuben A., *The Poetry of Robert Frost* (NY, Oxford UP, 1963).

Cooperman, Stanley, *World War I and the American Novel* (Baltimore, MD, Johns Hopkins UP, 1967).

Donaldson, Scott, *By Force of Will: The Life and Art of Ernest Hemingway* (NY, Viking, 1977; Penguin, 1978).

Fussell, Edwin S., *Edwin Arlington Robinson: The Literary Background of a Traditional Poet* (Berkeley, CA, U of California P, 1954).

Hoffman, Frederick J., *The Twenties: American Writing in the Postwar Decade* (NY, Free Press, revised edn., 1962).

Howe, Irving, *Sherwood Anderson* (NY, Sloane, 1951).

Kermode, Frank, *Wallace Stevens* (Edinburgh, Alexander and Boyd, 1960).

Lears, Jackson, *No Place of Grace: Antimodernism and the Transformation of American Culture, 1880–1920* (NY, Pantheon, 1981).

Lindberg-Seyersted, Brita, ed., *Pound/Ford: The Story of a Literary Friendship* (NY, New Directions, 1982). Reciprocal writings of Ezra Pound and Ford Madox Ford.

Ludington, Townsend, *John Dos Passos: A Twentieth-Century Odyssey* (NY, Dutton, 1980).

Perkins, David, *A History of Modern Poetry: From the 1890s to Pound, Eliot, Yeats* (Cambridge, MA, Harvard UP, 1976).

Pritchard, William H., *Frost: A Literary Life Reconsidered* (NY, Oxford UP, 1984).

Ruggles, Eleanor, *The West-Going Heart: A Life of Vachel Lindsay* (NY, Norton, 1959).

Ruland, Richard, *The Rediscovery of American Literature: Premises of Critical Taste, 1900–1940* (Cambridge, MA, Harvard UP, 1967).

Schorer, Mark, *Sinclair Lewis: An American Life* (NY, McGraw-Hill, 1961).

Tapscott, Stephen, *American Beauty: William Carlos Williams and the Modernist Whitman* (NY, Columbia UP, 1984).

Turnbull, Andrew, *Scott Fitzgerald* (NY, Scribner's, 1962).

Unterecker, John, *Voyager: A Life of Hart Crane* (NY, Farrar Straus and Giroux, 1969).

Vendler, Helen, *On Extended Wings: Wallace Stevens' Longer Poems* (Cambridge, MA, Harvard UP, 1969).

Weaver, Michael, *William Carlos Williams: The American Background* (NY, Cambridge UP, 1971).

Whipple, T. K., *Spokesmen: Modern Writers and American Life* (NY, Appleton, 1928).

CHAPTER XIII: SOUTHLAND

Among many useful commentaries by Louis D. Rubin, Jr., see his bibliographical essay, 'Scholarship in Southern Literature', in *American Studies International* 21, April 1983, pp. 3–34.

Bradbury, John M., *Renaissance in the South: A Critical History of the Literature, 1920–1960* (Chapel Hill, NC, U of N. Carolina P, 1963).

Brooks, Cleanth, *William Faulkner: The Yoknapatawpha Country* (New Haven, CT, Yale UP, 1963).

Cousins, Paul, *Joel Chandler Harris: A Biography* (Baton Rouge, LA, Louisiana State UP, 1968).

Faust, Drew G., *A Sacred Circle: The Dilemma of the Intellectual in the Old South, 1840–1860* (Baltimore, MD, Johns Hopkins UP, 1977). W. G. Simms, N. B. Tucker and others.

Gray, Richard, *The Literature of Memory: Modern Writers of the American South* (Baltimore, MD, Johns Hopkins UP, 1977).

Hobson, Fred C., *Serpent in Eden: H. L. Mencken and the American South* (Chapel Hill, NC, U of N. Carolina P, 1974).

Irwin, John T., *Doubling and Incest/Repetition and Revenge: A Speculative Reading of Faulkner* (Baltimore, MD, Johns Hopkins UP, 1975).

Karanikas, Alexander, *Tillers of a Myth: Southern Agrarians as Social and Literary Critics* (Madison, WI, U of Wisconsin P, 1966).

Kennedy, Richard S., *The Window of Memory: The Literary Career of Thomas Wolfe* (Chapel Hill, NC, U of N. Carolina P, 1966).

King, Richard H., *A Southern Renascence: The Cultural Awakening of the Modern South, 1930–1955* (NY, Oxford UP, 1980).

Mixon, W., *Southern Writers and the New South Movement, 1865–1913* (Chapel Hill, NC, U of N. Carolina P, 1980).

O'Brien, Michael, *The Idea of the American South, 1920–1941* (Baltimore, MD, Johns Hopkins UP, 1979).

Ridgely, Joseph V., *Nineteenth-century Southern Literature* (Lexington, KY, UP of Kentucky, 1980).

Rubin, Louis D., and Holman, C. Hugh, eds., *Southern Literary History: Problems and Possibilities* (Chapel Hill, NC, U of N. Carolina P, 1975).

Singal, Daniel J., *The War Within: From Victorian to Modernist Thought in the South, 1919–1945* (Chapel Hill, NC, U of N. Carolina P, 1982).

Taylor, William R., *Cavalier and Yankee: The Old South and American National Character* (NY, Braziller, 1961).

Weaver, Richard M., *The Southern Tradition at Bay: A History of Postbellum Thought* (New Rochelle, NY, Arlington House, 1968).

Woodward, C. Vann, *The Burden of Southern History* (Baton Rouge, LA, Louisiana State UP, 1960; revised edn., 1968).

CHAPTER XIV: AGAINST AND AFTER THE GENTEEL TRADITION

Abrahamson, Edward A., *The Immigrant Experience in American Literature* (BAAS Pamphlets in American Studies, no. 10, 1982).

Benson, Brian J., and Dillard, Mabel M., *Jean Toomer* (Boston, MA, Twayne, 1980).

Bigsby, C. W. E., *The Second Black Renaissance: Essays in Black Literature* (Westport, CT, Greenwood, 1980).

Bone, Robert A., *The Negro Novel in America* (New Haven, CT, Yale UP, 1958; revised edn., 1965).

Brawley, Benjamin, ed., *Early Negro American Writers* (1935; repr. NY, Dover, 1970).

Chametzky, Jules, *From the Ghetto: The Fiction of Abraham Cahan* (Amherst, MA, U of Massachusetts P, 1977).

Cooley, John, *Savages and Naturals: Black Portraits by White Writers in Modern American Literature* (Newark, U of Delaware P, 1982).

Fine, David M., *The City, The Immigrant and American Fiction, 1880–1920* (Metuchen, NJ, Scarecrow P, 1977).

Gates, Henry L. Jr., ed., *Black Literature and Literary Theory* (NY and London, Methuen, 1984).

Homberger, Eric, *American Writers and Radical Politics, 1900–1939: Equivocal Commitments* (London, Macmillan, 1985).

Huggins, Nathan, *Harlem Renaissance* (NY, Oxford UP, 1971).

Klein, Marcus, *Foreigners: The Making of American Literature, 1900–1940* (Chicago, IL, Chicago UP, 1981).

Lee, Robert A., *Black Fiction: New Studies in the Afro-American Novel Since 1945* (NY, Barnes and Noble, 1980).

Lewis, David L., *When Harlem Was in Vogue* (NY, Knopf, 1981).

O'Meally, Robert G., *The Craft of Ralph Ellison* (Cambridge, MA, Harvard UP, 1980).

Toomer, Jean, *The Wayward and the Seeking: A Collection of Writings by Jean Toomer*, ed. Darwin T. Turner (Washington, DC, Howard UP, 1980).

CHAPTER XV: MODERNIST AND POST-MODERNIST MODES

Also of use for ch. 17.

Aaron, Daniel, *Writers on the Left: Episodes in American Literary Communism* (NY, Harcourt Brace and World, 1961).

Baumbach, Jonathan, *The Landscape of Nightmare: Studies in the Contemporary American Novel* (NY, New York UP, 1965).

Bellamy, Joe D., ed., *American Poetry Observed: Poets on Their Work* (Urbana-Champaign, IL, U of Illinois P, 1984. Twenty-six interviews.

Berthoff, Warner, *A Literature Without Qualities: American Writing since 1945* (Berkeley, CA, U of California P, 1980).

Brookeman, Christopher, *American Culture and Society since the 1930s* (London, Macmillan, 1984).

Dickstein, Morris, *Gates of Eden: American Culture in the Sixties* (NY, Basic Books, 1977).

Eisinger, Chester E., *Fiction of the Forties* (Chicago, IL, Chicago UP, 1963).

Field, Andrew, *Nabokov: His Life in Part* (NY, Viking, 1977; Penguin, 1978).

Haffenden, John, *The Life of John Berryman* (London and Boston, MA, Routledge and Kegan Paul, 1982).

Hamilton, Ian, *Robert Lowell: A Biography* (NY, Random House, 1982).

Hendin, Josephine, *Vulnerable People: A View of American Fiction since 1945* (NY, Oxford UP, 1978).

Hoffman, Daniel, ed., *Harvard Guide to Contemporary American Writing* (Cambridge, MA, Harvard UP, 1979).

Hungerford, Edward B., ed., *Poets in Progress: Critical Prefaces to Thirteen Modern American Poets* (Evanston, IL, Northwestern UP, 1962, 1967).

Litz, A. Walton, ed., *Modern American Fiction: Essays in Criticism* (NY, Oxford UP, 1963). Emphasis on major figures up to *c.* 1950.

McConnell, Frank D., *Four Postwar American Novelists: Bellow, Mailer, Barth, and Pynchon* (Chicago, IL, Chicago UP, 1977).

McNally, Dennis, *Desolate Angel: Jack Kerouac, the Beat Generation and America* (NY, McGraw-Hill, 1979).

Malin, Irving, *New American Gothic* (Carbondale, IL, S. Illinois UP, 1962). The fiction of Capote, McCullers, Salinger, O'Connor, John Hawkes and James Purdy.

Manso, Peter, *Mailer: His Life and Times* (NY, Simon and Schuster, 1985).

Martin, Jay, *Always Merry and Bright: The Life of Henry Miller, An Unauthorized Biography* (Santa Barbara, CA, Capra Press, 1978).

Nicholls, Peter, *Ezra Pound: Politics, Economics and Writing: A Study of the Cantos* (London, Macmillan, 1984).

Rosenberg, Harold, *The Tradition of the New* (NY, Grove, 1961).

Rosenthal, M. L., *The New Poets: American and British Poetry since World War II* (NY, Oxford UP, 1967).

Sontag, Susan, *Against Interpretation* (NY, Farrar Straus and Giroux, 1966).

Stepanchev, Stephan, *American Poetry since 1945: A Critical Survey* (NY, Harper and Row, 1965).

Tanner, Tony, *City of Words: American Fiction, 1950–1970* (NY, Harper and Row, 1971).

Tompkins, Jane P., ed., *Reader-Response Criticism: From Formalism to Post-Structuralism* (Baltimore, MD, Johns Hopkins UP, 1980).

Vendler, Helen, *Part of Nature, Part of Us: Modern American Poets* (Cambridge, MA, Harvard UP, 1980).

Webster, Grant, *The Republic of Letters: A History of Postwar American Literary Opinion* (Baltimore, MD, Johns Hopkins UP, 1979).

Writers at Work: The Paris Review Interviews (NY, Viking, 1958; 2nd series, 1963; 3rd, 1967; 4th, 1974). Interviews with modern authors, mostly American.

CHAPTER XVI: THE AMERICAN THEATRE

Bigsby, C. W. E., *A Critical Introduction to Twentieth-century American Drama* (3 vols., Cambridge UP: vol. 1, *1900–1940*, 1982; vol. 2, *Tennessee Williams, Arthur Miller, Edward Albee*, 1985; vol. 3, *Beyond Broadway*, 1985).

Grimsted, David, *Melodrama Unveiled: American Theatre and Culture, 1800–1850* (Chicago, IL, Chicago UP, 1968).

Marker, Lise-Lone, *David Belasco: Naturalism in the American Theatre* (Princeton, NJ, Princeton UP, 1975).

Mathews, Jane D., *The Federal Theatre, 1935-1939: Plays, Relief, and Politics* (Princeton, NJ, Princeton UP, 1967, repr. NY, Octagon, 1980).

Moody, Richard, *America Takes the Stage . . . 1750–1900* (Bloomington, IN, Indiana UP, 1955); ed., *Dramas from the American Theatre, 1762–1909* (Cleveland, OH, World, 1966), a collection running from Francis Hopkinson to Clyde Fitch.

Poggi, Jack, *Theater in America: The Impact of Economic Forces, 1870–1967* (Ithaca, NY, Cornell UP, 1968).

Styan, J. L., *Modern Drama in Theory and Practice* (3 vols., Cambridge UP, 1981: vol. 1, *Realism and Naturalism*; vol. 2, *Symbolism, Surrealism and the Absurd*; vol. 3, *Expressionism and Epic Theatre*).

CHAPTER XVII: AMERICA AND THE WORD

Several Americans, including Brautigan, Doctorow and Vonnegut, are included in the *Contemporary Writers* series, ed., for Methuen, by Malcolm Bradbury and Christopher Bigsby.

Cain, William E., *The Crisis in Criticism: Theory, Literature, and Reform in English Studies* (Baltimore, MD, Johns Hopkins UP, 1984).

Donoghue, Denis, *Ferocious Alphabets* (NY, Columbia UP, 1984).

Fiedler, Leslie, *What Was Literature? Class Culture and Mass Society* (NY, Simon and Schuster, 1982).

Ketterer, David, *New Worlds for Old: The Apocalyptic Imagination, Science Fiction, and American Literature* (Bloomington, IN, Indiana UP, 1974).

Lynn, Kenneth S., *The Airline to Seattle: Studies in Literary and Historical Writing About America* (Chicago, IL, Chicago UP, 1983).

Marc, David, *Demographic Vistas: Television in American Culture* (Philadelphia, PA, U of Pennsylvania P, 1984).

Salmagundi, nos. 63–4, Spring–Summer 1984: special section by Charles Newman, 'The Post-Modern Aura' (also published as a book by Newman).

Sims, Norman, ed., *The Literary Journalists* (NY, Ballantine,1984).

Updike, John, *Hugging the Shore* (NY, Random, 1984).

DATES IN AMERICAN HISTORY

1584	Founding of the unsuccessful colony of Roanoke [North Carolina]
1607	Founding of Jamestown, by the Virginia Company of London
1619	Appearance of the first Negro slaves in North America (at Jamestown, brought by a Dutch ship)
1620	Founding of Plymouth Colony [Massachusetts] by the Pilgrims of the *Mayflower*
1630	Founding of the Massachusetts Bay Colony
1650	Anne Bradstreet, *The Tenth Muse*
1664	Capture of New Amsterdam [New York] from the Dutch
1681	Grant of Pennsylvania to William Penn
1702	Cotton Mather, *Magnalia Christi Americana*
1732	Grant of charter for the colony of Georgia to General James Oglethorpe
1741	Jonathan Edwards, *Sinners in the Hands of an Angry God*
1754–60	French and Indian War, culminating in the defeat of the French in North America and cession of French territories (by the Treaty of Paris, 1763)
1773	Phillis Wheatley, *Poems*
1775–83	American Revolutionary War; independence of the colonies formally recognized by the Treaty of Paris, 1783
1782	John Trumbull, *M'Fingal*
	Crèvecœur, *Letters from an American Farmer*
1787	Constitutional Convention held at Philadelphia
	Joel Barlow, *Vision of Columbus*
	Royall Tyler, *The Contrast*
1789–97	Presidency of George Washington
1792–1815	H. H. Brackenridge, *Modern Chivalry*
1798	C. B. Brown, *Wieland*
1801–9	Presidency of Thomas Jefferson
1803	Purchase from France of the Louisiana Territory (between the Mississippi and the Rocky Mountains), from which thirteen new states were eventually formed
1808	Further importation of slaves into the United States prohibited
1812–14	War of 1812 against Britain
1818	Northern boundary (from the Great Lakes to the Rocky Mountains) fixed at 49th parallel of latitude
1819	Purchase of Florida from Spain

	W. Irving, *The Sketch Book*
1820–21	Missouri Compromises over slavery (involving the admission to the Union of Missouri as a slave state, simultaneously with that of Maine as a free state)
1823	Announcement of the Monroe Doctrine (no further European colonization accepted on the American continent)
	J. F. Cooper, *The Pioneers*
1826	Cooper, *The Last of the Mohicans*
1829–37	Presidency of Andrew Jackson
1836	Declaration by Texas of independence from Mexico, and establishment of the 'Lone Star Republic'
	R. W. Emerson, *Nature*
1837	N. Hawthorne, *Twice-Told Tales*
1838	E. A. Poe, *Narrative of Arthur Gordon Pym*
1845	Annexation of Texas to the United States
1846	Acquisition of the Oregon Territory
	H. Melville, *Typee*
1846–8	Mexican War (acquisition from Mexico of territory between the Rocky Mountains and the Pacific, including the present states of California, Arizona, New Mexico, etc.)
1849	F. Parkman, *The Oregon Trail*
1850	Further compromise over slavery, after prolonged and heated debates between north and south
	Hawthorne, *The Scarlet Letter*
1851	Melville, *Moby-Dick*
	Hawthorne, *The House of the Seven Gables*
1852	H. B. Stowe, *Uncle Tom's Cabin*
1854	H. D. Thoreau, *Walden*
1855	W. Whitman, *Leaves of Grass*
	H. W. Longfellow, *Hiawatha*
1856	Republican party nationally organized (though a northern body, replacing the old Whig party in that section)
1859	John Brown's raid on Harper's Ferry, Virginia
1861–5	Presidency of Abraham Lincoln (Republican; assassinated 1865)
	Civil War, ending in Southern defeat
1867	Purchase of Alaska from Russia
1869	M. Twain, *Innocents Abroad*
	Completion of the first trans-continental railroad
1869–77	Presidency of General Ulysses S. Grant (Republican)
1876	Twain, *Tom Sawyer*
1881	H. James, *Portrait of a Lady*
1884	Twain, *Huckleberry Finn*

1885	W. D. Howells, *The Rise of Silas Lapham*
1888	E. Bellamy, *Looking Backward*
1890	Sherman Anti-Trust Act, designed to combat monopolistic practices in business
1891	Formation of the Populist party
1895	S. Crane, *The Red Badge of Courage*
1896	Klondike gold rush
1898	Spanish-American War (invasion of Cuba; occupation of the Philippines; annexation of Hawaii)
1900	T. Dreiser, *Sister Carrie*
1901–9	Presidency of Theodore Roosevelt (Republican)
1903	James, *The Ambassadors*
1904	Panama Canal begun (opened 1914)
1909	Henry Ford's Model T first produced
	J. London, *Martin Eden*
1912	Admission to statehood of New Mexico and Arizona, the 47th and 48th states of the Union
1913	W. Cather, *O Pioneers!*
1913–21	Presidency of Woodrow Wilson (Democrat)
1919	18th Amendment to the Constitution (prohibition; repealed by the 21st Amendment, 1933)
	S. Anderson, *Winesburg, Ohio*
1920	E. Wharton, *The Age of Innocence*
	19th Amendment (female suffrage)
1921–3	Presidency of Warren G. Harding (Republican)
1922	S. Lewis, *Babbitt*
1923–9	Presidency of Calvin Coolidge (Republican)
1924	E. O'Neill, *Desire Under the Elms*
1925	Dreiser, *An American Tragedy*
	F. Scott Fitzgerald, *The Great Gatsby*
1927	Execution of Sacco and Vanzetti
1929–33	Presidency of Herbert Hoover (Republican)
1929	E. Hemingway, *Farewell to Arms*
	T. Wolfe, *Look Homeward, Angel*
	W. Faulkner, *The Sound and the Fury*
	Collapse of New York stock market
1930	H. Crane, *The Bridge*
	S. Lewis receives Nobel prize
1932	Faulkner, *Light in August*
1933	Inauguration as President of Franklin D. Roosevelt (Democrat)
	Beginning of New Deal legislation
1935	J. Steinbeck, *Tortilla Flat*

	C. Odets, *Waiting for Lefty*
1936	R. Frost, *A Further Range*
	C. Sandburg, *The People, Yes*
	O'Neill receives Nobel prize
1938	T. Wilder, *Our Town*
	Pearl Buck receives Nobel prize
1939	Steinbeck, *The Grapes of Wrath*
	N. West, *The Day of the Locust*
1940	U.S. population 132 million (*c.* 17 million in 1840)
1943	T. S. Eliot, *Four Quartets*
1945	T. Williams, *The Glass Menagerie*
1946	R. P. Warren, *All the King's Men*
1948	T. S. Eliot receives Nobel prize
	N. Mailer, *The Naked and the Dead*
1950	Faulkner receives Nobel prize
1951	J. D. Salinger, *Catcher in the Rye*
1953	Inauguration as President of Dwight D. Eisenhower (Republican)
	Saul Bellow, *Adventures of Augie March*
1953–5	Rise and fall of Senator Joseph McCarthy
1954	Supreme Court directs end of racial segregation in public schools; rapid spread in next decade of Negro protests – ranging from non-violent demonstrations to extremist Black Muslim movement – against continued racial discrimination
	Hemingway receives Nobel prize
1956	J. Berryman, *Homage to Mistress Bradstreet*
	A. Ginsberg, *Howl*
1957	Inauguration for second and last term as President of Dwight D. Eisenhower (Republican)
1958	V. Nabokov, *Lolita*
1959	Admission to statehood of Alaska and Hawaii, the 49th and 50th states of the Union
	R. Lowell, *Life Studies*
1960	U.S. population 180 million
1961	J. Heller, *Catch 22*
1961–3	Presidency of John F. Kennedy (Democrat; assassinated November 1963; succeeded by his Vice-President, Lyndon B. Johnson)
1962	E. Albee, *Who's Afraid of Virginia Woolf?*
	Steinbeck receives Nobel prize
1968	Assassinations of Senator Robert F. Kennedy and the Rev. Martin Luther King
	Mounting protest at U.S. involvement in Vietnam
	Mailer, *Armies of the Night*

1969	Inauguration as president of Richard M. Nixon (Republican; re-elected 1972; obliged to resign over 'Watergate' scandals 1974; followed by his own nominee, Gerald R. Ford)
1970	U.S. population 203 million
1973	T. Pynchon, *Gravity's Rainbow*
	G. Vidal, *Burr*
	K. Vonnegut, *The Breakfast of Champions*
1975	E. L. Doctorow, *Ragtime*
1976	Bellow receives Nobel prize
1981	J. Updike, *Rabbit is Rich*
1982	L. Fiedler, *What Was Literature?*
1983	A. Walker, *The Color Purple*
1985	A. Clampitt, *What the Light Was Like*
1985	Inauguration for second and last term as president of Ronald W. Reagan (Republican)

INDEX